INTERNATIONAL TAX DIGEST

DANIEL E. FELD

Member, New York Bar

WARREN, GORHAM & LAMONT

How to Use This Book

International Tax Digest provides a comprehensive reference to important U.S. international taxation cases and rulings rendered since 1990. All relevant reported decisions of federal courts and the Internal Revenue Service have been carefully reviewed, selected, and edited to present concise and easily understandable abstracts of complex cases. Also included are digests of articles about international taxation published since 1990 in the following WG&L tax publications: *The Journal of Taxation, The Journal of International Taxation, Estate Planning*, and *U.S. Taxation of International Operations*. The digested articles include analysis of the tax laws of foreign countries as well as those of the United States.

Digest Contents and Citations. Each digest of a case or ruling summarizes the facts of the case or ruling and gives the holding of the court or the IRS on the important legal issues. Each digest closes with a citation that states the name of the case or ruling and the volume and page number of the law reporters where the decision is printed, the court, and the year the case was decided. Citations to reporters published by Commerce Clearing House and the Research Institute of America are provided for convenience. Each digest of a journal article includes the title of the article, the year of publication, a summary of the article, and a citation of the volume and page of the journal where the article was published.

Digest Organization. The digests are arranged topically into seven chapters. The following research tools are helpful in directing the reader to specific topics: a Table of Contents, a Table of Internal Revenue Code Sections, a Table of Treasury Regulations, a Table of Revenue Rulings, Revenue Procedures, and Other IRS Rulings, a Table of Cases, and an Index. In addition, a Bibliography of Research References at the end of each chapter directs the reader to other WG&L tax books where the topic of that section is discussed.

Letter Rulings. Digests of selected letter rulings and technical advice memoranda have been included for the reader's convenience. Section 6110(j)(3) states that unless the Secretary of the Treasury rules otherwise, a written determination made available for public inspection may not be used or cited as precedent. Regulation § 1.6662-

4(d)(3)(iii) states that with respect to the accuracy-related penalty, private letter rulings and technical advice memoranda issued after October 31, 1976, are counted in determining whether there is substantial authority for the tax treatment of an item. Under Regulation § 1.6694-2(b)(2), they also are authority for determining if a position on a tax return satisfies the realistic possibility standard.

Acknowledgments

Bruce A. Furst contributed digests to this volume. An important contribution was also made by Debbie Davis, the book editor, and Carol Andronofsky, the copy editor, who diligently edited a large manuscript in a short period. Prudence Conner provided clerical assistance.

Summary of Contents

Table of Contents

1   General Matters

2 U.S. Persons With Foreign Activities

3 Foreign Persons With U.S. Activities

4 U.S. Possessions

5 International Estate and Gift Taxation

6 Tax Treaties

7 Tax Laws of Foreign Countries

CHAPTER 1

General Matters

¶ 1.01 INTERNATIONAL TAXATION, GENERALLY[1]

"Withholding, other cross-border trading effects of the Revenue Reconciliation Act of 1993 (RRA 1993) remain unclear" (1993). RRA 1993 contains two categories of revenue-raising provisions aimed at the securities markets: (1) those attacking financial transactions "manufacturing" capital gains out of ordinary income and (2) those governing the computation of income of broker-dealers in securities (the mark-to-market and hedging rules). In addition, changes in marginal tax rates collaterally affect partnerships engaged in a U.S. trade or business that have foreign partners.

In this article, the authors discuss and illustrate the application of potential problems that may arise under these new provisions. First, they consider the "conversion transaction" rules of new Section 1258 and the stripped preferred stock provisions of new Section 305(e), as well as other "anti–capital gain manufacturing" rules. Next they explore Section 475, affecting the accounting method of broker-dealers. Last, they examine RRA 1993's effects on partnerships with foreign partners.

[RJ Shapiro & RD Lorence, 4 J. Int'l Tax'n 473.]

"A roadmap through the maze: *U.S. International Taxation* by Kuntz and Peroni" (1992). This article is a review of *U.S. International Taxation,* a treatise published by Warren Gorham Lamont in 1992.

[77 J. Tax'n 51.]

"New procedures for rulings, closing agreements, and technical advice memorandums" (1991). In Revenue Procedures 91-27 and 91-28, the IRS has updated its methods of handling various international matters. Revenue Procedure 91-27 governs rulings, information and determination letters, and closing agreements for issues under the jurisdiction of the Associate Chief Counsel (International). Revenue Procedure 91-28 revises the procedures for providing technical advice on such issues to various submitting offices, i.e., District Directors, the Assistant Commissioner (International), and appeals office chiefs. This article discusses the six changes to the previously published procedures for obtaining international rulings, the clarification of the definition of "technical advice," and the effective dates of the revenue procedures.

[75 J. Tax'n 256.]

"Revenue Reconciliation Act of 1990 (RRA 1990) changes affect cross-border transactions" (1991). This article discusses provisions of RRA 1990 affecting international taxation. These provisions were adopted as a result of a congressional perception that foreign-owned businesses are not shouldering their fair share of U.S. tax, because the IRS has been at a disadvantage in policing compliance provisions, especially with regard to transfer pricing abuses.

[SA Musher & JM Colon, 1 J. Int'l Tax'n 294.]

¶ 1.02 SOURCES OF INCOME AND DEDUCTIONS[2]

[1] Source Rules for Income

[a] Generally

"Source of income rules: the debits and credits of international taxation" (1993). The distinction between U.S.-source income and foreign-source income is important for many reasons. This article explores the Code's sourcing provisions and the manner in which they are affected by certain tax treaties.

After defining "United States" for purposes of the sourcing rules, the author considers the sourcing rules applicable to different categories of income. Specific discussion is provided of the rules for interest income; dividend income; personal service income; rental and royalty income; real estate gains; gains from the sale or exchange of personal property (including the different treatment of inventory sales, sales of depreciable/amortizable property, foreign affiliate stock sales, and other special treatment sales); underwriting income; transportation income; international communications income; income from space, the oceans, or Antarctica; and foreign currency transactions.

In the last part of this article, the author considers the interaction of the above source rules with various income tax treaty provisions. An appendix is provided where the statutory provisions for certain source rules are set forth with a brief explanation of their effects.

[ER Larkins, US Tax'n Int'l Operations ¶ 6006.]

"Proposed regulations answer some (but not all) questions about substitute payments" (1992). Recently issued proposed regulations under Sections 861, 871, 881, 894, and 1441, provide guidance on the source, character, and tax treaty treatment of substitute payments made in certain cross-border securities-lending transactions.

Securities-lending transactions can serve various nontax objectives. For example, securities are lent to brokers who use the borrowed securities to cover short sales and fail sales. The lender typically is compensated with a fee, as well as "substitute payments" equal to any interest or dividends that were paid with respect to the loaned securities during the period the securities were loaned. The author discusses the domestic taxation of substitute payments. The IRS did not focus its attention on cross-border issues related to securities lending until relatively recently. Prior to the proposed regulations on cross-border substitute payments, IRS guidance was limited to a few private letter rulings along with some narrow references in several sets of regulations. A review of the law prior to the proposed regulations then follows.

Rather than reconcile its conflicting impulses in the domestic and international contexts with a new unified theory for substitute payments, the IRS issued proposed regulations providing look-through treatment only for purposes of Sections 861,

862, 871, 881, 894, 1441, and 1442, while specifically reaffirming its denial of look-through treatment in the domestic context.

Proposed Regulations §§ 1.871-7(b)(2), 1.881-2(b)(2), and 1.1441-2(a)(1) reiterate the look-through characterization of substitute interest and dividend payments for purposes of Sections 871, 881, 1441, and 1442. Proposed Regulation §§ 1.881-7(b)(2) and 1.881-2(b)(2) also clarify that substitute interest payments made by U.S. persons to foreign persons with respect to transferred portfolio interest obligations may be treated as portfolio interest exempt from U.S. tax. A substitute interest payment will be so treated if the withholding agent receives a Form W-8 (or substantially similar form) that has been properly executed by the payee.

Proposed Regulation § 1.894-1 addresses the application of income tax treaties to substitute payments. To the extent that an income tax treaty refers to U.S. law for the definition of the term "dividend or interest," the substitute payment will be treated as a dividend or interest, as the case may be, for purposes of the treaty. It is not clear whether the proposed regulations will be disregarded in the case of substitute payments to residents of jurisdictions whose treaties with the United States define the terms "dividend" and "interest" in any manner other than by reference to the provisions of U.S. law.

The proposed regulations apply only to cross-border substitute interest and dividends payments (i.e., substitute payments made by a foreign person to a U.S. person, or vice versa). Fees paid in connection with securities loans are not covered.

The proposed regulations also apply only to securities-lending transactions described in Section 1058(a) and substantially similar transactions. The only guidance as to the scope of the substantially similar transactions language is the solicitation of comments in the preamble regarding the extent to which the regulations should apply to substitute payments made in connection with sale and repurchase agreements (repos).

In the context of loans by U.S. persons, the proposed regulations do not apply for purposes of various relevant sections of the Code, such as Section 902.

[JE Croker, Jr., 3 J. of Int'l Tax'n 40.]

[b] Gain From Sales of Personal Property

Regulations § 1.863-3(b)(2) Example (1) method of sourcing mixed-source income is applicable only when all prerequisites for its application are met, including the existence of a different country branch. Taxpayer sold products it manufactured in the United States to unrelated parties. Title to the products passed to the buyers outside the United States. During the years in issue, taxpayer did not maintain a selling or distributing branch outside the United States. The IRS determined that an independent factory price could be determined for the products sold by taxpayer outside the United States, and therefore taxpayer was required to source the income realized on these sales using the method prescribed in Example (1) of Regulation § 1.863-3(b)(2), as it ruled in Revenue Ruling 88-73. Taxpayer argued that use of the method set forth in Example (2) of that regulation was proper.

Held: For taxpayer. Example (1), while not elective, requires for its application that all its factual prerequisites be met. One of these is that the taxpayer have made the sale of goods outside the United States through a selling or distributing branch located outside the United States. The other is that an "independent factory price" exist with respect to the goods sold in the cross-border sale. The existence of only one of these does not permit application of the Example (1) method; otherwise no mixed-source income would result from taxpayer's cross-border sale.

[Intel Corp., 100 TC No. 39 (1993).]

Passage of title test satisfied by momentary holding of title; income was foreign-source income. A U.S. liquor distributor purchased goods from their U.K. producer for resale in the United States. The goods were delivered FOB in the United Kingdom to the distributor's customers. The IRS argued that the income was not foreign-source income, because title to the goods passed between taxpayer and its customers in the U.S.

Held: For taxpayer. The sale of the goods took place where the beneficial ownership and risk of loss passed to the buyer. In this case, title passed in the United Kingdom and the income was sourced there. Taxpayer's momentary holding of title was sufficient to transfer the rights, title, and interest in the property.

[Liggett Group, Inc., 58 TCM 1167, RIA TC Memo. ¶ 90,018 (1990).]

"Tax Court allows apportioning 50 percent of cross-border sales to foreign-source income" (1993). In *Intel Corp.*, a 1993 Tax Court decision, the court held that the taxpayer had to determine U.S.-source income from production and sale of inventory produced inside the United States, but sold outside the United States, using an independent factory price only where the cross-border sales were effected through a foreign distributing or selling branch of the taxpayer. This holding confirms a U.S. manufacturer's ability to generate low-taxed overall basket foreign-source income by simply transferring title and the other incidents of ownership of the inventory sold offshore. Thus, under the export sales source rule, a U.S. exporter of inventory can in many circumstances effectively apportion 50 percent of the income from cross-border sales to foreign sources.

[PM Daub, 4 J. Int'l Tax'n 468.]

[c] Natural Resources Income

Income from foreign sale of liquefied natural gas produced from U.S. wells is (1) sourced partly within and partly without the United States; (2) Section 907(c)(2) foreign oil related income to the extent attributed to a foreign source; and (3) apportioned in accordance with the manner set forth in Regulations § 1.863-3(b)(2). Taxpayer sold liquefied natural gas, produced and processed in Alaska, to Japanese customers. Under the contract for these sales, taxpayer owned the gas until it was delivered in Japan by tankers. On its returns for years 1976–1978, taxpayer treated income from these sales as earned partly within and partly without the United States, apportioned this income in accordance with Example (2) of Regulation § 1.863-3(b)(2), and considered the foreign-source income from these sales to be foreign oil related income. The IRS determined, under Regulation § 1.863-1(b), that all income from these sales was U.S. source because the gas was produced from wells located in the United States, that no part of such income was thus foreign oil related income, and that taxpayer was required to use the apportionment method prescribed in Example (1) of Regulation § 1.863-3(b)(2).

Held: For taxpayer, except as to the use of the Example (2) apportionment method. To the extent that Regulation § 1.863-1(b) requires worldwide income from U.S. natural resources be treated per se as U.S.-source income, it is invalid. It clearly conflicts with Section 863(b)(2), which states that income from the sale of personal property produced within the United States and sold without the United States shall be treated as mixed source. The liquefied natural gas sales by taxpayer came within the rule of Section 863(b)(2). To the extent that under this provision, the income realized by taxpayer is treated as foreign source, it is foreign oil related income. It is the source of the taxable income from sales of oil and gas, and not the location of the oil or gas wells, that determines foreign oil related income under Section 907. Finally, however, taxpayer's use of the apportionment method described in Example (2) of Regulation § 1.863-3(b)(2) was improper. Under this regulation, the methods described in its examples are not elective. As a matter of law, if all the factual prerequisites to the application of the Example (1) method are present, that method must be used.

[Phillips Petroleum Co., 97 TC 30 (1991).]

"Record-keeping, transfer pricing, and sourcing updates" (1991). In *Phillips Petroleum,* a 1991 Tax Court decision, Phillips extracted natural gas and processed it into liquefied natural gas (LNG) in Alaska. Phillips sold the LNG under a long-term contract to a Japanese gas company and a Japanese electric power company. Regulation § 1.863-1(b) provides that "[t]he income derived from the ownership or operation of any farm, mine, oil or gas well, other natural deposit, or timber, located within the United States, and from the sale by the producer of the products thereof within or without the United States, shall ordinarily be included in gross income from sources within the United States." In other words, the regulation would generally treat as exclusively from U.S. sources the income of a producer from sale outside the United States of natural resource products extracted inside the United States.

The majority of the court found the regulation to be contrary to the express statutory language in Section 863(b), as it read at the time, that "income . . . from the sale of personal property produced (in whole or in part) by the taxpayer within and sold without the United States . . . shall be treated as derived partly from sources within and partly from sources without the United States."

The authors analyze and comment upon the Tax Court's decision, concluding that the case may represent a hollow victory for the taxpayer, since the apportionment must be determined under the independent factory price method of the regulations, assuming its factual predicates are present. The taxpayer wanted to choose between that method and the more favorable "50/50 sourcing" method of the regulations.

[M. Abrutyn, SA Musher & GW Rubloff, 2 J. Int'l Tax'n 162.]

"Tax Court invalidates income-sourcing regulation" (1991). In *Phillips Petroleum* (1991), the Tax Court invalidated Regulation § 1.863-1(b), which treats income from natural resource operations located in the United States, and from the sale of the products inside or outside the United States, as U.S.-source income. Although the taxpayer was thus successful in being able to allocate the income to mixed sources, the IRS prevailed on the mandatory application of the apportionment method used in Regulation § 1.863-3(b)(2), Example (1).

[75 J. Tax'n 254.]

[d] Notional Principal Contracts

IRS issues final regulations concerning allocation of income attributable to certain notional principal contracts. The IRS has issued final regulations under Section 863(a), which set forth the source of income attributable to certain notional principal contracts (notional principal contract income).

[TD 8330, 1991-1 CB 105, Reg. § 1.863-7.]

"Final regulations issued on sourcing notional principal contracts" (1991). New Regulation § 1.863-7 provides rules for determining the source of income from notional principal contracts, commonly known as swaps. In general, a notional principal contract provides that in exchange for a lump-sum payment or a series of payments made by one party, another party will make a corresponding series of payments. These contracts are used as hedges against fluctuations in the interest rate, currencies, or commodity prices. This article discusses the sourcing rule for swap income, the qualified business unit (QBU) exception to this general sourcing rule, and the relationship between this new regulation and the Section 988 rules.

[75 J. Tax'n 116.]

"Sourcing rules for notional principal contracts modified" (1991). The IRS recently issued final regulations under Section 863, governing the sourcing of income on notional principal contracts, such as interest rate swaps, caps, and collars, in which one party makes payments at specified intervals based on one rate index and a hypothetical (notional) principal and the other party makes payments based on a different interest rate or index.

The new regulations extend these rules to notional principal contracts involving commodities swaps. Such income is sourced according to the recipient's residence, unless the income is earned by a qualified business unit (QBU), and, in a requirement imposed by the amended regulations, is properly reflected on its books. In that event, the income will be sourced by the QBU's residence, i.e., foreign.

[1 J. Int'l Tax'n 377.]

"U.S.-source rules under notional principal contracts" (1991). The last decade has been marked by a tremendous increase in the use of notional principal contracts, such as interest rate swaps, caps, floors, and collars, to manage interest rate risk on liabilities and assets.

An interest rate swap is a contract under which, over a specified period of time, each party makes payments to the other calculated on the basis of a different interest rate formula applied to an assumed or notional principal amount of debt. Typically, one party will make payments at a fixed interest rate while the other will make payments determined by a specified floating rate index, e.g., the prime or London Interbank offered rate. The notional principal amount only determines the amount of payments and is not actually exchanged between the parties.

An interest rate cap is a contract under which one party (purchaser) pays an initial "premium" for an agreement by the other party (writer) to make a series of payments equal to the excess, on each payment date, of a floating rate index over a specified fixed rate, as applied to a notional principal amount. Conversely, an interest rate floor is an agreement under which the writer makes payments to the purchaser based on the amount by which a floating rate index is less than a specified fixed rate on each payment date. A collar combines a cap and a floor.

Notional principal contracts may be entered into between U.S. taxpayers and foreign or domestic counterparties. The U.S. tax consequences to the parties will turn, in part, on whether income from the contract is deemed to derive from a U.S. source as opposed to a foreign source, and whether losses are allocated against U.S.- or foreign-source income.

For example, in the case of a foreign party that is not engaged in a U.S. trade or business, payments received under a notional principal contract that are U.S.-source income may be subject to a 30 percent U.S. withholding tax. If the foreign taxpayer is engaged in a U.S. trade or business, U.S.-source income derived from the contract will be subject to U.S. taxation on a net basis, at graduated rates, if the income is effectively connected with the conduct of a trade or business.

From the perspective of a U.S. taxpayer, payments made to a foreign counterparty that are U.S.-source income subject to U.S. withholding tax will expose the taxpayer to liability if the tax is not paid. Moreover, a U.S. taxpayer's foreign tax credit limitation depends on the net foreign-source income earned by the taxpayer during the year.

Thus, the credit limitation will be affected by the source of income received under a notional principal contract and by the source of income against which losses under the contract are allocated, regardless of the residence of the counterparty.

On January 11, 1991, the IRS promulgated, in final form, Regulation § 1.863-7, which provides source rules governing income earned under notional principal contracts that are denominated in the taxpayer's functional currency. Together with similar source rules under Temporary Regulation § 1.988-4T applicable to notional principal contracts denominated in nonfunctional currency, the regulations generally provide that income derived from a notional principal contract is sourced by reference to the residence of the taxpayer. Moreover, losses or expenses incurred under a notional principal contract by a U.S. taxpayer generally are allocated against U.S.-source income for foreign tax credit purposes.

This source rule generally avoids U.S. withholding tax on payments made by U.S. parties to foreign counterparties, and eliminates uncertainty as to the source of payments received under notional principal contracts for foreign tax credit purposes. The source rule, however, is subject to a number of important limitations and exceptions. Furthermore, the source rule generally does not apply to ancillary income derived from notional principal contracts, such as late payment fees.

Perhaps most important, allocation provisions under Temporary Regulation § 1.861-9T(b)(6), in part, supersede the residence-based source rule for purposes of determining a U.S. taxpayer's foreign tax credit limitation. Losses incurred under a notional principal contract entered into as a liability hedge generally must be allocated and apportioned against U.S.- and foreign-source income pursuant to the interest allocation provisions of Temporary Regulation § 1.861-9T. In addition, if the liability hedge is identified on the taxpayer's books, income from the notional principal contract may be applied as an offset against interest expense.

The source rule contained in Regulation § 1.863-7 is a modified version of the rule set forth by the IRS in Notice 87-4. In the notice, the IRS adopted the position that income derived from certain types of interest rate swaps is sourced by reference to the residence of the recipient of the income.

The authors discuss in detail the general source rule, and conclude that Regulation § 1.863-7, together with Temporary Regulation § 1.988-4T, provides a general residence-based source rule applicable to notional principal contracts. The rule excludes notional principal payments made by U.S. parties to foreign counterparties from U.S. withholding tax. The rule also treats payments received by U.S. taxpayers from foreign counterparties as U.S.-source income, which cannot be used to increase the taxpayer's foreign tax credit limitation. As discussed in the article, however, for credit limitation purposes but not for U.S. withholding tax purposes, this rule is substantially modified by the allocation provisions contained in Temporary Regulation § 1.861-9T(b)(6).

The authors also discuss in detail the rules with respect to the residence of a corporation for purposes of the source rule, the exception under which income from a notional principal contract is sourced by reference to the residence of a QBU of a taxpayer, and the "effectively connected" exception to the general source rule.

The recharacterization of a notional principal contract in whole or in part as a loan, with the portion of the payments recharacterized as interest sourced according to the residence of the payer, is then examined. After that, the allocation of losses as it affects the taxpayer's foreign tax credit limitation is discussed.

With respect to U.S. taxpayers, the general U.S.-source treatment of income and loss derived from notional principal contracts is substantially modified by Regulation § 1.861-9T(b)(6). The regulation provides that in the case of a taxpayer that is not a financial services entity or a dealer in financial products, any loss incurred on a financial product that alters the taxpayer's effective cost of borrowing with respect to an actual liability is treated as expense equivalent to interest for purposes of determining the taxpayer's foreign tax credit limitation. Thus, the loss must be allocated against U.S.-source and foreign-source income pursuant to the interest allocation provisions of Regulation § 1.861-9T. This result obtains regardless of whether the financial product is identified as a liability hedge on the taxpayer's books and records. Moreover, this rule applies in cases where the financial product is denominated in nonfunctional currency if the underlying liability is denominated in the same nonfunctional currency.

Lastly, the authors discuss when the new rules apply. These dates range from taxable income includable in income after December 23, 1986, to such income includable after February 12, 1991. There are also provisions for elections to have the new rules apply to income earned before the effective dates.

[PB Marrs & DM Crowe, 2 J. Int'l Tax'n 14.]

[e] Income Derived Partly From Within and Partly From Without United States (Section 863(b))

Regulations § 1.863-3(b)(2) Example (1) method of sourcing mixed-source income is applicable only when all prerequisites for its application are met, including the existence of a different country branch. Taxpayer sold products it manufactured in the United States to unrelated parties. Title to the products passed to the buyers outside the United States. During the years in issue, taxpayer did not maintain a selling or distributing branch outside the United States. The IRS determined that an independent factory price could be determined for the products sold by taxpayer outside the United States, and therefore taxpayer was required to source the income realized on these sales using the method prescribed in Example (1) of Regulation § 1.863-3(b)(2), as it ruled in Revenue Ruling 88-73. Taxpayer argued that use of the method set forth in Example (2) of that regulation was proper.

Held: For taxpayer. Example (1), while not elective, requires for its application that all its factual prerequisites be met. One of these is that the taxpayer have made the sale of goods outside the United States through a selling or distributing branch located outside the United States. The other is that an "independent factory price" exist with respect to the goods sold in the cross-border sale. The existence of only one of these does not permit application of the Example (1) method; otherwise no mixed-source income would result from taxpayer's cross-border sale.

[Intel Corp., 100 TC No. 39 (1993).]

Income from foreign sale of liquefied natural gas produced from U.S. wells is (1) sourced partly within and partly without the United States; (2) Section 907(c)(2) foreign oil related income to the extent attributed to a foreign source;

and (3) apportioned in accordance with the manner set forth in Regulations § 1.863-3(b)(2). Taxpayer sold liquefied natural gas, produced and processed in Alaska, to Japanese customers. Under the contract for these sales, taxpayer owned the gas until it was delivered in Japan by tankers. On its returns for years 1976–1978, taxpayer treated income from these sales as earned partly within and partly without the United States, apportioned this income in accordance with Example (2) of Regulation § 1.863-3(b)(2), and considered the foreign-source income from these sales to be foreign oil related income. The IRS determined, under Regulation § 1.863-1(b), that all income from these sales was U.S. source because the gas was produced from wells located in the United States, that no part of such income was thus foreign oil related income, and that taxpayer was required to use the apportionment method prescribed in Example (1) of Regulation § 1.863-3(b)(2).

Held: For taxpayer, except as to the use of the Example (2) apportionment method. To the extent that Regulation § 1.863-1(b) requires worldwide income from U.S. natural resources be treated per se as U.S.-source income, it is invalid. It clearly conflicts with Section 863(b)(2), which states that income from the sale of personal property produced within the United States and sold without the United States shall be treated as mixed source. The liquefied natural gas sales by taxpayer came within the rule of Section 863(b)(2). To the extent that, under this provision, the income realized by taxpayer is treated as foreign source, it is foreign oil related income. It is the source of the taxable income from sales of oil and gas, and not the location of the oil or gas wells, that determines foreign oil related income under Section 907. Finally, however, taxpayer's use of the apportionment method described in Example (2) of Regulation § 1.863-3(b)(2) was improper. Under this regulation, the methods described in its examples are not elective. As a matter of law, if all the factual prerequisites to the application of the Example (1) method are present, that method must be used.

[Phillips Petroleum Co., 97 TC 30 (1991).]

[2] Allocation and Apportionment of Deductions

[a] Generally

"New allocation and apportionment regulations contain contradictory approaches" (1991). On March 11, 1991, the IRS released three sets of regulations in the international area that provide guidance on apportioning expenses: (1) proposed regulations covering the controlled foreign corporation (CFC) netting rule; (2) proposed regulations regarding charitable contributions; and (3) final regulations concerning state income taxes, including state, local, and foreign income, war profits, and excess profits taxes. Each set of regulations is quite different in its approach to basically the same question: How are expenses allocated and apportioned in an international context?

The three sets of allocation regulations are a contrast in style and content. At one extreme, the charitable contribution regulations adopt a pragmatic approach while possibly violating the basic principle of Regulation § 1.861-8 that a deduction is allocated (and, if necessary, apportioned) based on the factual relationship of the deduction to gross income. At the other extreme, the state income tax regulations have adopted a defensive posture and use a strict technical approach in allocating and apportioning state income tax deductions. In between both extremes, the netting rule regulations take a middle ground approach that is somewhat sensitive to prior taxpayer criticism and pragmatically focuses on tax-motivated borrowing.

All three sets of regulations do have one thing in common: They provide taxpayers with the ability to affect the allocation of their deductions through careful tax planning.

[PM Bodner & TA Bryan, 75 J. Tax'n 112.]

[b] Interest

"Effectively connected income (ECI) interest deduction limited by proposed regulations" (1992). The IRS has proposed revisions to Regulation § 1.882-5, under which the allocation of interest expense to ECI is calculated. Section 882(a) taxes a foreign corporation on taxable income that is effectively connected with the conduct of a trade or business in the United States. To derive effectively connected taxable income, the Section 861 regulations generally allocate and apportion deductions. Regulation § 1.882-5, however, applies for computing a foreign corporation's interest deduction under Section 882(c).

Under Proposed Regulation § 1.882-5(a)(1), the maximum allocable interest expense is the amount allowed under Section 163(a). Amounts in excess of this are not allowed in prior or subsequent years. The preamble notes that regulations will be proposed under Section 265 on the disallowance of interest expense to a foreign corporation under Regulation § 1.882-5.

The regulation provides a three-step process for determining a foreign corporation's allocable interest expense.

[3 J. Int'l Tax'n 76.]

"Final regulations on interest allocation clarify the netting rule" (1992). Final regulations under Section 861, issued in April 1992, provide guidance on the allocation and apportionment of interest expense for a U.S. affiliated group under the "netting rule" of Section 864(e). This article examines the provisions of the final regulations, which are substantially similar to the proposed regulations issued in 1991.

Before discussing the step-by-step process required for calculating the allocation, the article explores the final regulations' failure to address the fungibility principle for debt incurred by related CFCs. Also addressed are the considerations involved in choosing the proper base period for the allocation calculation and the ratios used for both the current year and base period calculations. The regulations' provisions concerning the definition of assets used in determining the ratios are also examined. Last, certain legislative proposals that would modify the Section 864(e) interest allocation rules are discussed.

The article concludes that the netting rule has been drafted to eliminate various tax planning strategies. The rules suggest a layered approach to related-party lending. In the initial evaluation of the effective date for the rules, particular attention should be paid to electing the base period that provides the highest ratios. There may be a marginal benefit in bifurcating the year in which the initial borrowing and related party lending occurs (up to the point at which the antistuffing rule is not violated).

To identify potentially tax-motivated borrowing and on-lending, the regulations adopt a hindsight approach by comparing current-year ratios with historical base-period ratios. Ironically, the use of this approach puts taxpayers that engaged in tax-motivated borrowing and on-lending at an early stage in a better position vis-à-vis other taxpayers because of their relatively high base-period debt-to-asset ratios. Consequently, the netting rule favors the taxpayers whose activities precipitated the rule.

[77 J. Tax'n 176.]

"New interest expense allocation rules pose practical difficulties for foreign banks" (1992). Proposed regulations modify the rules under Regulation § 1.882-5 for determining the allowable allocation of interest expense to a foreign corporation's U.S. ECI attributable to a U.S. trade or business or permanent establishment. The rules generally would be effective for tax years beginning after the publication of final regulations in the Federal Register.

The proposals conform the existing regulations to subsequent statutory enactments, primarily relating to the branch profits tax (BPT) and branch-level interest tax provisions, and to the U.S. tax treatment of foreign currency transactions. In addition, they seek to clarify issues raised under Regulation § 1.882-5, and take into account the appropriate economic treatment of international financial market product developments (such as notional principal contracts) that were not considered when the existing regulations were adopted in 1980. Although primarily directed to banking institutions, the proposed regulations would apply to all foreign corporations that have ECI or income treated as ECI under Sections 882(a) and 882(d).

The authors provide an overview of the differences between the new proposed regulations and the existing regulations. Thereafter, they examine the proposed regulations' three-step process for computing allowable interest expense. In explaining Step 1, the authors cover coordination with the BPT rules, the treatment of U.S. real estate and stock, and other matters set forth in the proposed regulations. The potential effect of treaties in this area is also considered. Thereafter, the authors address Step 2 concerning U.S. liabilities, as set forth in the proposed regulations. They examine Step 3, concerning the determination of allocable interest expense. Thereunder, they discuss the treatment of booked liabilities, partnership liabilities, computation of the allowable interest expense deduction, applicability of the scaling ratio, treatment of excess interest expense, and the election of daily computation of the three-step formula.

The authors conclude that foreign banks would face many practical implementation difficulties under the proposed regulations in their current form. To obtain the highest allowable interest expense deduction, many foreign banks would be required to increase the frequency of their worldwide financial reporting and establish worldwide accounting records adjusted under U.S. tax principles that are not otherwise required or maintained in the ordinary course of business. Although the proposed regulations seek to apply a general principle of fungibility, arbitrary ceilings on the imputation of liabilities also depart from principles contemplated in the branch tax legislative history.

If the proposed regulations were to adhere more broadly to principles of parity and consistency under the Tax Reform Act of 1986 (TRA 1986) for the generation and deemed remittance of effectively connected earnings and profits under the BPT provisions, the rules could be simplified and a more efficient administration of IRS examinations might be facilitated. Placing a U.S. trade or business on a more equal footing with a U.S. subsidiary would remove much of the discrimination that currently remains and likely would induce more uniform application of the rules by all foreign taxpayers. Absent a more remedial approach, many treaty-based foreign taxpayers will have no choice but to invoke the full protection of their respective treaties, which may result in protracted competent authority proceedings or potential U.S. litigation. Finally, even non-treaty-based foreign taxpayers may have legitimate claims on statutory grounds that the IRS's failure to adhere to parity and consistency is beyond the scope of the regulatory authority for implementing revised interest expense allocation rules.

[PJ Connors, BE Blanco & PS Epstein, 77 J. Tax'n 368.]

"Proposed Regulation § 1.882-5 overhauls interest allocation rules for U.S. branches" (1992). In April 1992, the IRS published proposed amendments to Regulation § 1.882-5 on the interest deduction for foreign corporations engaged in business in the United States. The regulation applies only to foreign corporations having U.S. operations in branch form, primarily foreign banks and insurance companies and foreign corporations formed to make U.S. real estate investments.

Foreign banks and insurance companies typically adopt the branch format for nontax regulatory reasons, including reliance on worldwide capital as the basis for U.S. operations. Traditionally, U.S. real estate investments were made through foreign corporations in order to shield ultimate individual foreign owners from U.S. estate tax. Since 1986, however, such investments have tended to be structured or restructured through U.S. subsidiaries of foreign corporations to avoid the complications of the branch-tax rules, and some have eschewed the corporate form altogether to avoid potential double taxation.

The proposed regulations (1) seek to coordinate the interest allocation rules with the BPT rules; (2) attempt to take into account the effects of notional principal contracts as liability hedges; and (3) address a number of aspects of the current regulations that have led taxpayers to complain about the difficulty of applying the rules and the IRS to complain about the difficulty of examining taxpayer compliance with the rules.

[HJ Birnkrant, JE Croker, Jr. & SA Musher, 3 J. Int'l Tax'n 166.]

"Proposed regulations change rules for allocating interest to ECI" (1992). In proposed regulations, the IRS has revised the rules for determining the interest expense of a foreign corporation that is allocable to U.S. ECI and is deductible under Section 882(c). This article compares the proposed regulation provisions to the prior regulation provisions and examines the modifications made by the proposed regulations.

[77 J. Tax'n 52.]

"The CFC netting rule entangles U.S.-based multinationals" (1992). TRA 1986 significantly reduced the ability of U.S. taxpayers to claim foreign tax credit against their U.S. tax liability by expanding the number of baskets of income for which separate foreign tax credit limitations must be computed.

TRA 1986 also adopted the fungibility concept for the allocation and apportionment of interest expense to foreign-source income. This concept, embodied in Section 864(e)(1), generally requires the domestic members of an affiliated group to allocate and apportion interest expense to foreign-source income as if all members of the group were a single corporation. In addition, interest expense must generally be allocated on an assets basis (i.e., based on the relative value of assets that produce foreign-source income to the value of all assets), rather than on a gross income basis.

As a departure from the fungibility concept, however, Section 864(e)(5) requires interest expense of CFCs to be directly allocated to foreign-source income. As a further departure from the fungibility concept, under certain circumstances, interest expense of the affiliated group is directly allocated to foreign-source interest income from CFCs. This latter departure, known as the CFC netting rule, was not part of TRA 1986, but rather was adopted by the IRS in proposed and, later, temporary regulations.

In April 1992, final regulations on the CFC netting rule were published in the Federal Register, generally retaining both the rule and its more controversial aspects.

[AS Lederman & B. Hirsh, 3 J. Int'l Tax'n 69.]

"IRS's third try at CFC netting regulations" (1991). U.S. multinationals have traditionally financed overseas affiliates, generally CFCs, with intercompany loans rather than with third-party borrowing by the CFCs. Often, CFCs are minimally capitalized and cannot obtain funding in the local country. Therefore, they borrow from the U.S. parent or other members of the affiliated group.

The IRS believes that this approach to financing overseas affiliates constitutes an abuse, because taxpayers may manipulate borrowing by related CFCs to achieve both an increase in the foreign-source income and a reduction of the U.S.-source income of a U.S. affiliated group. Consequently, the IRS has issued regulations to limit the benefits flowing out of this financing approach. The latest (and third) version of these regulations is the subject of this article.

The proposed regulations apply the netting approach only when both of the following conditions occur:

1. The current-year average third-party borrowings of the U.S. group have increased over that of a five-year base period.
2. The current-year average loans from the U.S. group to foreign affiliates have increased over that same five-year base period.

Notably, an increase in both factors listed above must be present in the same year to invoke the new CFC netting rule. If the increase in third-party borrowing of the U.S. group exceeds the increase in the loans from the U.S. group to its foreign affiliates, then such excess is unrelated to the foreign affiliates and related to other needs of the group. Similarly, if the increase in loans from the U.S. group to its foreign affiliates exceeds the increase in third-party borrowing of the U.S. group, then such excess comes from sources other than third-party borrowing of the U.S. group.

The proposed regulations use a three-step method of allocating interest expense to interest received from related-party CFCs. Step 1 involves the computation of excess related-group indebtedness. "Excess related-group indebtedness" is the increase in lending by the U.S. group to its foreign affiliates. This increase is the amount lent by the U.S. group to its foreign affiliates that is potentially tax-motivated and is computed as the excess of the average current-year loans to foreign affiliates, over the "allowable related-group indebtedness."

"Allowable related-group indebtedness" measures what the current year's loans from the U.S. shareholder to its foreign affiliates would be if a historical average of such loans (over an established base period) were outstanding. This equals the current year's aggregate average of assets of the foreign affiliates, multiplied by an average of the preceding five years' ratios of loans (from the U.S. group to its foreign affiliates) to the average amount of foreign affiliate assets.

Step 2 involves the computation of excess U.S. shareholder indebtedness. Excess U.S. shareholder indebtedness is the increase in third-party borrowing by the U.S. parent. This increase is the amount of borrowing by the U.S. parent that is potentially tax-motivated, and is computed as the excess of the average amount of third-party borrowing in the current year over the allowable indebtedness. The allowable indebtedness measures what the current year's indebtedness of the U.S. group to unrelated parties would be if the base period historical average indebtedness of the U.S. group to unrelated parties were outstanding. The allowable indebtedness is the current-year average assets of the U.S. shareholder consolidated group (reduced by the excess related-group indebtedness), multiplied by the average of the preceding five years' unrelated-party debt-to-asset ratios of the U.S. shareholder.

Step 3 involves the direct allocation of interest expense. If both Steps 1 and 2 resulted in increases in a single year, the group has engaged in tax-motivated borrowing and on-lending. In such a case, some third-party interest expense of the U.S. parent must be directly allocated to the foreign-source interest income of the U.S. group. The amount so allocated equals the interest income on "allocable related-group indebtedness," as defined in the article.

If an affiliated group's excess U.S. shareholder indebtedness exceeds its excess related-group indebtedness in the current year, the entire excess related-group indebtedness has been financed with tax-motivated borrowing, and the taxpayer's allocable related-group indebtedness equals its excess related-group indebtedness. If an affiliated group's excess U.S. shareholder indebtedness does not exceed its excess related-group indebtedness, the taxpayer's allocable related-group indebtedness equals its excess U.S. shareholder indebtedness. Third-party interest expense of the U.S. affiliated group, in an amount equal to the interest income received by the group on allocable related-group indebtedness, must be allocated directly to foreign-source income of the U.S. affiliated group. The discussion then focuses on the allocation calculation.

In certain cases, equity contributions made in taxable years beginning after 1986 by a U.S. shareholder to a CFC will be recharacterized as related-group indebtedness. For this to apply, the CFC must meet certain conditions as described in the article. A U.S. shareholder must treat as related-group indebtedness its holding of stock in a related CFC if the related CFC claims a deduction under foreign law for distributions on such stock. This was inserted in the proposed regulations to prevent circumvention of earlier proposed regulations.

In determining the relevant historical base-period ratios, special rules are provided for corporate acquisitions and dispositions. The article concludes with brief discussions on certain mechanical problems. These problems concern effective dates, phantom interest, incorporation of a new CFC, and acquisition of an additional corporation.

[WT Kresge, Jr. & TJ Throndson, 2 J. Int'l Tax'n 156.]

"Taking advantage of exceptions to asset-based apportionment" (1991). One objective of multinational corporations is to generate foreign-source income in a manner that maximizes the corporation's foreign tax credit. The rules for allocating interest expense under Section 864(e) and numerous foreign tax credit limitation categories under Section 904(d) have placed most multinational taxpayers in an excess foreign tax credit position. These corporations must now seek ways to increase the foreign-source taxable income in the appropriate Section 904(d) category in order to use excess foreign tax credits.

One way is for multinational corporations to use the exceptions under Temporary Regulation § 1.861-10T, which deviate from the general rule that interest is a fungible expense and must be apportioned to all assets of certain related parties. Some of these exceptions to asset-based apportionment allow taxpayers to allocate interest expense to U.S.-source income or to a Section 904(d) category of foreign-source income that is not in an excess foreign tax credit position. These narrowly drawn rules apply to nonrecourse indebtedness and integrated financial transactions. In addition, multinational corporations should attempt to avoid the rule under Temporary Regulation § 1.861-10T(e) that requires allocation of interest expense to foreign-source income in the case of certain loans between the U.S. affiliated group and CFCs.

[TT Tuerff & KF Sellers, 1 J. Int'l Tax'n 261.]

"Interest expense allocations for foreign and domestic income" (1990). TRA 1986 revised the rules for computing source of income by clarifying the allocation of deductions, particularly for interest expense. The revised Code and regulations have significantly altered interest expense allocation between foreign- and domestic-source income by changing the method of apportionment, as well as the definition of "included interest." These changes have greatly reduced the flexibility available to taxpayers to apportion interest expense and thus maximize foreign tax credits. The TRA 1986 revisions focused on three areas of change: (1) the treatment of interest expense within an affiliated group; (2) the asset method of computation; and (3) the treatment of tax-exempt income.

Definition of "allocable interest expense." The revised Code and regulations adopt a broad view of interest. Specifically, an expense or loss that is incurred for the use of funds over time is treated as interest if the expense or loss is incurred substantially in consideration of the time value of money. In order for interest expense to be allocable and apportioned, it must be currently deductible. Temporary Regulation § 1.861-T(c) sets forth rules concerning this requirement. Certain items of deductible interest expense must be allocated separately, according to Temporary Regulation § 1.861-10T. This provision also contains special rules concerning the treatment of nonrecourse indebtedness.

Thus, in defining what is interest expense, the temporary regulations have restricted the ability of the taxpayer to avoid the disadvantageous application of the allocation and apportionment rules. Nevertheless, some planning possibilities exist with respect to those items exempt from the allocation and apportionment rules. Taxpayers may also plan transactions in such a way as to fall under the separate allocation of interest provisions.

Apportionment of interest. Prior to TRA 1986, taxpayers had the option of allocating interest expense on the basis of either assets or income. Now, most taxpayers are required to use the asset method.

To implement the asset method requires three basic steps. The taxpayer and its affiliates must first calculate values for all assets. Next, these asset values must be allocated to the various statutory groupings (foreign or domestic). Finally, qualifying interest expense is allocated to the various statutory groupings based on the average total value of assets within each grouping for the tax year. For determining average assets, taxpayers may elect to use either book values or fair market value. Once selected, the valuation method chosen can only be changed with the consent of the IRS. (This article discusses in-depth the application and use of both methods.)

In determining asset character, assets are characterized under Temporary Regulation § 1.861-9T(g)(3) according to the source and type of income they generate, have generated, or could reasonably expect to generate, regardless of their physical location. Generally, asset values are assigned to statutory and residual groupings by segregating assets into three categories: single category, multiple category, and support assets. The category assigned depends on whether the asset generates income and, if so, what types of income. For example, multiple category assets generate income in more than one category, and support assets either generate no identifiable income or contribute equally to the generation of all income to the taxpayer.

Temporary Regulation § 1.861-12T prescribes special characterization rules and adjustments for certain assets, i.e., primarily interests in nonaffiliated corporations, CFCs, and inventory. Additionally, Temporary Regulation § 1.861-11T provides, with respect to the treatment of loans between members of an affiliated group, that an indebtedness is not treated as an asset in the hands of the member lender. An exception to this rule exists in the case of indebtedness between a nonfinancial and affiliated financial corporation. In this case, the loan is treated as an asset in the hands of the financial lender and is characterized by reference to how the member-borrower allocates and apportions unrelated person interest expense.

Conclusion. Both Congress and the Treasury have emphasized the importance of the definition of ''interest expense'' and its allocation for the source of income rules, including valuation and characterization of assets. The allocation of interest expense for foreign-source income becomes more critical as corporations and individuals increasingly rely on financial leverage to fund business operations and growth. Also, as domestic corporations and other U.S. taxpayers enter into the global economy, more U.S. taxpayers will be affected by these rules.

[KF Sellers & DW Thomas, 1 J. Int'l Tax'n 152.]

"Rules for interest expense, derivative financial products" (1990). Temporary regulations set forth transition rules for allocation and apportionment of interest expense for purposes of the foreign tax credit, as well as rules concerning the treatment of financial products that alter the effective cost of borrowing.

Under Temporary Regulation § 1.861-9T(b), any expense or loss (to the extent deductible) incurred in a transaction or a series of transactions in which the taxpayer secures the use of funds for a period of time is subject to allocation and apportionment if the expense or loss is substantially incurred in consideration of the time value of money. The allocation and apportionment does not affect the characterization of the loss as capital or ordinary.

According to Temporary Regulation § 1.861-9T(b)(6)(i), derivative financial products (e.g., interest rate swaps, options, forwards, caps, and collars) that are part of such transactions can alter a taxpayer's effective cost of borrowing with respect to actual liabilities. Gains on such derivative instruments are defined by Temporary Regulation § 1.861-9T(b)(6)(ii) as the excess of the amounts properly taken into account under a financial product that alters the effective cost of borrowing over the amounts properly deductible in a taxable year. Loss refers to the excess of the amount properly allowed as a deduction under a financial product over the amount properly taken into income thereunder within a given taxable year.

Taxpayers other than financial services entities and dealers apportion losses on financial products in the same manner as interest expense, whether or not the product is identified as a liability hedge, according to Temporary Regulation § 1.861-

9T(b)(6)(iv). Gains reduce the taxpayer's total interest expense subject to apportionment, but only if the financial product is identified as a liability hedge. The reduction is accomplished by directly allocating interest expense to the income derived from the financial product.

[72 J. Tax'n 47.]

[c] Research and Experimental Expenditures

"RRA 1993 changes sourcing allocation percentages for research and experimental expenditures" (1993). RRA 1993 has amended Section 864(f)(1)(B) by changing the minimum allocation percentage for "qualified research and experimental expenditures" from 64 percent to 50 percent.

[4 J. Int'l Tax'n 477.]

"Taxpayers have a choice in research and development (R&D) expense allocation" (1992). Under Revenue Procedure 92-56, taxpayers may use, in allocating R&D expense between U.S.- and foreign-source income, either the Section 861 regulations or the expiring 64 percent rule of Section 864(f) for R&D expense incurred during the last six months of the first tax year beginning after August 1, 1991, and during the immediately succeeding tax year (the transition period). This article discusses the provisions of this revenue procedure concerning such allocations, including the allocation used where R&D is undertaken solely to meet legal requirements imposed by a political entity (i.e., the legal-requirement rules).

[77 J. Tax'n 178.]

[d] State, Local, and Foreign Taxes

IRS issues final regulations concerning allocation and apportionment of deduction for state income taxes. The IRS has issued final regulations relating to the allocation and apportionment of deductions for state income taxes in computing taxable income from sources inside and outside the United States.

[TD 8337, 1991-1 CB 92, Reg. § 1.861-8(e)(6).]

"Unresolved issues remain when apportioning state taxes to foreign income" (1990). Regulations under Section 861, concerning allocation and apportionment of expenses between foreign and domestic income, included two examples specifically pertaining to state income tax expense when they were issued in 1977. Regulation § 1.861-8(g), Examples (25) and (26), interrelated the tax consequences of state taxation with domestic- and foreign-source income for federal income tax purposes. However, these examples left unresolved a number of major issues in the context of interstate and international taxation. These issues were not resolved by the 1988 temporary regulations under Section 861. Instead, the temporary regulations provide taxpayers with more examples and still more issues.

Examples (25) and (26) of Temporary Regulation § 1.861-8T(g) are basically unchanged from the 1977 version. A modification indicates that for purposes of allocating the deduction for state income taxes, both federal and foreign-source taxable income are computed without taking into account such deduction. The temporary regulations also make clear that the examples merely illustrate reasonable methods of allocation and do not establish the methods used as substantive rules. On audits, the IRS has provided little leeway to change the suggested formula if the alternative method would revise the state tax allocation in the taxpayer's favor. These formulas are implicit, rather than stated in Examples (25) and (26).

Aggregate tax base. The allocation and apportionment regulations use the concept of aggregate tax base. Under this approach, the tax base for each state is added to the tax base of all the other states. An aggregate tax base is viable only if three conditions are met: (1) the starting point for each state's taxable income must be the Code; (2) taxable income may be adjusted by adding or subtracting enumerated items, but these adjustments must be minor in total; and (3) the adjusted taxable income must be apportioned by three equal factors; that is, property, payroll, and sales.

An aggregate tax base that is comparable to federal taxable income can rarely be achieved. Accordingly, the three preconditions present innumerable obstacles at a practical level to achieving a viable aggregate tax base.

The blended ratio. The allocation and apportionment examples in the regulations use a blended ratio that combines domestic-source income and the aggregate tax base for state income tax purposes. The formula produces results that are inherently defective. Misallocations occur in three primary areas: (1) U.S.-source income exceeds the aggregate state tax base; (2) negative U.S. income is more than the aggregate state tax base; and (3) foreign-source income is greater than the aggregate state tax base. TAM 8321008 addressed the first situation and did not allow the taxpayer to claim a negative state tax expense that yielded an increase to the foreign tax credit limitation. The preamble to the temporary regulations states that if aggregate state taxable income is not more than U.S.-source income, no state income tax expense is allocable to foreign-source income. The blended ratio can also cause adverse results to the taxpayer.

Conclusion. Allocations of state income taxes under the temporary regulations frequently produce inequitable results. A better approach is to allocate all such amounts as attributable to U.S.-source income. In 1990, bills in both the House Ways and Means Committee and the Senate Finance Committee were introduced that would mandate this treatment.

[R. Feinschreiber, 73 J. Tax'n 396.]

[e] Losses

In determining taxpayer's foreign tax credit, loss for worthlessness of foreign subsidiary's stock was allocated solely against taxpayer's foreign-source dividend income. In the 1970s, taxpayer formed a wholly owned Japanese subsidiary to compete with Japanese tool companies in Japan and worldwide. During its existence, taxpayer made an $8 million investment in the subsidiary before suspending its operations and liquidating its assets in 1981. The liquidation resulted in a worthless stock loss equal to the $8 million invested in the subsidiary. The IRS argued, and the Tax Court agreed, that this worthless stock loss was to be allocated by taxpayer solely against taxpayer's foreign-source dividend income in determining its foreign tax credit for 1981. Taxpayer appealed, arguing that the loss should be allocated to its worldwide income.

Held: Affirmed for the IRS. The international quality of taxpayer's investment in the subsidiary, based on its intent to use the subsidiary to protect its worldwide market share, is insufficient to support an allocation of the stock loss to its worldwide income. Moreover, under Regulation § 1.861-8 and the principles applied therein, the loss is related to the kind of income the investment was expected to yield for taxpayer, that is, foreign-source dividend income. The mere fact that the subsidiary never paid any dividends to taxpayer is irrelevant.

[Black & Decker Corp., 986 F2d 60, 71 AFTR2d 93-964, 93-1 USTC ¶ 50,125 (4th Cir. 1993).]

¶ 1.03 TRANSFER PRICING; REALLOCATIONS UNDER SECTION 482[3]

[1] Generally

Section 482 reallocation could not be made, since Spanish subsidiary's failure to pay royalties to U.S. parent was due to Spanish law. In 1968, when taxpayer formed its Spanish subsidiary, Spanish law provided broad authority for the regulation of payments from Spanish entities to residents of foreign countries. Governmental authorization was required before such payments could be made. Making payments without such authorization was a crime. In the Spanish government's approval letter allowing taxpayer to form a Spanish subsidiary the payment of royalties by the subsidiary to the U.S. parent for technical assistance was barred. The binding nature of this restriction was confirmed by taxpayer's Spanish legal counsel. Such counsel also advised that appeal of this payment restriction was futile. In 1985, economic changes in Spain presented an opportunity to revise the restriction and, in 1987, such restriction was removed. The IRS assessed deficiencies against taxpayer for years 1978 and 1979, which arose from its Section 482 reallocation of taxpayer's and its Spanish subsidiary's income to account for the nonpayment of royalties in those years. The Tax Court held that Section 482 could not be used to shift income where the payment of such income would be illegal under foreign law. The Tax Court also held that Section 482's blocked income provisions were inapplicable because, despite the restriction's removal in 1987, the restriction was a permanent (and not a temporary) prohibition when it was in effect.

Held: Affirmed for taxpayer. Here, the distortion of taxpayer's income by the nonpayment of royalties was due to the operation of foreign law and was not within taxpayer's control, as is required for readjustment under Section 482. Moreover, the Spanish subsidiary was not required to pay a disguised royalty through additional dividends when such payment would have been in violation of Spanish law. Finally, Section 482's "blocked income" provisions are inapplicable, as determined by the Tax Court, because the restriction on royalty payments as originally applied by the Spanish government was not intended to be temporary. Its subsequent removal was due to factors that arose after the years in issue.

[Procter & Gamble Co., 961 F2d 1255, 69 AFTR2d 92-1063, 92-1 USTC ¶ 50,209 (6th Cir. 1992).]

Under Section 482, royalty charged and transfer price paid between U.S. parent and foreign subsidiary each had independent significance; lack of sales and price guarantees prevented subsidiary from being a "contract manufacturer" of parent. Taxpayer formed an Irish subsidiary to manufacture contact lenses using taxpayer-parent's technology. Under the licensing agreement between taxpayer and the subsidiary, a royalty of 5 percent of the subsidiary's net sales (the maximum allowed under taypayer's agreement with the country of Ireland) was paid. Taxpayer was under no agreement to purchase the contact lenses manufactured by the Irish subsidiary, but, in fact, purchased between 50 and 60 percent of the subsidiary's output during the tax years before the court. The balance of the subsidiary's sales in these years were to overseas affiliates. Although there was no guaranteed contract price to be paid for lenses manufactured by the subsidiary, a sales price of $7.50 per lens was used for all sales in the relevant years. The IRS determined that the royalty charged and the intercompany transfer price paid required adjustment under Section 482 and proposed a combined adjustment of the royalty and transfer price that limited the Irish subsidiary's net profit before taxes to 20 percent of its sales. The Tax Court ruled first that a combined adjustment of the royalty and transfer price was improper and next that, while the transfer price did not require adjustment, the royalty should have been 20 percent of net sales despite taxpayer's agreement with Ireland.

　　Held: Affirmed for taxpayer. The subsidiary was not a "contract manufacturer" for taxpayer, as argued by the IRS, because taxpayer was not committed to purchase the subsidiary's entire production of contact lenses and there was no resale price guarantee for sales to taxpayer. Accordingly, the subsidiary was entitled to be paid more than a contract manufacturer's modest markup of its manufacturing costs. Moreover, this means there was a bona fide licensing of taxpayer's technology causing the royalty paid and transfer price charged to have independent significance. Under the "comparable uncontrolled price" method, the transfer price charged for the lenses did not require adjustment. However, as determined by the Tax Court, the royalty charged should have been 20 percent of the subsidiary's net sales.

[Bausch & Lomb, Inc., 933 F2d 1084, 67 AFTR2d 91-980, 91-1 USTC ¶ 50,244 (2d Cir. 1991).]

Since parent did not give foreign subsidiary any guarantees on the volume of products it would purchase nor the price it would pay for these products, subsidiary was not a "contract manufacturer" under Section 482. In 1975, taxpayer entered into a licensing agreement with its Singapore subsidiary under which it transferred to the subsidiary the right to use certain intangibles to make spare parts for taxpayer's products in exchange for the payment of a 2 percent royalty. Though there existed no agreement to do so, taxpayer purchased all of the subsidiary's output. Taxpayer paid the subsidiary taxpayer's catalog price less a 15 percent discount as established under a distributor agreement. The IRS determined that the subsidiary was a "contract manufacturer" for taxpayer and redetermined the subsidiary's income under Section 482 using the "cost-plus" method.

Held: For taxpayer. Taxpayer's Singapore subsidiary was not a "contract manufacturer" for taxpayer. There existed no guarantee that taxpayer would purchase the subsidiary's output and there was no certainty that taxpayer would pay any particular price for any output purchased. Accordingly, the subsidiary was entitled to more than a "cost-plus" payment for output sold to taxpayer. On the other hand, under the facts of this case, the royalty paid by the subsidiary and the purchase price paid by taxpayer were not arm's-length consideration. Thus, Section 482 adjustments of the royalty and transfer price were required.

[Sundstrand Corp., 96 TC 226 (1991).]

Reallocation of income from foreign parent to U.S. subsidiary was abuse of discretion. Taxpayer was the U.S. subsidiary of a foreign corporation. The foreign parent paid the subsidiary for R&D under a written contract using a cost-plus-fees formula. On the grounds that the payments were not made in an arm's-length transaction and were inadequate under Section 482, the IRS allocated additional fee income to the taxpayer.

Held: For taxpayer. The IRS abused its discretion because the fees charged by the subsidiary clearly reflected income. The IRS did not compare the taxpayer with similar companies and ignored its transactions with such companies. In addition, it used an improper salary multiplier in determining the fees that the taxpayer should have charged its parent.

[Westreco, Inc., 64 TCM 849, RIA TC Memo. ¶ 92,561 (1992).]

Estoppel did not prevent relitigation of allocation of income issues. Based on new evidence, the IRS sought reconsideration of an earlier Tax Court decision concerning reallocation of income between a parent corporation and its subsidiary. Taxpayer argued that the IRS was estopped from raising the issues.

Held: For the IRS (in part). The IRS was allowed to litigate the discount rate applied to the transfer prices, the charges for services rendered by taxpayer, and the arm's-length rate of interest on certain intercompany loans. The IRS could not relitigate the transfer prices that had been held to be reasonable and at arm's length.

[Sundstrand Corp., 63 TCM 2043, RIA TC Memo. ¶ 92,086 (1992).]

IRS issues intercompany transfer pricing temporary regulations. The IRS has issued temporary regulations relating to intercompany transfer pricing under Section 482. The regulations reflect TRA 1986, which amended Section 482 to require that consideration for intangible property transferred in controlled transaction be commensurate with the income attributable to the intangible.

[TD 8470, 1993-10 IRB 5, Temp. Reg. §§ 1.482-OT–1.482-7T.]

IRS issues proposed regulations concerning intercompany transfer pricing. The IRS has issued proposed income tax regulations relating to intercompany transfer pricing and cost sharing under Section 482. The proposed regulations reflect TRA 1986, which amended Section 482 to require that consideration for intangible property be commensurate with the income attributable to the intangible.

[INTL-372-88, INTL-401-88, 1992-1CB 1164; Prop. Reg. §§ 1.482-1, 1.482-2.]

"Better comparable analysis persuades Tax Court in *Westreco*" (1993). The significance of cross-border services involving related parties was highlighted by the Tax Court's 1992 memorandum decision in *Westreco, Inc*. The decision provides guidance regarding, among other things, methods that may be used to value cross-border services between related parties and what underlying empirical data will be considered by the Tax Court to be reliable and reasonable. In addition, *Westreco* decided certain procedural issues regarding a taxpayer's burden of proof in Section 482 cases that may significantly affect how the IRS international examiners develop cases at the audit level.

The authors of this article first review the facts of *Westreco*, focusing on the nature and terms of the contracts involved. Thereafter, they examine the IRS's initial audit position and Westreco's recomputation of its fee using a different salary multiplier than used by the IRS on audit. The IRS's trial position is also discussed and critiqued.

In the next section of this article, the authors focus on the Tax Court's reasoning and analysis of the issues presented. The authors provide specific discussion and commentary on the Tax Court's position on the valuation of integral services under Section 482, the functional analysis applied to the parties to the transaction, the meaning and determination of "comparable" companies, and certain procedural issues.

The authors conclude that because the Tax Court issued *Westreco* as a memorandum decision its value is uncertain. Nevertheless, it provides a good general framework for comparable company analysis in determining the validity of a transfer pricing policy. While limited to the area of services, the standards provided should be fairly similar for tangible and intangible property.

[MM Levey & CJ Schoen, 4 J. Int'l Tax'n 39.]

"Customs planning may avoid conflict with IRS transfer pricing rules" (1993). The Customs law and the income tax law pull the importer-taxpayer in opposite directions. Although the objectives of both the Customs Service and the IRS are identical—to collect revenue—the demands they make on the importer-taxpayer contradict each other.

The Customs Service wants the price paid for imported merchandise at the highest possible level, since the higher the value, the greater the duty collected. The IRS wants to ensure that transfer prices for inbound goods will be at the lowest justifiable level in order to maximize the taxable profit in the subsequent resale or other transfer in the United States. Importer-taxpayers get the best of both worlds when they bring in goods at a low dutiable value for Customs purposes if they can revalue the inventory basis to compute taxable profit.

The tax law recognizes these tensions. Under Section 1059A, the inventory cost for goods imported into the United States from a related party may not exceed the amount of such costs in computing Customs value. Nevertheless, the regulations under this section implicitly acknowledge that the Customs value may exclude cost elements generally taken into account in calculating inventory basis. This notion of separately allocated "off-invoice" costs creates opportunities in Customs planning.

The author first discusses the Customs valuation rules and their treatment of related-party transactions. Next, he explains the required additions to invoice price for Customs purposes. Thereafter, he explains the tax adjustments for inventory basis, including the required additions to Customs value and the treatment of commissions and assists. Beneficial use of the uniform capitalization rules for inclusion of inventory costs is then addressed.

The author concludes that any advice to an importing taxpayer affected by Section 1059A must begin with an understanding of what is dutiable under the Customs laws. Additionally, such taxpayers must avoid the "valuation vise," which can occur when the IRS adjusts the inventory basis of imported merchandise downward if it sees the transfer price as too high. This can occur despite earlier approval by Customs of the price as the basis for dutiable value.

[MK Neville, Jr., 4 J. Int'l Tax'n 70.]

"Intercompany transfer pricing: how Section 482 affects international allocations" (1993). Section 482 authorizes the IRS to reallocate items of gross income among related taxpayers. This section is usually aimed by the IRS at non-arm's-length transactions that shift profit from a U.S. taxpayer to a foreign affiliate outside the U.S. taxing jurisdiction. Its basic goal is to make a U.S. entity pay tax on net income that fairly reflects its own activities. In 1993, the IRS issued temporary and proposed regulations on intercompany transfer pricing and related penalties. This article concerns Section 482 and the regulations promulgated thereunder, as well as the problems they have created for taxpayers with foreign affiliates.

After briefly noting the basic aspects of Section 482, the authors discuss the rules governing specific transactions affected by Section 482 reallocations (i.e., interest payments, payments for services rendered, rent paid on tangible personal property, payments for the use of intangible property, and sales of goods). Next, the authors examine the determination of an arm's-length price under various methods.

A more extensive and detailed analysis is then provided for the 1992 proposed regulations on intercompany pricing and cost sharing, which seek to revise the methods used to determine an arm's-length price in light of the enactment of the "commensurate with income" standard in TRA 1986. Each of the provisions of the proposed regulations is explained and given critical commentary. The authors also discuss the special intercompany pricing rules for foreign sales corporations and domestic international sales corporations.

The authors go on to explore the interaction of the Section 482 adjustments and the foreign tax credit. Consideration is given to the consequences of Section 482 adjustments resulting in a constructive dividend. The effect of a foreign country's currency and payment of dividend restrictions on the operation of Section 482 is also considered.

In the last section of this article, the authors consider the approaches taken by the IRS and the courts in their application of Section 482. The authors conclude this article with a brief discussion of the interaction of Section 482 and the Code's nonrecognition provisions, the special Puerto Rican pricing rules, and the new regulations on application of the penalty provisions in this area.

[US Tax'n Int'l Operations ¶ 7521.]

"IRS seeks to reverse *Procter & Gamble* result with Section 482 proposed regulations" (1993). In November 1992, the IRS allowed its deadline to petition the U.S. Supreme Court for review of the Sixth Circuit's decision in *Procter & Gamble* (1992) to expire. The case involved the IRS's ability to allocate income under Section 482 where payment of the proposed allocation is prohibited by foreign law.

Although the court upheld the taxpayer's argument that the allocation was improper, the IRS continues its efforts to negate the effect of the decision in several other cases before the Tax Court and in the proposed regulations under Section 482 issued in January 1993.

[MM Levey & JP Clancy, 4 J. Int'l Tax'n 137.]

"New Section 482 regulations still favor the comparable profits method (CPM)" (1993). The transfer pricing regulatory package, issued in 1993, contains specific methods for determining an arm's-length charge for both tangible and intangible property transfers. The authors of this article first discuss the provisions of the new temporary regulations on transfers of tangible property. The following methods, set forth in the regulations, are discussed: the comparable uncontrolled price method, the resale price method, the cost-plus method, and other acceptable methods (including the profit-split method). In the course of their discussion, the authors compare the old and new regulations and discuss the implications of the changes made.

Next, the authors examine the new temporary regulations governing the pricing of intangible property. Despite changes made to the prior regulations, most taxpayers will still be forced into using the CPM analysis for the purpose of determining an acceptable licensing or transfer fee. This method and other methods prescribed by the regulations for determining an arm's-length transfer price (i.e., the comparable uncontrolled transaction method and other "reasonable" methods) are given specific discussion and critical commentary. Aspects of the CPM are then detailed, in conjunction with the authors' explanation of its six-step process. Also discussed are the concepts of "tested party," "business segment," "comparable companies," and "profit level indicators."

The authors' final comments on the temporary regulations cover the liberalization of the exceptions to the periodic adjustment requirements, the restatement of the developer-assister rules, and the rules addressing the form of a transfer of intangibles and the consideration paid therefor. The authors conclude that the temporary regulations under Section 482 represent an improvement over those proposed in 1992. Nevertheless, the IRS has not gone as far as it might have to provide flexibility and allow taxpayers to avoid the CPM, particularly for intangible property transfers. Practitioners must hope that the prescribed methods are applied in a way that practical solutions will be allowed.

[MM Levey, RR O'Haver & JP Clancy, 4 J. Int'l Tax'n 202.]

"New Section 482 regulations warn taxpayers to start gathering the data" (1993). In 1993, the IRS issued the most recent version of the Section 482 proposed and temporary regulations, along with proposed regulations under the transfer pricing–related penalty provisions of Section 6662(e). In this first part of a two-part article, the general principles of the regulations and their standards of comparability are analyzed.

First, in discussing the general principles, the authors examine the best method rule, which governs the selection of transfer pricing methods (TPMs) under the new temporary regulations. In so doing, they also discuss the scope of IRS review provisions in the regulations. Other provisions of the regulations, such as those concerning the same-year data requirement and the safe harbor for small taxpayers, are also explored.

Next, the authors review the regulations' standards of comparability, which are used to provide a reasonable benchmark to establish an arm's-length transfer price. Each standard is specifically discussed, along with the factors that must be considered (including function, risk, contractual terms, and economic conditions), the regulations' omission of company size as a factor, and the nature of the property and services offered. Thereafter, the authors consider certain allowable adjustments to these factors, such as those needed to reflect the differences between controlled and uncontrolled transactions. The regulations' "market strategy" rule, as well as the "location savings" and isolated transaction provisions, are also discussed.

The authors conclude that, while the general principles of the temporary regulations appear to provide guidance for arm's-length pricing, the import of these rules is deceiving. The rules require finite definitions of the functions, risks, and obligations of the parties, precise empirical and factual support for all aspects of the transaction, and documentation.

[MM Levey, RR O'Haver & JP Clancy, 4 J. Int'l Tax'n 148.]

"New transfer pricing regulations adhere more closely to an arm's-length standard" (1993). In 1993 temporary and additional proposed regulations under Section 482 were published. The temporary regulations require taxpayers to increase contemporaneous documentation of their TPMs, and reward such behavior with additional flexibility in establishing and using such methods. That "requirement/ reward" theme is also reflected in the new proposed regulations.

The authors first establish the background for these regulations, including a discussion of prior developments such as the White Paper, the advance pricing agreement (APA) procedures, court decisions, and the 1992 proposed regulations. Thereafter, they examine the provisions of the 1993 regulations, starting with the general rules of comparability and the five factors that are used for pricing comparisons. Other general concepts and principles set forth in the regulations are then addressed, including the "best method" rule, the "arm's-length range," compensating adjustments allowing taxpayers to correct pricing errors, the use of multiyear pricing data, and the small taxpayer safe harbor.

Next, the authors explore the regulations' provisions on allowable pricing methods for intangibles, including the comparable uncontrolled transaction method, the CPM, and other acceptable methods, as well as application of the commensurate with income rule to these methods. The allowable methods for tangibles are then addressed. Included therein is a discussion of the CUP method, the RPM, and the cost-plus method.

The authors then explore the regulations' approach to several areas of recognized abuse. These areas include the transfer of intangibles to foreign manufacturing subsidiaries by U.S. parents, the treatment of profits associated with location savings, prices associated with a market share strategy, and payments that are prevented owing to foreign legal restrictions (e.g., the Ninth Circuit's 1992 decision in *Procter & Gamble Co.*). Last, the authors discuss application of the Section 6662 accuracy-related penalty in this area and its special definition of "good faith" for Section 482 misstatements.

The authors conclude that the new regulations provide a much more palatable blend of uncertainty, incentive, and punishment than the 1992 proposed regulations did. A major purpose of the new regulations is to require taxpayers to accurately determine and document their transfer prices in the year their transactions occur, rather than when the IRS challenges the prices on audit or in court. Many methods described in the regulations require contemporaneous documentation, contemporaneous written agreements, and filing of timely elections. In all cases, taxpayers will benefit from additional transfer price planning. In many cases, written agreements relating to the functions to be performed and to the risks to be borne by each party to a controlled transition will be required in order to avoid larger Section 482 allocations and potentially crippling penalties.

Since the temporary regulations are effective, it is most important that taxpayers finally decide whether to obtain an advance ruling from the IRS, find true comparables, or engage an economist with access to a relevant data base to otherwise determine transfer prices in accordance with the new methods.

[PA Glicklich & SB Goldstein, 78 J. Tax'n 306.]

"Risk identification is a key component to a useful functional analysis" (1993). Consistent with the IRS announcements and proposed regulations, the 1993 temporary regulations under Section 482 highlight the importance of a functional analysis in determinining an arm's-length transfer price under any regulatory method. A crucial first step in such an analysis is examination of the economically significant functions performed, risks assumed, and assets used by each party to the transaction.

While the focus is often on actual "functions" performed, the importance of a detailed analysis of the relative risks assumed by each party should not be underestimated. These risks often account for key differences between the taxpayer's business and the comparable benchmark. In addition, risk analysis is central to each of the regulatory pricing methods. This article does not discuss the difficult issue of determining the appropriate methods for quantifying risk.

The authors first discuss the purpose of this risk analysis. Thereafter, they address the economic foundations or theory thereunder. The regulatory foundation of the risk analysis is then examined. Next, the authors explore, in particular, risk assessment under a risk analysis. Included within this discussion is an examination of inventory-related risks, supply-related risks (including key supplier and cost volatility factors), transactional risks (including those relating to direct and indirect foreign currency problems, commerical risk, product return risk, and warranty/product liability risks), and other market-related risks.

After discussing documentation of risk, the authors conclude that taxpayers must contemporaneously document the allocation of business risks and periodically review and update the documentation. An evaluation of relevant risks is essential for a thorough functional analysis and is a pervasive component of a taxpayer's defense in an audit.

[MM Levey & GE Hurowitz, 4 J. Int'l Tax'n 284.]

"Settlements in Maquiladora cases contain planning guidance" (1993). Two cases involving Mexican Maquiladora operations with significant cross-border Section 482 issues were recently settled at the IRS appeals level. The audit positions taken by the IRS in these cases illustrate typical issues currently raised, as well as the aggressive nature in which they are pursued, especially with Maquiladora operations. The actions of the Appeals Officer, however, offer some encouragement that the IRS adheres to established law in this area. The cases were *El Paso Maquila Sales Co.* and *Elamex Services, Inc.*

The authors first discuss the facts of the Maquiladora operations in these two cases. Thereafter, they discuss the assessments against the U.S. subsidiary involved in these cases as to interest income, rental income, and adjustments to the cost of goods sold. Next, the assessments against the parent, a British Virgin Islands corporation, are examined on the issue of ECI. The resolution of these cases, through settlement, is then addressed.

Planning considerations arising from the issues raised by the IRS in these cases and the manner in which they were resolved are then explored. The authors conclude that it is likely that cross-border transactions involving related parties will continue to be closely scrutinized for arm's-length transactions. In the Maquiladora-type transaction where equipment is provided at no charge, the IRS will likely impute income to the U.S. related party under Section 1059A. Where Section 482 will not support adjustments, the IRS will make adjustments under other sections such as Sections 162 and 882 and attach transactions under ECI or treaty permanent establishment theories. Future cross-border transactions should be carefully planned and should include the assumption that the transaction will be reviewed on audit. An advance transfer pricing policy should be considered.

[MM Levey & PR Gordon, 4 J. Int'l Tax'n 84.]

"Temporary and proposed regulations under Sections 482 and 6662 on intercompany transfer pricing and related penalties" (1993). In January 1993, temporary and proposed regulations were issued under Sections 482 and 6662. These regulations employ a more flexible approach to transfer pricing than the former proposed regulations, especially for transfers of tangible assets, and will allow taxpayers and the IRS greater freedom to tailor pricing methodologies to the particular facts and circumstances of a case. The cost of this greater flexibility is the need for increased taxpayer compliance. Sanctions for noncompliance include penalties and the denial of the regulations' benefits. APAs are available to provide taxpayers with greater certainty in this area.

The authors begin their article with a general discussion and a comparison between the old and new sets of regulations. New rules developed in response to major cases in this area are noted. Thereafter, the authors commence their analysis of the regulations. They first examine allocation of income and deductions under the regulations, including the new "best method" rule, the concept of comparability, the scope of IRS review, the making of collateral adjustments, and the safe harbor election for small taxpayers. Next, they specifically examine the regulations' provisions concerning the transfer of tangible property and the transfer of intangible property. Full discussion is provided of the following regulation methods: the CPM, the profit-split methods, and certain special methods and restrictions. Last, the authors discuss the Section 482–related provisions of the proposed regulations on the Section 6662 accuracy-related penalty and the regulations' effective date provisions.

[MF Patton, PD Quick & BJ Hawkins, US Tax'n Int'l Operations ¶ 7523.]

"The role of economic analysis in transfer pricing compliance, audits, and litigation" (1993). Two very different roles for economic analysis can arise in transfer pricing compliance, audits, and litigation. An economist may be involved as an expert witness or as an integrated member of the taxpayer's defense team. In this article, the author examines the role of the economist in an IRS intercompany transfer pricing inquiry. She first discusses the role of an economist who is an expert witness. Thereafter, she fully explores the role of an economist as a defense team member, that is, as an inside expert.

Thereafter, the author discusses the use of the economist's expertise before an audit (to ensure better compliance with the tax law) and during an audit to minimize taxpayer losses and penalties. The scope of the beneficial impact of such use and the areas that are affected by this impact are then addressed. Last, the author explores the use of the economist's expertise during the IRS appeals process and litigation, as well as during competent authority procedures.

[VL Amerkhail, US Tax'n Int'l Operations ¶ 7524.]

"Allocating exchange rate risk has tax effects for multinationals"(1992). A key element in a multinational firm's transfer pricing policy is which of the related entities will bear foreign exchange risk. The more risk an entity bears, the higher its profit should be. Typically, the tax planning process focuses exclusively on the currency in which the intercompany transaction will be invoiced. If the subsidiary is invoiced in its local currency, it is too often concluded that its foreign exchange exposure is automatically reduced or eliminated. A company's foreign exchange exposure, however, is more than transaction exposure. Foreign exchange exposure is determined by numerous factors, only one of which is the multinational's invoicing strategy. Construction of an intercompany pricing policy, which includes foreign exchange planning, must take into account all of these factors.

A proper definition of "exchange rate exposure" is broader than the concept of transaction exposure. In general, a firm faces foreign exchange exposure if changes in its profits are correlated with changes in the exchange rate. A company can be exposed to exchange rate fluctuations though none of its invoices are denominated in a foreign currency. Consequently, if a multinational desires to structure its transfer pricing policy to limit the subsidiary's exchange exposure and, thus, minimize profit variability, it must look beyond the direct exchange rate effect of the intercompany transaction. The choice of which currency should be used to invoice intercompany transactions must be viewed in terms of the entire exchange exposure of the subsidiary. Under certain circumstances, the subsidiary's exchange exposure may be reduced if the transfer price is denominated in currency other than the subsidiary's local currency.

The article concludes with a detailed tax planning example.

[BJ Cody, 3 J. Int'l Tax'n 156.]

"Application of Section 482 proposed regulations to transfers of intangibles is likely to create problems" (1992). In 1992, extremely complicated proposed regulations under Section 482 were issued. They focus on transfers of tangible and intangible property and introduce the comparable profit interval (CPI) concept.

The authors provide an overview of the proposed regulations, focusing on the three proposed methods of determining an acceptable transfer price for intangible property, i.e., the matching transaction method (MTM), the comparable adjustable transaction (CAT) method, and the CPM. The retention and expansion of the periodic adjustment concept of the Section 482 White Paper, by the proposed regulations in the "multiyear transfer" rules, is also discussed.

In the next section of the article, the authors explain application of the CPM. A step-by-step analysis is provided, which includes the determination of (1) the party to be tested; (2) the applicable business classification; (3) the constructive operating incomes; (4) the appropriate CPI; (5) the appropriate point interval; and (6) the transfer price.

The authors discuss some of the problems that may be encountered under the proposed regulations, focusing principally on the selection of comparable companies and the treatment of "service" and trading companies. The failure of the proposed regulations to recognize the importance of certain nontransfer-price "events" that can affect performance is also examined. Thereafter, the authors compare the CPM and the CAT method, specifically with regard to the impracticality of the proposed regulations' enhanced importance of the CPM and the lack of priority given the CAT method. The problems and difficulties that can arise because of this are explored. Next, the proposed regulations' limitation on the comparable profit split is discussed, both in terms of its application and complications.

The authors address the periodic adjustment rules, focusing on the exceptions provided in the proposed regulations as a response to the severe criticism of the "periodic adjustment" requirement set forth in the Section 482 White Paper. The authors address the difficult issues that may arise under the proposed regulations with regard to transfers of tangible property and the performance of services where an intangible property component may be included in the property or services transfer. Examples are given to illustrate these problematical issues.

The authors conclude that the Section 482 proposed regulations continue the evolution of transfer pricing. However, it is important for both the IRS and taxpayers to realize that statistics cannot be used blindly. This is particularly true when there is a broad range of constructed operating incomes. In such cases, there may be economic reasons justifying a result that is more appropriate than what would result under a purely statistical approach.

[MM Levey, RR O'Haver & JP Clancy, 77 J. Tax'n 308.]

"Claims Court holds no Section 482 charge for group market planning and pricing policy" (1992). How far can a U.S. parent corporation go in managing the affairs of a foreign corporation without subjecting itself to U.S. income tax on a portion of the income of the foreign subsidiary under Section 482? Can it provide group market planning and pricing policy to its vertical integrated subsidiaries and see to the execution of such group policy by its senior executives who sit on the boards of directors of the vertically integrated subsidiaries? This is the ultimate question raised by the 1991 Claims Court decision, *Merck & Co.*, which is discussed in this article.

[JE McDermott, Jr., 2 J. Int'l Tax'n 314.]

"IRS guidelines for cost-sharing arrangements provide insufficient certainty" **(1992).** Proposed regulations under Section 482 include rules for "qualified cost-sharing arrangements" (QCSAs), the sole alternative to the controversial transfer pricing rules applicable to intragroup transfers of intangibles.

In discussing the proposed regulations, the author provides a background for this area. He discusses treatment under the proposed regulations in absence of cost sharing, what is cost sharing, and prior developments in this area. The author focuses specifically on the proposed regulations. He discusses the cost-sharing rule thereunder, the requirements for QCSAs, and the character of payments pursuant to a QCSA. A table of the potential benefits and detriments of cost sharing is set forth in the article.

The author examines the "eligible participant" requirements under the proposed regulations, including the inclusion of cost-sharing subgroups and the effect of ineligibility of a participant in the QCSA. The scope of a QCSA is discussed in-depth.

Finally, other requirements and provisions of the proposed regulations are discussed. These include: (1) specification of a participant's legally enforceable interest in an intangible; (2) costs covered by the QCSA; (3) the determination of cost shares of participants; (4) the limited safe harbor for nonsubstantially disproportionate cost/income ratios among participants; (5) the deemed partial transfer for substantially disproportionate cost/income ratios; (6) the computation of cost/income ratios; (7) computation of a participant's "average cost shares" and "average operating incomes"; (7) the grossly disproportionate test for cost/income ratios; (8) the treatment of buy-in and buy-out payments; (9) the administrative requirements that assure that the arrangement is a QCSA and that a participant is an eligible participant; and (10) the desirability of developing an international standard for cost-sharing arrangements.

The author concludes that the proposed regulations create a variety of "moving target" uncertainties for taxpayers desiring to share costs. Nevertheless, the cost-sharing alternative should be seriously considered by taxpayers conducting business within and outside the United States. While the proposed regulations do not provide the kind of certainty achievable through an advance agreement with the IRS, perhaps that merely suggests the hidden agenda of the drafters. In the absence of an advance agreement, it is hoped that the IRS National Office will coordinate audit adjustments to provide some uniformity of result among the various IRS Districts and to facilitate operation of the mutual agreement mechanism to resolve tax issues that affect taxpayers operating in different jurisdictions.

Cost-sharing arrangements will be most attractive to U.S.-based multinationals, but they will experience problems in the absence of a private ruling. Foreign-based multinationals will continue to have more alternatives, including structuring acquisitions to avoid the necessity of cost-sharing arrangements, or entering into contract manufacturing arrangements with their U.S. affiliates. Foreign-based multinationals that do not enter into cost-sharing arrangements also will have practical advantages over their U.S.-based competitors, including fewer "U.S. participants," smaller cost-share adjustments, and fewer U.S. tax issues from any required buy-ins or buy-outs.

[PA Glicklich, 77 J. Tax'n 42.]

"No Section 482 allocation where foreign law prohibited payments" (1992). In the 1992 case of *Procter & Gamble Co.*, the Sixth Circuit held that a foreign law prohibition on payments from a subsidiary to its parent prevented the IRS from allocating income under Section 482. Since any income distortion was not caused by the taxpayer's control of its subsidiaries, allocation under Section 482 was unwarranted.

[77 J. Tax'n 50.]

"Objective test of transfer pricing proposed regulations require subjective determinations" (1992). Long-awaited proposed regulations provide guidance on the "commensurate with income" standard added to Section 482 by TRA 1986. Under that standard, income from the transfer of intangible property between controlled parties must be commensurate with the income attributable to the intangible. Detailed new rules would apply the standard to the transfer of intangible property and to cost-sharing arrangements. The commensurate with income standard is also proposed to apply to transfers of tangible property. Further, certain of the general rules of application of the current Section 482 regulations are modified.

The proposed regulations provide new objective tests in determining transfer prices for tangible and intangible property. Each objective test will require subjective determinations based on information that often will be difficult (if not impossible) to obtain. It is not yet clear whether the proposed regulations will achieve the certainty of result sought or will merely have the effect of creating or shifting, rather than resolving, transfer pricing controversies between taxpayers and the IRS.

[AW Granwell & K Klein, 76 J. Tax'n 308.]

"Practical problems remain under Section 482 proposed regulations—part I" (1992). Recently the IRS issued proposed regulations under Section 482. These proposals focus principally on the transfer of tangible and intangible property, the introduction of the CPI concept, and cost-sharing arrangements.

Part I of this article addresses transfers of intangible property and the new CPI concept. Part II addresses cost-sharing arrangements for intangible property, transfers of tangible property, and certain ancillary matters. The proposed regulations under Section 482 focus on transfers of intangible property. Three new methods of ascertaining the appropriate transfer prices or royalty rates under the arm's-length standard are set forth. The three proposed methods of determining an acceptable transfer price for intangible property, in order of priority, are the MTM, the CAT method, and the CPM.

Under the MTM, the appropriate transfer price is determined by reference to transfers of the same intangible under similar economic conditions and contractual terms. This method contemplates transfers of the "identical" intangible property, but permits variations in such things as geographic rights, product limitations, duration of the transferee's rights, and level of technical assistance provided. These variations must be accounted for by adjustments to reflect the amounts that unrelated parties would have charged. A transaction will be "matching" only if the differences in contractual terms and economic conditions have a minor effect on the consideration charged in the uncontrolled transaction and that effect is definite and precisely determinable. If these requirements are not satisfied, the MTM cannot be used.

The CAT method will apply whenever the identified uncontrolled transaction is similar, but not identical, to the taxpayer's transaction or there are more than minor differences in contractual terms or economic conditions between the controlled and uncontrolled transactions. This method requires two separate economic analyses to arrive at an arm's-length consideration because any transfer price derived from a similar transaction is acceptable only if it results in an operating profit for the tested party that falls within the CPI, discussed below. A taxpayer must first examine the similar transaction to identify the differences between it and the controlled transaction and quantify the effect of those differences on the consideration charged. Thereafter, the taxpayer must construct the CPI and determine whether the transfer price resulting from the comparability analysis produces operating profit within that interval.

In applying the CAT method, the uncontrolled transaction need only be sufficiently similar so that the effect of any material differences can be determined with reasonable accuracy. Similar to the MTM, the value of these differences must be reflected in adjustments to the purchase price. Those adjustments must reflect the amount the parties to the uncontrolled transfer would have charged had the terms of that transaction been the same as those of the controlled transfer. If more than one comparable transaction is identified, the most similar transaction must be used as the comparable in applying this method.

The cornerstone of the new proposed regulatory scheme is the CPI. This concept is applied to transfers of intangible property through the application of the CPM. This method focuses on the operating profit of the parties to an intangible transaction, rather than on any similar transactions involving unrelated parties. Adjusting for differences in assets and asset-related income and expenses, the CPI is the range of operating profits that the tested party would have earned had its economic performance matched that of companies performing similar functions. The tested party for this purpose is the party to the controlled transfer whose operating income can be verified with the most reliable data and the fewest and most accurate adjustments. For intangible transfers, this is most likely the licensee.

The proposed regulations measure economic performance for the purpose of this analysis by reference to the "profit level indicators" of companies similar to the tested party. These indicators refer generally to such financial measures as rates of return on assets (i.e., operating income over assets), margins such as operating income to sales, gross income to operating expenses (i.e., the Berry Ratio), and other economic relationships that provide reliable bases for splitting profits. These profit-splitting methods, known as comparable profit splits, must be derived from the combined operating income of uncontrolled taxpayers that entered transactions and performed functions similar to those of the members of the group of controlled taxpayers. The proposed regulations set forth two methods for determining comparable profit splits, the residual method and the overall profit split, which are explained by the authors.

When the CPM applies, the proposed regulations construct an incentive-based regimen for determining any tax adjustment that the IRS might impose. If the arm's-length consideration charged by the parties results in profits to the tested party that fall within the CPI, then the transaction will generally be treated as arm's-length and no adjustment will be proposed. If the controlled transaction produces profits that are outside, but close to, the interval, then the District Director has the discretion to limit the appropriate adjustment under Section 482 to one that brings the tested party's operating income within the interval, but not to the most appropriate point therein. If the operating income of the tested party is substantially outside the interval, then the adjustment will likely be one that brings the tested party's operating income to the most appropriate point (i.e., the "central tendency" of the result defining the interval) within the interval. "Operating income" is the net income before the interest and income taxes.

The authors discuss each step of the six-step process required by the CPM. These steps are selecting the tested party, determining the applicable business classification, computing constructive operating income, determining the appropriate CPI, determining the appropriate point interval, and determining the transfer price.

Part I of the article concludes with a discussion of the practicality of the proposed regulations.

[MM Levey, RR O'Haver & JP Clancy, 2 J. Int'l Tax'n 325.]

"Practical problems remain under Section 482 proposed regulations—part II" (1992). The proposed regulations significantly change the tangible property provisions of the existing regulations in an effort to conform with the newly proposed intangible-property rules. In general, the CPI is applied to verify the results of the RPM, cost-plus method, or any "fourth" method of determining transfer prices for tangible property. Transfer prices determined under these methods are not arm's length unless the operating profit of the tested party falls within the CPI.

The proposed amendments change the priority of TPMs. Although the CUP method remains preferred for tangible property, the RPM and cost-plus method now have equal priority. If both could apply, the one that relies on the most complete and accurate data, and requires the fewest and most readily quantifiable adjustments, should be used.

When none of the three specified methods apply, Proposed Regulation § 1.482-

2(e)(iv) allows as a "fourth method," any method that is reasonable under the facts and circumstances, provided that the transfer price results in operating profit for the tested party that falls within the CPI. The primary impact of the CPI is that it shifts the transfer pricing inquiry from an analysis of similar uncontrolled transactions to an examination of the financial performance of comparable uncontrolled companies. Net operating margins have been the IRS's primary concern over the past few years in auditing U.S. distribution affiliates of foreign multinationals. Thus, for transfers of tangible property, the IRS has accomplished its apparent goal of focusing on net operating margins instead of gross profit margins, as required under the current regulatory approach.

The proposed rules, as they apply to U.S. affiliates of foreign multinationals, fail to effectively coordinate with the Section 6038A regulations, which impose stringent reporting and record-keeping requirements on U.S. affiliates of foreign multinationals and foreign multinationals doing business in the United States. Perhaps the most controversial rule is the requirement that these companies maintain product line or industry segment profit and loss statements, to be provided to the IRS upon request.

The provisions governing cost sharing largely incorporate the requirements set forth in the White Paper for recognition of the arrangement for tax purposes. The arrangement will qualify if it meets the following requirements:

1. It includes at least two eligible participants.
2. It is recorded in writing contemporaneously with the formation of the arrangement.
3. It provides for sharing among eligible participants of the costs and risks of developing one or more intangibles in return for specified interests in those intangibles.
4. It reflects a reasonable effort to share the costs and risks of development in proportion to the benefits each participant expects to receive from the arrangement.
5. It meets administrative requirements.

Existing cost-sharing arrangements that were bona fide under the old regulations will be qualified arrangements under the new rules if conforming amendments are made within one year after final regulations are published in the Federal Register.

Whether costs are shared proportionately to anticipated benefits will be determined from the facts and circumstances, as discussed by the authors.

The administrative provisions of the proposed regulations add new reporting and record-keeping requirements for participants in a cost-sharing arrangement. These requirements are in addition to any reporting required under Sections 6038 and 6038A. Proposed Regulation § 1.482-2(g)(6)(iii) specifies the material provisions of an arrangement. The proposed cost-sharing provisions liberalize some recommendations of the White Paper. Gone is the troubling geographic-rights assignment requirement deemed so necessary in the White Paper. Also eliminated is the

White Paper's strict requirement that participants be limited to manufacturing affiliates. Perhaps the most welcome change is the allowance of cost-sharing arrangements for developing marketing intangibles. The proposed regulations also appear to have eliminated the need to consider the going-concern value of research facilities in structuring a buy-in payment. Another significant development is that affiliates using contract manufacturer agreements for the use of intangibles may participate in the arrangement.

The proposed regulations also seem to allow participants to use the research intangibles by licensing them to related parties, suggesting only that an intangible is not used in a trade or business if a substantial purpose for participating is to transfer the intangible to an uncontrolled taxpayer. These provisions appear to recognize the role intangibles may play in choosing between high and low tax jurisdictions outside of the United States.

The proposed regulations present major implementation issues, however. Possibly the most important issue in structuring a cost-sharing arrangement is the cost-sharing formula or method. The proposals require that the method allocate costs in proportion to anticipated benefits, which seems reasonable. Proposed Regulation § 1.482-2(g)(2)(ii) then provides that the method will be presumed unacceptable if the cost/income ratio of the U.S. party is grossly disproportionate to the combined ratio of the other parties to the arrangement.

The proposed regulations specify that the cost/income ratio refers to the average cost of developing intangible property divided by the average operating income of the participant attributable to intangibles developed under the arrangement. The average is computed using data from the current and the two preceding years. Problems seen by the authors are addressed, including those with the three-year averaging period, the cost/income ratio comparison, the use of average operating income in the method-testing presumption, and several specific definitions, including the definition of ''related-intangible development.''

Other troubling provisions concern the timing of allocations and the related computation of interests charges. Those provisions suggest that an allocation under a cost-sharing method must be included in income for the taxable year under review, even if the costs to be allocated were included in the prior taxable year. Appropriate interest adjustments must be made to account for prior years' cost allocations. The year under review appears to mean the year under examination by an IRS agent. This suggests that an international examiner who finds a problem with the formula can make retroactive adjustments in the year under examination that reallocate costs deducted by the participants in earlier years. It also suggests that these adjustments can be made even if the assessment period for those years is closed because the examiner logically would otherwise simply make the adjustment in the earlier open year. The apparent result is that the assessment period can never expire for reallocations of research costs where the cost-sharing method is inappropriate because the U.S. participant's cost/income ratio is merely disproportionate, rather than substantially or grossly disproportionate. This is, of course, contrary to the provisions of Section 6501, not to mention being an extremely broad, and perhaps unwarranted, reading of Section 482. It also creates double taxation problems for the foreign participants in the arrangement.

Despite some rather significant problems, cost sharing offers the advantage of enabling the transfer of intangibles to foreign affiliates without the risk of Section 482 adjustments. It may also provide the only reasonable means of avoiding application of the CPI analysis to transfers of intangible property, as matching transactions may be difficult to find.

[MM Levey, RR O'Haver & JP Clancy, 3 J. Int'l Tax'n 5.]

"Proposed cost-sharing regulations could change result in *Ciba-Geigy*" (1992). How should a multinational group determine intercompany ownership of geographical or other interests in intangible products developed by research in the group? How should such a group determine the sole ownership interest in products of foreign members of the group where U.S. members provide valuable developmental assistance? In such a circumstance, how should the group value the developmental assistance provided by U.S. members? Recently issued proposed regulations under Section 482 complicate the resolution of these questions.

Under the transfer price and cost-sharing regulations proposed in January 1992, joint ownership interests may be determined under the QCSA provisions of Proposed Regulation § 1.482-2(g) or under Proposed Regulation § 1.482-2(g)(2)(iii), which allows the IRS to apply such rules to any arrangement "that in substance constitutes a cost sharing arrangement."

In a QCSA, the determination of joint group ownership is complicated, but fairly certain. Under the de facto cost-sharing rules of Proposed Regulation § 1.482-2(g)(2)(iii), the determination of joint ownership is complicated, but fairly uncertain.

In the alternative, sole foreign ownership may be determined under the "developer-assister" provisions of Proposed Regulation § 1.482-2(d)(8), in which event the value of assistance provided by the U.S. member is determined under the "service" provisions of existing Regulation § 1.482-2(b) or, if any intangible property is transferred by the U.S. member in connection with providing assistance, under the "intangible property" provisions of Proposed Regulation § 1.482-2(d).

The proposals justify a second look at the 1985 Tax Court decision of *Ciba-Geigy*, in which the IRS first attempted, under Section 482, to assign a joint interest in a developed intangible to a U.S. member of a controlled group in a de facto cost-sharing arrangement. The facts and an analysis of the holding in *Ciba-Geigy* are discussed.

The joint research and development project conducted by the Swiss parent and the U.S. subsidiary in *Ciba-Geigy* is of renewed interest in light of the provision for a de facto cost-sharing arrangement contained in Proposed Regulation § 1.482-2(g)(2)(iii). This new provision undoubtedly arose from *Ciba-Geigy*, where the IRS could not make a de facto cost-sharing argument owing to the absence of such a provision. Now, the IRS has the discretion to find a de facto cost-sharing arrangement where applying the developer-assister provisions would not clearly reflect income. The proposed regulations continue the developer-assister provisions of the existing regulations. Most changes are for language that ties them into the de facto cost-sharing arrangement provisions. The language provides that when two or more members of a controlled group undertake the development of intangible property, except as provided in the cost-sharing rules, only one will be the developer; other members will be assisters. The developer becomes the owner under Section 482.

Proposed Regulation § 1.482-2(g)(2)(iii) provides that "in unusual circumstances" where the developer-assister rules "would not clearly reflect income of a member of a group of controlled taxpayers," the IRS may apply the cost-sharing rules "to any arrangement that in substance constitutes a cost sharing arrangement (notwithstanding a failure to comply with any requirement of this section)."

When is income not clearly reflected under the developer-assister rules? No test or guiding principles are specifically set forth. The author analyzes and argues that safe harbors should be devised.

[JE McDermott, Jr., 3 J. Int'l Tax'n 52.]

"Proposed Section 482 regulations attacked at hearings" (1992). Hearings held in August 1992, which are discussed in this article, addressed the proposed regulations under Section 482.

[MM Levey, 3 J. Int'l Tax'n 248.]

"International related-party debt: Part II" (1991). Section 482 grants the IRS the authority to allocate income, deductions, and credits among organizations that are owned or controlled, directly or indirectly, by the same interests in order to prevent the evasion of tax or to clearly reflect income. The propose of Section 482 is to place transactions between related organizations on the same basis as arm's-length transactions between unrelated taxpayers. The IRS will apply the Section 482 principles whether the non-arm's-length transactions were intentional or unintentional.

U.S. tax authorities are concerned with the use by a foreign subsidiary of funds belonging to its U.S. parent without adequate interest being paid to the U.S. parent for the use of the funds. The regulations provide that when a loan or advance is made between controlled entities, the IRS can make the allocations necessary to reflect an arm's-length rate of interest. This applies to loans, advances, and debts arising in connection with the sale, lease, or performance of services (i.e., intercompany trade receivables) between controlled organizations.

For debts arising after June 1988, the general rule is that interest must be charged from the day after the debt arises to the day the debt is satisfied. For purposes of determining the period an intercompany trade receivable is outstanding, payments and credits are applied against the oldest receivables on a first-in, first-out basis. Therefore, tracing payments to individual receivables is not required.

The Section 482 regulations specify safe harbor interest rates that taxpayers may charge to avoid interest from being imputed by the IRS. The safe harbor interest rules do not apply when the creditor is regularly engaged in the business of making loans, or when the principal or interest of the loan is expressed in a foreign currency. The authors then detail the safe harbor interest rates, grandfather rules, and penalty provisions under Sections 6662(b)(3) and 6662(e). Whenever the IRS adjusts the income of one member of a controlled group of taxpayers under Section 482, an appropriate "correlative adjustment" must be made to the income, deductions, or basis of the assets of other members of the affiliated group. When the IRS makes a Section 482 adjustment, it is required to furnish the U.S. parent with a written statement that contains the amount and the nature of the correlative adjustment deemed made to its CFC. Correlative adjustments are then discussed.

When a U.S. parent receives a dividend from its CFC, the U.S. parent is deemed under Section 902(a) to have paid a portion of the income taxes paid or accrued by the CFC with respect to the accumulated profits out of which the dividend is distributed. The deemed-paid foreign taxes and withholding taxes that a U.S. parent can claim as a tax credit in the United States are subject to additional computations under Section 904. The Section 482 regulations provide that where the other party to the transaction is a foreign organization, each U.S. shareholder must give full consideration to the impact of the correlative adjustment on the foreign subsidiary during the preparation of the U.S. shareholder's tax return. Accordingly, if a U.S. parent receives a dividend from its CFC in a year in which a Section 482 adjustment is made, the U.S. parent must take the adjustment into account in its deemed-paid foreign tax calculation.

Pursuant to a Section 482 adjustment, an organization can be taxed on income that it never actually received, or denied a deduction for expenses that it paid. If a foreign corporation reimburses its U.S. parent for the adjustment imposed by the IRS, the foreign government will likely treat the payment as a dividend subject to withholding. Where the U.S. corporation relies on the U.S. competent authority to negotiate a reduction in the tax paid in the foreign country, part of the agreement reached by the two governments may allow the foreign subsidiary to reimburse its U.S. parent. The reimbursement of interest that a domestic parent receives from its foreign subsidiary will be subject to a withholding tax imposed by the foreign government. Foreign tax withheld on income earned by the U.S. parent is an "in lieu of" income tax under Section 903 and can be included in the domestic parent's foreign tax credit calculation. The withholding tax may be reduced or eliminated, however, by a tax treaty between the United States and the foreign country.

When a loan or advance is subject to adjustment under Section 482 and the rules of another Code section also apply, only the interest that is charged on the debt is subject to adjustment under Section 482. If another section is used to determine any unstated interest, Section 482 will apply to the restated principal amount. The regulations under Section 482 provide that in addition to Sections 483, 1274, and 7872, Section 482 can be applied to loans and advances. Each of these provisions imputes interest or recharacterizes payments as interest where there are sales or loans between related parties. The authors then address loans at below-market interest rates (under Section 7872), original issue discount (under Section 1274), and imputed interest on deferred payments.

Under Section 904(d)(3)(C), interest income received or accrued from a CFC in which the taxpayer is a U.S. shareholder is separate basket income to the extent it is allocable to income of the CFC in such category. This rule is circumscribed, however, by Section 954(b)(5), which provides that a foreign subsidiary must allocate its interest expense incurred with respect to related-party loans to offset passive basket income to the full extent of the subsidiary's foreign personal holding company passive income. The special allocation rule of Section 954(b)(5) does not apply if the CFC earns less than the de minimis amount described in Section 954(b)(3)(A), i.e., less than the lower of $1 million, or 5 percent of gross income. How the interest is allocable to the passive and other income baskets at the CFC level is spelled out in Regulation § 1.904-5(c)(2), as discussed by the authors.

For taxable years beginning after 1990, if a loan is made to a foreign subsidiary when the U.S. parent has its own third-party debt on which it pays interest, consideration should be given to whether the interest paid on the U.S. parent's debt may be allocated directly against foreign-source income under the rules of Proposed Regulation § 1.861-10(e).

Interest received by a U.S. corporation from a CFC in which it is a U.S. shareholder is generally not treated as high withholding tax interest, regardless of the rate of withholding tax to which the interest is subject, because of the lookthrough rules of Section 904(d)(3). Interest received by a U.S. corporation from a foreign subsidiary that is not a CFC, however, is treated as high withholding tax interest under Section 904(d)(2)(B) to the extent the interest is subject to at least 5 percent withholding tax. In this case, the high withholding tax interest income is put into a separate basket for foreign tax credit limitation purposes, and only those withholding taxes to which the interest is subject may offset the U.S. tax on that interest income.

[F Windholtz & JE Bernot, 2 J. Int'l Tax'n 147.]

"Record-keeping, transfer pricing, and sourcing updates" (1991). Bausch & Lomb (B&L) has decisively won the second round in its Section 482 battle with the IRS. In a unanimous opinion, the Court of Appeals for the Second Circuit has affirmed a 1989 Tax Court ruling that reduced a $20 million allocation of 1981–1982 income to B&L, as proposed by the IRS, to just $5 million.

B&L, one of the world's leading manufacturers of soft contact lenses, has its principal production facilities in Rochester, N.Y. In 1980, it formed B&L Ireland to produce these lenses abroad. B&L granted its Irish subsidiary the right to use B&L patents and trademarks and its unique manufacturing technology to produce lenses at a cost far below that of competing manufacturers. In return, the subsidiary agreed to pay B&L a royalty equal to 5 percent of its net sales. Although the project's plan contemplated that all of B&L Ireland's production would be marketed in Europe through affiliates, the majority of its sales in both 1981 and 1982 were made to B&L for distribution in the United States. The transfer price for these intercompany sales was $7.50 per lens, plus freight and duty. Since B&L Ireland could manufacture lenses at a unit cost of only $1.50, it realized substantial profits from its sales to its U.S. parent, even after its payment of the 5 percent royalty.

At trial, the taxpayer showed that the prices other lens manufacturers were receiving from their independent distributors for these items were approximately the same as those B&L paid its Irish subsidiary.

The appellate court restated the proposition that a taxpayer may avoid a Section 482 adjustment if it can show that the prices paid for goods or services in a controlled context were comparable to those prevailing in arm's-length transactions, even though the circumstances in the two sets of transactions are not identical in all material respects. On the royalty issue, the court agreed with the Tax Court and its analysis, as discussed in the article. The authors comment on the importance of the case.

[M. Abrutyn, SA Musher & GW Rubloff, 2 J. Int'l Tax'n 162.]

"Transfer pricing guidance offered by *Sundstrand*" (1991). Since the 1986 enactment of the Section 482 superroyalty provisions, taxpayers have sought guidance on transfer pricing issues. First came the 1988 "A Study on Intercompany Pricing," often called the White Paper, which set forth the IRS's suggestions for addressing transfer pricing issues for intangible property and which, in practice, also has been applied to transfers of tangible property. Met with criticism and controversy, the White Paper left taxpayers with more bewilderment and insecurity than concrete wisdom or practical guidelines.

Next came the 1989 Tax Court decision in *Bausch & Lomb*, where White Paper principles were seemingly tested in a pre-1986 case. The Tax Court's analysis came under close scrutiny by taxpayers and commentators, especially given the court's strong admonishments concerning the White Paper arguments that were advanced by the IRS.

In the midst of these two significant events have come numerous audits of multinational corporations' transfer pricing programs, with the issues and the IRS's position varying with the nature of the corporations. The Tax Court's 1991 opinion in *Sundstrand* heavily relies on the CUP method to determine the appropriateness of a taxpayer's transfer price and royalty analysis and provides some guidance as to the standards that must be met for a corporation's pricing structure to be sustained.

[MM Levey & RR O'Haver, 2 J. Int'l Tax'n 69.]

"Intercompany pricing—the White Paper" (1990). Intercompany pricing has now become a major regulations project. The White Paper issued by the Treasury Department is one of the first of many studies made on the subject of transfer pricing. This article concerns the White Paper's analyses of the problems existing in this area and proposals for curing these problems.

The topics covered by the author include: the "commensurate with income" standard, the valuation of intangibles, and the pricing of tangibles. Analysis is also provided for determining the commensurate with income standard in the case of an intangible. Issues on timing and risk, high-profit intangibles, periodic review and adjustments, lump-sum payments, and safe harbors are explored. Also discussed by the author are the economic theories applied to implement Section 482 and the White Paper's proposals on the subject of cost sharing.

[R. Feinschreiber, US Tax'n Int'l Operations ¶ 7525.]

"Introduction to cost sharing" (1990). Cost-sharing arrangements permit parties to share costs and risks while developing intangible property. Cost sharing can be used between affiliates or unrelated entities. When cost sharing takes place between affiliates, intercompany pricing rules apply. The White Paper, issued by the Treasury Department in 1988, describes the IRS's proposed cost-sharing rules. In this article, the author examines these rules.

The author first provides a general discussion of the issues in this area, including the use of direct and in-kind payments by cost-sharing affiliates. Next, the author addresses the primary issues, i.e., those concerning selective inclusion of high-profit intangibles, proportionality in the bearing of costs and benefits by research associates, and delayed buy-in to research projects. Specific discussion is then provided on determining the proportionality of benefit and cost shares, including the periodic adjustment thereof.

The author explores the impact of geographic or worldwide rights in the determination of cost shares. This is of critical importance under the White Paper, which advocates the use of exclusive geographic rights rather than worldwide rights to predict the benefits share. Next, the author examines the issues that arise when a participant in the development of an intangible enters after research and development has started, such as in a buy-in arrangement.

Last, the author examines the changes suggested by the White Paper with regard to the administrative requirements for cost-sharing arrangements. In so doing, the author discusses the documentation requirements for cost-sharing agreements, including the effect of the "seeking to enter" test on such requirements, the formalities of the agreement, certain affiliation requirements, the "specifics" test applicable to documentation of the agreement, the "first return" requirements, and record-keeping rules.

[R. Feinschreiber, US Tax'n Int'l Operations ¶ 7526.]

"Tax Court restricts IRS's Section 482 powers" (1990). A number of important international tax issues have been the subject of recent litigation. One of the most noteworthy cases is the Tax Court's 1989 holding in *Bausch & Lomb, Inc.*

The *Bausch & Lomb* case, which involved the application of Section 482, required a determination of both an arm's-length price for tangible property and an arm's-length royalty for intangibles transferred between a U.S. parent corporation and its foreign subsidiary. Generally regarded as a victory for the taxpayer, *Bausch & Lomb* is being appealed to the Second Circuit by the IRS.

[GW Rubloff, 1 J. Int'l Tax'n 103.]

"Transfer pricing regulations contain many uncertainties for foreign-controlled corporations" (1990). Section 482 empowers the IRS to reallocate income among commonly controlled businesses in order to prevent tax avoidance or to clearly reflect income. Internationally, this authority has been employed to monitor the allocation of international income between commonly controlled domestic and foreign affiliates. The focus of Section 482 has been on foreign-controlled groups and imported products. This reflects changing international trade flows.

The IRS's statistics for 1985 showed that 36,700 foreign-controlled corporations reported $514 billion in receipts and $511 billion in deductions, of which $358 billion were costs of sales and operations, or 70 percent of total deductions. Such figures have resulted in congressional and IRS concerns that foreign-controlled U.S. corporations are underpaying U.S. tax owing to excessively high transfer prices. Congress has amended Section 482 with a view to having the United States capture a larger share of tax on the very substantial international trade revenue derived by foreign-controlled U.S. corporations from U.S. consumers. Foreign-controlled groups assert that transfer pricing rules are vague and unclear. Congress's response was to introduce HR 4308, one purpose of which was to make the enforcement provision, Section 6038A, retroactive to all open years.

The 1986 amendment to Section 482 qualified the existing principle that transfer prices be based on comparable arm's-length prices, with the requirement that transfer prices also be commensurate with income earned from the sale of the products. It appears that the IRS wants foreign-based multinationals to make available books and records of the full product line so that it can determine product line net income and its allocation within and without the United States.

According to the Treasury's White Paper, the CUP method is the best evidence of arm's-length prices that are commensurate with income. Under Regulation § 1.482-2(e), products do not have to be identical to be comparable, only "so nearly identical the difference can be reflected by a reasonable number of adjustments to price." In *Eli Lilly*, a 1985 Tax Court case, pain killer tablets containing the same active ingredient as Lilly's Darvon were deemed comparable for purposes of the CUP method. So long as the products compete, in terms of a demand and price relationship, they should be identical products.

Under Regulation § 1.482-2(e), the RPM can be used in support of the CUP method if the distributor has not added substantial value through alteration of the physical property or by the addition of intangible property. The RPM avoids the same property issue, since it compares gross profit margins that depend on similarity of function rather than property. Under *El DuPont de Nemours & Co.*, a 1979 Court of Claims case, the RPM has been held not to be valid unless the taxpayer can also demonstrate that the companies compared have similar expense to gross profit ratios. The White Paper dealt very little with the RPM and its place in the future is unclear.

It is expected that the Second Circuit will affirm the Tax Court's denial of the contract manufacturer theory, which automatically denies controlled foreign production units ownership of intangible property. The regulation should put an end to the contract manufacturer theory if controlled foreign production units are valid owners of intangible property. The microeconomic approach to transfer price analysis, as it applies to foreign-controlled groups, should be dealt with in the forthcoming regulations.

Definite limitations should be placed on books and records requirements under the Section 6038A regulations. The IRS has made it clear that product line net income is the focus of the books and records requirements under Section 6038A. This section provides that companies dealing with the U.S. corporations and all related foreign entities will have to designate the U.S. reporting corporation as agent for the service of summons.

In addition to clarifying geographic and entity limitations on the books and records requirements and on the agency requirement, the regulations will also have to specify what financial data will be required. One major aspect of the books and records requirement that the regulations need to address is attorney-client privilege and attorney work-product privilege.

The profitability of foreign-controlled U.S. corporations is an issue that will be considered not only in the context of filing returns for 1990 and future years, but also in the context of an audit of all open years of the past decade. When regulations are issued under Section 482, they will relate to all years since the 1986 amendment.

[JE McDermott, Jr., 1 J. Int'l Tax'n 50.]

[2] Advance Pricing Agreements

IRS issues revenue procedure concerning APAs. This revenue procedure tells how to secure an APA from the office of the IRS Associate Chief Counsel (International) covering the prospective determination and application of TPMs for certain international transactions of foreign or domestic taxpayers. An APA is an agreement between the IRS and the taxpayer on the TPM to be applied to any apportionment or allocation of income, deductions, credits, or allowances between or among two or more organizations, trades, or businesses owned or controlled, directly or indirectly, by the same interests. An APA may relate to any transaction between related parties that raises such apportionment or allocation issues.

[Rev. Proc. 91-22, 1991-1 CB 526.]

"Culbertson discusses APA program" (1993). This short article summarizes the content of the speech given by Robert E. Culbertson, Associate Chief Counsel (International), at the NYU Tax Institute on Federal Taxation in November 1992. His discussion concerned the current status of the IRS's APA program.

[4 J. Int'l Tax'n 48.]

"Intercompany transfer pricing and APAs" (1992). The IRS has broad authority to challenge the arm's-length character of a U.S. taxpayer's transfer prices in intercompany transactions with foreign related parties, under Section 482. Frequently, conflicts involving transfer pricing are very expensive and time-consuming. This article examines how Revenue Procedure 91-22 facilitates the use of APAs, which can mitigate the adverse effects of these conflicts, and what information is required for their use.

The author begins by discussing a number of different aspects of intercompany pricing, including the new reporting requirements, regulations, and the *Ash* decision, a 1991 Tax Court case. Next, he explores the use of an APA to avoid conflicts concerning intercompany pricing, the benefits of an APA, and the prerequisites to a successful APA. Thereafter, the author discusses the principles applied in the APA process, proposed TPMs, "critical assumptions," the nature of compensating adjustments, competent authority considerations, confidentiality considerations, and the legal force and effect of APAs.

In the second part of this article, the author explains the content of an APA request and the procedure for such a request. Specific discussion is provided of prefiling conferences, the general requirements for a request, factual guidelines for pricing methodologies, considerations associated with cost-sharing arrangements, and the processing of an APA request by the IRS (including evaluation, withdrawal, and use of independent expert opinions). Last, the author considers administration of an existing APA, including required annual reports, IRS examination, record retention requirements, revocation or cancellation of the APA for cause, and APA renewal.

The author concludes that the APA process provides a potentially superior approach to resolving cross-border, intercompany transfer pricing disputes than the traditional administrative, judicial, and treaty resolution procedures currently available to multinational corporate taxpayers. This process, as explained in this article, is particularly valuable to a taxpayer who views itself as a mere stakeholder in a pricing dispute between two jurisdictions. The ultimate success of the APA process will depend to a significant extent on the willingness of the IRS, taxpayers, and the United States's treaty partners to experiment with new approaches to transfer pricing issues.

[JR Mogle, US Tax'n Int'l Operations ¶ 7522.]

"Two banks sign APAs" (1992). APAs have been signed between two international financial institutions, the IRS, and the United Kingdom's Inland Revenue.

[MM Levey, 3 J. Int'l Tax'n 248.]

"APAs provide a safe harbor" (1991). The IRS has issued Revenue Procedure 91-22, on how to secure an APA. This definitive path-breaking procedure has been developed as an alternative to Section 482 audits for future taxable years.

Solving pricing issues by agreement with respect to future transactions involves somewhat different considerations than are involved when dealing with audits of past years. Revenue Procedure 91-22 generally attempts to address these distinctions. First, the taxpayer must provide complete factual and financial information concerning its proposed TPM. Second, flexibility is required to allow for changes in business conditions occurring during the term of an APA, such as the recession now in progress. Third, as a matter of practical necessity (and good theory), there generally must be a range of permissible prices or results that will be considered consistent with arm's-length pricing.

APAs should enable taxpayers and the IRS to reach agreement on a nonadversarial basis with respect to Section 482 allocation issues, including cost-sharing arrangements. An APA need not cover all of a taxpayer's Section 482 pricing arrangements. Instead, the revenue procedure gives the taxpayer flexibility to limit its APA request to specified affiliates and specified intercompany transactions. APAs may cover a spectrum of different types of interaffiliate transactions, both outbound and inbound, involving the transfer of goods, services, or intangibles.

The APA process is intended to result in an agreement among the parties on:

1. An appropriate TPM;
2. The factual nature of the relevant transactions; and
3. The expected range of results of the TPM.

The taxpayer and the IRS are essential parties; foreign competent authorities may also be parties.

Revenue Procedure 91-22 reflects the view that, absent a single perfect comparable, there is no one correct transfer price, but rather a range of arm's-length prices. The authors then detail the range concept and TPM.

The final procedure evidences a continuing emphasis on a search for suitable comparables. Happily, the concept of comparables is applied broadly. First, attention is directed at finding comparable transactions. Failing this, a new area of focus, clearer in practice than in the revenue procedure, is an attempt to identify comparable companies or businesses. The idea is to develop a result-oriented TPM from the experience of such businesses.

The revenue procedure lists examples of possible adjustment factors that could be used to create the required parity. The examples are listed in the article.

Revenue Procedure 91-22 requires the taxpayer to illustrate a proposed TPM by applying it, in a consistent format, to the prior three years' data. Hypothetical data may be used in the absence of appropriate historical data, as may a period other than three years if more appropriate.

The critical assumptions are the boundaries of the APA, as agreed to by the parties and specified in the APA. The need to introduce these boundaries stems from the application of a TPM to future transactions. A critical assumption is any fact that, if changed, would significantly affect the substantive terms to which the IRS and the taxpayer were willing to agree. A critical assumption may be either a business fact within the taxpayer's control or economic circumstances beyond its control.

An actual change in critical assumptions will require that the parties return to the table and attempt to appropriately revise or, absent agreement, cancel the APA. If the IRS finds that a change in critical assumptions resulted from circumstances within the taxpayer's control, and not occurring for good faith business reasons, it may revoke or cancel the APA. Thus, the critical assumptions represent protections and risks for all parties to the APA. Accordingly, special attention must be devoted to their formulation.

The parties may agree to permit the taxpayer and its related foreign affiliate to make compensating adjustments if actual results fall outside the agreed-upon range, as detailed by the authors. Revenue Procedure 91-22 requires a thorough and careful description of the facts, search for comparables where available, and analysis. Therefore, an APA remains costly.

The final procedure, like the draft, seeks an explanation of the taxpayer's and the IRS's positions on previous and current issues at the examination, appeals, court, or competent authority levels (and possibly similar information regarding such issues before foreign tax authorities), but only to the extent that these "relate to the proposed TPM." At the expense of the taxpayer, an independent expert who has not participated materially in development of the request may be required to review and opine on the proposed TPM.

Annual reports by the taxpayer are required to demonstrate that the actual results of the TPM for the year conform to the terms and conditions of the APA, to alert the IRS as to whether any critical assumptions have changed, and to set forth adjustments that must be made in compliance with the terms of the APA.

The revenue procedure requires the taxpayer to maintain sufficient records for the IRS to verify compliance with the APA. Generally, upon IRS request, records must be provided within sixty days, and translations must be provided within thirty days. The taxpayer may include with the APA a Section 6038A record retention agreement related to the subject matter of the APA.

The taxpayer and the IRS must agree to an initial APA term appropriate to the industry, product, or transaction involved. Three years is given as an example rather than (as in the draft procedure) specified as the norm. Under the draft procedure, failure to revise an APA required by a change in a critical assumption gave only the IRS an option to cancel the APA. The final procedure gives both parties the ability to force a cancellation in this situation. The IRS may (but is not required to) revoke an APA for fraud, malfeasance, or disregard, as detailed in the article. The authors then discuss in detail the important role of IRS field examiners and the balanced approach in relation to the APA years that the revenue procedure achieves.

The IRS prefers that an APA be trilateral among the taxpayer, the IRS, and the foreign competent authority, or multilateral where more than one foreign competent authority has potential jurisdiction over the relevant transactions or affiliates. Nevertheless, an affirmative request by the taxpayer is necessary for a competent authority process to be initiated with respect to the granting of an APA. Any such competent authority agreement will be concluded only with the taxpayer's consent. The final procedure takes the position that APAs fall within the category of return information subject to the confidentiality requirements of Section 6103.

The article concludes with the authors' view of the outlook for success of the APAs, concluding that for both the IRS and taxpayers, APAs may, in appropriate cases, avoid protracted and expensive disputes, streamline ongoing audits, and eliminate the need for litigation.

[M. Abrutyn, RT Cole & SA Musher, 2 J. Int'l Tax'n 5.]

"Use of APAs enhanced by new revenue procedure" (1991). In Revenue Procedure 91-22, the IRS set forth the procedures for taxpayers to enter into APAs with the IRS. An APA is an agreement on TPMs to be applied to any apportionment or allocation of income, deductions, credits, or allowances in connection with international transactions of U.S. taxpayers with organizations, trades, or businesses under common control or ownership, within the meaning of Section 482.

The APA revenue procedure has been much in discussion ever since a draft version, dated April 27, 1990, was circulated among certain practitioner groups for comment. The final procedure differs considerably from the earlier draft. In particular, the final procedure is significantly less burdensome to taxpayers and provides more flexibility with regard to the scope and duration of an APA. The new APA rule, particularly if combined with a competent authority agreement, may be useful to large corporations.

After discussing the standards for an APA, the author examines the necessary contents of an APA request, as set forth in Revenue Procedure 91-22. He also discusses the revenue procedure's coverage of establishing the arm's-length basis of the proposed TPM, the term of the APA, the objective business and economic criteria that must be proposed, competent authority agreements, the provision of an annual report, and the required list of nonfactual representations or submissions. The utility and right to request prefiling conferences is also addressed.

Thereafter, the author examines the IRS's evaluation of the request for an APA. Other considerations are also examined: (1) compensating adjustments; (2) the legal effect of an APA; (3) the revocation or cancellation of an APA; (4) changes in assumptions or law that affect any matter covered by the APA; (5) record retention requirements; and (6) disclosure concerns and confidentiality of information received or generated during the APA process.

In the second part of the article, the author discusses the advantages and disadvantages of the procedure. The author notes that one of the principal advantages of entering into an APA is the avoidance of interest and penalties on tax deficiencies attributable to Section 482 adjustments. An additional benefit discussed is the potential for the APA procedure to enable taxpayers to reach agreement in advance among competent authorities to avoid double taxation of income that has not yet been earned. Thus, corporations concerned with avoiding double taxation should consider whether the APA process can be used to recruit the IRS as an ally in treaty partner discussions.

On the other hand, the author notes that there are several drawbacks to engaging in the APA process. First, the APA process is a red flag to the IRS that there may be Section 482 issues on a corporation's past and present returns. Second, the APA procedure requires a large volume of information and documentation. Third, there is the concern of how binding an APA will really be: It seems clear that the IRS will not sign an APA on a closing agreement, which is the only Code-sanctioned way to enter into a binding agreement with the IRS. Additionally, the revenue procedure allows the IRS several avenues to escape being bound by the results of the APA.

The author concludes that the APA process is new, and that only a few U.S. corporations have begun to experiment to see if it is worthwhile. The process is expensive and not for everyone. The benefits in avoiding future disputes with treaty partners over double taxation, however, may justify the use of the APA procedure for certain major corporations that regularly face Section 482 audits.

[CM Smith, 74 J. Tax'n 374.]

[3] Enforcement and Penalties

"Proposed regulations apply accuracy-related penalty to transfer price adjustments" (1993). Proposed regulations applying the Section 6662 accuracy-related penalty to "substantial" and "gross" valuation misstatements of transfer price results were published in 1993. The revised regulations contain several discrete methodologies for determining arm's-length transfer prices, as well as a coherent compliance format based on taxpayer contemporaneous documentation of TPMs— documentation prepared and executed by the date of filing the tax return.

The author first discusses the contemporaneous documentation compliance format reflected throughout the temporary and proposed Section 482 regulations, which were part of the package that included the Section 6662 proposed regulations. The author next addresses the recognition of business realities, especially with regard to the manner in which transfer prices are actually determined, built into the provisions of the regulations. The author then focuses on the proposed regulations concerning the accuracy-related penalty, including the manner in which the penalty is assessed.

Thereafter, the author discusses substantial and gross valuation misstatements, including the threshold levels applicable to such misstatements. Last, the author examines the "reasonable cause and good faith" defense to the penalty and its elements.

The author concludes that the temporary and proposed Section 482 regulations provide a menu of flexible and user-friendly pricing methods. Together with those proposed under Sections 6662(e) and 6662(j), and Section 6664, these regulations incorporate a coherent compliance format where none previously existed. The compliance expected is reasonably within the function of the tax department of a multinational corporation. This format has two legs—contemporaneous documentation requirements and the accuracy-related penalty. The entire effort suggests that the Treasury and the IRS are attempting to solve an enforcement problem with a compliance solution, rather than through threat of litigation.

[JE McDermott, Jr., 4 J. Int'l Tax'n 100.]

"Transfer pricing penalty proposed regulations limit reasonable cause exception" (1993). The accuracy-related penalty for transfer pricing misstatements, Sections 6662(e) and 6662(h), reflects Congress's concern that foreign-controlled corporations were regularly failing to comply with documentation and record-keeping requirements and prompt production of pricing data. In 1993, proposed regulations were issued interpreting these penalty provisions.

In this article, the author first examines the general features of the accuracy-related penalty, and the reasons for its application to erroneous transfer price valuations. A general review is then provided of the proposed regulations concerning the transfer pricing penalty. Thereafter, he considers in detail the "reasonable cause" exception in Section 6664(c). With regard to the regulations on the transfer pricing penalty, this involves the meaning of the requirements that the taxpayer show it made a "reasonable effort to accurately determine proper tax liability" and that it had a "reasonable belief" that the TPM used produced an arm's-length result. The author discusses what constitutes "reasonable effort" and "reasonable belief," the issues these standards create, and whether the use of these standards is consistent with the "reasonable cause" exception in Section 6664(c).

Based on his analysis in this article, the author concludes that the proposed regulations on the reasonable cause exception to the transfer pricing penalty will impose on taxpayers the dual obligation to (1) prepare contemporaneous studies to support transfer prices, applying the temporary regulations under Section 482 and (2) produce those studies on international examiners' demand (not summonses). This two-fold obligation for documentation has not been associated with the reasonable cause exception of Section 6664(c), which applies to the other accuracy-related penalties. As a result, the proposed regulations conflict with the legislative history of the transfer price misstatement penalty. The proposed regulations also take a view of the reliance defense that is more stringent than has been applied by the courts, especially in negligence penalty cases involving valuation misstatements.

Additionally, the proposed regulations can be criticized for adopting a rather idiosyncratic view of reasonable cause at odds with the application of that standard to other types of taxpayer conduct. There is also a confusion of purpose: a penalty that punishes taxpayer conduct in taking certain return positions is transformed into a document-production penalty. These policy choices might have been modified in final regulations or struck down by the courts. For tax years beginning after 1993, however, these controversial proposals have received statutory blessing. RRA 1993 modifies the accuracy-related penalty for transfer price misstatements by adding two alternative requirements before a net Section 482 transfer price adjustment will be reduced and the penalty potentially avoided.

It is discouraging to note that these alternatives for reducing the transfer price penalty are "coordinated" with the reasonable cause exception of Section 6664(c) in such a way that the section no longer applies to transfer price adjustments. Thus, one of the cornerstones of the 1989 penalty reform—a single reasonable cause standard for all taxpayer penalties—has been removed only four years after it was put in place. Where transfer price adjustments are made, the reasonableness of the taxpayer's conduct is not the issue. Rather, it is the taxpayer's compliance with the Section 482 regulations and with the Section 6038A regulations concerning document creation, retention, and production. Dubious policy decisions formerly reflected only in proposed regulations for pre-1994 years are enshrined in the Code for post-1993 years. How taxpayers facing transfer price adjustments for post-1993 years will be treated under the amended penalty cannot be predicted with certainty. It can be said, however, that disputes over the penalties, including the transfer price misstatement penalty, will increase, with taxpayers having to bear a heavy burden of proof. This will encourage examiners to use the penalty as a bargaining chip in the audit and on appeal—a situation that already exists with the substantial understatement penalty. In addition, the statutory validation of these decisions may make it tempting to incorporate them in final regulations for pre-1994 years.

[MI Saltzman, 79 J. Tax'n 252.]

"IRS audit process for intercompany transfer pricing" (1992). This article reviews the IRS's audit procedures when examining intercompany transfer pricing arrangements between U.S. and foreign related persons. The author first discusses the coordinated examination program used for large corporations. Operation of this program is explained and its interaction with the APA procedure and industry specialization program is discussed. The IRS's use of the economic assistance program and foreign international support team is also noted.

Thereafter, the author discusses the enforcement authority of the IRS, particularly with regard to record-keeping requirements, and the IRS's general summons power. Additionally, the author examines other means by which the IRS gathers information, such as through its review of Forms 5471 and 5472, review of foreign records kept in accordance with Sections 6038A and 6038C, use of a Section 982 formal document request, use of exchange of information provisions in tax treaties, use of treaty-authorized summonses, use of the provisions of the Convention of Mutual Administrative Assistance in Tax Matters, and use of the "designated summons" to toll the statute of limitations (under Section 6503(k)). The use of letters rogatory by the IRS to acquire foreign evidence is also discussed.

Relevant penalties associated with transfer pricing problems are also reviewed. The use of mutual assistance in criminal tax matters and grand jury (or trial) subpoenas for information gathering is also examined.

[W. O'Connor, US Tax'n Int'l Operations ¶ 7528.]

"Enforcement focuses on imported products" (1990). The House Ways and Means Committee hearings in July 1990, raised the question of whether the method of determining transfer prices of imported products under Section 482 and the enforcement effort is adequate to assure the United States its fair share of tax revenue from the inbound trade. While the 1986 amendment appears adequate to prevent U.S. multinationals from transferring income abroad, Congress now doubts whether its prevents foreign-based multinationals from doing so. Congress has inquired whether Section 482 should be amended again to substitute a formulary method, in lieu of the existing arm's-length method, for determining transfer prices of inbound trade. The formula would allocate, presumptively, at least 50 percent of the income from the product line to the United States.

IRS officials believe that efforts should be directed toward enforcement and not toward the amendment of Section 482. The IRS favors retaining the arm's-length method as the only practical method for allocating international income. The IRS maintains that Section 6038A, accompanied by adequate funding, enables them to effectively audit prices in international trade.

Section 6038A, as amended in 1989, provides the IRS with authority to specify the books and records that must be maintained in the United States to support transfer prices. In addition, each foreign entity trading with a controlled U.S. affiliate must designate the U.S. affiliate as its agent for the service of summons under Section 7602, and the U.S. affiliate must report transfer price transactions with foreign affiliates with the specificity required by the IRS. Failure to properly report the transactions or to properly meet the books and records requirements results in substantial monetary penalties. Further amendments proposed in 1990 extend the provisions of Section 6038A to U.S. branches, suspend the statute of limitations for three years on all open years, and tax gains of foreign persons on sales and exchanges of shares in U.S. corporations in which their interests are at least 10 percent.

Foreign reaction to the threat to amend Section 482 has been immediate, in the form of correspondence from Germany and an offer from the United Kingdom (which the United States has accepted) to participate in a joint study with the United States on the scope of the transfer price problem. In Europe, the European Economic Community members have affirmed their confidence in the arm's-length method and have agreed on a procedure to resolve major disputes. The arbitration principle has also been incorporated in the provisions of the impending U.S.-German income tax treaty.

The threat of foreign retaliation to unreasonable legislation cannot be ignored and is another argument against amending Section 482. Allocating income from international trade by market forces and not by arbitrary formulary methods is the only method that will work when the principal trading nations are equals. The United States, Europe, and the Pacific Rim countries identify the problem as being the enforcement effort and not the allocation method.

The principal defect in enforcing Section 482 appears to be the failure to provide detailed instructions on how to apply the complex pricing methods generally stated in the regulations. Employees of multinationals lack a coherent blueprint for analyzing and documenting transfer prices. In its manual, the IRS has methodically attempted to work out analytical patterns for the application of the arm's-length method in all three of its traditional variations. Instructions in the IRS training manual could be used to form the basis of a revenue procedure, which would provide taxpayers with much needed clarification in order to comply with the law as interpreted by the IRS and to identify points of dispute.

The United States represents the principal consumer market in the world. Yet its tax authorities have devised a theory of income allocation developed when the United States was the major exporting nation that assigns the principal portion of income from the sale of products to U.S. consumers to the foreign parent corporation of the multinational producing the product. This residual income theory shows the dangers in adopting arbitrary methods of income allocation that depart from market forces as a guide and should be repudiated.

A modern competent authority procedure is also needed for more effective enforcement. The main ingredient of a modern compentent authority procedure is an efficient and open dispute resolution process at which the taxpayer is truly represented. A dispute cannot be resolved without the consent of all the parties: the taxpayer, the United States, and the foreign country of consumption or production. The existing competent authority procedure is an anachronism from the days when the United States stood alone as the principal trading nation, when most conflicts over the allocation of income from international trade could be resolved in the head office of the corporate group involved. Today, the transfer price examination is conducted much more at arm's length. A revised competent authority procedure to provide a modern, high-level dispute resolution forum greatly enhances enforcement efforts and resolves conflicts over the allocation of income from international trade.

[JE McDermott, Jr., 1 J. Int'l Tax'n 240.]

¶ 1.04 FOREIGN CURRENCY TRANSACTIONS[4]

IRS issues revenue ruling concerning repayment of nonfunctional currency denominated mortgage loan. The IRS ruled that gain or loss realized by a U.S. citizen from the sale of a personal residence may not be offset by loss or gain realized from the repayment of a nonfunctional currency denominated mortgage loan used to finance the purchase of the residence.

[Rev. Rul. 90-79, 1990-2 CB 187.]

IRS issues final regulations concerning Section 988 transactions. The IRS has issued final regulations relating to the taxation of gain or loss from certain foreign currency transactions (Section 988 transactions).

[TD 8400, 1992-1 CB 101, Reg. §§ 1.988-0–1.988-5.]

IRS issues final regulations concerning definition of "QBU." The IRS has issued final regulations relating to the definition of a QBU under Section 989, effective for taxable years beginning after December 31, 1986. The regulations expand the definition of "QBU" to include partnerships, trusts, and estates. In addition, a branch of a partnership, trust, or estate may qualify as a QBU. Because a partnership, trust, or estate is treated as a QBU of each of the partners or beneficiaries, Section 987 (relating to branch transactions) may apply to remittances from a partnership, trust, or estate to partners or beneficiaries. A QBU also includes activities that produce income or loss effectively connected with a U.S. trade or business.

The regulations provide that a trade or business for purposes of Section 989(a) is generally any specific unified group of activities that constitute (or could constitute) an independent economic enterprise carried on for profit, the expenses related to which are deductible under Sections 162 or 212 (rather than only Section 162). Thus, all activities engaged in for profit are eligible for QBU status.

[TD 8279, 1990-1 CB 151, Reg. § 1.989(a)-1.]

"Changes to rules on functional currency, branch accounting" (1993). Final regulations under Section 985, issued in 1993, affect taxpayers with QBUs that change functional currency, and contain special rules for QBUs operating in a hyperinflationary environment that use the dollar approximate separate transactions method (DASTM) for the first post-1986 tax year. In addition, proposed regulations discuss the adjustments required when a QBU that used the profit and loss method of accounting in a post-1986 tax year changes to DASTM.

[78 J. Tax'n 177.]

"Computing foreign currency gains and losses on branch transactions" (1993). Sections 985 through 989 establish a statutory framework for the treatment of foreign currency transactions. Proposed and final regulations under Section 987 were issued to deal with the currency translation issues of a QBU. In some situations, these rules may be unduly burdensome to smaller taxpayers and may require clarification by the IRS.

After providing background for the topic of this article, the authors discuss the meaning of QBU as set forth in Section 989 and the regulations thereunder, including a discussion of the presumption of the U.S. dollar as the functional currency in certain cases, the translation rules, and operational rules. Next, the authors examine the regulations' provisions concerning equity and basis pools and certain other rules applicable in this area. Last, the authors examine the transition rule set forth in Regulation § 1.987-5 for a U.S. taxpayer's QBU that uses a functional currency other than the U.S. dollar and that used the profit and loss method of accounting or a net worth method of accounting prior to 1987.

The authors conclude that the regulations under Section 987 go a long way toward clarifying the complex operation of accounting for foreign currency transactions of foreign branches of U.S. corporations. Some issues, however, were not addressed by the regulations. The tax treatment of U.S. QBU branches of foreign taxpayers was not outlined. Also, the preamble to the proposed regulations under Section 987 noted that some industries, such as life insurance and regulated investment companies, may require special treatment.

In addition, the regulations are not yet integrated with the partnership tax rules. Currently, under Regulation § 1.989(a)-1(b)(2), a partnership is a QBU branch of each of its partners. Therefore, an actual distribution (i.e., remittance) may result in exchange gain or loss to the partner even though, under normal partnership rules, no taxable event has occurred. The regulations also do not address the termination of a QBU branch before the effective date of the proposed regulations. In terms of additional taxpayer burdens, the regulations require two sets of books for each QBU (one in the taxpayer's functional currency and the other in the QBU's functional currency), and taxpayers must track the relevant exchange rates daily for each QBU. Since one of the stated goals of the regulations was to simplify the tax treatment of QBU transactions, perhaps the regulations should be amended to assist smaller taxpayers that begin new ventures in overseas markets.

[DT Williamson & RZ Law, 78 J. Tax'n 172.]

"Final and proposed regulations describe functional currency changes" (1993). Final regulations on changes in functional currency under Section 985, adopted in 1992, contain guidance for taxpayers with QBUs that change their functional currency or that elect the dollar as functional currency in a hyperinflationary environment for the first taxable year after 1986. In addition, proposed regulations under Section 985 were issued for QBUs that change methods of accounting from the profit and loss method to the DASTM.

[4 J. Int'l Tax'n 192.]

"Character, source, and integration rules are provided for currency transactions" (1992). The first part of this article describes the transactions covered by the final Section 988 regulations and the basic timing and calculation rules. The second part of the article discusses the character and source rules, foreign tax credit effects, integration of hedging transactions, and the new proposed Section 988 regulations.

Although Section 988 usually requires ordinary income treatment, taxpayers can elect capital treatment for certain transactions. Rules for integrating hedging transactions have been refined, but not significantly expanded, by the final regulations. Fortunately, advance rulings will now be allowed.

[DM Crowe & DM Ring, 3 J. Int'l Tax'n 140.]

"Computing branch income subject of new regulations" (1992). Proposed regulations under Section 987 explain the calculation of income attributable to a taxpayer's QBU branch, including currency gains and losses on remittances from and terminations of branches. The rules also provide guidance on characterization of the gains and losses for purposes of the foreign tax credit limitation. In addition, final regulations provide transition rules for QBU branches using the profit and loss or net worth method of accounting for tax years beginning before 1987. The final regulations generally are effective for tax years beginning after October 24, 1991.

This article discusses the proposed and final regulations, including an examination of the proposed regulations' requirement that taxpayers use the profit and loss method of accounting in computing the income attributable to a QBU branch, the rules for gains and losses on property transferred from a QBU branch in a remittance or termination, the provisions concerning termination of a QBU branch, and the transition rules contained in the final regulations.

[76 J. Tax'n 31.]

"Final and proposed regulations expand available foreign currency hedging opportunities" (1992). Proposed and final regulations relating to the taxation of foreign currency transactions under Section 988 were issued by the IRS in March 1992. The final regulations adopt the same basic approach as the temporary regulations issued in September 1989, but generally simplify the calculation of foreign exchange gain or loss and substantially liberalize the foreign currency hedging provisions. The proposed regulations expand into new issues and provide special rules, including a mark-to-market election for taxpayers.

In the aggregate, these regulations create greater conformity between the financial accounting and tax treatment of foreign currency transactions, although significant differences still remain (most notably, with respect to the types of transactions that qualify for "hedge" treatment). Nevertheless, corporations cannot automatically rely on the financial accounting treatment of foreign currency hedging transactions in order to determine the proper tax treatment of these hedging transactions.

[BH Weinrib, TJ Driscoll & PJ Connors, 77 J. Tax'n 110.]

"Final currency regulations alleviate restrictions of the temporary regulations" (1992). For U.S. tax purposes, a taxpayer or its business unit has a single "functional currency" in which gains or losses are taxed by the United States. Under Section 985, the functional currency for most individuals and other U.S. resident taxpayers is the U.S. dollar.

Section 988 was introduced by TRA 1986 to provide specific rules for determining the character, source, and timing of the exchange gain or loss. Section 988(a) generally provides ordinary treatment for foreign currency gain or loss and sources such gain or loss to the residence of the taxpayer or the QBU of the taxpayer on whose books the item is reflected. Section 988 generally defers to other sections of the Code for the timing of the gain or loss in covered transactions. Section 988(d) offers integrated tax treatment for qualified foreign currency hedging transactions.

Temporary Section 988 regulations issued in 1988 resolved basic timing, character, and source issues and enabled a U.S. resident corporation that had acquired a foreign currency denominated debt instrument issued by a foreign corporation to determine

1. The portion of payments received under the debt obligation attributable to foreign currency gain or loss;

2. The portion of payments characterized as interest;
3. When total gain or loss on the transaction was to be taken into income;
4. Whether any loss on the transaction was subject to allocation and apportionment rules; and
5. Whether gain or loss was to be sourced to the United States.

In March 1992, the Section 988 regulations were issued in final form. The final regulations, with some notable exceptions, follow the structure and general substance of the temporary regulations and attempt to simplify calculation of exchange gain and loss. On the same date, the IRS also issued proposed Section 988 regulations on several issues left open in the final regulations.

With the final Section 988 regulations, the IRS has generally resisted suggestions to broaden covered transactions and has been given greater latitude in determining whether intrataxpayer transfers are to be treated as dispositions. The final regulations, however, facilitate a taxpayer's calculation of exchange gain and loss by making changes to the definition of "spot rate," the fair market value calculation, the calculation of interest on the extension of the maturity date of a financial instrument, the translation of interest income and expenses, and the definition of "currency swaps."

[DM Crowe & DM Ring, 3 J. Int'l Tax'n 98.]

"Fine tuning for hedging and marking-to-market is found in Section 988 package" (1992). In March 1992, the IRS issued proposed regulations dealing with several foreign currency issues, primarily marking-to-market and hedging, and final regulations completely superseding the Section 988 temporary regulations. This article discusses three aspects of the regulations: hedging, marking-to-market, and debt instruments in multiple currencies or that contain embedded options.

[RJ Shapiro & RD Lorence, 3 J. Int'l Tax'n 58.]

"Proposed Section 987 regulations expand coverage of QBUs" (1992). Section 985 provides when a domestic corporation with a foreign branch can make federal income tax determinations in the foreign currency of the economic environment in which a significant part of the branch's activity is conducted. Generally, this accounting method is available when the branch operation is a QBU and books and records are kept in the identified currency. Taxpayers who meet the requirements of Section 985 must then look to Section 987 to make determinations relating to

1. Computing taxable income derived through QBUs;
2. Accounting for foreign taxes when a foreign tax credit is claimed;
3. Timing the recognition of exchange gain or loss on QBU assets and earnings (i.e., Section 987 gain or loss); and
4. Characterizing and sourcing Section 987 gain or loss.

In September 1991, the IRS issued proposed regulations under Section 987 that address these issues for QBUs other than those operating in hyperinflationary economies.

[LG Stodghill, 2 J. Int'l Tax'n 300.]

"Translating foreign currency into U.S. tax sense" (1992). Whenever a U.S. taxpayer becomes involved in a foreign business or investment activity a very significant consideration is the stability of the currency used in that business or investment transaction. A U.S. taxpayer that engages in international transactions in currency other than U.S. dollars will have currency exchange gains or losses. This article examines the tax rules related to currency exchange problems and the techniques used to minimize currency fluctuation risks, such as futures, swaps, and hedging.

The authors first discuss the concepts of QBU and functional currency. Next, they consider the election of the U.S. dollar as the functional currency of a QBU whose functional currency would otherwise be a hyperinflationary currency. The reporting of foreign transactions in U.S. dollars is then explained, along with the currency translation required for the foreign tax credit.

In the next part of the article, the authors examine the treatment of foreign currency transactions, including transactions under Section 988 generally, those involving branch transactions (under Section 987), multiple QBU transactions, and Section 988(c) and 988(d) transactions. Thereafter, they discuss translating debt instruments in complex situations, such as where original issue discount (OID) is paid on a nonfunctional currency instrument, where market discounts are determined in nonfunctional currency units, and where nonfunctional currency debt is swapped for the debtor's stock.

In the last part of this article, the authors examine the tax treatment of transactions entered into to minimize risks associated with foreign currency transactions, that is, forward, futures, and option contracts that call for future delivery of a nonfunctional currency. In this regard, notional principal contracts and currency swaps are also discussed. Thereafter, hedging transactions and the seven criteria used to determine if a qualifying debt instrument and a hedge are an integrated economic transaction are considered. The taxation of qualified hedging transactions (including hedged executory contracts) is explained. Last, the character and source of Section 988 gains and losses are reviewed.

[ML Moore & S. Lassar, US Tax'n Int'l Operations ¶ 5018]

"Typical foreign currency trading strategies are nightmares under Section 988 rules" (1992). The Section 988 temporary regulations that were first promulgated on September 20, 1989, attempted to provide broad guidance on the tax consequences of foreign currency transactions involving nonfunctional currencies. While addressing the taxation of certain foreign currency related financial instruments, these temporary regulations seemed to be particularly directed toward the corporate treasury function as it relates to operating transactions (e.g., receivables and payables in nonfunctional currencies). The Treasury was far less focused, however, on the often complex problems raised by stock and security traders on a global basis, e.g., traders with the U.S. dollar as the functional currency that buy and sell in numerous nonfunctional currencies, hedge currency and market-price exposure, and finance their activities through margin accounts. While the tax issues of purely domestic traders can be complex, this column illustrates the heightened tax problems that face an international trader operating in nonfunctional currencies as well as the U.S. dollar.

[RD Lorence & RJ Shapiro, 2 J. Int'l Tax'n 374.]

"Foreign currency bonds raise many U.S. tax issues" (1991). In its massive set of Section 988 regulations, the IRS gave short shrift to several critically important issues for U.S. investors in foreign-currency-denominated bonds. Particularly troublesome is the treatment of market discount, premiums for both OID and non-OID bonds, and conversions into and exchanges of bonds for the obligor's stock.

The Section 988 regulations fail to adequately apply many of the fundamental concepts in the taxation of debt instruments to foreign-currency-denominated bonds. The administrative burdens placed by the regulations on U.S.-regulated investment companies that are international bond funds are obvious. The treatment of Section 988(d) hedges under Regulation § 1.988-5T is necessarily similarly flawed, as the synthetic debt instrument is subject to OID and related rules. Therefore, reformation of these basic rules should be made before the IRS addresses the treatment of the ever-increasing array of exotic financial products in the marketplace, such as floating rate bonds denominated in European currency units.

[RJ Shapiro & RD Lorence, 2 J. Int'l Tax'n 124.]

"Two tax-efficient investments in foreign equities" (1991). A critical federal income tax issue is whether foreign equity index options (warrants) are classified as Section 1256 contracts and thus governed by the mark-to-market rules of that section, subject to certain exceptions (such as for dealers). Resolution depends on whether there is a designation of a contract market by the Commodities Futures Trading Commission (CFTC) for a futures contract based on the index or, alternatively, a determination by the Treasury that the option qualifies for such a designation. No such Treasury designation has been made for the warrants. If there is a CFTC designation, under rules enacted in 1981, each warrant is treated as sold for its market price on the last day of the taxable year. The holder recognizes capital gain or loss equal to the difference between that market price and its basis. Such gain or loss is 60 percent long-term and 40 percent short-term. This is, of course, a major exception to the general rule that paper (unrealized) profits and losses are not given effect for tax purposes.

Under the Section 1256 rules, the tax treatment turns upon whether the warrants should be treated as nonequity options. A nonequity option is any option (these warrants clearly are options, although settled in cash rather than by delivery of property) listed on an exchange (here, the American Stock Exchange), that is not an equity option. An equity option is any option to buy or sell stock or based on the value of a stock or stock index (as here) unless there is a CFTC designation (as there is for certain foreign index contracts). Thus, under the statutory terminology, a stock index option becomes a nonequity option.

The attractive feature of foreign index warrants from a federal income tax standpoint is the avoidance of numerous complex technical issues attendant to transactions in foreign equity products. First, because the options are settled in dollars, there are no foreign currency translation issues under Section 988. This is an important concern, because the index warrants are settled by reference to the value of the local currency in which the bourse is located. Any transaction in which the taxpayer is entitled to receive an amount determined by reference to the value of one or more nonfunctional currencies (e.g., Japanese yen, British pound, French franc to most U.S. investors) is a Section 988 transaction if it involves gross income to be paid at a later date or is an option or similar financial instrument, unless an exception applies. If acquisition of a warrant were a Section 988 transaction, the foreign currency gain or loss (based on movements in the yen, pound, or franc) against the dollar during the optionee's holding period would have to be separately accounted for and generally treated as ordinary. Second, because the warrants are derivative products and not the underlying foreign equities, no foreign taxes are due. This eliminates foreign tax credit issues. This is important because the sales would not generate foreign-source income, increasing the likelihood that the foreign taxes would not currently be usable.

Overall, the foreign index products present the U.S. investor with a means of speculating on the direction of a foreign bourse's equities and the foreign currency's movement against the dollar in a highly tax-efficient structure.

The equity securities of numerous foreign companies are listed on U.S. markets in the form of American Depositary Receipts (ADRs). An ADR is a security issued by a depositary bank in the United States that evidences a right to a particular number or fraction of shares of a specified class of the foreign corporation. The actual shares are held by the depositary and can be used in exchange for the ADR.

In effect, the ADR is a sophisticated warehouse receipt. Although traded on U.S. markets, for tax purposes an ADR is stock of the foreign corporation, and dividends are subject to withholding for foreign taxes by the depositary. Because most ADRs represent shares of corporations of treaty countries (e.g., Australia, the United Kingdom, Japan), the U.S. holder generally is entitled to reduced treaty rates. The typical rate is 15 percent for portfolio dividends (that is, the holder generally has under 10 percent of the payor's equity). Similarly, no local gains tax would be levied by any treaty country. Thus, ADRs are in essence foreign equities in U.S. packaging.

[RJ Shapiro & RD Lorence, 1 J. Int'l Tax'n 314.]

"Functional and nonfunctional currency regulations" (1990). The IRS has issued Regulation §§ 1.985-1 through 1.985-4 concerning the determination of functional currency, the election by QBUs to use the U.S. dollar as their functional currency, and QBU accounting methods. Additional temporary regulations under Section 985 also explain the adjustments that must be made to determine U.S. taxes when there is a change in functional currency.

The IRS has also issued Temporary Regulation §§ 1.988-1T through 1.988-5T on nonfunctional currency transactions. These regulations cover the timing, character, and source of gain or loss owing to exchange rate fluctuations. Rules for integrated hedging transactions are also provided. Some of these rules are effective prospectively.

[72 J. Tax'n 48.]

"New foreign currency regulations provide guidance under Section 988" (1990). Subpart J (Sections 985 through 989) was added by TRA 1986 to provide rules for the treatment of foreign currency transactions. The cornerstone of Subpart J is Section 988, which provides rules for determining the timing, amount, character, and source of gain or loss owing to fluctuations in exchange rates (exchange gain or loss) for Section 988 transactions, i.e., transactions denominated in or determined by reference to the value of a taxpayer's nonfunctional currency. Section 988 also provides rules for Section 988(d) hedging transactions.

This article discusses Section 988 and the temporary regulations issued under Section 988 on September 20, 1989. The article gives particular attention to (1) the definition of "Section 988 transactions"; (2) the timing and amount of exchange gain or loss; (3) the character of exchange gain or loss; (4) the source of exchange gain or loss; and (5) Section 988(d) hedging transactions.

The article concludes that the temporary regulations contain a few gaps (such as the determination of exchange gain or loss from debt instruments denominated in more than one currency) and some surprises (such as the treatment of debt-to-equity conversions as taxable events), but overall provide ample guidance, particularly through the use of numerous examples.

[RM Wilson & RG Nassau, 72 J. Tax'n 96.]

"QBUs include trusts, estates, and partnerships" (1990). The definition of "QBU" has been expanded by an amendment to Regulation § 1.989(a)-1 (TD 8279), to include partnerships, trusts, and estates. Special rules are also provided for treating as a separate QBU any activity engaged in for profit that is effectively connected with a U.S. trade or business. Under the amendment, effective for tax years beginning after 1986, partnerships, trusts, and estates (or their branches) may qualify as QBUs. Thus, Section 987, dealing with branch transactions, may apply to remittances from partnerships, trusts, or estates to partners or beneficiaries. To qualify as a QBU, the activities of the partnership, trust, or estate must constitute a trade or business for which a separate set of books and records is maintained.

Activities carried on for profit (wherever conducted and regardless of their frequency) that are, or are treated as, effectively connected with the conduct of a trade or business within the United States are separate QBUs, provided separate books and records are used to determine their income or losses. Books of original entry and ledger accounts (both general and subsidiary) or similar records will suffice.

[72 J. Tax'n 170.]

"Regulations expand the Subpart J foreign currency rules" (1990). Enactment of the foreign currency rules in Sections 985 through 989 by TRA 1986 imposed structure on an increasingly complex area of sophisticated financial transactions. The statutory definitions contained in Sections 985 and 989(a) provide that all income tax determinations are to be made in the taxpayer's functional currency. Many companies may have one currency as their financial reporting currency and another as their Subpart J functional currency. All taxpayers must use the dollar, except for a QBU that operates in an economic environment where a significant part of its activities are conducted, and which keeps its books and records in a foreign currency. Although Section 989(a) refers to a QBU as "any separate and clearly identified unit of trade or business of a taxpayer which maintains separate books and records," the regulations provide that any income-generating activity is a QBU. Thus, a parent corporation, a branch, a subsidiary, or an individual's investment activities, can be a QBU. In addition, the regulations provide that any activity generating ECI is a QBU, whose functional currency is always the dollar. The result of these regulations is that a U.S. taxpayer can be required to apply Subpart J to a wide variety of entities.

The taxpayer's selection of the proper functional currency for the parent corporation and each of its subsidiary corporations and foreign branches is essential for two reasons. First, the adoption of a functional currency is treated as a method of accounting. Thus, a change in functional currencies is a change in accounting methods requiring IRS consent. Second, the choice of functional currency determines whether the transactions are Section 988 transactions involving nonfunctional currencies. These would be subject to transaction-by-transaction segregation and to special treatment of currency gain or loss from gain or loss on the underlying transaction involved.

The regulations' and legislative history's favor of the dollar as the functional currency appears to be intended to trap as many transactions as possible under Section 988. The dollar is required in the case of the following taxpayer or activities:

1. An individual;
2. A QBU resident in the United States, or its possessions;
3. A QBU electing the dollar;
4. A QBU that does not keep its books and records in the foreign currency in which a significant part of its activities are conducted;
5. An activity that produces ECI; and
6. A QBU conducting activities primarily using the dollar.

The eight nonexclusive criteria examined under the facts and circumstances test are:

1. The currency of the country in which the QBU is resident;
2. The currencies of the QBU's cash flows;
3. The currencies in which the QBU generates revenues and incurs expenses;
4. The currencies in which borrowing and lending are made;
5. The currencies of the QBU's sales markets;
6. The currencies in which pricing and other financial decisions are made;
7. The duration of the QBU's operations; and
8. The significance or volume of the QBU's independent activities.

Of major importance is the rule found in Regulation § 1.985-1(c)(5) that the Financial Accounting Standards Board Standard 52 functional currency ordinarily will be the Subpart J functional currency, if the criteria in the regulations are employed.

The generally accepted accounting principles (GAAP) need not be followed if the factors used were not similar to the regulation's factors and do not provide any real guidance on this issue because no explanation is furnished. Even where the GAAP functional currency is based on factors similar to those set forth in the regulations, the QBU can opt to use local currency as its functional currency if the factors are sufficiently split, provided the QBU keeps its books and records in the local currency.

The regulations further provide that although the IRS can presume that a QBU keeps its books in the currency of the economic environment in which a significant part of its activities is conducted, the QBU cannot use this presumption affirmatively. The regulations' approach leads to divergence of GAAP and tax accounting, creating substantial compliance burdens for the taxpayers where no significant tax policy appears to be in jeopardy.

Because the regulations provide that a foreign corporation and each of its branches can qualify as a QBU, a method is provided for determining a corporation's functional currency when it has two or more branches with different functional currencies. The corporation must make an independent fact and circumstances analysis to determine the dominant currency.

[RJ Shapiro & RD Lorence, 1 J. Int'l Tax'n 55.]

"U.S. treatment of foreign currency transactions modified" (1990). A taxpayer who normally deals in U.S. dollars has an exchange gain or loss for book accounting purposes from a foreign currency demoninated transaction whenever there is a change in the U.S.-dollar value of the foreign currency. For federal income tax purposes, only in a Section 988 transaction is exchange gain or loss accorded independent significance. Section 988 applies to

1. Determine the timing of exchange gain or loss;
2. Prescribe ordinary (as opposed to capital) characterization; and
3. Source or allocate such gain or loss by reference to the taxpayer's residence.

Temporary Regulation §§ 1.988-1T through 1.988-5T address the threshold issue regarding the definition of a "Section 988 transaction." Generally, statutory ambiguities are clarified in favor of an expansive scope. At the same time, both the temporary regulations and the statute provide rules of convenience and other exceptions that limit the operative rules of Section 988. As a result, even when transactions fall within the statutory definition of a "Section 988 transaction," taxpayers may not be required (or permitted) to account separately for exchange gain or loss. Conversely, in view of the regulatory refinements, Section 988 may come into play to alter the tax consequences of certain transactions that are not specifically described in Section 988.

In any transaction involving a currency other than the U.S. dollar, the temporary regulations should be carefully reviewed to determine the applicability of Section 988. While the temporary regulations are generally effective for transactions occurring after 1986, various provisions set forth special effective dates.

[LG Stodghill, 1 J. Int'l Tax'n 28.]

¶ 1.05 CLASSIFICATION OF ENTITIES[5]

German business organization classified as association taxable as corporation. The IRS ruled that a German business organization (GmbH) formed under German law possessed the corporate characteristics of centralized management, limited liability, and free transferability, but not continuity of life. Therefore, the GmbH was classified as an association taxable as a corporation.

[Rev. Rul. 93-4, 1993-3 IRB 5, modifying and superseding Rev. Rul. 77-214, 1977-1 CB 408.]

Chinese joint venture entity taxed as U.S. corporation. This letter ruling held that an entity formed under the joint venture law of the People's Republic of China (PRC) would be classified as a corporation for U.S. tax purposes. One joint venturer is a U.S. corporation; the other is a PRC municipal corporation. The entity had the corporate characteristics of centralized management and limited liability. The ruling also concluded that the entity had the corporate characteristic of continuity of life.

The entity's articles of association provide that either party may bring the entity to an early termination in certain situations, one of which is the bankruptcy, etc., of either joint venturer. The entity's articles of association state that such a bankruptcy constitutes grounds for termination "without any further action by the board of directors." The U.S. company represented in this regard that "upon the demand of the appropriate party . . . the board of directors will unanimously pass a resolution to submit an application for dissolution of [the entity] to the appropriate authorities."

Under Regulation § 301.7701-2(b)(1), an organization has continuity of life if the bankruptcy, etc., of a member will not cause a dissolution of the organization. The IRS apparently felt that bankruptcy, etc., would not cause a dissolution of the PRC entity because its articles merely *empower* a member to cause dissolution.

The IRS also held that Regulation § 301.7701-2(b)(3) did not apply. Under that provision, an organization lacks continuity of life if the agreement establishing the organization provides that the organization can be terminated by the will of any member. The IRS apparently concluded that the PRC joint venture entity could not be terminated by the "will" of either member, because the specified event (bankruptcy, etc.) must occur before either of the members has the power to cause a dissolution. Thus, the power is conditional.

[Priv. Ltr. Rul. 9152009.]

U.K. unlimited liability company is partnership. This letter ruling characterizes a U.K. unlimited liability company as a partnership for U.S. tax purposes. It states that the U.K. entity will lack the corporate characteristics of limited liability and free transferability of interests. The latter conclusion is based on the entity's Articles of Association, which state that three specified corporations are its only permitted "shareholders." Its shares are not transferable to anyone other than those shareholders under any circumstances.

[Priv. Ltr. Rul. 9132054.]

"Hybridizing foreign entities can cause disaster" (1993). In Revenue Ruling 93-4, the IRS has made it easier for a foreign entity to be classified as a partnership for U.S. tax purposes. Some of these entities may nevertheless be taxable as corporations in their home country.

The authors first discuss use of a hybrid entity (i.e., an entity that is taxed in the United States as a partnership even though it is a corporation for other purposes) to avoid restrictions under the indirect foreign tax credit and S corporation rules. Thereafter, they discuss certain tax disadvantages caused by dealing with a hybrid entity. The situations examined here are (1) the transfer of a foreign hybrid between members of a U.S. consolidated group; (2) the merger of a hybrid foreign entity into a foreign corporation (as a partnership liquidation followed by an asset transfer, an asset transfer followed by a liquidation, and a transfer of partnership interests followed by the liquidation); (3) the merger of a foreign corporation into the hybrid foreign entity (as an asset transfer followed by a corporate liquidation, a corporate liquidation followed by an asset transfer, and a transfer of shares followed by a corporate liquidation); and (4) a Section 304 transaction involving hybrid foreign entities. With regard to each of these situations, the authors discuss the attending tax consequences.

Next, the authors review Revenue Ruling 93-4 and its rejection of the "single economic interest" theory previously used to determine the entity status of foreign business organizations. In discussing this ruling, the authors indicate its impact on the holdings of Revenue Ruling 77-214 on the corporate factors of continuity of life and free transferability. Last, the authors consider planning under Revenue Ruling 93-4. Here, the tax planning problems discussed are the effect of a foreign law provision requiring entity dissolution on the bankruptcy of an equity holder in the entity, U.S. tax partnership classification of a foreign entity with only a single owner, and the foreign tax credit consequences of converting a foreign corporation to a foreign hybrid.

[JS Karls & CM Siegel, 4 J. Int'l Tax'n 340.]

"IRS modifies rules for classifying in-house joint ventures" (1993). In Revenue Ruling 93-4, the IRS issued its long-awaited ruling revising its position on whether affiliated corporations can form a limited liability company that is treated as a partnership for U.S. tax purposes. Although Revenue Ruling 93-4 reaches the same answer as its predecessor (Revenue Ruling 77-214) on the particular facts, its modified analysis provides a road map showing how a GmbH could have qualified as a partnership for U.S. tax purposes merely by adding an appropriate clause to its organizational documents. Recent letter rulings confirm that such a clause will work in the same manner for other foreign in-house joint ventures or for an in-house joint venture conducted as a U.S. entity.

The author first analyzes Revenue Ruling 77-214 and the "separate interest" analysis used by the IRS during the period from 1977 to 1992. In this regard, additional concerns raised by the decision in *MCA, Inc. & Universal City Studios, Inc.*, a 1982 Ninth Circuit case, are explored.

Next, the author considers Revenue Ruling 93-4. Specific discussion is provided on this ruling's consequences for the formation of in-house foreign joint ventures that will gain U.S. partnership classification. Thereafter, he explores the question, raised by Revenue Ruling 93-4, of whether a GmbH could be classified as a branch (i.e., permanent establishment) for U.S. tax purposes rather than as a corporate subsidiary of a U.S. corporation.

The author then reviews the impact of Revenue Ruling 93-4 on U.S. in-house joint ventures. He concludes that this ruling reaffirms the holding of its predecessor. However, unlike its predecessor, it provides guidance on what clauses to include in the organizational documents to cause a GmbH or other joint venture entity to be classified as a partnership, even if it is owned solely by affiliated corporations.

[BN Davis, 4 J. Int'l Tax'n 76.]

¶ 1.06 INTERNATIONAL TAXATION OF PARTICULAR OCCUPATIONS

[1] Teachers, Students, and Researchers

IRS issues revenue procedure concerning representations alien must make to claim withholding exemption under certain treaties. This revenue procedure modifies two earlier revenue procedures by providing the representations that an alien must make to claim a withholding exemption under certain newly ratified income tax treaties. Under most U.S. income tax treaties, an alien student, teacher, or researcher at a U.S. university or other educational institution who receives income for personal services is generally exempt from income tax provided certain requirements are met. These requirements include a limited number of years in which the alien can claim the exemption and a maximum dollar amount for the exemption in a taxable year. Normally, the payor of compensation for personal services is required under Section 1441 or Section 3405 to withhold and pay over federal taxes on such income. However, withholding is not required if the income is exempt under treaty. In order to claim the withholding exemption, the alien must submit Form 8233 to the withholding agent certifying that the income is exempt from taxation under treaty. This revenue procedure provides the representations that an alien must include in Form 8233 to claim a withholding exemption under the newly ratified treaties with Germany, India, Indonesia, Spain, and Tunisia. This revenue procedure also modifies the representations in a prior revenue procedure pertaining to the treaty with the former Soviet Union. This revenue procedure obsoletes representations in two prior revenue procedures pertaining to the earlier treaty with Finland, which has been replaced by a newly ratified treaty that does not exempt income earned within the United States by alien students, teachers, or researchers. This revenue procedure also modifies a prior revenue procedure with respect to the maximum annual exemption allowed students under the Cyprus treaty.

[Rev. Proc. 93-22, 1993-18 IRB 15, modifying Rev. Proc. 87-8, 1987-1 CB 336, and Rev. Proc. 87-9, 1987-1 CB 368.]

"Teachers and scholars get tax benefits here and abroad" (1992). The cross-cultural exchange of knowledge between people of various nationalities has historically been valued by the international community. This belief is embodied in the Code and in rulings that affect foreign teachers and scholars in the United States and U.S. teachers and scholars abroad. Additionally, most income tax treaties to which the United States is a party contain specific exemptions for amounts received by teachers and scholars.

Special exceptions from the general residency rules for domestic income tax purposes apply for visiting teachers and scholars, and IRS rulings provide special sourcing rules for income received by these individuals. U.S. teachers and scholars abroad may usually receive significant exemptions or deductions for U.S. tax purposes. These benefits may often be combined with exemptions under income tax treaties to significantly reduce the worldwide tax burden imposed on income from academic pursuits.

Section 7701(b)(1) defines "resident status" for U.S. tax purposes. U.S. citizens, individuals who are lawful permanent residents of the United States, and individuals who meet the "substantial presence" test are subject to U.S. tax on worldwide income. Special exceptions to the substantial presence test apply to visiting teachers and scholars. U.S. days of J-1 visa holding teachers, researchers, and trainees temporarily in the United States are not counted for determining residence, pursuant to Section 7701(b)(3)(C). This exemption applies for two out of six calendar years. The exemption increases to five years for foreign students.

Status as a nonresident alien individual does not exempt the visiting teacher or scholar from paying U.S. income tax. Compensation paid to such individual for U.S. personal services is subject to 30 percent withholding at the source, unless subject to wage withholding. Because the compensation is ECI, a refund of a portion of this tax can usually be claimed by filing Form 1040NR.

In Revenue Ruling 89-67, the IRS addressed the question of how to determine the source of a fellowship or scholarship. According to that ruling, payments for fellowships or scholarships are not compensation for personal services because no services are performed. The ruling then states that it is more appropriate to source these payments at the residence of the payor, where the principal economic nexus with the payment exists. Under Revenue Ruling 89-67, nonresident aliens who perform research or studies in the United States are not subject to U.S. income tax on amounts received from foreign payors, even if a U.S. agent disburses the funds on behalf of the foreign payor. U.S. payors of grants and scholarships to nonresident alien individuals for study outside the United States must now withhold U.S. income tax from grant or scholarship payments. The nonresident alien individual is subject to U.S. tax and must file Form 1040NR, even though such individual may never have set foot in the United States.

A U.S. scholar who receives a grant or scholarship for study overseas is generally subject to U.S. income tax on the full payment. Pursuant to Revenue Ruling 89-67, the scholar would not be providing personal services and therefore would not be entitled to a Section 911 exclusion.

The scholar may exclude from gross income the portion of the grant or scholarship that represents "qualified scholarship" payments under Section 117. "Qualified scholarship" payments are defined under Proposed Regulation § 1.117-6 as amounts received for tuition, related fees, books, supplies, and equipment, if the recipient is a candidate for a degree at an educational institution. Amounts received for room and board, travel, or research, are not eligible for the gross income exclusion, even if such items are included in the grant or scholarship award.

Compensation received by a teacher who is a citizen or resident of the United States is subject to U.S. income tax, regardless of where services are performed. In many institutions, however, the U.S. teacher abroad will be entitled to either the Section 911 exclusion or a deduction for "away from home" expenses. Such expenses are discussed.

Income tax treaties have historically provided liberal rules for teachers and scholars, in order to limit double taxation. This has been based in part on the importance given to the free exchange of knowledge and ideas. Income tax treaties to which the United States is a party almost universally exempt from income tax grants or scholarships that are paid from abroad. To qualify for the exemption, the recipient usually must be a student or trainee, and must not provide personal services on behalf of the payor. Most income tax treaties to which the United States is a party also include a separate article that exempts income received by teachers if they meet a number of requirements, which are discussed by the author.

Both the Organization for Economic Cooperation and Development (OECD)

Model Income Tax Treaty and the U.S. Model Income Tax Treaty exempt from income taxation payments received from abroad for education or training by students or apprentices who are present here for such purposes. This basic rule is found in various forms in all student and trainee treaty articles. Some of these treaty articles provide for additional exemptions that are usually more liberal than the basic provision.

The OECD and U.S. model treaties do not include a provision for teachers or researchers. Nevertheless, a majority of treaties to which the United States is a party include articles that exempt income earned by teachers and researchers.

A U.S. teacher may claim the Section 911 income exclusion for U.S. tax purposes even though such individual also obtains an exemption from foreign income tax under a teacher treaty article.

[DM Cordova, 2 J. Int'l Tax'n 343.]

[2] Athletes

"U.S. taxation of athletes in United States and abroad" (1990). U.S. federal income tax laws affect U.S. citizen athletes performing abroad, resident alien athletes performing in the United States, and nonresident alien athletes performing in the United States on professional teams, as well as performers in other mediums of entertainment. Section 871 provides that U.S. citizens and resident aliens are to be taxed on their worldwide income according to the general graduated rate scheme.

A "resident alien" is defined, under Section 7701(b), as a non–U.S. citizen who is a lawful U.S. permanent resident (i.e., has a green card) or meets the substantial presence test. There is an exception to the substantial presence test for a non–U.S. citizen athlete who was present in the United States for less than 183 days in the current year and who had a tax home in a foreign country.

Section 871(a)(1) taxes nonresident aliens on income from sources within the United States at a flat 30 percent rate unless the income is effectively connected with a U.S. trade or business. Income that is effectively connected with the conduct of a U.S. trade or business is subject to the same graduated tax rates that apply to U.S. citizens and resident aliens. The performance of professional athletic services in the United States has been held to qualify as a trade or business. Under Section 864(c)(4)(B), nonresident athletes are not subject to tax on compensation earned for services rendered outside the United States.

The general treatment discussed previously is subject to any overriding provisions of income tax treaties between the United States and a foreign country. An examination is provided of treaties with the United Kingdom, France, Canada, Italy, and Germany, those countries that commonly have their athletes perform in the United States. The current tax treaty between the United Kingdom and the United States provides a special rule for athletes and artists who receive compensation either as employees or independent contractors, which takes precedence over its general provisions. Their income is taxed in their country of residence as well as in the country where their services are performed unless their gross receipts (including reimbursed expenses) derived from such activities in the taxable year do not exceed $15,000 or its equivalent in pounds sterling. A corporation carrying on a trade or business in a country other than the country where it has a principal place of business is taxed on the profits it receives only if it carries on the business through a permanent establishment, as defined in Article 5 of the treaty. Since the income may be taxed in both the United States and United Kingdom, the treaty provides for foreign tax credits (FTCs) and also has a nondiscrimination provision that precludes each country from imposing higher taxes on nonresident aliens than on citizens. Rules for determining the residence of an individual are also included in the treaty.

The tax treaties between Italy and the United States and France and the United States are virtually identical to the U.S.–U.K. tax treaty, with a few major differences in provisions concerning the level of gross receipts and number of days of presence permitted before athletes are taxed in the country where their services are performed.

The various tax treaties provide some opportunity to engage in tax planning by shopping for the best location of residence for an athlete. For example, an athlete in either Canada or the United Kingdom, who rendered services in the United States, is not subject to tax in the United States on the income earned if it did not exceed $15,000 (or its foreign equivalent). If the athlete resided in France, the income is taxed if it exceeded $10,000. In Italy, $12,000 applies, and under the new German treaty, the annual compensation threshold is $20,000.

Another tax planning tool often mentioned is the establishment of a corporation in the athlete's country of residence that furnishes the athlete's services in the country of nonresidence. The tax treaties generally exempt from taxation the fees received by such a corporation for the athlete's services if the corporation engages in a trade or business in the country of nonresidence and does not have a permanent establishment there. Caution must be exercised in this area and a review of all the pertinent cases and rulings must be made because the IRS and the courts have disregarded the existence of a corporation where it has no meaningful purpose other than to obtain tax savings. A corporation that loans out the services of numerous athletes, handles their promotion, negotiates their endorsements, and does more than just book their events most likely could qualify for an exemption.

Where the nonresident alien athlete performs services in both the United States and a foreign country, the compensation (salary and bonuses) must be allocated between the two countries. The compensation effectively connected to a U.S. trade or business is determined by multiplying the total compensation received by the total days of performance in the United States, divided by the total days of performance for such year. A signing bonus is subject to the flat 30 percent tax to the extent it is sourced in the United States, unless a tax treaty provides otherwise.

Unless protected by a treaty, nonresident aliens should attempt to ensure they receive non-U.S.-source income before they become resident aliens of the United States because any income from sources outside the United States that is not effectively connected with the taxpayer's conduct of a U.S. trade or business is taxable if received while an individual is a resident of the United States, even if earned earlier.

An amount an employer promises to pay in future years for future services is not includable in income of the athlete if (1) the promise is unfunded or the amount is reachable by a general creditor of the team owner and (2) the athlete has no immediate present right to recover the amount set aside. Under Regulation § 1.451-2, a bonus paid in escrow that can be drawn on without substantial restrictions constitutes constructive receipt and is income to the taxpayer.

Whether they are U.S. citizens, resident aliens, or nonresident aliens, athletes providing services for professional teams can deduct all of their ordinary and necessary business expenses, subject to the 2 percent of adjusted gross income and itemized deduction limitations. Although unreimbursed expenses for travel away from home are allowed, an athlete's principal place of business has been held to be the location of the professional team, so unreimbursed travel expenses in that city, such as rent and commuting costs, are not deductible. Under Section 874(a), a nonresident alien athlete can claim deductions only for expenses that are connected with the conduct of such trade or business in the United States, under the constraints of Form 1040NR.

A U.S. citizen or resident alien athlete who receives compensation for services rendered in a foreign country can claim an FTC, a $70,000 earned income exclusion, or foreign tax deduction under Sections 901, 911, and 275(a)(4).

[P. Weisman & R. Rale, 1 J. Int'l Tax'n 218.]

¶ 1.07 INTERNATIONAL TAX EXAMINATIONS

[1] Generally

"How international tax examinations affect U.S. and foreign companies" (1992). This article examines the special problems that arise during international tax examinations. The first problem area addressed by the author concerns intercompany transfer pricing compliance. Consideration is given to the imposition of accuracy-related penalties for Section 482 disputes and Sections 6038A and 6038C's reporting and document maintenance requirements. Next, the author examines the application for and use of APAs. He reviews the required content of a request, use of expert opinions on pricing and value matters, certain prefiling matters, and the IRS's processing of an APA request.

Thereafter, the author considers relief measures for taxpayers facing the threat of double taxation or discriminatory tax treatment. In this area, he explains how to obtain competent authority assistance and how to use the mutual agreement procedures authorized by Revenue Procedure 65-17.

In the last section of this article, the author examines the IRS's response to attempts by foreign-based companies to strip earnings out of U.S. subsidiaries. Current law restrictions on the amount of debt that can be held in such subsidiaries by foreign persons are reviewed by the author. Other approaches challenged by the

IRS, such as the "superroyalty," are noted. The author concludes his article with a discussion of a number of common issues taxpayers have faced in foreign tax audits. These include transfer pricing, the classification of capital vs. ordinary expenses, the deduction of travel and entertainment expenses, depreciation, income inclusion for employee benefits, parent company management fees, expense accrual, the distinction between capital gains and ordinary income, the distinction between debt and equity investments, and the use of multiple taxpayers to reduce the effective rate of a foreign tax.

[W. O'Connor, US Tax'n Int'l Operations ¶ 7530.]

"Key issues in international tax examinations" (1992). International tax examinations by the IRS frequently include issues arising from the foreign tax credit rules, Subpart F, and intercompany pricing arrangements. In this article, the author discusses the manner in which these issues are dealt with by the IRS.

The author first discusses issues arising in the foreign tax credit area. Specific discussion is provided on problem areas with respect to interest expense and allocating R&D expenses. Next, he addresses significant Subpart F issues. Thereafter, he provides an in-depth analysis of the many issues that commonly arise with regard to intercompany pricing. Key areas include TPM, sales of tangible property, and the transfer or use of intangible property.

In the last section of this article, the author discusses recent case law developments in the targeted issues areas. Cases examined include *Sundstrand Corp.* (a 1991 Tax Court case concerning Section 482) and *Procter & Gamble* (a 1990 Tax Court case also involving Section 482).

[W. O'Connor, US Tax'n Int'l Operations ¶ 7529.]

[2] Obtaining Evidence Abroad

"United States is changing its approach to obtaining evidence abroad" (1991). Private litigants, as well as prosecutors, have traditionally employed several different techniques to obtain information from sources outside the United States. These have included the use of letters rogatory, the Hague Convention, mutual legal assistance treaties, interim executive agreements, and bilateral income tax treaties. Each of these methods has its uses, but also its limitations, in obtaining information abroad. The author discusses each of the preceding traditional techniques to obtain information from sources outside the United States, including the advantages and disadvantages of each technique.

A relatively new technique is the issuance of a summons or subpoena directly to a foreign bank or other entity for its records, by serving a branch of that bank or a subsidiary or parent of the entity located in the United States. Noting that foreign governments have strongly objected to such subpoenas (contending that they constitute an improper exercise of U.S. jurisdiction), the U.S. *Attorney's Manual* (USAM) requires prosecutors to obtain the approval of the Office of Internal Affairs of the Department of Justice (OIA) prior to issuing a subpoena for records located in a foreign country.

The USAM then provides that in considering whether to approve the issuance of such a subpoena, OIA will take the following factors into account:

1. The availability of alternative methods for obtaining the records in a timely manner, such as use of mutual assistance treaties, tax treaties, or letters rogatory;

2. The indispensability of the records to the success of the investigation or prosecution; and

3. The need to protect against the destruction of records located abroad and to protect the ability of the United States to prosecute for contempt or obstruction of justice for such destruction.

OIA concurrence also must be obtained prior to serving a subpoena to testify on an officer of, or attorney for, a foreign bank or corporation who is temporarily in, or passing through, the United States when the testimony relates to the officer's or attorney's duties in connection with the operation of a bank or corporation.

The failure to follow the procedures outlined in the USAM does not create any enforceable rights for a taxpayer. Where counsel learns of, or anticipates a request for, foreign records, counsel should nevertheless argue that USAM procedures must be followed. In some instances, OIA may well refuse to permit the issuance of a subpoena after a prosecutor's request.

With respect to the issuance of an IRS summons for offshore records, no preissuance procedures exist in the IRS *Special Agent's Handbook*. If a bank refuses to comply with a summons, however, the IRS must ask the Department of Justice to enforce it. At this stage, the USAM procedures outlined above should become applicable and should require a review prior to an enforcement action being commenced.

The article also addresses the issue of obtaining personal jurisdiction over the subpoenaed or summoned party. Once jurisdiction has been established, the critical issue becomes whether compliance with the subpoena or summons can be compelled when that compliance would result in the violation of the laws of another country. The U.S. Supreme Court and several appellate courts have held that such a violation of a foreign country's laws is not sufficient, by itself, to prevent compliance with a request for documents issued by a U.S. court.

The author also discusses the 1987 U.S. Supreme Court decision in *Society Nationale Industrielle Aerospatiale,* and how other cases have approached the issue. More case law is then analyzed in the author's discussion of summonses enforced and summonses denied. He then concludes this analysis by stating that based on prosecutors' perceptions that difficulties will be encountered if offshore records are subpoenaed or summonsed, prosecutors have begun to use yet another investigative technique, which avoids, for the most part, the problems arising in litigating issues relating to foreign law.

In the 1988 U.S. Supreme Court case of *Doe,* Doe was a target of a federal grand jury investigating possible offenses arising from manipulation of oil cargoes and the failure to report income. Doe was subpoenaed to produce records of accounts at banks in the Cayman Islands and Bermuda. The prosecutor was unable to obtain the records from the banks, because both the governments of Bermuda and the Cayman Islands objected to disclosure. Doe claimed his Fifth Amendment privilege against self-incrimination when questioned about the accounts. In an attempt to avoid time-consuming litigation with respect to compelling the banks to produce records, the IRS filed a motion seeking to compel Doe to sign twelve forms consenting to disclosure of the bank records relating to twelve different accounts where the IRS knew or suspected Doe had account control.

The issue on appeal was whether the signing of the consent forms violated Doe's Fifth Amendment privilege. The Court found that the contents of foreign bank records were not privileged under the Fifth Amendment and that the banks themselves could not invoke the Fifth Amendment, since the privilege does not extend to artificial entities. The Court also stated that the Fifth Amendment did not prevent the banks from disclosing account records, since the Constitution does not proscribe incriminating statements elicited from another.

[IM Comisky, 1 J. Int'l Tax'n 334.]

BIBLIOGRAPHY OF RESEARCH REFERENCES

[1]J. Kuntz & R. Peroni, U.S. International Taxation, (Warren Gorham Lamont 1992).

S. Singer, U.S. International Tax Forms Manual, (Warren Gorham Lamont 1993).

B. Bittker & J. Eustice, Federal Income Taxation of Corporations and Shareholders ch. 15 (Warren Gorham Lamont, 6th ed. 1994).

[2]J. Kuntz & R. Peroni, U.S. International Taxation ch. A2 (Warren Gorham Lamont 1992).

S. Singer, U.S. International Tax Forms Manual ¶ 1.03, ch. 6 (Warren Gorham Lamont 1993).

B. Bittker & J. Eustice, Federal Income Taxation of Corporations and Shareholders ¶ 15.02[1] (Warren Gorham Lamont, 6th ed. 1994).

[3]J. Kuntz & R. Peroni, U.S. International Taxation ch. A3 (Warren Gorham Lamont 1992).

S. Singer, U.S. International Tax Forms Manual ¶ 2.02, ch. 7 (Warren Gorham Lamont 1993).

B. Bittker & J. Eustice, Federal Income Taxation of Corporations and Shareholders ¶¶ 13.20–13.22 (Warren Gorham Lamont, 6th ed. 1994).

[4]J. Kuntz & R. Peroni, U.S. International Taxation ¶ A2.03[16] (Warren Gorham Lamont 1992).

S. Singer, U.S. International Tax Forms Manual ¶ 4.03 (Warren Gorham Lamont 1993).

B. Bittker & J. Eustice, Federal Income Taxation of Corporations and Shareholders ¶ 15.02[5] (Warren Gorham Lamont, 6th ed. 1994).

[5]J. Kuntz & R. Peroni, U.S. International Taxation ¶¶ B2.02, C3.02 (Warren Gorham Lamont 1992).

CHAPTER 2

U.S. Persons With Foreign Activities

¶ 2.01 DEFINITIONS OF "U.S. CITIZEN," "RESIDENT ALIEN," AND "DOMESTIC CORPORATION"[1]

[1] Generally

U.S. author living in Ireland was liable for self-employment tax where he failed to renounce his U.S. citizenship. Taxpayer, an author, lived in Ireland and claimed that he was a naturalized Irish citizen not subject to U.S. tax on his royalty income. The IRS argued that he was a U.S. citizen when he received the income, and imposed self-employment tax and penalties.

Held: For the IRS. Taxpayer failed to officially renounce his U.S. citizenship for the years in question. Thus, he remained liable for U.S. taxes during that time.

[Dacey, 63 TCM 2584, RIA TC Memo. ¶ 92,187 (1992).]

British citizen was a U.S. resident despite frequent absences. The English-born taxpayer maintained a U.S. residence, owning a condominium and other property in Florida. He also had significant business activities in the United States. Taxpayer traveled frequently outside the United States, however, and claimed that he was a nonresident alien.

Held: For the IRS. Taxpayer spent more time in the United States than in other countries and had significant connections here, including his children, property, and business.

[Bigio, 62 TCM 119, RIA TC Memo. ¶ 91,319 (1991).]

IRS issues final regulations concerning definition of "resident alien." The IRS has issued final regulations relating to the definition of a "resident alien" under Section 7701(b) and various other provisions of the Code.

[TD 8411, 1992-1 CB 254, Reg. §§ 301.7701(b)-1–301.7701(b)-9.]

IRS issues proposed regulations concerning dual-status alien who is S corporation shareholder. Proposed regulations under Section 7701(b) provide that for purposes of determining the U.S. income tax liability of a dual-status alien who is a shareholder of an S corporation, the trade or business or permanent establishment of the S corporation shall be passed through to the dual-status alien pursuant to Section 1366(b).

[INTL-121-90, 1992-1 CB 1198; Prop. Reg. § 301.7701(b)-7.]

"U.S. taxation of resident and nonresident aliens" (1993). This article examines the differences in U.S. tax treatment between resident aliens and nonresident aliens and the determination of "U.S. resident" status. The author first discusses the Section 7701(b) definition of "resident alien" for U.S. tax purposes. Included in this discussion is his analysis of the "lawful permanent resident" and "substantial presence" tests applied thereunder. The "first-year" election by certain nonresident aliens resident in a subsequent year and the "closer-connection" exception to resident alien status are also reviewed.

The author then considers the U.S. tax treatment of resident aliens, including the availability of the Section 911 foreign earned income exclusion. The U.S. tax treatment of a resident alien holding a "U.S. real property interest" is noted for resident aliens who intend to become nonresident aliens.

Next, the author discusses the U.S. tax treatment of nonresident aliens. Separate discussions are included of the U.S. tax treatment of income not effectively connected with the conduct of a trade or business in the United States, and effectively connected income (ECI). Such discussions explain the determination of the type of income involved and the deductions and credits that may be available. The treatment of gains on the disposition of "U.S. real property interests" under Section 897, that is, the Foreign Investment in Real Property Tax Act (FIRPTA), is also explained. The U.S. estate tax treatment of nonresident aliens is reviewed.

Last, the author addresses certain special issues in this area, including: (1) a dual-resident taxpayer's resident status in determining if a corporation meets the S corporation requirements; (2) the implications for controlled foreign corporation (CFC) designation and shareholder taxation when a nonresident alien becomes a resident; and (3) the deemed disposition of a passive foreign investment company (PFIC) when a shareholder ceases to be a resident.

[HF Wunder, US Tax'n Int'l Operations ¶ 15,508.]

"New regulations define 'resident alien' " (1992). The IRS has issued final regulations, which expand the definition of "resident alien" under Section 7701(b)(1). The regulations revise proposals issued in 1987, and are generally effective after 1984.

[3 J. Int'l Tax'n 24.]

"New tax planning opportunities for U.S. resident and nonresident aliens" **(1992).** An alien's U.S. income tax liability can vary greatly depending on whether the person is a resident alien or nonresident alien. This article examines the determination of U.S. resident status for aliens. The authors first discuss the definition of "resident alien" in Section 7701(b). The "lawful permanent resident" and "substantial presence" tests thereunder are given detailed examination. Exemptions from the "substantial presence" test are then enumerated and discussed. Thereafter, special rules for applying these tests are considered, including the tax avoidance rule. Next, the authors explore the election by a nonresident alien to be treated as a resident alien under both the "first-year election to be treated as a resident" and the "joint return with resident spouse" election. The impact of income tax treaties on dual-resident taxpayers is then examined. Last, the authors cover various tax planning pointers for scenarios in which a choice of resident or nonresident alien status is available. Planning into and away from the "resident alien" definition is illustrated.

[RJ Rizzo & CD Daniel, US Tax'n Int'l Operations ¶ 15,507.]

"U.S. tax residency rules broadened in final regulations" (1992). Whether an alien is a U.S. resident for tax purposes is crucial to determining the alien's U.S. tax liability. Resident aliens are generally taxed at graduated rates on their worldwide income in the same manner as U.S. citizens. By contrast, nonresident aliens are subject to tax at graduated rates only on net income effectively connected with a U.S. trade or business and at a flat rate on the gross amount of certain other U.S.-source income. In April 1992, the IRS adopted final regulations under Section 7701(b), which amplify the operation of the statutory tests for residency of both aliens and citizens.

The authors provide a background discussion of this area, which includes an examination of the scope of the regulations and use of the "green card" test. Also addressed is the "substantial presence" test, the 121-day safe harbor thereunder for aliens without a green card, the determination of excluded days despite physical presence in the United States (and the four grounds for exclusion), and the "closer connection" exception for aliens present in the United States at least 183 days based on the weighted formula, but actually present for less than 183 days during the current year.

Next, the authors discuss the duration of U.S. residency, including the regulation provisions concerning starting and termination dates, dual-status years, breaks in U.S. residency, and dual residences. Certain other considerations are also discussed by the authors. These considerations include the regulations' procedural requirements (which apply in connection with the claiming of the "closer connection" exception and the exclusion of "U.S. days"), the treatment of illegal aliens, effective dates, and proposed rules for S corporations with dual-resident shareholders.

The authors conclude that the final regulations strictly limit the availability of the closer connection exception, the medical exception, and certain other exceptions to substantial presence. Moreover, the regulations require current reporting and substantiation to qualify for such exceptions. To avoid the risk of U.S. residency and the reporting requirements, many aliens will prefer to confine their actual presence to the 121-day safe harbor or to otherwise not exceed the 183-day threshold, without the necessity of relying on the exceptions to substantial presence. Of perhaps most interest to tax advisers are the new opportunities presented by the potential ability of certain treaty-country residents to become S corporation shareholders.

[AS Lederman & B. Hirsh, 77 J. Tax'n 152.]

[2] Loss of Citizenship

IRS issues revenue ruling concerning individuals who lost U.S. citizenship and subsequently had their citizenship retroactively restored. This revenue ruling, which involves four fact situations, provides guidance concerning several categories of individuals who have failed to file past years' federal income and gift tax returns, including individuals who lost their U.S. citizenship and subsequently had that citizenship retroactively restored. The IRS ruled, among other things, that individuals who lost their U.S. citizenship and had it retroactively restored before January 1, 1993, will not be held liable for federal income taxes as U.S. citizens between the date they lost their U.S. citizenship and the beginning of the taxable year when their citizenship was restored, and will not be held liable for federal gift taxes as U.S. citizens between the date they lost their U.S. citizenship and January 1 of the calendar year when their citizenship was restored. Individuals who lost their U.S. citizenship and have it retroactively restored after December 31, 1992, will not be held liable for federal income taxes as U.S. citizens between the date they lost their U.S. citizenship and the beginning of their first taxable year beginning after December 31, 1992, and will not be held liable for federal gift taxes as U.S. citizens between the date they lost their U.S citizenship and January 1, 1993.

[Rev. Rul. 92-109, 1992-2 CB 3.]

"Expatriation of U.S. individuals—a tax planning alternative" (1993). When individuals abandon their U.S. citizenship, several income, estate, and gift tax advantages may arise. This article focuses on the tax advantages to the former U.S. citizen (the expatriate) who becomes a nonresident alien for U.S. income, estate, and gift tax purposes. Adverse U.S. consequences are also considered from the loss of U.S. citizen status. The author first discusses the "expatriation to avoid tax" provision of the Code (Section 877), which subjects the expatriate to U.S. tax on income, though not in the same manner as U.S. citizens and residents. Certain aspects of Section 877's tax avoidance rules are discussed, including exceptions for cause (i.e., the automatic, nonvoluntary loss of U.S. citizenship occurring under the immigration rules). Thereafter, he examines proof of no tax avoidance purpose in the loss of U.S. citizenship through analysis of case law. The method of alternative income taxation applied under Section 877 is then explained, along with its gross income limitations and special source rules. Various cases and rulings on expatriating to gain tax treaty benefits are then discussed. Last considered in this part of the article is income tax planning for both U.S. citizens and nonresident aliens thinking of becoming U.S. citizens. In the second part of this article, the author examines the estate tax avoidance rule for expatriates. The author considers application of the "expatriation to avoid tax" provision and the generally less favorable treatment accorded nonresident aliens under the U.S. estate tax provisions. Thereafter, he examines U.S. estate taxation of the estates of U.S. expatriate-decedents to whom the "avoidance" rules apply. Next, the estate tax benefits of expatriation are noted. Thereafter, the author discusses the gift tax avoidance rules to the extent that they differ from the estate tax rules. Planning in this area is also considered.

[M. Rosenberg, US Tax'n Int'l Operations ¶ 15,503.]

"IRS gives expatriates income and gift tax relief" (1993). In Revenue Ruling 92-109, the IRS considered the issue of income and gift tax relief for individuals in four categories who had not filed tax returns for years in which they were (or thought they were) not U.S. citizens, or were U.S. citizens who lived abroad. This article first sets forth the four fact patterns considered in the ruling. Thereafter, the applicable gift tax and income tax return filing requirements are reviewed, along with the rules on the relinquishment of U.S. citizenship. Last, the IRS's analysis of each situation is examined and commentary is offered on some of the ruling's ramifications.

[20 Est. Plan. 179.]

"Ruling provides filing relief for expatriates" (1993). According to Revenue Ruling 92-109, individuals who performed expatriating acts and lost their U.S. citizenship are not liable for income or gift taxes as citizens during the expatriation period. The ruling also discusses possible relief for individuals who performed such acts but did not lose their U.S. citizenship, or were unable to file during a period of foreign residence owing to extenuating circumstances.

[78 J. Tax'n 138.]

¶ 2.02 U.S. PERSONS WORKING ABROAD[2]

[1] Generally

"Tax planning for Americans working overseas" (1992). U.S. citizens or residents who live and work abroad, though subject to U.S. tax on their worldwide income, may be able to exclude from gross income foreign earned income and a certain amount of employer-provided foreign housing costs. A deduction may also be available for housing costs incurred directly by the employee. This article addresses qualification for these exclusions, their elements, the deduction for foreign housing costs, and preparation of the returns on which they are claimed.

The authors first discuss qualification for the deduction or exclusion under Section 911. Specific attention is given to the meaning of "tax home" and how one is established abroad, qualification under the bona fide residency test (and the meaning of "resident" and "resident alien"), qualification under the "physical presence" test, and the "restricted country" limitation. Revenue Procedure 92-63, which waives the time requirements in the above tests for certain countries suffering internal strife, is also discussed. The effects of certain tax treaties on these tests are also explained.

Next, they discuss the election and computation of the Section 911 foreign earned income exclusion, the Section 911 foreign housing exclusion, and the foreign housing cost deduction, including the carryover of deductible amounts. Thereafter, the authors examine the use of the U.S. foreign tax credit (FTC) by U.S. employees living and working abroad. They also consider the Code's denial of a deduction or credit attributable or allocable to excluded income.

In the last part of this article, the authors review the tax treatment of moving expenses associated with a foreign move, the determination of estimated taxes and withholding for U.S. employees working abroad, the effect of having a foreign tax home on the gain rollover for sales of personal residences (Section 1034), the rental of an employee's U.S. residence, the exclusion of employer-furnished meals and lodging, the payment of Federal Insurance Contributions Act (FICA) tax by the U.S. employee while abroad, and the reporting of foreign bank accounts. The authors consider the tax return procedure, including automatic extensions, applicable to U.S. employees working abroad.

[US Tax'n Int'l Operations ¶ 13,507.]

"Understanding tax reimbursement policies" (1992). Most companies have some type of policy to address the needs of their expatriate employees. This article concerns how U.S. employees are "reimbursed" for expenses and taxes paid when living and working abroad.

The author first explains the U.S. tax treatment of U.S. employee expatriates. In doing so, he discusses the foreign earned income exclusion and the foreign housing cost exclusion. Next, he considers certain tax reimbursement policies whereunder employers attempt to equalize the tax burden of U.S. expatriate employees through tax equalization and tax protection schemes. The different means of carrying out these schemes and their tax consequences are reviewed by the author.

Thereafter, he considers tax reimbursement methods, including payment of an employee's additional tax burden through a gross-up and a rollover of such tax burden as an additional compensation in the following year. An example is provided illustrating the operation of each of these methods. Last, he discusses other common allowances and reimbursements provided to expatriates. Specific attention is given to allowances for goods and services, housing, and moving expenses.

In the appendix of this article, the author has provided forms for calculating allowances and tax liabilities for expatriates.

[EB Andrew, US Tax'n Int'l Operations ¶ 13,506.]

"Planning for state and local taxation of U.S. expatriates" (1991). In this article, the authors examine the state income tax implications of a U.S. citizen or resident working abroad for an extended period. An in-depth review is provided of the taxing systems of New York, California, and Illinois, as well as the federal system that impacts state income tax computations. The authors first discuss a state's basis for taxing a U.S. expatriate. Within this discussion, the authors consider the U.S. residency tests and the Section 911 exclusions. Next, they discuss state residency tests and the variations that exist among the states. Thereafter, the authors specifically review California, New York, and Illinois tax rules. With respect to each state they consider the residency test applied to U.S. expatriates, the impact of the federal exclusions under Section 911, the effect of the federal FTC, as well as other state tax implications. Last, they discuss tax planning in this area, at both the state and federal levels.

The authors conclude that for a company attempting to design a uniform policy for compensating its expatriate employees, the varying state rules create uncertainties and complexities that can easily result in inequitable consequences for particular expatriates. To alleviate any undue burden on its expatriates, compensation policies should provide compensation at an amount that is determined after taking into account all federal and state tax costs. To do so requires a sophisticated understanding of the federal and state tax rules applicable to expatriates.

[W. Zink, ST Ryan & G. Thornton, US Tax'n Int'l Operations ¶ 13,509.]

Determination that Panama Canal Commission was U.S. agency resulted in loss of taxpayer's Section 911 foreign earned income exclusion. In 1981 and 1982, taxpayer was employed by the Panama Canal Commission (PCC). One of the grounds upon which taxpayer excluded income received from the PCC was the Section 911 foreign earned income exclusion. The IRS determined that the PCC was a U.S. agency and therefore the foreign earned income exclusion was not available to taxpayer. The district court agreed with the IRS and held that the PCC was a U.S. agency. Taxpayer appealed.

Held: Affirmed for the IRS. The PCC is a U.S. agency under the test set forth in *Kalinski*, 528 F2d 969 (1st Cir. 1976). Applying this three-part test, it was determined that the United States "controlled" the PCC, established it to effectuate U.S. government purposes, used it to generate government (not private) revenue, and limited employment by the PCC to government-connected personnel.

[Payne, 980 F2d 148, 71 AFTR2d 93-323, 92-2 USTC ¶ 50,609 (2d Cir. 1992).]

[2] Exclusions From Gross Income Under Section 911

Nonappropriate fund instrumentality (NAFI) personnel were employees of U.S. agency for foreign exclusion purposes. Taxpayers worked for NAFIs in West Germany. NAFIs are U.S. government agencies providing services to U.S. military personnel. The Tax Court upheld the disallowance of the foreign earned income exclusion.

Held: Affirmed for the IRS. Under some federal laws, NAFI personnel are independent contractors. For purposes of the Section 911 exclusion, however, there is no indication that Congress intended "employee" to have any meaning other than its normal common-law definition.

[Matthews, 907 F2d 1173, 66 AFTR2d 90-5282, 90-2 USTC ¶ 50,363 (DC Cir. 1990).]

Grandfathered higher pre-1962 limit on foreign income exclusion was not applicable. Taxpayer worked overseas for thirty years until retiring in 1982. He claimed the maximum foreign earned income exclusion available for that year under Section 911, $75,000. He then filed an amended return to also exclude certain housing and moving expense reimbursements that he claimed were exempted from the limitation under a grandfather clause in the 1962 act that first placed a cap on the foreign earned income exclusion. The IRS claimed that the grandfather clause no longer applied.

Held: For the IRS. Section 911 as in effect in 1962 was repealed by substitution when the Foreign Earned Income Act of 1978 revised Section 911, and the grandfather clause then expired by its own terms.

[Foreman, 26 Cl. Ct. 553, 69 AFTR2d 92-1399, 92-1 USTC ¶ 50,295 (Cl. Ct. 1992).]

After determining that taxpayer was independent contractor for U.S. agency, Tax Court holds that foreign earned income exclusion was available though no tax was paid to foreign country in which he worked. Taxpayer was a U.S. citizen and a civil engineer. In November 1983, taxpayer contracted with the U.S. Agency for International Development, a federal agency, to work as a civil engineering consultant on an emergency disaster relief project in Ecuador. Taxpayer worked in Ecuador for this agency in 1984 and 1985. Although taxpayer filed a W-4 form with the agency, the agency did not issue taxpayer a W-2 nor withhold or pay employment taxes for taxpayer in 1984 or 1985. On his 1984 and 1985 returns, taxpayer excluded all amounts paid to him by the agency under the Section 911 foreign earned income exclusion. Such income was reported by taxpayer as nonemployee compensation and an offsetting deduction was then claimed under the exclusion. Taxpayer did not pay any Ecuadorean taxes on this income because he believed that the grant agreement between the U.S. and Ecuador for disaster relief exempted his compensation from such taxation. The IRS determined that taxpayer was an employee and not an independent contractor for the agency, and thus did not qualify for the exclusion. Additionally, the IRS determined that even if the exclusion were available it would not be allowed, because taxpayer did not pay Ecuadorean taxes on his compensation from the agency.

Held: For taxpayer. In determining whether a person is an employee or an independent contractor, the primary test is whether the person for whom the work is performed has the right to control the activities of the individual whose status is in issue, not only as to the result but also as to the means and method to be used for accomplishing the result. This is the same common-law employee status test that is applied in determining whether an individual is an employee of the federal government under Section 911. Under the facts, despite the type of contract used by the agency, the agency did not have the right or ability to control taxpayer in such a manner as to render him an employee. This conclusion is supported by other factors, such as the failure to issue a W-2 form and withhold or pay employment taxes for taxpayer, all of which indicate that the agency did not view taxpayer as its employee. Finally, there is no requirement that a person claiming the foreign earned income exclusion under Section 911 pay income tax to a foreign country. Taxpayer's position that his income was exempted under the agreement between Ecuador and the United States was not inconsistent with respect to his position that he was an independent contractor qualifying for the earned income exclusion.

[DeTorres, 65 TCM 2381, RIA TC Memo. ¶ 93,161 (1993).]

Professor on one-year sabbatical did not qualify for foreign earned income exclusion. Taxpayer, a college professor, took a one-year sabbatical from teaching in order to travel. He worked temporarily in Australia and New Zealand. The IRS denied the foreign earned income exclusion.

Held: For the IRS. Taxpayer failed to qualify for the exclusion because his leave was not indefinite and he failed to establish a foreign tax home.

[Gelhar, 63 TCM 2466, RIA TC Memo. ¶ 92,162 (1992).]

International pilot denied earned income exclusion despite family outside United States. Taxpayer, a pilot, was employed by a U.S. airline and was based at Kennedy airport in New York, although he flew only intra-European assignments. His family lived in Mexico. The IRS denied a foreign earned income exclusion.

Held: For the IRS. Taxpayer's tax home was in the United States, since his principal place of business was in New York.

[Dougherty, 62 TCM 680, RIA TC Memo. ¶ 91,442 (1991).]

Pilot based in Japan allowed earned income exclusion despite family residing in United States. Taxpayer was employed by a California company that provided crews for international flights. He accepted a permanent transfer to Japan while his wife and children remained in the United States. The IRS disallowed the foreign earned income exclusion, contending taxpayer's home was in the United States. In Japan, he lived near the airport in a hotel owned by the Japanese airline for which he flew. Taxpayer argued that the nature of Japanese society did not allow him to integrate into the community and that he could not afford to buy property in Japan.

Held: For taxpayer. Taxpayer's principal place of business was the airport, and his tax home was therefore in Japan.

[Cobb, 62 TCM 408, RIA TC Memo. ¶ 91,376 (1991).]

Worker at overseas U.S. agency denied foreign earned income exclusion. Taxpayer worked in Peru under a contract with the U.S. Agency for International

Development. He characterized himself as an independent contractor and claimed the foreign earned income exclusion. The IRS denied the claim, contending he was an employee of the U.S. agency and thus not entitled to the exclusion.

Held: For the IRS. Taxpayer was an employee of the agency, based on its right to control the manner and means of his activities.

[Marckwardt, 62 TCM 262, RIA TC Memo. ¶ 91,347 (1991).]

Flight engineer denied foreign earned income exclusion. Taxpayer was a flight engineer on an international cargo service. Although his base station was in New York, he rented an apartment in the Bahamas. The IRS denied the foreign earned income exclusion.

Held: For the IRS. Taxpayer's principal place of business was his base station and thus his tax home was in New York.

[Wojciechowski, 61 TCM 2758, RIA TC Memo. ¶ 91,239 (1991).]

Employee of U.S. agency abroad denied foreign earned income exclusion. Taxpayer lived in Haiti and worked there for the U.S. Agency for International Development under a personal services contract. Taxpayer argued that he was an independent contractor and claimed the foreign earned income exclusion. The IRS denied the exclusion.

Held: For the IRS. Taxpayer was an employee within the common-law meaning of that term. Under Section 911(b)(1)(B)(ii), foreign earned income does not include payments by the United States or its agencies to an employee.

[Juliard, 61 TCM 2683, RIA TC Memo. ¶ 91,230 (1991).]

Economic, familial, and personal ties determine situs of Section 911 "tax home" of U.S. citizen employee. Taxpayer, a U.S. citizen, was employed abroad by various employers from 1965 until June 1984. During 1984, the year in question, taxpayer was provided free housing in Brunei by his then employer. Taxpayer's wife and child maintained their sole residence in Texas in 1984. Taxpayer's work schedule allowed him to return to Texas every twenty-eight days to be with his wife and child. Each stay in Texas was twenty-eight days long; then he returned to Brunei for another twenty-eight-day work period. Taxpayer was registered to vote in Texas and his sole bank account was in a Texas bank. On his 1984 return, taxpayer claimed the Section 911 foreign earned income exclusion. The IRS determined he did not qualify for the exclusion, because taxpayer did not establish a "tax home" in Brunei.

Held: For the IRS. To qualify for the Section 911 exclusion, a taxpayer must establish a "tax home" in a foreign country. An individual is not treated as having a tax home in a foreign country for any period for which his abode is within the United States. Here, taxpayer's economic, familial, and personal ties were all with Texas and his contacts with Brunei were transitory at best. Because taxpayer had no "tax home" in Brunei, it was unnecessary to determine whether he qualified for the Section 911 exclusion under the bona fide residence or physical presence tests.

[Dye, 60 TCM 446, RIA TC Memo. ¶ 90,420 (1990).]

Employee of U.S. agency denied foreign earned income exclusion. Taxpayer was an economic advisor working overseas for the U.S. Agency for International Development. She claimed to be an independent contractor and excluded her income under the foreign earned income exclusion.

Held: For the IRS. The agency had significant control over taxpayer's activities. As a U.S. employee, she was not entitled to the exclusion.

[Matt, 59 TCM 472, RIA TC Memo. ¶ 90, 209 (1990).]

Oil rig worker denied earned income exclusion. Taxpayer was a U.S. citizen working on an oil rig located off the coast of Chile. He worked rotation shifts of twenty-eight days on and twenty-eight days off. Taxpayer had minimal contact with Chile and generally spent his off period in the United States, where he maintained significant financial and personal contacts. The IRS disallowed his foreign earned income exclusion.

Held: For the IRS. Taxpayer was neither a bona fide resident of Chile nor did he establish a tax home there.

[Harper, 58 TCM 1509, RIA TC Memo. ¶ 90,094 (1990).]

Foreign earned income exclusion denied. Taxpayer worked in Angola providing technical assistance and advice on oil and gas exploration. He worked on a rotational basis, spending twenty-eight days on and twenty-eight days off. While in Angola, he stayed in the company camp. During his off period, he returned to the United States, where he maintained significant ties. The IRS disallowed taxpayer's foreign earned income exclusion.

Held: For the IRS. Taxpayer failed to establish a tax home in Angola. Thus, he was not a qualified individual for exclusion purposes. The civil unrest in Angola was not the cause for taxpayer's failure to establish a tax home.

[Billeaud, 58 TCM 1348, RIA TC Memo. ¶ 90, 059 (1990).]

Foreign earned income exclusion denied. Taxpayer worked in Saudi Arabia on a rotating shift basis: forty-two days on and twenty-one days off. During his off shifts, taxpayer left Saudi Arabia and returned to his family in the United States. While in Saudi Arabia, taxpayer had no contact with local towns or people. The IRS denied taxpayer's claimed foreign earned income exclusion.

Held: For the IRS. Taxpayer did not satisfy the bona fide residence test. He was essentially a global commuter.

[Woodward, 58 TCM 1133, RIA TC Memo. ¶ 90,007 (1990).]

IRS rules that nationals of United Kingdom who are residents in United States may qualify for benefits provided by Section 911 by satisfying bona fide residence test of Section 911(d)(1)(A). The IRS ruled that nationals of the United Kingdom who are residents of the United States within the meaning of Section 7701(b) may qualify for the exclusions and deduction provided by Section 911 by establishing to the satisfaction of the IRS that they have been bona fide residents of a foreign country or countries under the residency rules of Regulation § 1.871-2(b) for a period that includes an entire taxable year. The conclusions reached in this revenue ruling are also applicable to all U.S. income tax treaties now in effect, which are listed in the revenue ruling.

[Rev. Rul. 91-58, 1991-2 CB 340.]

IRS issues revenue ruling concerning revocation of elections under Section 911. The IRS ruled that a qualified individual's claiming of an FTC with respect to foreign earned income that is eligible for exclusion under Section 911 and that the taxpayer has elected to exclude is inconsistent with the previously made election or elections and generally will result in the revocation of one or both elections.

[Rev. Rul. 90-77, 1990-2 CB 183.]

"Residence test applies to all U.S. treaty countries" (1992). According to Revenue Ruling 91-58, citizens of a treaty country who are U.S. residents under Section 7701(b) may qualify for the foreign earned income exclusion by establishing residence in a foreign country for at least one tax year. U.S. resident aliens are subject to the same rules as U.S. citizens and may exclude income under Section 911 by meeting either the bona fide residence test or the physical presence test. This article discusses this revenue ruling, the meaning of qualified individual under Section 911 as it applies to resident aliens, and the impact of U.S. tax treaty nondiscrimination clauses.

[76 J. Tax'n 34.]

"Ruling demonstrates power of nondiscrimination provisions" (1992). Section 911(a) provides that a qualified individual may elect for any taxable year to exclude from gross income foreign earned income and a housing cost amount. A "qualified individual" is an individual whose tax home is in a foreign country and either (1) is a U.S. citizen who has been a bona fide resident of a foreign country for an uninterrupted period that includes an entire taxable year or (2) is a U.S. citizen *or resident* who is present in a foreign country during at least 330 full days during any twelve consecutive months. The first test is sometimes referred to as the bona fide residence test, and the second as the physical presence test. "Tax home" is defined in Section 911(d)(3) as an individual's home for purposes of Section 162(a)(2) (relating to traveling expenses while away from home). Under current law, an individual can be a resident alien for U.S. income tax purposes *and* a "bona fide resident'' of another country under the principles of Section 871. In Revenue Ruling 91-58, X is a U.S. corporation providing services in the United States and foreign countries. Nationals of the United Kingdom whose tax homes are in the United Kingdom or other foreign countries are employed by X and are residents of the United States for income tax purposes under Section 7701(b). The issue addressed by the ruling is whether those employees who are earning income from employment outside the United States may qualify for the Section 911 exclusion under the bona fide residence test. The ruling addresses the question of whether Article 24 of the U.S.-U.K. treaty allows resident aliens of the United States who are U.K. nationals to qualify for the Section 911 exclusion under the "bona fide residence test."

The IRS held that Article 24 of the U.S.-U.K. treaty requires nationals of the United Kingdom to be treated as "qualified individuals" for purposes of Section 911 if they satisfy the bona fide residence test. The ruling extends its holding to thirty-eight income tax treaties, other than the U.S.-U.K. treaty, to which the United States is a party. The article closes with a discussion of the implications of the revenue ruling on the effect of treaty nondiscrimination clauses on U.S. internal tax law.

[RE Andersen, 2 J. Int'l Tax'n 317.]

"U.S. partners going overseas can plan ahead for tax breaks" (1992). Among U.S. tax benefits for citizens and residents residing and working overseas are the rights to

1. Exclude annually up to a maximum of $70,000 of foreign earned income from gross income;
2. Exclude or deduct a portion of foreign housing costs; and
3. Use foreign taxes paid or accrued as a credit against U.S. tax liabilities.

Frequently, a partnership (law firm, engineering firm, accounting firm, and so on) sends partners on a foreign assignment. Such individuals may be entitled to the benefits enumerated above, but their status as partners rather than employees creates unique concerns. In order to be entitled to the $70,000 foreign earned income exclusion, an individual's tax home must be in a foreign country. In addition, Section 911(d)(1) provides that citizens of the United States qualify if either (1) they are bona fide residents of a foreign country or countries for an uninterrupted period that includes an entire tax year or (2) during any twelve-month period they are physically present in a foreign country or countries at least 330 full days. This limitation can be significant for partners who report their distributable share of their partnership's income. Section 911(d)(6) disallows deductions and credits to the extent attributable to excluded income. In Revenue Ruling 75-86, the IRS argued that the foreign earned income exclusion is claimed against partnership gross income and partnership deductions are disallowed accordingly.

A partner is entitled to an unadjusted exclusion to the extent foreign earned income is represented by a guaranteed payment for services rendered. Under Section

707(c), a guaranteed payment is a payment to a partner for services determined without regard to the income of the partnership. Such payments are considered as made to one who is not a member of the partnership and, accordingly, are treated as compensation for services. To the extent attributable to foreign services, such amounts are eligible for exclusion under Section 911. The method of sourcing a guaranteed payment is based on the partner's percentage of foreign days. Sourcing part or all of the guaranteed payment as foreign earned income has an adverse effect on the partnership. Specifically, this amount becomes a foreign-source deduction to the partnership, thereby reducing the other partners' ability to use FTCs. A guaranteed payment must be properly structured to assure full benefit of the foreign earned income exclusion.

U.S. citizens and residents residing overseas can under Section 911(a) exclude or deduct a portion of their housing costs. An exclusion is available for any individual qualifying for the foreign earned income exclusion whose housing is "employer provided." The exclusion is the lesser of excess housing costs or foreign earned income.

The disallowance rule of Section 911(d)(6) also applies to the FTC. The disallowed portion is computed by multiplying the foreign taxes by a fraction. The numerator of the fraction is the foreign earned income and housing exclusions, the denominator is foreign earned income less properly allocable deductible expenses. The housing cost deduction is a deductible expense properly allocable to foreign earned income. It is sometimes advantageous to forgo the election to claim the foreign earned income exclusion.

Frequently, a partnership's activities will create a state tax liability for nonresident partners. For example, New York and California require that nonresident partners report their share of partnership income from sources within the state. In determining income sourced to these states, a guaranteed payment is included as an amount subject to allocation or apportionment. There are procedural and mechanical nuances associated with the integration of the foreign exclusion provisions of Section 911 and the partnership provisions. The primary focus of planning is to assure the full benefit of the relief provisions provided by U.S. income tax law.

[LJ Bardoff, 3 J. Int'l Tax'n 20.]

"Foreign earned income exclusion" (1991). Section 911 permits U.S. citizens who are bona fide residents of foreign countries to exclude foreign earned income from gross income. Foreign earned income generally includes compensation for personal services, but does not include amounts that represent a distribution of earnings or profits.

In *Davis*, a 1990 Tax Court case, the taxpayer, a U.S. citizen living in Israel, owned a 66 percent share each in a U.S. accounting firm and a U.S. investment firm. When the taxpayer moved to Israel in 1982, his clients generated approximately 50 percent to 60 percent of the accounting firm's gross receipts. In 1984, the taxpayer performed services for the accounting firm by meeting with clients in

Israel and consulting with the firm on customer relations with the existing client base. He personally kept in contact with many of his clients, advised his co-owner on collection matters, and was responsible for developing new clients.

Also, during 1984, the taxpayer performed client relations services and sought new clients for the investment firm. He also worked on projects in the development stage, including projects located in Israel. The taxpayer received $81,400 for the services that he performed in 1984. Apparently, the IRS introduced no evidence that the amounts the taxpayer received from the accounting firm or the investment firm represented a distribution of earnings and profits (E&P), and the Tax Court found no basis for rejecting the testimony of the taxpayer or his co-owner.

Regulation § 1.911-2(b)(3) provides that professional fees constitute earned income, although the taxpayer employs assistants to perform part or all of the services rendered, provided that the taxpayer's clients look to the taxpayer as the person responsible for the services rendered. In *Davis*, the IRS took the position that work performed for the taxpayer's clients by other individuals could not be attributed to the taxpayer unless the other individuals looked to the taxpayer for guidance. Because the taxpayer was physically located in Israel, the IRS argued that such a result was precluded. The Tax Court rejected this argument, pointing out that the IRS's reliance on the regulatory rule was misplaced, because it is the clients, not the taxpayer's assistants, who must look to the taxpayer as the person responsible for the services rendered. Under these circumstances, the Tax Court concluded that the taxpayer had satisfied the requirements of Section 911 and could exclude the amounts received in 1984 as foreign earned income.

[1 J. Int'l Tax'n 365.]

"How to establish foreign residency" (1991). Under Section 911, a qualifying individual can elect to exclude $70,000 of foreign earned income and a certain amount of housing costs. To qualify for these benefits, the individual must have a "tax home" in a foreign country and the individual must be (1) in the case of a U.S. citizen, a bona fide resident of a foreign country for an uninterrupted period that includes one tax year or (2) in the case of a U.S. citizen or resident, present in a foreign country for at least 330 days in a period of twelve consecutive months.

The authors first address the meaning of "tax home" and the determination of "abode within the United States." Next, they explore the determination of residency and the effects of visits to the United States. Thereafter, they review and explain the factors the courts have used to determine residency. Documenting the satisfaction of these factors is then discussed with respect to the intention of the taxpayer. Specific problem areas of concern to war workers, technicians, and foreign career workers are discussed. Next, the authors discuss how to establish a "home" in a foreign country. They consider such factors as local community involvement; business motives for being abroad; temporary visits to the United States; payment of taxes and the extent of economic ties; registration as a resident in a foreign country and other acts indicating non-U.S. residency; domicile of spouse and other family members; and the nature and term of the contract for foreign employment. Last, the authors discuss the impact of treaty provisions on the determination of residency status.

The authors conclude that establishing a "tax home" in and becoming a resident of a foreign country requires careful planning. The framework of factors (discussed in this article) required to establish residency must be considered and supported by as much evidence as possible. Letters, memos, and other written documentation prepared before a confrontation with the IRS occurs will be invaluable in supporting the taxpayer's case.

[ML Moore & CC Vines, US Tax'n Int'l Operations ¶ 13,505.]

"Revocation of elections" (1991). In Revenue Ruling 90-77, the IRS considered circumstances in which a revocation of an election to exclude foreign earned income or housing costs from gross income will be deemed to have occurred. In Situation 1, an individual made a valid election to exclude foreign earned income and claimed the exclusion for the 1984 and 1985 taxable years. In his tax return for 1986, however, the individual reported all foreign earned income and claimed a foreign tax credit for foreign taxes paid with respect to that income, without filing a statement to revoke his earlier election. The IRS ruled that the regulations do not purport to provide an exclusive method for revoking the election. The claiming of an FTC, which is inconsistent with a previously made election, also revokes an election.

The facts in Situation 2 were the same, except that the individual also made a valid election to exclude his housing costs for 1984 and 1985. Here, the IRS ruled that although the Section 911 regulations require a separate revocation for each Section 911 election, whether the claiming of the FTC will result in the revocation of one or both of the elections depends on the amount of the claimed FTC. Thus, where an FTC that is claimed equals the sum of the foreign earned income and housing cost exclusions the individual is eligible to claim, claiming the FTC will serve to revoke both elections.

In Situation 3, an individual miscalculated and claimed a smaller housing cost exclusion than that to which he was entitled. As a result, the individual claimed an FTC against foreign earned income that was excludable but, because of the miscalculation, was not excluded. Here, the IRS ruled that good faith errors in determining excludable foreign earned income may affect the allowable FTC, but will not revoke an earlier election.

[1 J. Int'l Tax'n 365.]

"Waiver of foreign residency requirement" (1991). Section 911 generally imposes a residency requirement: either bona fide residence in a foreign country for an uninterrupted period that includes an entire taxable year or presence in a foreign country during at least 330 full days during twelve consecutive months. There is an exception to the residency requirement where an individual present in a foreign country is required to depart because of war, civil unrest, or similar adverse conditions that preclude the normal conduct of business by the individual. Revenue Procedure 90-55 updates the list of foreign countries in which adverse conditions exist, adding Burma, China, Haiti, Liberia, Panama, Peru, and Yemen, and specifying the relevant time periods for purposes of this waiver.

[1 J. Int'l Tax'n 366.]

"Foreign earned income exclusion regulation is valid" (1990). A taxpayer employed overseas who failed to file returns in the belief that the foreign earned income exclusion covered his earnings was held ineligible for the exclusion in *Faltesek*, a 1989 Tax Court case. According to the Tax Court, Regulation § 1.911-7(a), which requires the exclusion to be affirmatively elected on a properly filed return, is valid. In 1982 and 1983, the taxpayer was employed in two foreign countries. In addition to his earnings from employment abroad, he earned rents from two properties in Texas, but filed no returns until a deficiency notice was issued. He contended that Regulation § 1.911-7(a), which requires a taxpayer to elect to exclude foreign earned income on Form 2555 or a comparable form, was invalid.

Regulation § 1.911-7(a) states that an individual must elect the Section 911(a)(1) exclusion for foreign earned income on Form 2555 or a comparable form. A taxpayer who does not elect the exclusion can take the foreign tax paid on the earned income as an FTC. Under Section 911(e), if the exclusion election is revoked, the taxpayer must wait five years to make another election. The court explained that permitting the taxpayer to make the election in 1987, five years after the income was first earned, is equivalent to permitting retroactive tax planning. Regulation § 1.911-7(a), which prevents this by establishing time limits, was thus manifestly reasonable.

[72 J. Tax'n 49.]

[3] Exclusions for Certain Government Employees Under Section 912

U.S. government employee's lodging excluded from gross income. Taxpayer was a principal representative of the United States stationed in a foreign country. In accordance with the Administrative Expenses Act of 1946 and various State Department regulations, the government provided taxpayer with an official residence and paid both usual and unusual residence expenses. Five percent of taxpayer's salary was withheld to defray the costs of usual expenses. Taxpayer met the conditions specified in Section 119 for exclusion from gross income of lodging furnished by an employer. Section 912(1)(D) provides that in the case of employees of the U.S. government, certain amounts received as allowances under the act are excludable from gross income. In the instant case, the value of the lodging was excludable from taxpayer's gross income under Section 119. The payments of unusual expenses incident to the operation and maintenance of the official residence were excludable under Section 912(1)(D). The 5 percent of salary paid by taxpayer, however, was a charge for neither lodging nor those unusual expenses, but rather was payment for ordinary and everyday living expenses and was not excludable from gross income.

[Rev. Rul. 90-64, 1990-2 CB 35.]

[4] Social Security

"Social Security strategies for U.S. employees working abroad" (1991). The Social Security consequences of employment abroad differ, depending on whether or not there is a totalization agreement in effect with the host country. If such an agreement does not exist, the type of employer becomes the predominant factor that determines the applicable rules. Coverage and benefits vary for U.S. individuals employed by U.S. employers, 10 percent foreign affiliates for which a special election is made, and other foreign employers. There are planning techniques for avoiding double Social Security taxation while retaining full Social Security benefits. From an employment tax perspective, two issues are apparent each time a U.S. person works abroad. First, the foreign country of destination may impose an employment tax in addition to the FICA tax imposed by the United States, resulting in double taxation on the same wages. Second, FICA benefits may be lost because of the term abroad. Simply avoiding either the U.S. FICA tax or the foreign Social Security tax may not be a satisfactory solution.

The United States has concluded totalization agreements with the following twelve countries: Belgium, Canada, France, Germany, Italy, the Netherlands, Norway, Portugal, Spain, Sweden, Switzerland, and the United Kingdom. Upon becoming effective, these agreements override conflicting statutory and administrative rules. The purpose of these agreements is two-fold. First, they assign Social Security coverage to only one of the agreement partners. The double taxation problem for most U.S. persons employed in these countries, therefore, is minimized. Second, these agreements provide for a totalized benefit whenever an individual's period of employment in a country is insufficient by itself to qualify for benefits.

Generally, Social Security coverage is assigned to the country where the services are performed. Under this general rule, a U.S. individual performing services in the host country pays Social Security taxes only to that country. Because no double taxation problem arises, these levies are not creditable or deductible on a U.S. return. The detached worker exception to this general rule is then discussed, as are other issues relating to totalization agreements.

Absent a totalization agreement, a U.S. citizen or resident alien who is employed outside the United States by a U.S. employer is subject to FICA coverage on wages. U.S. employers include:

1. The U.S. government;
2. An instrumentality of the United States;
3. A U.S. resident as defined in Section 7701(b);
4. A partnership where two thirds of the partners are U.S. residents;
5. A trust in which all of the trustees are U.S. residents; and
6. A domestic corporation.

Since the U.S. FICA tax is imposed on both the employee and the employer, a potential double taxation problem arises for the employee, the employer, or both when a foreign government also imposes its Social Security tax on the same wages.

U.S. individuals abroad who do not work for a U.S. employer or who work in a country that has concluded a totalization agreement with the United States are normally exempt from FICA coverage. A U.S. employer can elect, however, to cover U.S. citizens and residents of one or more of its 10 percent–owned foreign affiliates. This election, known as a Section 3121(*l*) agreement or FICA election, is made through a contractual arrangement with the IRS. Once elected, the agreement cannot be terminated by the U.S. employer.

All agreements specify that the U.S. employer must pay both the employer and the employee portions of FICA tax, including interest and penalties and any other additions to tax, on behalf of all U.S. citizens and resident aliens employed by the designated foreign affiliate. Whether the employer is reimbursed by the covered employees for their portion of the FICA payment is left to those parties. All U.S. citizens and residents employed by the particular foreign affiliate are covered under the agreement, even if some of these are hired at a later date. The Social Security Act Amendments of 1983 extended the opportunity to engage in a FICA election (i.e., Section 3121(*l*) agreement) to all U.S. employers. Further, the election can now be made for any foreign affiliate, whether corporate or noncorporate. A by-product of the FICA election is that the agreement enables the U.S. employer to cover U.S. citizens and residents of its foreign affiliates under its qualified pension, profit-sharing, stock bonus, or annuity plan. In order to obtain this extended coverage, the qualified plan must expressly state that U.S. employees of foreign affiliates that are covered by a Section 3121(*l*) agreement are entitled to retirement contributions or benefits.

Absent a totalization agreement, U.S. citizens and residents working abroad for a foreign entity (whether affiliated or not) for which a FICA election is not in force may lose significant U.S. Social Security benefits. As noted in this article, the employer can compensate the employee for these losses through additional remuneration or the provision of private insurance. Alternatively, coverage through a foreign Social Security program may be available. Depending on the vesting period and the employee's time abroad, however, amounts paid into a foreign system may be forfeited without qualifying for any program benefits. For this reason, U.S. employees have some incentive to maintain their FICA coverage while abroad.

Several strategies are available that allow U.S. citizens or resident aliens working abroad to secure or to continue FICA coverage on at least a portion of their compensation. Generally, these strategies involve arranging the employment relationship so that the individual will be considered an employee of a U.S. employer or a 10 percent–owned foreign affiliate.

Some multinational companies keep U.S. employees on the payroll of their U.S. home office and loan or second them to their related businesses abroad on a consignment basis. This is a common means to continue employee benefit plan and FICA coverage for overseas employees. Variations of this arrangement exist.

Another method used by U.S. multinationals to retain FICA coverage for their employees transferred abroad is to place them on a split payroll. Essentially, this means that part of their compensation will be paid by the U.S. home office, and the remainder will be paid by the foreign employer. The author continues this discussion by addressing other methods currently in use. The article then turns to a general discussion of U.S. taxation of Social Security benefits. Whether working abroad for a U.S. or a foreign employer, U.S. employees are faced with Social Security implications that demand careful attention. The immediate concern is to ensure that salary or wages are not subject to Social Security taxation both in the United States and in the foreign host country. As important as this concern might be, the issue of future benefits might prove to be even more significant. Lack of foresight can result in the partial or total loss of Social Security benefits from either the United States or a foreign country in which the employee has worked.

[ER Larkins, 2 J. Int'l Tax'n 220.]

¶ 2.03 COMPENSATION OF EMPLOYEES OF FOREIGN GOVERNMENTS OR INTERNATIONAL ORGANIZATIONS (SECTION 893)[3]

Wages were not excludable under Section 893 when waiver was executed under immigration statute. Taxpayers were a husband, who was a citizen of Jamaica, and a wife, who was a citizen of the Philippines. They were employed by the United Nations and were permanent residents of the United States. As a condition to obtaining this status, they filed waivers of rights, privileges, and exemptions with the Immigration and Naturalization Service. They excluded their wages from income under Section 893 (compensation of employees of foreign governments or international organizations) notwithstanding the waivers.

Held: For the IRS (in part). Salary received by non–U.S. citizen employees of the United Nations, who as a condition for permanent resident status execute a waiver of rights, is not eligible for exclusion under Section 893. As a citizen of the Philippines, however, the wife is specifically eligible for exclusion under Section 893(a)(1), notwithstanding the waiver.

[Ying, 99 TC 273 (1992).]

¶ 2.04 DUAL-RESIDENT CORPORATIONS[4]

IRS issues final regulations concerning dual consolidated losses. The IRS has issued final regulations implementing Section 1503(d), which was added to the Code by the Tax Reform Act of 1986 (TRA 1986) and amended by the Technical and Miscellaneous Revenue Act of 1988 (TAMRA). Section 1503(d) generally provides that a dual consolidated loss of a dual-resident corporation may not be used to offset the taxable income of any domestic corporate affiliate. These regulations generally affect domestic corporations that are subject to an income tax of a foreign country on their worldwide income or on a residence basis.

[TD 8434, 1992-2 CB 240; Reg. § 1.1503-2.]

"Final dual consolidated loss regulations still have some high hurdles" (1993). In 1992, the IRS issued final regulations under Section 1503(d) to restrict use of a dual consolidated loss. These replace temporary regulations issued in 1989 and in some respects relax the prior rules. For certain structures and transactions, however, the final rules apply stricter guidelines and the treatment of foreign operations conducted through branches, partnerships, and trusts, in particular, contain unexpected results and unanswered questions.

The authors of this article first discuss those abuses involving dual-resident corporations that Congress intended to impede by enacting Section 1503(d). Examples are given by the authors illustrating certain abuses and the corrective effect of Section 1503(d). Next, the authors discuss the provisions of the new final regulations. Specific discussion is provided of the regulations' definition of "dual-resident corporation" (and the treatment of separate business units and branches, partnerships, and hybrid entities thereunder); the "no foreign-use" exception (including the antimirror legislation rule, the meaning of "foreign use," regulatory "no foreign-use" exceptions, and "no foreign-use" certification); and the calculation of dual consolidated losses (including the modification of certain basis adjustments and the "antistuffing" provision authorized under Section 1503(d)(4)).

Thereafter, the authors discuss the final regulations' effective date and transitional relief provisions. The authors conclude that the final regulations, although an improvement, are a tightly drawn set of difficult to administer rules that attempt to deny any double benefit of a single net operating loss. It is questionable whether the objective is worth the administrative burden where taxpayers are engaged in foreign active business operations. Taxpayers will have to learn to live with these rules, however, since it is unlikely that they will be revised in the near future.

[SE Shay & RP Watson, 4 J. Int'l Tax'n 52.]

"Dual consolidated loss regulations have broad reach" (1990). In 1986, Congress limited the deductibility of dual consolidated losses, i.e., losses used, through tax consolidation, to offset income in both the United States and a foreign country. Section 1503(d) was a response to transactions in which taxpayers had isolated expenses (especially interest deductions from debt incurred to finance cross-border acquisitions) in dual-resident companies, thereby obtaining a double tax benefit. Temporary Regulation § 1.1503-2T, which implements this legislation, goes well beyond the section and may affect the U.S. tax planning for numerous other transactions involving foreign losses. The temporary regulations often extend beyond the apparent intent of Section 1503(d) to produce surprising and sometimes harsh results. Therefore, taxpayers should consider the possible impact of these rules on all transactions involving foreign losses. In particular, because of the recapture rules, strategies that exploit the time value of foreign losses should be reexamined.

[JR Wilson, 1 J. Int'l Tax'n 78.]

¶ 2.05 FOREIGN CORPORATIONS OWNED BY U.S. PERSONS[5]

[1] Generally

"Structuring foreign sales" (1993). U.S. manufacturers selling in international markets through exporting or doing business abroad can gain substantial U.S. tax savings if they properly structure their export and foreign sales activities. Proper structuring, as explained in this article, minimizes U.S. tax burdens and maximizes potential tax-saving benefits. This article examines both U.S. and foreign tax problems and benefits when exporting or doing business abroad. It also highlights the tax effects of different forms of overseas operations.

The first format discussed by the author is direct export sales by the U.S. manufacturer. Taxation of the U.S. manufacturer by the customer's country and the use of a foreign branch or subsidiary by the U.S. manufacturer are examined. The use of interest-charge domestic international sales corporations (DISCs) is also considered in this section of the article. The author next examines the use of a foreign sales corporation (FSC). The requirements for such classification and the restrictions placed thereon are discussed. The advantages gained by such classification are also reviewed. Next, the author examines qualification and use of a "possessions corporation," which like the "FSC," offers tax incentives to U.S. manufacturers that establish active business operations outside the continental United States.

The use of CFCs by the U.S. manufacturer is then considered and explained. A brief discussion of the subpart F provisions applicable to such corporations is also provided. The advantages to be gained from judicious use of the FTC are then reviewed, along with the restrictions and limitations on its availability. Last, the author considers intercompany allocation problems faced by U.S. manufacturers using related entities to carry out foreign sales. The impact of Section 482 and Regulations § 1.861-8 in this context are explored. The author concludes this article with a summary checklist of the types of business structures that may be used when exporting or doing business abroad.

[KR Bindon, US Tax'n Int'l Operations ¶ 5004.]

"Setting up your foreign subsidiary" (1992). In this article, the authors consider the relevant policies, procedures, and planning guidelines for organizing a foreign manufacturing subsidiary, with particular emphasis on the tax consequences for U.S. persons operating through such a subsidiary. The authors first review many of the incentives and deterrents likely to be faced by U.S. persons operating businesses in foreign lands. Next, they consider the general effects of the various U.S. tax treaties and planning considerations thereunder: A table is included listing the status of all tax treaties to which the United States is a partner. The European Community is also briefly discussed. Next, the authors explain various employment factors considered by employees faced with the opportunity to relocate outside the United States. The generally allowable forms for doing business outside the United States and other business factors, such as inflation, are also addressed.

The authors then discuss certain U.S. considerations associated with the formation and capitalization of a foreign subsidiary, including coverage by Sections 367 and 1491. U.S. reporting requirements are also reviewed with respect to (1) officers, directors, and significant shareholders of foreign corporations and (2) shareholders of a CFC. A copy of Form 5471 is included. Last, the authors examine relevant U.S. tax considerations, including the consequences of CFC status, the treatment of a CFC's earnings, the FTC, intercompany pricing and charges, and the filing of a consolidated return with certain Canadian and Mexican subsidiaries.

[US Tax'n Int'l Operations ¶ 7506.]

"Choosing the best way to enter a foreign market" (1991). Although an international presence can be structured in a number of ways, three common methods of doing business abroad are an FSC, a joint venture, and a foreign manufacturing subsidiary of a U.S. corporation. An FSC is a special entity created by Congress to encourage U.S. export sales by reducing federal corporate income tax. It avoids the need to make a substantial capital investment in the foreign market, and can generally be arranged so that its income is exempt from foreign taxation. Potential drawbacks to an FSC are stringent import quotas, restrictions, duties, and tariffs.

A joint venture is a contractual arrangement, partnership, or other unincorporated form of foreign business, organization, or entity that is treated as a partnership for U.S. tax purposes. The primary advantage of the joint venture is its ability to combine both U.S. product technology and capital with the market knowledge of the foreign joint venture partner. Backed by the financial and management resources of the two companies, a venture generally also meets the local ownership requirements of most foreign countries. The venture's profits and losses are included with the other corporate taxable income of its U.S. partner (a U.S. corporation) and are not subject to foreign withholding taxes. On the other hand, day-to-day operations and dissolution are subject to the local laws of the foreign jurisdiction, and, as an unincorporated entity, a joint venture generally exposes the principals to unlimited legal liability.

A foreign manufacturing subsidiary offers all the advantages of a corporation, including limited liability and the ability of the parent to retain control of the foreign business and related assets, while allowing it to enjoy the full benefits of the overseas profits. The earnings of the subsidiary are generally not subject to U.S. tax until they are repatriated in the form of dividends. Of course, as with all forms of doing business abroad, manpower, administrative responsibility, and the burden of U.S.

tax compliance are a number of the drawbacks to using a subsidiary. Also, some foreign countries may require significant local ownership and not allow a foreign subsidiary to repatriate profits.

A portion of the FSC's export gross profit and distributions to its corporate shareholders is exempt from federal taxation if the Section 922 tests relating to foreign presence and stockholder requirements are met. Certain U.S. corporations may also elect to be treated as a small FSC under Section 922(d) if they are not members, at any time during the taxable year, of a controlled group of corporations that includes a regular FSC. The benefits of the small FSC and the exclusion under Section 924(b)(2)(B)(i), apply only to the first $5 million of foreign trading gross receipts, aggregated from among the entire control group.

Any foreign corporation where more than 50 percent of the voting power or value of such stock is owned directly, indirectly, or constructively by U.S. shareholders on any day during the taxable year is a CFC under Section 957. Generally, under Section 951, U.S. shareholders are taxed on their pro rata share of the CFC's current Subpart F income, as defined in Section 952, as if it had been distributed on the last day of the CFC's taxable year. A foreign manufacturing subsidiary, however, while offering all of the advantages of corporate limited liability and U.S. control of the foreign business, also provides for deferral of taxation on current earnings until they are repatriated in the form of dividends under Regulation § 1.954-3(a)(4).

The remainder of this article is built around how the three different structures would apply to a hypothetical corporation in (1) a high tax rate country with a 50 percent tax and a tax treaty with the United States; (2) a low tax rate country with a 25 percent tax and a tax treaty with the United States; (3) a high tax rate country with a 50 percent tax but no tax treaty with the United States; and (4) a low tax rate country with a 25 percent tax but no tax treaty with the United States. The authors conclude by stating that whether a domestic corporation seeking to do business abroad should enter the local market as an FSC, joint venture, or foreign manufacturing subsidiary requires consideration of both the business and tax aspects. The practical, as well as financial, considerations of each particular venture must be carefully weighed.

[RE Meldman & S. Ziemer, 1 J. Int'l Tax'n 350.]

"Foreign finance subsidiaries are still useful after TRA 1986" (1990). Prior to TRA 1986, many U.S.-based multinationals established a European subsidiary to perform banking, currency management, and administrative functions for their foreign affiliates. These subsidiaries (called headquarter companies, finance subsidiaries, or coordination centers, depending on the specific functions undertaken), made sense not only for business reasons but also for foreign and U.S. tax reasons. Although the determination depends on each taxpayer's particular facts, a group finance subsidiary is still a good idea for many U.S.-based multinationals. All the business and tax reasons for their use before TRA 1986 remain, and several TRA

1986 and associated changes—lowering of U.S. corporate rates, amendments to the high-tax and de minimis Subpart F exceptions, enactment of PFIC legislation, the amendment of regulations relating to rents—make their use more desirable than ever. The repeal of the chain deficit rule and amendment of the regulations that implement the same-country interest rule may require some attention, but certainly not wholesale junking of the finance subsidiary concept. Only the rules relating to foreign currency under Sections 954 and 988 require consideration of major structural changes.

[PM Daub, 1 J. Int'l Tax'n 69.]

[2] Foreign Personal Holding Companies

IRS issues revenue procedure concerning foreign personal holding companies. This revenue procedure provides guidance for foreign personal holding companies with respect to the designation of certain dividends paid as being taken into account under Section 563(c).

[Rev. Proc. 90-26, 1990-1 CB 512.]

[3] Passive Foreign Investment Companies

IRS issues proposed regulations concerning PFICs. The IRS has issued proposed regulations under Sections 1291, 1293, 1295, and 1297 concerning the taxation of shareholders of certain PFICs upon payment of distributions by such companies or upon disposition of the stock of such companies.

[INTL-941-86, INTL-656-87, INTL-704-87, 1992-1 CB 1124, Prop. Reg. §§ 1.1291-0–1.1291-10, 1.1293-1, 1.1295-1.]

"New PFIC regulations have strong impact on active foreign subsidiaries" (1992). On March 31, 1992, the IRS issued substantive proposed regulations and procedural temporary regulations dealing with PFICs. This article reviews the effect of the PFIC rules on active foreign subsidiaries and therefore on their U.S. parents. The most important point is that careful planning can allow U.S. parents to avoid the rules.

The PFIC rules deal with foreign corporations regardless of the level of U.S. ownership. A foreign corporation is a PFIC if, for any taxable year, either (1) 75 percent or more of its gross income is passive or (2) 50 percent or more of its assets would produce passive income. In general, passive income includes dividends, interest, rents, and royalties, although there are significant exceptions for such income received from a corporation at least 25 percent owned by the recipient or from other related parties. If a foreign corporation is a PFIC, each U.S. shareholder elects either to be taxed currently on its proportionate share of all the PFIC's income or to be subject to interest on the tax liability deferred until earnings are distributed or the stock disposed of. The foreign and U.S. tax liability and U.S. interest may exceed 100 percent of the distribution.

Section 1297(a) as enacted by TRA 1986 provided rules for attributing to a U.S. person the stock of a PFIC that the U.S. person held indirectly. This alone produced no tax as Section 1291 only imposes an interest charge where the U.S. person actually receives a distribution from a PFIC or disposes of its stock. Section 1297(b)(5) states that "under regulations," however, distributions from PFICs viewed as indirectly held under the Section 1297(a) attribution rules will be treated, in proportion to the indirect ownership, as distributions received directly by the U.S. person. A corresponding rule was also provided for dispositions.

Proposed Regulation § 1.1291-3(e)(2) defines "indirect dispositions" to include not only a disposition of stock of a PFIC where ownership of the stock had been attributed to the U.S. shareholder, but also any transaction that reduces or terminates an indirect shareholder's ownership. Proposed Regulation § 1.1291-3(d) indicates that a pledge is a disposition on the first date the stock is used as security or the beginning of the taxable year that the corporation becomes a PFIC. The deemed consideration is the lesser of the unpaid principal secured or the value of the stock. If the latter, an increase in value does not trigger a new deemed disposition unless additional principal is secured.

Proposed Regulation § 1.1297-2(b)(3) provides that there may be an excess distribution to the extent that Section 304 treats the sales proceeds as a distribution of earnings of a PFIC. In addition, the preamble to the proposed regulations points out that if the company being sold is a PFIC, there has been a disposition of its stock that must be recognized under the PFIC rules, and if the purchasing corporation is a PFIC, the amount paid may be an excess distribution.

Section 1297(a)(4) of the attribution rules provides that, "to the extent provided in regulations," an option or series of options to acquire stock will be treated as actual ownership. This, of course, can apply not only to stock of a PFIC but also to stock of any foreign corporation by virtue of which ownership of PFIC stock would be attributed to a U.S. shareholder. Proposed Regulation § 1.1291-1(d) provides that the holder of an option to acquire PFIC stock is the owner of the PFIC stock itself and, on disposition of the option other than by exercise, the gain will be subject to the interest-charge rules. Where an option is exercised, the holding period of the PFIC stock includes the holding period of the option. The consequences of this rule are then examined. Section 1291(f) provides that, "to the extent provided in regulations," any nonrecognition provision applying to the transfer of stock of a PFIC will be overridden. Proposed Regulation § 1.1291-6 overrides *all* nonrecognition provisions, itself allowing for nonrecognition in certain situations. Those situations are

1. Where the shareholder receives in exchange for the PFIC stock a direct or indirect interest in a PFIC of equivalent value, or
2. Where the transferee is a U.S. person answerable for the latent PFIC consequences to the transferor because the basis has not been increased and the holding period has been tacked.

The proposed regulation, however, states that these exceptions to gain recognition do not apply unless another nonrecognition provision outside the PFIC rules applies. If no such nonrecognition provision is available, there will be gain recognition on transfer of stock in a PFIC. The possibility that affirmative use of the Subpart F rules might be the key for CFCs to avoid the PFIC rules is then explored. The new proposed regulations increase the number and magnitude of disasters that await the active foreign subsidiary that inadvertently meets the PFIC tests, which is quite easy to do. Nevertheless, the proposed rules provide an escape route so that a U.S. parent can avoid PFIC consequences for its CFCs.

[JS Karls, 3 J. Int'l Tax'n 133.]

"PFICs" (1992). Congress, in 1986, enacted the PFIC rules to prevent U.S. taxpayers from deferring U.S. tax on "passive income" by investing through a foreign corporation held in such a manner as to avoid the CFC and foreign personal holding company provisions. This article explains the operation of the PFIC provisions and examines the principal issues that arise in their application.

The authors first review the definition of a "PFIC," including the income or assets tests, the various categories of passive income, the look-through rule for subsidiary corporations, and the special rules of Notice 88-22 on what constitutes passive income–producing assets. Next, they show how a corporation regularly engaged in a trade or business can fall victim to PFIC categorization. In so doing, they address some of the problems with the current PFIC rules, such as distortions introduced by the gross income test, the treatment of mining companies, and the treatment of loss corporations. The "start-up" and "changing business" exceptions are also discussed.

In the next part of this article, the authors discuss the tax consequences for a PFIC that does not elect qualified electing fund (QEF) status, that is, a nonqualified PFIC with "excess distributions." Specifically, they discuss the punitive rules applicable to "excess distributions" from a nonqualified PFIC, including the tax on excess distributions, the definition of "excess distribution," the treatment of gain as an excess distribution, the claiming of an FTC by a PFIC, the PFIC taint on stock, and the income inclusion election for CFCs. Next, they examine the QEF election, the requirements and procedure for election, the current taxation of a U.S. shareholder on PFIC income, as well as other consequences of this election.

Last, the authors discuss the special stock ownership and attribution rules applicable in this area, reporting by PFICs, and planning strategies available to shareholders of a PFIC to avoid or defer some of the tax disadvantages of owning PFIC stock. In concluding, the authors review provisions of proposed tax legislation that would overhaul the PFIC rules and summarize many of the weaknesses inherent in the PFIC rules.

[RS Rich & LE Nemirow, US Tax'n Int'l Operations ¶ 6050.]

"Regulations affecting PFICs ensure acceleration of income" (1992). In 1992, temporary and proposed regulations, generally effective April 1, 1992, were issued that affect the taxation of shareholders of PFICs and provide guidance as to the elections available to those shareholders. The proposed regulations are the most significant set of guidelines since TRA 1986 established special rules for the taxation of U.S. persons owning shares in PFICs. Determination of PFIC status, however, is not addressed in these regulations.

The authors provide an overview of the PFIC rules. Within this framework, PFIC status and types of PFICs are also discussed. Next, the authors address certain elections, i.e., the deemed dividend election, the deemed sale election, and the "QEF" election under Section 1295. Distributions by a Section 1291 fund are discussed, including an examination of the regulation provisions concerning the taxation of excess distributions, the annualization of certain distributions, the use of a foreign currency in the determination of both nonexcess distributions and total excess distributions, the taxation of nonexcess distributions, and indirect distributions.

Thereafter, the authors discuss the regulations' provisions concerning dispositions of stock of a Section 1291 fund, including a disposition that occurs upon change in residence or citizenship status to a nonresident alien and a pledge of Section 1291 fund stock. Other subjects covered within this section of the article are indirect dispositions, indirect dispositions via S corporations, transfers within a consolidated group, installment sales, the inapplicability of Sections 1246 and 1248, and nonrecognition transfers of Section 1291 fund stock.

The last part of the article is dedicated to certain other important matters, including the "deferred tax amount" under Section 1291, holding period rules, FTC determinations, mark-to-market elections by regulated investment companies (RICs) holding stock in PFICs, and proposed legislation in this area.

The authors conclude that the temporary and proposed regulations provide significant guidance to PFIC shareholders, but that there are a few exceptions. Further, the rules may bring some harsh results to investors unaware of these provisions. While most of the elections are only proposed, the interpretive and definitional provisions contained in these regulations also afford an important indication of the IRS's views. Nevertheless, more changes will be forthcoming if pending legislation is enacted.

[WE Smith & JN Calvin, 77 J. Tax'n 242.]

"Applying PFIC rules to RICs can cause double taxation" (1991). The PFIC provisions (Sections 1291 through 1297) were enacted in 1986 to eliminate a tax advantage enjoyed by U.S. taxpayers who invested in passive assets through foreign investment companies, relative to the treatment of U.S. investors in domestic investment companies. The broad scope of the PFIC rules, however, produces anomalous, and perhaps unintended, tax consequences for taxpayers other than those who are invested in foreign mutual funds. In fact, the PFIC rules appear to penalize investors in domestic mutual funds, the very taxpayers to whom Congress looked as models for the proper treatment of PFIC shareholders.

Normally, a mutual fund that qualifies as a RIC and meets prescribed income, asset diversification, and distribution requirements is a conduit for federal income tax purposes under Sections 851 through 855. The fundamental premise of conduit treatment is that the RIC's income should be taxed only once at the RIC shareholder level, rather than at the RIC level. Nevertheless, the application of the PFIC rules to RICs holding PFIC stock raises the possibility of a double tax at both the RIC and the RIC shareholder levels.

The technical problem under current law is due to the imposition of the PFIC tax directly on the RIC, with no provision for passing the character of the tax and related income through to RIC shareholders.

The author examines the problem in detail and discusses the chances for legislative reform. The author concludes that RICs holding PFIC stock have two basic options. First, a RIC could simply divest itself of stock that would attract the tax. Alternatively, the RIC could hold on to the stock, with the possibility that legislative or administrative relief will be forthcoming. The second option may be most attractive where no current PFIC dividends are paid, because no immediate tax consequences will result from the decision to hold. No one can predict, however, whether corrective legislation will be retroactive or only prospective. Further, given the competing concerns of other victims of the PFIC rules and the various proposed solutions, it is difficult to determine what the shape of any corrective PFIC legislation might take.

[LG Stodghill, 2 J. Int'l Tax'n 100.]

"PFIC/passive foreign corporation planning for active foreign subsidiaries" **(1991).** For foreign incorporated companies that are active, including wholly owned foreign marketing or manufacturing subsidiaries of a U.S. parent corporation, the PFIC rules can present some very nasty surprises.

The PFIC rules deal with foreign corporations regardless of the level of U.S. ownership. A foreign corporation is a PFIC if, for any taxable year, either 75 percent or more of its gross income is passive, or 50 percent or more of its assets would produce passive income. These two tests are discussed in detail.

Satisfying either of the PFIC tests subjects the U.S. shareholder to the unhappy choice of being taxed under an interest-charge regime or under a current-inclusion regime. Under the interest-charge regime, when a U.S. taxpayer receives a distribution from (or recognizes a gain on sale or exchange of stock of) a foreign corporation that was a PFIC during any post-1986 year, the portion of the distribution or gain exceeding 125 percent of the average distributions during the three preceding years is allocated ratably over the days in the taxpayer's holding period for the stock. The tax on the portion of the distribution or gain allocated to any taxable year, beginning with the first year for which the PFIC tests were first satisfied, is subject to interest from that year to the year of the distribution or gain. The result is:

1. The distribution or gain allocated to this period is excluded from taxable income;
2. A special tax is computed on the portion of the distribution or gain allocated to each year during the period at the highest marginal tax rate applicable to the taxpayer under Section 1 or Section 11;

3. The special tax computed for each year can be offset by FTC that would ordinarily be generated by the portion of the distribution or gain allocated to that year; and

4. Interest is computed on the after-credit special tax at the rates applicable to tax deficiencies.

Section 1291(a)(1) provides that the interest-charge period starts with the earlier of the first day in the taxpayer's holding period or the first day of the first taxable year for which the PFIC tests are satisfied. Another ramification of the method of allocating income under the interest-charge rules is that a repatriation of all earnings to date in the interest-charge period does not prevent part of a later excess distribution from being allocated back to the earlier years. Although the Section 1291(a)(1) interest-charge period may start with the first day of the first taxable year for which the PFIC tests are satisfied, there is no requirement that the PFIC tests continue to be satisfied. Indeed, Section 1297(b)(1) confirms this fact.

One nasty surprise is that the current PFIC rules can apply to U.S. CFCs that are already subject to the Subpart F rules. The lack of coordination is somewhat surprising, because Subpart F rules are also aimed, in part, at the current inclusion of passive income.

There are two provisions that supply partial coordination. Section 951(f) provides that if an amount is includable in the income of a U.S. shareholder under both the current-inclusion regime of the PFIC rules and the Subpart F rules, it will be includable under Subpart F. This does not help the shareholder that has chosen the PFIC interest-charge regime, however. In addition, the PFIC current-inclusion regime taxes the U.S. parent on all of the foreign subsidiary's income, including active income. Accordingly, Section 951(f) does not limit the U.S. parent to being taxable on only the subsidiary's passive income. Rather, the U.S. parent is taxed on the subsidiary's passive income under Subpart F, while the subsidiary's active income is recognized under the PFIC current-inclusion regime.

The second provision that affords partial coordination is Section 1291(b)(3)(F). It calls for a "proper adjustment" by regulation to the excess distribution subject to the interest-charge regime, to take into account distributions of income that were previously taxed under the Subpart F rules and, therefore, excluded from gross income under Section 959(a).

The U.S. shareholder of a PFIC has the choice of being taxable under the interest-charge regime or electing to be taxable under a current-inclusion regime. There are a number of disadvantages to the current-inclusion regime. The U.S. shareholder would be taxable on its share of all of the corporation's income, not just its share of the passive income. Also, the current-inclusion regime taxes electing shareholders on their share of the corporation's income but gives them no benefit for their share of the corporation's losses. Obvious planning possibilities include preventative measures to avoid ever satisfying either the gross income test or the asset test.

Similarly, strategies that might be employed with respect to the asset test include maintaining high levels of trade receivables and avoiding cash. After offering several of these strategies, the author notes that because many, if not most, of these types of planning possibilities will not be acceptable from a business viewpoint, consideration should be given to electing the current-inclusion regime, keeping in mind its disadvantages, as discussed in the article.

The author continues with a discussion of the Tax Simplification Bill of 1991 and how it would modify the PFIC rules, if enacted.

[JS Karls, 2 J. Int'l Tax'n 205.]

"PFICs pose significant hazards for U.S. investment companies" (1991). A foreign investment company is essentially a foreign corporation that is engaged (or holds itself out as engaged) in the business of investing or trading in securities or commodities when it is at least 50 percent–owned (by vote or value) by U.S. persons.

A PFIC generally includes any foreign corporation if either: (1) At least 75 percent of its gross income (not gross receipts) is passive income under Section 954(c) (the Subpart F definition of "foreign personal holding company income") or (2) at least 50 percent or more of the average value of its assets produce or are held for the production of passive income.

There are exceptions for the income and assets pertaining to an active banking or insurance business. Under a look-through rule, direct or indirect ownership of at least 25 percent (by value) of another corporation's stock results in the pro rata share of the lower-tier company's assets and income being treated as owned by the upper-tier company. The authors then provide an example.

The federal income tax results to the PFIC shareholder are unpleasant: An excess distribution, which includes all gain on disposition plus actual distributions in excess of 125 percent of the three-year average (or shorter holding period), is spread out over the shareholder's portion of the holding period (except for the current year) that the distributor was a PFIC.

The PFIC provisions contain some very quirky rules that are at odds with both the Code's general scheme of taxation and the rules of taxation of RICs. Particularly odd is the result that a taxpayer is taxed (at maximum statutory rates, which are 34 percent for a RIC) and subject to an interest penalty on distributions that are a return of capital, solely because they are in excess of the 125 percent three-year average.

The PFIC rules can turn a foreign operating company into a passive vehicle in three ways. First, because the income test is based on 75 percent of the gross income for any year, the test is easy to fail for any producer or distributor that has a poor year (because gross income is gross receipts less cost of goods sold and returns).

Second, any long-standing profitable foreign subsidiary that accumulates earnings may readily meet the asset test. Assets must be valued quarterly, without regard to liabilities, although appraisals will generally not be required. An optional (and easier) method provided by Section 1296(a) uses adjusted tax basis as the value.

Third, under the look-through rule, if an operating company owns 25 percent of another foreign corporation, the assets of the upper-tier company and the pro rata share of the subsidiary are aggregated. Thus, all of the assets of the group and minority subsidiaries must be evaluated. Because of these rules, the absence of detailed regulatory guidance, and the fact that a foreign corporation's financial statements (if published or otherwise available to the RIC) will almost certainly be based on non-U.S. accounting principles, may be in a foreign language, and will probably be based on a foreign reporting currency, ascertaining whether a foreign corporation is a PFIC will be no easy task.

The authors end the article with a discussion of proposed legislation.

[RJ Shapiro & RD Lorence, 2 J. Int'l Tax'n 185.]

"PFIC tax implications when investing in a non-CFC" (**1990**). Use of a non-CFC may be advisable in certain circumstances, such as for sheltering income earned outside the United States. However, to avoid adverse tax consequences, the non-CFCs being used must be closely monitored. One of the more significant adverse tax consequences to be avoided is characterization as a PFIC, which results in shareholders being taxed on corporation income when earnings are realized. This article examines some PFIC-related problems that a tax planner may encounter when deciding whether an individual should invest in a non-CFC. After providing a general discussion of the PFIC rules, the author details the consequences of PFIC status. Thereafter, he discusses Letter Ruling 9007014 in light of the post-1986 rules for PFICs.

[WL Raby, US Tax'n Int'l Operations ¶ 7505.]

[4] Domestic International Sales Corporations

DISC regulation establishing limit on marginal costing allocation method upheld. A DISC and its parent corporation filed returns consistent with Regulation § 1.994-2(b)(3), regarding marginal costing, which limited the income that could be allocated to the DISC based on the DISC's profit percentage realized on all of its worldwide sales of a particular product. Under the limitation, indirect costs are generally allocated to the exported product if the profit margin using only direct production costs would exceed the worldwide profit margin for all product sales. The parent subsequently filed amended returns claiming that the regulation was invalid, and allocating more taxable income to the DISC. The Claims Court upheld the regulation and denied the refund.

Held: Affirmed for the IRS. Congress gave the IRS wide discretion to establish rules regarding the use of the marginal costing method. The regulation was a reasonable implementation of that method.

[Dow Corning Corp., 984 F2d 416, 71 AFTR2d 93-624, 93-1 USTC ¶ 50,042 (Fed. Cir. 1993).]

Workpaper entries did not support collection of DISC's receivables. Qualified export assets must account for 95 percent of a DISC's assets. Accounts receivable from the DISC's parent qualify if they are paid within sixty days after the end of the DISC's fiscal year. Taxpayer, organized as a DISC, had commissions receivable on its books. Instead of recording collection of the commissions and redistributing the funds to the parent corporation as a dividend, however, taxpayer's CPA made a workpaper entry eliminating the commissions and dividends payable and receivable from the companies' consolidated financial statements. The district court found that the elimination entries did not affect the underlying accounts and thus could not effect payment of those accounts.

Held: Affirmed for the IRS. The CPA's workpapers were not sufficiently detailed and complete to constitute a part of taxpayer's regular books of account.

[TSI, Inc., 977 F2d 424, 70 AFTR2d 92-5838, 92-2 USTC ¶ 50,521 (8th Cir. 1992).]

Taxpayer filing as a DISC but failing to qualify could not later claim such status. Taxpayer's subsidiary elected to be a DISC. Nevertheless, the DISC's original returns indicated it did no business as a DISC, and neither the DISC nor its parent reported any commission income or expense. Amended returns were filed, however, reporting DISC commissions. Taxpayer conceded the subsidiary did not qualify as a DISC solely under Section 992(a), but claimed it qualified under Section 992(a)(2) in conjunction with Regulation § 1.992-1(g), which concerns when a corporation, having filed a DISC return, will be treated as a DISC despite failing to meet some statutory or regulatory requirement. The Claims Court upheld denial of DISC treatment.

Held: Affirmed for the IRS. Regulation 1.992-1(g) covers only taxpayers that, after having claimed DISC status, seek to avoid such treatment.

[Stokely–Van Camp, Inc., 974 F2d 1319, 70 AFTR2d 92-5649, 92-2 USTC ¶ 50,459 (Fed. Cir. 1992).]

Worldwide gross receipts of DISC's shareholders include excise tax receipts. Taxpayer conducted its liquor export sales through a DISC. For purposes of computing the overall profit percentage limitation under Regulation § 1.994-2(b)(3), taxpayer reduced worldwide gross receipts by the federal excise tax paid. The IRS disallowed the reduction and the Tax Court held for the IRS.

Held: Affirmed for the IRS. Regulation § 1.993-6(a), which defines "gross receipts," plainly includes the excise tax in "total amounts received."

[Brown-Forman Corp., 955 F2d 1037, 69 AFTR2d 92-579, 92-1 USTC ¶ 50,075 (6th Cir. 1992).]

DISC's commission received on 65th day disqualifies election. On the 65th day following the close of the taxable year, taxpayer, a DISC, received from its parent the maximum commissions allowable. The district court determined that because they were not received by the 60th day, the unpaid commissions were not qualified export assets. As a result, taxpayer was disqualified as a DISC.

Held: Affirmed for the IRS. As logical as taxpayer's 2½-month rule would be, the IRS has authority to prescribe a sixty-day rule.

[L&F Int'l Sales Corp., 912 F2d 377, 66 AFTR2d 90-5487, 90-2 USTC ¶ 50,472 (9th Cir. 1990).]

In determining "combined taxable income" under DISC provisions, nonspecific interest expense is allocated on a net (and not gross) basis, but deduction for discount losses on receivables transferred to DISC is allocated directly to gross export income. In 1972, taxpayer established a commission DISC. In 1976 and 1977, taxpayer had both interest income and interest expense, none of which was directly traceable to export sales made through its DISC in those or any other years. Also, in 1976 and 1977, taxpayer had losses on the sales of export receivables to the DISC. The DISC realized discount income from the collection of these receivables in 1976 and 1977. In calculating "combined taxable income," taxpayer allocated its interest income and expense on a net basis to the dollar volume of domestic and export sales. While initially allocating the deduction for the discount losses on export receivables to export sales income, taxpayer later sought to allocate this deduction to income from both domestic and export sales in computing "combined taxable income." The IRS contested taxpayer's allocation of interest on a net basis and the deduction of the discount loss on export receivables to domestic sales income. The Tax Court ruled in favor of the IRS on both allocation issues, and taxpayer appealed.

Held: Reversed for taxpayer on the interest allocation issue, but affirmed for the IRS on the allocation of discount loss. Since taxpayer's interest expense was not attributable to a specific business activity, taxpayer was permitted to net its interest income and interest expense, and then allocate the net interest expense to its DISC for purposes of computing "combined taxable income." This conclusion is supported by *General Portland Cement Co.*, 628 F2d 321 (5th Cir. 1980) and is not, as suggested by the Tax Court, irreconcilable with Regulation § 1.861-8's expense allocation provisions. With respect to the discount losses, Regulation § 1.994-1(c)(6)(v) allocates the deduction for discount losses attributable to the transferred receivables to gross export income for the purposes of calculating "combined taxable income." This regulation is legislative in nature and its requirements and effect have not been shown by taxpayer to be arbitrary or contrary to the governing statutory provisions.

[Dresser Indus., Inc., 911 F2d 1128, 66 AFTR2d 90-5637, 90-2 USTC ¶ 50,505 (5th Cir. 1990).]

No loss regulation for DISC intercompany pricing held invalid. Taxpayer, a parent corporation of a DISC, filed returns and paid tax in accordance with Regulation § 1.994-1(e)(1)(i), which limits the use of the 4 percent gross receipts and combined taxable income methods of intercompany pricing when such methods would result in a loss to the supplier of a DISC (the "no loss" rule). Taxpayer claimed the regulation was invalid.

Held: For taxpayer. Regulation § 1.994-1(e)(1)(i) exceeds the grant of Section 994(b) to issue regulations by adding a requirement to the statute without a valid reason.

[Archer-Daniels-Midland Co., 798 F. Supp. 505, 92-2 USTC ¶ 50,612 (CD Ill. 1992).]

Continental shelf use of cranes on offshore drilling platform was use outside of United States for purposes of determining DISC's sales of export property. Taxpayer sold cranes to U.S. companies, which used the cranes on offshore oil drilling platforms. In all cases, these platforms were attached to the Outer Continental Shelf of the United States in the Gulf of Mexico, more than 3 miles, but less than 200 miles, from the U.S. coastline. Taxpayer made these sales using its "commission" DISC and paid the DISC commissions on the sales of these cranes. Taxpayer treated the cranes as being used outside the United States and as export property. Therefore, commissions it paid to its DISC were deducted under Section 994 on its 1978, 1980, and 1982 returns. The IRS determined that the cranes were not used by the purchasing companies outside the United States, and therefore the cranes were not export property under the DISC provisions. This determination led to deficiencies being assessed against taypayer arising from the disallowance of the deduction of the commissions paid to the DISC.

Held: For the IRS. Only commissions paid to a DISC on the sale of export property are deductible. Export property is property that is sold by a DISC for use, consumption, or disposition outside the United States. In this case, the Section 7701(a)(9) definition of "United States" is supplemented by Section 638, which includes within the definition of "United States" adjacent territorial waters, seabed, and subsoil of the submarine areas with regard to which the United States has exclusive exploration and exploitation rights. Section 638, which applies with respect to mines, oil and gas wells, and other natural deposits, is triggered in this instance because taxpayer's cranes were used by the purchasers of these cranes to drill oil and gas wells. Accordingly, because of this use, the Outer Continental Shelf is not outside the "United States" for purposes of determining taxpayer's export property. Despite taxpayer's arguments to the contrary, it is proper to examine the buyer's post-sale use of the property in determining whether such property constitutes export property. Finally, *Ocean Drilling & Exploration Co. v. United States,* 24 Cl. Ct. 714 (1991), *aff'd,* 988 F2d 1135 (Fed. Cir. 1993), relied on by taxpayer, is distinguishable. In that case, the Claims Court held that Section 638 did not expand the definition of "the United States" to include the Outer Continental Shelf in determining whether premiums received from insuring oil platforms on the Outer Continental Shelf constituted income derived from the insurance of U.S. risks. The basis of the court's decision was that Section 638 only applied when the income was derived directly from the exploitation of oil and gas wells. Insurance premiums were not derived directly from this activity. In DISC cases, the purchaser's use of the property is controlling, and therefore Section 638 includes the Outer Continental Shelf.

[FMC Corp. & Subsidiaries, 100 TC No. 38 (1993).]

Tax Court explains aggregation requirements for base-period exports receipts of acquired DISC and for those generated by business discontinued by DISC. In 1976, taxpayer acquired all the stock of a DISC in which it previously held a 50 percent interest. Once taxpayer acquired complete ownership, this DISC was kept inactive and received only interest income. Also, during the years in issue, taxpayer sold some of its business divisions whose products were previously sold by taxpayer's DISCs. The IRS determined (1) that in calculating deemed distributions from taxpayer's DISCs for 1976 and subsequent years, taxpayer was required to aggregate the now inactive DISC's export receipts for the base-period years with the export receipts of taxpayer's other DISC's for the base-period years and (2) that in calculating taxpayer's increased export receipts and deemed distributions for 1976 and subsequent years, taxpayer was also required to aggregate the export receipts generated by each of the sold corporate divisions in the base-period years.

Held: For the IRS. Aggregation is required, as argued by the IRS, even though the underlying business of a DISC is separated from the DISC itself and the DISC, after it is acquired, ceases any active export activity, and no related DISC carries on the same or a related export activity. Acquisition of the DISC for the purpose of reducing the amount of deemed distributions to be calculated under Section 995(e)(8) is not required. With respect to the businesses sold and discontinued by taxpayer, taxpayer must include in its base-period export receipts the base-period export receipts generated by its DISC, including those attributable to corporate divisions sold by taxpayer prior to and during the years in issue. Regulation § 1.995-7(e)(1), which requires this result, is valid, as argued by the IRS.

[FMC Corp. & Subsidiaries, 100 TC No. 38 (1993).]

Regulation § 1.933-6(e)(1) is invalid to the extent it requires DISC to use same accounting method as its parent-supplier in computing qualified export and gross receipts. During the years in issue, taxpayer's parent employed two methods of accounting for income tax purposes. For some transactions, it used the accrual method, and for eligible long-term contracts, it used the completed contract method. Nevertheless, taxpayer's parent deducted the commissions payable to taxpayer for all contracts in the year accrued. In determining its qualified export and gross receipts, taxpayer included receipts attributable to long-term contracts that its parent had not yet reported under the completed contract method. The IRS reduced the amount of qualified export receipts reported by taxpayer by the amount of receipts (attributable to long-term contract receipts) that had not yet been included in the parent's income under the completed contract method. This reduction resulted in taxpayer's failure to qualify as a DISC.

Held: For taxpayer. Section 993 is silent on whether a DISC or its related supplier's accounting method should be utilized in applying the "95 percent gross receipts" test. The regulations under Section 993, as argued by the IRS, require that a commission DISC use the same accounting method as its related supplier in computing its gross receipts. This requirement is invalid. The same accounting method must be used to determine both qualified export receipts and gross receipts for purposes of the gross receipts test. Moreover, a DISC is a separate corporation from its related supplier, and as such may choose its own accounting method. The legislative history under the DISC provisions does not indicate any intent to revise this aspect of a DISC's separate entity status. Finally, if any timing benefit is achieved by this mismatching of accounting methods, Code provisions other than the gross receipts test are a more appropriate vehicle for addressing this issue.

[Hughes Int'l Sales Corp., 100 TC 293 (1993).]

Corporation did not qualify as DISC. Taxpayer, a DISC, was a wholly owned subsidiary of *D*. *D* purchased a helicopter under a conditional sales agreement, and transferred it to taxpayer. Following financial difficulties, *D* was in default and the helicopter was transferred back to the seller, who in turn subsequently exported it to Europe. Taxpayer filed as a DISC, but the IRS determined it had failed to maintain its status, since the helicopter was not disposed of for use outside the United States within one year of the sale to *D*.

Held: For the IRS. Regulation § 1.993-3(d)(2)(i)(*b*), containing the one-year limitation, is valid. There is no exception because of the default and involuntary retransfer. Taxpayer's failure to satisfy the requirement that a U.S. purchaser of export property from a DISC resell it for use outside the United States within one year of the purchase resulted in loss of its DISC status.

[Sim-Air, USA, Ltd., 98 TC 187 (1992).]

DISC and supplier's combined income to be computed with allocation of research and development (R&D) expense. Taxpayer supplied medical products to its related DISC. Both entities computed the allowable transfer price under the 50/50 combined taxable income method. Taxpayer failed to allocate R&D expenses as required under the regulations, however, believing the Economic Recovery Tax Act of 1981 moratorium on allocating and apportioning R&D expense applied.

Held: For the IRS. The moratorium applied if geographic sourcing of income was relevant. Geographic sourcing is not an element in the computation of combined taxable income, and thus the moratorium did not apply to a DISC.

[St. Jude Medical, Inc., 97 TC 457 (1991).]

"Combined taxable income" of U.S. parent and its DISC, using full cost accounting, must be reduced by full amount of discount on export receivables transferred by parent to DISC. Taxpayer formed a commission DISC. In 1981, taxpayer and its DISC entered into an agreement under which the DISC purchased, at a discount, undivided interests in taxpayer's receivables from export sales made through the DISC. Taxpayer used full cost accounting to calculate "combined taxable income." Taxpayer allocated its discount loss on the transfer of its export receivables to all of its income. The IRS argued such treatment was improper and that the discount should have been allocated exclusively to the product lines generating the export receivables as per *Dresser Industries, Inc.*, 911 F2d 1128 (5th Cir. 1990).

Held: For the IRS. Allocation of the discount losses to domestic product lines and other income was improper in the determination of "combined taxable income." Such discount is incorporated into the computation of the overall profit percentage limitation by subtracting the discount from "combined taxable income" (determined using full costing) in the numerator of the overall profit percentage.

[Computervision Corp., 96 TC 652 (1991).]

Subsidiary failed to qualify as DISC. Taxpayer purchased grain from growers. It cleaned, dried, aerated, fumigated, and graded the grain at its grain elevators, and then exported it. Taxpayer obtained what it considered producer's loans from its wholly owned subsidiary, a DISC. Taxpayer used the mark-to-market inventory valuation method. At year-end, any open forward contracts to buy and sell grain were marked-to-market with the net gain or loss recorded on its balance sheet. The IRS determined taxpayer was not a producer and the subsidiary was not a DISC.

Held: For the IRS. Taxpayer was not engaged in the production or growing of export property. Therefore, the loans did not qualify as producer's loans within the meaning of Section 993. Taxpayer's grain elevator operations generally were not considered production in the grain industry, but rather were classed as assembly or packaging. In addition, the net gain or loss on open forward contracts should be disregarded in computing taxpayer's investment in export-related assets.

[Garnac Grain Co., 95 TC 7 (1990).]

DISC commission expense deduction cannot be calculated by using a country-by-country grouping. Taxpayer formed a DISC to act as its commission agent for sales of its products. The products manufactured by taxpayer constituted a single product line. In computing its deductible DISC commission expense, taxpayer separately determined on a country-by-country basis its total DISC commission expense under the gross receipts method and its total DISC commission expense under the taxable income method. The IRS determined that the country-by-country method used by taxpayer was not permitted under Section 994 and Regulations § 1.994-1.

Held: For the IRS. Regulations § 1.994-1 is a legislative regulation and is thus entitled to greater weight than an interpretive regulation. Under this regulation, the grouping of transactions is only permitted (1) on a transaction-by-transaction basis or (2) on the basis of products or product lines. No other method, including one using a country-by-country analysis, is allowed.

[Napp Sys., Inc., 65 TCM 2567, RIA TC Memo. ¶ 93,196 (1993).]

Disqualification of DISC results in reallocation of income to subsidiaries. The IRS determined that taxpayer did not qualify as a DISC and reallocated the income among taxpayer's subsidiaries. The grounds for disqualification were that the producer's loans on the DISC's tax return were really nonqualified export assets. Taxpayer argued that the item was actually a distribution to the DISC's parent.

Held: For the IRS. The item was not a producer's loan, because there was no written note evidencing the obligation. In addition, the argument that the item was mischaracterized was rejected.

[McCoy Enters., Inc., 64 TCM 1449, RIA TC Memo. ¶ 92,693 (1992).]

IRS issues final regulations concerning requirements of DISCs. The IRS has issued final regulations relating to DISCs. These regulations remove the requirements that a DISC have "paid-in" capital and that a DISC maintain a bank account. The Tax Court held these requirements invalid in *Durbin Paper Stock Co.*, 80 TC 252 (1983). The regulations are amended to reflect this holding.

[TD 8371, 1991-2 CB 347; Reg. § 1.992-1(d)(1).]

IRS issues final regulations concerning apportionment of expenses in FSC and DISC contexts. The IRS has issued final regulations relating to apportionment of expenses in the FSC and DISC contexts. The IRS took this action in order to discontinue the apportionment of expenses of the related supplier of a DISC or FSC to dividends from the DISC or FSC. The regulations are necessary to prevent a second apportionment to the dividend from an FSC or DISC of expenses already apportioned to determine the combined taxable income of the FSC or DISC and its related supplier.

[TD 8286, 1990-1 CB 138; Reg. § 1.861-8(f).]

[5] Foreign Sales Corporations

IRS issues revenue ruling concerning FSCs. The IRS ruled that an FSC and a small FSC may both be members of a controlled group of corporations provided that they do not exist at the same time during the taxable year of the controlled group. When switching from a small FSC to an FSC, the corporation has thirty days from the effective date of the FSC election to establish a principal FSC bank account.

[Rev. Rul. 90-108, 1990-2 CB 185.]

IRS issues final regulations concerning apportionment of expenses in FSC and DISC contexts. The IRS has issued final regulations relating to apportionment of expenses in the FSC and DISC contexts. The IRS took this action in order to discontinue the apportionment of expenses of the related supplier of a DISC or FSC to dividends from the DISC or FSC. The regulations are necessary to prevent a second apportionment to the dividend from an FSC or DISC of expenses already apportioned to determine the combined taxable income of the FSC or DISC and its related supplier.

[TD 8286, 1990-1 CB 138; Reg. § 1.861-8(f).]

"Introduction to FSCs" (1992). To encourage U.S. exports, the Tax Reform Act of 1984 (TRA 1984) created the FSC and partially exempted its export income from U.S. tax. This article covers the FSC provisions and provides a basic understanding of their operation.

The author first compares the tax treatment of an FSC with a non-FSC. Thereafter, he provides a glossary of the terms and concepts needed to understand and apply the FSC provisions. Next, he explains how to create and organize a corporation that will satisfy the FSC requirements. Subsequent events resulting in the loss of such status are also reviewed. The author then considers the so-called foreign presence tests, i.e., the foreign management test and the economic processes test. Pitfalls and planning opportunities related to the economic processes test are discussed. The detailed definition, as well as other requirements, for export property are also considered.

In the second half of this article, the author explains the treatment of FSC income. Relevant terms and concepts are reviewed, along with the calculation of foreign trade income and the determination of allowable deductions and credits. The treatment of shareholder distributions is also discussed. An illustration is then provided in which these calculations are highlighted.

In the last part of this article, the author discusses the provisions concerning the small FSC and the interest change DISC, the transition rules for DISCs and export trade corporations, and other provisions, such as those concerning qualified agricultural cooperatives, the disallowance of treaty benefits, and exclusion from the branch profits tax (BPT). In the appendix of this article are various IRS forms and instructions pertaining to FSCs.

[WW Wondolowski, US Tax'n Int'l Operations ¶ 9511.]

"Converting from a small FSC to a regular FSC" (1991). Many practitioners have discovered the procedural pitfalls created by the mechanical, yet substantive, foreign presence and other requirements for qualifying the receipts of an FSC for the partial U.S. tax exemption provided by Sections 921 through 927.

As one example, Section 924(c)(2) requires that an FSC maintain a principal bank account in a qualifying foreign country at all times during the taxable year. Similarly, Section 922(b)(2) bars qualification as a small FSC (eligible for certain procedural exceptions, e.g., the absence of a principal bank account requirement) if a regular FSC is a member of the same group of controlled corporations.

In Revenue Ruling 90-108, the IRS took a refreshingly practical approach to determining the efficacy of certain self-help measures to convert a small FSC to a regular FSC, obviating certain technical issues presented by the form in which the conversion was effectuated by the taxpayers.

[1 J. Int'l Tax'n 366.]

"Choosing the best FSC pricing options" (1990). Exporters who qualify can claim favorable tax benefits under the FSC provisions by establishing a separate entity that meets organizational and operative requirements under Sections 922 and 924, respectively. If the entity qualifies as an FSC, it can then use one or more transfer pricing options contained in Section 925, and taxes are imposed at a lower rate for a portion of the income.

An FSC must meet four principal operative requirements contained in Section 924 on a continual or recurrent basis: export property, foreign management, sales activities, and direct costs. Pricing rules, related to those of its predecessor, the DISC, enable an FSC to benefit from safe-haven pricing, and provide some measure of certainty between the U.S. manufacturer or other related supplier and the FSC.

Two of the transfer pricing rules for FSCs derive from the former DISC safe-haven alternatives. Under Section 925(a)(1), an FSC can earn 1.83 percent of the foreign trading gross receipts, including total receipts from the sale, lease, or rental of property in the ordinary course of a trade or business, and gross income from all other sources, determined on a transaction-by-transaction basis or on a grouping basis.

Under the 23 percent combined taxable income method of Section 925(a)(2), the taxable income of the FSC and its related supplier are combined on a transaction-by-transaction basis or a grouping basis. Combined taxable income is computed by determining foreign trading gross receipts and then subtracting the sum of the cost of goods sold (including inventory amounts, noninventory costs, and uniform capitalization rules amounts), related supplier's expenses, and the FSC's direct and indirect expenses.

The gross receipts computation is limited to twice the combined taxable income or 46 percent of combined taxable income under Section 925(d). The FSC income is the lower of the gross receipts amount or the gross receipts limitation, or the higher of these two amounts and the 23 percent of combined taxable income amount, analogous to the former DISC rule. If the related supplier and FSC have negative combined taxable income, the related supplier incurs the entire portion of the loss and the FSC breaks even.

Under Section 925(a)(3), the transfer price or the commission may be determined under Section 482 in lieu of the 1.83 percent rate or 23 percent rate and all of the usual rules of Section 482 apply according to Regulation § 1.925(a)-1T(a)(3). If an FSC earns profit that exceeds the profit under the administrative-pricing rules, the IRS is likely to object to this pricing split and give special scrutiny to such transaction.

Comparing the gross receipts method, the combined taxable income method, and the combined taxable income limitation method, the best method depends on the profit margin. For high-profit transactions, the 23 percent of combined taxable income alternative is preferable. For low-profit transactions, the optimal approach is to use the gross receipts method subject to the combined taxable income limitation.

Marginal costing can be used as an alternative to conventional FSC pricing according to Regulation § 1.925(b)-1T. Subject to certain limitations, it is often not advantageous except where export sales are less profitable than domestic sales of the same product.

Grouping by product or product line is accepted by the IRS if the pricing conforms to recognized trade or industry usage or falls within a major group based on the government's standard industrial classification manual. The related supplier may use a product grouping with respect to one product but use the transaction-by-transaction method for another product within the same taxable year. Transactions in which combined taxable income is negative can be excluded from FSC computations or included.

Because there are so many variations of grouping, whether or not to group must be decided by each company, depending on the circumstances of the transactions involved. Grouping FSC transactions to minimize computations and paperwork may not be advantageous when it does not maximize FSC benefits. Examples are provided of situations where grouping is advantageous or disadvantageous, calculating FSC income under the pricing alternatives on both a grouped and ungrouped basis.

[R. Feinschreiber, 1 J. Int'l Tax'n 213.]

"Introduction to FSC marginal costing" (1990). FSCs can often increase their income from export sales by using marginal costing. Marginal costing uses certain costs when determining the combined taxable income of an FSC and its related supplier. Marginal costing enables an FSC and its related supplier to eliminate fixed costs and a significant portion of their other costs and expenses. This strategy increases combined taxable income, which can then increase FSC income. These FSC benefits are often substantial, but require careful structuring of intercompany pricing. This article discusses the marginal costing rules for increasing allowable FSC profits.

The author first discusses the prerequisite for marginal costing by an FSC, that is, that the FSC must be seeking to establish or maintain a market for export property. Thereafter, he explains the treatment of costs and expenses under the marginal costing rules. The determination of direct production costs—the only costs used in determining combined taxable income—is given in-depth explanation.

Next, the author considers the "overall profit percentage limitation," which restricts marginal costing benefits. Determination of the limitation and planning in this area are explained by the author. Last, the author discusses the two "no loss" rules applicable to FSC income, the "no profit" exception provided by each, and grouping for marginal costing.

[R. Feinschreiber, US Tax'n Int'l Operations ¶ 7527.]

[6] Controlled Foreign Corporations

[a] Generally

"Stapled stock rules expand CFC restrictions" (1992). Under a "stapled stock" arrangement, shares of stock of two corporations are paired or linked so that neither can be traded or disposed of without simultaneous transfer of the other. These arrangements were initially used to avoid banking regulations. In recent years, however, they have been associated more frequently with CFCs.

Section 269B(a)(1), enacted in 1984, indicates generally that if a domestic corporation and a foreign corporation are stapled entities, the foreign corporation is treated as a domestic corporation for all purposes under the Code. This means that the stapled foreign corporation is subject to U.S. tax on its worldwide income, thereby preventing avoidance of the subpart F rules. In addition, for purposes of the Section 1563 controlled group definition, stock in a corporation that constitutes a stapled interest with respect to the stock of another corporation is treated as owned by the other corporation.

The stapling of a foreign corporation's stock to the stock of its U.S. parent originated as a means of avoiding the subpart F provisions. Section 269B, however, has created new tax policy questions. The primary question that has been decided concerns whether the conversion of a foreign corporation into a domestic corporation as a result of stapling is an F reorganization. With Revenue Ruling 89-103, the IRS ruled that it is.

Because of the substantially higher tax cost imposed by Section 269B when paired stock is used to acquire an interest in a foreign corporation, the paired stock technique has declined in use since 1984. Taxpayers who staple stock should be aware of the problems involving worldwide taxation of the foreign corporation's income, problems arising because treaty provisions may be overriden, and problems resulting when the foreign corporation is unstapled from its domestic counterpart.

[RS Ross & JL Kramer, 3 J. Int'l Tax'n 78.]

"International related-party debt: Part I" (1991). In a previous article, the authors examined the tax treatment under Section 956 of direct and indirect investments that a CFC has in "U.S. property." These rules are designed to prohibit a U.S. parent from using the earnings of its CFC without paying U.S. tax on those earnings. The increase in earnings of a CFC invested in U.S. property is treated as if the CFC had paid a dividend to its U.S. parent.

As promised in response to a letter from a reader commenting on the fact that the authors' earlier article did not cover all other possible tax consequences regarding inbound related-party debt, the following discussion presents an overview of other possible tax considerations that may arise when a U.S. parent owes money to a CFC. It is the first part of a two-part article that focuses on the U.S. tax considerations relative to intercompany related-party debt. Part one addresses the U.S. tax considerations of inbound intercompany related-party debt, and part two addresses the tax considerations of outbound intercompany related-party debt. The article is meant to provide practitioners with a "checklist" of issues that should be addressed.

Debts between a U.S. parent corporation and its CFC arise in many different ways, including loans or accounts payable resulting from intercompany transactions involving the sale of goods or services, interest, rents, royalties, and similar transactions. In addition to U.S. considerations, a U.S. parent and its CFC must consider the impact of the laws of the country in which the CFC operates and tax treaties between the United States and the foreign jurisdiction.

The authors conclude that in order to determine the costs and benefits of the intercompany debt on the U.S. parent and its CFC, the following questions need to be answered:

1. Is any interest paid deductible and at what tax rate, and is any interest income taxable and at what tax rate?

2. Are there any currency restrictions that limit the currency in which the loan can be denominated or prohibit the payment of interest?

3. Will foreign exchange gain or loss be subject to taxation and at what rate?

4. What withholding tax rate will be applied to interest payments and what compliance is necessary to secure a treaty-reduced withholding tax rate?

5. What is the impact on the FTC calculation for each company? Can withholding taxes be claimed as a tax credit, and what is the tax impact on the U.S. parent if the loan is an investment in U.S. property for U.S. tax purposes?

6. What is the impact on each company if the interest rate is above or below the arm's-length rate that the lender would charge to an unrelated organization?

After gathering answers to these questions, the after-tax impact of the intercompany debt on the U.S. parent and its CFC can be compared to other borrowing alternatives to provide management with information with which to make informed decisions.

[JE Bernot & TF Windholtz, 2 J. Int'l Tax'n 85.]

"Public companies can avoid current tax on Subpart F income" (1991). Many public corporations, or corporations that expect to go public, plan to operate abroad or to export their products at some time. Many of these public corporations are formed under U.S. state law (U.S. corporations). Under Sections 951(b) and 957(a), a foreign subsidiary of such a U.S. corporation would be a CFC, i.e., a foreign corporation more than 50 percent of whose stock, by vote or value, is controlled by U.S. persons owning 10 percent or more of the foreign corporation's voting stock (U.S. shareholders). The U.S. corporation, as a U.S. shareholder, would be subject to U.S. tax on any Subpart F income earned by the CFC, according to Section 951. On the other hand, some, and in many cases all, types of Subpart F income would not be subject to U.S. tax, and could be earned in a tax haven, if the public company were formed under foreign law rather than under U.S. state law.

A public foreign-parent corporation (FHC) would not be a CFC and its U.S. shareholders would not be subject to tax under Subpart F if U.S. persons that each owned more than 10 percent of the FHC's stock did not own, collectively, more than 50 percent of the FHC's stock. This is quite often the case with public corporations. With such an ownership structure in place, the FHC would organize foreign subsidiaries in tax havens. These foreign subsidiaries could then purchase supplies, or sell products for, related U.S. corporations or related foreign subsidiaries organized in taxable foreign jurisdictions. The tax-haven foreign subsidiaries would earn a commission or a gross profit (foreign base sales income) for these related-party transactions. In addition to foreign base sales income, under Sections 952(a) and 954(a), the tax-haven foreign subsidiaries could earn the following U.S. tax-deferred income:

1. Related-party service income;
2. Shipping income (including any income derived from a space or oceanic activity);
3. Insurance income;
4. Banking income; and
5. Oil-related income.

A foreign subsidiary also can make a loan to any U.S. subsidiary of the FHC without triggering U.S. tax under Section 956, since no foreign subsidiary would be a CFC. The author sets out the preferred organizational structure in an exhibit.

The article then examines the PFIC provisions concerning passive income. A long analysis follows involving the question as to whether a separate U.S. subsidiary should be formed if U.S. operations are intended. The author advises that a separate U.S. subsidiary should be formed, and details several strategies to set up the corporations. Next, the author suggests a recapitalization/dividend strategy by way of example for a U.S. public corporation that (1) owns existing CFCs that earn Subpart F income or (2) wants to obtain funds that were already earned by a CFC and that were subject to a low foreign tax. An exhibit helps illustrate the structure.

An examination of the arm's-length-pricing risks ensues, focusing on the use by the IRS of Section 482 to reallocate all or a portion of the foreign subsidiary's income to the U.S. corporation, where it would be subject to U.S. tax under the theory that the excess purchase price paid by the U.S. corporation or the reduced sales price received by the U.S. corporation represents a constructive dividend to the foreign-parent corporation, which would be subject to U.S. withholding tax. In this regard, an arm's-length selling commission is often 10 percent of the ultimate sales price. The IRS might also attempt to reallocate income from a tax-haven foreign subsidiary to a high-tax foreign subsidiary and assert that the income reallocation constitutes a constructive dividend.

The article then discusses other considerations in organizing the foreign corporation: (1) what to look for in a country of organization; (2) possible Securities and Exchange Commission (SEC) reporting or filing requirements; and (3) the risks of expropriation if the foreign country becomes politically unstable.

[MA Masek, 1 J. Int'l Tax'n 342.]

"Pre-sale loan from CFC can reduce or eliminate gain" (1990). A U.S. corporate shareholder that plans to sell a CFC should consider a temporary pre-sale loan from the CFC, repaying the loan before the CFC stock is sold. In many cases, such a loan can reduce or eliminate any tax arising from the sale of the appreciated CFC stock.

Moreover, a pre-sale loan could generate a capital loss that would offset capital gain from any other capital assets sold by the U.S. shareholder. If these asset sales are coupled with a leaseback, a large loan would permit the U.S. shareholder to receive tax-free funds that would be deductible when repaid.

Finally, if the stock of a U.S. corporation that owns a CFC is sold, a pre-sale loan allows the purchaser to step-up the U.S. corporation's assets to fair market value at a reduced tax cost and thus circumvent the repeal of the *General Utilities* doctrine.

[MA Masek, 73 J. Tax'n 256.]

"Should your foreign corporation be a CFC?" (1990). To discourage U.S. taxpayers from deferring U.S. tax by operating through foreign base companies, Congress enacted Subpart F of the Code (Sections 951 through 964), creating the concept of a CFC. The classification of a foreign entity as a CFC (or non-CFC) is critical in analyzing the U.S. income tax consequences of an international structure.

Under Section 951(a)(1)(A), U.S. shareholders are taxed currently on their pro rata share of the foreign corporation's Subpart F income and on the corporation's increase in earnings invested in U.S. property even if no distributions are made. Exchanging U.S. shareholders may be required to treat their proportionate share of the CFC's E&P as a dividend in order to qualify the CFC for a tax-free reorganization. Gain recognized by a U.S. shareholder upon liquidation of a CFC or a sale of its shares may be recharacterized as dividend income under Section 1248(a).

For purposes of applying the FTC limitation, look-through rules under Section 904(d)(3) apply in determining the appropriate FTC limitation category in which to include dividends, interest, rents, and royalties received from a CFC.

The first step in determining whether a foreign entity is a CFC is to establish whether it is a corporation (versus a partnership) for U.S. tax purposes. Under Regulations § 301.7701-2, referred to as the regulatory resemblance test, an organization is treated as a corporation if it has a majority of the following corporate characteristics:

1. Limited liability;
2. Continuity of life;

3. Representative centralized management; and
4. Free transferability of interests.

In creating a foreign entity, it may be possible to modify certain provisions of its organizing documents to achieve, for U.S. tax purposes, corporate or noncorporate status depending on the result desired. Where a foreign entity is effectively controlled by a single economic interest, the IRS may contend it possesses the characteristics of free transferability of interests and continuity of life despite provisions to the contrary in the entity's governing documents (as in Revenue Ruling 77-214).

Identifying the foreign corporation's U.S. shareholders is a key step in determining CFC status because the statutory definition focuses on whether these shareholders in the aggregate own more than 50 percent of the voting power or value of the stock. There is little guidance in determining the value of a foreign corporation's stock for purposes of the CFC definition, and the definition of a "U.S. shareholder" focuses solely on voting power. Under Section 951(b), a U.S. shareholder is a U.S. person (i.e., U.S. citizen, resident alien, domestic partnership, corporation, estate, or trust) that owns directly, indirectly or constructively 10 percent or more of the total combined voting power of a foreign corporation's stock. Regulation § 1.951-1(g)(2)(i) provides that if a corporation has more than one class of stock outstanding, a U.S. person holds the percentage of voting power equal to the proportionate share of the percentage of directors his or her class may elect. However, a U.S. person is deemed to own 10 percent or more of the total combined voting power if such person owns directly, indirectly, or constructively 20 percent or more of the total number of shares of a class of stock that has the right to elect, appoint, or replace a majority of the board of directors, break a corporate deadlock, or elect, appoint, or replace the sole manager who exercises the powers ordinarily exercised by a board of directors.

Under Section 958(a), stock owned directly or indirectly by a foreign corporation, partnership, trust, or estate is considered as owned proportionately by its shareholders, partners, or beneficiaries. Attribution under the rule stops with the first U.S. person in the chain of ownership from foreign entities. The constructive ownership rules of Section 958(b) incorporate the Section 318(a) constructive ownership rules with certain modifications in the family and attribution-from-entity rules. For the purposes of Section 958(b), options to acquire stock are treated as ownership; warrants and convertible debentures exercisable at will (although not a right of first refusal) are treated as options. However, stock constructively owned under the family attribution rule or attribution-to-entity rule may not be reattributed to other family members or under the attribution-from-entity rules.

Arrangements to shift formal voting power away from U.S. shareholders is not respected if, in reality, substantive voting power is retained. Regulation § 1.957-1(b)(2) provides a three-part test indicating when such arrangements are disregarded. In several landmark cases, including *Garlock, Inc.* (1972), *Kraus* (1973), and *Estate of Weiskopf* (1975), the Tax Court upheld CFC status despite attempts by U.S. shareholders to decontrol their existing CFC by issuing a new class of voting preferred stock to non-U.S. shareholders. The district court's holding in *Koehring Co.* (1977) was similar and affirmed by the Seventh Circuit in 1978. However, in *CCA, Inc.* (1975) a parent corporation successfully decontrolled its Swiss CFC, where the Tax Court found no voting restrictions on the new preferred shareholders and the board members representing them had significant powers over corporate affairs.

Corporations planning to avoid CFC status could disperse the foreign corporation's voting stock so that U.S. persons individually own less than 10 percent of the voting power (directly, indirectly, or constructively). CFC status also may be avoided by dispersing the corporation's voting power among various classes of stock, so that no one class has any of the three powers specified in Regulation § 1.957-1(b)(1). Control may be indirectly vested with U.S. shareholders who own no more than 50 percent of a foreign corporation's stock if these shareholders have the power to make major decisions in the event of a deadlock. To obviate against any notion of control, arbitration provisions should be included in the shareholders' agreements to address potential deadlocks.

Since expansion of the number of FTC limitation categories by TRA 1986, U.S. shareholders often want to convert a non-CFC into a CFC to avoid the non-controlled Section 902 FTC limitation category under Section 904(d)(1)(E). Where a foreign coventurer wishes to remain an equal partner, converting a foreign corporate joint venture into a CFC by placing certain elements of control within the hands of the U.S. shareholder might be difficult. One way of establishing CFC status that might not be objectionable from the foreign owner's viewpoint would be for the U.S. shareholder to acquire an option to purchase additional shares of the foreign joint venture corporation, causing it to be treated as owning more than 50 percent of the stock for U.S. tax purposes under the constructive ownership rules. Alternatively, a 50/50 foreign corporate joint venture could issue additional non-voting preferred shares to the U.S. shareholder, increasing its ownership to more than 50 percent of the value of the stock, while the foreign coventurer would remain an equal voting partner.

[MM Levey & LA Pollack, 1 J. Int'l Tax'n 204.]

[b] Insurance Income (Section 953)

IRS issues proposed regulations concerning insurance income of CFC. The IRS has issued proposed regulations relating to the definition and computation of the insurance income of a CFC. The proposed regulations also contain definitions and rules applicable to certain captive insurance companies.

[INTL-939-86, 1991-1 CB 902; Prop. Reg. §§ 1.953-0–1.953-7.]

"U.S. insurers face tax barriers to international expansion" (1992). In contrast to the general treatment of U.S. corporations doing business abroad, a U.S. insurance company must wind its way through a maze of specialized rules. These rules often result in the imposition of current taxes that would be deferred if the underlying income were earned from wholly domestic insurance operations. Thus, while tax planning for a noninsurance multinational focuses on identifying opportunities for deferral of U.S. tax, a U.S. insurer seeking to enter foreign markets must concern itself with avoiding an increase in its overall U.S. tax expense. This column surveys difficulties in minimizing the U.S. tax burden on transnational insurance activities.

As an exception to the general rule that defers U.S. tax on a CFC's earnings, income from certain activities is taxed currently to U.S. shareholders under Sections 951 through 964 (Subpart F). The application of Subpart F to a U.S. property and casualty or life insurer that operates through a CFIC was modified by TRA 1986. First, the definition of a "CFIC's Subpart F income" was expanded to include all income from issuing insurance, reinsurance, or annuity contracts, with the exception of underwriting income derived from insuring risks in the CFIC's home country. Income derived from investment of a CFIC's unearned "home-country" premiums is also includable as Subpart F income under the definition of "foreign personal holding company income" in Section 954(c).

A second 1986 amendment introduced the rule for captive foreign insurance companies (captives) in Section 953(c). Subject to the home-country exception, underwriting income from related parties is treated as Subpart F income if the aggregate holdings of U.S. persons (determined without regard to individual ownership percentages) exceed 25 percent of a captive's vote or value.

Proposed Section 953 regulations (issued April 17, 1991) would give rules for computing a CFIC's Section 953 insurance income and address the treatment of captives.

The author discusses in detail the following issues: calculating Subpart F insurance income (including identification of reserve factors and branching out), fitting in exceptions to Subpart F, CFIC investments (including the "hopscotch" effect and indirectly owned PFICs), captives insuring related-party risks (including the BPT), the FTC, U.S. consolidated groups, and U.S. withholding.

In conclusion, the author writes that whether a U.S. insurer operates through a CFC or a branch, the taxpayer must be wary of incurring U.S. tax costs that are not borne by domestic insurers or foreign competitors. While the IRS may clarify certain issues (such as the scope of various U.S. tax definitions), only Congress can remove obstacles such as the limited scope of the home-country exception. In the former case, taxpayers may be justified in relying on reasoned legal opinions as to unresolved issues.

[LG Stodghill, 3 J. Int'l Tax'n 172.]

[c] Foreign Base Company Income (Section 954)

[i] Foreign base company sales income (Section 954(d))

Wholly owned subsidiary of CFC cannot be Section 954(d)(2) "branch or similar establishment" of such CFC. Taxpayer, a U.S. corporation, owned all the stock of a Swiss corporation. This Swiss CFC owned all the stock of a U.K. corporation. Under a license from taxpayer, the Swiss CFC sold oil drilling equipment and other products designed and manufactured by taxpayer for use in North Sea oil exploration and production. Among these products were pipe and pipe connectors, which the U.K. CFC manufactured for sale to the Swiss CFC. The U.K. CFC invoiced the Swiss CFC for the pipe and pipe connectors at a price equal to costs for fabrication services plus a 5 percent markup. The IRS determined that the U.K. subsidiary should be treated as a "branch" of the Swiss subsidiary under Section 954(d)(2).

Held: For taxpayer. The "branch" rule of Section 954(d)(2) merely supplies the relationship required to bring an otherwise unrelated party within the spectrum of Section 954(d)(1). In operation, it was meant to prevent CFCs from avoiding Section 954(d)(1) when there was no transaction with a related person within the meaning of Section 954(d)(3). It does not apply to persons who are related, such as subsidiaries of a CFC. As a matter of law, a person who is related to a CFC under the provisions of Section 954(d)(3) cannot be a "branch" of that CFC under Section 954(d)(2).

[Vetco, Inc., 95 TC 579 (1990).]

Tax court considers scope of "branch or similar establishment" and determines it is to be given its customary business meaning. Taxpayer was the U.S. parent of a CFC organized in Liberia. The CFC did not manufacture any products, but sold personal property it acquired from *T*, a Belgium corporation unrelated to the CFC and any of its affiliates. The products sold by the CFC were manufactured by *T* outside of Liberia and sold for use outside Liberia. The agreement between the CFC and *T* required twelve months notice for termination; otherwise, there existed no specific termination date, and in fact, the agreement remained in force for many years. Under this agreement, the CFC transferred all proprietary technical information required to manufacture these products to *T*. *T* purchased all the materials needed to make these products. The selling price for the products *T* made for the CFC was determined by a formula under which *T* received the cost of the raw materials and packaging plus a "conversion fee," which included labor, overhead, financing, and profit. Thus, if the products were made satisfactorily, *T* was guaranteed a return of its costs and a profit. The agreement also required *T* to deliver the products to whomever the CFC designated, including the CFC's customers. While 80 percent of the CFC's income was attributable to the resale of products manufactured by *T*, only 8 percent of *T*'s gross sales were attributable to products it manufactured for the CFC. The IRS determined that *T* was a "branch or similar establishment" of the CFC under Section 954(d)(2), and thus the manufacture of products by *T* for the CFC and the subsequent sales by the CFC to unrelated third parties resulted in foreign base company sales income.

Held: For taxpayer. The critical issue was whether *T* was, under Section 954(d)(2), a "branch or similar establishment" of the CFC. To find that it was would require a reading of the statute that goes far beyond its actual wording. The legislative history of Section 954(d)(2) indicates that Congress intended that the term "branch" be given its ordinary meaning in a business and accounting sense. The inclusion of the phrase "or similar establishment" was intended to bring within the phrase establishments that bear the typical characteristics of an ordinary-usage branch, yet go by another name for accounting, financial reporting, local law, or other purposes. It does not, as argued by the IRS, apply to any arrangement that results in a proscribed tax effect. Here, T was unrelated to the CFC, its U.S. parent, and any of their affiliates. Moreover, T was a separately incorporated manufacturing entity operating pursuant to an arm's-length agreement with the CFC. Finally, the degree of the CFC's control over T's manufacturing operations and the degree of risk borne by the CFC relative to T under their agreement along with the anticipated length of their relationship were irrelevent considerations. T was not a "branch or similar establishment" of the CFC within the meaning of Section 954(d)(2).

[Ashland Oil, Inc., 95 TC 348 (1990).]

"Tax Court refuses to extend definition of 'branch' in two cases" (1991). In *Ashland Oil* and *Vetco,* two 1990 cases, the Tax Court rejected the IRS's broad approach to the branch-tax rule and found that the entities in question were not branches. In *Ashland,* the court held that a foreign entity that manufactured under contract with a CFC was not a branch of the CFC. In *Vetco,* the court did not even consider whether the independent manufacturer was a branch, because the IRS did not properly raise the issue. The court did, however, hold in *Vetco* that a wholly owned subsidiary of the CFC was not a branch.

[75 J. Tax'n 118.]

"Tax Court restricts CFC branch rule" 1991). The tax Court restricted the scope of the "branch rule" under Section 954(d)(2) in two 1990 cases, *Ashland Oil* and *Vetco.*

A U.S. shareholder of a CFC generally must include in gross income a pro rata share of the CFC's Subpart F income for the taxable year, including foreign base company sales income. Under the branch rule, foreign base company sales income includes certain income derived by a CFC "through a branch or similar establishment outside the country of incorporation" of the CFC where the activity has substantially the same effect as if the branch were a wholly owned subsidiary. While the term "branch or similar establishment" is not defined by statute, the regulations test for branch/subsidiary equivalency by reference to whether there is a disparity in tax rates between manufacturing and sales locations.

The *Ashland Oil* case involved Drew Ameroid International (Drew Ameroid), a Liberian CFC of Drew Chemical Corp. (Drew Chemical). Drew Ameroid and an unrelated manufacturer, Societe Des Products Tensio-Actifs et Derives, Tensia S.A. (Tensia), entered into a manufacturing, license, and supply agreement pursuant to which Drew Ameroid transferred proprietary information for Tensia's use in manufacturing products for Drew Ameroid. There was no ownership interest directly or indirectly between Drew Chemical or Drew Ameroid and Tensia. Tensia's principal place of business was Belgium, the effective tax rate of which was substantially greater than that of Liberia. Nevertheless, the IRS contended that Drew Ameroid's sales of products manufactured by Tensia resulted in foreign base company sales income, on the theory that Tensia was a branch or similar establishment of Drew Ameroid.

The Tax Court determined that the legislative history indicates that the term "branch" was intended to have its ordinary meaning, and thus concluded that the arrangement between Drew Ameroid and Tensia did not fall within the branch rule, because it involved an unrelated corporation operating under an arm's-length contract.

The *Vetco* case addressed the issue of whether a wholly owned subsidiary of a CFC can be a branch for purposes of applying the branch rule. The case involved an arrangement between a Swiss CFC and the CFC's wholly owned U.K. subsidiary. Under a license from its U.S. parent, the Swiss CFC sold pipe connectors to unrelated customers. An unrelated corporation manufactured the pipe connectors and shipped them to the U.K. subsidiary. The U.K. subsidiary assembled the pipes and stored them until shipment to the CFC's customers.

The IRS did not argue that the Swiss CFC ran afoul of Section 954(d)(1), which defines "foreign base company sales income" to include income generated by certain transactions involving a CFC and related parties. Rather, the IRS took the position that the U.K. subsidiary was no different from a branch, within the meaning of Section 954(d)(2). The Tax Court, however, concluded that the branch rule was not intended to be a backstop to the rule for related-party transactions in Section 954(d)(1), and therefore did not apply to treat income derived by a CFC's subsidiary as foreign base company sales income.

[LG Stodghill & ND O'Neil, 1 J. Int'l Tax'n 364.]

"Contract manufacturer not 'branch or similar establishment' for CFC" (1990). Through Subpart F, the income of a CFC may be taxed directly to its U.S. shareholders. One type of income that can be taxed directly is foreign base company sales income, which is a form of Subpart F income. In a 1990 Tax Court decision, *Ashland Oil, Inc.*, the court, in determining a CFC's foreign base company sales income, considered the threshold issue of whether products purchased by a CFC from a Belgium manufacturer were purchased from a related party within the meaning of the Section 954(d)(2) "branch" rule.

After discussing the facts of this case, the author examines the arguments made by the IRS in favor of the application of this rule. Next, the author reviews the Tax Court's decision in favor of the taxpayer. Thereafter, the author comments on the court's treatment of this case.

[WL Raby, US Tax'n Int'l Operations ¶ 6030.]

[ii] Foreign base company shipping income (Section 954(f))

"Income from floating casinos was space or ocean activity" (1993). U.S. share-holders of CFCs that operated gambling casinos and food and beverage concessions aboard cruise ships were engaged in space or ocean activity, the income of which was foreign base company shipping income under Section 954(f). The IRS reached this result as to casinos in Technical Advice Memorandum 9327001 and as to beverage and food concessions in Technical Advice Memorandum 9327003. In both cases, the taxpayer argued that the income from the activities was transportation income under Section 863(c)(3), and not income from space or ocean activity under Section 863(d).

[4 J. Int'l Tax'n 404.]

[iii] Foreign base company oil related income (Section 954(g))

IRS issues final regulations concerning foreign base company oil related income. The IRS has issued final regulations concerning taxation of foreign base company oil related income. The regulations, which provide guidance needed to comply with changes made by the Tax Equity and Fiscal Responsibility Act of 1982 (TEFRA) and TRA 1984, affect CFCs with foreign oil related income and their U.S. shareholders.

[TD 8331, 1991-1 CB 146; Reg. § 1.954-8.]

[d] Earnings Invested in U.S. Property (Section 956)

IRS issues revenue ruling concerning U.S. real property owned by partnership in which CFC is partner. The IRS ruled that real property located in the United States that is owned by a partnership in which a CFC is a partner constitutes U.S. property held by the CFC for purposes of Section 956(b).

[Rev. Rul. 90-112, 1990-2 CB 186.]

"IRS curbs parent's ability to roll over loans from a CFC" (1990). In Revenue Ruling 89-73, the IRS rejected yet another method used by taxpayers to avoid the deemed dividend consequences of Section 956. That ruling deals with the rolling over of short-term loans or advances made by a CFC to its U.S. parent, whereby the parent repays the loan before the CFC's year-end with the understanding that the CFC will relend the funds to the parent shortly after the CFC's year-end. Prior to the ruling, this allowed the CFC's earnings to be repatriated on a long-term basis while avoiding Section 956.

Revenue Ruling 89-73 concludes that a short period of interruption between loans is disregarded, so that even if there were no formal Section 956 investment in U.S. property at the end of the CFC's taxable year, a continuous investment is deemed to occur. Through the combination of this ruling and the repeal of the one-year rule of former Regulations § 1.956-2(d)(2)(ii), the IRS believes that it has successfully attacked Section 956 rollover loans.

The objective of Section 956 is to prevent the repatriation of income to the United States in a manner that avoids U.S. taxation. The section taxes the profits of a CFC that are indirectly repatriated when the CFC acquires U.S. property in lieu of making a distribution.

Numerous practitioner comments received by the IRS indicated that because the one-year rule allowed short-term obligations to span the CFC's year-end, it was used not to avoid taxes but to aid in year-end financial planning. The rule had been useful for companies that sought to improve their credit ratings by replacing third-party debt at year-end (and at the end of each quarter) with short-term borrowing from their CFCs that reduced debt-to-capital ratios and lowered borrowing costs.

By switching from third-party debt to related-party debt just prior to financial reporting dates, corporations could improve their financial picture. The loan proceeds were used to repay commercial paper or to make deposits with lenders of long-term debt, eliminating outside debt from the balance sheet. Such planning is not prohibited by the SEC and was not barred by the IRS until the repeal of the one-year rule.

The IRS recognized that Section 956 was not intended to combat this type of situation. It addressed some of the business reasons for short-term borrowing between CFCs and their U.S. shareholders in Notice 88-108. The notice permits very limited categories of short-term obligations to remain outstanding at the CFC's year-end without being obligations for purposes of Temporary Regulation § 1.956-2T(d)(2).

The preamble to Treasury Decision 8209 states that the IRS was concerned that CFCs might make successive loans, each with maturities of less than one year, as a means of loaning their earnings to related U.S. corporations on a de facto, long-term basis in avoidance of Section 956. However, the Section 956 temporary regulations address only loans that are outstanding when the snapshot is taken (i.e., loans that span year-end).

The issue in Revenue Ruling 89-73 is whether purchases of new debt may be considered together with the debt previously held so as to constitute a continuous investment by a CFC of its earnings in U.S. property as of its year-end.

The ruling states that Section 956 was adopted to prevent the indirect repatriation of foreign earnings that have been deferred from U.S. taxation. To achieve this objective, the analysis under Section 956 examines the substance of a transaction, not its form. According to the ruling, the facts and circumstances of each case must be reviewed to determine if, in substance, there has been a tax-free repatriation of the CFC's earnings.

Not surprisingly, the ruling concludes that if a CFC lends its earnings to its U.S. shareholders "interrupted only by brief periods of repayment" that include the last day of the CFC's taxable year, in substance a repatriation of those earnings to the U.S. shareholders has occurred for purposes of Section 956. It is considered to be a continuous investment in U.S. property, and the obligation is thus treated as outstanding at the close of the CFC's taxable year for purposes of computing the earnings invested in U.S. property under Section 956(a)(1)(A).

Although the substance-over-form doctrine theoretically ensures that the economic realities of rollover transactions govern the tax consequences, the logic of Revenue Ruling 89-73 may fail in the context of other changes made to Section 956. The rulings approach—focusing solely on the period of disinvestment—coupled with the elimination of the one-year rule, indicates that the IRS may have engaged in overkill of the perceived abuse.

If the ruling's substance-over-form rule were evenly applied, it appears that there was no need to eradicate the one-rule rule. The IRS simply could have applied Revenue Ruling 89-73 to all obligations (whether they mature before or after year-end).

The elimination of the one-year rule and the issuance of Revenue Ruling 89-73 have created an unbalanced application of the substance-over-form doctrine. Without the one-year rule, the period of investment by the CFC may be sufficiently brief when considered along with the period of disinvestment so that the substance of the transaction in effect would be a continuous period of disinvestment with no indirect repatriation of earnings. Thus, a brief period of investment (by holding U.S. obligations), even if at year-end, should be evidence of no intent to repatriate earnings. The application of Revenue Ruling 89-73 in a consistent manner supports this conclusion.

With the repeal of the one-year rule and the issuance of Notice 88-108 and Revenue Ruling 89-73, U.S. taxpayers have only limited repatriation alternatives available that avoid Section 956 deemed dividend consequences.

[H. Morgenson & P. Rogers, 72 J. Tax'n 44.]

"Taxing amounts owed foreign subsidiaries by U.S. parents" (**1990**). Tax authorities in the United States are concerned with the use by a U.S. parent corporation of its foreign subsidiaries' earnings without the payment of U.S. tax on those earnings. To prevent the avoidance or evasion of tax, Section 956 provides that a loan from a foreign subsidiary to a U.S. parent is treated as if the foreign subsidiary paid a dividend to its U.S. parent.

Temporary regulations that were issued in June 1988 made significant changes to the Section 956 regulations for investments made after June 13, 1988, and the IRS has issued several rulings, discussed in this article, that have far-reaching implications for planning Section 956 transactions. U.S. parents should review their loans and accounts payable with their foreign subsidiaries to ensure that unexpected tax results do not occur.

[TF Windholtz & JE Bernot, 1 J. Int'l Tax'n 92.]

[e] Earnings Invested in Excess Passive Assets (Section 956A)

"CFC deferral dwindles, while CFC-PFIC overlap increases" (**1993**). In Section 956A, the Revenue Reconciliation Act of 1993 (RRA 1993) took another step toward the repeal of the U.S. tax deferral for undistributed earnings of U.S. CFCs. Section 956A eliminates deferral of a CFC's post-1993 E&P invested in passive assets to the extent such assets exceed 25 percent of the CFC's total assets. RRA 1993 also changes the Section 956 amount of earnings invested in U.S. property that will be included in a U.S. shareholder's income. It treats certain inclusions of subpart F income and Sections 956 and 956A amounts as distributions for PFIC purposes, and it eliminates the fair market value method of measuring assets for determining PFIC status of CFCs. Finally, RRA 1993 enacts several other changes to the taxation of CFCs and their U.S. shareholders, with the general effect of increasing U.S. shareholders' current U.S. tax liability.

The authors first review the development of the antideferral measures enacted as subpart F and the changes made to its provisions since 1962 (including the PFIC rules). Next, they specifically examine new Section 956A and its application. The meaning of key terms, such as "excess passive assets," and concepts, such as the grouping of CFCs and the decontrol of foreign corporations, are discussed.

Thereafter, the authors consider the changes made by RRA 1993 to Section 956 to parallel the Section 956A rules for measuring tainted investment of a CFC's E&P. The operation of amended Section 956 is explored by the authors, along with the coordination of income inclusions under Sections 956A and 956 and the new ordering rules of Section 959(c). Next, the authors examine the changes made in the PFIC provisions (specifically Section 1296(a)) and the likelihood that more CFCs will fall into PFIC status. Last, the authors consider other changes made by RRA 1993, which affect CFCs, including changes concerning income from timber cutting, the working capital of oil and gas and shipping companies, and the FTC limitation of U.S. shareholders. The authors conclude this article with a discussion of planning considerations, particularly those directed to avoiding Section 956A.

[B. Hirsh & AS Lederman, 4 J. of Int'l Tax'n 436.]

"Excess passive asset rules of RRA 1993 require current inclusion in income" (1993). RRA 1993 has established a new constraint on the tax deferral otherwise available to a U.S. taxpayer operating abroad through a CFC. Specifically, Section 956A, added to Subpart F by RRA 1993 Section 13231, generally taxes U.S. shareholders on their CFC's investment in "excess passive assets." The ostensible purpose of such current taxation is to encourage reinvestment of income in domestic business by eliminating the preexisting U.S. tax deferral accorded to excessive foreign accumulations of passive assets held by CFCs. Congress recognized that other statutory regimes regulated tax deferral and the accumulation of foreign earnings, including the PFIC provisions of Sections 1291–1297 and the accumulated earnings tax. Nevertheless, Congress quite reasonably viewed the accumulated earnings tax as insufficiently objective; it somewhat more surprisingly dismissed the PFIC provisions as insufficiently restrictive.

As discussed in this article, two fundamental premises underlie Section 956A: (1) tax deferral is appropriate only with respect to "active" business operations and (2) assets that generate passive income are presumptively not active business assets, at least to the extent that they exceed 25 percent of the business's total assets. These principles square well enough with prior law's taxation of current passive earnings to a CFC's U.S. shareholders, but Section 956A goes further: it terminates tax deferral with respect to prior earnings invested in the income-generating assets themselves, even if those prior earnings derived from active business operations. Essentially, it is a restriction on *foreign* investment of previously accumulated tax-deferred earnings, just as Section 956 restricts their *domestic* investment. Hence, although prospective in its characterization of investments as active or passive (and thus potentially taxable), Section 956A operates retroactively, effectively recapturing tax deferral sanctioned under prior law.

Specific attention is given to issues arising under the "aggregation rule," the "look-through rule," the antiavoidance provisions, and the potential application of the PFIC rules (as amended by RRA 1993). Thereafter, the author provides a detailed example illustrating the operation of these rules. The author concludes with a discussion of various strategies for minimizing the impact of Section 956A.

[CJ Burke, 79 J. Tax'n 314.]

[f] Computation of Earnings and Profits (Section 964)

IRS issues revenue ruling concerning E&P of CFC. The IRS ruled that E&P of a CFC are decreased by amounts previously included in gross income of the transferor-shareholder as a dividend under Section 1248. The decrease occurs at the time of the actual distribution of the Section 951(a)(1)(A) amount attributable to such Section 1248 dividend.

[Rev. Rul. 90-31, 1990-1 CB 147.]

IRS issues proposed regulations concerning E&P of foreign corporations. The IRS has issued proposed regulations relating to the computation of E&P of foreign corporations. The proposed regulations would simplify the computation of E&P of foreign corporations by largely eliminating required book-to-tax adjustments attributable to depreciation and to the uniform capitalization rules of Section 263A.

[INTL-18-92, 1992-2 CB 757, Prop. Reg. §§ 1.952-2, 1.964-1.]

IRS issues temporary regulations concerning E&P of CFCs. The IRS has issued temporary regulations relating to the election or adoption of tax accounting methods affecting the computation of E&P of a CFC in post-1986 taxable years. The temporary regulations reflect changes to the applicable law made by TRA 1986.

[TD 8283, 1990-1 CB 148; Temp. Reg § 1.964-1T.]

"E&P computation for foreign corporations changed by IRS" (1992). Under the Section 964 proposed regulations issued in July 1992, the computation of E&P for foreign corporations would be simplified by eliminating the required book-to-tax adjustments attributable to depreciation and the uniform capitalization rules under Section 263A. Additional new proposed regulations would amend the filing requirements for Form 5471 and would permit U.S. taxpayers to report E&P of CFCs in the corporation's functional currency. This article discusses the elimination of these adjustments under the proposed regulations, as well as the proposed amendments to the information reporting rules.

[77 J. of Tax'n 177.]

"Foreign E&P calculations simplified" (1992). New proposed regulations will simplify computation of E&P for reporting inventories and depreciation. Adjustments resulting from book/tax differences have been eliminated in many cases, allowing conformity with generally accepted accounting principles (GAAP) rather than U.S. tax accounting rules. Proposed Regulation § 1.952-2 has been revised to clarify that the new rules apply to E&P only and not the computation of a foreign corporation's taxable income, Subpart F income, or ECI. Changes are effective for tax years beginning after 1991.

Although adopting the procedures of the proposed regulations involves a change in accounting method, the IRS says it will not require the filing of a Form 3115 if the change is made in the first tax year beginning after 1991. The IRS also indicates that any Section 481(a) adjustment is to be taken into income ratably, generally over a six-year period beginning with the year the change is made. Proposed Regulation § 1.964-1(c)(1)(ii)(B) provides that for taxable years beginning after 1991, the uniform capitalization rules will not be applied to require that inventory costs be capitalized in excess of those required by GAAP.

The regulations under Section 964 presently require foreign corporations receiving less than 20 percent of their gross income from U.S. sources to compute depreciation under Section 167. Proposed Regulation § 1.964-1(c)(1)(iii)(D) will permit such corporations to compute depreciation for tax purposes based on GAAP useful lives, conventions, and recovery methods for taxable years beginning after 1991. Depreciable bases of assets for book purposes may be used if they do not differ materially from amounts computed under tax accounting principles. Proposed Regulation § 1.964-1(c)(1)(iii)(D) states that use of the "push-down" and "purchase" methods is generally not allowed in determining the basis of an asset of an acquired foreign corporation.

[3 J. Int'l Tax'n 154.]

"Understanding currency exchange restrictions and blocked foreign income" (1992). When income is derived from investing or operating a business in a foreign country and the use of the local currency or its conversion into U.S. dollars is restricted, this income is considered blocked. In such cases, the blocked foreign income rules may permit the deferral of tax on this income. This article examines the treatment of blocked foreign income and related deductions (and credits) for U.S. tax purposes.

After discussing Revenue Ruling 74-351, which sets out the basic treatment for blocked foreign income, the authors examine what constitutes blocked income. In this regard, the authors discuss *International Mortgage & Investment Corp.* (1937), a leading Board of Tax Appeals case in this area. Also discussed are the classification of blocked income and blocked Subpart F income. Next, the authors examine accounting for blocked income, deductions, and credits under Revenue Ruling 74-351, including the election of deferrable income status, when to make the election, and when deferral ceases. The ruling's treatment of expenses and credits relating to blocked income is also discussed.

Thereafter, the authors address blocked E&P of CFCs. Specific attention is given to the calculation of E&P and of foreign personal holding company income in a blocked income situation. The authors then discuss the blocked income rules as an exception to antideferral provisions in the Code, such as Sections 482 and 367 in the case of outbound transfers of intangibles.

[DW Nelson & RA Mikita, US Tax'n Int'l Operations ¶ 6019.]

"Regulations may require earlier accounting elections by CFCs" (1990). Under Section 964, as revised by TRA 1986, a CFC must make tax accounting elections when its E&P first becomes relevant for U.S. income tax purposes. Recently issued temporary regulations make it clear that the previous definition of what is a "significant event" is an illustrative, rather than an exclusive, list. The temporary regulations also cover other aspects of the election and, in Temporary Regulation § 1.964-1T(g)(6), provide five examples illustrating the new rules. In addition, Regulation § 1.964-1(c)(6) lists five events, the occurrence of any one of which requires that accounting elections be made by a CFC. After 1989, other events may also require such an election, according to Temporary Regulation § 1.964-1T(g)(2).

If the election is not made when required and the failure is not due to reasonable cause, E&P is computed in accordance with any permissible method, not requiring an election, reflected on the books of the CFC. Any change in this method requires the consent of the IRS.

Under Temporary Regulations § 1.964-1T(g)(4), a minority U.S. shareholder may have to compute a CFC's E&P before the corporation or its controlling U.S. shareholders are required to make the accounting election. In that event, the computation is made as previously stated, that is, using any permissible accounting method not requiring an election and reflected on the books of the CFC. However, a later, properly filed election by or for the CFC will not be a change in accounting method.

Once an election is made, it binds both the CFC and its U.S. shareholders regardless of the following:

1. When the election or adoption of an accounting method was made;
2. Whether the corporation was a CFC at the time of the election;
3. When ownership was acquired; and
4. Whether the U.S. shareholder received the written notice required by Regulation § 1.964-1(c)(3).

[72 J. Tax'n 252.]

[7] Taxable Year of Certain Foreign Corporations (Section 898)

IRS issues revenue procedure concerning taxable year of certain foreign corporations. This revenue procedure provides guidance with respect to the required taxable year of certain foreign corporations for U.S. tax purposes under Section 898(a) and the election set forth in Section 898(c)(1)(B).

[Rev. Proc. 90-26, 1990-1 CB 512.]

IRS issues proposed regulations concerning taxable year of certain foreign corporations. The IRS has issued proposed regulations setting forth the required taxable year for specified foreign corporations for taxable years of those foreign corporations beginning after July 10, 1989. The proposed regulations reflect the Revenue Reconciliation Act of 1989 (RRA 1989), which added Section 898 to the Code. The purpose of Section 898 is to eliminate the deferral of income and, therefore, the understatement in income, by U.S. shareholders of certain CFCs and foreign personal holding companies, referred to in the statute as specified foreign corporations. Deferral results when certain income earned by these corporations is subject to U.S. income tax in a taxable year of the U.S. shareholder subsequent to the taxable year during which it was earned. The elimination of deferral is accomplished by requiring a specified foreign corporation to conform its taxable year to the required year, which is generally the majority U.S. shareholder year, for taxable years of specified foreign corporations beginning after July 10, 1989.

[INTL-848-89, 1993-5 IRB 17; Prop Reg. §§ 1.898-0–1.898-4.]

"Proposed regulations conform tax years of foreign corporations, shareholders" (1993). The required tax year for foreign corporations in tax years beginning after July 10, 1989, is the subject of proposed regulations, issued in 1993, under Section 898. That section, added by RRA 1989, generally requires that the tax year of a CFC or foreign personal holding company conform to the tax year of its majority U.S. shareholder in order to eliminate the shareholder's deferral of income.

[78 J. Tax'n 178.]

"Tax year proposed regulations issued" (1993). This article examines Section 898 and the proposed regulations issued thereunder in 1992 designed to eliminate deferral of income by U.S. shareholders of certain foreign corporations. The targeted deferral resulted when income earned by such a corporation was subject to U.S. income tax in a tax year of the U.S. shareholder subsequent to the year during which it was earned. This article discusses the regulations' provisions concerning affected corporations, exemptions from coverage, the meaning of "required year," relevant procedures, mismatches between Section 898 accrual and Section 960 credit, and effective date provisions.

[4 J. Int'l Tax'n 60.]

[8] Returns and Information Reporting (Sections 6035, 6038, 6038B, 6046)

Reporting requirements eased for U.S. owners of dormant foreign corporations. Under Sections 6038(a)(1), 6038(a)(4), and 6046(a)(3), certain U.S. shareholders of CFCs must file Form 5471 to report various financial information with respect to the CFC. If the CFC is a dormant corporation, however, a summary filing procedure may be used in lieu of preparing a complete Form 5471. In addition to the names, addresses, and ID numbers of the U.S. person and the CFC, generally only the shareholder's stock ownership percentage and the CFC's accounting period and date and country of incorporation need be reported. To be a dormant corporation, the CFC must meet maximum income, expense, and asset limits, and satisfy certain other requirements. The procedure is effective for reports due (including extensions) after September 14, 1992.

[Rev. Proc. 92-70, 1992-2 CB 435.]

Changes in currency translation conventions and other rules for reporting on CFCs. Proposed regulations clarify various reporting requirements under Sections 6035, 6038, and 6046 affecting U.S. shareholders that file Form 5471 in connection with their CFCs. Under the proposal, certain financial statement information would be expressed in U.S. dollars translated in conformity with U.S. GAAP and also, with respect to the profit and loss statement required by Regulation § 1.6038-2(g)(1), in the CFC's functional currency. Under Proposed Regulation § 1.6038-2(h), certain E&P amounts may be reported in the functional currency, and a uniform translation convention is provided for related-party transactions reportable on Form 5471 Schedule M.

[INTL-79-91, 1992-2 CB 749; Prop. Reg. §§ 1.6035-1, 1.6038-2, 1.6046-1.]

"Functional currency rules added for CFCs reporting" (1992). The IRS has proposed several changes to the regulations under Section 6038 to clarify information reporting requirements on Form 5471, "Information Return of U.S. Persons With Respect to Certain Foreign Corporations." The changes would permit some items to be reported using a functional currency.

[3 J. Int'l Tax'n 155.]

¶ 2.06 FOREIGN TAX CREDITS[6]

[1] Generally

"Introducing the FTC—part I" (1992). Because U.S. persons are subject to U.S. taxation on their worldwide income, and the foreign income of such persons will most likely also be taxed in the foreign country in which it arises, a U.S. FTC is made available to counterbalance this double taxation. The availability of this credit is subject to complex rules restricting, and in certain cases precluding, the use of this credit. These rules, which were completely reshaped in 1986, are the subject of this article.

The author first provides a background discussion illustrating the types of credits allowed (direct and indirect), source of income issues, and the impact of tax treaties. Thereafter, the author examines the decision to claim the FTC or deduction. Here, consideration is given to the limitations on the credit and its election. Thereafter, the impact of electing the credit is illustrated by several examples.

In the next part of this article, the author examines who can claim the credit in a discussion of the applicable eligibility rules. The issues surrounding the determination of foreign taxpayer status are also explored. The procedure for electing use of the foreign credit is then explained, along with the election by cash-basis taxpayers to accrue foreign taxes.

In the third part of this article, the author discusses what constitutes a creditable foreign tax. Specific attention is given to the issues of what is a tax, whether the tax is levied on income, whether the tax is compulsory, and the treatment of taxes imposed in lieu of income taxes. The effect of Section 482 allocations on the credit are also explored. The author lists the U.S. taxes against which the Code does not permit the credit to be claimed. Also provided is a list of noncreditable foreign tax items.

Last, the author explains the classification of income associated with foreign taxes into separate categories of income. These "baskets" of income are then matched with a portion of the foreign taxes paid, which portion then is a limitation on the amount of the credit that can be claimed with respect to that income on the taxpayer's U.S. return.

[A. Sofer, US Tax'n Int'l Operations ¶ 5056.]

"Introducing the FTC—part II" (1992). In the second installment of this article on the FTC, the author focuses on the indirect (or deemed paid) FTC, the allocation and apportionment of deductions in connection with determining the FTC limitation, the special FTC rules applicable to PFICs, and the application of the foreign tax redetermination rules.

The first section of this part concerns the so-called deemed-paid tax credit. Specific discussion is provided on the topics of claiming the credit, pooling, stock ownership requirements, the amount of foreign taxes deemed paid, qualifying dividends (which carry the deemed-paid taxes), accounting for E&P, the treatment of deficits in E&P, and the Section 78 dividend gross-up rule.

Next, the author examines the complex issues associated with the allocation and apportionment of deductions in determining the amount of the taxpayer's U.S.-source and foreign-source incomes. Special FTC rules for PFICs are then reviewed and explained. These rules subject U.S. taxpayers owning any amount of stock in any foreign corporation generating primarily passive income to one of two alternative regimes: (1) an interest charge regime or (2) a current inclusion regime. Qualification as a PFIC, as well as treatment under either of these regimes, is given full consideration by the author.

The last part of this article concerns the application of the foreign tax redetermination rules, which are triggered when a foreign tax liability for which a credit was claimed is ultimately redetermined. Specific topics covered are the meaning of foreign tax redetermination, currency translation problems, specific rules for both the direct and indirect credit, and operative adjustments affecting foreign tax pools.

[A. Sofer, US Tax'n Int'l Operations ¶ 5057.]

"Some FTC adjustment rules suspended" (1990). In Notice 90-26 the IRS has suspended a portion of the temporary regulations (Treasury Decision 8210) covering credit adjustments for foreign tax redeterminations in years beginning after 1986.

In general, under Temporary Regulation § 1.905-3T, an adjustment regarding FTCs previously claimed is required where there is a subsequent refund of foreign taxes. An adjustment is also required if there is an over- or under-accrual owing to differences in units of foreign currency or fluctuations in exchange rates.

The IRS announced the suspension, effective as if originally not in the temporary regulations, of Temporary Regulation § 1.905-3T(d)(2)(ii)(A), which required U.S. corporations to adjust their FTCs claimed for a tax year if there was a foreign tax redetermination that (1) affected the foreign taxes deemed paid under Section 902 or Section 960 for such year and (2) occurred more than ninety days before the due date (including extensions) and before the filing date of the return for that year.

[72 J. Tax'n 372.]

[2] Taxes That May Be Credited

Foreign borrowers' letters stating foreign tax was withheld and paid to foreign taxing authorities from interest payments made to taxpayer under net loan arrangements does not prove payment of foreign tax for FTC purposes. Taxpayer made net loans to a number of foreign borrowers. Under these loans, the borrower either paid taxpayer interest due net of foreign withholding tax or assumed taxpayer's obligation to pay such tax (thereby assuring taxpayer a certain after-tax rate of return). In years 1977–1979, taxpayer claimed FTCs with respect to the foreign tax on the net loans. The IRS disallowed these credits for lack of substantiation. Taxpayer argued that letters from its borrowers indicating that the foreign tax on interest was withheld and paid was sufficient proof of foreign tax payment. The Tax Court held for taxpayer.

Held: Reversed in part for the IRS. The borrowers' letters do not meet the substantiation requirements of Regulation § 1.905-2. Contrary to taxpayer's argument, the FTC does not attach to the withholding of tax (evidenced by the borrowers' letters) but to the payment or the accrual of payment of the foreign tax. Here, no adequate proof of the borrowers' payments, e.g., tax receipts, was submitted. On the other hand, the IRS cannot require that taxpayer include in income the grossed up interest amount that accounted for the borrowers' assumptions of taxpayer's foreign tax liability. Judicial estoppel prevents the IRS from arguing that for income purposes it is to be assumed that the foreign taxes were paid by the borrowers.

[Continental Ill. Corp., 998 F2d 513, 72 AFTR2d 93-5308, 93-2 USTC ¶ 50,400 (7th Cir. 1993).]

FTC allowed for withholding tax paid by borrowers. Taxpayer, a U.S. bank, made net loans to Brazilian borrowers. Net loans require the borrower to withhold and pay the tax on the interest directly to the Brazilian government. The IRS denied taxpayer's FTCs for the withholding.

Held: For taxpayer. The taxpayer was legally liable for the tax and thus was allowed the FTCs. The credits were reduced, however, by Brazilian government subsidies to the Brazilian borrowers.

[Norwest Corp., 63 TCM 3023, RIA TC Memo. ¶ 92,282 (1992).]

U.S. bank allowed credit for foreign taxes on nonresident alien borrowers' interest. Taxpayer, a U.S. bank holding company, made loans from its U.S. banking subsidiary to Brazilian borrowers. Remittance of funds and currency conversions took place through Brazilian banks. Brazil withheld taxes from the interest paid by the borrowers to the Brazilian banks, which remitted the net interest to the U.S. bank. The Brazilian borrowers received subsidies from Brazil equal to a portion of the tax withheld. Taxpayer claimed FTCs for the tax withheld.

Held: For taxpayer. The U.S. bank was liable for the Brazilian withholding tax and hence was entitled to an FTC. The credit was reduced, however, to reflect the subsidies paid.

[First Chicago Corp., 61 TCM 1774, RIA TC Memo. ¶ 91,044 (1991).]

IRS issues revenue rulings concerning FTC. Revenue Ruling 92-62 provides guidance relating to transition issues that arise when a foreign country ceases to be described in Section 901(j). Revenue Ruling 92-63 lists countries the income from which is subject to certain special tax rules under Sections 901(j) and 952(a)(5). The ruling also lists countries subject to Section 911(d)(8).

[Rev. Rul. 92-62, 1992-2 CB 193; Rev. Rul. 92-63, 1992-2 CB 195.]

IRS rules that interaction of Mexican assets tax and Mexican income tax will not affect creditability of Mexican income tax under Section 901. The IRS ruled that assuming that the Mexican income tax is otherwise creditable under Section 901 or Section 903, the amount of the income tax paid or accrued will not be reduced under Regulation § 1.901-2(e)(4) by any amount of Mexican assets tax liability for that taxable year. The IRS further ruled that any Mexican assets tax that is refunded for a taxable year under Article 9 of the Mexican Assets Tax Law because the taxpayer's income tax liability exceeds its assets tax liability in a subsequent taxable year will not reduce the amount of Mexican income tax paid in that subsequent year.

[Rev. Rul. 91-45, 1991-2 CB 336.]

IRS issues revenue ruling concerning Brazilian investment certificates. This revenue ruling describes the FTC consequences attendant to the receipt and disposition of Brazilian investment certificates. The IRS ruled that the amount of creditable foreign tax deemed paid for Sections 901 and 902 purposes is the initial amount of tax paid, reduced by the fair market value (FMV) of the investment certificate ascertained at the time of payment of the tax.

[Rev. Rul. 90-107, 1990-2 CB 178.]

IRS issues revenue ruling concerning South Africa. The IRS ruled that the FTC allowed under Section 901 is denied for taxes paid on income derived in South Africa attributable to taxable years beginning after December 31, 1987. The IRS also ruled that Section 952(a)(5) applied to income derived from sources inside South Africa and, therefore, such income is Subpart F income.

[Rev. Rul. 90-53, 1990-2 CB 178.]

IRS issues final regulations concerning denial of FTCs for government provided subsidies. The IRS has issued final regulations relating to denial of FTCs for subsidies provided by foreign governments through the use of taxing systems.

[TD 8372, 1991-2 CB 338, Reg. § 1.901-2(e)(3).]

"FTC not allowed on net loans" (1993). A bank could not determine FTCs on taxes paid by borrowers on "net loans," the Seventh Circuit held in *Continental Illinois Corp.* (1993). The court based its decision largely on the bank's failure to establish that the taxes had in fact been paid, and thereby avoided the question of whether the IRS had changed its position to allow calculation of FTCs in net-loan arrangements. For certain loans to Brazil, the credit was allowable, but only to the extent that the Brazilian government did not rebate the taxes.

In a net loan, the borrower pays the lender interest net of any taxes due on the loan. This is a means of insulating the lender from any changes in the tax rates of a foreign country.

[4 J. Int'l Tax'n 405.]

"FTC requires strict substantiation" (1993). The Seventh Circuit decided a number of FTC issues in *Continental Illinois Corp.* (1993). The case illustrates the necessity of a taxpayer in providing adequate substantiation, as discussed in this article.

[79 J. Tax'n 318.]

"IRS approves crediting taxes for Kazakhstan venture" (1993). In Letter Ruling 9326044, the IRS ruled that profits and withholding taxes to be paid in Kazakhstan would generally qualify for FTC treatment under Sections 901 and 903.

[4 J. Int'l Tax'n 414.]

"No credit when foreign tax used for subsidies" (1992). Regulation § 1.901-2(e)(3) clarifies what are subsidies under Section 901(i). That section bars credits for foreign taxes that are used by the foreign country to provide a subsidy to (1) the taxpayer; (2) a related party; or (3) any party to the transaction or to a related transaction. Under the final regulation, a "subsidy" is any benefit granted, directly or indirectly, by the foreign country to the taxpayer or to any of the other parties described in the statute. The existence of a subsidy is governed by substance over form, and it is irrelevant whether the U.S. taxpayer derives a benefit therefrom. A subsidy may be provided by any method.

The regulations adopt the holding of Revenue Ruling 84-143 in providing that a subsidy does not include the use of an official foreign government exchange rate where a free exchange rate also exists, provided that

1. The economic benefit of the official exchange rate is not related to transactions that give rise to the FTC;
2. The economic benefit of the official exchange rate applies to a broad range of international transactions based on the total to be paid, regardless of whether the payment represents income or is subject to tax; and
3. Any decrease in the overall cost of the transaction is coincidental to the operation of the official exchange rate.

An FTC is barred to the extent of any indirect subsidy provided to a taxpayer by means of a direct subsidy from the government to any person with whom it deals or that is a party to a related transaction. Accordingly, Regulation § 1.901-2(e)(3)(iv), Examples (4) and (5) have been added to clarify the treatment of "dual-capacity taxpayers" as defined in Regulations § 1.901-2(a)(2)(ii).

[2 J. Int'l Tax'n 349; 76 J. Tax'n 175.]

"How to identify creditable foreign taxes" (1991). The Code allows taxpayers a credit against their U.S. tax liability for foreign taxes paid or accrued to avoid double taxation of income. However, not all foreign taxes are so creditable. The determination of whether a so-called foreign tax is creditable for U.S. income tax purposes can involve complex and difficult issues. This article provides an in-depth guide to the considerations involved in determining whether a foreign tax is a tax and whether it is creditable.

The author first provides a general discussion of the U.S. tax treatment of creditable foreign taxes. Included therein is a discussion of what is a "tax" and whether a tax is a "tax on income." Also discussed is the "soak-up tax" prohibition, that is, the denial of a credit for a foreign tax that is imposed only if a credit for such tax is available in another country. The determination of whether a foreign tax is being used as a subsidy to the taxpayer or a related person, and thus is disqualified from creditability, is examined in light of the 1991 final regulations. The treatment of noncompulsory payments to foreign governments and contested taxes are also reviewed.

Next, the author examines the special rules applicable to dual-capacity taxpayers, that is, taxpayers who while paying taxes to a foreign country also receive a specific economic benefit from that country. Here, the problem is knowing what portion of the levy on the taxpayer is a creditable tax. The considerations associated with this problem and the interaction of various tax treaty provisions in making this determination are explained by the author.

Last discussed is the Section 903 credit for taxes paid in lieu of income taxes. The creditability requirements for such a tax are considered. The author provides a table of countries and their creditable taxes in the appendix of the article.

[VA Gosain, US Tax'n Int'l Operations ¶ 5017.]

[3] Indirect Foreign Tax Credit Under Section 902

Pre-1986 Section 1248 dividend sourced, for Section 902 credit purposes, using method set forth in Revenue Rulings 74-550 and 87-72, and not "pooling" method adopted by Congress in 1986. Taxpayer formed a wholly owned U.K. subsidiary in 1967. During the period 1967–1982, the subsidiary incurred foreign taxes and paid no dividends despite having E&P in some of those years. In 1982, taxpayer made a taxable exchange of the subsidiary's stock for stock in another corporation. This exchange resulted in a Section 1248 dividend to the extent of the subsidiary's accumulated E&P. Taxpayer claimed a Section 902 credit for the foreign taxes paid by the U.K. subsidiary, based on its recognition of the Section 1248 dividend. The IRS challenged the method under which taxpayer determined the foreign taxes attributable to the Section 1248 dividend. Specifically, the IRS, in calculating taxpayer's FTC under Section 902, used the attribution method set forth in Revenue Rulings 74-550 and 87-72. Under this method, later-year earnings by the subsidiary offset earlier-year deficits, and thus the earnings in those years could not be viewed as a source of the Section 1248 dividend. Unfortunately for taxpayer, sizable foreign taxes were paid in those "earnings" years, and this offset resulted in a significant decrease in the foreign taxes creditable by taxpayer.

Held: For the IRS. Dividends are deemed paid out of the most recently accumulated profits of a foreign corporation. If a dividend received by the U.S. corporation exceeds the foreign subsidiary's accumulated profits of the most recent year, any excess is sourced to the accumulated profits of prior years in reverse chronological order. The foreign taxes paid by the subsidiary in this case are sourced in the same manner. The carryforward of creditable foreign taxes attributable to such accumulated earnings would be similarly determined. The approach argued by taxpayer, that is, "pooling" or aggregating earnings and foreign taxes from all years, while adopted by Congress after the years here in issue, was made effective prospectively only.

[Brunswick Corp., 100 TC 6 (1993).]

"Accumulated profits" for purposes of the indirect FTC included only that portion of foreign corporation's profits attributable to its U.S. shareholders. Taxpayer owned a 48 percent stock interest in a Saudi Arabian corporation that operated in Saudi Arabia. Under that country's laws, income tax was imposed only on that portion of the corporation's profits allocable to shareholders who were not Saudi nationals. Nationals instead paid a tax based on the net equity of the corporation. When a Saudi corporation has both national and nonnational shareholders, the corporation's pre-tax profits are allocated among the shareholders based on percentage stock ownership and are then recorded as allocated in separate accounts for each shareholder. Each account is then debited for the tax paid on the shareholder's share of profits and dividend distributions to the shareholder. On its 1983 and 1984 returns, taxpayer claimed a Section 902 deemed-paid credit for Saudi Arabian taxes paid by the Saudi corporation. In determining the Saudi Arabian tax allocable to taxpayer's stock interest, taxpayer multiplied the Saudi Arabian tax paid by a fraction; the numerator of which was the dividends paid during the year out of profits for the year and the denominator of which was that portion of the corporation's pre-tax profits allocable to U.S. shareholders as reduced by the corporation's Saudi Arabian income taxes paid for the year. The IRS redetermined taxpayer's FTC attributable to the Saudi corporation by changing the denominator of taxpayer's fraction to include all of the corporation's pre-tax profits (including profits allocated to the Saudi shareholders).

Held: For taxpayer. While Goodyear Tire & Rubber Co., 493 US 132 (1989), requires that "accumulated profits" for the Section 902 credit be determined in accordance with U.S. tax principles, it does not address whether all or a portion of such profits are to be included in the formula for determining the Section 902 credit. Moreover, such inclusion is not required under the Code. If, in this case, taxpayer were required to include all of the Saudi corporation's accumulated profits in the denominator, a portion of the Saudi income taxes paid by the corporation would not be recoverable through the FTC. Since the purpose of the credit is to avoid or limit the double taxing of the same income by the United States and a foreign jurisdiction, the policy underlying the Section 902 credit dictates that the fraction used by taxpayer be deemed proper.

[Vulcan Materials Co., 96 TC 410 (1991), aff'd without published opinion, 959 F2d 973 (11th Cir. 1992).]

IRS issues revenue ruling concerning indirect FTC and Section 304. The IRS ruled that a domestic corporation may compute foreign taxes deemed paid under Section 902 on deemed dividend distributions from foreign corporations under Section 304 if the domestic corporation owns, directly or by attribution, 10 percent of the voting stock of the distributing foreign corporation.

[Rev. Rul. 92-86, 1992-2 CB 199, modifying and amplifying Rev. Rul. 91-5, 1991-1 CB 114.]

IRS issues revenue ruling concerning FTC and income allocation from foreign subsidiary to domestic parent. The IRS ruled that the allocation of income from a foreign subsidiary, in a country with which the United States has an income tax convention, to its domestic parent under Section 482 reduces the amount of the foreign tax paid by the subsidiary to be used in computing the parent's deemed-paid FTC under Section 902 in the absence of efforts by the subsidiary and the domestic parent, including competent authority consideration, to reduce the subsidiary's foreign income tax liability.

[Rev. Rul. 92-75, 1992-2 CB 197.]

"Limits of deemed FTC defined by Tax Court" (1991). The Tax Court has addressed the deemed FTC in two 1991 decisions. In *First Chicago,* the court barred a consolidated group from combining stock ownerships to meet the 10 percent test required for the deemed FTC. In *Vulcan Materials,* the court allowed a full credit on a tax imposed only on non–Saudi Arabian shareholders, without requiring income attributable to Saudi Arabian shareholders, which was not subject to tax, to be taken into account.

This article reviews the requirements for the deemed-paid credit and examines (1) the 10 percent ownership requirement in terms of the *First Chicago* decision and Revenue Ruling 85-3 (which was directly on point with the issue in that case) and (2) the accumulated profits issue in *Vulcan Materials* and Revenue Ruling 87-14, upon which the IRS relied in that case.

[75 J. Tax'n 117.]

"Recent ruling allows FTC for cash repatriations" (1991). In a significant recent ruling, the IRS has answered an important question regarding cash repatriations from foreign affiliates to U.S. affiliates of U.S.-based multinational groups. This article theorizes about the reasoning behind the ruling and points up many issues yet unresolved. It also examines the legislative history and past decisions relating to the issues involved.

In Revenue Ruling 91-5, the IRS allowed a U.S. subsidiary of the parent of a U.S.-based multinational group a deemed-paid FTC under Section 902(a) of the Code for taxes paid by a foreign affiliate that purchased the stock of another foreign affiliate owned by the U.S. subsidiary. The transaction resulted in a dividend under Section 304 from the acquiring and acquired affiliates to the selling U.S. affiliate.

In Revenue Ruling 91-5, *P*, a domestic corporation, owns all the outstanding stock of *DX*, a domestic corporation, with which it files a consolidated federal income tax return, and all the outstanding stock of *FX*, a foreign corporation. *DX* owns all the stock of *FY*, a foreign corporation. One half of the outstanding stock of *FX* is voting stock and one half is nonvoting stock. *DX* has a basis of $100*x* in its *FY* stock, which has a FMV of $200*x*. The FMV of the *FX* stock owned by *P* is $200*x*. *FY* has $110*x* of post-1986 undistributed earnings on which it has paid foreign taxes of $25*x*. *FX* has $90*x* of post-1986 undistributed earnings on which it has paid foreign taxes of $20*x*. *DX* sells all of its *FY* stock to *FX* for $200*x*.

The ruling first concludes that the sale is a transaction described in Section 304(a)(1): *DX* controls both *FY* and *FX*, and one of these corporations (*FX*) acquires stock in the other (*FY*) in return for property (cash). The $200*x* received by *DX* is a distribution in redemption of the *FX* stock. Whether Section 301 applies to the distribution in redemption is determined by reference to the stock in *FY*. *DX* owned directly 100 percent of the *FY* stock before the transaction and by attribution 100 percent after the transaction. Thus, the redemption is a Section 301 distribution rather than payment in exchange for stock under Section 302(b). Since the $200*x* distribution equals the combined E&P of *FY* and *FX* ($110*x* and $90*x*), the distribution is treated as a dividend in its entirety: first, as a dividend from *FX* to the extent of its E&P ($90*x*) and then as a distribution from *FY* to the extent of its E&P ($110*x*). The ruling treats the deemed dividends as paid directly by *FX* and *FY* to *DX*, apparently for all Code purposes, including the basic determination of which entity includes the dividends in income.

Respecting the FTC, Revenue Ruling 91-5 holds that *DX* may compute foreign taxes deemed paid of $25*x* with respect to the dividend that is received from *FY*. Reversing the position in Letter Ruling 8515041, the ruling goes on to hold that *DX* "shall be considered to own at least 10 percent of the voting stock of *FX* for purposes of section 902(a)," and that it may compute foreign taxes deemed paid of $20*x* with respect to the dividend that is considered received from *FX*. Although the basis for the ruling is thus very unclear, the result of the ruling should undoubtedly be welcome to taxpayers, since it maps out a tax-effective mechanism for repatriating cash from foreign subsidiaries.

Revenue Ruling 91-5 leaves a number of unresolved questions the resolution of which may depend on the unstated reasons for the result in the ruling. One set of questions relates to how the ruling's result may be extended to the application of the dividends received deduction and the 30 percent withholding tax imposed on foreign corporations on U.S.-source income not effectively connected with the conduct of a U.S. trade or business.

Another lingering issue arising from the ruling relates not to the deemed-paid credit but to the capital contribution aspect of a Section 304 transaction.

Although the IRS's rationale for Revenue Ruling 91-5 is unclear and its utility for taxpayers is therefore limited to transactions deviating only slightly from the facts in the ruling, the ruling does present U.S.-based multinationals with an opportunity to move cash from foreign subsidiaries to the United States or to other foreign subsidiaries without incurring foreign withholding taxes. With the IRS's allowance of a deemed-paid credit with respect to the acquiring company in Revenue Ruling 91-5, its adherence in that ruling to the Section 304 analysis of Revenue Ruling 70-496, and the contemporaneous decision in *First Chicago*, however, practitioners must now travel a legal landscape even more confused than before when dealing with Section 902 stock-ownership issues and Section 304 in the international context.

[PM Daub, 2 J. Int'l Tax'n 30.]

"*Goodyear* affirms supremacy of U.S. tax accounting rules" (1990). The Supreme Court's 1989 decision in *Goodyear Tire & Rubber Co.* lays to rest one of the last lingering doubts surrounding the mechanical application of the deemed-paid formula. While the impact of *Goodyear* is arguably of limited importance owing to the fact that Congress, as part of the TRA 1986, rewrote the statutory definition that was at the core of the case, it nonetheless confirms the validity of the IRS's long-standing view that U.S. tax accounting rules are the standard to be used in measuring the income that is earned by U.S. taxpayers outside the United States. The Supreme Court's decision in *Goodyear* does, however, have a very direct influence on the computation of the deemed-paid credit formula for future years. This is because pre–TRA 1986 rules continue to apply to future distributions to the extent that they relate to earnings by foreign subsidiaries prior to 1986.

Most practitioners and taxpayers believed that while there were differences between the terms "accumulated profits" and "E&P" computed pursuant to Section 964, the general principle that U.S. tax accounting rules applied was common to both approaches. Goodyear challenged this assumption because two extremely generous provisions under the former U.K. tax law allowed Goodyear-U.K. to transform what would have been a year with positive earnings into one that generated a substantial loss. This U.K. tax loss became available for carryback. The principle that a carryback could indeed adjust the positive earnings of prior years for U.S. tax purposes had, for the most part, been settled by *Champion*, a 1985 Tax Court case. The issue was not whether the carryback was a legitimate adjustment to the denominator of the deemed-paid formula, but whether there was a carryback at all by U.S. standards.

What Goodyear essentially challenged was the idea that conformity with U.S. tax accounting principles was not an absolute tax policy objective. Goodyear's principal argument was that such conformity should be overridden by the principle that the numbers in applying the deemed-paid formula should be adjusted in such a way as to minimize the risk of double taxation. Goodyear held out an argument that was in many ways novel, conforming the term "accumulated profits" to taxable income determined under foreign tax law, as opposed to U.S. computational principles, to minimize the likelihood of double taxation. The Supreme Court rejected Goodyear's challenge by agreeing with the IRS that the policy objective of conforming the tax treatment of foreign branches and subsidiaries outweighed the risks of double taxation.

[R. Henrey, 72 J. Tax'n 164.]

"Indirect FTC based on U.S. income concepts" (1990). The Supreme Court's decision in *Goodyear Tire & Rubber Co.* (1989) resolved the question of how to calculate "accumulated profits" under the indirect FTC for pre–TRA 1986 years. This article is a brief review and summary of the way in which the FTC works— with particular reference to the indirect FTC as interpreted by the Supreme Court in this case.

The author first provides a background for this area, which includes an explanation of the issues in the *Goodyear* case. He then examines the arguments made in this case and compares U.S. and U.K. tax law on the computation of E&P. Thereafter, the author reviews the Court's decision in *Goodyear*, as well as its effect on the application of the FTC rules.

[WL Raby, US Tax'n Int'l Operations ¶ 6026.]

"IRS wins on FTC" (1990). A number of important international tax issues have been the subject of recent litigation. One of the most noteworthy cases is the Supreme Court's 1989 decision in *Goodyear Tire & Rubber Co.*

The *Goodyear* case represents a final and decisive win for the IRS. In *Goodyear*, the Supreme Court unanimously ruled that U.S., not foreign, tax principles govern in computing a foreign corporation's accumulated profits for purposes of the Section 902 indirect FTC.

[GW Rubloff, 1 J. Int'l Tax'n 103.]

[4] Section 904 Limitations on Use of Foreign Tax Credits

IRS issues final regulations under Section 904. The IRS has issued final regulations relating to the application of Section 904 with respect to income received or accrued by a taxpayer consisting of income described in Section 904(d). The regulations affect individuals and entities claiming the FTC.

[TD 8412, 1992-1 CB 271; Reg. §§ 1.904-4–1.904-7.]

IRS issues final regulations concerning Section 904(f) transition rules. The IRS has issued final regulations relating to transition rules for implementing the changes made to Section 904(f) by TRA 1986. These final regulations provide rules for the recapture of overall foreign losses incurred in taxable years beginning before January 1, 1987, and rules for the treatment of overall foreign losses that are part of net operating losses incurred in taxable years beginning after December 31, 1986, which are carried back to taxable years beginning before January 1, 1987.

[TD 8306, 1990-2 CB 179; Reg § 1.904(f)-12.]

"CFC allowed to average pre-acquisition earnings of subsidiaries" (1993). In Letter Ruling 9324023, the IRS ruled that when a U.S. corporation transferred its stock in eight foreign subsidiaries to a U.S. subsidiary, the U.S. subsidiary was not required to treat the pre-acquisition earnings of the eight foreign subsidiaries as dividends received from noncontrolled Section 902 corporations. In reaching this conclusion, the IRS permitted the taxpayer to use an exception contained in the proposed regulations under Section 904.

[4 J. Int'l Tax'n 479.]

"Separate basket rules reduce incentives for international lending" (1993). The author of this article first provides a discussion of the problems addressed by Congress in enacting Section 904(d)(1)(B), i.e., the separate basket U.S. foreign tax credit rule for high withholding tax interest. These problems are illustrated in a detailed example. Next, the author discusses another problem addressed by this section, which involved certain actions by foreign governments permitting a gross-up of the foreign interest withholding tax, without the foreign borrower bearing all of the economic burden of the gross-up. The Brazilian tax-sparing system is offered as an example of this problem.

The author then discusses the separate basket rule. Included is a discussion of the definition of "high withholding tax interest." The author concludes that the FTC rules prevent U.S. lenders from generating excess credits on international loans that can then offset other foreign-source income. The separate basket rule limits use of the credits generated by high withholding tax interest income to offset only other high withholding tax interest income. The rule may have less impact than it first appears, since "high withholding tax" is defined as a tax of 5 percent or more. Lenders need to consider their tax positions to maximize potential benefits.

[DE Spencer, 4 J. Int'l Tax'n 89.]

"New rules on FTC limitations" (1992). The IRS has adopted final regulations on the application of the Section 904 FTC limitation to separate income categories under Section 904(d). It has also issued proposed regulations containing additional rules on the Section 904 limitation, as well as rules for allocating affiliated group interest and other expenses.

[77 J. Tax'n 118.]

"Dealing with foreign losses in consolidated returns" (1991). Tax professionals may very well remember the 1980s as the time during which their technical skills became globalized or internationalized. Of particular concern is an understanding of the Section 901 FTC and the Section 904 FTC limitation. A significant but often overlooked aspect of the FTC limitation is a concept referred to as the overall foreign loss (OFL).

The FTC limitation provides that the FTC cannot exceed:

$$\text{Precredit U.S. tax} \times \frac{\text{Foreign-source taxable income}}{\text{Worldwide taxable income}}$$

The numerator of the fraction, foreign-source taxable income, is a product of the complex and controversial sourcing and apportionment rules. The OFL provisions generally diminish or eliminate an FTC by reducing foreign-source taxable income. This reduction is accomplished through a resourcing mechanism (i.e., the conversion of foreign-source income into domestic-source income).

Regulation § 1.1502-9 provides guidance for the application of the OFL rules within the context of U.S. consolidated tax returns. Appreciation of these OFL rules will be enhanced, if one is familiar with the net-operating-loss separate-return-limitation-year rules. OFLs may arise in taxable years in which taxpayers have not credited foreign taxes. Because of the cumulative nature of these rules, an OFL will carry forward to subsequent years, at which time the FTC limitation will be adversely affected. In addition, the presence of an OFL could cause a taxpayer to realize income in a transaction that would otherwise be exempt from current taxation. For these and other reasons, taxpayers with international operations should not overlook the OFL rules.

[BD Brier & SL Berkowitz, 2 J. Int'l Tax'n 78.]

"Coping with separate FTC limitations" (1990). Since the U.S. tax system subjects U.S. citizens and residents to tax on their worldwide income, income they earn outside the United States has a real potential for international double taxation, once by the United States and a second time by the country in which it is earned. The FTC was introduced to eliminate such double taxation, and the limitation on the credit was intended to prevent use of such taxes as a credit against the tax on U.S.-source income. Over time, the limitation calculations have become increasingly complex, with the most significant changes coming with TRA 1986.

TRA 1986 introduced an unprecedented number of separate FTC limitations, in Section 904(d), for specific types of income. These limitations restrict a taxpayer's ability to generate low-taxed foreign-source income of one type that can be combined with high-taxed foreign-source income of another type to maximize the use of FTCs and therefore minimize U.S. tax.

Congress thus expected the new limitations to increase federal revenues. Regardless of this expectation, a major effect of TRA 1986 has been to so complicate the FTC that the calculations, including such auxiliary calculations as the allocation and apportionment of deductions, can no longer be effectively accomplished without the use of sophisticated computer software. Some are of the opinion that the new limitations have placed many U.S. multinationals at a disadvantage in competing with their foreign counterparts.

The separate limitation category created for dividends from noncontrolled foreign corporations is probably of the greatest concern as it is the most restrictive and difficult category.

[RM Hammer & WN Riemer, 1 J. Int'l Tax'n 5.]

"Final regulations clarify foreign-source loss recapture rules" (1990). Final regulations provide transition rules regarding (1) the recapture in tax years beginning after 1986 (post-effective date years) of overall foreign losses incurred in tax years beginning before 1987 (pre-effective date years) and (2) the treatment of overall foreign losses that are part of net operating losses incurred in post-effective date years and carried back to pre-effective date years. The final regulations are substantially unchanged from the temporary regulations. The final regulations implement the changes to Section 904(f) enacted by TRA 1986 and, in general, explain the categories of income from which particular categories of foreign-source losses are recaptured. The final regulations are effective for tax years beginning after 1986. Under Regulation § 1.904(f)-12(f), for tax years beginning before 1990, taxpayers may rely on Temporary Regulation § 1.904(f)-13T.

[73 J. Tax'n 399.]

"Safe harbors provided for loss reserve reporting" (1990). Revenue Procedure 90-14 provides safe harbors for meeting the loss reserve reporting requirements of Section 7404(c) of RRA 1989. This allows taxpayers that comply to continue to qualify for transition relief from the separate FTC limitation in Section 904(d)(1)(B) applicable to foreign taxes paid with respect to high withholding tax interest.

RRA 1989 extended transition relief beyond 1989 if (1) the taxpayer files a financial statement for regulatory purposes for a quarter ending during March 31, 1989, to December 31, 1989, and (2) the statement shows loss reserves equal to 25 percent of the taxpayer's qualified loans.

A taxpayer that must file a call report with a Federal Reserve District Bank, the Federal Deposit Insurance Corporation, the Office of the Comptroller of the Currency, or a state bank regulatory agency, satisfies the safe harbor if the call report reserves ratio for any qualifying quarter is at least 25 percent.

A taxpayer that is required to file quarterly and annual reports (Forms 10-Q and 10-K) with the SEC during 1989 qualifies for a safe harbor if the recomputed reserve ratio with respect to such qualifying quarter is at least 25 percent.

[72 J. Tax'n 252.]

"S corporations can make maximum use of tax treaties, FTCs" (1990). A closely held service corporation's movement into the international arena requires a reexamination of the decision to be a C corporation versus an S corporation. By making an S election, a service corporation and its shareholders may make more efficient use of FTCs, particularly if the corporation conducts operations in both tax treaty and non–tax treaty countries. The tax savings from the S election occur because a foreign tax payment on income, earned and taxed overseas and in the United States, passes through to the shareholders under Section 1366 and is available as a credit at the shareholder level. If 100 percent of a C corporation's earnings can be comped out for U.S. tax purposes in the form of deductible salaries and bonuses, the corporation's U.S. tax liability is zero, and any corporate-level FTC is wasted.

The source of income rules under Section 904(a) provide that income arising from services performed in the United States is domestic-source income and an FTC is not available to offset foreign taxes on the income. Regulation § 1.861-4(b)(1) permits the allocation of income between U.S. and foreign sources "on the basis that most correctly reflects the proper source of income under the facts and circumstances of the particular case," a lack of regulatory guidance that leaves some room for tax planning. The parties might allocate the compensation under the contract between on-site services in the foreign country and engineering and design services in the U.S. home office, which are generally higher paid.

The corporation could be exposed to double taxation if the United States and the foreign country apply inconsistent sourcing rules, resulting in each country claiming to be the source of the same income. If an income tax treaty is in effect between the foreign country and the United States, the foreign country typically is not permitted to tax the corporation's service income unless the corporation has a permanent establishment in the foreign country, unlikely on a one-project contract. In such circumstances, the traditional method of comping out all earnings and remaining a C corporation may be viable because no corporate level taxes are paid abroad or in the United States.

Although the United States has income tax treaties with virtually all of its major trading partners, it has few tax treaties with developing countries, where much of the need for the expertise of service providers arises. Because the vast majority of the income is earned in the developing country, the traditional treaty approach of the source country's ceding taxing jurisdiction to the country of residence has been unacceptable because it would result in a revenue sacrifice. In order to rescue developing nations from this dilemma, the United Nations produced in 1980 a Model Income Tax Treaty between Developed and Developing Countries (U.N. Model) whereby the developed country compensates the developing country for its revenue loss by providing an incentive tax credit, known as tax sparing. The United States has permitted developing countries to negotiate provisions that allow source-country taxation of U.S companies using time and activity thresholds lower than those found in traditional tax treaties. The political reality is that U.S. companies continue to pay significant levels of foreign income taxes on services rendered in developing countries regardless of whether a tax treaty exists between the United States and the country in question. This reality, coupled with the operation of the Section 904(a) limitation, ensures that S elections continue to greatly benefit numerous U.S. service corporations and their shareholders.

Under Section 904(a), the United States grants its taxpayers a credit for foreign income taxes only up to the effective rate on the taxpayer's foreign-source income. If an S corporation performs services in both tax treaty and non–tax treaty countries, it is averaging no-tax foreign-source income with high-tax foreign-source income, effectively increasing its Section 904(a) limitation. S shareholders may be able to use excess FTCs generated in a nontreaty country to offset their U.S. taxes on income earned in a second foreign country, even though no foreign taxes were paid in the second country.

Developing countries may tax service income on a gross basis without allowance of any deductions, particularly for compensation paid to nonresident personnel, who generally escape foreign taxation on that income. Employees of foreign corporations that do business in the United States are theoretically subject to U.S. taxation on their U.S.-source compensation. However, their U.S. taxes are not paid, owing to the administrative difficulties in determining the amount of compensation attributable to services performed in the United States and lack of an effective enforcement mechanism. Most U.S.-source business income earned by foreigners is earned through U.S. corporations. Moreover, the vast majority of inbound transactions by foreign corporations involve sales of goods rather than performance of services. Thus, the United States has focused on transfer pricing issues under Section 482, rather than on untaxed compensation income.

[WW Bell & DB Shoemaker, 1 J. Int'l Tax'n 197.]

[5] Special Rules for Foreign Oil and Gas Income (Section 907)

IRS issues final regulations concerning limitation of FTC for foreign oil and gas taxes. The IRS has issued final regulations relating to the amendments made to Section 907 by TEFRA and TAMRA. The amendments made by TEFRA require that foreign oil and gas extraction income and losses from all foreign countries be aggregated before computing the limit on creditability of foreign taxes. The amendments also repeal the separate application of the FTC limitation to taxes on foreign oil related income. The amendments made by TAMRA remove dividends paid by a domestic corporation from inclusion within foreign oil related income.

[TD 8338, 1991-1 CB 115; Reg. §§ 1.907(a)-0–1.907(f)-1.]

[6] Foreign Tax Credits Under Alternative Minimum Tax (Section 59)

Taxpayer's alternative minimum tax (AMT) FTC limited despite treaty. Taxpayer, a U.S. citizen, resided and worked in Switzerland. He paid income tax to Switzerland and claimed an FTC to fully offset his U.S. tax liability. The IRS determined that the credit offset only 90 percent of his AMT liability.

Held: For the IRS. Under Section 59(a)(2), the AMT FTC is available to offset only 90 percent of AMT. Under TAMRA, the limitation applies notwithstanding the U.S.-Switzerland treaty prohibiting double taxation.

[Lindsey, 98 TC 672 (1992).]

"AMT FTC limit overrides treaty" (1992). A U.S. citizen residing in Switzerland was liable for AMT in *Lindsey,* a 1992 Tax Court decision, because of the limitation in Section 59(a)(2) of the AMT FTC to 90 percent of the AMT liability. This limitation was applied despite the fact that the treaty between the United States and Switzerland prohibits double taxation and provides for full credit for Swiss taxes paid against a taxpayer's U.S. liability. The taxpayer had only foreign-source income, all taxable in Switzerland. His total FTC was sufficient to reduce his regular U.S. tax to zero. The IRS computed his tax under the AMT rules and assessed a deficiency based on the limited FTC available under Section 59(a)(2).

[3 J. Int'l Tax'n 147.]

[7] Effect of Treaties on Foreign Tax Credits

"FTC cases address true and false treaty-statute conflicts" (1992). Two 1992 court decisions address the interaction of income tax treaties with the FTC rules of the Code. Since most treaty provisions for eliminating double taxation explicitly refer to the law of the contracting states, questions frequently arise as to the application of the U.S. FTC in a treaty context.

The author discusses the Tax Court's decision in *Lindsey*. In that case, the Tax Court was faced with an apparent conflict between the provisions of the U.S.-Switzerland treaty and the limitation on the FTC for purposes of a U.S. taxpayer's AMT liability. The author sets forth the facts of this case and examines the IRS's position and the court's holding.

Next, the author discusses the Claims Court's *Snap-On Tools, Inc.* decision. In that case, the court resolved a potential treaty-statute conflict in the FTC area by finding that no conflict in fact existed. The facts of this case, the IRS's position, and the court's reasoning are examined.

The author concludes that, in *Lindsey*, the Tax Court was faced with a clear treaty-statute conflict situation in which Congress explicitly directed that the statute overrides inconsistent treaty provisions. By contrast, in *Snap-On Tools*, the treaty was silent on whether a Code provision from which a taxpayer received a benefit was applicable. The Claims Court held that no conflict existed between the statute and the treaty. Both decisions provide potentially valuable insight into the interpretation of treaties and resolution of treaty-statute conflicts.

[RE Andersen, 3 J. Int'l Tax'n 253.]

¶ 2.07 ORGANIZATION, LIQUIDATION, AND REORGANIZATION OF FOREIGN CORPORATIONS[7]

[1] Generally

Domestic corporations were formed principally to hold stock of foreign subsidiaries. Taxpayer held stock in two domestic corporations that manufactured electronic goods in the Far East. Two foreign subsidiaries were created to facilitate the sale of the products to a national retail chain that wanted to maintain situs control over the manufacturing process. Taxpayer sold his interests in the domestic corporations. The IRS argued that the corporations were formed principally to hold stock in the foreign subsidiaries under Section 1248(e) and that the gain was ordinary dividend income.

Held: For the IRS. For purposes of Section 1248(e), "principally" is given its everyday meaning.

[Teller, 64 TCM 166, RIA TC Memo. ¶ 92,402 (1992).]

Regulation allows double benefits on foreign subsidiary's liquidation. A U.S. parent corporation's wholly owned subsidiary (Sub 1) held all of the outstanding stock of a foreign subsidiary (Sub 2). Sub 2 had always been a nonresident foreign corporation and was at no time engaged in a U.S. trade or business and never had any U.S.-source income.

In June 1979, Sub 2 was liquidated into Sub 1. Except as provided by Section 367, the transfer of assets by Sub 2 to Sub 1 qualified as a liquidation under Section 332(a). Pursuant to Temporary Regulation § 7.367(b)-5(b), taxpayer elected not to include in income the all E&P amount, thereby rendering Section 332(a) inapplicable. As a result of this election, taxpayer recognized gain on the liquidation of Sub 2.

Sub 1 took a carryover basis in the property received from Sub 2, asserting that, under Section 334(b)(1), a carryover basis still resulted even though Section 332(a) was not applicable to the transaction. Because the assets had depreciated in value, the domestic subsidiary's gain on this transaction was significantly less than the amount that Sub 1 would have been required to have included in income if it had elected an otherwise tax-free liquidation under Section 332(a).

After the liquidation, Sub 1 continued to operate the foreign business until the end of 1982. The U.S. parent consolidated group used the carryover basis to depreciate the assets of Sub 2 that Sub 1 had received in the transaction. The carryover basis was also used by the parent to compute the loss under Section 1231 on the sale of the foreign subsidiary's property at the end of 1982.

The IRS District Director argued that Section 334(b)(1) is inapplicable to determine the basis of the distributed property, since Section 332(a) did not apply to the distribution. The District Director contended further that even if taxpayer had a carryover basis in the distributed property under Section 334(b)(1), the basis of such property should be limited to its FMV as of the date of the distribution for purposes of computing depreciation and gain or loss on a subsequent disposition. Otherwise taxpayer would get a double benefit, since taxpayer already had effectively recognized a loss associated with the low FMV of the property distributed by Sub 2 to Sub 1.

In ruling for taxpayer, the IRS explained that when a wholly owned foreign subsidiary liquidates into its domestic parent, the foreign corporation is viewed as a corporation for purposes of Temporary Regulation § 7.367(b)-5(b). This temporary regulation, the IRS noted, does not condition the applicability of Section 334(b)(1) on whether the basis of the distributed property is less than or greater than its FMV.

While acknowledging that the domestic subsidiary did receive a double benefit because it obtained a high carryover basis in the distributed property for depreciation purposes and also recognized a limited gain on the distribution as a result of the assets' reduced FMV, the IRS concluded that Temporary Regulation § 7.367(b)-5(b) definitely allows such a result. This is because the temporary regulation provides that the liquidating foreign corporation is viewed as a corporation for purposes of all the provisions of the Code other than Section 332.

[TAM 9003005.]

"Deemed dividend comes first from previously taxed income in stacking CFCs" **(1993).** In two letter rulings (9313013 and 9325040), the IRS outlined a number of tax consequences for a transaction in which a parent corporation sold its stock in one CFC to another of its CFCs.

[4 J. Int'l Tax'n 384.]

"IRS clarifies redemptions through related corporations in cross-border transactions" **(1993).** Revenue Rulings 92-85 and 92-86 are the IRS's latest attempts to provide guidance on the application of Section 304 in an international context. These rulings are unlikely to be the last word.

When a corporation purchases stock of another corporation directly or indirectly from persons that directly or indirectly control both corporations, Section 304 recharacterizes the sale as two separate constructive transactions, thereby preventing sale or exchange treatment for what otherwise may be very similar to disguised dividends. In one of the constructive transactions, the transfer of the stock in the issuing (acquired) corporation to the acquiring corporation is a contribution to capital. In the other, the acquiring corporation's transfer of its property to purchase the stock is a distribution in redemption of stock. Such constructive distributions generally are dividends to the extent of the E&P of the acquiring and issuing corporations.

In a cross-border transaction, the operation of Section 304 is complicated by Code provisions that govern the U.S. taxation of distributions of profits from foreign corporations to U.S. persons, distributions of profits from U.S. corporations to foreign persons, and contributions of capital to foreign corporations. The interplay of these rules has been made even more complex by the IRS's published interpretation of Section 304, in Revenue Ruling 70-496, as creating dividend and capital contribution transactions directly between the selling corporation and the acquiring corporation even absent the selling corporation's direct ownership of stock in the acquiring corporation.

At the same time, the use of Section 304 as an affirmative tax planning tool has increased in recent years. Given the excess FTC position of most U.S. multinationals (and the absence of foreign counterparts to Section 304), the ability to repatriate foreign earnings (and foreign taxes) through stock sales without a foreign dividend withholding tax (which has an immediate effect on the bottom line) represents an enticing opportunity.

Revenue Ruling 92-86 modifies and amplifies the IRS's analysis of the interaction between Sections 304 and 902 in Revenue Ruling 91-5. Revenue Ruling 92-85 involves two transactions in which part of the deemed dividend distributions under Section 304(a)(1) is made from U.S. corporations to foreign corporations. The ruling confirms that Section 304 applies to such transactions and focuses on the related-dividend withholding obligations.

[HJ Birnkrant & JE Croker, Jr., 78 J. Tax'n 38.]

"IRS recasts spin off of foreign subsidiary in reorganization" (1993). In Letter Ruling 9245024, the IRS ruled that a separation of two U.K. businesses owned by a U.S. parent, structured to avoid U.K. taxes, was tax-free under U.S. law as a "D" reorganization followed by a double spin off of the transferred business. In so doing, the IRS ignored the liquidation of a U.K. holding company and its simultaneous transfer of its assets to a new holding company.

The result of the ruling was to permit the U.S. parent to use one of its two businesses to acquire a 91.5 percent stock interest in a corporate joint venture that acquired a target corporation from the coventurer group for stock and cash.

[4 J. Int'l Tax'n 185.]

"IRS refines approach to cross-border related corporation sales" (1993). Recent IRS rulings have clarified the application of Section 304 in the international context. The first ruling examined by the author is Revenue Ruling 91-5. In this ruling, the IRS permitted a U.S. subsidiary of the parent of a U.S.-based multinational group to claim a Section 902 deemed-paid FTC for taxes paid by a foreign affiliate, which purchased the stock of another foreign affiliate owned by the U.S. subsidiary in a transaction that resulted in a dividend under Section 304 from the acquiring and acquired affiliates to the selling U.S. affiliate.

The author next discusses Revenue Ruling 92-86, which deals with the same situation as Revenue Ruling 91-5, with its facts slightly altered to clarify certain issues left open by Revenue Ruling 91-5. Here, there was no direct ownership between the acquiring U.S. subsidiary and the selling foreign affiliate. Nevertheless, the IRS ruled that the domestic subsidiary was deemed to have paid the foreign taxes paid by the selling foreign affiliate. The author explores, in detail, the IRS's reasoning in reaching this conclusion. Thereafter, he discusses a variety of situations in which this ruling would support a credit for "attributed" foreign taxes. Additionally, through certain private letter rulings, the author addresses other issues existing in this area, such as the capital contribution aspect of the ruling's holding and the treatment of earnings associated with income that has, prior to the Section 304 transaction, been taxed under Subpart F to U.S. shareholders of a foreign corporation involved in the Section 304 transaction.

In the next section of this article, the author examines Revenue Ruling 92-85, in which the IRS extended its international Section 304 analysis to foreign-owned

U.S. multinationals. Here, the focus shifted to the 30 percent U.S. withholding tax imposed by Sections 881 and 1442 on the U.S.-source dividends paid to a foreign corporation not engaged in a U.S. trade or business. The author reviews the facts and analyzes the IRS's holding in this ruling. In doing so, the author discusses the possibility that the IRS may be implying a new "conduit" treaty analysis that goes beyond prior published and private rulings. Additionally, the author discusses the fact that constructive ownership under Section 304 was apparently sufficient to support the application of the relevant Code and treaty provisions. Other issues concerning the IRS's analysis, especially with regard to the holding period and the treatment of gains under a treaty, are thereafter explored. Last addressed is the question of whether the IRS might have ruled differently if the domestic subsidiary were a U.S. real property holding corporation.

The author concludes that certain issues remain open. In the case of U.S.-owned multinationals, the analysis of the capital contribution leg of the Section 304 transaction, especially under Section 367 and related provisions, is still very unclear. In the case of foreign-owned multinationals transferring subsidiaries that could give rise to a withholding tax under Section 304, the effect of income tax treaties requires further clarification.

[PM Daub, 4 J. Int'l Tax'n 4.]

"Buying and selling foreign businesses under Section 338" (1992). TRA 1986 drastically increased tax exposure for corporations and their shareholders under Section 338. Under this section, an acquiring corporation can elect to treat stock purchases as asset acquisitions, but upon such election the target corporation will realize gain or loss on the deemed sale of its assets. In 1992, the IRS issued proposed regulations under Section 338 that significantly altered that section's consistency rules, particularly in the foreign area. This article examines the transformation of Section 338 and several international aspects to transactions that trigger this section.

After discussing the enactment of Section 338 in 1982, the authors examine the general provisions of Section 338. Next, they explain the operation of the Section 338 election. Election by an affiliated group, deemed elections, target affiliate rules and the consistency requirement, and the effect of an election are also discussed.

In the next part of this article, the authors consider the international tax aspects of Section 338. Last, the authors review the proposed regulations. Specific discussion is provided of the proposed regulations' narrowing of situations in which the consistency rules apply, the differences between the proposed regulations and the current temporary regulations, and the international impact of the proposed regulations.

[US Tax'n Int'l Operations ¶ 6021.]

"Proposed regulations rethink deemed asset sales—part I" (1992). Nothing in the statutory framework of Section 338 indicates how its deemed sale rules apply to foreign target corporations. Under the proposed regulations, any gain or loss arising in a foreign corporation as a result of a Section 338 deemed sale results in gain or loss under otherwise applicable rules of the Code. The proposed regulations cover rules applicable to foreign personal holding companies under Section 551, subpart F income under Section 951, and PFICs treated as QEFs under Section 1293, with a minimum of corrective adjustment.

In a transaction involving a target that is a CFC, the proposed regulations seek to charge a selling U.S. shareholder with an "appropriate" portion of the foreign target corporation's E&P under Section 1248(c), including E&P resulting from a deemed asset sale. While the calculation is generally straightforward where all the target CFC's stock is sold on the acquisition date, staggered stock sale rules apply under the proposed regulations to deal with sales before the acquisition date. This general rule of Proposed Regulation § 1.338-5 provides that the gain or loss from a deemed sale of assets, as well as resulting E&P, are taken into account by both the foreign target and its shareholders in determining their respective tax liabilities. In determining the tax liability of the shareholders, however, any shareholder who sells target stock on the acquisition date is treated as owning that stock at the close of that date. Similarly, to the extent the purchasing corporation holds stock of the foreign target that was acquired before the acquisition date, regardless of its inclusion as part of the qualified stock purchase, the purchasing corporation is treated as owning that stock as of the close of the acquisition date. For purposes of Section 1248, these new rules would charge the selling U.S. shareholders with only that portion of the E&P of the target CFC attributable to their ownership of the target, and then only for the period they actually owned target stock. Thus, the deemed asset sale could only create additional E&P for those selling shareholders who owned stock of the target CFC during the tax year of the target ending on the acquisition date.

The proposed regulations provide special rules to account for stock of the target CFC that either is not acquired by the purchasing corporation as part of the qualified stock purchase of a foreign target (a retained minority interest) or was historically held by the purchasing corporation (nonrecently purchased stock) and for which no gain recognition election has been made. Under Proposed Regulation § 1.338-5(b)(3), such stock is "carryover foreign target stock." This is stock in a corporation that (1) was a CFC at any time during the foreign target's twelve-month acquisition period that ends on the acquisition date and (2) was owned as of the beginning of the day after the acquisition date by a person other than the purchasing corporation or was owned by the purchasing corporation and is nonrecently purchased stock for which no gain recognition election is made.

The E&P of the target and associated foreign taxes attributable to such stock, adjusted to reflect the deemed sale gain, will carry over to the post-acquisition date target, subject to similar limitations. The carryover can thus characterize an investment of earnings in U.S. property as income under Sections 951 and 956.

For subpart F purposes, a selling U.S. shareholder will have to recognize subpart F income relating to either (1) transactions occurring during the tax year of the target CFC ending on the acquisition date or (2) the effects of the deemed asset sale only with respect to stock of the target CFC sold by such shareholder on the acquisition date. The purchasing corporation, if it is a U.S. shareholder subject to the income inclusion rules of subpart F, will have to recognize subpart F income on shares of the foreign target acquired before the acquisition date.

The purchasing corporation must generally file a Section 338 election for a foreign target by the statutory due date, which means by the fifteenth day of the ninth month after the month in which the foreign target is acquired. Where neither the foreign target nor a foreign purchasing corporation are subject to U.S. tax, the election due date is the earlier of (1) three years after the acquisition date or (2) the 180th day after the close of the taxable year in which a post-acquisition date member of the purchasing corporation's affiliated group becomes subject to U.S. tax. A corporation subject to U.S. tax is expanded by the proposed regulations to include the period during which a foreign corporation is a PFIC for which a Section 1295 election to be taxed as a QEF is in effect.

Owing to potential U.S. tax consequences of a Section 338 election for a foreign target that was owned by selling U.S. shareholders, reporting requirements are imposed on the purchasing corporation to inform such shareholders of the election.

A discussion of these reporting requirements under the proposed regulations concludes this article.

[DE Rossi, 3 J. Int'l Tax'n 160.]

"Proposed regulations rethink deemed asset sales—part II" (1992). The proposed Section 338 regulations simplify a number of matters considered in the current temporary regulations and discuss other issues that were ignored by earlier regulations. In this second part of a two-part article on the regulations, the author discusses the major changes made in the consistency rules.

After briefly discussing the replacement of the temporary regulations' provisions on ECI by legislative changes of the income sourcing and taxation of ECI rules, the author examines the proposed regulations provisions concerning the allocation of foreign taxes and the FTC. Next, he reviews the provisions concerning the consistency rules, focusing on asset consistency, stock consistency, and the special consistency rules applicable when a CFC is involved.

The author concludes that the revised consistency rules will greatly enhance acquisition flexibility in both the domestic and foreign target contexts and remove a potential consistency trap for the less sophisticated corporate buyer. Some rethinking may, however, be warranted on penalizing the buyer for potential abuse by the seller.

[DE Rossi, 3 J. Int'l Tax'n 204.]

"Transferring shares in Section 304 cross-border transactions" (1992). Section 304 was enacted to prevent shareholders from bailing out corporate earnings at capital gains rates by selling stock of one commonly controlled corporation to another. It does this by characterizing the sale as a dividend. The drafters of Section

304 did not consider the ramifications of this characterization beyond the limited tax avoidance area on which they focused. In a cross-border context this characterization creates a number of problems. This article explores the tax ramifications of Section 304 when one or more of the following parties to a Section 304 cross-border transaction are not U.S. persons: the corporation whose shares are being acquired, the holder of these shares, and the related corporation that acquires the shares.

The author first discusses Section 304's provisions and its operation with respect to brother-sister and parent-subsidiary transactions. The meanings of "control" and "property" for Section 304 purposes are also discussed. Thereafter, he examines cross-border Section 304 imputed dividends and capital contributions in the context of outbound transactions (i.e., the deemed dividend paid to a foreign person or the deemed capital contribution to a foreign corporation) under Sections 1441, 1442, 1491, 1248, and 367(a); inbound transactions (i.e., the deemed dividend or capital contribution traveling to a U.S. person from a foreign person) under Sections 902 and 959; and foreign-to-foreign transactions. Next, the author analyzes the different cross-border transaction rules in the following cases: direct stock ownership in the issuing corporation and the indirect ownership of such stock.

The author concludes that, as shown in this article, the application of Section 304 to cross-border transactions is very complex. It was not until 1991, many years after the enactment of Section 304, that the IRS began to address these issues. And, even after the issuance of Revenue Ruling 91-5 and Letter Ruling 9131059 (discussed in this article), there are still unanswered questions, especially with regard to Section 959 issues.

[RJ Ruble, US Tax'n Int'l Operations ¶ 9536.]

"Foreign qualified stock purchases require careful planning" (1990). When a foreign corporation is acquired directly or indirectly through a qualified stock purchase under Section 338(d)(3), many planning considerations must be balanced in deciding whether to make a Section 338 election. Such an election reflects the cost of the target corporation's stock in the tax basis of the target's underlying assets.

For the purchaser in a typical situation where the target has unrealized appreciation with respect to its assets on an overall basis, one basic strategy might be to make the Section 338 election in order to increase the elective rate of FTC on future target dividends. Since the election is not recognized by foreign taxing jurisdictions, the foreign tax is undisturbed, while earnings from a U.S. tax perspective are reduced owing to the increased depreciation and amortization.

An alternative strategy for the U.S. purchaser of the foreign target is to refrain from making a Section 338 election in order to preserve tax basis in the target's stock. For many U.S. purchasers, a high effective rate of FTC on dividends is not enticing because they already have excess FTCs, and the Section 338 election does two things that are potentially very damaging to preserving the U.S. parent's tax basis in the target's stock.

First, the high effective rate of credit is produced, not by reducing the foreign income tax, but by reducing the earnings from a U.S. tax perspective. Where the U.S. parent intends to repatriate a significant portion of cash flow, these reduced earnings cause any excess of cash flow repatriations over the reduced earnings to erode the U.S. parent's tax basis in the target's stock, pursuant to Section 301(c)(2).

Second, a Section 338 election eliminates the accumulated earnings that existed on the acquisition date, because Section 338(a)(2) treats the target as a new corporation, that is, New Target, that purchases all of Old Target's assets for FMV. This may be damaging if repatriations exceed post-acquisition earnings. If the pre-acquisition earnings have been erased by a Section 338 election, the excess of repatriations over post-acquisition earnings erodes the U.S. parent's tax basis in its target stock. Although pre-acquisition earnings are placed in a separate basket for which FTC is computed separately, the separate basketing should not be a problem if those earnings have been taxed at an effective rate that at least equals the U.S. rate.

The article discusses other international aspects of Section 338, all of which are exceedingly complex. The considerations discussed in the article must be taken into account based on the facts of each case in order to determine the proper strategy.

[JS Karls, 1 J. Int'l Tax'n 142.]

[2] Section 367

Effect of converting French corporation into partnership. This letter ruling addresses the conversion of a French SA (societe anonyme) into an SNC (societe en nom collectif). The SA was presumed to be a corporation for U.S. tax purposes. The SNC is a partnership for U.S. tax purposes because it lacks the corporate characteristics of limited liability and continuity of life. Continuity of life is lacking because the bankruptcy or incapacity of a member will cause the dissolution of the SNC.

The IRS treated the conversion as the liquidation of a French corporation (the SA) into its U.S. shareholder, following which the assets were deemed contributed to a French partnership (the SNC).

Taxpayer represented that the U.S. group did not have an overall foreign loss under Section 904(f), the U.S. company would transfer assets that include "tainted" property described in Section 367(a)(3)(B) (inventory, foreign currency, and so on), and the U.S. parent had licensed certain intangibles to the SA that would be licensed to the SNC in a manner that reflected the economic substance of the transaction or terms that would be obtained between unrelated parties. (The latter representation was made to avoid issues under Section 367(d).) The assets would be used in the active conduct of a trade or business.

The parent was required to include in its gross income on the liquidation of the SA the "all E&P amount" under Section 367(b). The U.S. transferor also was required to include in gross income the appropriate amounts on the transfer of the tainted property described in Section 367(a)(3)(B). It was required to file Form 926 and elect under Section 1492 to apply principles similar to the principles of Section 367 to the transfer before making the transfer.

[Priv. Ltr. Rul. 9252033.]

IRS issues final regulations concerning certain corporate distributions to foreign corporations under Section 367(e)(1). The IRS has issued final regulations relating to the distribution of stock and securities under Sections 355 and 367(e)(1) by a domestic corporation to a person who is not a U.S. person. The regulations, which reflect TRA 1986's addition of Section 367(e)(1) to the Code, provide rules concerning the recognition of gain by a domestic corporation on a distribution that qualifies for nonrecognition under Section 355 of stock or securities of a domestic or foreign corporation to a person who is not a U.S. person. The regulations provide, as a general rule, that gain recognition is required on such a distribution. However, the final regulations follow the proposed regulations, with certain modifications, in providing three exceptions to this rule in the case of distributions of stock or securities of domestic controlled corporations: the U.S. real property holding corporation exception, the publicly traded exception, and the five-year gain recognition agreement exception.

[TD 8472, 1993-12 IRB 4; Reg. § 1.367(e)-1.]

IRS issues final and temporary regulations concerning certain exchanges involving a foreign corporation. The IRS has issued final and temporary regulations concerning requirements relating to certain exchanges involving a foreign corporation pursuant to Section 367(b).

[TD 8397, 1992-1 CB 144; Reg. §§ 1.367(b)-2, 1.367(b)-7, 1.367(b)-8, 1.367(b)-9.]

IRS issues proposed regulations concerning transfers of stock or securities by U.S. persons to foreign corporations. The IRS has issued proposed regulations under Section 367 relating to transfers of stock or securities by U.S. persons to foreign corporations pursuant to the corporate organization, reorganization, or liquidation provisions of the Code. The proposal also includes proposed regulations setting forth rules for exchanges described in Sections 332, 351, 354, 355, 356, or 361 that involve one or more foreign corporations. The proposed regulations provide guidance for taxpayers engaging in the specified exchanges in order to determine the extent to which gain or income shall be recognized and the effect of the transaction on E&P, basis of stock or securities, and basis of assets.

[INTL-54-91, INTL-178-86, 1991-2 CB 1070; Prop. Reg. §§ 1.367(a)-3, 1.367(a)-8, 1.367(b)-0–1.367(b)-6.]

"Final Section 367(e) regulations improve on temporary regulations, but policy concerns remain" (1993). The IRS recently issued final regulations under Section 367(e)(1) on Section 355 distributions of stock and securities to foreign distributees.

These regulations are effective for distributions after January 16, 1993, but a corporation may elect to apply them to Section 367(e)(1) distributions after February 15, 1990. The IRS also announced that regulations under Section 367(e)(2) will be made final.

Before discussing the final regulations, the author discusses Section 367(e) and its legislative history. In doing so, the author also discusses the application of Sections 355, 1248(f), and 1291(f). Thereafter, the author makes a detailed examination of the final regulations. First addressed is the regulations' general recognition rule for gain by the distributing corporation in a Section 355 transaction; a comparison to the temporary regulations' rules is also made. Next, the author discusses exceptions to this general rule, including the exceptions for distributions for U.S. real property holding corporations and publicly traded stock distributions. Also discussed is the important "five-year gain recognition agreement" exception. Conditions for qualification under this exception are explained.

[SE Shay, 4 J. Int'l Tax'n 244.]

"Final Section 367(e) regulations offer only limited restructuring options" (1993). In 1993, the IRS issued final regulations under Section 367(e)(1) governing distributions to foreign shareholders that otherwise qualify as tax-free Section 355 distributions. Before discussing these final regulations, the author first discusses outbound spin-offs under Sections 355 and 367(e)(1). Thereafter, he discusses the final regulations' provisions covering gain recognition in this instance. Included within this discussion are examinations of the final regulations' provisions on mandatory basis averaging, distributions to pass-throughs, and abusive distributions to U.S. corporations.

Next, the author discusses the regulations' exceptions to gain recognition. The treatment of U.S. real property holding corporations, distributions to public shareholders, and gain recognition agreements are given specific attention, along with the effect of subsequent nonrecognition transfers. The author last considers the regulations' effective date provisions and the election to apply the final regulations to previously filed returns.

[BW Reynolds, 78 J. Tax'n 368.]

"How to structure inbound transfers under Section 367" (1993). In this article on Section 367, the author focuses on Section 367(b), the final regulations issued thereunder in 1992, the temporary regulations issued in 1977, and the proposed regulations issued in 1991.

In the first part of this discussion, the author considers the types of transactions to which Section 367(b) is applicable. Thereafter, he examines the definitions and special rules set forth in the temporary regulations applicable to Section 367(b) transactions. Terms that were redefined or introduced in the later issued proposed regulations are then explored.

Next, the inbound transactions requiring current inclusion under Section 367(b) by U.S. shareholders holding interests in CFCs are discussed (i.e., liquidation of a foreign subsidiary by a domestic parent; liquidation of a foreign subsidiary by a foreign parent; exchange of first-tier CFC stock for non-CFC stock; exchange of second-tier CFC stock for non-CFC stock; and the exchange by a U.S. shareholder of foreign investment company stock for U.S. stock). Thereafter, the author examines transactions which under Section 367(b) result in deferred inclusion, namely, exchanges by a U.S. shareholder of CFC stock for other stock as to which it is a U.S. shareholder. A discussion of required basis adjustments and elections available in this circumstance is followed by a detailed example that illustrates application of all of these rules.

The proposed regulations, which apply to acquisitions by a domestic corporation of foreign corporate assets in a Section 332 liquidation or tax-free reorganization, are discussed with regard to asset repatriations and acquisitions by a foreign company of a foreign target's assets in a Section 351 transaction or a non-"A" type tax-free reorganizaiton. Application of the temporary regulations and proposed regulations to divisive reorganizations under Section 355 is then addressed. In the last part of this article, specific attention is given to corporate level adjustments (E&P and basis) and shareholder level adjustments under these provisions. Many examples are used to illustrate the application of these rules to various corporate transactions.

[VA Gosain, US Tax'n Int'l Operations ¶ 7504.]

"How to structure outbound transfers under Section 367" (1992). Section 367 may require a taxpayer to recognize gain on a corporate formation, liquidation, or reorganization that is otherwise entitled to nonrecognition treatment under the Code. This article provides a guide to the application of Section 367(a) in "outbound" transfer situations.

The author first discusses the legislative purposes for the enactment of Section 367 and its predecessors, the 1968 guidelines issued by the IRS on its application, and the changes made to Section 367 by TRA 1984. Next, he considers post-1984 outbound transfers under the temporary regulations promulgated under Section 367, including their treatment of indirect transfers and the application of the "stock or securities" and "trade or business" exceptions. The trade or business exception is given extensive consideration by the author. One of the problems addressed by the author is a transfer to a foreign corporation by a foreign branch that has incurred losses previously deducted by a U.S. person. Notice 87-85, which simplifies stock transfer rules under the temporary regulations, is also discussed.

In the next section of this article, the author discusses the provisions of the proposed regulations. Specific attention is given to their application to various transfers of stock to a foreign corporation, their expansion of the temporary regulations' provisions on indirect transfers of stock, and their provisions on gain recognition agreements. Section 367(d), which contains special rules on the transfer of intangibles under Sections 351 and 361, is given careful examination. Next, the author discusses Section 367(e) with respect to outbound Section 355 distributions, distributions by liquidating subsidiaries, and foreign corporation to foreign corporation liquidations. Outbound transfer notification requirements, under Section 6038B and its regulations, are then reviewed.

In the last section, the author examines a number of cases decided under Section 367 prior to the TRA 1984 changes. The impact of TRA 1984 changes on the holdings of these cases is then discussed.

[VA Gosain, US Tax'n Int'l Operations ¶ 7503.]

"New rules for foreign transfers simplify some aspects, complicate others" (1992). Proposed regulations under Sections 367(a) and 367(b) were issued on August 23, 1991, and relate to the income tax treatment of transfers of property to and from foreign corporations.

The author examines the provisions of the proposed regulations, which concern Section 367(a)(1). He notes the ways in which the proposed regulations follow the rules in Notice 87-85 and the ways in which they differ. He also compares the provisions of the proposed regulations with the temporary regulations. Specific discussion is provided on the proposed regulations' provisions concerning indirect transfers, deemed dispositions, and gain recognition agreements.

The author then discusses the provisions of the proposed regulations that concern Section 367(b). He explains the general rules, including the exchange notice filing requirements, effective date provisions, and the omission of the temporary regulations' extensive record-keeping requirement. Specific discussion is provided of (1) the provisions concerning the repatriation of assets (including the determination of the "all E&P amount," the deemed dividend rules, the new currency exchange gain and loss rules, and the election of taxable exchange treatment); (2) foreign-to-foreign transfers (including the problems of loss of Section 1248 shareholder status and excessive shifting of E&P, the determination of the Section 1248 amount deemed dividend, and the special rules for subsequent exchanges); (3) Section 355 distributions (including the treatment of distributions by a domestic corporation and CFCs, the election to treat the distributions as taxable, and the rules for adjustments to E&P); and (4) the special rules for F reorganizations, Section 367(b) exchanges involving differences in functional currencies, and the ownership of stock or securities by noncorporate entities. Finally, the author examines the overlap of Sections 367(a) and 367(b) under the proposed regulations.

The author concludes that the proposed regulations provide some welcome simplification to the rules governing Section 367 exchanges. In particular, the absence of the attribution regime and its related record-keeping requirement will provide relief to many taxpayers. One potential area of complexity added by the proposed regulations, however, is the requirement that the currency exchange gain or loss be recognized in asset repatriation under Section 367(b). In addition, the overlap between Sections 367(a) and 367(b) under the proposed regulations is troubling. Some taxpayers previously subject to only one set of rules will now find themselves subject to both, required to enter into a gain recognition agreement under Section

367(a) and taxable on a deemed dividend under Section 367(b). This adds a layer of complexity that is arguably unnecessary, particularly in the absence of any meaningful differential between the income tax rates on ordinary income and capital gains.

[Q. Cotton, 76 J. Tax'n 24.]

"Proposed Section 367 regulations—a Trojan horse of simplification" (1992). In August 1991, the IRS published proposed regulations under Section 367, relating to international organizations, reorganizations, and liquidations, and to the transfer of stock or securities by U.S. persons to foreign corporations.

The proposed regulations, which are discussed in this article, would replace the "stock or securities" rules of the Section 367(a) temporary regulations and all the Section 367(b) temporary regulations. Although they would eliminate many complexities, they would tax certain transfers that qualify for nonrecognition today.

[B. Hirsh & RD Lorence, 2 J. Int'l Tax'n 261.]

"New temporary regulations on outbound distributions and liquidations" (1990). New temporary regulations implement Sections 367(e)(1) and 367(e)(2) governing, respectively, outbound Section 355 distributions and Section 332 liquidating distributions to a foreign shareholder-distributee. These regulations generally require gain to be recognized by a distributing or liquidating domestic corporation or, in certain cases, a liquidating foreign corporation, and also affect the taxability of the foreign shareholder-distributee.

Owing to the new regulatory exceptions to gain recognition, all outbound liquidations of U.S. and foreign subsidiaries (completed and contemplated) should be reviewed. A review should be made of prior year outbound liquidations involving corporations the assets of which continue to be used in a U.S. business, to determine if an amended return may be filed in order to claim nonrecognition treatment for the transaction. The amended return would be due before July 17, 1990.

The temporary regulations under Section 367(e) are particularly significant. They close the window of opportunity that had remained open after TRA 1986 and limit the availability of nonrecognition treatment for some previously accomplished outbound liquidations to those reported on amended returns filed before July 16, 1990.

[H. Mogenson & P. Rogers, 72 J. Tax'n 304.]

¶ 2.08 INTERNATIONAL BOYCOTTS[8]

Treasury Department publishes list of countries requiring cooperation with international boycott. In order to comply with the mandate of Section 999(a)(3), the Department of the Treasury regularly publishes a current list of countries that may require participation in, or cooperation with, an international boycott within the meaning of Section 999(b)(3). The list published in this notice includes the following countries: Bahrain; Iraq; Jordan; Kuwait; Lebanon; Libya; Oman; Qatar; Saudi Arabia; Syria; United Arab Emirates; and Republic of Yemen.

[Notice 93-56, 1993-35 IRB 21.]

"Understanding the Code boycott provisions" (1992). The United States has enacted legislation limiting the ability of foreign governments to use U.S. businesses as a means of enforcing boycotts. The most far-reaching attempt is Section 999. It requires reporting by persons having operations in or related to a boycotting country and imposes the loss of tax benefits on persons that comply with an international boycott. This article examines the Code's antiboycott provisions.

The author first distinguishes between those boycotts that will trigger the penalty provisions and those that will not. The procedure for obtaining an IRS ruling on whether the boycott will result in a loss of tax benefits and other restrictions is noted. Thereafter, the author considers the reporting requirements imposed under Section 999. Particular terms and concepts, including certain exemptions, are then considered. What constitutes a "boycotting country," and the countries that the IRS has already determined qualify, are discussed.

Next, the author explains in-depth the concept of "participation in or cooperation with a boycott." In so doing, he reviews general prohibitions and lists permissible and tainted activities. Thereafter, he discusses the presumption that participation in a boycott extends to all the taxpayer's activities in the country. The author concludes this article with a discussion of the method for computing the loss of tax benefits under both the "specifically attributable taxes and income" method and the "international boycott factor" method.

[PK Freeman, US Tax'n Int'l Operations ¶ 9523.]

BIBLIOGRAPHY OF RESEARCH REFERENCES

[1]J. Kuntz & R. Peroni, U.S. International Taxation ¶ B1.02 (Warren Gorham Lamont 1992).

B. Bittker & J. Eustice, Federal Income Taxation of Corporations and Shareholders ¶ 15.01[3] (Warren Gorham Lamont, 6th ed. 1994).

[2]J. Kuntz & R. Peroni, U.S. International Taxation ¶ B1.04 (Warren Gorham Lamont 1992).

S. Singer, U.S. International Tax Forms Manual ¶¶ 9.03–9.08 (Warren Gorham Lamont 1993).

[3]J. Kuntz & R. Peroni, U.S. International Taxation ¶ B1.03[3] (Warren Gorham Lamont 1992).

[4]J. Kuntz & R. Peroni, U.S. International Taxation ¶ B1.05 (Warren Gorham Lamont 1992).

[5]J. Kuntz & R. Peroni, U.S. International Taxation, Chapters B2, B3 (Warren Gorham Lamont 1992).

S. Singer, U.S. International Tax Forms Manual, ¶¶ 2.03–2.07 (Warren Gorham Lamont 1993).

B. Bittker & J. Eustice, Federal Income Taxation of Corporations and Shareholders ch. 15 (Warren Gorham Lamont, 6th ed. 1994).

[6]J. Kuntz & R. Peroni, U.S. International Taxation ch. B4 (Warren Gorham Lamont 1992).

S. Singer, U.S. International Tax Forms Manual ch. 5 (Warren Gorham Lamont 1993.)

B. Bittker & J. Eustice, Federal Income Taxation of Corporations and Shareholders ¶ 15.21 (Warren Gorham Lamont, 6th ed. 1994).

[7]J. Kuntz & R. Peroni, U.S. International Taxation ¶ B2.04, chs. B5, B6 (Warren Gorham Lamont 1992).

S. Singer, U.S. International Tax Forms Manual ¶ 4.04 (Warren Gorham Lamont 1993).

B. Bittker & J. Eustice, Federal Income Taxation of Corporations and Shareholders ¶¶ 15.80–15.85 (Warren Gorham Lamont, 6th ed. 1994).

[8]J. Kuntz & R. Peroni, U.S. International Taxation ¶ B1.08[2] (Warren Gorham Lamont 1992).

S. Singer, U.S. International Tax Forms Manual ¶ 1.11 (Warren Gorham Lamont 1993).

B. Bittker & J. Eustice, Federal Income Taxation of Corporations and Shareholders ¶ 15.24 (Warren Gorham Lamont, 6th ed. 1994).

CHAPTER 3

Foreign Persons
With U.S. Activities

¶ 3.01 TAXATION OF FOREIGN PERSONS WITH U.S. ACTIVITIES, GENERALLY[1]

"Tax planning for foreign investors in the United States" (1990). This article can be divided into two parts. The first part reviews and explains the rules covering U.S. taxation of foreign investors in the United States. Both U.S. income tax consequences and U.S. estate and gift tax consequences are discussed. With respect to the U.S. income tax consequences, attention is given to the general rules in the Code, the net income basis election, the sale or exchange of U.S. real property under the Foreign Investment in Real Property Tax Act of 1980 (FIRPTA), the withholding rules and exemptions, and various filing requirements, as well as the impact of tax treaties on these provisions. The second part concerns planning techniques.

[AM Curtis, 1 J. Int'l Tax'n 160.]

¶ 3.02 INCOME NOT EFFECTIVELY CONNECTED WITH U.S. TRADE OR BUSINESS (INCLUDING PORTFOLIO INTEREST)[2]

"Withholding net will now catch more debt arrangements" 1993. In response to complaints by U.S. corporations that they were unfairly being kept out of the Eurobond financing market, Congress enacted Section 871(h) to provide an exemption (i.e., the portfolio interest exemption) from the 30 percent U.S. withholding tax on U.S.-source income earned by a nonresident alien individual or foreign corporation that is not effectively connected with the conduct of a U.S. trade or business. However, Congress thereafter was concerned that, because the FIRPTA rules do not tax an interest held solely as a creditor, it might be possible for foreign investors to structure investments in U.S. real property by providing for equity participation rights so that their investment returns would be characterized as interest income exempt under Section 871(h). In response to this concern, Congress enacted Section 871(h)(4), which makes the portfolio interest exemption inapplicable to certain contingent interest income received by foreign persons. It was through the use of such contingent interest arrangements that FIRPTA was being avoided and the exemption of Section 871(h) was being abused.

    In this article, the author discusses the application of new Section 871(h)(4) and the transactions excepted from its application. Changes made to the estate tax provisions with regard to covered debt instruments are also considered. Last, revisions in planning Eurobond transactions are discussed in light of these statutory changes. In conclusion, the author discusses new Section 7701(1), which authorizes regulations to recharacterize any multiple-party financing transaction as a transaction directly among any two or more parties where recharacterization can prevent U.S. tax avoidance. The likely scope of these regulations is also explored.

[AI Appel, 4 J. Int'l Tax'n 464.]

"Introduction to the portfolio interest exemption" (1991). In 1984, the portfolio interest exemption was enacted, in Sections 871(h) and 881(c), primarily to simplify U.S. companies' access to the Eurodollar market without use of international finance subsidiaries.

In the first part of this article, the author provides a background to the enactment of the portfolio interest exemption. Additionally, he discusses the basic taxing scheme for payments of interest by U.S. debtors to foreign lenders, directly and through use of a finance subsidiary.

Next, the author provides an overview of the portfolio interest exemption. He reviews both the statutory and regulatory requirements for exemption. A detailed discussion is then provided of the requirements applicable to debt instruments issued in registered form to foreign persons, including those issued or guaranteed by the United States. The purpose and requirements of the registered form obligation are examined. The exemption's certification requirements (i.e., as to the holder's foreign status) and problems likely to be faced thereunder are then discussed. The application of these requirements in the case of foreign-targeted issues, as well as the applicable filing, information reporting, and back-up withholding rules, are also explained.

The last section of this article is dedicated to the rules applicable in the case of obligations issued in bearer form (i.e., unregistered form). Specific attention is given to the foreign-targeting requirements in Section 163(f)(2)(B). The three tests for satisfying the targeting condition are set forth. The different rules for obligations issued on or before September 8, 1990, and those issued after September 8, 1990, are considered. The "interest payment condition," that is, that interest be payable only outside the United States and its possessions, and the means for its satisfaction are also addressed. Last, the author enumerates the various filing, information reporting, and back-up withholding rules applicable to bearer obligations.

[MJA Karlin, US Tax'n Int'l Operations ¶ 5014.]

"Using the portfolio interest exemption" (1991). U.S. issuers wishing to have access to international capital markets may find that the portfolio interest exemption is not available in certain cases. Where the exemption does not apply, several alternatives may be available to permit foreign lenders to avoid the 30 percent withholding tax on interest. This article examines the exceptions to the portfolio interest exemption and explores planning alternatives when the exemption is not available.

Even if the generally applicable requirements for the portfolio interest exemption can be met, the exemption is not available in certain cases. The first of these, discussed by the author, is where portfolio interest is paid to a 10 percent–shareholder of the payor. The rules for determining whether an interest recipient is such a shareholder, including stock ownership attribution, are discussed by the author. The next case in which the exemption is lost is where the interest is received by a controlled foreign corporation (CFC) from a related person. The author discusses how to establish that a bondholder is not a 10 percent–shareholder or a related person of a CFC. A third case, addressed by the author, is when interest is paid to a foreign bank corporation on a loan made in the ordinary course of its business. In this regard, the author discusses the prohibited use of so-called back-to-back loans to avoid the 10 percent–shareholder or foreign bank restrictions.

In the next part of this article, the author explains the special rules applicable to international finance subsidiaries (particularly those formed in the Netherlands Antilles), pass-through certificates in grantor trusts holding a pool of mortgages or similar obligations, and interest paid to CFCs.

In the last section of this article, the author provides several planning options. First addressed are alternatives to the portfolio interest exemption, including use of revolving underwriting facilities, note issuance facilities, and other similar techniques that take advantage of the exemption from withholding tax available for original issue discount (OID) on short-term obligations. Also considered are use of a U.S. branch of a foreign bank in certain circumstances to effectively connect the U.S. interest, use of an 80-20 company lender, and back-to-back loans that fall outside the currently broad IRS rules. Next considered is use of a small private offering of registered form obligations. Last examined are the many issues concerning the withholding agent's responsibilities, including Chapter 3 withholding and back-up withholding.

[MJA Karlin, US Tax'n Int'l Operations ¶ 5015.]

"Final regulations ease rules for portfolio bearer debt offerings" (1990). Final regulations substantially revise the requirements for issuing bearer debt in the Eurobond market, free of U.S. withholding taxes. On May 10, 1990, final Regulation § 1.163-5(c)(2)(i)(D) was issued with respect to registration required obligations. These regulations represent a substantial improvement over the 1989 proposed regulations.

The most important modification was the elimination of the possibility of tainting an entire issue for failure to meet specific requirements. Although the statutory language is broad enough to allow regulations that would create such "death penalty" type provisions, the final regulations wisely moved away from such action. They provide a general safe harbor under which an issuer can be assured of meeting the requirements of the regulations.

If the general safe harbor is not met, other specific requirements are provided and apply only on an obligation-by-obligation basis. Thus, only the obligations that fail those requirements are subject to denial of interest deductions, potential excise taxes under Section 4701, withholding tax liability under Sections 871(h) and 881(c), and possible contractual penalties owed to investors. Unlike the initial regulations, both the final and proposed regulations remove the ability to rely on a written opinion of securities counsel.

[PJ Connors & PF Hiltz, 73 J. Tax'n 166.]

"Final regulations on foreign bearer bonds improve access to Eurobond market"(1990). Significant changes have been made in final regulations governing the requirements that issuers and distributors of bearer bonds offered to foreign persons must observe to qualify the bonds as portfolio interest obligations. Qualification offers two major tax benefits: (1) interest is deductible by the issuer and (2) interest is not taxable in the hands of unrelated foreign holders. The regulations substantially modify the highly restrictive and cumbersome proposed regulations and, in general, are a reasonable compromise between the competing interests of facilitating U.S. borrowers' access to the Eurobond market and the prevention of tax evasion by U.S. taxpayers. The final regulations also establish workable procedures to be followed by the issuer and the distribution syndicate in order to obtain the desired tax benefits.

Nevertheless, there are some problem areas under these regulations. For example, the definition of offer or sale to "a person who is within the United States" or to a "U.S. person" is ambiguous. Such an offer or sale occurs if the offeror or seller has an address within the United States or its possessions for the offeree or buyer of the obligation. The regulation could be read to mean that any U.S. address for the buyer taints the transaction, so that if a foreign corporate purchaser has a U.S. branch with an address known to the seller, this buyer taints the entire distribution. The regulations should be clarified so that the address in question is that given on the purchase form.

The regulations' ambiguity should be contrasted with Securities and Exchange Commission (SEC) Regulation S § 230.902(i), defining "offshore transaction," which contains detailed guidance on the effectuation of offshore securities offerings. Particularly important is the SEC's rule that a transaction executed on a foreign securities market is by definition an offshore sale unless the seller or a member of the distribution syndicate knows that the sale has been prearranged with a U.S. buyer (which would necessarily be an abusive case by using the foreign exchange to conceal the U.S. buyer's disqualified status).

A major problem in the proposed regulations is the requirement that a purchaser provide a certificate that it is not a disqualified person by the tenth day after the end of the restricted period. This would have imposed a deadline on the issuer and distributors that in practice would have been difficult to meet. Under the regulations, the certification must be given by the earlier of the first interest payment or the issuance of definitive bearer securities—that is, the purchaser or its nominee or custodian must provide a certification before it receives the bonds or interest payment. The certification must state that the purchaser is a qualified purchaser (a non-U.S. person, a qualifying U.S. person such as the foreign branch of a U.S. bank purchasing for its own account, or a financial institution such as a broker that further certifies that it will not resell to a U.S. person). An issuer having actual knowledge that a certificate is false cannot rely on it.

The result of having both SEC's Regulation S and the final treasury regulations is that Eurobond offerings are subject to two separate qualification procedures, which are by no means congruent. Since the issuer must comply with both, the more restrictive provisions of each regime govern. In the critical area of certification, Regulation S § 230.903(c)(2) does not require certification of non-U.S. status in offshore offerings of debt securities by issuers subject to the SEC's reporting regime, but only that a confirmation be sent to the purchaser during the forty-day restricted period notifying the purchaser that it is subject to the same restrictions as the distributor with respect to offers or sales to U.S. persons.

The regulations also provide guidance on the deductibility of interest on regular interests (essentially, a mortgage-backed bond) in a real estate mortgage investment conduit (REMIC) and qualification as a portfolio interest obligation for REMIC regular interests and residual interests (essentially, the REMIC's equity). The regulations treat the REMIC regular interests as securities distinct from the REMIC's portfolio of mortgage securities, so that the REMIC securities must qualify on their own if issued in bearer form. Moreover, an antiavoidance rule under Regulation § 1.163-5T(e) is intended to prevent the use of REMICs to issue nonqualifying bearer bonds where the portfolio consists of qualifying regular interests in another REMIC.

The regulations provide that regular interests are subject to the same portfolio interest qualification requirements as any other debt obligations. (The REMIC security, not the underlying mortgages, is tested.) Interest paid on residual interests is looked through to the underlying mortgages to determine whether they qualify (as either registered or bearer) and were issued after July 18, 1984 (the effective date for issuance of portfolio debt).

The final regulations are a major advance over the unduly restrictive proposed regulations, which could, if not modified, have led to choking off access by U.S. issuers to the Eurobond market. The proposed regulations' dropping of the existing reasonably designed standard (which tracked the statute) in favor of a standard approaching absolute liability was simply unworkable and subject to attack as an override of the congressional intent.

[RJ Shapiro & RD Lorence, 1 J. Int'l Tax'n 185.]

"Portfolio interest exception is affected by recent ruling" (1990). U.S. investments are often structured to qualify a foreign investor's return as portfolio interest, eligible for an exception to the 30 percent U.S. federal withholding tax (30 percent tax) on fixed or determinable annual or periodical income.

The recent revocation of Letter Rulings 8819027 and 8705058 by Letter Ruling 9028094 highlights the absence of guidance regarding the threshold issue of whether a payment is viewed as interest for purposes of the portfolio interest exception to the 30 percent tax. The issue whether a payment is properly characterized as portfolio interest is presented by a variety of international transactions that may not be labeled as financings—such as investments arranged as cross-border leases or corporate securities with both debt and equity features.

Absent a statutory or regulatory definition under Section 871(h) or Section 881(c), the threshold determination regarding the nature of portfolio interest is made by reference to the historical and commonly understood definitions. For general federal income tax purposes, taxpayers rely on a facts and circumstances determination regarding whether a payment satisfies the basic definition of interest as "compensation for the use or forbearance of money." In addition to technical requirements and limitations, "portfolio" interest generally is defined as interest paid on certain bearer or registered obligations. Once it is determined that an amount constitutes interest, the existence of an obligation is assumed to have been established.

Based on Revenue Ruling 68-54 and other rulings, there are minimum standards that should be met to establish the elements of a debtor-creditor relationship. For example, the obligation should have a fixed maturity date for the repayment of an identifiable principal amount. Similarly, the arrangement should provide customary legal remedies upon the occurrence of defaults, and the guaranteed annual return should approximate the annual return on comparable instruments.

[LG Stodghill, 1 J. Int'l Tax'n 229.]

"Structuring foreign investment in U.S. portfolio securities" (1990). Portfolio investment in the United States offers many attractive features to foreign investors. U.S. taxation of foreigners on investment income affects the actual return on foreign investment. This article concerns the significant U.S. tax and investment considerations for foreign investors, as well as tax strategies aimed at reducing U.S. tax rates on dividends and interest, gaining deductions for investment expenses, and preserving the tax advantages available for capital gains.

The following non-U.S. tax considerations are discussed by the author: anonymity, exchange controls, and home country taxation. After briefly noting U.S. estate and gifts tax considerations, the author provides an in-depth examination of the following U.S. income tax aspects: the exemption for portfolio interest, the U.S. trade or business determination of the foreigner's investment, and the impact of tax treaties.

In the next part of this article, the author considers planning for a U.S. investment by a foreigner. Specific discussion is provided of the basic objectives for such a plan, considerations for passive and unleveraged portfolios and active portfolios, the consequences of achieving U.S. trade or business status, and the effects of investment through a U.S. or foreign corporation. The beneficial effects of investment under tax treaties are also considered. The minimum tax and branch profits tax (BPT), to the extent a consideration for foreign investors, is also discussed. The author concludes by summarizing the numerous complex rules that can result in adverse tax consequences for foreign investors.

[KP Brewer, US Tax'n Int'l Operations ¶ 6015.]

¶ 3.03 INCOME EFFECTIVELY CONNECTED WITH U.S. TRADE OR BUSINESS[3]

[1] Definition of "Trade or Business Within the United States"

IRS issues revenue ruling concerning barter transactions of foreign persons. The IRS ruled that foreign persons who engage in U.S. barter transactions through a partnership or through a dependent agent are subject to U.S. tax on gain from such transactions.

[Rev. Rul. 90-80, 1990-2 CB 170.]

Foreign insurer was engaged in U.S. trade or business. This ruling involved a U.S. person (*X*) who owned both corporation *A*, which conducted a retail car sales business in the United States, and corporation *C*, a foreign corporation that the IRS assumed qualified as a life insurance company for U.S. income tax purposes.

Corporation *B*, which was unrelated to *A* and *C*, provided credit life insurance on the lives of car purchasers, all of whom were U.S. citizens. The insurance was sold through *A*, which retained 40 percent of the gross premiums paid for life insurance sold to its customers and remitted the balance to *B*. *B* was the issuer of the credit life insurance policies, and only *B*, *X*, and two employees of *A* were licensed to sell insurance in the state. *C* was not so licensed, but reinsured 90 percent of *B*'s risk with respect to *A*'s customers.

C conducted all of its business in the offices of its sister corporation, *A*, but did not pay *A* for space, use of equipment, or salaries for persons who performed services for *C*. *C*'s books and records were maintained in the United States. Its tax returns were prepared in the United States, its reinsurance contracts were negotiated in the United States, and its board of directors and shareholder meetings were conducted in the United States. *C* conducted no activities in its country of incorporation or anywhere else outside the United States.

The IRS was asked whether corporation *C* was engaged in the conduct of a trade or business in the United States. This issue consists of two elements, i.e., whether there is a trade or business and, if so, where such trade or business is conducted. The examining agent stated that since *C* was not licensed to sell insurance in the United States, *C* should not be treated as engaged in a trade or business in the United States.

The IRS stated that the fact that *C* was not licensed in the United States did not compel the conclusion that it was not engaged in a trade or business. *C* reinsured the risks assumed by *B*, and no license was required. Further, the activity itself may be characterized as a trade or business activity. All of corporation *C*'s (limited) activities were conducted in the United States.

Having determined that *C* is engaged in a trade or business, it followed that the location of that trade or business must be within the United States. The location of the insured risk had no bearing on the determination that *C* was engaged in a trade or business or that such trade or business was located in the United States. It was the activity of *C* itself that was relevant to the determination of the location of *C*'s trade or business.

[TAM 9209001.]

"Investing in U.S. securities and commodities through partnerships" (1990). The investment or trading partnership presents an attractive vehicle for pooled, professionally managed foreign investment in the U.S. securities market. Unless engaged in a U.S. trade or business, nonresident aliens and foreign corporations are generally not taxed on their U.S.-source capital gains other than from U.S. real estate. Dividends are taxable to the foreign investor at a 30 percent withholding rate on the gross amount, which may be reduced, typically to 15 percent, but as low as zero in some cases, under an applicable income tax treaty.

Income effectively connected with the conduct of a trade or business within the United States is subject to taxation at graduated rates on a net basis under Sections 871(b) and 882. Trading (but not dealing) in commodities for the foreign taxpayer's own account is excluded from trade or business status. There is also a general exclusion under Section 864(b)(2) for trading in stocks, securities, or commodities through a resident independent agent, provided that at no time during the taxable year does the foreign taxpayer have a U.S. office that directs the transactions.

Regulation §§ 1.864-2(c)(2) and 1.864-2(d) do not adequately distinguish between trading, investing, and dealing in stocks, securities, and commodities. However, the 1987 Tax Court decision in *King* found that a trader is engaged in the trade or business of frequent and substantial buying and selling, seeking to profit from short-term price swings, and not from the sale of inventory (like dealers) or from dividends (like investors). It is clear that a partnership that is a trader in stocks, securities, or commodities is engaged in a trade or business and that, generally, the foreign partners of a domestic or foreign partnership engaged in such U.S. trading would be subject to U.S. tax on a net basis on the income from such activities. Section 875(a)(1) provides that a nonresident alien or foreign corporation is engaged in a U.S. trade or business if it is a member of a partnership that is so engaged. The stakes are raised by the fact that treaty protection is likely to be unavailable to the partners.

Partners in trading partnerships can take comfort from the safe harbor provided in Regulation § 1.864-2(c)(2)(ii). A foreign partner is not treated as engaged in a U.S. trade or business merely because the partnership engages in trading for its own account in U.S. stocks or bonds, whether through an agent or otherwise. The safe harbor is inapplicable to dealers or to a partnership whose principal office is in the United States at any time during the year. There is an exception to this exception whereby the safe harbor is again made applicable to a partnership that at any time during the last half of the taxable year had more than 50 percent of either capital or profits owned directly or indirectly by five or fewer partners who are individuals.

Regulation § 1.864-2(c)(2)(iii) provides considerable guidance in determining whether a foreign corporation's principal office is in the United States or abroad. Even though most or all of its investment activities are carried on within the United States, if all or a substantial portion of the enumerated managerial functions are carried on at a foreign office, the principal office is not in the United States. Where the 50 percent plus test cannot be met, the partnership must be careful that its principal office not be located in the United States.

In view of the lack of certainty regarding many of the issues, the investor or trader partnership structure is best advised to follow either the two-tier partnership in which the upper tier is foreign and its office is offshore or the foreign partnership/domestic independent agent route.

The IRS has stated in Revenue Procedure 89-6 that it will not ordinarily rule on requests after February 26, 1989, on whether income is effectively connected or whether a taxpayer trading in stocks, securities, or commodities is engaged in a trade or business within the United States under Regulation § 1.864-2(c). Although the use of tiered partnerships was approved in Letter Rulings 8916004 and 8916005, there can be no assurance that the results there were correct or apply to a particular taxpayer's situation, given the lapse in dealing with the issue of the imputation of the operating partnership's office to the upper-tier partnership. The principal office limitation, in any event, can be readily avoided by using a U.S. independent agent, such as a trust company, to perform day-to-day administrative functions.

Foreign partners are subject to withholding at 30 percent for noneffectively conected U.S.-source fixed or determinable annual or periodical income, principally dividends, and on a foreign partner's share of effectively connected income (ECI).One of the difficulties created by this withholding regime for partnerships is the rule under Section 865(i)(5) that the source of income from the sale of personal property is determined at the partner level unless as-yet unissued regulations provide to the contrary. If a nonresident maintains a U.S. office, gains from sales of personal property attributable to such office are U.S.-source and withholding may not be avoided. If no U.S. office of the partnership directs the transaction, then gain should be foreign-source under Section 865.

[RJ Shapiro & RD Lorence, 1 J. Int'l Tax'n 246.]

"U.S. taxation of nonresident alien partner in U.S. partnership" (1990). This article examines the issue of whether a nonresident alien partner is engaged in a U.S. trade or business or has a permanent establishment in the United States merely by being a partner in a partnership that is itself engaged in a U.S. trade or business or has a permanent establishment in the United States.

The author first examines the facts and the reasoning of the Tax Court in *Unger*, a 1990 decision. The IRS's arguments based on the Ninth Circuit's 1962 opinion in *Donroy, Ltd.* are also discussed. Last, the author examines the court's application of the aggregate theory to find Unger, though merely a limited partner, had a U.S. permanent establishment in the United States by reason of his interest in a partnership with a permanent establishment in the United States.

[WL Raby, US Tax'n Int'l Operations ¶ 15,520.]

[2] Definition of "Effectively Connected Income"

[a] Generally

IRS issues revenue ruling concerning partnership ECI. The IRS, in a revenue ruling involving three fact situations, ruled that gain or loss of a foreign partner from a disposition of an interest in a partnership that conducts a trade or business through a fixed place of business or has a permanent establishment in the United

States is gain effectively connected with such trade or business (or loss allocable to such gain) or is gain attributable to a permanent establishment (or loss allocable to such gain).

[Rev. Rul. 91-32, 1991-1 CB 107.]

"Foreign corporations in the United States must be wary of ECI" (1992). This article discuss the ECI rules of the United States and compares them to those of the 1977 Organization for Economic Cooperation and Development (OECD) model convention. After a discussion of the OECD approach, the author turns to the U.S. approach.

Section 864 and the regulations thereunder govern ECI. A foreign corporation doing business in the United States should not presume that the tax treaty between the United States and its country of residence offers a safe harbor from the regulations. First, the treaty is probably no more explicit than the OECD model convention. When the treaty is not precise enough, it is a principle of international tax law that the internal law of the contracting countries applies.

Also, pursuant to Section 7852(d)(1), "neither the treaty nor the law shall have preferential status by reason of its being a treaty or law." In the United States, Congress is free to override treaties with new legislation, contrary to most developed countries. In any doubtful situation, a cautious foreign corporation will thus assume that the U.S. law applies. Under Section 864(b), a prerequisite to having ECI is to have a trade or business in the United States.

Fixed or determinable annual or periodical (FDAP) income is defined in Section 881(a). It consists mainly of interest, dividends, rents, salaries, and other pre-determinable (upon a known basis) periodical (whatever the period over which the income is paid) income. Foreign corporations most frequently have interest and fee income of this type. Whether FDAP income is ECI depends on satisfaction of the asset use test or the business activities test. Under the asset use test, if an asset is used in the conduct of the foreign corporation's U.S. trade or business, the income generated by the asset is ECI. This test applies to passive income. Such use is made of an asset if it has a direct relationship with the U.S. business. Such a relationship implies that the asset is needed for the present U.S. business and is probable if the asset is acquired with funds generated by the U.S. business. The business activities test applies to income generated by the U.S. trade or business. Income qualifies as ECI under this test if it is derived directly from the active conduct of the U.S. trade or business. In other words, the U.S. trade or business must be a material factor in the realization of the income.

Since FDAP income is the major source of income of the banking business, the regulations include a special set of tests regarding ECI generated by banks. The article goes on to discuss ECI generated by banks in detail, including a section devoted to compliance problems.

Except for real estate income, all U.S.-source income other than FDAP income is effectively connected to a U.S. trade or business.

A foreign corporation can also have effectively connected foreign-source income. This can easily generate double taxation as the residence country will most likely enforce worldwide taxation or tax income sourced within its border in the case of territorial taxation.

To tax foreign-source income in the United States, the regulations require the presence of a U.S. office. The threshold for a U.S. office is higher than the threshold for a U.S. trade or business. The regulations provide that foreign law is irrelevant in determining whether there is a U.S. office. Any fixed place of business used with some degree of continuity is a U.S. office. Only part of the foreign-source income may be ECI. Rent, royalties, dividends, interest, gain from sale of stocks and securities, and insurance income will be subject to U.S. tax if attributable to the U.S. office.

The remainder of the article deals with compliance difficulties and contains a number of examples. In addition to the above-mentioned banking discussion, the discussions deal with the asset use test and investing in the United States, the material factor test, and practical considerations.

[C. Bouvier, 2 J. Int'l Tax'n 287.]

"Look-through rule applied to sale of partnership interest" (1992). Characterization of the gain realized by a foreign partner disposing of its interest in a partnership engaged in a trade or business through a U.S. fixed place of business or permanent establishment turns on application of the look-through rule, according to Revenue Ruling 91-32. The gain is effectively connected—and thus taxable at regular U.S. rates—to the extent that the partner's distributive share of unrealized gain of the partnership is attributable to U.S.-source partnership property. In essence, the partner is treated as disposing of an aggregate portion of the partnership's underlying property.

[2 J. Int'l Tax'n 293.]

"What is ECI" (1992)? A nonresident alien or foreign corporation engaged in business in the United States during the tax year is subject to U.S. tax on income that is "effectively connected" with the conduct of a trade or business within the United States. This concept of ECI is relevant in the following situations: when U.S. tax is owed by the nonresident alien or foreign corporation; when a foreign corporation has U.S. shareholders; when U.S. income of a foreign person must be withheld; and when dividends are paid by a foreign corporation. This article addresses the determination of whether income is "effectively connected" and the consequences of that determination.

The author first examines taxation of a foreign person who has ECI. In so doing, he compares the treatment of the foreign person with taxation of a U.S. person, explaining the similarities and differences. Next, he addresses the impact of a U.S. tax treaty on the taxation of such a foreign person. Last, within this section, he compares the taxation of a foreign person in the absence of any ECI.

Next, the author notes the interaction between the ECI rules and the rules concerning CFCs, when a foreign subsidiary of a U.S. corporation has ECI. The author then considers the exemption from withholding for ECI. The sourcing of dividends and interest from a foreign corporation is then explained when such corporation realizes ECI.

In the next section of the article, the author examines how to determine whether income is "effectively connected." Within this part, the author discusses this determination with respect to various types of income, including ordinary U.S.-source business income, U.S.-source fixed or determinable income and capital gains, foreign-source income, transportation income, and U.S. real property income. The special rules for determining the ECI character within each of these special categories of income is given detailed examination.

[J. Harllee, Jr., US Tax'n Int'l Operations ¶ 5001.]

[b] Election to Treat Real Property Income as Effectively Connected With U.S. Trade or Business (Sections 871(d) and 882(d))

IRS issues revenue ruling concerning election under Section 882(d). Section 882(d) allows a foreign corporation to elect to have certain income from real property held for the production of income treated as if it were effectively connected with the conduct of a trade or business within the United States. This revenue ruling explains the income tax consequences of an election under Section 882(d).

[Rev. Rul. 92-74, 1992-2 CB 156.]

"Consequences of election to treat realty income as ECI" (1993). Revenue Ruling 92-74 explains the tax consequences in various situations when a foreign corporation elects to treat income from U.S. real property as effectively connected with a trade or business in the United States. The ruling specifically addresses the computation of net operating losses and capital gains and losses on the disposition of such property.

[78 J. Tax'n 45.]

[3] Deductions

IRS rules that foreign persons who purchase real estate that produces no gross income may not capitalize interest, taxes, and other carrying charges that are otherwise not deductible. The IRS ruled that a nonresident alien individual or foreign corporation may not make an election under Section 871(d) or Section 882(d) for a taxable year in which the foreign taxpayer does not derive income from U.S. real property. The IRS also ruled that a nonresident alien individual or foreign corporation may not make an election under Section 266 to capitalize real estate taxes, mortgage interest, and other carrying charges attributable to unimproved and unproductive U.S. real property if, during the taxable year in which such expenses are incurred, such expenses are not allowable deductions under Section 873(a) or Section 882(c).

[Rev. Rul. 91-7, 1991-1 CB 110.]

IRS issues final regulations concerning denial of deductions and credits because of untimely filing of income tax returns by nonresident alien individuals and foreign corporations. The IRS has issued final regulations under Sections 874 and 882 relating to denial of deductions and credits to nonresident alien individuals and foreign corporations that do not file true and accurate income tax returns by the time limits set forth in the final regulations.

[TD 8322, 1990-2 CB 172, Reg. §§ 1.874-1, 1.882-4.]

"Regulations on timely filed returns changed" (1991). Final regulations change the definition of "timely filed return" for the first year a return is due from a nonresident individual or a foreign corporation. This article discusses (1) the foreign person's need for a timely filed return to gain the benefit of U.S. deductions and credits and (2) when a foreign person's return is deemed timely filed under the regulations. The fact that the deductions and credits need not be claimed on the timely filed return is also noted, along with the extension of the timely filed return requirement for a corporation claiming deductions and credits for accumulated earnings tax purposes.

[75 J. Tax'n 119.]

"Lack of income bars capitalization election of Section 266" (1991). Real property must actually produce income before an election may be made to treat such income as effectively connected with a U.S. trade or business, according to Revenue Ruling 91-7. Therefore, when property did not produce any income, the election was unavailable. As a result, taxpayers also could not elect to treat the carrying charges of the property as capital expenses under Section 266.

The basis of the IRS's position was that the property that does not produce income during the year was not held for production of income. Therefore, the investors in the property could not elect to treat the investment as a trade or business. As to the carrying charges, since no deductions would have been permitted, the foreign taxpayers could not elect capitalization of the carrying charges.

This article concludes that this ruling may be applicable only where land is being held without any effort at further development. The capitalization election should be available during the construction period or when the property is undergoing preparations to ready it for its intended use, even though a deduction would still not be available for such costs.

[74 J. Tax'n 385.]

¶ 3.04 BRANCH-LEVEL TAXES FOR CERTAIN FOREIGN CORPORATIONS, INCLUDING BRANCH PROFITS TAX (Section 884)[4]

IRS issues final regulations concerning branch level profits. The IRS issued final regulations under Section 884 relating to the BPT, branch-level interest tax (BLIT), and qualified resident rules.

[TD 8432, 1992-2 CB 157, Reg. §§ 1.884-0, 1.884-1, 1.884-4, 1.884-5.]

"Branch's excess interest is tax-free under treaty" (1993). In Letter Ruling 9327073, the IRS ruled that a foreign bank with a U.S. branch was able to take advantage of a treaty provision and avoid taxation of its excess interest under Section 884(f)(1)(B).

[4 J. Int'l Tax'n 477.]

"Final BLIT regulations add sourcing rules, planning elections" (1993). Section 884 imposes the BPT, provides rules for sourcing interest paid by a foreign corporation's U.S. trade or business (the branch interest rules), and imposes a tax on a foreign corporation's "excess interest." Temporary regulations issued in September 1988 were made final in September 1992, and additional proposed regulations were promulgated then. This article discusses the Regulation § 1.884-4 BLIT regulations, which set forth the branch interest and excess interest tax rules, and also discusses the BPT and BLIT effective date rules.

The author first discusses the BLIT, along with the applicable provisions of the final regulations. Next, the author examines the determination of "excess interest" and the manner of its taxation. Additionally, the author explains the "interest shortfall rules" set forth in the regulations. Then, the author reviews miscellaneous provisions of the BLIT regulations.

The author then discusses the final BPT regulations' election by a foreign corporation to reduce its U.S. tax liabilities for purposes of the BPT. He also examines the impact of this election on the BLIT. Last discussed is the treatment of interest paid by partnerships to foreign corporations, proposed amendments to the BLIT regulations, and the effective date provisions of the BPT and BLIT regulations.

The author concludes that the final BLIT regulations contain helpful provisions for taxpayers. In particular, the election to reduce liabilities provides a mechanism for taxpayers to avoid or limit their excess interest tax liability. In addition, when the proposed regulations become final, significant simplification will be obtained as a result of coordinating the BLIT rules with Regulation § 1.882-5.

[KR Silbergleit, 4 J. Int'l Tax'n 123.]

"Final BPT regulations modify U.S. asset, qualified resident rules" (1993). Section 884 imposes the BPT, provides rules for sourcing interest paid by a foreign corporation's U.S. trade or business (branch interest rules), and imposes a tax on a foreign corporation's "excess interest." Temporary regulations issued in September 1988 were made final in September 1992, and additional proposed regulations were promulgated.

The author first discusses application of the BPT. Specific attention is given to the effect of terminations, liquidations, reorganizations, and incorporations of foreign corporations on the BPT. The reporting of a complete termination is also discussed.

Next, the author examines exemption under the BPT for "qualified residents" of a country whose income tax treaty with the United States prohibits its imposition. He also examines the consequences of the exemption. Within this part of the article, the author also discusses the regulations' provisions concerning attribution rules for determining ownership by "qualifying shareholders," the "publicly traded stock" exception, the "active trade or business" exception, the rulings procedure on "qualified resident" status, and the reporting of stock ownership. Application of the BPT to foreign governments is discussed in the last part of this section of the article.

In the next section of the article, the author discusses the final regulations' revisions to the U.S. liability rules and the treatment of specific U.S. assets under the temporary and final regulations. The specific assets discussed are money and bank deposits, installment obligations, and accounts and notes receivable. Planning for U.S. assets determinations is then addressed.

In the last section of the article, the author examines the proposed regulations. Specific discussion is provided on the provisions concerning partnership interests and interests in trusts as U.S. assets.

The author concludes that the IRS has learned from experience with the temporary regulations and thus the final regulations are clearer and easier to operate under. Some additional refinement is suggested in the proposed regulations, many of which will also be useful for the practitioner.

[KR Silbergleit, 4 J. Int'l Tax'n 18.]

"Final branch regulations fail to clear the thicket of complexity" (1993). In 1992, final and temporary regulations under Section 884 on the BPT and the BLIT were adopted. They replace temporary regulations issued in 1988 and incorporate the Technical and Miscellaneous Revenue Act of 1988 (TAMRA) amendments to the branch-tax rules. Issued simultaneously were proposed amendments to certain of these rules and those under Section 864 relating to the determination of ECI.

In this article, the authors first review the purposes and application of the BPT. Thereafter, they compare and analyze the differences between the new regulations and the 1988 temporary regulations with respect to the following aspects of the BPT: (1) the definition of "U.S. assets" (including the treatment of real property interests, inventory, installment obligations, receivables, cash and marketable securities, expansion capital, and partnerships and trust interests); (2) the definition of "U.S. liabilities" (including the election to reduce U.S. liabilities); and (3) the interaction of treaties and the BPT.

Next, the authors examine the BLIT rules, including the TAMRA expansion of these provisions. The new regulations' provisions covering the BLIT are then explained. The authors then examine the new regulations' provisions on the three alternative tests for determining whether a foreign corporation is a resident of a country with which the United States has an income tax treaty, as well as the provisions that permit a ruling in lieu of meeting these tests. Each of these tests, as modified by the new regulations, and the requirements for a "qualified resident" ruling are specifically discussed.

The authors last discuss certain other matters, including application of the BPT and BLIT to foreign governments and the earnings stripping rules under the new regulations. The authors conclude that foreign corporations that are qualified residents of jurisdictions with tax treaty relief from the BPT and BLIT will welcome the regulations' effort to simplify the attribution rules and documentation requirements. Other foreign corporations, however, may be disappointed. The guidelines for obtaining a "qualified resident" ruling are vague. The expansion of the rules to foreign governments could result in unexpected and controversial application. But most of all, for the typical foreign corporation, the IRS's final rules leave the computation of branch taxes entwined in a thicket of complexity.

[AS Lederman & B. Hirsh, 78 J. Tax'n 110.]

"Qualified resident status reduces BPT" (1993). Two private letter rulings (9322021 and 9323008) indicate some of the factors on which the IRS may rely in determining whether a corporation can take advantage of treaty benefits as a qualified resident of a treaty country under Section 884(e)(4). In both rulings, the IRS exercised its authority under Section 884(e)(4)(D) to rule that a taxpayer was a qualified resident of a treaty partner. In one ruling, however, an anti–treaty shopping provision was inserted.

[4 J. Int'l Tax'n 363.]

"Operating under the BPT" (1992). In 1986, the BPT provision (Section 884(a)) was enacted to create parity in tax treatment between the U.S. branch and subsidiary operations of foreign corporations. Before enactment of this provision, profits from a U.S. branch to a foreign head office could be repatriated without taxation, since this transfer occurred within a single entity. Now, Section 884(a) subjects the repatriation of earnings from a U.S. subsidiary or U.S. branch to the foreign parent to a withholding tax.

The author first explains the operation of the BPT. Important concepts thereunder, such as the "dividend equivalent amount" and the definition of "U.S. assets and liabilities," are given detailed examination. The "effectively connected earnings and profits adjustment" for changes in the foreign corporation's U.S. net equity is also discussed.

The author then considers the effects of income tax treaties on the BPT. Those countries whose qualified residents are exempted from this tax are listed and the meaning of "qualified resident" is explained. Avoidance of the BPT through complete termination of the foreign business' U.S. trade or business is examined. Specific discussion of the meaning of "complete termination" is also provided.

The application of the BPT in the year in which the foreign business undergoes a liquidation or reorganization is then discussed by the author. Specific attention is given to the carryover of tax attributes, including the dividend equivalent amount and earnings and profits.

The next technique discussed by the author is the domestic incorporation of the U.S. branch of the foreign enterprise. The changes made in the computation of the "dividend equivalent amount," after such incorporation are discussed in light of certain elections available to the newly formed corporation.

The author last discusses the BLIT under Section 884(f)(1). The impact of this provision on the sourcing of interest paid by a U.S. trade or business, along with the definition of "branch interest," is examined by the author.

[HF Wunder, US Tax'n Int'l Operations ¶ 5005.]

"Treaty excuses branch from excess-interest tax" (1992). A treaty served to excuse a foreign bank from tax on "excess interest" in Letter Ruling 9218032. The taxpayer was a foreign bank with a branch operation in the United States that expected to have excess interest under Section 884(f)(1)(B). Part of the excess interest was excused under Notice 89-80, which indicates that a portion of excess interest is treated as interest on deposits, exempt under Section 881(d). Under Article 11(3) of the U.S. income tax treaty with the taxpayer's resident country (several U.S. treaties, such as the treaty with Belgium, fit the description of the ruling), interest derived by a resident of one contracting state from sources in the other is exempt from tax by the other contracting state if it is interest paid between banks, except on loans represented by bearer instruments. In Letter Ruling 9218032, the IRS concluded that the treaty did apply to excuse the excess-interest tax.

[3 J. Int'l Tax'n 85.]

¶ 3.05 GAINS AND LOSSES FROM DISPOSITIONS OF U.S. REAL PROPERTY INTERESTS (SECTION 897)[5]

IRS issues revenue ruling concerning foreign corporation's gain on distribution in liquidation of U.S. real property interest acquired in another liquidation from purchased foreign corporation. The IRS ruled that a foreign corporation must recognize gain on the distribution of a U.S. real property interest under Temporary Regulation § 1.897-5T(c)(2)(ii)(B) as in effect prior to August 1, 1989, where the foreign corporation acquired the U.S. real property interest in a liquidating distribution under Section 332(a) from another foreign corporation, the stock of which it purchased from a foreign person or entity that was not subject to U.S. income taxation on the disposition. This holding also applies to any liquidation after July 31, 1989, if the rules of Temporary Regulation § 1.897-5T(c)(2)(ii)(B), as in effect prior to August 1, 1989, apply to such liquidation. See Notice 89-85, 1989-2 CB 403. The result would be similar under the modified provision of Temporary Regulation § 1.897-5T(c)(2)(ii)(B) as in effect after July 31, 1989.

[Rev. Rul. 90-76, 1990-2 CB 176.]

IRS finds Congress's intent as to FIRPTA in later history. A nonresident alien formed a wholly owned corporation in a foreign country (F-1). That corporation formed another corporation in a different country (F-2). In 1980, F-2 purchased an option to acquire certain U.S. real property in 1980. F-1 incorporated four U.S. corporations on June 25, 1980. F-2 transferred the option to them, and they exercised the option and bought U.S. realty on June 30, 1980.

F-2 formed a wholly owned subsidiary (F-3) in a third country (presumably the Netherlands). F-3 bought the stock of the four U.S. companies on November 24, 1980, effective July 1, 1980, from F-1 in exchange for a note. F-3 was in the process of incorporation on July 1, 1980. It could contract, and if it later ratified the contract, the corporation would be bound. F-3's incorporation was completed on December 10, 1980.

On December 5, 1980, FIRPTA was enacted effective as of June 18, 1980. The new law provided for the continued application of treaties until 1985. The third foreign country involved in the restructuring exempted capital gains from U.S. tax.

Each of the four U.S. corporations adopted Section 337 plans of liquidation, sold their U.S. real property, and distributed the cash proceeds to F-3. All three foreign corporations were liquidated within twelve months pursuant to the plan (necessary to qualify under prior Section 337(c)(3)).

The IRS held that taxpayer was subject to U.S. tax under Section 897 on the four corporations' distributions of the cash proceeds from the sale of the U.S. realty. F-3 was not entitled to rely on FIRPTA's five-year treaty override provision, because F-3 was not a resident of its foreign country on FIRPTA's effective date. The IRS also disregarded the sale of the four U.S. corporations by F-1, stating that the sale lacked substance, and citing National Lead Co., 336 F2d 134 (2d Cir. 1964). According to IRS, the transaction must be treated as though F-1 never parted with the stock of the four U.S. corporations.

The IRS relied on statements in the Economic Recovery Tax Act of 1981 conference report to determine the intent of Congress in enacting FIRPTA in 1980. That report states that the FIRPTA treaty override was intended to apply to foreign investors who were residents of their treaty countries on the date Section 897 became effective. It states that it was not Congress's intent to grant such an exemption to a foreign investor who, after the enactment of Section 897, rearranged his investments so as to come under a treaty that would exempt the gain from U.S. tax.

[TAM 9214003.]

FIRPTA consequences of trust's distribution. An individual who is not and never was a U.S. resident or citizen created a trust in the United States in 1939. The trust's situs was transferred to Canada in 1955. Control over the trust was exercised by a U.S. advisor until 1978, when control was transferred to a Canadian advisor. The trust advisor has the sole discretion to distribute trust income and corpus during the life of the stated beneficiary (the child of the trust's grantor) and any of the beneficiary's descendants. The trust's annual income consists primarily of U.S.-source interest and dividend income that is subject to U.S. withholding and Canadian income tax. The trust is not a grantor trust.

The trust owns 69 percent of the common stock of a corporation. It has been proposed that the trust distribute to its beneficiaries all of the shares it holds in the corporation. The beneficiaries will remain beneficiaries of the trust, which will continue to conduct investment activities. Immediately after the distribution, each beneficiary will transfer his or her shares to a specified Canadian corporation solely in exchange for shares of that corporation. The trust will not make an election to recognize gain under Section 643(e).

The IRS held that the trust and the beneficiaries will not recognize any gain under Section 897(e)(1) on the distribution of the first corporation's shares to the beneficiaries. The IRS also ruled that, provided that the basis of the first corporation's stock in the hands of the beneficiaries is the same as the basis of the stock in the hands of the trust, the beneficiaries will be entitled to claim the benefits of Article 13(9) of the U.S.-Canada income tax treaty.

These rulings were conditioned on compliance with the filing requirements of Temporary Regulation § 1.897-5T(d)(1)(ii), as clarified by Notice 89-57, 1989-1 CB 698. The IRS based its holding on the assumption that the first corporation will be treated as a U.S. real property holding company under the provisions of Section 897(c).

The ruling was issued under Announcement 89-124, 1989-40 IRB 31. The IRS stated there that it would consider, on a case-by-case basis, requests for private rulings dealing with the extent to which nonrecognition provisions will apply under Section 897(e) to a foreign trust and to foreign beneficiaries of a foreign trust on the distribution of a U.S. real property interest by the trust.

[Priv. Ltr. Rul. 9152014.]

"Foreign investment in U.S. real property" (1993). In this article, the authors examine the application and operation of Section 897 concerning the U.S. taxation of U.S. real property gains by foreign investors. After discussing the general effects of Section 897, the authors focus on the definition of its three key terms: "real property," "U.S. real property interest," and "U.S. real property holding corporation." In discussing the meaning of each of these terms, the authors consider the complex issues that arise in determining whether specific property is included within the applicable term's definition. Additionally, in-depth attention is given to the regulation provisions pertaining to these terms.

Next, the authors consider Section 897's treatment of dispositions of U.S. real property interests. The types of transactions that qualify as a "disposition" are explored, e.g., distributions by domestic corporations to nonresident alien shareholders and subsidiary liquidations. The treatment of nonrecognition exchanges is also considered, along with inbound reorganizations, foreign-to-foreign corporation reorganizations, and Section 355 distributions. The treatment of dispositions of interests in personal residences, partnerships, estates, trusts, and REITs is also examined.

The withholding rules of Section 1445 applicable to Section 897 transactions are then addressed. The liability of the transferee of a U.S. real property interest to withhold and qualification for withholding exemptions are given detailed consideration. Special withholding rules for partnerships, trusts, estates, and corporations with foreign interest holders are explained.

Next discussed is the Section 897(i) election by a foreign corporation to be treated as a domestic corporation. The various conditions, requirements, and consequences of this election are explained, including the antiabuse rule set forth in the regulations. Next, the authors discuss the interaction of FIRPTA and the BPT. Last, the authors consider planning for investments in U.S. real property in light of the partial termination of the U.S.–Netherlands Antilles income tax treaty and enactment of the U.S. BPT. Four alternative structures for foreigners who want to hold a U.S. real property interest are analyzed under current law.

[L. De Vos & WL Blum, US Tax'n Int'l Operations ¶ 9528.]

"An overview of FIRPTA" (1992). In 1980, FIRPTA was enacted to reduce the overall tax advantage of a foreign person's investment in U.S. real property. It does this by taxing the foreign person's gains from the sale of U.S. real property as if the gain arose from the conduct of a U.S. trade or business. In this article, the author provides an overview of the operation of Section 897 and some of the significant issues that now exist in this area.

The author first examines what constitutes a U.S. real property interest. In this regard, he discusses both direct interests and indirect interests, such as those held through corporations and partnerships. Creditor and noncreditor interests are distinguished. The inclusiveness of FIRPTA's definition of "real property" is also discussed. The special rules applicable to U.S. real property holding corporations are then reviewed, along with important issues that arise in their application. These concern derivation of the U.S. real property holding corporation "determination fraction," the "look-through" rules, termination of U.S. real property holding corporation status, key dates in the determination of U.S. real property holding corporation status, annual reports of non–U.S. real property holding corporation status, and interests in U.S. real property holding corporations that are not U.S. real property interests.

Next, the author discusses taxable dispositions under FIRPTA and the application of the Code's nonrecognition provisions. FIRPTA's interaction with certain treaty provisions is also reviewed. Thereafter, the author discusses the Section 897(i) election by foreign corporations to be treated as a U.S. corporation. Whether this election truly avoids any discriminatory effects attributable to the application of the FIRPTA provisions is then discussed. The requirements for making this election are set out by the author.

[BW Reynolds, US Tax'n Int'l Operations ¶ 9524.]

"FIRPTA and state tax liability" (1992). FIRPTA treatment of U.S. real property gains has some specific implications for state tax liability. By adding a new class of federal taxable income for foreign persons, FIRPTA may have conceivably created a state tax liability these taxpayers would not otherwise have borne. Forty-six states and the District of Columbia conform their tax bases to the federal standard. This article addresses the state tax issues that have arisen or may arise because of FIRPTA's operation in those states that conform to the federal standard.

The author first discusses whether the holding of a U.S. real property interest in a state creates a state tax nexus. He also discusses whether a nexus results if such interest is otherwise considered an intangible, e.g., a noncreditor debt interest. Next, the author examines the varying effects FIRPTA may have at the state tax level depending on whether the state conforms to the federal tax base using the federal gross, adjusted, or taxable income. In some states, the wording of their statutes may, as discussed by the author, give rise to exemption of gains from the sale of a U.S. real property interest. In other states the same argument may be based on the state tax regulations or other official announcements. Consideration is also given by the author to specific exemptions in some states' laws for types of foreign income. Last, the author discusses whether and how income from a U.S. real property interest can be allocated or apportioned to another state jurisdiction.

[BW Reynolds, US Tax'n Int'l Operations ¶ 9526.]

"Closing agreement can avoid U.S. real property interest gain recognition" (1990). Temporary Regulation § 1.897-5T(c)(2)(ii)(B) requires that gain be recognized on distribution of a U.S. real property interest by a foreign corporation to a domestic corporation in certain Section 332 liquidations if there have been dispositions of the foreign corporation's stock in the preceding five years. The IRS now permits nonrecognition in certain situations. Revenue Procedure 90-19 sets forth the requirements.

[72 J. Tax'n 371.]

"How a foreign corporation is taxed on gain from a real property disposition" (1990). Nonresident aliens and foreign corporations are, as a result of FIRPTA, subject to U.S. tax on dispositions of U.S. real property interests. As of 1984, FIRPTA also requires the buyer in such transactions to withhold U.S. tax and to remit such withholding to the IRS. This article examines whether the sale of a note received upon the sale of a U.S. real property interest was subject to U.S. tax as capital gain or ordinary income.

The author discusses *Botai Corp, NV*, a 1990 Tax Court memorandum case. In this case, the taxpayer, a foreign corporation, sold an installment note that it had received on the sale of a U.S. real property interest. The taxpayer argued that the gain realized on the sale of the note was ordinary income exempt under the U.S.-U.K. tax treaty. After holding that the gain was capital and thus not exempt, the court noted that the note might have escaped taxation as a Section 897 disposition of a real property interest if it had qualified as an "interest solely as a creditor." Here, however, the taxpayer had not initially elected out of installment sale treatment. The author discusses this reasoning and the possibility that FIRPTA can subject a foreign corporation to the BPT. Last, the 1984 withholding rules are reviewed by the author.

[WL Raby, US Tax'n Int'l Operations ¶ 9520.]

¶ 3.06 TRANSPORTATION INCOME (SECTION 887)[6]

IRS issues revenue procedure concerning tax on gross transportation income of nonresident aliens and foreign corporations. Nonresident aliens and foreign corporations are subject to a 4 percent tax on their U.S.-source gross transportation income under Section 887 for taxable years beginning after December 31, 1986. This revenue procedure advises such foreign persons on the proper procedure for computing, reporting, and paying the 4 percent tax under Section 887, and for claiming exemption from the 4 percent tax under an income tax convention or under Section 872(b) or Section 883.

[Rev. Proc. 91-12, 1991-1 CB 473.]

"Locating a transportation company offshore may still be the best route" (1992). By adopting a source rule for transportation, the Deficit Reduction Act of 1984 transformed substantial amounts of foreign-source income into US.-source income. The Tax Reform Act of 1986 (TRA 1986) expanded the sourcing rules, imposing a 4 percent excise tax on the gross income of some offshore transportation companies and restricting the statutory exemption of transportation income to "residents" of qualified countries.

The author covers the category of exemptions from U.S. taxation concerning international operation of aircraft and ships. Reciprocity agreements in this area are also discussed. The scope of the statutory exemption in the Code and its look-through rule are also examined.

Next, the author discusses the transportation excise tax imposed by Section 887(a). The definition of "transportation income" and the issues concerning personal services related to the use of a vessel or aircraft are explored. The sourcing of transportation income for purposes of this tax is discussed. The author concludes this section of the article with a discussion of planning in this area, including a specific discussion of certain allocation problems that must be faced.

The last section of this article is dedicated to an examination of the U.S. reporting requirements, both with regard to foreign parties claiming exemption and foreign parties with U.S.-source gross transportation income. Other reporting requirements are also discussed.

The author concludes that the 4 percent excise tax on U.S.-source gross transportation income allows the United States to tax offshore transportation companies, even when they have no net profit. New reporting and record-keeping requirements represent major changes for many offshore companies that formerly did not file U.S. tax returns. The significant penalties for noncompliance mean that offshore transportation companies should not ignore these administrative demands.

[ER Larkins, 3 J. Int'l Tax'n 218.]

"Tax agreements facilitate international transportation" (1991). The United States uses the beginning and ending points of transportation to determine the source of income derived therefrom. Under Section 863(c)(1), income derived from transportation between two U.S. points is entirely U.S.-source income. Where transportation begins or ends, but does not both begin and end, in the United States, Section 863(c)(2) provides that 50 percent of the income derived from the transportation activity is from U.S. sources. Transportation between two non-U.S. points generates wholly foreign-source income.

In the absence of an applicable exemption, the United States taxes U.S.-source transportation income in one of two ways:

1. Such income earned by a nonresident alien or foreign corporation that is effectively connected with the conduct of a U.S. trade or business is taxed under Sections 871(b) and 882.

2. U.S.-source transportation income of foreign persons not effectively connected with the conduct of a U.S. trade or business is subject to a 4 percent gross basis tax under Section 887.

Transportation income derived from U.S. sources by foreign persons can be exempt from U.S. tax in three ways. The classic formulation of the exemption for transportation income found in most income tax treaties to which the United States is a party is echoed in Article 8 of the OECD model treaty. This deceptively simple provision, providing a blanket exemption from source-state taxation for shipping and aircraft income derived by a resident of the other treaty country, conceals several items of considerable interest. The author discusses these items.

Second, not all income tax treaties are created equal with respect to shipping and aircraft income. Although the most recent treaties to which the United States is a party grant the U.S. tax exemption to a resident of the treaty-partner country, some older treaties grant the exemption on the basis of the flag of the carrier. This can provide a surprising (and disadvantageous) result, as the author describes. The United States has nearly thirty transportation tax agreements in effect (including those that cover shipping or aviation). The transportation income articles of income tax treaties do not necessarily supplant transportation tax agreements, nor is the converse true. The United States has both treaty-based and agreement-based transportation provisions in force with Belgium, Cyprus, Denmark, Finland, Greece, and Sweden.

Transportation tax agreements differ from treaty-based transportation income provisions generally by being more generous in granting the exemption.

Another way in which transportation tax agreements can be more generous than income tax treaties is in their scope. A corporation organized in a country with which the United States has an agreement in force frequently need not be resident there for an agreement-based exemption to apply, even if an income tax treaty exemption would not be available to that corporation because of its nonresidence.

[RE Andersen, 2 J. Int'l Tax'n 189.]

¶ 3.07 WITHHOLDING[7]

[1] Withholding on Payments to Foreign Persons, Generally (Sections 1441 and 1442)

Corporation was responsible for withhholding tax on interest paid to nonresident. Taxpayer, a domestic corporation, was organized by a Canadian citizen who was not a U.S. resident, to market time-share units in a condominium. The Royal Bank of Canada had made substantial loans to the shareholder to finance the venture. The shareholder in turn held a promissory note from taxpayer. The Bank of California collected the proceeds from the time-share sales for taxpayer. To satisfy the obligation to the Royal Bank, taxpayer, by the Canadian shareholder, directed the Bank of California to remit to the Royal Bank directly the net proceeds of the time-share notes that were due to it. Taxpayer failed to withhold tax on the interest portion of the notes, and the IRS determined that taxpayer was responsible as a withholding agent under Section 1441 for withholding tax on the shareholder's interest income.

Held: For the IRS. Under Section 1441, all persons that have the control, receipt, custody, or payment of income items of nonresident aliens are required to withhold tax on such income items. The shareholder constructively received the interest income when taxpayer directed that the money be expended on his behalf.

[Casa De La Jolla Park, Inc., 94 TC 384 (1990).]

IRS issues revenue ruling concerning withholding on deemed dividend distribution to foreign corporation. The IRS ruled that a Section 304 deemed dividend distribution to a foreign corporation by a domestic or foreign corporation is subject to federal income tax and therefore Section 1442 withholding to the extent the distribution is from sources within the United States. The 30 percent statutory with-holding tax rate may be reduced under the appropriate income tax treaty to the treaty withholding tax rate for dividends paid to 10 percent or greater corporate share-holders.

[Rev. Rul. 92-85, 1992-2 CB 69.]

"Withholding on alimony paid to nonresidents" (1992). In the 1992 Tax Court memorandum case of *Housden*, the court held that a U.S. resident alien was required to withhold U.S. tax from alimony payments to his former wives, who were non-resident aliens at the time of the payments. The court held that such payments constituted "fixed or determinable annual or periodic income." This article dis-cusses this case, focusing on how the taxpayer met the source and control require-ments for withholding. The article also addresses why the court did not impose penalties on the taxpayer and the effect of the new alimony provision in the U.S.-Canada tax treaty, which was not effective during the years before the court.

[77 J. Tax'n 51.]

"Form 1001 need not be filed before payment" (1991). The IRS has acquiesced in the 1986 Tax Court decision in *Casanova*. There, the taxpayer made interest payments to a foreign corporation in 1980 but did not obtain Form 1001, Ownership, Exemption or Reduced Rate Certificate, from the foreign corporation until 1985. Under Sections 1441 and 1442, a taxpayer generally is required to withhold U.S. income tax at the rate of 30 percent on any interest payments to a foreign person not engaged in a U.S. trade or business, unless the rate is reduced or eliminated by an income tax treaty with the foreign country of which the recipient is a resident.

In order to claim the benefits of an applicable treaty, the recipient must file a Form 1001 with the withholding agent. With respect to the time for filing Form 1001, the regulations under Section 1441 merely provide that the form "shall be filed as soon as practicable." The Tax Court concluded that nothing in the Code, the regulations, or the applicable income tax treaty imposed the requirement that the Form 1001 must be filed with the withholding agent prior to the time the interest in question is paid.

[1 J. Int'l Tax'n 366.]

"Withholding required despite oral denial" (1991). A domestic corporation that failed to withhold tax of 30 percent because of verbal representations that the payee was not a foreign corporation was found liable for the tax in Technical Advice Memorandum 9103002. The IRS also concluded that the domestic payor would not be indemnified under Section 1461, if it withheld more than 30 percent from future payments.

[75 J. Tax'n 116.]

"Failure to properly file Form 4224 can trigger corporate liability for withholding tax on interest paid to a nonresident alien" (1990). In 1990, the Tax Court decided *Casa De La Jolla Park, Inc.* In this case, the court had to determine whether taxpayer, a U.S. corporation, was a withholding agent as to its sole shareholder, a nonresident alien. This withholding agent issue arose with respect to payments made by taxpayer directly to a bank owed money by the sole shareholder. On the corporation's books, these payments were recorded as payments of interest on a loan made by the shareholder to taxpayer.

The author discusses the arguments made by both taxpayer and the IRS. He also analyzes the court's holding with respect to the impact that a timely filed Form 4224 would have had in this case. Also discussed is the issue of whether the sole shareholder, under the facts of this case, could be said to have received the interest payments while engaged in a U.S. trade or business.

[W. Raby, US Tax'n Int'l Operations ¶ 15,513.]

[2] Withholding on Dispositions of U.S. Real Property Interests (Section 1445)

IRS issues final regulations concerning withholding by publicly traded partnerships, publicly traded trusts, and REITs. The IRS has issued final regulations under Section 1445 relating to the withholding that is required upon the disposition of a U.S. real property interest by publicly traded partnerships, publicly traded trusts, and REITs. These final regulations enable publicly traded partnerships, publicly traded trusts, and REITs, by meeting certain notice requirements, to shift the responsibility for withholding on proceeds from the disposition of U.S. real property interests to a nominee where such an entity does not make a payment directly to a foreign person.

[TD 8321, 1990-2 CB 201, Reg. § 1.1445-8.]

"FIRPTA withholding and reporting requirements" (1992). When it was first enacted, FIRPTA relied for enforcement on voluntary tax returns and information reporting identifying U.S. real property interests owned by foreign persons. Congress determined that these procedures were ineffective and enacted new reporting and withholding requirements. This article reviews the application of these reporting and withholding rules.

The author first discusses the FIRPTA withholding requirement placed on transferees of U.S. real property interests. The types of transactions affected by the withholding requirement and the persons required to withhold are enumerated. Thereafter, the author considers exemptions from withholding. While all eight exemptions are explained, a more detailed discussion is provided of the exemptions for (1) publicly traded stock and partnership or trust interests; (2) foreclosures on a U.S. real property interest; and (3) "nonforeign" affidavits by the transferor. Payment requirements are then reviewed, along with the withholding certificate procedure (as set forth in Revenue Procedure 85-41).

The author then considers the special entity withholding rules for unincorporated entities, such as partnerships and trusts, which are triggered when a foreign person holds an interest in the entity. Next, the author discusses the tax return and payment requirements imposed on the foreign transferor of a U.S. real property interest. The appendix of this article has various forms for use in seeking an exemption from withholding.

[BW Reynolds, US Tax'n Int'l Operations ¶ 9525.]

[3] Partnership Withholding on Foreign Partners' Shares of Effectively Connected Taxable Income (Section 1446)

"How to minimize withholding for foreign partners" (1991). Federal withholding taxes on nonresident aliens and foreign corporations are applied to partnerships with foreign partners based on the type of income involved. The types of income included: (1) FDAP income; (2) income attributable to a U.S. real property interest; and (3) income effectively connected with a U.S. trade or business.

As a general rule, income earned by a partnership that is allocable to the foreign partner and not otherwise exempt from tax will be subject to the withholding for one of these types. To the extent income allocable to a foreign partner is not subject to U.S. income tax, however, no withholding applies. For example, because capital gains and certain income from trading in stocks or securities and commodities are not taxable to foreign partners, such items are not subject to withholding. Since different rules apply to each of the withholding provisions, the determination of the type of income is crucial in determining the responsibilities of the withholding agent.

With the enactment of Section 1446, Congress has subjected all taxable income allocable to foreign partners to withholding. Because separate rules apply to each of the different withholding provisions, compliance requires an understanding of each of the withholding provisions. More important, an understanding of the rules enables the tax practitioner to minimize their impact.

[TS Wisialowski, 1 J. Int'l Tax'n 268.]

[4] Withholding From Wages

IRS issues revenue procedure concerning representations alien must make to claim withholding exemption under certain treaties. This revenue procedure modifies two earlier revenue procedures by providing the representations that an alien must make to claim a withholding exemption under certain newly ratified income tax treaties. Under most U.S. income tax treaties, an alien student, teacher, or researcher at a U.S. university or other educational institution who receives income for personal services is generally exempt from income tax provided certain requirements are met. These requirements include a limited number of years in which the alien can claim the exemption and a maximum dollar amount for the exemption in a taxable year. Normally, the payor of compensation for personal services is required under Section 1441 or Section 3405 to withhold and pay over federal taxes on such income. However, withholding is not required if the income is exempt under treaty. In order to claim the withholding exemption, the alien must submit Form 8233 to the withholding agent certifying that the income is exempt from taxation under treaty. This revenue procedure provides the representations that an alien must include in Form 8233 to claim a withholding exemption under the newly ratified treaties with Germany, India, Indonesia, Spain, and Tunisia. This revenue procedure also modifies the representations in a prior revenue procedure pertaining to the treaty with the former Soviet Union. This revenue procedure ob-soletes representations in two prior revenue procedures pertaining to the earlier treaty with Finland, which has been replaced by a newly ratified treaty that does not exempt income earned within the United States by alien students, teachers, or researchers. This revenue procedure also modifies a prior revenue procedure with respect to the maximum annual exemption allowed students under the Cyprus treaty.

[Rev. Proc. 93-22, 1993-18 IRB 15, modifying Rev. Proc. 87-8, 1987-1 CB 336 and Rev. Proc. 87-9, 1987-1 CB 368.]

IRS issues revenue ruling concerning withholding of income, Federal Insurance Contributions Act (FICA), and Federal Unemployment Tax Act (FUTA) taxes. In this revenue ruling the issue was as follows: Are amounts paid by an employer in the situations described in the ruling "wages" for purposes of FICA, FUTA, and the collection of income tax at source on wages (Chapters 21, 23, and 24, Subtitle C of the Code)? In situation 1, a U.S. citizen or resident performs services outside the United States, but not in a U.S. possession, as an employee of a U.S. person. In situation 2, the facts are the same as in situation 1 except that the employer is a foreign person. In situation 3, a nonresident alien performs work within the United States as an employee of a U.S. person. In situation 4, the facts are the same as in situation 3 except that the employer is a foreign person. For purposes of the ruling, there is no applicable tax treaty or Social Security agreement to which the United States is a party and no applicable statutory or regulatory provision dealing with a specific type of employee.

    The IRS ruled that remuneration for services paid to the employee who is a U.S. citizen in situations 1 and 2 are wages for income tax withholding purposes to the extent that they exceed the amount of the exclusion that the employee is entitled to under Section 911 and are not subject to withholding under the laws of a foreign country. In the case of wages paid to a U.S. resident, no exception from income tax withholding is available for the amount of the exclusion that the employee is entitled to under Section 911. In situation 1, the remuneration for services paid to the employee are also wages for FICA purposes. The U.S. employer is also liable for taxes imposed under FUTA with respect to U.S. citizens. The IRS further ruled that in situation 2, a foreign person is not an "American employer" as defined in Sections 3121(h) and 3306(j)(3). Because the individual is performing services outside the United States, and the individual's employer is not an "American employer," services performed by an employee are not included within the definition of "employment" for FICA and FUTA purposes. Therefore, remuneration paid the employee is not wages for FICA and FUTA purposes.

The IRS also ruled that the wages paid to the nonresident aliens in situations 3 and 4, with respect to services performed in the United States, are effectively connected with the conduct of a trade or business in the United States. Assuming the exception in Section 864(b)(1) for services performed within the United States for a nonresident alien individual or foreign corporation by a nonresident alien individual temporarily present in the United States for ninety days or less during the taxable year and whose compensation is $3,000 or less in the aggregate does not apply to situation 4, the wages are subject to graduated tax rates under Section 871(b) and to income tax withholding under Section 3402(a).

The IRS ruled that in both situations 3 and 4, the services for which the compensation is paid are performed in the United States, and therefore, the employer must withhold FICA taxes under Sections 3101(a) and 3101(b). The employer is also subject to the FICA and FUTA taxes imposed under Sections 3111(a), 3111(b), and 3301.

[Rev. Rul. 92-106, 1992-2 CB 258.]

¶ 3.08 U.S. CORPORATIONS OWNED BY FOREIGN PERSONS[8]

[1] Deductions for Interest and Original Issue Discount

[a] Generally

"Final regulations issued on amounts owed foreign related parties" (1993). In 1993, the IRS issued final regulations under Sections 163 and 267 that specify when OID and other amounts owed to related foreign persons may be deducted. Also, Revenue Procedure 93-13 sets forth steps to be followed by taxpayers required to change accounting methods to comply with the final regulations.

After discussing the general OID rules, this article examines the exceptions set forth in the regulations from the general rule requiring the cash method for OID paid to related foreign persons. Thereafter, the new Section 267 regulations covering the matching principle where the person to whom certain payments are made is not a U.S. person are discussed. Exceptions to this principle, as well as remaining opportunities for mismatching deductions and accruals, are noted. Last, the provisions of Revenue Procedure 93-13 are reviewed.

[4 J. Int'l Tax'n 74.]

"New procedures for deducting debts owed to foreign persons" (1993). Final regulations, issued in 1993, govern the timing of deductions under Sections 163 and 267 for amounts owed to related foreign persons. Additionally, Revenue Procedure 93-13 provides guidance for U.S. taxpayers required to change their method of accounting.

[78 J. Tax'n 178.]

"Maximizing interest capitalization planning opportunities" (1992). In TRA 1986, uniform cost capitalization rules were enacted in Section 263A. This section embodies the full absorption concept of capitalization. Two other Code sections interact with Section 263A in the case of foreign-owned U.S. corporations engaged in U.S. manufacturing operations. These are Section 267(a)(3), which matches the deduction and payment of interest to foreign persons, and Section 163(j), which contains the earnings stripping rules. Planning in this area is the subject of this article.

The author first examines the operation of Section 263A, especially with regard to the capitalization of interest. Next, interest capitalization, as set forth in Notice 88-99, is considered. The "traced debt" calculation and the "avoided cost" method set out in the notice are highlighted. Thereafter, the author explores the interaction of Sections 267(a)(3) and 263A. Problem areas are discussed and planning considerations are noted. The earnings stripping rules are then explained and the effect of Section 263A on the earnings stripping provision is examined. This interaction is illustrated by a hypothetical problem.

The author concludes that interaction of the discussed Code provisions creates complex problems. For example, the effective interest rate planning used to avoid capitalization may contradict planning necessary to decrease the related-party interest expense deferral under the earnings stripping provision. Accordingly, careful consideration, along with unique planning strategies, must characterize a tax professional's work in this area.

[D. Karnuta, US Tax'n Int'l Operations ¶ 9507.]

"Cash method of OID if holder is related foreign person" (1991). Proposed Regulation §§ 1.163-12 and 1.267(a)-3 implement the Deficit Reduction Act of 1984 and TRA 1986 changes deferring the current deduction for OID by an instrument's issuer when the holder is a related foreign person. The regulations generally require taxpayers to use the cash method, and affected taxpayers will have to follow the change in method procedures under Section 446.

This article discusses the new proposed regulations, focusing on (1) the matching principle under Section 267(a)(2) as extended to foreign payees; (2) application of the OID rules to foreign payees; (3) the definition of "OID" as set forth in the new proposed regulations; (4) the application of the payment rule to amounts described in Sections 871(a)(1) and 881(a), as well as foreign-source interest; (5)

exceptions to the payment rule; and (6) the effective dates of the proposed regulations.

[75 J. Tax'n 118.]

[b] Limitations on Earnings Stripping (Section 163(j))

"Earnings stripping proposal has U.S. subsidiaries looking to replace parent-guaranteed debt" (1993). For foreign investors, one of the most significant Clinton administration tax proposals is to enhance the earnings stripping rules under Section 163(j). The rules, enacted in 1989, have been avoided by some foreign-controlled U.S. corporations by substitution of unrelated-party debt guaranteed by the foreign parent for a borrowing by the U.S. corporation from its foreign parent, itself financed by a borrowing by the foreign parent from an unrelated party. The chief aim of the proposal is to foreclose a foreign-controlled U.S. corporation from using this option for financing without subjecting the U.S. corporation to the earnings stripping rules. The proposal is poor tax policy as it will adversely affect transactions that do not run afoul of the purpose of the original earnings stripping legislation, is unlikely to raise much, if any, revenue, and will violate many U.S. income tax treaties and thus invite foreign retaliation against U.S.-owned multinationals.

The author first examines current Section 163(j) and the nature of the recently proposed change. Specific aspects of the proposed change are then examined, including the "guarantee rule" and its anticipated consequences. Last, the author examines the breadth of the proposed change and offers his criticisms.

[PM Daub, 4 J. Int'l Tax'n 330.]

"How the earnings stripping provision limits interest deductions—part I" (1992). In an attempt to halt the eroding tax base of U.S. and foreign corporations who deduct interest paid to tax-exempt related parties, Congress enacted the earnings stripping provision of Section 163(j) in 1989. This provision limits the interest deductions of U.S. corporations when paid to tax-exempt related entities. In this article, the authors examine this provision and the proposed regulations issued thereunder in 1991.

The authors first consider the typical fact patterns for operation of the earnings stripping limitation. Thereafter, they discuss various aspects of this provision, including the debt-equity ratio, which triggers application of the provision, the meaning of "exempt related-party interest expense," and the determination of "related-party" status. Next, they examine how the relevant debt-equity ratio is determined. This examination includes a discussion of the meaning of "debt" and "equity" for purposes of the limitation. In this regard, special rules such as the antirollover rule and antiabuse rule are also discussed. Next reviewed is the calculation of excess interest expense. The determination of net interest expense and adjusted taxable income for this purpose is also explored. The various aspects of this calculation are illustrated by the authors through a series of examples.

[WJ Lazar, Jr. & J. Stenstrom, US Tax'n Int'l Operations ¶ 9504.]

"How the earnings stripping provision limits interest deductions—part II" **(1992).** In this article, the authors examine how the earnings stripping provision is applied to both foreign and domestic corporations. Also, they explore the provision's effect on corporations that are members of the same affiliated group.

The authors first review application of the earnings stripping rules, including the determination of deductible interest expense with regard to all of the Code's limitations, the calculation of the amount of disallowed interest expense, and application of these provisions when interest is exempt under the Code or a treaty. Next, they examine application of the earnings stripping provision when an affiliated group is involved. To this end, they discuss the consolidated return rules and the consequences of an admission or acquisition of a new member by the group.

Thereafter, the authors discuss application of the earnings stripping provision in the case of foreign corporate debtors. The treatment of guarantees and back-to-back loans not otherwise subject to the earnings stripping provision as loans subject to such limitation is explored. The authors then provide a comprehensive example illustrating the application and interaction of earnings stripping rules. The authors conclude this article with a discussion of whether the earnings stripping provision does, in fact, violate nondiscrimination clauses in various tax treaties and the position of Congress and the IRS that it does not.

[WJ Lazar, Jr. & J. Stenstrom, US Tax'n Int'l Operations ¶ 9505.]

"New issues raised by earnings-stripping proposed regulations" **(1992).** The so-called earnings stripping rules of Section 163(j) limit the deductibility of interest paid by U.S. corporate taxpayers to related foreign parties. Section 163(j) was enacted in 1989, in response to the perception that foreign companies were abusing the tax advantages of capitalizing U.S. subsidiaries with debt rather than equity.

Congress concluded that the corporate tax base was being eroded by allowing unlimited deductions for interest payments made to foreign related parties who are exempt from U.S. withholding tax on the interest received. Congress decided that limitations should apply when the U.S. subsidiary is thinly capitalized and its overall interest expense is high in relation to its cash flow.

In June 1991, the IRS issued proposed regulations under Section 163(j), which are discussed in this article. While they resolve a number of issues raised by the statute, some of the approaches taken raise new questions.

[PH Spector, 2 J. Int'l Tax'n 272.]

"Earnings stripping proposed regulations raise the level of complexity for related-party debt" **(1991).** The earnings stripping rules in Section 163(j), added by the Revenue Reconciliation Act of 1989 (RRA 1989), were enacted to address perceived excessive erosion of the U.S. tax base through intercompany debt financing. These rules can limit the deductibility of interest paid to related persons that are exempt from U.S. tax or subject to reduced U.S. tax rates on interest income.

In Section 163(j)(7), Congress granted the Treasury broad authority to prescribe appropriate rules, and proposed regulations were issued June 12, 1991. The IRS reserved two important issues: guaranteed debt and interest equivalents. The IRS's failure to address these issues continues the uncertainty that has hindered the structuring of various transactions. Moreover, in several instances, the proposed regulations introduce a degree of complexity neither mandated by the statute nor warranted by policy concerns. Finally, the IRS has stretched, if not surpassed, the limits of its regulatory authority in its controversial treatment of disallowed interest carried forward to years in which the debtor's debt-equity ratio does not exceed the safe harbor level of 1.5:1.

The first part of this article focuses on the general operating rules of Section 163(j) as interpreted in the proposed regulations. The author first examines the operation of Section 163(j) and the impact of the proposed regulations, covering the definitions of "interest income" and "expense," the coordination of Section 163(j) with other limitation provisions (e.g., the passive activity loss rules), the computation of adjusted taxable income, and the proposed regulations' provisions concerning related persons and exempt interest (including treaty-reduced tax rates on interest and interest indirectly subject to U.S. tax, as in the case of CFCs, passive foreign investment companies, and foreign personal holding companies).

Next, the debt-equity ratio rules under the proposed regulations are addressed, including the timing and computation of the debt-equity ratio and safe harbor planning. The last part of this installment of the article addresses the IRS's reservation of sections for guarantees and back-to-back loans, and the House and Conference Reports comments on these matters, as well as the effective date provisions and the treatment of grandfathered debt.

[JE Croker, Jr. & HJ Birnkrant, 75 J. Tax'n 244.]

"Earnings stripping rules are even more complex for affiliated corporations" **(1991).** The first part of this article described the general operating rules of Section 163(j), as interpreted in the proposed regulations. This part focuses on the complicated affiliated group rules and the application of the earnings stripping rules to foreign corporations engaged in business in the United States.

The authors first review the rules concerning affiliated groups. They conclude that as applied to related U.S. corporations, the proposed regulations are complex and, especially with regard to related corporations not filing consolidated returns, are likely to impose a significant compliance burden. Stand-alone application of the earnings stripping rules is denied to any corporation that is a member of an "affiliated group" (as defined in the proposed regulations) on the last day of the corporation's taxable year, whether or not it joins in a consolidated return. The authors examine the proposed regulations' definition of "affiliated group" and the determination of the affiliated group's debt-equity ratio for the earnings stripping rules.

The authors next discuss the proposed regulations' fixed stock write-off method, pursuant to which an affiliated group can, under certain circumstances, elect to substitute the purchasing shareholder's purchase-price basis in the stock of a target corporation for the target corporation's basis in its assets. The authors note that this method was provided by the IRS in response to the inequity of comparing acquisition debt to a target's historic basis in its assets. However, the narrow scope of this method will, according to the authors, likely attract justifiable criticism (for reasons explored in this article).

Next, the authors examine in-depth the affiliated group rules for consolidated groups provided in the proposed regulations, including the computation of adjusted taxable income and the treatment of exempt person related expense, the dissallowed interest expense carry-forward, and the excess limitation carry-forward. Thereafter, the authors focus on the treatment of nonconsolidated affiliated groups, including the computations that must be made by them.

In addition to the specific limitations on carry-forwards, the proposed regulations include a catchall to the effect that the same item of income or expense may not be taken into account more than once to the extent such treatment would be inconsistent with the principles of Section 163(j). Within this context, the authors examine the disallowed interest expense carry-forward and the excess limitation carry-forward.

Last, the authors examine the treatment of foreign corporations and the special rules provided in the proposed regulations for foreign corporations with ECI. The authors explain the proposed regulations' incorporation of the BPT rules, including the interaction of those rules with the earnings stripping rules.

The authors conclude that in many respects, the proposed regulations reflect a commendable effort to balance simplicity with rational interpretations of the statute. However, they believe that the complexity of the affiliated group provisions could be replaced with general antiabuse rules.

It appears, according to the authors, that both Congress and the IRS are aware that Section 163(j) needs to be amended. Congress and the IRS have taken the position that Section 163(j) does not violate the nondiscrimination provisions in income tax treaties. However, their arguments that foreign corporations are properly compared to U.S. tax-exempt organizations is particularly unconvincing. Nevertheless, it is expected that amendments to the proposed regulations will be influenced substantially by nondiscrimination considerations. Additionally, it is hoped that such considerations lead to broader availability of the debt-equity safe harbor. Substantial simplification of the consolidated group's adjusted taxable income determination, however, is not likely to occur.

[JE Croker, Jr. & HJ Birnkrant, 75 J. Tax'n 318.]

[2] Information and Record-Keeping Requirements Under Sections 6038A and 6038C

IRS issues revenue procedure concerning Section 6038A agreements. This revenue procedure provides a procedure whereby a reporting corporation may request that the IRS enter into a Section 6038A agreement under Regulation § 1.6038A-3(e). A reporting corporation is either (1) a U.S. corporation that is owned by a 25 percent–foreign shareholder or (2) a foreign corporation that is engaged in a trade or business within the United States at any time during a taxable year. Under Sections 6038A and 6038C, a reporting corporation is subject to specific record maintenance requirements. These record maintenance requirements, in addition to other matters, may be varied by an agreement between a reporting corporation and the IRS District Director. The IRS provides this procedure to encourage the clarification by mutual agreement of the application of the record maintenance requirements of the Sections 6038A and 6038C regulations to the case of a particular reporting corporation.

[Rev. Proc. 91-38, 1991-2 CB 692.]

IRS issues final regulations concerning information with respect to certain foreign-owned corporations. The IRS has issued final regulations relating to information that must be reported and records that must be maintained by certain foreign-owned corporations under Section 6038A.

[TD 8353, 1991-2 CB 402, Reg. §§ 1.6038A-0–1.6038A-7.]

"Foreign-owned U.S. corporations: the reporting requirements" (1993). Foreign-owned U.S. corporations must comply with onerous reporting requirements under Section 6038A. Inadequate compliance with these requirements can result in loss of deductions and imposition of penalties. This article addresses the reporting and other requirements imposed under Section 6038A.

The author first examines the Form 5472 reporting requirements with respect to intercompany transactions between a corporation required to report and a "related party." Next, the author considers whether a transaction is reportable and the manner in which monetary consideration from a "foreign related party transaction" must be reported. The reporting of nonmonetary transactions is also examined. Next, the author discusses additional information required to be reported and the use of reasonable estimates where exact amounts cannot be determined at the time the Form 5472 is required to be filed. Last, the author notes other requirements for Form 5472, such as use of U.S. dollars and the English language, as well as exemptions from reporting for certain transactions.

[US Tax'n Int'l Operations ¶ 9533.]

"Triple penalties affect foreign-controlled U.S. corporations" (1993). The regulations under Section 6038A establish three tiers of penalties for foreign-controlled U.S. corporations that fail to meet certain reporting and record maintenance requirements: (1) initial penalties; (2) additional penalties; and (3) noncompliance penalties.

The author first examines the "initial penalties" imposed on the failure to furnish information required on Form 5472, the failure to comply with the record maintenance rules, and the failure to produce records maintained outside the United States within the required time. The standards for these penalties, as set forth in the regulations under Section 6038A, are also discussed. Avoidance of the penalty by a showing of reasonable cause is then examined, along with the notion of "substantial compliance." Thereafter, the author examines the exemption for "small transactions." Next, the author discusses certain issues concerning the "failure" standard applied in the regulations, consolidation of penalties, and the application of the effective date provisions. The author then reviews the so-called additional penalties for continued failure to comply with reporting requirements after the IRS has notified the taxpayer of the initial failure. Application of the "additional penalties" in the case of record maintenance failures is also reviewed. Last, the author examines the noncompliance penalties imposed for the failure of a foreign related party to authorize a reporting corporation to act as its agent or to furnish required information. When these penalties apply, some or all of the intercompany deductions subject to reporting requirements may be disallowed.

[US Tax'n Int'l Operations ¶ 9534.]

"Final regulations modify reporting and record-keeping obligations of foreign-owned corporations" (1991). Final regulations under Section 6038A cover reporting, record maintenance, and agency authorization requirements for related-party transactions of foreign-owned U.S. corporations and foreign corporations engaged in a U.S. trade or business. This article examines the final regulations and compares the provisions of the final regulations to those of the proposed regulations. Topics specifically covered include Section 6038A reporting (including the definitions of "reporting corporation" and "related party"), the small business and other exceptions, record maintenance requirements (including the safe harbor thereunder, the keeping of records abroad, and agreements that alter the scope of such requirements), monetary penalty provisions, the authorization of agents for foreign parties, enforcement procedures, and effective date provisions.

The authors conclude that the Section 6038A final regulations respond to many of the concerns expressed by corporations subject to its provisions. By deleting the requirements of an affirmative election to maintain records outside the United States and of an annual filing of agency authorization, the final regulations eliminated the potential for many inadvertent violations of the record maintenance and agency authorization rules. They also eliminated a source of administrative burden for reporting corporations.

The burden placed on large foreign-owned multinational corporations was, however, not otherwise significantly reduced. The changes made to the requirements for material profit-and-loss statements will have only a limited effect on reporting corporations subject to the record maintenance requirements. Such corporations will still be required to undertake laborious calculations to determine the reasonable level of specificity of significant industry segments that results in the greatest number of separate segments in comparison to other possible classifications. Moreover, by explicitly providing that the Section 6038A record maintenance requirements are equivalent to the requirements of Section 6001 and that the safe harbor places a cap on these requirements, the final regulations preclude reporting corporations from electing out of the safe harbor. Furthermore, the final regulations expanded the exemptions for small corporations and for corporations with de minimis related-party transactions from the record maintenance and agency authorization requirements of Section 6038A. While these corporations may avoid monetary penalties, the final regulations have put such corporations on notice that they may be required under Section 6001 to maintain cost records sufficient to substantiate the propriety of the transfer pricing used in related-party transactions. They may prove particularly burdensome to smaller corporations.

The final regulations' changes to the Section 6038A enforcement procedures generally will be favorably received by reporting corporations. Specifically, the final regulations should alleviate concern that the IRS would routinely issue large numbers of summonses directed at foreign related parties pursuant to agency authorizations as a first step in an audit of a reporting corporation's related-party transactions. Such regulations did not, however, address the concern of certain closely held reporting corporations, particularly those with owners from countries that have, or have pending, a tax treaty or tax information exchange agreement with the United States.

Under the final regulations, the role of Section 6038A may well be as a weapon maintained in reserve by the IRS to encourage voluntary compliance by large foreign-owned corporations with information document requests and reasonable settlement of transfer pricing disputes. A collateral effect of the final regulations may be to foster cooperation by both the IRS and large foreign-owned corporations through the record maintenace agreement procedure and advance pricing agreements.

[AS Lederman & B. Hirsh, 75 J. Tax'n 158.]

"Final reporting and record-keeping rules address enforcement issues" (1991). The IRS recently issued final regulations under Section 6038A. In this comprehensive article, the author begins with a discussion of transfer pricing enforcement problems under Section 482.

Although issued under Section 6038A, the related-party reporting and record maintenance rules of the Section 6038A final regulations also apply to related-party transactions with U.S. branches that are subject to Section 6038C. In view of the focus of Section 6038A on "reporting corporations" and transactions with "related parties," definitions of these terms set forth in Regulation § 1.6038A-1 become critical. Under Section 6038A, a reporting corporation is a U.S. corporation with at least one foreign shareholder that owns, in terms of vote or value, at least 25 percent of its stock. The ownership requirements are determined with reference to the direct and indirect ownership rules of Section 318. As of December 10, 1990, a reporting corporation under Section 6038C is a foreign corporation with a U.S. branch. The indirect ownership rules of Section 318 apply in determining whether a corporation is a reporting corporation.

The final regulations provide two exceptions to the definition of "reporting corporation." Foreign corporations with U.S. branches that do not possess a U.S. permanent establishment under an applicable treaty are not reporting corporations. In addition, foreign corporations with U.S. branches engaged in international transportation that are exempt from tax under Section 883 are not reporting corporations. Banks and other financial institutions previously exempt from reporting requirements are covered by the final regulations.

Every reporting corporation is obligated to file Form 5472 with respect to each related party, foreign or domestic, with which it has had reportable transactions during the taxable year. The Form 5472 must be filed even though it may not affect the amount of any tax due. The Form 5472 must be filed with the U.S. corporation tax return for the taxable year. If the return is untimely filed, the Form 5472 must be timely filed. A copy of Form 5472, with attachments, must also be filed with the IRS service center in Philadelphia.

Five classes of information are required to be provided on the Form 5472. Class 1 is information about the reporting corporation and 25 percent–foreign shareholders. Class 2 is information about the related party to which the Form 5472 pertains. Classes 3 and 4 are information on transactions with foreign related parties. The transitional information required to be reported follows existing regulations and is essentially the same as was required before the 1989 legislation. Class 5 is Customs-related information relevant to the limitation of tax basis or inventory cost in determining Customs value under Section 1059A.

The author discusses who must file the form and what information must be supplied. Thereafter, the penalty for not filing and for not maintaining proper records, including a reasonable-cause and good faith defense, are discussed.

Regulation § 1.6038A-3 contains the record maintenance and production requirements relating to "relevant" records and "foreign" records. Each reporting corporation must maintain or cause another to maintain records sufficient to establish the correctness of the federal tax return of the corporation, including information, documents, or records to the extent that they may be relevant to determine the correct U.S. tax treatment of transactions with related parties. A detailed discussion follows concerning what records must be maintained and a safe harbor defining "records relevant to transactions between the reporting corporation and related parties." An exhibit illustrates the various material profit-and-loss tests based on the example provided in Regulation § 1.6038A-3(c)(8).

In addition to defining "relevant records," the final regulations also define "foreign records" and require their maintenance and production in the United States for tax examinations. The maintenance requirement includes not only records of the reporting corporation itself but also records of any foreign related party that may be relevant to determine the U.S. tax treatment of transactions between the reporting corporation and foreign related parties, including records that are directly or indirectly related to such transactions. A discussion of indirect foreign records and where records must be kept, including outside the United States, follows.

The regulations contain threshold levels of related-party payments that have to be exceeded in order for a reporting corporation to be subject to the record maintenance requirements. The threshold levels that will excuse record maintenance are gross payments that do not exceed $5 million and are less than 10 percent of U.S. gross income. Both of these standards must be met. Because of the strictness of the threshold exemption, the final regulations include a small corporation exemption from record maintenance requirements. A reporting corporation that has less than $10 million in U.S. gross receipts for a taxable year is not subject to the record maintenance requirements. The threshold and small corporation exemptions apply only to record maintenance, and not to reporting requirements.

The author then discusses the noncompliance penalty and the increased jurisdiction of the federal district courts, including summonses for foreign executives. The article concludes with a discussion about changes made by the final regulations to the proposed regulations under Section 6038A.

[JE McDermott, Jr., 2 J. Int'l Tax'n 133.]

"Foreign-owned corporations face new record-keeping duties under the Revenue Reconciliation Act of 1990 (RRA 1990) and proposed regulations" (1991). On December 10, 1990, the IRS published proposed regulations interpreting Section 6038A, as amended by RRA 1990. These rules will also apply generally to corporations subject to Section 6038C.

After providing background information concerning Sections 6038A and 6038C and the proposed regulations, the article addresses specific aspects of the proposed regulations. First, the authors address the applicability of Section 6038A. Within this section, they cover the topics of qualification as a reporting corporation, identification of related parties, and the consequences of attribution. Next, the authors discuss certain of the requirements imposed by the proposed regulations, including reporting and record maintenance requirements, exceptions from the record maintenance requirements, the categories of records that must be kept, and the three tests used to determine whether profit-and-loss statements are material.

The next section of the article concerns the monetary penalties imposed for the failure to file a substantially complete Form 5472 and the appointment of the reporting corporation as agent for related foreign corporations. Other enforcement elements are also discussed, such as nonmonetary penalties for failure to furnish summonsed information or noncompliance with agency authorization requirements. Enforcement alternatives, such as those provided under various tax treaties and exchange-of-information agreements, are also discussed. Related RRA 1990 provisions are discussed in this article, namely, the Section 6662 penalty for certain 482 adjustments, the Section 6503(k) statute-of-limitations extension, and disclosure of tax return information under Section 6103(n).

In conclusion, the authors note that under the proposed regulations, U.S. corporations with a 25 percent or greater foreign owner that engage in more than minimal transactions with foreign related parties will face burdensome new reporting, record-keeping, and jurisdictional requirements. In many cases, there appears to be no justification for many of the records outlined under the Section 6038A proposed regulations. Additionally, the extensiveness of the required records is overwhelming and may cover virtually every piece of paper produced by related parties. Moreover, small corporations are not immune from this burden. Finally, concern has been expressed that Section 6038A violates the nondiscrimination provision of certain U.S. treaties.

[AS Lederman & B. Hirsh, 74 J. Tax'n 186.]

"Minimizing IRS scrutiny under high-profit test" (1991). High-profit segments of a multinational business are subject to special scrutiny under the record maintenance rules for foreign-owned corporations. The final regulations under Section 6038A amplify and expand these rules to encompass "industry segments" that would not otherwise constitute the broader category of "significant industry segments." If an industry segment is "highly profitable," as defined by these regulations, a combined profit-and-loss statement must then be prepared when requested by the IRS. This financial statement must reflect the intercompany transactions encompassing the reporting corporation and its foreign related parties. This statement may then be used by the IRS as part of its Section 482 audit to allocate income between the U.S. and the foreign jurisdiction.

Segmental profit-and-loss statements are required by the regulations but not directly by Section 6038A. The IRS established industry segment rules under Regulation §§ 1.6038A-3(c)(5) and 1.6038A-3(c)(6) to delineate the boundaries for disclosure purposes. The reporting corporation has considerable discretion within these boundaries, however, to select crucial aspects of the database, including the related products or services to determine the segments. Most reporting corporations consider high-profit segments as waving a red flag, and seek to avoid their disclosure. Selective grouping and ungrouping of these industry segments may achieve this objective in some situations.

The high-profit test of Regulation § 1.6038A-3(c)(6) focuses on "U.S.-connected products or services within a single industry segment." Regulation § 1.6038A-3(c)(7)(i) defines "U.S.-connected products or services," as products or services that are imported to or exported from the United States through intercompany transactions. An "industry segment," as defined by Regulation § 1.6038A-3(c)(7)(ii), is a segment of the "related party group's combined operations" comprising the reporting party and all related parties on a combined basis.

A profit-and-loss statement is material and, as such, is necessary as a part of the records that must be created or maintained, if the industry segment is a high-profit segment. The statements must reflect the profit and loss of the related-party group that is attributable to the U.S.-connected products or services within a single industry segment, with or without constituting a significant industry segment. Narrower industry segments must be tested for this purpose.

The remaining high-profit tests are quantitative: To constitute a high-profit segment, the gross revenue of the industry segment must be earned by the related-party group from U.S.-connected products or services within this industry segment, and such gross revenue must be $100 million or more in the taxable year. In addition, the segment must meet the complex return-on-assets test.

The return-on-assets test is the third phase of the high-profit test and the most complex because divided significant industry segments must be tested against ratios of operating profit and identifiable assets. Under the high-profit test, significant industry segments would previously have been ascertained using the required level of specificity of Regulation § 1.6038A-3(c)(5)(iv), and these significant industry segments must be redivided to comply with the high-profit test of Regulation § 1.6038A-3(c)(6). Narrower segments must be used for this purpose, assuming the $100 million in gross revenue threshold has been satisfied, even if the narrower segments would not meet the significant industry segment test.

An industry segment (which might be a division of a significant industry segment) must determine its return on assets of the related-party group using the worldwide operations within the industry segment. An industry segment is a high-profit segment if the rate of return exceeds 15 percent and is at least 200 percent of the return on assets earned by the related-party group in all industry segments on a combined basis. The return-on-assets ratio, for purposes of the high-profit test, is the "operating profit" of the industry segment divided by the "identifiable assets" of the industry segment. Both of these terms are defined under the foreign-owned-corporation reporting provisions of Regulation § 1.6038A-3(c)(7), as explained in detail.

The regulations provide the reporting party with considerable power to ascertain its industry segments. While "industry segment" is defined under Regulation § 1.6038A-3(c)(7)(ii) as "a segment of the related party group's combined operations that is engaged in providing a product or service or a group of related products or services," "related products or services" are defined under Regulation § 1.6038A-3(c)(7)(vii) as "groupings of products and types of services that reflect reasonable accounting, marketing, or other business practices within the industries in which the related group operates." The reporting corporation has the option to select any such method to determine industry segments within these boundaries. Using these boundaries to group or ungroup industry segments can be advantageous for related-party groups. Selection of industry segments could enable the reporting corporation to avoid preparing profit-and-loss statements that would otherwise be required under the high-profit test. The remainder of the article describes an application of the new regulations to a complex hypothetical situation.

[R. Feinschreiber, 2 J. Int'l Tax'n 143.]

"New reporting and record rules increase burdens" (1991). In 1989 and 1990, Congress broadened the functions of Section 6038A of the Code, and, in 1990, it enacted Section 6038C with a view to changing the rules under which the IRS conducts international tax examinations of U.S. affiliates and branches of foreign corporations, in particular with respect to transfer price and other transactions with foreign related parties. Proposed Regulation §§ 1.6038A-1 through 1.6038A-7 and

Proposed Regulation § 1.6038C-1, issued on December 4, 1990, flesh out the changed rules. The changes reflect a new approach to international tax enforcement. The author then discusses the traditional enforcement tools and the problems with them, including the two 1983 California federal district court decisions in *Toyota Motor Corp.*

Sections 6038A and 6038C take a different approach to such tax examinations in the case of related-party payments. On the one hand, these sections seek to implement the traditional approach under which summonses are enforced by the IRS through the federal district court. Acting under authority conferred by these sections and Section 6001, the IRS has designated specific categories of records that must be maintained and produced for the IRS in the United States in a form usable for tax examinations. Technically, this obligation is placed on the U.S. related party. As a practical matter, however, this obligation is placed on foreign related parties to the extent it relates to records that are owned by and in the possession of foreign related parties.

In addition, in an effort to avoid lengthy court fights over the production of foreign records, the U.S. "reporting corporation" must maintain the foreign records in the United States, or elect to maintain them outside of the United States, in return for an annual commitment to produce them for examination in the United States. Also, the foreign related parties must authorize their U.S. affiliates to act as agents for the service of IRS summonses for records and testimony relevant to related-party transactions.

Sections 6038A and 6038C also provide the IRS with an alternative to having the summons enforced by the federal district court: The IRS can exact a noncompliance penalty. Under this penalty, the U.S. taxpayer's deduction for the related-party payment can be determined in the IRS's sole discretion, from its own knowledge or from such information as it may choose to obtain. Thus, the IRS bypasses the federal district court unless the taxpayer seeks the protection of the court to prevent imposition of the noncompliance penalty.

The new rules apply to foreign related party groups and only with respect to related-party transactions. Section 6038A applies to foreign related party groups with a U.S. corporate affiliate. Section 6038C applies to foreign related party groups with a U.S. branch of a foreign corporation. Proposed Regulation §§ 1.6038A-1 through 1.6038A-7 apply the new rules to related-party transactions with the U.S. corporate affiliate. Proposed Regulation § 1.6038C-1 applies the same rule to related-party transactions with a U.S. branch. There is an important exception to the above provisions. Section 6038C also applies to such non-related-party transactions as may be designated by the IRS. The sections function by addressing the U.S. corporate affiliate under Section 6038A and the U.S. branch of a foreign corporation under Section 6038C (reporting corporations).

After discussing the definition of "reporting corporations," the article points out that Proposed Regulation § 1.6038A-3 applies the basic principle of Section 6001 to related-party transactions. All records relevant to the correct tax treatment of related-party transactions must be maintained and produced, including records of foreign related parties. "Relevant" records are those bearing upon or related to the related-party transaction. A safe harbor is provided under which a corporation that maintains or causes another person to maintain the records listed therein will be deemed to have met the record maintenance requirement. Another safe harbor is for corporations with a de minimis value of related-party transactions.

The author then discusses the basic accounting records that must be maintained in the United States of the reporting corporation and the foreign related parties. Material profit-and-loss records that show the profit and loss of the related-party group with respect to U.S.-connected products or services are addressed. This requirement targets transfer price transactions for imported products.

An annual election on Form 5472 allows foreign related parties to maintain or to cause another to maintain the records outside of the United States subject to an agreement to produce them in the United States at the request of the IRS. An annual authorization of agency is required under Proposed Regulation § 1.6038A-5. Unless the de minimis exception, described above, applies, the foreign related party must authorize the reporting corporation with which it engages in a related-party transaction to act as its limited agent for purposes of service of IRS summonses under Sections 7602, 7603, and 7604.

A noncompliance penalty of $10,000 is discussed in the proposed regulations with respect to each related party for each taxable year, with an additional $10,000 penalty for each thirty-day period that the violation continues, beginning ninety days after the IRS provides written notice of the violation. For multiple violations with respect to a related party, one penalty, subject to thirty-day extensions, will be imposed. Multiple penalties are possible, and a provision is made for an affirmative showing of reasonable cause.

The noncompliance penalty provides that the IRS may determine the deduction for related-party payments, in its sole discretion, from its own knowledge or from such information as it may choose to obtain from testimony or otherwise. The proposed regulations make it clear that in determining the deductions under the noncompliance penalty, the IRS may disregard any information, documents, or records submitted by the reporting corporation if, in its sole discretion, it deems that they do not have significant or sufficient value to the resolution of the issue. The noncompliance penalty can be imposed where a foreign related party fails to authorize the reporting corporation to act as agent for the service of summonses, and where the agency authorization has been made and a summons issued, but it is not substantially complied with or cannot be substantially complied with because the designated records have not been maintained or have been destroyed. The IRS is still entitled to pursue enforcement of the summons in the federal district court.

Finally, the author makes some planning suggestions after suggesting that many decisions will be easy to make, since, for example, it should prove impractical to maintain foreign related party records in the United States. Therefore, most foreign related parties will require the reporting corporations to make the election on Form 5472.

As to foreign records, consideration should be given to their content and effect on the tax or Customs treatment of related-party transactions. Internal storage records of relevant foreign related parties should be reviewed as these are certain to be requested in any serious tax examination.

Material profit-and-loss statements present the most difficult decisions. It seems premature to make decisions in this respect until revised Section 482 regulations are issued.

[JE McDermott, Jr., 1 J. Int'l Tax'n 325.]

"Record-keeping, transfer pricing, and sourcing updates" (1991). Revenue Procedure 91-38 describes how to secure a Section 6038A record-keeping agreement with the District Director having audit jurisdiction over the taxpayer. Jurisdictionally, this is different than an advance pricing agreement, which is negotiated with the IRS. The purpose of a Section 6038A agreement is to clarify and to ease the burden of the record keeping required under Section 6038A for foreign-based groups with U.S. operations.

Revenue Procedure 91-38 and the regulations give the District Director broad authority to depart by negotiated agreement from the general record-keeping rules (which records, how maintained, where, how long, by whom), agent authorization, time periods for production and translation of documents, material profit-and-loss statements, and effective dates. The revenue procedure specifically contemplates the possibility of a Section 6038A agreement being obtained in conjunction with an advance pricing agreement on the anticipated range of arm's-length transfer prices under an appropriate transfer pricing methodology. If an advance pricing agreement is not desired, it may be possible to reach a Section 6038A agreement with the District Director on one or perhaps two relevant methodologies for purposes of record keeping.

The revenue procedure emphasizes that the District Director has discretion whether to enter into or to revoke a Section 6038A agreement, and is not obligated to vary the otherwise applicable Section 6038A rules. In determining whether to enter a Section 6038A agreement, the District Director is directed to consider the prior examination history of a taxpayer. Change of circumstances may warrant modification of a Section 6038A agreement. Withholding consent unreasonably to such a modification may justify the District Director's revoking a Section 6038A agreement prospectively, as would disregard of the agreement by the reporting corporation. A Section 6038A agreement would ordinarily not be retroactively revoked absent bad faith, material misstatement, or omission of fact. The revenue procedure contemplates that District Directors or Industry Specialization Programs may develop model agreements for particular industries that would provide the starting point for negotiation of particular Section 6038A agreements.

[M. Abrutyn, SA Musher & GW Rubloff, 2 J. Int'l Tax'n 162.]

"Reporting eased for foreign-owned corporations" (1991). Revenue Procedure 91-55 eases one of the more controversial requirements of the recently adopted

Section 6038A regulations. Specifically, under the procedure, foreign-owned corporations can satisfy their reporting obligations under Regulation § 1.6038A-2(b)(1)(ii) without identifying every indirect 25 percent–foreign shareholder. This article discusses the requirements of Section 6038A and the regulations thereunder, as well as the requirements of Revenue Procedure 91-55.

[75 J. Tax'n 327.]

"Reporting rules made tougher for multinationals" (1990). Although on its face Section 6038A, as amended by RRA 1989, deals only with information reporting and record keeping, the amendments can result in substantially different tax treatment for taxpayers that run afoul of its provisions than those that comply. To a large extent, the revision of Section 6038A is an outgrowth of IRS frustration in seeking transfer pricing and other Section 482 adjustments against U.S. corporations that are controlled by a foreign entity.

Section 6038A places a premium on good record retention by foreign parties related to a reporting U.S. corporation and on their being able to produce evidence quickly to support intercompany transactions. It is therefore essential for taxpayers to maintain memorandums regarding their transfer pricing policies, to support these policies with comparable or empirical data, and to continually monitor these policies with their advisors to ensure that they reflect contemporary facts and views.

Given the drastic consequences that can occur to a noncomplying corporation, the IRS must take special care in defining the types of records it expects taxpayers to maintain. If it wants product-specific or product-line data, it should specify this with detailed guidance and not leave generalized and ambiguous rules that are susceptible to controversy.

[MF Patton & MM Levey, 1 J. Int'l Tax'n 19.]

¶ 3.09 FOREIGN BANKS

"Foreign banks can be caught between banking and IRS rules" (1993). All U.S. branches and agencies of foreign banks must file detailed schedules of their assets and liabilities on a quarterly basis. The quarterly report (FFIEC-002) contains a variety of schedules. A new supplement to this report (FFIEC-002S), issued in 1992, may put some foreign banks into a difficult position with the IRS. This supplement will require reporting information on the assets and liabilities of any non-U.S. branch that is "managed or controlled" by a U.S. branch or agency of a foreign bank. The problem arises because this management or control may be read by the IRS to mean that the non-U.S. branch has income effectively connected with the U.S. branch or agency.

The author discusses, in detail, the considerations involved with this problem, particularly with regard to how this problem can arise under the U.S. tax laws. He also explores the interaction between the U.S. tax laws and banking rules. The author concludes that the new information requirements for non-U.S. branches that are managed or controlled by a U.S. branch or agency may require some foreign banks to provide information that will ultimately attract the attention of the IRS. Fortunately, both the banking and IRS rules contain exceptions, and foreign banks should determine if they fit within these exceptions. Unfortunately for practitioners, a number of crucial terms still remain vague. Nevertheless, planning will have to be done within reasonable interpretation of the rules.

[DE Spencer, 4 J. Int'l Tax'n 190.]

"New interest expense allocation rules pose practical difficulties for foreign banks" (1992). Proposed regulations modify the rules under Regulation § 1.882-5 for determining the allowable allocation of interest expense to a foreign corporation's U.S. ECI attributable to a U.S. trade or business or permanent establishment. The rules generally would be effective for tax years beginning after the publication of final regulations in the Federal Register.

The proposals conform the existing regulations to subsequent statutory enactments, primarily relating to the branch profits tax (BPT) and branch-level interest tax provisions, and to the U.S. tax treatment of foreign currency transactions. In addition, they seek to clarify issues raised under Regulation § 1.882-5, and take into account the appropriate economic treatment of international financial market product developments (such as notional principal contracts) that were not considered when the existing regulations were adopted in 1980. Although primarily directed to banking institutions, the proposed regulations would apply to all foreign corporations that have ECI or income treated as ECI under Sections 882(a) and 882(d).

The authors provide an overview of the differences between the new proposed regulations and the existing regulations. Thereafter, they examine the proposed regulations' three-step process for computing allowable interest expense. In explaining Step 1, the authors cover coordination with the BPT rules, the treatment of U.S. real estate and stock, and other matters set forth in the proposed regulations. The potential effect of treaties in this area is also considered. Thereafter, the authors address Step 2 concerning U.S. liabilities, as set forth in the proposed regulations. They examine Step 3, concerning the determination of allocable interest expense. Thereunder, they discuss the treatment of booked liabilities, partnership liabilities, computation of the allowable interest expense deduction, applicability of the scaling ratio, treatment of excess interest expense, and the election of daily computation of the three-step formula.

The authors conclude that foreign banks would face many practical implementation difficulties under the proposed regulations in their current form. To obtain the highest allowable interest expense deduction, many foreign banks would be required to increase the frequency of their worldwide financial reporting and establish worldwide accounting records adjusted under U.S. tax principles that are not otherwise required or maintained in the ordinary course of business. Although the proposed regulations seek to apply a general principle of fungibility, arbitrary ceilings on the imputation of liabilities also depart from principles contemplated in the branch tax legislative history.

If the proposed regulations were to adhere more broadly to principles of parity and consistency under the Tax Reform Act of 1986 (TRA 1986) for the generation and deemed remittance of effectively connected earnings and profits under the BPT provisions, the rules could be simplified and a more efficient administration of IRS examinations might be facilitated. Placing a U.S. trade or business on a more equal footing with a U.S.subsidiary would remove much of the discrimination that currently remains and likely would induce more uniform application of the rules by all foreign taxpayers. Absent a more remedial approach, many treaty-based foreign taxpayers will have no choice but to invoke the full protection of their respective treaties, which may result in protracted competent authority proceedings or potential U.S. litigation. Finally, even non-treaty-based foreign taxpayers may have legitimate claims on statutory grounds that the IRS's failure to adhere to parity and consistency is beyond the scope of the regulatory authority for implementing revised interest expense allocation rules.

[PJ Connors, BE Blanco & PS Epstein, 77 J. Tax'n 368.]

BIBLIOGRAPHY OF RESEARCH REFERENCES

[1]J. Kuntz & R. Peroni, U.S. International Taxation ch. C1 (Warren Gorham Lamont 1992).

S. Singer, U.S. International Tax Forms Manual chs. 10–13 (Warren Gorham Lamont 1993).

[2]J. Kuntz & R. Peroni, U.S. International Taxation ¶ C1.03 (Warren Gorham Lamont 1992).

S. Singer, U.S. International Tax Forms Manual ch. 10 (Warren Gorham Lamont 1993).

B. Bittker & J. Eustice, Federal Income Taxation of Corporations and Shareholders ¶ 15.03 (Warren Gorham Lamont, 6th ed. 1994).

[3]J. Kuntz & R. Peroni, U.S. International Taxation ¶ C1.04 (Warren Gorham Lamont 1992).

S. Singer, U.S. International Tax Forms Manual ch. 11 (Warren Gorham Lamont 1993).

B. Bittker & J. Eustice, Federal Income Taxation of Corporations and Shareholders ¶¶ 15.02[2], 15.02[3] (Warren Gorham Lamont, 6th ed. 1994).

[4]J. Kuntz & R. Peroni, U.S. International Taxation ¶ C1.05 (Warren Gorham Lamont 1992).

S. Singer, U.S. International Tax Forms Manual ¶ 11.09 (Warren Gorham Lamont 1993).

B. Bittker & J. Eustice, Federal Income Taxation of Corporations and Shareholders ¶ 15.04[2] (Warren Gorham Lamont, 6th ed. 1994).

[5]J. Kuntz & R. Peroni, U.S. International Taxation ¶ C1.06 (Warren Gorham Lamont 1992).

S. Singer, U.S. International Tax Forms Manual ¶ 10.04[2] (Warren Gorham Lamont 1993).

B. Bittker & J. Eustice, Federal Income Taxation of Corporations and Shareholders ¶ 15.85 (Warren Gorham Lamont, 6th ed. 1994).

[6]J. Kuntz & R. Peroni, U.S. International Taxation ¶ C1.07 (Warren Gorham Lamont 1992).

[7]J. Kuntz & R. Peroni, U.S. International Taxation ch. C2 (Warren Gorham Lamont 1992).

S. Singer, U.S. International Tax Forms Manual ¶¶ 10.03, 13.04 (Warren Gorham Lamont 1993).

[8]J. Kuntz & R. Peroni, U.S. International Taxation ch. C3 (Warren Gorham Lamont 1992).

S. Singer, U.S. International Tax Forms Manual ch. 12 (Warren Gorham Lamont 1993).

CHAPTER 4

U.S. Possessions

¶ 4.01 POSSESSIONS TAX CREDITS (SECTION 936)[1]

Taxpayers may change methods in connection with possessions tax credit. A taxpayer who elected the cost-sharing method under Section 936(h)(5)(C)(i) for tax years beginning before 1987 may change to another acceptable method on an amended return for the possessions corporation's first tax year beginning after 1986. The amended return must be filed by the due date (including extensions) for the corporation's return for its fifth tax year beginning after 1986. For cost-sharing elections made for tax years beginning after 1986, the amended return must be filed by the due date (including extensions) for the corporation's return for its last tax year beginning before 1992. In addition, the taxpayer must agree to an extension of the statute of limitations.

[Notices 87-27, 1987-1 CB 471, 88-97, 1988-2 CB 421, and 89-82, 1989-2 CB 402, are modified, as are Rev. Procs. 89-61, 1989-2 CB 782 and 90-50, 1990-2 CB 624. Rev. Proc. 91-53, 1991-2 CB 782.]

IRS issues final regulations concerning requirements for investments to qualify as investments in qualified Caribbean Basin countries. The IRS has issued final regulations relating to the requirements that must be met for an investment to qualify under Section 936(d)(4) as an investment in qualified Caribbean Basin countries. Subject to such conditions as are prescribed by regulation, funds of possessions corporations that are invested by financial institutions in active business assets or development projects in a qualified Caribbean Basin country are to be treated as used in Puerto Rico for purposes of Section 936(d)(2). The regulations prescribe the conditions for such an investment to qualify as for use in Puerto Rico under Section 936(d)(4).

[TD 8350, 1991-1 CB 135; Reg. § 1.936-10(c).]

"New rules affect taxable income, research and development (R&D) of possessions corporations" (1993). Two revenue procedures issued in 1992 modify the rules for Section 936(h) possessions corporations. Revenue Procedure 92-68 provides guidance for taxpayers seeking to change from the cost-sharing method of computing taxable income. Revenue Procedure 92-69 addresses the allocation and apportionment of R&D expenses.

[78 J. Tax'n 44.]

"Possessions corporations face two new limitations" (1993). The Revenue Reconciliation Act of 1993 (RRA 1993) imposes two alternative limitations on the credit allowed under Section 936. The new limitations add an additional layer of complexity in the statute. The requirements of pre-RRA 1993 Section 936 remain in place and the calculations required to compute the taxable income of the possessions corporation remain the same.

The authors first discuss Section 936 and its requirements for election of the possessions credit. Next, they discuss the two limitations placed on the credit by RRA 1993: the economic-activity limitation and the percentage-income limitation. They then consider which limitation a taxpayer must use, as well as the application and computations required under each limitation. Key terms and phrases used in the statutory language for these limitations are explored.

The authors conclude that the two alternative limitations on the Section 936 credit will result in substantially reduced benefits for many taxpayers. The choice of limitations will be an arithmetic exercise with the result dictated by the particular taxpayer's circumstances. All the complex rules relating to the computation of the Section 936 credit under cost-sharing, profit-split, or Dole methods still apply and must be observed. The new limitations in no way simplify the operation of Section 936 and, in fact, add an additional layer of complexity. The benefits are still substantial, however, and compliance with these new limitations in addition to all of the old rules will be very rewarding for many taxpayers.

[MT Adams & JA Riedy, 4 J. Int'l Tax'n 445.]

"Accounting changes issued for possessions corporations" (1992). The IRS is allowing, under Revenue Procedure 92-68, possessions corporations that have elected the cost-sharing method additional time to change to the profit-split method or other acceptable method under Section 936(h). Also, in Revenue Procedure 92-69, the IRS provides specific guidance on treatment of R&D expenditures for corporations with income from U.S. possessions.

[3 J. Int'l Tax'n 255.]

"Final regulations liberalize Caribbean Basin financing" (1992). Section 936 of the Code permits U.S. corporations with manufacturing facilities in Puerto Rico (Section 936 corporations) to avoid U.S. tax on their income. The Puerto Rico

Industrial Incentives and Tax Acts provide similar corporate tax exemptions. As a result, billions of dollars in Section 936 funds have been accumulated.

Section 936, and similar provisions of the Puerto Rico tax laws, exempt from corporate tax not only the direct sales income of the Section 936 corporations, but also the interest income they earn on deposits of Section 936 funds in Puerto Rico financial institutions. For the interest earned on deposits to qualify for corporate tax exemption, however, Section 936 and the Puerto Rico tax rules require that the Puerto Rico financial institution lend the Section 936 funds for certain qualifying uses in Puerto Rico and the Caribbean Basin.

Section 243(b)(1)(B)(ii) permits the U.S. parent corporation, if it is not in a corporate alternative minimum tax position, to completely avoid U.S. corporate tax on its receipt of dividends from its Section 936 corporation subsidiary. The Puerto Rico Industrial Incentives and Tax Acts likewise generally permit a U.S. parent to almost entirely avoid Puerto Rico dividend withholding tax on its receipt of dividends from a Section 936 subsidiary, provided the distributed funds have been placed in the Section 936 funds market by the Section 936 corporation for a certain number of years prior to the dividend. Thus, there is both a Section 936 corporation and U.S. parent corporate tax exemption offered, by both the United States and Puerto Rico, on the interest yields on the Section 936 funds. This corporate tax exemption, and the large supply of Section 936 funds relative to the demand for new qualifying loans in Puerto Rico and the Caribbean by creditworthy borrowers, have caused interest rates on deposits and loans of Section 936 funds to be approximately one-fifth lower than Eurodollar yields of comparable maturities. Because of the interest expense savings, businesses that can profitably invest large amounts of borrowed funds in Puerto Rico and the Caribbean have closely followed the U.S. and Puerto Rico tax regulations to qualify their projects for Section 936 funding. Section 936(d)(2) and the regulations thereunder contain the federal tax rules governing the permissible uses in Puerto Rico of funds loaned by Section 936 corporations, directly or through deposits in Puerto Rico financial institutions that then make the loans. Temporary and proposed regulations governing Section 936(d)(2) were issued several years ago, and final regulations governing Section 936(d)(2) are expected in 1992.

Section 936(d)(4) governs the permissible uses, outside Puerto Rico but within the Caribbean Basin, of Section 936 funds. On May 13, 1991, Regulation § 1.936-10(c) (Treasury Decision 8350), interpreting Section 936(d)(4), was adopted.

Section 936(d)(4) requires that, to be tax-exempt, the interest income of a Section 936 corporation must be received from a qualified "financial institution," and *not* directly from the ultimate borrower. Temporary Regulation § 1.936-10T(c)(3) generally limited a qualified financial institution to a Puerto Rico corporation, or a Puerto Rico branch of a U.S. corporation or other non–Puerto Rico corporation, that engaged in an active banking, financing, or similar business with the general public.

The government of Puerto Rico formed the Caribbean Basin Projects Region Financing Authority in 1990, presumably to provide access to the Section 936 funds bond issue market by Caribbean Basin borrowers, to reduce administrative costs, and to eliminate duplicative credit enhancement costs.

The final regulations, like the temporary regulations, permit newly constructed building and new equipment used in an active business in a qualified Caribbean Basin country to qualify for Section 936(d)(4) financing. Inventory or other working capital can also be financed by the Section 936(d)(4) funds, but generally only in an amount equal to 10 percent of the investment in fixed assets to be financed by Section 936(d)(4) funds. The final regulations expand the working capital allowance to 50 percent of fixed assets if the operation is "manufacturing" under Regulation § 1.954-3(a)(4), provided the excess over the 10 percent is used to finance inventory.

Jets and ships are particularly attractive candidates for Section 936(d)(4) financing, because they typically involve large absolute and percentage amounts of debt financing.

In order for projects located in a Caribbean Basin country to qualify for Section 936(d)(4) financing, the country must be a beneficiary of the Caribbean Basin Initiative Customs duty program, and must execute a tax information exchange agreement with the United States.

Since February 1990, Costa Rica, Honduras, St. Lucia, and Trinidad and Tobago have executed tax information exchange agreements with the United States. These countries join Barbados, Dominica, the Dominican Republic, Grenada, and Jamaica as Caribbean Basin Initiative beneficiary countries in which projects qualify for Section 936(d)(4) loans.

The most logical candidates for Section 936(d)(4) financing include strong-credit multinationals with capital intensive operations in the Caribbean Basin. Credit is a crucial consideration because Section 936(d)(4) does not grant any Caribbean Basin borrower the right to obtain a loan from a Puerto Rico financial institution or provide for any credit enhancement.

The huge pool of funds available at below Eurodollar rates makes Section 936 funds an attractive source for financing captial intensive projects. The increasing number of countries eligible for such financing and the liberalized final regulations should make Section 936 funds a popular source of financing for companies with major operations in the Caribbean Basin.

[AS Lederman, 2 J. Int'l Tax'n 350.]

"Obtaining tax-advantaged financing for investments in the Caribbean Basin" **(1990).** U.S. manufacturing subsidiaries that operate in Puerto Rico (Section 936 corporations) have accumulated approximately $10 billion in excess cash, in part because of the generous intercompany pricing policies, U.S. corporate tax exemption under Section 936, and Puerto Rican tax exemptions. Section 936(d)(4) makes this excess cash available to provide below-market-rate financing for qualifying projects in the Caribbean Basin. Temporary Regulation § 1.936-10T(c), prescribing the circumstances under which such financing will be available, was adopted by Treasury Decision 8268 on September 21, 1989.

Under Section 936(d)(4) and the newly adopted temporary regulation, qualifying Puerto Rican financial institutions can act as intermediaries by borrowing low-cost funds from Section 936 corporations and then lending the funds at a low interest rate to businesses located in qualified countries in the Caribbean Basin. The interest received by the Section 936 corporations from these financial institutions is qualified possessions-source income that is not subject to U.S. corporate tax. The Section 936 corporations are thus able to accept lower yields, and the Puerto Rican financial institutions can pass on these savings to their Caribbean Basin borrowers in the form of low interest rates.

This article discusses the following aspects of Section 936(d)(4) financing: (1) qualification for financing; (2) the assets and projects that may be financed; (3) the Puerto Rican regulations governing this financing; and (4) restrictions on Puerto Rican and other financial institutions eligible to obtain this financing.

At present, only Caribbean Basin businesses located in Barbados, Dominica, the Dominican Republic, Grenada, Jamaica, and the U.S. Virgin Islands can obtain Section 936(d)(4) loans. Other Basin countries will be added to this list when they enter into tax information sharing agreements with the United States and are declared eligible by the president of the United States. Section 936(d)(4) financing is available to any "person," as defined in Section 7701(a)(1), as well as to a local government. Section 936(d)(4) loans may be guaranteed, without risk of disqualification of the borrower, in the event the borrower has weak credit.

Under Temporary Regulation § 1.936-10T(c)(4), Section 936(d)(4) loans may be used to finance capital expenditures incurred in establishing or conducting an active business in a Caribbean Basin country. In addition, Section 936(d)(4) financing can be used in conjunction with other provisions of the Caribbean Basin Initiative, such as those allowing duty-free importation of products into the United States. Section 936(d)(4) loans may not be used to finance inventory, since the regulation under such section specifically makes Section 1221 dealer personal property ineligible. It is nevertheless possible to use a portion of the Section 936(d)(4) loan to finance inventory under the 10 percent working capital allowance exception.

Under the temporary regulation, financing is intended to promote new investment rather than recycle existing investment. For example, with respect to existing buildings, financing is available for rehabilitation or improvement, but not for the existing building or the land on which it is situated. Similarly, property purchased in a sale-and-leaseback arrangement is not eligible for financing and an existing non–Section 936(d)(4) loan cannot be refinanced by a Section 936(d)(4) loan. Special rules are provided for the refinancing of existing Section 936(d)(4) loans with new Section 936(d)(4) loans. Finally, because of the problem of financing existing assets, Section 936(d)(4) loans cannot be used to finance the leveraged buyout of an existing qualifying business.

In addition to active business ventures, the temporary regulation permits financing for development projects, i.e., ventures that support economic development in an area and are available to the general public (e.g., public utilities or low-income housing). Development projects are entitled to somewhat greater amounts of financing under Section 936(d)(4) than active businesses.

Under the temporary regulation, new real estate (residential or commercial) qualifies for Section 936(d)(4) financing. However, the new real estate must be actively managed by the owner (or its employees) rather than by unrelated independent contractors. Accordingly, a net leased commercial building is not an active business, and will not qualify for Section 936(d)(4) financing. Since the disqualification for inventory and other Section 1221 dealer property extends only to personal property, it appears that Section 936(d)(4) financing is available for real estate developed for sale by the owner. However, because of Puerto Rican regulations, the availability of such financing for buildings other than factories and hotels is uncertain.

Finally, in the area of eligible assets, the temporary regulation sets forth special rules for the financing of jets and ships under Section 936(d)(4). This article gives attention to the financing of jets and ships because they are particularly attractive candidates for Section 936(d)(4) financing.

The temporary regulation provides that a Section 936(d)(4) loan must receive the prior approval of the Commissioner of Financial Institutions of Puerto Rico, pursuant to Puerto Rican regulations. Accordingly, Section 936(d)(4) financing is limited by the stricter of the Section 936 regulations or the Puerto Rican regulations governing the assets or project to be financed. At present, the Puerto Rican regulations appear to be stricter than U.S. regulations as to the types of businesses or activities that can be financed. This problem is discussed in-depth in this article.

This article discusses the problems of banks using Section 936(d)(4) to finance other loans, the manner in which back-to-back funding can be obtained using Section 936(d)(4) loans, and the means by which the eligibility of the ultimate borrower may be ensured. Finally, the article discusses the problems confronted in proving interest received by the Section 936 corporation qualifies for the U.S. corporate tax exemption.

[AS Lederman, 72 J. Tax'n 104.]

¶ 4.02 VIRGIN ISLANDS²

Virgin Islands surtax of 10 percent of the federal income tax payable to the Virgin Islands was not tax deductible under Section 164. In 1986, 1987, and 1988, taxpayer paid a 10 percent corporate surtax on income imposed by the Virgin Islands and deducted this tax in determining its taxable income for these years. The Virgin Islands determined deficiencies against taxpayer for the years in question on the ground that the surtax was not deductible, as claimed by taxpayer, under Section 164 (applicable in the Virgin Islands under the "mirror system" of taxation). The district court held for taxpayer upon determining that the surtax was deductible under Section 164.

Held: Reversed for the Virgin Islands Bureau of Internal Revenue. Section 164, which permits a deduction of state and local taxes, applies in the Virgin Islands under the "mirror system" of taxation. In determining the deductibility of the surtax, the critical issue is whether this tax is a "state or local" tax or is in the nature of a federal income tax. The Virgin Islands is permitted by Congress to impose both types of taxes. In this case, the 10 percent surtax was imposed by the Virgin Islands pursuant to congressional permission allowing such a surtax of up to 10 percent on federal income taxes payable to the Treasury of the Virgin Islands. While this grant of authority was enacted in 1975, Congress, in 1986, also permitted the Virgin Islands to impose local income taxes without regard to the 10 percent limitation. Taxpayer argued that the surtax is deductible under the "equality principle," i.e., without the deduction the tax payable to the Virgin Islands would be greater than the amount of income tax that would be payable to the U.S. Treasury if the taxpayer were residing in the continental United States. However, unlike state or local taxes imposed in the continental United States, the surtax here is paid to the same treasury as the income tax on which it is based. Since both taxes are paid to the same treasury, the equality principle is inapplicable and the surtax is not deductible under Section 164 even if it is in the nature of a Section 164 tax.

[Abramson Enters., Inc. v. Government of VI, 71 AFTR2d 93-2054, 93-1 USTC ¶ 50,321 (3d Cir. 1993).]

IRS lists obsolete revenue rulings concerning Virgin Islands. In this revenue ruling the IRS declares that the following revenue rulings, which deal with taxation in the Virgin Islands, are obsolete: Revenue Ruling 60-291, 1960-2 CB 291; Revenue Ruling 73-315, 1973-2 CB 225; and Revenue Ruling 80-318, 1980-2 CB 247. In addition, the portion of Revenue Ruling 85-200, 1985-2 CB 307, that applies to citizens of the Virgin Islands is obsolete; the remainder of that revenue ruling remains in effect. These rulings are not determinative with respect to events occurring after November 23, 1992. They apply to events before this date during any period in which the particular statutes on which they are based were in effect.

[Rev. Rul. 92-103, 1992-2 CB 323.]

IRS declares that revenue procedure concerning Virgin Islands is obsolete. In this revenue procedure the IRS declares that Revenue Procedure 81-20, 1981-1 CB 690, is obsolete. Revenue Procedure 81-20 sets forth a procedure to eliminate withholding on payments to Virgin Island residents who were exempt from U.S. tax under the "inhabitant rule," repealed in 1986. Revenue Procedure 81-20 applies to U.S. citizens who are permanent inhabitants of the Virgin Islands. It provides a procedure for them to notify U.S. payors of income not to withhold pursuant to Section 1441. The Tax Reform Act of 1986 repealed the inhabitant rule and added Section 932(a)(3), which states that the term "United States" shall include the Virgin Islands. U.S. citizens whose permanent residence is in the Virgin Islands must now pay their income taxes to the U.S. Treasury and are not subject to Section 1441.

[Rev. Proc. 92-96, 1992-2 CB 510.]

U.S.–Virgin Islands realty swap is proper under Section 1031. Prior to the Revenue Reconciliation Act of 1989, it made no difference where real property that was the subject of a Section 1031 exchange was located. It was, for example, possible to swap U.S. realty for realty located in a foreign country and obtain Section 1031 nonrecognition (see Rev. Rul. 68-363, 1968-2 CB 336). The 1989 legislation changed the law with the enactment of Section 1031(h), which provides that U.S. real property and real property located outside the United States are not like-kind property. In view of the specific definition of "United States" in Section 7701(a)(9)—the states and the District of Columbia—the question arises regarding the extent to which U.S. realty can be exchanged tax free for property in a U.S. possession. As this letter ruling indicates, the only remaining opportunity outside the United States is an exchange for Virgin Islands real property.

[Priv. Ltr. Rul. 9038030.]

BIBLIOGRAPHY OF RESEARCH REFERENCES

[1]J. Kuntz & R. Peroni, U.S. International Taxation ¶ B1.06, Chapter D1 (Warren Gorham Lamont 1992).

S. Singer, U.S. International Tax Forms Manual ch. 8 (Warren Gorham Lamont 1993).

B. Bittker & J. Eustice, Federal Income Taxation of Corporations and Shareholders ¶ 15.22 (Warren Gorham Lamont, 6th ed. 1994).

[2]J. Kuntz & R. Peroni, U.S. International Taxation ¶¶ D1.04–D1.07 (Warren Gorham Lamont 1992).

CHAPTER **5**

International Estate and Gift Taxation

¶ 5.01 ESTATE AND GIFT TAXATION OF NONRESIDENT ALIENS, GENERALLY[1]

U.S.-France tax treaty does not permit nonresident alien to claim the greater U.S. unified estate tax credit available to U.S. residents. The decedent was a nonresident alien domiciled in France at the time of his death. His estate filed a U.S. estate tax return because the decedent owned real property in the United States. On this return, the estate claimed the marital deduction and the larger unified credit available to U.S. citizens and residents. The IRS challenged the estate's use of the larger credit and the Tax Court agreed with the IRS, holding that the estate was only entitled to claim the unified credit applicable to nonresident aliens and that the U.S.-France tax treaty did not require otherwise. The estate appealed.

Held: Affirmed for the IRS. Article 11(2) of the U.S.-France tax treaty specifically requires that a French domiciliary be allowed the same marital deduction as if domiciled in the United States. It does not make the same express grant with regard to the unified credit. It merely states that the applicable tax rates shall be the same as those that would be applicable if the decedent were domiciled in the United States. Taxpayer argued that upon electing the marital deduction under this treaty provision it became subject to the higher U.S. estate tax rates imposed on U.S. citizens and residents and therefore should be allowed the same unified credit as a U.S. citizen or resident. This, however, is not supported by the treaty provision. The only relevant effect of the provision is to permit the estate of a nonresident alien to claim the marital deduction as if it were a domestic estate, at the cost of being subject to higher estate tax rates. The treaty does not, explicitly or implicitly, provide the estate of a French nonresident with the option of having its tax computed as if it were the estate of a U.S. citizen or resident.

[Estate of Arnaud, 895 F2d 624, 65 AFTR2d 90-1196, 90-1 USTC ¶ 60,006 (9th Cir. 1990).]

Nonresident aliens allowed portion of unified credit. In Rev. Rul. 81-303, 1981-2 CB 255, the IRS ruled that the term "specific exemption" referred to in the U.S.-Switzerland Estate and Inheritance Tax Convention did not include the Section 2010 unified credit. Thus, a Swiss resident was entitled to only the smaller exemption allowed under Section 2102(c)(1). The IRS has ruled that as a result of the 1988 amendments to Section 2102(c) (effective for decedents dying after November 10, 1988), a credit is allowed in an amount that bears the same ratio to $192,800 as the value of the gross estate situated in the United States at the time of death bears to the value of the entire gross estate. This ruling applies to any treaty with language similar to the U.S.-Swiss Convention, e.g., those with Australia, Finland, Greece, Italy, Japan, and Norway.

[Rev. Rul. 90-101, 1990-2 CB 315.]

No deduction for charitable bequest by nonresident alien. The will of a nonresident alien decedent permitted the executor to designate both domestic and foreign charitable beneficiaries. Within nine months after the decedent's death, the executor made a distribution to a domestic charity. The estate tax return claimed a charitable deduction of $1,450,000. The assets included in the domestic estate were $2.7 million. The IRS held that the decedent did not qualify as having made a bequest to a domestic charitable beneficiary for purposes of Section 2106(a)(2).

The IRS cited Mississippi Valley Trust Co., 72 F2d 197 (8th Cir. 1934), which held there was no enforceable intent on the part of the decedent to make a charitable donation where the decedent's sons could choose whether or not to do so. At the date of death, it was uncertain whether any charitable contribution would ever be made.

The IRS also held that the executor, while terminating his power to choose a foreign charity by transferring assets to a domestic charity, was not in a position to make disclaimers on behalf of all of the potential foreign charities. He also was not able to disclaim his fiduciary power to choose foreign charities. Rev. Rul. 90-110, 1990-2 CB 209, holds that a trustee acting solely in a fiduciary capacity cannot disclaim a power to invade corpus for the benefit of a specific beneficiary where neither local law nor the governing instrument authorizes the trustee to make a unilateral disclaimer of a fiduciary power.

[TAM 9135003.]

"Factors affecting the estate and gift taxation of a nonresident alien decedent/ transferor" (1992). A number of U.S. tax considerations come into play upon the death of a nonresident alien who has significant holdings in the United States. Similarly, many of these same considerations arise when a nonresident alien makes a gift of a U.S. holding. In this article, the authors examine these considerations through the use of an extended hypothetical situation. The fact pattern used by the authors involves a nonresident alien holding various items of property.

The authors first discuss the alien status of the hypothetical client and the application of the situs rules with respect to each of the items of property owned by the client. These items include real and personal property located in the United States, stock in U.S. companies, insurance with U.S. companies, notes from U.S. debtors, cash in a U.S. safety deposit box, Treasury bills, and executory contract rights, as well as many other property items that raise issues as to the U.S. taxability of their transfer.

Next, the authors prepare the estate tax return covering this property. In doing so, they consider the various deductions and credits allowed to nonresident aliens, including the marital deduction and the unified credit. The consequences of hypothetical lifetime gifts are also explored.

In conclusion, the authors briefly note the ways in which a tax treaty might affect the considerations discussed in this article.

[M. Rosenberg & D. Ginsburg, US Tax'n Int'l Operations ¶ 15,502.]

"Introducing U.S. estate and gift taxation of nonresident aliens" (1992). The estate of a nonresident alien is generally subject to U.S. estate tax on any U.S. property includable in the gross estate. Resident status is determined by the situs of the nonresident alien's domicile. If a decedent is a nonresident alien, a special U.S. estate tax rate and method for figuring estate tax is applicable. This article is a general overview of the taxation of estates of nonresident aliens.

The authors first examine the meaning of "domicile," including that of an expatriate who gave up U.S. citizenship. Thereafter, they discuss the determination of a nonresident alien's gross estate. In doing so, they specifically consider what constitutes U.S. property includable in the nonresident alien's U.S. gross estate. Special cases are explored (e.g., partnership interests, stock in U.S. corporations, revocable trust interests, community property, notes of U.S. debtors, joint property, foreign corporation stock held by expatriates, etc.). Next, the authors explain the computation of the nonresident alien's estate tax. In doing so, they specifically review available deductions and usage of the unified credit.

The potential effects of various tax treaties on the determination of a nonresident alien's U.S. estate tax liability are discussed. A list of those countries whose treaties with the United States are likely to have impact are enumerated. Last, the authors compare the gift tax treatment of gift transfers by U.S. citizens (or residents) and nonresident aliens. A sample Form 706NA, completed based on hypothetical facts, has also been included by the authors.

[EH Desany & S. Auderieth, US Tax'n Int'l Operations ¶ 15,501.]

"U.S. transfer taxes on estates of nonresident aliens: Part I" (1990). Changes made in the Technical and Miscellaneous Revenue Act of 1988 (TAMRA) significantly increased the tax imposed on estate, gift, and generation-skipping transfers of nonresident aliens. Where the nonresident alien used to be subject to a much lower tax rate than that of citizen or resident, now the applicable rates are the same for both groups. This change was made to treat nonresident aliens more like citizens and residents.

Another estate tax change under TAMRA involves the marital deduction. A marital deduction is now permitted where the surviving spouse is a U.S. citizen. However, the marital deduction is still disallowed for property passing from a U.S. citizen or resident to an alien surviving spouse. The rules determining the tax imposed on nonresident aliens are similar to those applying to citizens and residents, except for two differences. First, only property situated or deemed situated in the United States is subject to U.S. transfer tax. Second, the credits allowed against the tax are lower in most cases.

Section 2101(a) imposes the estate transfer tax on "every decedent nonresident not a citizen of the United States." It does not use the term "nonresident alien." For the purposes of the estate tax, such a decedent is an alien "who, at the time of his death, has his domicile outside the United States." A person acquires a domicile in a place by living there, for even a brief time, with no definite present intention of leaving and establishing a domicile elsewhere. Residence without the requisite intent to remain indefinitely does not constitute domicile, nor does an intent to change effect a change in domicile unless accompanied by actual removal. In determining the domicile of a deceased person, the courts have considered the location of the decedent's business interest, the location and relative sizes of the decedent's homes and the nature of their respective locales, and statements made by the decedent to immigration officials during the decedent's lifetime.

"Residency" is defined very differently for estate tax purposes than for income tax purposes. An alien becomes a resident of the United States for estate tax purposes only if he establishes residence in the United States with the intent to remain permanently, that is, if he establishes a domicile in the United States.

The gross estate of aliens includes only property situated in the United States at the time of death. The value of a nonresident alien decedent's gross estate includes (1) property beneficially owned by the decedent at the time of death; (2) property transferred in contemplation of death; (3) property in which the decedent retained a life interest or power of appointment; and (4) property held jointly with others, for which the decedent provided consideration. To determine beneficial ownership of a nonresident alien decedent, it is sometimes necessary to analyze foreign laws.

Another issue that may arise is whether a married decedent who is a national and resident of a community property country owns all of an interest in U.S. situs property or only half of it. In general, community property laws provide that the property acquired by a couple after marriage becomes community property. A deceased resident in a noncommunity property country who owned jointly held property in the United States is treated differently from other nonresident alien decedents. Such property is fully includable in the decedent's gross estate unless it can be proven that the co-owner contributed a part of the consideration with which the property was acquired. Consequently, the resident of a community property country enjoys a distinct tax advantage over a resident of a noncommunity property country.

Where property owned by the nonresident alien is situated is governed primarily by the Code and regulations, but sometimes foreign laws and tax treaties may determine the issue. The general rules are

1. Real property located in the United States is includable in the gross estate of a nonresident alien. Generally, mortgages and liens on real property are not real property. However, in *Perigny*, a 1947 Tax Court case, the transfer of ninety-nine year leases, exchangeable at the lessee's option for 999-year leases, of property in Kenya Colony is essentially a transfer of real property. In determining the decedent's includable gross estate, the value of real property is ordinarily not reduced by the amount of any liens of mortgages on it. These are deductible from the gross estate only to the extent of the ratio of the nonresident alien decedent's includable U.S. situs property to his total worldwide property. A nonrecourse debt is an exception to this general rule.

2. The situs for tangible personal property is determined by its physical location at the time of death. Exceptions to this are works of art on public loan to a U.S. gallery or museum, and personal property accompanying an individual who happens to be in the United States temporarily. The concept of situs involves some degree of permanence analogous to the notion of domicile.

3. The situs of intangible property generally is determined by the domicile of the property's issuer or entity against which the decedent's claim would be enforced. Debt obligations, regardless of form, of a U.S. person or governmental unit have a situs in the United States. Several exceptions specifically deemed to have non-U.S. situs are deposits with domestic banks, amounts held by an insurance company under agreement to pay interest, deposits in a foreign branch of a U.S. bank, and debt obligations of any domestic corporation that derives less than 20 percent of its gross income from the United States during the three years prior to the nonresident alien's death.

[D. Ryan & C. Strobel, 1 J. Int'l Tax'n 35.]

"U.S. transfer taxes on estates of nonresident aliens: Part II" (1990). The Code imposes a transfer tax on the estate of every decedent nonresident not a citizen of the United States. This tax is imposed only on property interests that have a situs in the United States. Determination of the situs or beneficial ownership of property is often difficult because foreign decedents may have a variety of property interests connected with other countries that require an understanding and analysis of foreign laws and customs.

In addition, there are a number of differences in the manner in which the tax is imposed on the estates of foreign decedents as compared to those of citizens and residents. These differences include a much smaller tax credit (the U.S. estate of a nonresident alien decedent generally is entitled only to a $13,000 general credit) and a marital deduction only in cases where the surviving spouse is a U.S. citizen. Because of these differences and TAMRA, the effective tax rate on nonresidents is generally higher than on residents.

[D. Ryan & C. Strobel, 1 J. Int'l Tax'n 87.]

¶ 5.02 MARITAL DEDUCTION WHERE SURVIVING SPOUSE IS NOT U.S. CITIZEN[2]

IRS issues proposed regulations concerning restrictions on allowance of marital deduction if surviving spouse is not U.S. citizen. In response to changes to the marital deduction provisions of the estate and gift tax chapters of the Code made by TAMRA, the Revenue Reconciliation Act of 1989 (RRA 1989), and the Revenue Reconciliation Act of 1990 (RRA 1990), the IRS has issued proposed regulations concerning restrictions on allowance of the marital deduction if the surviving spouse is not a U.S. citizen.

Prior to the enactment of TAMRA, Section 2056 of the Code provided an unlimited estate tax marital deduction for estates of U.S. citizens or residents regardless of the citizenship of the surviving spouse. Similarly, under Section 2523, the gift tax marital deduction was allowable for transfers by a U.S. citizen or resident to a spouse, regardless of the citizenship of the spouse. TAMRA placed restrictions on the availability of the estate tax marital deduction if the surviving spouse is not a U.S. citizen and eliminated the gift tax marital deduction if the donee spouse is not a U.S. citizen. These new rules are generally effective with respect to estates of decedents dying after November 10, 1988, and for gifts made on or after July 14, 1988. However, RRA 1989 (as amended by RRA 1990) limited the application of these rules in the case of certain estate and gift tax transfers otherwise covered by certain tax treaties.

With respect to the estate tax, in the case of decedents dying after November 10, 1988, the marital deduction is allowable for property passing to a noncitizen spouse only if the property passes (or is deemed to have passed) in a "qualified domestic trust" (QDOT). An exception to this rule is provided if the surviving spouse becomes a citizen of the United States before the estate tax return is filed and the spouse was a resident of the United States (as defined for estate tax and not for income tax purposes) at all times after the date of the decedent's death and before becoming a U.S. citizen. Further, with certain exceptions, a deferred estate tax under Section 2056A(b) is imposed on distributions of corpus from the QDOT during the spouse's lifetime and on the balance of the corpus held in the trust at the spouse's death.

[PS-102-88, 1993-4 IRB 48, Prop. Reg. §§ 20.2056A-0–20.2056A-13.]

"Marital deduction planning for noncitizen spouses" (1993). In general, if a surviving spouse is not a U.S. citizen at the time of the decedent's death, the estate cannot claim the marital deduction unless either (1) the property passes to or is treated as passing to the noncitizen spouse in a QDOT or (2) the noncitizen spouse (a) becomes a U.S. citizen before the date on which the decedent's federal estate tax return is made and (b) was a U.S. resident at all times after the date of the decedent's death and before becoming a U.S. citizen.

The authors of this article first discuss the improbability of a noncitizen spouse meeting the requirements of exception (2) if the U.S. naturalization process did not begin before the decedent's death. Thereafter, their discussion focuses solely on exception (1). They begin by examining the requirements for a QDOT. Next, they discuss the transfer of property to a QDOT. In doing so, certain unanswered questions are explored. The IRS's analysis in Letter Rulings 9032014 and 9109021 are also discussed. Taxation of a QDOT is then addressed along with certain other issues in this area. Last, they discuss the tax consequences of the death of the noncitizen spouse under the Code and a treaty (if applicable). The authors conclude with postmortem planning suggestions on using a QDOT and the reformation of testamentary trusts to satisfy QDOT requirements.

[RM Fijolek & JM Miller, 20 Est. Plan. 20.]

"Proposed regulations clarify QDOTs but add new requirements" (1993). In 1992, the IRS issued proposed regulations regarding the estate and gift tax marital deduction for transfers to a noncitizen spouse. In general, under these rules, property inherited or passed from a decedent's estate to a noncitizen spouse qualifies for the marital deduction only if (1) the property passes to, or is treated as passing to, the noncitizen spouse in a QDOT or (2) the noncitizen spouse (a) becomes a U.S. citizen before the date on which the decedent's federal estate tax return is filed and (b) was a U.S. resident at all times after the decedent's death and before becoming a U.S. citizen. As can be seen, the QDOT exception will become the most useful in obtaining the marital deduction. Although the proposed regulations clarify the statutory requirements for treatment as a QDOT, they also impose certain additional conditions for such treatment.

The authors first discuss the QDOT requirements as set forth in Section 2056A. In doing so, they also review the provisions of the proposed regulations, including those aspects of the proposed regulations that are likely to pose problems for taxpayers. Thereafter, they consider the making of the QDOT election under the proposed regulations. Explanation is also provided of the proposed regulations' provisions on the assignment and transfer of property to a QDOT and conforming marital trusts and nontrust marital transfers to the requirements of a QDOT. Special rules that permit nonassignable annuities, such as survivor benefits from annuities or retirement plans, to qualify for QDOT treatment are then discussed.

Last, the authors discuss the imposition of the deferred QDOT tax, including the nature of the tax, the triggers for its imposition, and various other rules included in the proposed regulations, such as those increasing basis for QDOT taxes and those concerning effective dates.

[RM Fijolek & JM Miller, 20 Est. Plan. 195.]

"Using QDOTs to secure marital deduction for noncitizens" (1993). In 1992, proposed regulations were issued that provide guidance on the availability of the estate and gift tax marital deduction where the recipient spouse or the donee spouse is not a U.S. citizen. In an effort to ensure collection of the deferred estate tax imposed on QDOTs, however, the proposed regulations impose burdensome information and record-keeping requirements on QDOT trustees. In addition, the proposed regulations contain numerous "governing instrument" requirements, and the absence of any such provision in the governing documents of the trust may prevent a trust from qualifying as a QDOT, even if the trust complies with the regulatory requirements.

The author first discusses the proposed regulations' requirements for an estate tax marital deduction for property passing to or from a non–U.S. citizen. Thereafter, he examines the three categories of tests for ensuring that a trust qualifies as a QDOT, i.e., the marital deduction requirements, the statutory requirements, and the requirements to ensure collection of the QDOT tax imposed under Section 2056A(b)(1). The provisions concerning nonprobate property are also discussed. Next, the author considers the proposed regulations' provisions on the treatment of annuities and similar arrangements, both with respect to assignable and nontransferable annuities and payments.

Imposition of the QDOT tax under the proposed regulations is then discussed, including use of Form 706-QDT, liability for the tax, the meaning of "designated return filer," the adjustment to the basis of distributed property, the effect of a change in the surviving spouse's citizenship, computation of the QDOT tax, and the special treatment of jointly held property affected by the tax. Last, the author considers the gift tax marital deduction under the proposed regulations generally and with regard to the creation of a joint tenancy.

[DL Siegler, 78 J. Tax'n 352.]

"The estate and gift tax impact of TAMRA and Omnibus Budget and Reconciliation Act of 1989 on the availability of the marital deduction to a noncitizen spouse" (1990). Before passage of TAMRA, the inter vivos gifts and bequests and other nontestamentary dispositions passing at death to a noncitizen spouse of a U.S. citizen or resident were treated in the same manner as a bequest or gift to a spouse who was a U.S. citizen for federal estate and gift tax purposes. That is, the decedent's estate or donor received an unlimited estate or gift tax marital deduction provided the property passed or was given to the surviving spouse either outright or in an otherwise qualifying manner.

TAMRA drastically limited the availability of the federal estate and gift tax marital deduction for transfers from a U.S. citizen or resident to a noncitizen spouse. Under TAMRA, the estate tax marital deduction is no longer available for property passing to a noncitizen spouse unless it passes in a QDOT. After discussing the general consequences of the changes made to the marital deduction in the case of noncitizen spouses, the author examines the new QDOT provisions. The nature and requirements of QDOTs and the manner of their taxation for estate tax purposes are explained. Various problems, such as the treatment of a QDOT on the noncitizen spouse's death, are also explored.

Next, the author examines the $100,000 gift tax exclusion for gifts made to noncitizen spouses. Certain problems associated with its application are considered. In addition to reviewing certain planning factors in the use of QDOTs, the author also notes the effect treaties may have in this area and discusses qualification for a charitable deduction on a QDOT remainder passing to charity.

[SJ Schlesinger, US Tax'n Int'l Operations ¶ 13,520.]

¶ 5.03 GENERATION-SKIPPING TRANSFER TAX AS APPLIED TO NONRESIDENT ALIENS[3]

"Proposed regulations provide guidance on generation-skipping transfer tax planning for nonresident aliens" (1993). In this article, the author discusses proposed regulations, issued in 1992, concerning the treatment of transfers by nonresident aliens under the generation-skipping transfer tax. The author first reviews the basic features of the generation-skipping transfer tax and the Code's provisions regarding nonresident aliens, their estates, and their gift transfers. Next, the author examines the proposed regulations' situs rule, which operates generally to limit the scope of the generation-skipping transfer tax to transfers by nonresident aliens of U.S. situs property. The author then considers the "deemed transferor," rule which can operate as an exception to the situs rule. Examples are given illustrating the operation of these principles. Additionally, some problem areas and open issues under the "deemed transferor" rule are also discussed.

In the last part of this article, the author discusses other issues under the proposed regulations. These include existing uncertainty in application of the situs rule because of an antiabuse provision included in the proposed regulations, allocation of the generation-skipping transfer tax exemption, and the consequences of certain tax treaties. The author concludes that the proposed regulations provide welcome guidance in the area of generation-skipping transfer tax planning for nonresident aliens. Nevertheless, their scope is overly broad, and in some areas they create, rather than resolve, uncertainty. Moreover, as examined in this article, by taxing certain transfers based solely on the status of the skip person beneficiary and the intervening generation, the proposed regulations place a premium on proper tax planning before the immigration to the United States of the potential transferor and any of his or her descendants.

[CJ Perry, Jr., 20 Est. Plan. 140.]

¶ 5.04 FOREIGN TRUSTS[4]

Foreign trust income was taxable to grantor. Taxpayer was a beneficiary of a trust established in the Cayman Islands. The trust owned 100 percent of the stock in a Cayman corporation, which was organized to operate taxpayer's international travel business. Part of the corporation's income was transferred to the trust. The taxpayer argued that the transferred amounts were not taxable distributions, because they were dividends constructively received in prior years or previously taxed Sub-part F income, or because the corporation had no income and could not pay a dividend.

Held: For the IRS. The deposits in the foreign trust were taxable distributions to the taxpayer under the grantor trust rules.

[Lewis, 64 TCM 117, RIA TC Memo. ¶ 92,391 (1992).]

IRS issues revenue ruling concerning foreign trusts. The IRS ruled that if a foreign trust accumulates income, changes its situs so as to become a domestic trust, and then makes a distribution that under the accumulation distribution rules of Section 666 is deemed to have been made in a year in which the trust was a foreign trust, the distribution is treated as a distribution from a foreign trust for purposes of the accumulation distribution rules of Sections 665 through 668.

[Rev. Rul. 91-6, 1991-1 CB 89.]

"Using foreign situs trusts for asset protection planning" (1993). Asset protection planning emphasizes lifetime planning to preserve assets from various identifiable risks, the most significant of which is the possibility of protracted, costly, aggravating, and demeaning litigation that could devastate one not only emotionally but financially as well. Asset protection planning is simply the process of organizing one's assets in advance to safeguard them from loss or dissipation by reason of potential risks to which they would otherwise be subject.

The author first examines the various asset protection tools available to planners, including the "asset protection trust," which the author considers "the most impervious, yet flexible, asset protection planning tool available." Thereafter, he compares the "asset protection trust" to other protection arrangements, such as a limited partnership. Next, he explains why foreign situs trusts are better than domestic trusts for asset protection. After detailing his preference for foreign situs trusts, he examines selection of the appropriate foreign jurisdiction for the formation of the trust and the location of its assets. Last, the author considers the tax ramifications associated with the establishment of a foreign trust, the fraudulent conveyance issues that can arise upon transfers of assets to the trust, and the avoidance of certain practical risks connected with the use of foreign trusts.

[BS Engel, 20 Est. Plan. 212.]

"U.S. taxation of foreign trusts and U.S. and non–U.S. trust grantors" (1991).
A foreign trust can be a valuable means of arranging the disposition and administration of the assets of a nonresident alien grantor having non–U.S. beneficiaries and U.S. beneficiaries. A foreign trust can also be utilized by a nonresident alien grantor for business purposes, such as investment in real estate or operating a business. In either case, the tax rules associated with foreign trusts must be carefully reviewed.

The author first discusses the creation of a foreign trust. Specific attention is given to the definitions of "trust" and "foreign." Suggested guidelines in the formation of such a trust are provided. Next, the author considers U.S. taxation of foreign trusts and nonresident alien grantors. First, he explains the considerations involved with the formation of nonresident alien nongrantor and grantor trusts. Next, he addresses the general tax consequences associated with such trusts, including the determination of its resident status and the 1990 amendments to Section 672(f). Thereafter, he examines U.S. taxation of foreign trusts created by U.S. grantors having U.S. beneficiaries. Within this part of the article, the author explores the operation of Sections 1491 and 679, exceptions to Section 679, and the determination of the existence of a U.S. beneficiary under Section 679. Other grantor trust rules are then discussed, including the operation of Sections 672 through 677 and Section 644 for gains on transfers to foreign trusts.

The author thereafter provides an in-depth discussion of Section 1491, which imposes an excise tax on transfers to avoid income tax by a U.S. person. Specific discussion is included on its application to related-party installment sales and private annuities. Planning considerations and Section 1491's interaction with the election to recognize gain under Section 1057 are also discussed.

Next, the author examines the U.S. estate and gift tax consequences associated with the formation of a foreign trust. First considered are the provisions of the Code applicable to U.S. citizens and residents. Next, application of these provisions, and certain special provisions, are examined with respect to nonresident aliens. The author follows this discussion with a review of the forms required to be filed by U.S. persons as to foreign trust transactions, Forms 3520 and 3520-A.

[EL Wyckoff, Jr., US Tax'n Int'l Operations ¶ 6013.]

"U.S. taxation of foreign trusts: U.S. and non–U.S. beneficiaries" (1991). In this article, the author discusses the U.S. tax treatment of a foreign trust's beneficiaries. The author begins this discussion with an explanation of the basic rules applicable to the taxation of trust beneficiaries of simple and complex trusts. The concepts of trust income and the treatment of trust gains under the throwback rules are reviewed. Throughout this discussion, the author provides illustrative examples and planning pointers with regard to the application of these basic rules, as well as certain special provisions, to foreign trust beneficiaries.

Next, the author explains the computation of a U.S. beneficiary's tax on a Section 666 foreign accumulation distribution. Examples are given illustrating the various steps in the process. Generation-skipping transfers are then considered. A review of the generation-skipping transfer tax provisions and the considerations they raise in this area are set forth by the author. Last, the author considers the special reporting requirements for beneficiaries of foreign trusts. Both general requirements and a specimen form are presented.

[EL Wyckoff, Jr., US Tax'n Int'l Operations ¶ 6014.]

BIBLIOGRAPHY OF RESEARCH REFERENCES

[1]R. Stephens, G. Maxfield, S. Lind, & D. Calfee, Federal Estate and Gift Taxation chs. 6, 7 (Warren Gorham Lamont, 6th ed. 1991).

[2]R. Stephens, G. Maxfield, S. Lind, & D. Calfee, Federal Estate and Gift Taxation ¶ 6.06[3] (Warren Gorham Lamont, 6th ed. 1991).

D. Westfall & G. Mair, Estate Planning Law and Taxation ¶ 13.05[1] (Warren Gorham Lamont, 2d ed. 1989).

[3]R. Stephens, G. Maxfield, S. Lind, & D. Calfee, Federal Estate and Gift Taxation ¶ 18.03 (Warren Gorham Lamont, 6th ed. 1991).

[4]J. Peschel & E. Spurgeon, Federal Taxation of Trusts, Grantors and Beneficiaries ch. 15 (Warren Gorham Lamont, 2d ed. 1989).

CHAPTER **6**

Tax Treaties

¶ 6.01 INCOME TAX TREATIES, GENERALLY[1]

IRS issues revenue procedure concerning representations alien must make to claim withholding exemption under certain treaties. This revenue procedure modifies two earlier revenue procedures by providing the representations that an alien must make to claim a withholding exemption under certain newly ratified income tax treaties. Under most U.S. income tax treaties, an alien student, teacher, or researcher at a U.S. university or other educational institution who receives income for personal services is generally exempt from income tax provided certain requirements are met. These requirements include a limited number of years in

6-1

which the alien can claim the exemption and a maximum dollar amount for the exemption in a taxable year. Normally, the payor of compensation for personal services is required under Section 1441 or Section 3405 to withhold and pay over federal taxes on such income. However, withholding is not required if the income is exempt under treaty. In order to claim the withholding exemption, the alien must submit Form 8233 to the withholding agent certifying that the income is exempt from taxation under treaty. This revenue procedure provides the representations that an alien must include in Form 8233 to claim a withholding exemption under the newly ratified treaties with Germany, India, Indonesia, Spain, and Tunisia. This revenue procedure also modifies the representations in a prior revenue procedure pertaining to the treaty with the former Soviet Union. This revenue procedure obsoletes representations in two prior revenue procedures pertaining to the earlier treaty with Finland, which has been replaced by a newly ratified treaty that does not exempt income earned within the United States by alien students, teachers, or researchers. This revenue procedure also modifies a prior revenue procedure with respect to the maximum annual exemption allowed students under the Cyprus treaty.

[Rev. Proc. 93-22, 1993-18 IRB 15, modifying Rev. Proc. 87-8, 1987-1 CB 336, and Rev. Proc. 87-9, 1987-1 CB 368.]

"IRS uses expanded conduit principle to limit treaty shopping" (1992). In Technical Advice Memorandum 9133004, the IRS expanded the conduit principle to break through the "equity wall" generally thought to establish the outer boundary of its application. The usual application of the conduit principle had been to treat the intermediary as a conduit in back-to-back loan transactions. In the technical advice memorandum, the IRS looked through a finance and holding company subsidiary to treat its sole shareholder as the owner of loans the finance subsidiary made to its own U.S. subsidiary, where the shareholder had funded the loans through *equity contributions* to the finance subsidiary. The finance subsidiary was incorporated in a country (apparently the Netherlands) that had a treaty with the United States that exempted from U.S. withholding tax interest received from a U.S. subsidiary. The U.S. treaty with the country where the finance subsidiary's parent was incorporated (apparently Canada), however, merely reduced the withholding rate. Accordingly, the IRS determined that the U.S. withholding tax exemption was not available and that tax should have been withheld at the parent's country treaty rate.

The authors discuss this technical advice memorandum and the implications it might have if construed broadly to encompass more than solely inbound treaty shopping arrangements of foreign investors.

In this article, the authors examine the tax law in this area, focusing on the 1971 Tax Court *Aiken Industries, Inc.* case; Revenue Rulings 84-152, 84-153, 85-163, and 87-89; the anti–treaty shopping provisions of Sections 884(e) and 884(f)(3); and other authority (e.g., Section 163(j)'s earnings-stripping rules and General Counsel Memorandums 39845 through 39851.) Thereafter, the authors discuss Technical Advice Memorandum 9133004. The IRS's reasoning is thoroughly analyzed. Additionally, the authors explore alternative theories that the IRS might have used (i.e., sham, nominee characterization, tax avoidance purpose, and effectively connected income characterization) and the difficulties the IRS would have had in attacking the treaty exemption under such theories. Finally, the authors examine other implications that use of the conduit theory might have in this area and the uncertainties created. Additional problems are noted if use of the conduit theory is made by foreign governments.

The authors conclude that if the main purpose for the technical advice memorandums expansion of the conduit theory is to limit inbound treaty shopping, a better approach would appear to be renegotiating stronger limitation-of-benefits articles in U.S. tax treaties. However, because of certain geopolitical concerns, such articles are unlikely to be renegotiated nor are tax treaties likely to be terminated. Accordingly, adoption of the expanded conduit principle seems to be the only available approach.

[AS Lederman & B. Hirsh, 76 J. Tax'n 170.]

"Tax reclamation is too often slow and difficult" (1992). One of the major headaches in global investing is obtaining the benefit of reduced withholding rates provided by income tax treaties for dividend and interest payments. Although virtually every income tax treaty provides for such reduced withholding rates (with generally even lower rates for intercorporate dividends), implementation generally remains in the control of the tax authorities of the treaty partner. A survey of treaty implementation reveals a variety of reclamation procedures with differences in promptness of payment. There often is a substantial gap between the theory of the treaty rules and actual practice.

Tax reclamation is an area in which the United States is a world leader both for the simplicity of its procedures for providing payment of the net amount without requiring a refund claim and for the relative promptness in payment on claims (filed after the close of the tax year). The focus of this article is on dividends, where procedures are often complex. Most countries have a zero withholding rate on interest payments to nonresident portfolio debtholders regardless of treaty benefits.

Dividend and interest taxes on nonresidents are generally withheld at source as a percentage of the gross amount. The withholding tax is a final tax—i.e., no further tax is due; no refunds based on allowances, reliefs, or expenses are permitted; and, typically, no return is due. Because a 25 percent or 30 percent gross withholding rate is a deterrent to inbound investment, income tax treaties provide for reduced rates of taxation on portfolio investments in stocks (typically 15 percent) and debt instruments (typically zero to 15 percent), and a lower rate for intercorporate dividends (typically 5 percent to 15 percent).

Rate reduction procedures can generally be placed in three broad groups:

1. The "blanket" exemption (under which a form provides preclearance for the payor to pay a net amount based on the treaty rate);

2. The payment-by-payment preclearance method, which is used in Italy, the Netherlands, and Spain; and

3. The credit refund method, used by France and the United Kingdom.

[RJ Shapiro & RD Lorence, 3 J. Int'l Tax'n 121.]

"Mutual assistance convention has its limitations" (1991). The convention on mutual administrative assistance in tax matters (convention) was prepared jointly by the Council of Europe and the Organization for Economic Cooperation and Development (OECD), and was opened for signature on January 25, 1988. The convention is supplemented by an explanatory report prepared by the committee of experts drafting the convention. The United States signed the convention and the Senate has ratified it, with reservations (as permitted by the convention).

Scope of convention. The convention, dealing solely with mutual administrative assistance in tax matters, is more complete than the mutual agreement procedure, exchange of information, and administrative assistance provisions of the OECD and U.S. model income and estate tax treaties. The purposes of the convention are to provide exchange of information and administrative assistance with regard to assessment, examination, collection, recovery, and enforcement of a tax covered by the convention.

Although the convention is a major development in international tax cooperation and enforcement, there are several limitations on its effectiveness. Some of the provisions of the convention, such as those on automatic exchange of information, simultaneous tax examinations, and tax examinations abroad, are not obligatory but require additional agreement by the respective governments. Even with regard to those provisions of the convention that are obligatory, the convention is subject to national law and reciprocity: It does not specify a required minimum level of mutual assistance by governments but requires assistance only to the extent that the laws and practices of both the applicant state and requested state provide for such procedures.

The forms of assistance provided by the convention include exchange of information (Articles 4 through 10) and assistance in recovery (Articles 11 through 16). This administrative assistance will be provided whether the person affected is a resident or national of a party or of any other state. Thus, one party (the applicant state) can request of another party (the requested state) information about a taxpayer, or other assistance under the convention, although the taxpayer is a resident or national of a third state (whether or not a party to the convention). A "national" of a party includes any individual possessing the nationality of that party, and all legal persons, partnerships, associations, and other entities deriving their status as such from the laws in force in that party.

Provisions relating to all forms of assistance. Articles 18 through 23 of the convention are provisions relating to all forms of assistance: both exchange of information and assistance in recovery. Some of these provisions are merely procedural, such as Articles 18, Information to Be Provided by Applicant State, and 20, Response to the Request for Assistance. Article 18 details the information to be provided by the applicant state in its request for information, for assistance in recovery, for measures of conservancy, or for the service of documents, in order for the requested state to determine whether each request is within the scope of the convention. Article 20 covers generally the procedures for the requested state to respond to the applicant state's request for assistance.

Application of convention. With regard to the administration of the convention, Article 24, Implementation, provides for "a coordinating body composed of representatives of the competent authorities of the Parties to monitor the implementation and development of the convention, under the aegis of the OECD." This coordinating body would transmit information among the parties and encourage the production of uniform solutions to problems in the application and interpretation of the convention. A state could request the coordinating body to give opinions on the interpretation of the convention. Such body would, however, have only an advisory function and would not settle disputes. Article 24(4) refers to the attempt by states to resolve, by mutual agreement, difficulties or doubts about the interpretation or implementation of the convention, but does not provide for a formal dispute resolution procedure.

Conclusion. The convention, in spite of understandable limitations, is a significant development in the traditionally sensitive area of international tax cooperation and enforcement. It will be interesting to follow the ratification process and to see if the convention serves as a model for other agreements on mutual administrative assistance in tax matters.

[DE Spencer, 1 J. Int'l Tax'n 284.]

"OECD convention update" (1991). The U.S. Treasury announced on February 20, 1991, that the U.S. Mission to the OECD had deposited with that institution the U.S. instrument of ratification of the OECD/Council of Europe convention on mutual administrative assistance in tax matters. Deposit of that instrument was the last act required to formalize the U.S. adoption (with permitted reservations) of the convention.

The convention by its terms will enter into force with respect to ratifying nations after five members of either the OECD or the Council of Europe have ratified the convention.

[2 J. Int'l Tax'n 64.]

"OECD mutual assistance convention to amplify members' tax treaties" (1990). On September 18, 1990, the U.S. Senate ratified a multilateral treaty as the Council of Europe–OECD. The convention, drafted jointly by the Council of Europe and the OECD, becomes effective on the first day of the calendar month that is three months after the date on which instruments of ratification, acceptance, or approval have been deposited with the Secretary General of the Council of Europe or of the OECD (depositary) by five members of either body. If and when the convention becomes effective, it will be the first multilateral treaty among Council of Europe or OECD members providing for mutual administrative assistance in tax matters and an important milestone in the evolution of international cooperation.

The convention contains three broad divisions: (1) exchange of information; (2) recovery of taxes; and (3) service of documents. These provisions are flanked by introductory and definitional sections at the beginning of the convention and implementation provisions at the end. All signatories are required to provide administrative assistance, including judicial action, to each other in civil and, to a limited extent, criminal tax matters, regardless of the citizenship or residence of the taxpayer with respect to whom assistance is sought. Such assistance is mandated with respect to national income, profits and capital gains taxes, and net wealth taxes.

The convention requires parties to exchange any information that is foreseeably relevant to the assessment and collection of tax or the recovery and enforcement of tax claims. Although parties are generally free to exchange information on whatever form desired, the convention lists six types of information exchange pursuant to which most assistance is likely to be given: (1) on request; (2) automatically, by bilateral or mutual agreement; (3) spontaneously, in certain ennumerated circumstances; (4) through simultaneous audits of the same taxpayer, where the parties have common or related interests with respect to the taxpayer; (5) through overseas audit by an applicant state's representatives; and (6) if one party receives information from another that conflicts with information already in the recipient's possession, it must notify the supplier of that information of the conflict.

The convention provides that a requested state must take measures permitted under its internal laws to recover tax claims of an applicant state as though such claims were its own and to serve documents of the applicant state in accordance with the requested state's laws in the lawful manner most resembling the applicant state's instructions. Under the reservation mechanism, the United States will not apply (and will not receive the benefits of) Article 17 of the convention, other than under an additional provision permitting service by mail.

A requested state may decline to honor an otherwise qualifying application by an applicant state under the following circumstances:

1. The applicant state has not pursued all available means in its own territory.
2. Granting the request would contravene the laws or administrative practices of either party, or would contravene the public policy or essential interests of the requested state.
3. The request seeks information not obtainable under the laws of either the requested state or the applicant state.
4. The request seeks information that is a trade secret or process.
5. Granting the request would lead to discriminatory treatment by the applicant state of a national of the requested state.
6. The requested state considers the taxation of the applicant state to be contrary to generally accepted taxation principles or to a treaty between the two parties.

With limited exceptions, the convention allows parties adopting it to choose among certain of its rules by signifying reservations to any of the following provisions (no other reservations are permitted and reservations can be made or withdrawn by notice to a depositary):

1. Assistance with respect to taxes not on the mandatory list.
2. Assistance in the recovery of tax claims.
3. Assistance relating to any claim in existence on the date the convention becomes effective with respect to the requested state.
4. Assistance with respect to service of documents.
5. Permission for service of documents by mail.

There is much scope for disagreement among the countries in the implementation of the treaty provisions, and it will be interesting to observe how disputes will be resolved. A potentially far-reaching provision of the convention is the one that allows a requested state to decline to honor an otherwise valid request for assistance if the requested state considers the tax system of the applicant state to be contrary to generally accepted taxing principles or to an applicable treaty. The United States may find itself unexpectedly vulnerable on this issue because another party to the convention might decline to honor a U.S. request for assistance on the grounds that the U.S. policy of unilateral treaty overrides is contrary to general principles of taxation.

[RE Andersen, 1 J. Int'l Tax'n 252.]

"Senate hearings focus on policies toward developing nations and treaty overrides" (1990). On June 14, 1990, the Committee on Foreign Relations of the U.S. Senate held hearings on six bilateral income tax treaties signed by the United States since early 1989. These hearings concerned the proposed treaties with the Federal Republic of Germany, Finland, India, Indonesia, Tunisia, and Spain.

Because of the rapid pace of recent changes in U.S. taxation of foreign taxpayers and international operations, as well as the relatively large number of treaties under consideration and the economic diversity of the prospective treaty partners involved, the six income tax treaties under committee consideration provide an interesting perspective on U.S. tax treaty policy and the political dimension of international investment. The two principal themes of the hearings were: (1) the differences in U.S. tax treaty practice and policy in dealing with developed countries and developing countries and (2) the relationship between the executive and legislative branches of the U.S. government in the matter of tax treaties and U.S. tax law.

Developing countries. In his prepared statement to the committee, Assistant Secretary Gideon described the differences in form and objectives between U.S. income tax treaties with developed countries and those with developing countries. In treaties with industrialized countries, capital and technology (and the income therefrom) tend to flow in both directions in a roughly reciprocal fashion. Therefore, as a general matter, two developed countries negotiating a tax treaty have roughly the same objectives in mind. The economic relationships between the United States and developing countries, on the other hand, are quite different. Since most of the capital and technology flows from the United States to a developing country, most of the income flows from the developing country to the United States. Consequently, the developing country must bear the revenue cost of reducing its taxes on cross-border income flows to attract needed U.S. capital. This tension is reflected in the proposed treaties pending before the committee in the rates of source-state with-holding tax and the treatment of international container leasing. For example, the rates of source-state withholding tax are substantially higher in the proposed U.S.-India treaty than in the U.S. model or in the majority of the income tax treaties to which the United States is a party. Also, as a concession to India's concern for preserving its scarce revenues, the proposed U.S.-India income tax treaty contains a broadened definition of "permanent establishment," which includes (unlike the U.S. model) an agent who habitually secures orders in the source jurisdiction wholly or almost wholly for the enterprise.

Another area of treaty policy tension that appears to be especially relevant to developing countries is source-country taxation of international container-leasing income. In the proposed treaties with India and Indonesia, container-leasing income would generally be treated as royalty income rather than as shipping income. In each case, the treaty partner is permitted to impose a 10 percent withholding tax on the gross rent paid to a container lessor. By contrast, rentals by a shipping company that owns its own containers and leases them would be exempt from taxation by India or Indonesia.

The issues raised in the proposed treaties with West Germany and Finland reflect that U.S. treaties with industrialized countries address different objectives than those with developing countries. With respect to both of the proposed treaties, one of the main issues is the effect of integrated corporate taxation on U.S. share-holders in West German or Finnish corporations. The proposed U.S.-West Germany income tax treaty would reduce the existing rate of dividend withholding tax between the two countries. The stated reason for this reduction is to simulate the shareholder-level benefits of the West German imputation system, which by its terms does not apply to nonresidents.

Finland has begun to implement an integrated corporate taxing regime that, like West Germany, provides an imputation credit to resident shareholders. How-ever, unlike the proposed treaty with West Germany, the proposed U.S.-Finland treaty provides no mechanism whereby U.S. investors could be granted some tax benefit designed to substitute for the unavailability under internal Finnish tax law of an imputation credit. The Finnish tax treaty negotiators indicated to their U.S. counterparts that it is Finnish policy that treaty benefits to compensate for the un-availability of an internal Finnish imputation credit would be limited to countries that themselves use an imputation system and that provide reciprocal benefits to Finnish shareholders.

Legislative overrides of tax treaties. A second theme present throughout the committee's considerations of the six pending tax treaties was the interplay of the executive and legislative branches of the U.S. government. Much publicity has surrounded the increasing propensity of the U.S. Congress to override existing tax treaty obligations by unilateral action.

One of the committee's members questioned whether the administration's concern over its ability to negotiate future treaties in light of the increasing congressional propensity to override U.S. treaty obligations was overstated, since the legislative trend has been present for a sufficient period of time to put prospective treaty partners on notice that such overrides are possible. Not surprisingly, the comment provoked substantial negative reaction from representatives of some U.S. treaty partners.

Another interesting question arises from the anticipated unification of Germany, that is, whether the proposed U.S.–West Germany income tax treaty would be applied to states that currently make up East Germany would depend on the manner in which such East German states were eventually unified with West Germany. In at least one scenario, Assistant Secretary Gideon suggested that the treaty as proposed automatically applies to taxpayers in currently East German states.

Conclusion. Deliberations on the ratification of proposed income tax treaties usually provide illuminating insights into U.S. tax treaty policy and the often differing views of the executive and legislative branches on that policy in particular. When, as in these hearings, so many treaties with such widely disparate treaty partners are under consideration, the process takes on even greater interest.

[RE Andersen, 1 J. Int'l Tax'n 189.]

¶ 6.02 ESTATE AND GIFT TAX TREATIES, GENERALLY[2]

"Treaties can alleviate harsh Code rules for nonresidents' estates" (1991). Although they are not as numerous as income tax treaties, by the end of 1990, the United States was a party to seventeen estate tax treaties (some covering gift taxes as well). These treaties can mitigate the otherwise adverse rules of the Code that are applicable to the estates of nonresident alien decedents that hold property situated in the United States. The author explains U.S. treatment of foreign estates, concluding that the effect of the foregoing is to subject U.S. and non–U.S. decedents (assuming estates consisting exclusively of U.S.-situs assets) to disparate estate tax treatment, to the detriment of the nonresident alien decedent.

Several estate tax treaties to which the United States is a party modify the ability of either country to tax property on the basis of its situs. For example, the U.S.-German estate and gift tax treaty prohibits the United States from taxing the value of shares or debt obligations of a U.S. corporation owned by a German decedent. Similar rules exist under the U.S. estate tax treaties with Denmark, the Netherlands, Sweden, and the United Kingdom. The treaty provisions discussed by the author do not modify the situs determination rules of U.S. or foreign law but merely allocate the right to tax between the jurisdictions. While some treaties provide special situs rules of their own, others are silent (and therefore refer impliedly to local law). This distinction can be important where a treaty taxing rule is directly or indirectly affected by subsequent legislation.

Congress amended Section 2102(c) in 1988 to require the Section 2010 credit to be used wherever called for by a U.S. treaty obligation.

The degree to which the gross estate of a nonresident alien decedent can be reduced by the value of bequests to the decedent's surviving spouse under the marital deduction provisions can vary significantly with the circumstances. Under the Code, no marital deduction is allowable for U.S. estate tax purposes unless the surviving spouse is a U.S. citizen (regardless of domicile). Since the enactment of the Revenue Reconciliation Act of 1989 (RRA 1989), however, the disallowance of the U.S. marital deduction will apply to bequests to noncitizen spouses only to the extent it does not violate an estate tax treaty.

Not all residents of treaty countries are similarly affected by RRA 1989. For example, the U.S.-German treaty excludes from the U.S. gross estate of a German decedent 50 percent of the value of a marital bequest otherwise taxable by the United States under the other provisions of that treaty, regardless of the surviving spouse's citizenship. On the other hand, the U.S. estate tax treaty with the United Kingdom does not appear to prevail over the Section 2056(d) requirement that the surviving spouse be a U.S. citizen for the U.S. marital deduction to be allowed.

[RE Andersen, 2 J. Int'l Tax'n 62.]

¶ 6.03 MODEL TREATIES[3]

"New OECD model expands scope, conduit, limitation-on-benefits principles" **(1993).** On July 23, 1992, the Council of the OECD adopted a revised model income tax treaty. This 1992 model replaces the 1977 version. In this article, the author examines the provisions of the new model treaty and contrasts them with certain provisions of the 1977 version. The provisions discussed by the author include the types of taxes covered, the territories covered, and the persons covered.

[RE Andersen, 4 J. Int'l Tax'n 46.]

"New OECD model updates employment, self-employment provisions" (1993). This article focuses on the most prominent changes made by the 1992 OECD model income tax treaty to the 1977 model income tax treaty in the taxation of employment and self-employment income. In discussing these changes, the author first addresses the treatment of "commercial travelers" and hired-out labor. Thereafter, the treatment of pension contributions is given an in-depth discussion. Last, he focuses on the changes made in the area of self-employment.

The author concludes that the growing volume of cross-border service activities and relationships calls for a modern and comprehensive approach to apportioning the taxation of income among the parties involved. Many existing income tax treaties have antiquated or ambiguous provisions dealing with these important issues. Nevertheless, the 1992 model provides a guide that will allow renegotiating such treaties in order to reflect contemporary economic realities.

[RE Andersen, 4 J. Int'l Tax'n 94.]

"New OECD model updates leasing and licensing provisions to reflect business realities" (1993). In this article, the author describes the substantial modernization made by the 1992 revised OECD model income tax treaty. First, the author examines the changes made to the treaty provisions affecting the leasing of personal property. In doing so, he compares the old model's provisions with the new model's provisions. Next, the same comparative analysis of provisions and their effect is provided by the author for computer software licensing transactions.

The author concludes that given the large and growing volume of cross-border leasing and licensing activities among OECD member countries, the 1992 model's revisions to Article 12 rank among the most significant changes made to the 1977 model. Although various OECD members have expressed reservations concerning one or more of the changes, on balance the revisions can be expected to have a substantial leveling effect on these important facets of international trade. This trend, if confirmed, can only be viewed as helpful to the growth of the global economy.

[RE Andersen, 4 J. Int'l Tax'n 334.]

"The OECD model tax convention is revised" (1993). After discussing the operations of the OECD, particularly with regard to international taxation, the author focuses this article on the revisions made to the OECD model tax convention. Specific discussion is made of the changes to the convention's articles and commentary thereto.

[J. Sasseville, 4 J. Int'l Tax'n 129.]

"American Law Institute (ALI) study recommends changes in U.S. tax treaty policy" (1991). On June 13, 1991, the ALI approved a report concerning U.S. income tax treaties.

The study is divided into four parts. In each part, the study analyzes the standard provisions of, and policy considerations behind, income tax treaties as reflected for the most part in the OECD, U.S., and United Nations model treaties, and makes recommendations that are often incongruent with existing U.S. tax treaty policy.

The study highlights the careful balance that must be struck between two tax treaty partners as they compromise their respective, and jealously guarded, taxing powers when attempting to alleviate double taxation that would otherwise cripple cross-border trade and investment.

The main compromise is between jurisdiction and revenue: The source state is usually granted primary taxing jurisdiction over nonresidents, but with a substantial reduction in the tax it can collect on their taxable activities. Consistent with this compromise, the principal exception to tax reduction, that the source state may impose its full tax on taxable business profits, carries with it the major inhibition on the source state's taxing jurisdiction, namely, that those business profits must be attributable to a permanent establishment in the source state.

Several observations and recommendations of the study flow from the recognition of this important allocation of taxing power between treaty partners, as are discussed in this article.

The study examines in some detail the appropriate use of extrinsic materials in the interpretation of income tax treaties. Predictably, the study addresses, and generally opposes, the growing trend of Congress to unilaterally override existing treaty obligations by subsequent tax legislation.

The study addresses the so-called cherry-picking problem (i.e., the concurrent application of a treaty and internal law) in some detail. The ALI's reporters recommend that income be separated into broadly defined categories that treat items differently without undue distortions to the country's overall taxing system and that taxpayers be allowed to choose yearly either treaty or statutory treatment for each category.

The study makes several recommendations designed to improve the administration and enforcement of income tax treaties. They include:

1. Reciprocal recognition and enforcement of treaty partner tax judgments;
2. Mediation or arbitration as alternative dispute resolution mechanisms; and
3. Broadening the typical exchange of information provisions to facilitate disclosure of taxpayer information to treaty partners in appropriate circumstances, subject to notice to the affected taxpayer.

Part two of the study discusses several knotty issues in the current U.S. tax treaty policy debate, under the general rubric of "Issues Arising in the Treaty Reduction of Source-Based Taxation." Two of the most important of these issues involve the determination of who is a resident and treaty shopping.

Part three of the study, entitled "Issues Relating to Residence Country Taxation," contains the fewest recommendations for change. Traditionally, the three most controversial issues in this area have been the savings clause, the inconsistent classification of foreign entities, and tax sparing. The ALI reporters recommend no change in the U.S. position on the savings clause and, while discussing the remaining two issues in some detail, make few specific suggestions for improvement in those areas.

In part four, "Non-Discrimination," the ALI reporters set out guiding principles that should apply in determining whether a particular tax-related requirement violates a tax treaty's nondiscrimination article. These principles, which seem to reflect a restrained use of treaty nondiscrimination provisions, are set forth in this article.

The study is a clearly written and well-reasoned think piece that represents an important step in the debate over U.S. tax treaty policy. By focusing on the basic premises of tax treaties and their impact on the U.S. position in the global economy, the ALI reporters have contributed meaningfully to the evolution of U.S. policy.

[2 J. Int'l Tax'n 253.]

¶ 6.04 SOCIAL SECURITY TOTALIZATION AGREEMENTS

"Administrative matters under Social Security totalization agreements" **(1991).** To gain the benefits of Social Security totalization agreements, which allow workers who have worked under more than one system to aggregate their periods of coverage so that they are eligible to receive Social Security benefits when they ordinarily would not qualify for them, a claimant must apply to the Social Security administrative bodies that will be paying the benefits and demonstrate eligibility under their administrative rules. Totalization agreements coordinate this process and allow the competent authorities to exchange information about the claimant.

From the claimant's perspective, an application for totalized benefits differs from a wholly "domestic" application in only one way: The foreign coverage periods must be mentioned during the application process for them to count towards eligibility. Doing so brings into play the totalization agreement's administrative provisions, which are the subject of this article.

The author first discusses the ways in which the totalization agreement's administrative provisions are triggered by the claimant's application for Social Security benefits. Administrative cooperation between countries is then discussed, along with the possibility of appealing the foreign country's unfavorable determination of coverage. The author then discusses the creditability of Social Security tax paid to a foreign country that does not have a totalization agreement with the United States.

The lack of creditability of the employer's Social Security payment on behalf of the employee is also examined. Procedures for obtaining refunds of excess Social Security tax paid by both employees and employers are reviewed by the author. The article concludes with a discussion of U.S. income taxation of Social Security benefits and the effect thereon of various income tax treaties.

[BW Reynolds, US Tax'n Int'l Operations ¶ 5023.]

"Totalization of Social Security benefits" (1991). Totalization agreements affect two aspects of Social Security benefits: (1) eligibility and (2) computation of the actual benefits. This article concerns the mechanics of determining eligibility and totalizing benefits.

The author first examines the way in which totalization agreements operate to determine a worker's qualification for Social Security benefits. Under these agreements, foreign periods of coverage are converted into comparable domestic periods of coverage, whether or not they would count if the worker had worked under the domestic system. The following steps necessary to make this determination are reviewed and explained by the author: compliance with domestic threshold coverage requirements; conversion of foreign coverage periods to domestic equivalent units; assignment of foreign coverage periods to fill gaps; elimination of foreign periods of coverage that are not needed to qualify; and determination of the totalization agreement providing the most favorable treatment.

Next, the author discusses how totalized benefits are computed. The three basic computation methods ("local earnings," "pro rata," and "ratable accrual") are explained. The last part of this article addresses how benefits are paid. Specific issues considered therein are the independence of each country's Social Security payment and the waiver of alien nonpayment provisions by totalization agreements.

[BW Reynolds, US Tax'n Int'l Operations ¶ 5022.]

"Working with Social Security totalization agreements" (1991). Social Security laws can present hidden issues of surprising importance to an international business. This article explains how U.S. totalization agreements reduce double Social Security coverage.

The author first presents the general problems faced by employers and employees engaged in foreign business, including double Social Security taxation and loss of benefits. To resolve these problems, international Social Security agreements, i.e., totalization agreements, were used to specifically address issues concerning cross-border Social Security coverage. The author provides a list of the existing U.S. totalization agreements and the countries that are signatories.

Next, the author examines the nature of the double coverage problem, both for aliens working in the United States and U.S. employees working abroad. Thereafter, he explains the ways in which totalization agreements have been designed to reduce the problems of double coverage, including adoption of the territorial approach, the temporary assignment exception (which allows portable coverage), and the use of competent authority procedures to work out special deals. The author provides, in chart form, a detailed summary of the specific temporary assignment provisions for each of the U.S. totalization agreements. Other exceptions to the territorial approach are then discussed and illustrated in chart form, including the government employee exception, the transportation employee exception, and the rule for self-employed individuals. Special provisions unique to particular totalization agreements are also discussed, along with the treatment of second-tier employees (i.e., employees who shift employment to a subsidiary or an affiliate of the home country employer when they accept foreign assignments). Last, proofs of coverage and related matters are discussed in connection with employees covered by one of the above exceptions.

The author then explores the scope of U.S. totalization agreements. Specific discussion is provided of the programs not covered under such agreements, e.g., the health or Medicare portion of the Federal Insurance Contributions Act, the Federal Unemployment Tax Act, and state programs. Other sources of relief from double Social Security taxation, such as income tax treaties and other treaties, are noted.

[BW Reynolds, US Tax'n Int'l Operations ¶ 5021.]

¶ 6.05 COMPETENT AUTHORITY PROCEDURES[4]

Injunctive relief not available to force competent authority assistance. Taxpayer contended that the IRS and other officials abused their discretion by refusing to enter into negotiations with Japan when the taxpayer invoked the U.S.-Japan convention (the double tax treaty). It sought a declaratory judgment that the double tax treaty had been violated and an order compelling the IRS to consider the merits of taxpayer's request for negotiations. Taxpayer also sought to enjoin (1) interference with the treaty process and (2) Tax Court litigation already underway. The IRS moved to dismiss for lack of jurisdiction.

Held: IRS motion granted. The underlying purpose of taxpayer's suit is to restrain the assessment or collection of taxes. It clearly seeks to proceed through the competent authority mechanism because it has determined this to be the best way to limit its tax liability. Accordingly, the court lacks jurisdiction under the Anti-Injunction and Declaratory Judgment Acts, since the taxpayer did not demonstrate that (1) under no circumstances could the IRS prevail and (2) it faced irreparable injury.

[Yamaha Motor Corp., USA, 779 F. Supp. 610, 69 AFTR2d 92-524, 92-1 USTC ¶ 50,025 (DDC 1991).]

IRS issues revenue procedure concerning competent authority assistance. This revenue procedure sets forth the procedures concerning requests for assistance of the U.S. competent authority (USCA) in resolving instances of taxation in contravention of the provisions of an income, estate, or gift tax treaty to which the United States is a party.

[Rev. Proc. 91-23, 1991-1 CB 534, clarified by Rev. Proc. 91-26, 1991-1 CB 543.]

"Treaty Division chief discusses competent authority" (1993). Christine Halphen, Acting Chief of the IRS Tax Treaty Division, speaking on a panel at the ABA Tax Section meetings in Washington, D.C., on May 7, 1993, stated that Revenue Procedure 91-23 is being studied for revision. The procedure, which describes how to request the assistance of USCA, will be made, according to Ms. Halphen, "more user-friendly." The revision will simplify the manner in which a request to competent authority can be made. For example, in certain instances a simple letter can be accepted as a request for intervention by competent authority. She noted that the revised procedure is likely to give some guidance on foreign tax credits.

[4 J. Int'l Tax'n 283.]

"How to get competent authority relief" (1992). In both unauthorized and double taxation cases, a taxpayer may apply to the USCA for assistance under the mutual agreement procedure (MAP) article of an applicable tax treaty. Procedures for requesting USCA assistance are outlined in Revenue Procedure 91-23. As of late, recourse to competent authority may be more than just optional—current IRS practice is to deny or postpone foreign tax credits (FTCs) on reallocated Section 482 income unless the taxpayer has pursued competent authority relief. This article fully explores the USCA procedure, from the origins of a request through its processing.

The first part of this article provides general information about the USCA, including the IRS officials involved, the types of cases considered (allocation and nonallocation), the meaning of "double taxation," and taxpayers eligible for USCA assistance. The MAPs are next examined. Specific discussion is provided of the MAP article in existing tax treaties, procedural problems that arise with respect to older treaties, and the situation that exists in the absence of a tax treaty. The authors then consider the types of competent authority cases and the manner in which they arise, including IRS examination of multinational U.S. taxpayers and the affirmative raising of fraud and similar issues by the USCA.

In the next part of this article, the procedures for requesting competent authority assistance are detailed. Specific attention is given to making such requests in domestic allocation cases, cases in litigation, refund claims, closed cases, foreign allocation cases, and nonallocation cases. The procedure for appealing a competent authority request or challenging a refusal by the USCA to act are also explained.

Next, the authors detail the processing of the competent authority request through the following stages and actions: initial review, economic analysis, case study and disposition, a unilateral withdrawal of the proposed allocation by the IRS, intergovernmental consultation, required taxpayer disclosures, case completion, taxpayer nonacceptance, and competent authority settlements. The filing of a protective refund claim in conjunction with the competent authority request is also considered.

Thereafter, the authors examine the extent to which taxpayers must take action in a foreign country to protect the availability of their U.S. FTCs. The extent to which these foreign mitigation of double taxation efforts must go is examined from both the IRS's and Tax Court's views. The last part of this article concerns the current use of the competent authority procedures by taxpayers and simultaneous examination cases.

[US Tax'n Int'l Operations ¶ 5020.]

"IRS reorganizes competent authority process" (1991). The IRS has issued Revenue Procedure 91-22, containing the rules for advance pricing agreements, and Revenue Procedures 91-23 and 91-24, relating to the competent authority process.

Revenue Procedure 91-23 combines in one revenue procedure a comprehensive set of rules regarding competent authority assistance under the MAPs of income tax treaties to which the United States is a party.

Revenue Procedure 91-23 divides the competent authority process into four parts:

1. General principles;
2. Rules for U.S. taxpayers seeking competent authority assistance in connection with U.S. initiated adjustments;
3. Rules for U.S. taxpayers seeking competent authority assistance in connection with foreign initiated adjustments; and
4. Small case procedures.

Under Revenue Procedure 91-23, only U.S. persons may file for competent authority assistance and only if there is an applicable income tax treaty in force. Under the MAP in income tax treaties to which the United States is a party, the treaty partners agree to consult to prevent their residents and nationals from being subject to double taxation or other taxation not in accord with the treaty. Revenue Procedure 91-23 applies to all proposed adjustments that threaten double taxation or taxation not in accord with the treaty. It is acknowledged, however, that transfer price adjustments that threaten double taxation will constitute the basis for the greatest number of requests. The arm's-length principle of the Section 482 regulations govern the resolution of allocation disputes.

Revenue Procedure 91-23 acknowledges that the USCA is the Assistant Commissioner (International), who is assisted by the Tax Treaty Division of the IRS. In administering or interpreting treaties, the competent authority acts only with the concurrence of the Associate Chief Counsel (International). The competent authority process is a government activity, and the taxpayer is not allowed to participate in the negotiations. The taxpayer may prepare position papers, however, and must cooperate in providing factual information and otherwise as required under Revenue Procedure 91-23.

The revenue procedure acknowledges that the treaty provisions take precedence over the revenue procedure whenever there is a conflict.

In the event of a U.S.-initiated adjustment proposed under Section 482, the competent authority process may be a better alternative than the domestic appeal/litigation route.

Revenue Procedure 91-23 advises a taxpayer faced with a U.S.-initiated adjustment to consider a laundry list of issues. Among the most important are the following:

1. When to include a request for relief under Revenue Procedure 65-17 (U.S. parent corporation–foreign subsidiary) or Revenue Procedure 82-80 (foreign parent–U.S. subsidiary);
2. Whether the MAP of the relevant treaty contains relief from procedural laws

of the treaty partners, e.g., interest, penalties, and statutes of limitations; and

3. The need to include a confidential disclosure statement and its consequences.

In the case of foreign-initiated adjustments, a U.S. taxpayer faces a somewhat different analysis. The United States has accepted or at least acquiesced in the taxable income as reported by the U.S. taxpayer. In this respect, their interests are allied rather than hostile as in the case of a U.S.-initiated adjustment. Revenue Ruling 91-23 sets forth issues to be considered and acts to be taken by a U.S. taxpayer filing for competent authority assistance in such a case.

[JE McDermott, Jr., 2 J. Int'l Tax'n 55.]

"New competent authority procedure allows for increased flexibility" (1991). On March 19, 1991, the IRS issued Revenue Procedure 91-23, restating, in one document, the procedures to be followed for requests to the USCA for assistance in resolving cases of double taxation and other instances of taxation in contravention of U.S. tax treaties. This procedure provides an administrative mechanism for taxpayers to present such claims for resolution by one or both competent authorities. Since the taxpayer's approval of the agreement reached by the tax authorities is generally needed for the taxpayer to be bound, the procedure is, in effect, trilateral. Where a treaty has special procedures, however, they will take precedence over the provisions in the revenue procedure.

In and of themselves, the changes made by Revenue Procedure 91-23 are of limited importance. The issuance of that revenue procedure at this time, however, combined with other initiatives of the IRS and other U.S. governmental authorities, makes what has long been an important but unappreciated and under-used tax procedure even that much more useful. Important new aspects of the competent authority process include the following: (1) The competent authority mechanism is a major component of the advance pricing agreement procedure put into effect by the IRS in Revenue Procedure 91-22; (2) the very issuance of Revenue Procedure 91-23 demonstrates a renewed commitment by the United States to the competent authority process; (3) Revenue Procedure 91-23 appropriately continues to recognize that one of the three main functions of the tax treaties is avoiding double taxation; (4) the new U.S.-German income tax treaty (awaiting ratification) contains a voluntary arbitration mechanism that is available when the competent authorities cannot agree; (5) as a negative aspect, the revenue procedure (as modified by Revenue Procedure 91-26) provides that the consent of the Chief Counsel to proceed with competent authority assistance is required for any case that has been designated for litigation; (6) under Revenue Procedure 91-24, where the United States has an income tax treaty with a MAP, relief is available only in conjunction with a request for assistance from the USCA, and thus the competent authority has to be involved. The author discusses each of these aspects.

Next, the author addresses the status of the advance pricing agreement as a competent authority matter. The author thereafter compares the significant differences between Revenue Procedure 91-23 and its predecessors. The areas discussed are (1) the elimination of the review panel; (2) small case procedure; (3) the relationship between the competent authority and IRS appeals; (4) the interaction of competent authority proceedings and court litigation; (5) protective measures under the revenue procedure and the waiver of procedural barriers under a tax treaty; (6) the effect of the failure to request competent authority assistance on the FTC; and (7) the conduct of the taxpayer required to obtain competent authority assistance.

Last, the author provides a discussion of the status of the competent authority process. Topics covered are the use of the competent authority process in transfer pricing disputes and other types of cases, interest on deficiencies and refunds arising from the competent authority process, and the utility of the competent authority process in resolving or avoiding transfer pricing disputes and other matters.

The author concludes that the procedural rules (such as those under the MAP) and the substantive rules (such as those set forth in the Section 482 regulations) need to work together. He also notes that to the extent that the U.S. transfer pricing and cost-sharing arrangement regulations depart from international norms, it will be much more difficult for the USCA to negotiate agreements under the MAP. Accordingly, as the United States develops proposed regulations under Section 482, consultation with its major trading partners would be very desirable so that whatever emerges in the United States has international acceptability. That would give much more assurance that the competent authority mechanism will continue to be effective in reaching agreements and avoiding double taxation.

[RT Cole, 74 J. Tax'n 380.]

¶ 6.06 DISCLOSURE OF TREATY-BASED RETURN POSITIONS (SECTIONS 6114 AND 6712)[5]

IRS issues proposed regulations concerning treaty-based return positions. Proposed regulations under Section 6114 provide that reporting is specifically required if the residency of an individual is determined under a treaty and apart from the Code. The proposed regulations implement Section 6114 in cases in which a resident alien who claims treaty benefits as a resident of the other treaty-partner's country (dual-status alien) fails to file a statement as required by the regulations under Section 7701(b).

[INTL-121-90, 1992-1 CB 1198, Prop. Reg. § 301.6114-1.]

IRS issues final regulations concerning treaty-based return positions. The IRS has issued final regulations under Sections 6114 and 6712 relating to the requirement that any taxpayer who takes a position that a treaty of the U.S. overrules or otherwise modifies an internal revenue law of the United States shall disclose such position.

[TD 8292, 1990-1 CB 180, Reg. §§ 301.6114-1, 301.6712-1, amended by TD 8305, 1990-2 CB 257.]

"Final regulations on reporting treaty-based positions" (1990). On March 14, 1990, the IRS issued final regulations (Treasury Decision 8292) under Sections 6114 and 6712, which require a taxpayer to indicate reliance on a treaty that provides protection from U.S. tax. There are penalties for failure to make a required disclosure.

These regulations apply retroactively to a position taken during any taxable year for which the due date of a return (without extensions) occurs after 1988. In Notice 90-40, the IRS announced that the final regulations would be amended to waive, in certain circumstances, reporting that a treaty exempts the taxpayer from the excise tax imposed by Section 4371 for policies issued by foreign insurers. Also, certain premiums may be reported as a single payment or income item within specified categories.

[LG Stodghill, 1 J. Int'l Tax'n 110.]

"Final regulations on reporting treaty-based positions are amended" (1990). The final regulations under Section 6114 requiring the reporting of treaty-based positions have been amended to clarify and liberalize the rules dealing principally with insurance risks. The amendments to the final regulations appeared on July 12, 1990 (Treasury Decision 8305). In general, the amendments exempt insureds and U.S. and foreign brokers of insurance risks from filing information reports, and clarify the classes of related persons who must file reports.

Areas affected by the amendments are the following. First, the amending regulations redefine the foreign persons obliged to file the disclosure report. Second, the amending regulations make technical drafting additions to clarify that independent personal services income—which under a treaty is not subject to tax on a net basis, because it is effectively connected, but it is attributable to a U.S. permanent establishment of fixed base of operations—is subject to the Section 6114 reporting requirements. Third, the amending regulations have relieved an insured and a U.S. or foreign broker of insurance risks from the requirement of reporting that a treaty exempts insurance policies from the excise tax imposed under Section 4371; the preamble to the amendments explains that the reason for this exemption is that reporting could best be provided by foreign insurers and reinsurers. Fourth, the amending regulations specify how reporting with regard to premium payments is to be made. Finally, amended Regulations § 301.6114-1(c)(7)(iii) adds a new de minimis exception waiving the reporting requirement for an individual where the payments or income received by the individual during the year do not exceed $10,000 in the aggregate.

The disclosure of treaty-based return positions, primarily directed toward foreign nationals, is one of a number of recent legislative enactments intended by Congress to stem what it perceives to be a flow abroad of U.S. untaxed revenue. Some examples include the superroyalty amendment to Section 482, access to foreign records and testimony through a domestic subsidiary concerning intercompany transactions under Section 6038A, inadmissibility in litigation of foreign-based documentation under certain circumstances as described in Section 982, and statutory support under Section 7852(d) to justify treaty overrides.

[M. Abrutyn, 1 J. Int'l Tax'n 172.]

"Regulations on treaty-based return positions amended" (1990). Final regulations on treaty-based return positions issued in March were amended July 11, 1990. Regulation § 301.6114-1(c) now provides that individuals who receive payments that do not exceed $10,000 for the taxable year are not required to report treaty-based return positions.

Under Regulation § 301.6114-1(b)(4)(ii) foreign persons who receive from a U.S. person annual or period income subject to withholding must report when a treaty either exempts these payments from tax or reduces the withholding rate. Foreign person includes: (1) a controlled foreign corporation under Section 957 with a U.S. shareholder; (2) a foreign shareholder of the U.S. person that is controlled by the foreign shareholder (for tax years beginning before July 11, 1989) or is 25 percent–owned by the foreign shareholder (for tax years beginning after July 10, 1989); and (3) after October 10, 1990, a foreign related party to the U.S. person.

Regulation §§ 301.6114-1(b)(5) and 301.6114-1(c)(1) have been revised to clarify that income derived from certain independent personal services must be reported under Section 6114.

The final regulations limit to foreign insurers and reinsurers only the class of persons required to report an exemption from the Section 4371 excise tax on insurance premiums. Such reporting is waived for insureds under Section 4372(d) and for U.S. or foreign insurance brokers. Language added to Regulation § 301.6114-1(d) provides that reporting with respect to premiums must be made for each of three specified categories, as described in Section 4371(a), and that aggregation of payments within each category is permitted. Reports with respect to insurance payments made during calendar years 1988–1990 may disclose for each category the total premiums derived by a foreign insurer or reinsurer in U.S. dollars even though a portion relates to non-U.S.-situs risks. Reports for years thereafter must disclose for each category the total premiums that are derived with respect to U.S.-situs risks. Reasonable estimates will suffice.

[73 J. Tax'n 172.]

¶ 6.07 TREATIES BETWEEN UNITED STATES AND PARTICULAR COUNTRIES[6]

[1] Argentina

IRS issues revenue ruling concerning effect of U.S.-Argentina agreement on U.S. taxation of gain from disposition of U.S. real property interest. The IRS ruled that gain from the disposition of a U.S. real property interest derived by an

Argentine enterprise engaged in the international operation of ships and aircraft is not excluded from U.S. taxation under Section 897 by Article 2(2) of an executive agreement between the United States and Argentina, concluded under Sections 872(b) and 883(a).

[Rev. Rul. 90-37, 1990-1 CB 141.]

[2] Australia

"Australia enters multilateral advance pricing agreement" (1991). The Australian Commissioner of Taxation has announced what he states is the world's first advance determination on intercompany transfer pricing between tax authorities. The agreement is between the Australian Taxation Office (ATO), the IRS, and Apple Computer Australia (Apple Australia).

Article 24 of the Australia-U.S. income tax convention, entitled "Mutual Agreement Procedure," provides for a procedure whereby the competent authorities of both countries may agree to the same attribution of income, deductions, credits, or allowances between a head office and a branch, or between different persons, one located in Australia and one located in the United States.

On August 16, 1990, Australia and the United States signed a competent authority agreement pursuant to Article 24 of the convention. The agreement is effective for tax years beginning thereafter.

Upon a request by a taxpayer in Australia or the United States (or both), the ATO and the IRS will consult with each other to arrive at a prospective agreement of an acceptable allocation of income, deductions, credits, or allowances between the countries.

Under the advance determination, Apple Australia, Apple Computer, Inc., the ATO, and the IRS agreed on a methodology for calculating Apple Australia's intercompany transfer pricing for the next four years.

In order to obtain the determination, a functional analysis of Apple Australia and its parent was developed. This analysis detailed the pricing arrangements between both companies, analyzed the arrangements in relation to each country's tax laws, and reviewed comparable transactions in accordance with those laws.

Because of the novelty of advance determinations and a desire by the ATO to avoid scaring off potential applicants, it appears that the ATO will take a flexible approach in determining a suitable transfer pricing methodology. Australia has not yet signed any MAPs with countries other than the United States.

There is no doubt that an advance determination will prove attractive for many multinational corporations. Prior to participating in an advance determination request, however, a corporation should conduct an audit of its own past transfer pricing arrangements to ensure that they fall within the accepted range for such arrangements; corporations should adopt one of the commonly used methodologies. The time and expense involved in obtaining an advance determination will be similar to a company's tax audit of international transactions.

The volume of information and data to be presented will be virtually identical, although the atmosphere will usually be one of willing cooperation rather than fear of penalty.

Where large multinationals have a long history of intercompany transactions of the same or similar goods or services, and an appropriate transfer pricing methodology may be found, an investment in seeking an advance determination may prove worthwhile. The insurance obtained will allow the company group to be secure in its knowledge that it will pay tax on its profits in only one country and will not face the prospect of double taxation or, perhaps just as important, will be unlikely to face large penalties upon the occurrence of a future audit.

[S. Phillipson, 2 J. Int'l Tax'n 116.]

[3] Canada

United States can tax Canadian's share of U.S. partnership capital gain. Taxpayer, a Canadian resident, was a limited partner in a U.S. partnership that generated a long-term capital gain on the sale of U.S. real estate. Taxpayer claimed that his share of the income was exempt because he had no permanent U.S. establishment. The Tax Court held that under the U.S.-Canada treaty, taxpayer had such an establishment, since the partnership had one.

Held: Affirmed for the IRS. Taxpayer had a permanent establishment owing to his interest in a company that maintained U.S. offices.

[Unger, 936 F2d 1316, 68 AFTR2d 91-5204, 91-2 USTC ¶ 50,328 (DC Cir. 1991).]

"Canada steps up use of information exchange agreements" (1993). Increasing globalization of trade and investment has caused a corresponding increase in the need for information to enforce Canada's tax laws in international transactions. One of the principal tools for gathering such information is the exchange of information network established in Canada's double taxation treaties. The authors of this article first discuss the treaty provisions covering the exchange of information between competent authorities regarding the tax liabilities of resident taxpayers. The scope of these provisions is explored under various treaties. Also considered are automatic exchanges of information, "spontaneous" exchanges, specific information requests, and simultaneous audits of the same taxpayer. Next, the authors discuss confidentiality requirements imposed on exchanged information and the limitations imposed on disclosure, applicable administrative procedures, and barriers to disclosure of trade or business secrets.

The authors also discuss enforcement under the convention on mutual administrative assistance in tax matters to which Canada is not yet a party. Last, requests for information under Canada's domestic law directed towards persons who have a nexus with Canada are examined. The authors conclude that although the exchange of information under Canada's treaty network is at present limited, the volume of exchanges is bound to increase. Taxpayers must be aware of this increasing tendency of countries to request and share information and their rights to protect against the possible misuse of such information by foreign competent authorities.

[AH Kingissepp & M. Biringer, 4 J. Int'l Tax'n 388.]

"Residence determines Canadian tax liability in recent cases" (1993). Several recent tax decisions in the Canadian courts have dealt with the question of residence for treaty purposes and whether or not a foreign corporation was liable for Canadian tax. In these decisions, the place of doing business, location of management, and permanent establishment were key factors.

The cases examined by the author of this article are *Crown Forest Industries, Ltd. v. The Queen* and *Placrefid, Ltd. v. The Queen.* In *Crown Forest Industries,* a corporation was found to be a U.S. resident under the Canada-U.S. treaty, thereby qualifying for a reduced tax rate. The corporation had both its place of management and place of business in the United States.

In *Placrefid,* Canada argued that the taxpayer was doing business in Canada or had disposed of an interest in Canadian real estate subject to Canadian tax under the Canada-Switzerland treaty. It was held that the taxpayer was not conducting business and had no permanent establishment in Canada where it was only conducting negotiations through an agent. Place of business and permanent establishment, as well as residence, were held to be in Switzerland.

Since the entity that granted the "option" to the taxpayer did not own the real estate at the time, it could not grant a valid option and the taxpayer's interest was not an interest in Canadian real property that would have been taxable in Canada.

[J. Bernstein, 4 J. Int'l Tax'n 325.]

" 'Permanent establishments' for partners under treaties found from (somewhat) analogous Code provisions" (1992). Two developments during 1991 demonstrate the difficulty of reconciling the notion of "permanent establishment" under income tax treaties with the "fixed place of business" and "engaged in U.S. trade or business" concepts of the Code.

Article I of the 1942 income tax convention between the United States and Canada provided that a Canadian enterprise was not subject to U.S. taxation on its industrial or commercial profits "except in respect of such profits allocable . . . to its permanent establishment in the [U.S.]."

In *Unger,* the U.S. Court of Appeals for the District of Columbia upheld the determination of the Tax Court that a Canadian individual limited partner in a Massachusetts limited partnership was taxable on his distributive share of a capital gain derived by the limited partnership from its sale of U.S. real estate. The Tax Court held that a partnership is not legally a separate entity, but rather the aggregate of its individual partners. Accordingly, the limited partnership's gain was gain derived proportionately by each of its partners (whether general or limited), and the partnership's fixed place of business was likewise attributed to its partners.

Consequently, the court held that the capital gain deemed derived by the partners was properly allocable to their U.S. permanent establishment (consisting of the partnership's fixed place of business). The author discusses the arguments of the parties and the court's reasoning.

In Revenue Ruling 91-32, the IRS held that a foreign partner is taxable on its sale of an interest in a partnership engaged in a U.S. trade or business through a fixed place of business, as though there had been a sale of the underlying partnership assets allocated to the selling partner. The argument made by the IRS was tripartite:

1. Section 875 attributes both a U.S. trade or business and a U.S. fixed place of business of a partnership to its partners.
2. An interest in such a partnership is personal property attributable to the partnership's U.S. trade or business.
3. The measure of gain or loss on a sale of an interest in such a partnership by a foreign partner is the gain or loss inherent in assets of the partnership that are attributable to that U.S. trade or business. The author analyzes the holding and discusses some possibly unintended results arising from it.

[RE Andersen, 3 J. Int'l Tax'n 62.]

"Permanent establishments in Canada" (1992). The concept of permanent establishments is central to the application of the business profits provision of Canadian tax treaties. Foreign enterprises eligible for treaty protection are subject to Canadian income tax on their business profits earned in Canada only if they have a permanent establishment in Canada. This column focuses on the Canadian jurisprudence concerning the term "permanent establishment" in Canadian tax treaties.

The provisions of Canadian treaties entered into after 1977 generally parallel those of the 1977 OECD model double taxation convention on income and on capital (OECD model convention).

In general, business profits earned in Canada by nonresident enterprises are not subject to Canadian income tax unless the enterprises "carried on business in Canada" under Paragraph 2(3)(b) of the Income Tax Act (the act). At common law, this threshold test is very low. In addition, Section 253 of the act has expanded the concept of carrying on business in Canada by a deeming provision. Consequently, the threshold is easily crossed by any trading operation undertaken in Canada by a foreign enterprise.

As a result, nonresident enterprises seeking to transact business in Canada will most often have to rely on the business profits provision of a Canadian tax treaty to protect their business income from Canadian income taxation. It is for this reason that the existence or nonexistence of a permanent establishment is so crucial to nonresident business entities.

The protection afforded by Canadian tax treaties does not extend to income tax liability under provincial law in Canada, however, since Canadian provinces are not bound by Canada's tax conventions.

In general, under Canadian tax treaties there must be a "fixed place of business" for there to be a permanent establishment. The commentary to the OECD model convention sets out three requirements for the existence of a permanent establishment of an enterprise:

1. There must be a place of "business."
2. The business must be "fixed."
3. The business activities must occur at the fixed place of business.

The author turns to the requirements for there to be a place of business, including that (1) there be business from which income is derived; (2) the activities of a business be undertaken with a reasonable expectation of profit; and (3) the office, premises, facilities, or installations be used or be capable of being used in the taxpayer's business.

With respect to the requirement that there be a fixed place of business, it is clear that there must be a link between the place of business and a specific geographical point, although no element of the place of business need be actually fixed to the ground. What is unclear is the degree of permanence this link must have. The commentary suggests that as long as the place of business was not set up for purely temporary purposes, a very short period of time may be all that is required where the activity of the enterprise has a special nature or where the place of business is prematurely liquidated owing to special circumstances. This interpretation of "fixed" apparently found favor in Canadian case law.

The third requirement of a permanent establishment is that the business must be carried on through the fixed place of business. According to the commentary to the model treaty, this usually means "that persons who, in one way or another, are dependent on the enterprise (personnel) conduct *the business of the enterprise* in the State in which the fixed place is situated." It is difficult to predict how a Canadian case involving a rental property or even a factory managed by an independent management company would be decided.

The OECD model convention also requires that the business be wholly or partly "carried on" through the fixed place of business. The language of "carrying on" business strongly suggests continuity and regularity. This interpretation finds support in *Tara Exploration & Development Co.*, where the Exchequer Court took the position that one could not "carry on" an isolated adventure in the nature of trade, since "carrying on" necessitated continuity.

In the author's experience, however, the administrative practice of Revenue Canada has been restrictive on this issue. Revenue Canada has, for example, indicated that a permanent establishment exists when a touring rock band performs two or three concerts in Canada.

[RG Tremblay, 2 J. Int'l Tax'n 305.]

"Canadian securities are good tax prospect for U.S. investors" (1991). The application of current Canadian tax rules as modified by the current U.S.-Canadian treaty (1984) to three types of Canadian investment securities issues (those traded on U.S. exchanges, Canadian-listed securities, and Canadian and U.S. mutual funds investing in Canadian securities) is discussed in this article.

Numerous Canadian corporations have obtained access to U.S. capital markets by registering their securities with the Securities and Exchange Commission, thereby achieving dual listings. Canadian shares represent direct ownership rather than an American Depositary Receipt for the shares of European or Japanese corporations.

Under Article X of the treaty, only a 15 percent tax may be withheld on portfolio dividends (10 percent where the U.S. person beneficially owns at least 10 percent of the Canadian payor), and the holding of the securities is not connected with a Canadian "permanent establishment" as defined in the treaty's Article V. The author describes the procedures to take advantage of the treaty.

Gains on disposition of the securities of Canadian issuers by portfolio investors, i.e., those not connected with a Canadian permanent establishment, are not taxed by Canada and, in any event, are protected under treaty Article XIII. Moreover, U.S.-listed Canadian securities are U.S.-dollar denominated, so there would not be any currency gain or loss. The result for U.S. investors is a 15 percent withholding tax on dividends, which is placed in the Section 904(d)(1)(A) passive income basket for FTC purposes.

A unique provision in the treaty, Article XXI, entitles U.S. tax-exempt organizations to receive dividends and interest from a Canadian payor free of Canadian tax if such income would be exempt in the United States.

Under Article XI of the treaty, interest on government bonds or governmental-organization-guaranteed obligations is subject to a zero rate, and interest on other obligations is subject to a 15 percent rate.

The rules applicable to U.S.-listed equities (and to gains on disposition of debt obligations or other financial instruments) apply to Canadian-listed securities, except that, in addition, the payment and receipt of Canadian funds raises the issue of foreign currency gain or loss and the Subpart J rules, especially Section 988. These complex rules are likely to apply only to acquisition of a Canadian-dollar denominated debt obligation or trading in options to purchase Canadian currency or options on Canadian-dollar-denominated debt instruments. Under Section 988(e), however, the Section 988 rules apply to U.S. individuals only if the transaction generates expenses deductible under Section 162 or Section 212.

If the Section 988 rules do apply, exchange gain or loss may arise in certain cases, e.g., an accrual-method obligee, as a result of the difference in exchange rates when interest payments are accrued and when payments are received. Such gain or loss generally would be interest income or loss and be U.S. source, assuming the U.S. obligee is a portfolio investor. This may mean that the U.S. investor suffers a Canadian withholding tax on what is recharacterized in part as U.S.-source ordinary loss.

Investors in a U.S. mutual fund holding Canadian securities receive treaty protection to the same extent as if they had purchased the securities directly. Canadian taxation of U.S. investors in Canadian-listed mutual fund trusts, i.e., unit investment trusts, operates under a modified look-through rule as though the U.S.

holder received directly each component of the fund's distribution (dividends or gain).

[RD Lorence, 1 J. Int'l Tax'n 376.]

[4] Czech Republic

IRS announces new tax treaty between United States and Czech Republic. A news release announces that copies of a new tax treaty between the United States and the Czech Republic are now available from the Treasury Public Affairs Office. The treaty, designed to avoid double taxation of income and capital and to prevent fiscal evasion, was signed September 16, 1993. The treaty, which is subject to ratification, would be the first such treaty between the two countries.

[Treasury Dep't News Release LB-402 (Sept. 29, 1993); 93(13) Stand. Fed. Tax Rep. (CCH) ¶ 46,358.]

[5] France

U.S.-France tax treaty does not permit nonresident alien to claim the greater U.S. unified estate tax credit available to U.S. residents. The decedent was a nonresident alien domiciled in France at the time of his death. His estate filed a U.S. estate tax return because the decedent owned real property in the United States. On this return, the estate claimed the marital deduction and the larger unified credit available to U.S. citizens and residents. The IRS challenged the estate's use of the larger credit and the Tax Court agreed with the IRS, holding that the estate was only entitled to claim the unified credit applicable to nonresident aliens and that the U.S.-France tax treaty did not require otherwise. The estate appealed.

Held: Affirmed for the IRS. Article 11(2) of the U.S.-France tax treaty specifically requires that a French domiciliary be allowed the same marital deduction as if domiciled in the United States. It does not make the same express grant with regard to the unified credit. It merely states that the applicable tax rates shall be the same as those that would be applicable if the decedent were domiciled in the United States. Taxpayer argued that on electing the marital deduction under this treaty provision, it became subject to the higher U.S. estate tax rates imposed on U.S. citizens and residents, and therefore should be allowed the same unified credit as a U.S. citizen or resident. This, however, is not supported by the treaty provision. The only relevant effect of the provision is to permit the estate of a nonresident alien to claim the marital deduction as if it were a domestic estate, at the cost of being subject to higher estate tax rates. The treaty does not, explicitly or implicitly, provide the estate of a French nonresident with the option of having its tax computed as if it were the estate of a U.S. citizen or resident.

[Estate of Arnaud, 895 F2d 624, 65 AFTR2d 90-1196, 90-1 USTC ¶ 60,006 (9th Cir. 1990).]

[6] Germany

IRS issues revenue procedure concerning U.S.-Germany tax treaty. This revenue procedure provides instructions for claiming a refund of an overpayment of excise tax on insurance policies when the claim is based on the convention between the United States and the Federal Republic of Germany for the avoidance of double taxation and the prevention of fiscal evasion with respect to taxes on income and capital and to certain other taxes. The treaty was signed at Bonn, Germany, on August 29, 1989, and entered into force on August 21, 1991.

[Rev. Proc. 92-14, 1992-3 IRB 31.]

"United States and West Germany sign new ground-breaking tax treaty" (1990). On August 23, 1989, the United States and the Federal Republic of Germany signed a new income tax treaty (New Treaty) to replace the one in effect since 1954 (Old Treaty). The New Treaty contains a number of provisions reflecting recent developments in U.S. tax treaty policy, as well as several that are without precedent among the U.S. tax treaties.

In its definition of "residence," the New Treaty differs markedly from the Old Treaty, since the latter does not define the term at all. The New Treaty definition resembles the 1981 U.S. model definition, which in turn is very similar to the 1977 OECD model provision. Article 4(3) of the New Treaty, the final tie-breaker provision, treats nonindividual taxpayers as residing in neither country for New Treaty purposes if none of the preceding tie-breaker rules apply.

The most important changes wrought by the New Treaty are those dealing with corporate income taxation and taxation of dividends. Article 10(8)(a) of the New Treaty expressly permits the United States to impose its branch profits tax after 1990 on the dividend equivalent amount of West German corporations having effectively connected U.S. earnings and profits. The Old Treaty, by virtue of its nondiscrimination and second-tier withholding rule, bars the U.S. branch profits tax.

The New Treaty's provisions on corporate dividends represent the cutting edge of U.S. treaty positions on this issue, largely because they address several policy aims at once. The United States had long sought to reduce the level of West German withholding tax on dividends paid to U.S. shareholders because the West German corporate tax system is integrated. The West German system allows a West German resident shareholder to claim a credit for corporate-level taxes paid on distributed profits, but denies that credit to nonresident shareholders. Other U.S. treaties mitigate this discrimination by providing a cash payment to be made by the treaty partner to a U.S. shareholder who would be entitled to the credit if he were a resident of the treaty-partner country. The New Treaty addresses this problem by reducing the rate of West German withholding tax on corporate dividends to certain U.S. shareholders.

Under the New Treaty, companies of one country holding at least 10 percent of the voting shares of a company residing in the other country are subject to a 10 percent tax on dividends paid or credited between January 1, 1990, and December 31, 1991. As long as a West German individual is entitled to a tax credit for West German corporate-level taxes paid, Article 10(2)(b) states that the West German withholding rate on dividends to U.S. shareholders is limited to 10 percent, but is treated as 15 percent for U.S. income tax purposes. The effect of this is to create a deemed dividend to the U.S. shareholder, taxable by the United States, and equal to the forgone West German withholding tax. Thus, the New Treaty provides for a U.S. tax-sparing credit on dividends not eligible for intercorporate relief. It also modifies these rules with respect to tax-advantaged companies. Distributions from a U.S. regulated investment company to a West German shareholder, as well as those from a West German investment fund to a U.S. shareholder, are subject to the 15 percent source-country withholding rate regardless of the degree of share of ownership, and no portion of the West German withholding tax is forgone under the special provision. West German shareholders in U.S. real estate investment trusts (REITs) are denied the 5 percent rate in all cases, and the 15 percent rate is available only if the beneficial owner is an individual owning a less-than-10-percent interest in the REIT.

The New Treaty contains a number of antiabuse provisions designed to curb certain practices that have developed under the Old Treaty. Article 28 contains limitations on the persons who may claim treaty benefits. This is based on the qualified residence rules, which require residents of a treaty partner to meet certain tests in their country of residence before being able to claim New Treaty benefits. These tests are (1) they actively conduct a noninvestment business; (2) their shares are actively traded on a recognized securities exchange; (3) they are a tax-exempt nonprofit organization; and (4) more than half of their interests are held by U.S. citizens or persons otherwise entitled to New Treaty benefits.

Other New Treaty provisions designed to close loopholes include the express permission for either country to tax participating debt and similar obligations under its own rules, regardless of the regular rules of the dividend and interest articles, if payments are deductible by the payor. Some other provisions are designed to close a long-standing opportunity under the Old Treaty that takes advantage of the general method of West German tax relief, namely, exemption with progression. This system confers a substantial advantage over the FTC system to West Germans, since income taxable to them by the United States at its relatively low rates is completely sheltered from the higher West German corporate and individual income tax rates.

Under Article 21 of the protocol to the New Treaty, West Germany may apply a credit system, rather than its exemption rules, to an item of income. If the two countries place the item under different treaty provisions, the discrepancy cannot be reconciled, and the result is either double taxation or too little taxation. Article 23(2) of the New Treaty also permits West Germany to apply an FTC, rather than the exemption method, to certain dividends, directors' fees, and gains from dispositions of U.S. real property. The effect of these exceptions to the exemption method is that West German taxpayers wind up bearing the higher West German tax rates on income items covered by the credit method.

The New Treaty contains an arbitration provision for any disagreements that cannot be resolved by competent authorities. The decision of the arbitral tribunal is binding on both countries as to the case before them. Some additional changes contained in the New Treaty include the omission of the option by West German residents to elect annually to be taxed on a net basis on income from real property located in the United States. The New Treaty covers the same taxes as the Old Treaty except now foreign insurers' premiums for insuring or reinsuring U.S. risks are exempt from U.S. tax unless attributable to a U.S. permanent establishment. The New Treaty provides explicit rules for handling refunds of tax where a treaty country requires full withholding on income that is entitled to a reduced or zero rate of withholding under the New Treaty.

[RE Andersen, 1 J. Int'l Tax'n 60.]

[7] India

IRS issues revenue procedure concerning U.S.-India tax treaty. This revenue procedure sets forth the exemptions, reliefs, or reductions in respect of taxes on income from grants, scholarships, and employment that are available under Article 21(2) of the U.S.-India income tax treaty to an Indian student or business apprentice who is present in the United States for educational or training purposes.

[Rev. Proc. 93-20, 1993-13 IRB 10.]

"Treaty benefits clarified for Indian students, apprentices" (1993). In Revenue Procedure 93-20, the IRS explained the exemptions and deductions allowable by reason of the U.S.-India tax treaty to Indian students or business apprentices temporarily in the United States for education or training.

[4 J. Int'l Tax'n 163.]

[8] Israel

"The U.S.-Israel tax treaty, bearing two protocols, moves toward ratification" (1993). One of the main reasons that a tax treaty between the United States and Israel had been so long in the making was Israel's fear that signing a treaty with a disclosure of information clause might deter U.S. investment in Israel. In 1985, however, the United States and Israel signed a free trade area agreement to remove Customs and non-Customs barriers to trade between the two countries. This raised the absurd situation of there being a trade agreement without a tax treaty to prevent double taxation. Accordingly, the United States and Israel signed a protocol in 1993 amending the original draft of their 1975 proposed tax treaty. Though this treaty has not been ratified as of June 1993, the Israeli Tax Commission has indicated its ratification is imminent. The principal issues now involve whether the treaty will resolve problems that U.S. investors encounter in Israel and those Israeli investors face in the United States.

The authors of this article first discuss Israel's taxation of businesses, particularly with respect to foreign investors. Its tax rates and special tax incentives for certain approved enterprises are also examined. Next, they address the anticipated effects of the proposed tax treaty between the United States and Israel. Specific attention is given to the applicable rates under the treaty and the manner in which the U.S. and Israeli systems will interact. Exhibits are provided by the authors that illustrate some of the points discussed in the text of the article.

Next, the authors examine the taxation of Israeli investors in the United States. The authors conclude that the treaty may eliminate the current double taxation on capital gains of U.S. residents and on persons engaged in a trade or business without a permanent establishment. Owing to the lack of a tax-sparing provision, the treaty does not reduce taxes for U.S. investors who invest in an approved enterprise in Israel. For U.S. investors considering an investment in Israel, the same results can be achieved without a tax treaty by having the U.S. investors form an S corporation to open a branch in Israel.

[Z. Holender & Al Appel, 4 J. Int'l Tax'n 292.]

[9] Mexico

"Exchange of information agreement used for documents before treaty was in effect" (1993). In *Barquero*, a 1993 case, a district court concluded that the agreement between the United States of America and the United Mexican States for the exchange of information and with respect to taxes allowed the IRS to use its summons power to obtain a Mexican citizen's bank records held by a U.S. bank, even though such records were created before the 1990 effective date of this agreement.

[4 J. Int'l Tax'n 478.]

"U.S.-Mexico tax treaty complements North American Free Trade Agreement (NAFTA)" (1993). In 1992, the United States and Mexico signed the first income tax treaty and accompanying protocol between the two countries. This followed the negotiation of NAFTA by the United States, Mexico, and Canada. NAFTA phases out barriers to trade in goods and services in North America, eliminates investment barriers, and strengthens the protection of intellectual property rights. Because NAFTA generally does not apply to taxation measures, the Treasury views the treaty as a significant complement to NAFTA that, among other things, would establish clear rules of taxing jurisdiction, reduce the overall tax on investment income flowing between the two countries, and grant relief from double taxation. Aside from certain references to NAFTA in the limitations of benefits article, however, the treaty is not based on NAFTA. Rather, it is similar to the income tax treaty with India, another developing country, signed in 1989. In the event of an inconsistency between NAFTA and a tax treaty, the treaty will prevail.

The authors first review the treaty's provisions for income not attributable to a permanent establishment, including dividends, interest, securities gains, real estate and equipment rents, and royalties. Next, they examine the treaty's provisions affecting personal services, as well as the taxation of personal service income in the United States and Mexico.

The authors then consider the treaty's provisions on permanent establishments. Last, they review other provisions of the treaty, including those concerning charitable organizations, shipping income, creditable taxes, source rules, consolidated groups, treaty beneficiaries, limitations on benefits, mutual agreement (i.e., arbitration) procedures, and termination.

The authors conclude that the treaty is generally consistent with historic U.S. treaty policies, yet takes into account both the nuances of Mexican tax law and the overall free trade spirit of NAFTA. The treaty will tend to make income taxes a neutral factor when a U.S. individual or business is deciding whether to invest in the United States or Mexico. This treaty may well serve as a model for future U.S. treaties with less-developed countries, particularly with those Caribbean, Central American, and South American countries that may join NAFTA as part of the proposed Enterprise for the Americas Initiative.

[AS Lederman & B. Hirsh, 79 J. Tax'n 100.]

"U.S.-Mexico treaty combines developed and developing country models" **(1992).** On September 18, 1992, the United States and Mexico signed the first comprehensive income tax convention (treaty) between the two countries. Although the treaty reflects current U.S. income tax policy in many respects, the historical relationship between the United States and Mexico, Mexico's status as a developing country, and the new realities of international trade in the western hemisphere influence a number of aspects of the treaty and introduce several idiosyncrasies.

Mexico generally has preferred to follow the 1977 OECD model income tax treaty in recent negotiations with the United States and European countries—a model designed to establish a bilateral relationship between two developed or highly industrialized countries. In certain circumstances, however, Mexico has recognized a fundamental imbalance in investment flows between its more developed treaty partners and itself and, in such instances, looks more to the United Nations model.

In this article, the authors analyze some of the principal points in the treaty that will affect trade and investment relations between the United States and Mexico. The authors discuss the permanent establishment and business profits provisions of the treaty and the fact that such provisions reflect Mexico's need to be viewed as a developing, and not a developed, country. Next, they discuss the treaty's provisions concerning taxation of income, as well as the series of compromises reached between the two countries in formulating these provisions. Specific discussion is provided on the subjects of royalties, dividends, interest, capital gains, and other income.

Thereafter, the authors address special situations covered by the treaty, i.e., exempt organizations and transportation income. Next, they examine the treaty provisions on the avoidance of double income taxation, which contains the standard

U.S. transfer pricing provisions, and the unusual extent to which the internal law of each country governs its application. An extensive discussion on the treaty's limitation on benefits article is provided. The authors finish the article with a short discussion of the treaty's MAP and exchange of information provisions.

The authors conclude that the unique relationship between the United States and Mexico generated some unusual provisions in the treaty. Whether some of the treaty's more radical departures from typical U.S. treaty practice represent changes in policy or merely concessions to a valued neighbor must await the publication of future U.S. tax conventions with other countries.

[BM Cass & RE Andersen, 3 J. Int'l Tax'n 197.]

"U.S.-Mexico tax information exchange agreement" (1990). Fiscal relations between the United States and Mexico have entered a new era, and the pace of developments in this area is accelerating. Although many years will pass before the full impact of these changes can be assessed, recent developments have proved to be a watershed in U.S.-Mexican tax matters.

On November 9, 1989, the United States and Mexico signed an agreement "for the exchange of information with respect to taxes" between the two countries. The agreement, which became effective on January 18, 1990, permits a significant flow of tax-related information between the two countries. This article summarizes the agreement and discusses key issues under the agreement.

[RE Andersen, 1 J. Int'l Tax'n 126.]

[10] Netherlands

"Benefits under new U.S.-Dutch treaty are limited by complicated tests" (1993). The U.S.-Dutch treaty, signed in 1992, contains complicated provisions for the elimination of double taxation and a limitation-on-benefits article that is longer than some treaties. Some of the complications reflect the differing views of the two countries concerning who should receive the benefits of the treaty. Others probably reflect the trend towards increasing specificity in international taxation treaties. In any event, the treaty is being looked at carefully for signs of what may be contained in the U.S. model treaty expected to be released in late 1993.

The authors first discuss the treaty's provisions concerning the elimination of double taxation. The specific methods set forth in the treaty are examined, including those covering triangular corporate arrangements. Next, the treaty's limitation-on-benefits provision is explored. Specific attention is given to the eleven categories of companies that qualify under this article for treaty benefits and its antiabuse provisions. Last, the authors discuss miscellaneous provisions of the treaty concerning offshore activities, tax-exempt organizations, and certain procedural rules.

[PH Sleurink & RE Andersen, 4 J. Int'l Tax'n 212.]

"U.S.-Dutch treaty reflects changed policies and economic forces" (1993). In 1992, the Netherlands and the United States signed a new double taxation convention, with a memorandum of understanding attached. The new treaty represents a compromise between two opposing views on the scope of double taxation treaties. The official policy of the Netherlands traditionally extends the benefits of a tax treaty to anyone who meets the basic residency test and, for certain types of income, is the "beneficial owner." On the other hand, the U.S. favors a narrower view as to which residents are entitled to the benefits and protection of a double taxation treaty. Under this view, a corporate resident must demonstrate a sufficient nexus with the resident country to be a "qualifying resident."

After discussing the more important ways in which this treaty is unique, the authors focus their examination of the treaty on its articles individually. An explanation and commentary are provided for most of the treaty's articles. The author concludes that the new treaty reflects the changes in the economic relations between the United States and the European Community countries, and indicates the increasing importance of streamlined dispute resolution mechanisms. Though the new treaty has not yet been ratified, it is likely to indicate how the treaty negotiators will be dealing with a number of important issues in other treaties still under negotiation.

[PH Sleurink & RE Andersen, 4 J. Int'l Tax'n 104.]

[11] Russia

"U.S.-Russian treaty provides new exemptions for construction activities" (1993). U.S. companies supplying big-ticket equipment items and engaging in turnkey projects on an international basis are going through a trying phase. They must deal with new players and increasing international competition across the board, and some of these competitors are taxed under more favorable tax regimes. In addition, local tax authorities are becoming more aggressive by deeming activities to constitute a taxable permanent establishment under the relevant treaty, expanding the concept of effectively connected income to include results of associated but distinct contracts, and disallowing deductions clearly related to gross taxable income, however determined.

Companies that would enter into international construction and assembly projects are immediately faced with several complex tax issues in the jurisdiction of the project host country—how the income from the project will be taxed, and how the employees assigned to the project will be taxed. These host-country tax issues must be addressed at three distinct stages.

1. When bidding on the project (usually with inadequate information and under extreme time constraints);
2. When negotiating the terms of the contracts (for companies lucky enough to be successful bidders); and
3. When managing the project to completion.

Given the burden of submitting timely bids (many of which will not be successful) for a number of different projects, the onus of the tax research and planning (and of the eventual impact of the taxes on the project) usually will depend on the availability of a tax treaty with the host country with terms that allow carrying out the project with minimum corporate and individual filing and tax obligations. Where there is no treaty in effect with the host country, or where the host country requires filing to report an activity that does not constitute a permanent establishment under the treaty, the tax costs in the host country become much more difficult to calculate accurately.

This article first examines treaty treatment of construction projects. Specific attention is given to treaty construction provisions and the treatment of employee costs thereunder. Next, the author examines the specific provisions affecting construction projects under the U.S.-Russia tax treaty. In addition, proposed model treaty changes in this area are discussed.

[BL Patton, Jr., 78 J. Tax'n 118.]

"U.S.-Russia convention follows pattern of recent U.S. treaties" (1992). On June 17, 1992, Presidents Bush and Yeltsin signed a new comprehensive income tax treaty between the United States and the Russian Federation. The treaty, intended to replace the existing convention between the United States and the former Soviet Union, conforms generally to the modern U.S. and OECD models but contains several novel provisions that reflect the special situation facing Russia.

The author reviews the provisions of the treaty conforming to those usually adapted from the U.S. and OECD models, including the scope provisions and the general taxing pattern.

Of great value is Article 22, which provides a credit for U.S. tax purposes of the Russian income taxes covered by the convention. The protocol (Articles 8(b) and 8(c)) clarifies that interest (up to the higher of the maximum interest deduction allowed under Russian law or the London Interbank offered rate plus a reasonable risk premium set forth in the debt documents) and wages generally will be deductible by Russian entities in computing tax on Russian profits, as long as they are at least 30 percent U.S.-owned and have capital of at least $100,000.

The United States was successful in getting its treaty priorities into the new treaty. For example, Article 10(5) expressly permits imposition of the U.S. branch profits tax, and Article 19(3) treats stock of a real property holding company as real property for purposes of taxing its disposition.

The new treaty contains the full-fledged limitation-of-benefits article (here, Article 20) that is a hallmark of recent U.S. income tax treaties.

The U.S.-Russia treaty, when ratified, will harmonize certain tax aspects of U.S. investment in Russia with investment elsewhere in the world. This will provide certainty for U.S. investors and should help attract capital for Russia's economic development plans.

[RE Andersen, 3 J Int'l Tax'n 191.]

¶ 6.08 TREATIES NOT DIRECTLY INVOLVING UNITED STATES

"Trade, regional interests drive 1992 global tax treaty developments" (1992). In 1991, the most striking trend may have been the negotiation of new or revised tax treaties corresponding to the creation or solidification of regional or trade relationships in various parts of the world.

The author briefly surveys tax treaty developments in many countries and regions, including Australia, China, Japan, Latin America, Mexico, Scandinavia, the Netherlands, and Germany.

The foregoing developments show that international tax trends generally, and changes affecting the tax treaty network in particular, mirror the political and economic forces affecting nations and regions. As trading blocs become ever larger factors in the area of international business, tax treaty developments can be expected to track these regional trends.

[RE Andersen, 2 J. Int'l Tax'n 379.]

"Last year's treaty developments bode well for investors" (1991). Significant treaty developments have occurred during 1990 that have not directly involved the United States as a treaty partner. These developments have implications, however, for the United States and its residents to the extent that they affect the investment climate in the relevant jurisdictions or hint at issues that may arise in future treaty negotiations with the United States.

Nordic Treaty. Since the start of 1990 (1991 for taxes on capital), a new multilateral tax convention (Nordic treaty) became effective for Denmark, the Faroe Islands, Finland, Iceland, Norway, and Sweden. The Nordic Treaty replaced its 1987 predecessor (1987 treaty), which was itself a revision of the original 1983 treaty, which was the world's first comprehensive multilateral tax convention.

The Netherlands. The Netherlands signed a new tax treaty and protocol with Norway in January 1990, replacing the current treaty signed in 1966. Although generally similar to the terms of the 1977 OECD model, the new treaty contains an unusual provision concerning source-state withholding taxes on dividend distributions. The new treaty generally allows Norway to impose a 15 percent withholding tax on dividends paid by a 25 percent Norwegian subsidiary to its Dutch parent. That rate will drop to zero, however, when the Norwegian tax on distributed profits is no longer lower than the rate on retained profits. Until that event occurs, the Netherlands may impose a 10 percent withholding tax on dividends paid by 25 percent–Dutch subsidiaries to their Norwegian parents.

France. On April 4, 1990, the Supreme Administrative Court reiterated its prior position that a disguised dividend, as determined under internal French tax law, is not a dividend for French tax treaty purposes in the absence of a specific treaty provision. Thus, a disguised dividend from a French company to a Portuguese shareholder was not subject to French dividend withholding tax under the French-Portuguese income tax treaty. The decision rested on the classification of the disguised dividend as "other income," which only the contracting state of the recipient's residence has the right to tax under Article 23 of that treaty.

On February 16, 1990, the Supreme Administrative Court ruled that interest paid by a French subsidiary to its Swedish parent was partially nondeductible. The ruling was based on a provision of internal French tax law that disallows certain interest paid to controlling shareholders but does not disallow interest paid by a French company to its French parent. The Court rejected the argument that the nondiscrimination provision (Article 16) of the French-Swedish income tax treaty required allowance of the full interest payment as a deduction.

France levies a 3 percent annual tax on the value of French situs real estate held by foreign corporations, unless (among other exceptions) the owning corporation resides in a country with which France has an income tax treaty containing a nondiscrimination clause based on Article 24 of the OECD model. Court decisions rendered during 1989 broadened the treaty exception beyond the position taken by the French tax authorities, particularly with regard to the use of interposed "convenience country" companies.

Legislation introduced by the French government as part of the 1990 Finance Act was designed to overrule those court rulings, in particular by providing that even if the ultimate beneficial corporate owner of French situs real estate resides in a country with which France has entered into an income tax treaty of the type contemplated in the original rule, use of a lower-tier entity (even one that is still above the actual owner of the real estate in the chain of ownership) will automatically disqualify all members of the chain for the benefits of the treaty exemption. This change and the others made to Code General des Impots Articles 990D through 990F are retroactive and make careful planning for foreign ownership of French real estate even more important than formerly.

[RE Andersen, 1 J. Int'l Tax'n 318.]

"Transfer pricing European style" (1991). European Community member states have executed a unique multilateral treaty on the elimination of double taxation in connection with the adjustment of profits of associated enterprises. The convention was signed in Brussels on July 23, 1990, and published on August 20, 1990.

The convention represents a remarkable development in dealing with double taxation within the European Community; first, because it is a multilateral treaty on the subject, and second, because it proposes to adopt a form of arbitration between tax authorities in settling transfer pricing issues.

Article (1) of the convention specifies that the convention applies to "an enterprise of a contracting state." Presumably, this will mean that the application will be somewhat uneven depending on the countries concerned, particularly in relation to partnerships and joint ventures. Article 1(2) states that a permanent establishment of an enterprise of a contracting state situated in another contracting state is deemed to be an enterprise of the state in which it is situated. The definition thus excludes the application of the convention to residents of third states.

The convention applies generally to the taxes on the income of individuals and companies that are imposed by member states of the community and where adjustments are made to profits of an enterprise in a contracting state, either under its domestic law or under the transfer pricing principles established in the convention. The convention is applicable only to taxes on income as specifically set out and any identical or similar taxes that may be imposed by member states.

The arm's-length standard set out in Article 4 of the convention requires the profits of a permanent establishment to be determined on a separate-enterprise basis. The convention adopts a single standard as to when profits of associated enterprises are subject to adjustment. It thus applies where an enterprise of a contracting state participates directly or indirectly in the management, control, or capital of an enterprise in another contracting state. Alternatively, it applies where the same persons participate directly or indirectly in the management, control, or capital of an enterprise in two different contracting states. Thus, the European subsidiaries of U.S. corporations will clearly be subject to adjustment in accordance with these provisions.

The convention treats double taxation of profits as having been eliminated if either the profits are included in the computation of taxable profits in one state only or the tax chargeable on those profits in one state is reduced by the tax chargeable on them in another.

Transfer pricing adjustments are commenced by notification by a contracting state to the taxpayer of its intention to make adjustments. If the other state and the taxpayer agree to the adjustment, no arbitration takes place.

A taxpayer who claims the arm's-length principles of the convention have not been properly applied may submit a case to the appropriate competent authorities pursuant to the convention, irrespective of any other remedy provided under domestic law. If the competent authorities jointly fail to resolve the matter by agreement that eliminates double taxation, they must establish an advisory commission in accordance with the convention's procedures. If agreement is reached, the competent authorities must implement it even if time limits under domestic laws have expired.

The competent authorities are not required to initiate arbitration proceedings if domestic, legal, or administrative proceedings against the taxpayer have resulted in a final ruling that one of the enterprises is liable for a serious penalty by virtue of an action giving rise to an adjustment or transfer of profits. A schedule to the convention details what each member state regards as a serious penalty. Typically, these relate to fraudulent or criminal conduct.

The term "arbitration" does not appear in the convention. The advisory commission is the panel established on an ad hoc basis to hear disputes under the convention. The opinion of the advisory commission is to be adopted by simple majority and must be delivered not more than six months from the date on which the matter was referred to it. A decision that will eliminate double taxation must be taken within six months of the date on which the advisory commission delivers its opinion. The competent authorities may take a decision that deviates from the advisory commission's opinion, but if they fail to reach agreement, they are required to act in accordance with that opinion.

The convention is to enter into force on the first day of the third month following that in which the instrument of ratification is deposited by the last signatory state. It is to endure for six years from entry into force.

[JS Schwarz, 2 J. Int'l Tax'n 120.]

"Worldwide treaty network expands during 1990" (1991). The dominant trend in the tax treaty area during 1990 was the accelerating rate of expansion of the global network to encompass developing nations. The most notable of these countries to enter into tax treaties has been India.

The author discusses a number of the India-Japan treaty provisions, especially the FTC articles. Here, he notes that the Indian-U.S. treaty was held up for over thirty years because of India's request that the United States grant tax-sparing credits to its investors in India, i.e., allowing a credit within the normal confines of Section 904 for Indian taxes that would normally be imposed but are abated or refunded pursuant to Indian tax incentive legislation. Although India dropped that request in its negotiations with the United States, it was successful in persuading Japan to allow tax-sparing credits in the Indian-Japanese treaty. The allowance of tax-sparing credits by the Japanese tax authorities gives prospective Japanese investors in India a substantial pricing advantage over their competitors from other countries that do not permit such phantom taxes to be credited.

Mexico is in the forefront of this worldwide trend, having recently signed a tax information exchange agreement with the United States and having begun negotiations with the United States concerning a possible comprehensive income tax treaty. Other Latin American nations have also been active in expanding their tax treaty networks. The author focuses on Brazil and Ecuador. On March 16, 1990, Canada signed a tax information exchange agreement with Mexico and, three months later, announced the beginning of negotiations between the two countries on a comprehensive income tax treaty. New treaties entered into force between Canada and Poland, Papua New Guinea and Zambia; and a Social Security totalization agreement with the Netherlands, signed on February 26, 1987, entered into force on October 1, 1990.

[RE Andersen, 1 J. Int'l Tax'n 380.]

BIBLIOGRAPHY OF RESEARCH REFERENCES

[1]J. Kuntz & R. Peroni, U.S. International Taxation ch. C4 (Warren Gorham Lamont 1992).

S. Singer, U.S. International Tax Forms Manual ¶ 1.06 (Warren Gorham Lamont 1993).

B. Bittker & J. Eustice, Federal Income Taxation of Corporations and Shareholders ¶ 15.02[4] (Warren Gorham Lamont, 6th ed. 1994).

[2]R. Stephens, G. Maxfield, S. Lind, & D. Calfee, Federal Estate and Gift Taxation ch. 7 (Warren Gorham Lamont, 6th ed. 1991).

[3]J. Kuntz & R. Peroni, U.S. International Taxation ¶ C4.01[5] (Warren Gorham Lamont 1992).

[4]J. Kuntz & R. Peroni, U.S. International Taxation ¶ C4.21[1] (Warren Gorham Lamont 1992).

[5]J. Kuntz & R. Peroni, U.S. International Taxation ¶ C4.22 (Warren Gorham Lamont 1992).

[6]J. Kuntz & R. Peroni, U.S. International Taxation ch. C4 (Warren Gorham Lamont 1992).

CHAPTER 7

Tax Laws of Foreign Countries

¶ 7.01 AFRICA

"French-speaking Africa is slow to modernize the colonial tax system" (1992).
There are fourteen former French colonies in West and Central Africa. All have
designated French as their official language—hence, "Francophone Africa." Because Niger shares common economic and tax characteristics with the other
Francophone countries, it serves as a basis for comparison in this article.

In an effort to attract foreign investment and to encourage the private sector,
all the Francophone countries are now dismantling their post-independence systems
of socialist control. All have granted tax holidays, although many insist on a minimum investment before such tax advantages are available. In Niger, the minimum
is $150,000 and benefits last from four to ten years, depending principally on the
size of the investment. Benefits include exemptions from (1) income taxes; (2)
import duties and fees; and (3) value-added tax (VAT). Since benefits are often
negotiated, agreement should be reached before the investment is begun.

There have been few major tax innovations in the Francophone African countries since their independence from France in 1960. The main change has been
introduction of the VAT, and many countries can be expected to switch to this form
in the near future. Some consolidation of other taxes may be attempted, but the
experience thus far suggests that this may be a slow process.

[R. Barlow & W. Snyder, 3 J. Int'l Tax'n 86.]

¶ 7.02 AUSTRALIA

"Foreign investment fund regime targets passive investments, large offshore holdings" (1993). Australia's new foreign investment fund (FIF) regime, effective January 1, 1995, addresses the problem of income deferral by Australian residents with offshore interests that are not Australian-controlled. The authors of this article discuss the FIF regime and its application. They provide specific discussion of the following: (1) the definition of "FIF"; (2) exemptions from the FIF regime; (3) calculation of the FIF tax; and (4) anti–double taxation provisions.

The authors conclude that the FIF regime will discourage certain Australian residents from making certain kinds of overseas investments, and consequently will discourage certain enterprises from seeking investors in Australia. The numerous exemptions, however, will prevent taxation of interests in active businesses or taxation of those interests that are held by small investors.

[D. Lockie & M. Brown, 4 J. Int'l Tax'n 178.]

"Australian interests in foreign investment funds to be taxed" (1992). During the past few years, the Australian government has introduced a controlled foreign corporation (CFC) regime. Now, as an adjunct to the CFC legislation, the government has released proposals for dealing with noncontrolling investments by Australian tax residents in foreign corporations and offshore investment bodies and trusts.

The proposed FIF tax regime is designed to counter the sheltering of passive income in nonresident entities. It is effective for taxable years beginning July 1, 1992, and is intended to complement CFC measures contained in the Taxation Laws Amendment (Foreign Income) Act 1990. The FIF measures apply to investment in entities that are principally engaged in activities earning passive income and that are not subject to the CFC measures.

The FIF regime will affect investments by Australian resident companies or individuals in all offshore companies and trusts earning passive income. The new measures will not apply to direct investments by Australian residents in foreign companies or trusts engaged principally in "active business" operations.

The FIF measures will tax income and gains from all Australian-held interests in offshore entities on a current basis (i.e., accrual, rather than cash), unless one of three exclusions detailed in the article applies. These exclusions are (1) a de minimis exclusion; (2) an Australian resident has interests in foreign entities that are already currently taxable under existing CFC measures; and (3) interests in companies engaged principally in "active business," as defined, if certain requirements are met as set forth by the authors.

Special provisions will also be developed to exclude holding companies with subsidiaries principally engaged in active business activity.

FIF income of a resident taxpayer will be calculated by the aggregate change in the market value of the taxpayer's FIF interests over the taxable year—with appropriate allowance for losses.

The FIF measures will apply on a worldwide rather than jurisdictional basis. This approach has been adopted by other countries with FIF regimes. Unlike the CFC rules, there will be no broad exemption for investments in countries with a tax system and tax rate comparable to Australia.

Investors in large funds or multinational trusts operating on a feeder fund arrangement will be affected by the new regime. Such arrangements include those in which money is raised from Australian investors, nominally situated in an Australian-based international trust or fund, and channeled to an overseas-based fund for investment.

Australian-based international funds that invest money directly in overseas assets, such as shares in overseas companies listed on a stock exchange or overseas fixed-interest securities, will not be taxed under the FIF rules. Investments directly in overseas business assets will also not be taxed. The assets acquired by the investment fund, however, must be assets of a company engaging in active business.

[S. Phillipson & C. Faulkner, 2 J. Int'l Tax'n 311.]

"Australia overhauls tax system with self-assessment approach" (1992). On May 26, 1992, the Australian government introduced the Taxation Laws Amendment Bill into Parliament, completing reforms of Australia's existing self-assessment regime.

The changes to the law made by the Self-Assessment Act are effective July 1, 1992 (i.e., fiscal 1993). The changes are as follows:

1. Introduction of a system of binding public rulings from the Australian Taxation Office (ATO);
2. Introduction of system of binding private rulings from the ATO;
3. Introduction of rights of review and appeal of private rulings;
4. Overhaul of penalty tax provisions;
5. Streamlining of the interest regime; and
6. Introduction of a self-assessment framework, with extended review rights.

The lodgement process for eligible taxpayers—companies and superannuation funds—has the following key elements:

1. All entities deriving Australian source income, including capital gains, are required to lodge an income tax return annually with the ATO.
2. For eligible entities, lodgement of an income tax return is an income tax assessment by the ATO.
3. The taxpayer, and the ATO, have four years from the deemed assessment to amend the income tax return.
4. The taxpayer has four years from the date of assessment to lodge an objection against the assessment.
5. The ATO may not alter a taxpayer's assessment of tax if the taxpayer has lodged its income tax return because of a binding public or binding private

ruling. If there are conflicting rulings, assessment is made under the ruling resulting in the lowest tax.

The Australian Tax Act prescribes circumstances under which taxpayers may be penalized for understated tax (tax shortfalls), stipulating additional penalty taxes for breaches of these provisions, subject to increase or decrease under specific rules, or remission at the discretion of the ATO. The new penalties and their amounts are then set out and discussed by the author.

The most significant change to Australia's taxation procedures is the introduction of a system of binding public rulings and binding and reviewable private rulings.

The Commissioner of Taxation can now issue (and withdraw) public rulings binding on the ATO. A public ruling is the commissioner's opinion on the way a tax law would apply to a class of people or arrangements, or the way in which the commissioner would exercise his discretion. To be binding, the commissioner must state that the ruling is a public ruling when it is published.

Taxpayers may now apply for a binding private ruling from the ATO.

The changes of the self-assessment act are a fundamental transformation of Australian tax procedures, significantly increasing the burdens and risks for taxpayers. The changes also portend new and vigorous audit activity by the taxation office.

[D. Lockie, 3 J. Int'l Tax'n 180.]

"Australia expands use of taxpayer identification numbers" (1991). As part of the economic statement issued by the Treasurer in May 1988, the Australian government chose to proceed with an ATO proposal to extend the use of the existing tax file number (TFN) system to make it more effective in combating tax evasion.

Under the new requirements for use of the TFN, effective July 1, 1991, all taxpayers with bank accounts, interest-bearing deposits, shares in public companies, unit trust investments, government body bonds, or deposits with solicitors need to provide their TFN if they want to earn interest or be paid dividends without being subject to taxation at the highest marginal tax rate (currently 48.25 percent).

The most significant extension of the use of the TFN has been since July 1, 1991. If a person has not provided a TFN to the appropriate public company or investment body, income is taxed at the highest marginal tax rate of 48.25 percent, if it is earned on

1. Investments in interest-bearing accounts;
2. Deposits;
3. Shares in public companies;
4. Units in unit trusts (mutual funds);
5. Government and semi-government bonds; and
6. Deposits of money with a solicitor.

If a taxpayer earns $120 or more a year in interest from any bank or similar account and has not provided a TFN, the bank must deduct 48.25 percent of such income and remit it to the ATO. If tax is taken out of any payment pursuant to the TFN provisions, taxpayers may claim a credit for that deduction on their tax returns but must wait until the end of the financial year to do so.

Nonresidents who earn income subject to interest or dividend withholding tax need not obtain or quote a TFN. They are required, however, to advise the relevant investment body that they are nonresidents and to provide their names and addresses. Quoting a TFN is always voluntary. There is no offense for failing to quote a TFN when requested, although there is an offense for deliberately quoting an incorrect TFN. As mentioned, however, if a person does not quote a TFN, a 48.25 percent tax is deducted from income. This financial sanction usually ensures compliance. Privacy safeguards are incorporated in the TFN legislation as part of the Privacy Act 1988, which is discussed in detail.

The article ends with a detailed discussion of a May 1991 submission by the Taxation Institute of Australia to the government and the ATO proposing an Australian residents withholding tax on interest income.

[S. Phillipson, 2 J. Int'l Tax'n 243.]

"Australia to expand full self-assessment tax system" (1991). The government of Australia has now decided, in principle, that full self-assessment should be extended progressively to all taxpayers, possibly commencing with returns filed for individuals by registered tax agents for the 1992–1993 income year and processed in the 1993–1994 year.

The Treasurer of Australia acknowledged that in moving to a full self-assessment system, a number of the administrative provisions of the law associated with self-assessment will need major amendment.

The treasurer announced that the key features of the new full self-assessment system will be

1. Faster issuing of tax refunds;
2. Payment of interest by the ATO on refunds not issued to taxpayers within a short period of the filing of a tax return;
3. Development of simpler tax return forms, with less information required with the return; and
4. Provision of rulings binding on the Commissioner of Taxation and subject to review by administrative tribunals and the courts.

The author discusses the government's proposals issued in a consultative document.

The second area of tax simplification announced by the treasurer relates to the tax rules for employment income earned in other countries by Australian taxpayers. These rules are to be changed, retroactively, from July 1, 1990. The previous provisions in this area involved significant compliance and administrative costs. To simplify these rules, the government has extended the existing exemptions and altered the method of calculating tax on other income for taxpayers with exempt foreign employment income. Retroactive to July 1, 1990, foreign employment income derived from more than ninety days of continuous foreign service will be exempt from Australian tax, unless the income is exempt from tax in the foreign country under either a double taxation agreement or the other country's tax laws.

For taxpayers with exempt foreign income, the method of taxing other assessable Australian income will be modified by applying a notional average tax rate computed on the sum of exempt and nonexempt income and applied to the nonexempt component. This method is consistent with the Australian foreign tax credit (FTC) system and will simplify the calculation of tax payable on nonexempt income. The treasurer has stated that no taxpayer will be disadvantaged by the change of the calculation method.

[S. Phillipson, 2 J. Int'l Tax'n 47.]

¶ 7.03 BELGIUM

"Belgium offers major tax incentives for holding companies" (1992). In October 1991, the Belgian Parliament adopted legislation making Belgium a highly attractive jurisdiction in which to establish holding companies. This legislation, which came about in connection with the implementation of the European Community (EC) Council Parent-Subsidiary Directive, goes far beyond the requirements of the directive. In fact, the Belgian government has taken the opportunity to establish an entirely revised system for the taxation of dividends and capital gains on shares.

The new law of October 23, 1991 (the law), amends the participation exemption, a Belgian tax law provision that partially exempts dividends derived from qualifying equity participations from corporate income tax. In addition, the law extends the participation exemption to capital gains realized on qualifying participations. Moreover, the Royal Decree of October 14, 1991, amends the withholding tax system on the distribution of dividends to parent companies established within the EC. The law is generally applicable from assessment year 1992 (accounting periods ending on December 31, 1991, or later), whereas the Royal Decree applies from October 15, 1991.

[V. Sway, 3 J. Int'l Tax'n 148.]

¶ 7.04 BERMUDA

"Bermuda—a base for international operations and investment" (1990). Bermuda is internationally recognized as a favorable base for foreign operations. It provides the technical and professional assistance needed to minimize business risks and, although it has never held itself out as a tax haven, it has no income taxes and virtually no other taxes.

In this article, the authors discuss the advantages of operating a business or investing in Bermuda. First, they provide general background information on Bermuda, including a brief history and discussion of its governmental operations. Next, they address various tax and other specific business benefits associated with operating in Bermuda. Taxes imposed by Bermuda on estates and payrolls, its general living conditions, and the available labor and professional services in the resident populations are also given consideration. Thereafter, the authors explain the various available forms for doing business in Bermuda. Of the corporate forms discussed are Bermuda companies, permit companies, and companies limited by guaranty. The Bermuda business law requirements and corporate formation fees are also discussed.

Specific discussion is then provided on operating an insurance or reinsurance business in Bermuda, including a captive insurance company. Operating a shipping business (including registration under the British flag) in Bermuda is then discussed. Incorporation of a U.S. tax-advantaged foreign sales corporation (FSC) in Bermuda is also addressed.

Other subjects covered by the authors in this article are the formation and operation of mutual funds out of Bermuda, Bermuda as a site for research and development, and the use of Bermuda trusts for foreign beneficiaries. Bermuda's laws applicable to such trusts are also briefly reviewed. Last, the authors consider the establishment of employee benefit plans in Bermuda for non-U.S. employees working outside of the United States. The Bermuda laws that affect such plans and trusts are reviewed.

[CM Collis & JA Ellison, US Tax'n Int'l Operations ¶ 8401.]

¶ 7.05 BRAZIL

"Brazilian indexing system can only approximate a stable economy" (1993). Inflation, characterized by a continuing increase in the price of goods and services due to excess money in circulation, triggers distortions in economic relationships, particularly between creditors and debtors. Monetary correction seeks to allow long-term transactions in spite of inflation and gains and losses that would occur in pure cash dealing are minimized or eliminated. Monetary correction involves the use of an index showing price variations to adjust the values of goods and services over a period. With inflation indexing, the value of goods and services for long-term payments, rather than being expressed in currency, is regularly adjusted under an index chosen by the parties. Price indexes thereby determine a constant value that ensures a lasting nature to long-term business relationships. Use of indexes thus makes it possible to enter into long-term contracts that would otherwise not be feasible.

The authors first discuss inflation in Brazil and the various laws and decrees issued by the Brazilian government to help stabilize transactions within the international economy and the taxation of such transactions. Thereafter, the authors examine the use of indexing in Brazil with respect to the following: financial statements and reports by corporations, taxes, contracts, wages, savings, and insurance. The authors then consider the various difficulties that constant monetary correction causes.

The authors conclude that the monetary correction system requires complicated and cumbersome administration. Even individuals feel this when filing income tax returns; which have to be calculated using an index rate, not in currency. This administrative cost makes consumer products more expensive.

Monetary correction also generates deceptive gains and gives the impression that it is beneficial. High inflation, together with manipulation of indexes and restrictions on the use of certain indexes has meant that Brazil no longer has a constant and trusted currency, making it practically impossible to engage in long-term business dealings. Real estate and an increasing number of consumer products are advertised with a U.S. dollar price, despite doubts as to the legality of doing this.

It is essential to "disindex" the Brazilian economy and return to a stable currency. This cannot be done artificially, however, having already been tried and failed. "Disindexing" is only viable in an economy without—or with very low—inflation. There are no secret formulas for wiping out inflation, but there is no doubt among the informed sectors of the population of the absolute need to eliminate it.

[A. Mendes & LR Galhardo, 4 J. Int'l Tax'n 394.]

"Brazil revises its tax system to attract foreign capital" (1993). There are three tiers of taxation in Brazil—federal, state, and municipal. Under Brazil's new Constitution of 1988, changes in the tax distribution structure affected each of these tiers. The new Constitution "decentralized" revenue distribution from the federal government to the states and municipalities, without decreasing the corresponding administrative expenditures. This imbalance in the tax structure considerably increased the country's public deficit. Excessive public spending also increased the public finance gap.

Attempting to correct this imbalance, the federal government drastically increased the corporate tax burden, resorting to both direct and indirect taxes. New taxes and parafiscal contributions were established, and rates were increased. Various economic plans aimed at doing away with the inflationary system weakened the economy and increased social inequalities. Inflation and the country's instability were used to justify further additions to the tax burden.

The author first discusses corporate taxation under Brazilian law. Specific examination is given to determining real values (for computing taxable income) in an inflationary economy, corporate tax rates, Social Security contributions, and current reform proposals. Next, the author discusses the taxation of gains from foreign investment in Brazil. The change in the treatment of royalties from technology transfers and franchising is also explored with respect to the deductibility of royalty payments to foreign persons. Last discussed are taxation of foreign investment income from fixed-yield (or equivalent) transactions by Brazilian domiciliaries and foreign investment in the Brazilian capital markets.

The author concludes that Brazil is struggling to make its tax system less burdensome to foreign investors and foreign corporations with operations in Brazil. The country's economic system is in rapid change, and further changes in the tax law will follow political developments as Brazil takes its place in international markets.

[LR Galhardo, 4 J. Int'l Tax'n 119.]

¶ 7.06 CANADA

"Canadian tax reform proposals will affect cross-border investors" (1993). At the end of 1992, the Canadian Department of Finance released draft legislation with a substantial number of proposed amendments to the Canadian Income Tax Act. Some aspects of this legislation could affect the Canadian activities of nonresidents. In this article, the author examines some important aspects of this proposed legislation.

The first area covered is the suggested changes in the tax treatment of "butterfly reorganizations," that is, a divisive reorganization that enables a Canadian corporation to spin off assets to one or more of its Canadian corporate shareholders on a tax deferred basis. Tax planning for nonresidents in light of this proposed amendment is also discussed. Next addressed is the proposed change in treatment in prepayment of shareholder loans. Planning pointers in light of this possible change are provided. Last discussed are the proposed amendments to the tax treatment of employee stock options and changes of Canadian residence.

The author concludes that the draft legislation contains proposals that restrict certain planning opportunities but add others. For instance, the option available to U.S. shareholders of disposing of Canadian real property tax-free through the use of a butterfly reorganization would be ended. On the other hand, removing foreign exchange fluctuations from tax calculations in the exercise of stock options is beneficial to many employees.

[F. Ahmed, 4 J. Int'l Tax'n 236.]

"Despite antiavoidance rules, Canadian tax havens find many uses" (1993). Tax havens offer planning opportunities for Canadian individuals and corporations. U.S. corporations may also benefit from international operating companies owned through a Canadian subsidiary where Subpart F does not apply. The use of Canada as an intermediary may also reduce foreign withholding tax.

The author first considers countries that are tax havens for Canadian taxpayers. Next, the author explains Canada's foreign accrual property income rules, which were enacted to prevent tax deferral where passive income is earned by an offshore corporation or trust. These rules tax undistributed income of the offshore entity from dividends, rents, royalties, interest, and other income not related to an active business, including capital gains from the sale of passive investments. Planning in this area is possible through exceptions to these rules for active business income, inter-affiliate dividends, and capital gains from the sale of a foreign affiliate's stock. The author then reviews, in respect of these exceptions, Canada's treatment of offshore dividends and the meaning of the phrase "active business" under Canadian law. Next, he examines application of the antiavoidance rule enacted to prevent avoidance of stock control requirements under the foreign accrual property income rules.

Thereafter, the author discusses Canadian benefits of using foreign operating companies. Intercompany pricing restrictions are also noted. Specific attention is given to reasons for establishing an offshore operating company, including reduction of withholding taxes. Use of foreign licensing and manufacturing companies is also explored by the author, along with use of offshore companies by star entertainers and athletes or as captive insurers.

Next, the author considers use of foreign holding companies and the interaffiliate dividend exemption from the foreign accrual property income rules. Last, the author discusses some final considerations, such as the level of substance of the offshore entity, the choice of location for the offshore company's operations, and recent Canadian government challenges to offshore entities.

The author concludes that opportunities still exist for using offshore trusts, holding companies, and operating companies located in countries that either are pure tax havens or offer certain tax advantages. There are, however, numerous anti-avoidance rules, as well as the risk of challenge from the Canadian tax authorities, and such investments should be carefully evaluated.

[J. Bernstein, 4 J. Int'l Tax'n 416.]

"Emigration to United States can benefit Canadian corporations and U.S. shareholders" (1993). Emigration to the United States by a Canadian corporation, whether governed by the Canadian Business Corporations Act or the provincial business corporation laws, involves numerous tax considerations. Corporate emigration may provide the following advantages to a Canadian corporation (Canco) and its shareholders where a significant portion of the corporation's operations and shareholders are in the United States:

1. A more active market and increased attractiveness to U.S. institutional investors of Canco shares;
2. Easier access to U.S. capital markets for debt and equity;
3. Avoidance of Canadian tax on income from non-Canadian operations;
4. Avoidance of Canadian withholding tax and more favorable U.S. tax treatment of distributions by Canco to its non-Canadian shareholders; and
5. A potentially more favorable legal and regulatory environment, depending on the state(s) in which the corporation will operate.

The most straightforward alternative is to "continue" Canco from its governing province into a U.S. state that permits such a continuance, but adverse Canadian tax consequences may result from this approach. Thus, a three-cornered amalgamation, which avoids some of these problems, is often preferable to a simple continuance.

The author first examines the alternative of corporate continuance. The benefits and drawbacks of this alternative are set forth. Specific discussion is provided of this alternative's adverse tax consequences for the Canadian corporation, shareholders, and creditors. Thereafter, the author offers a possible solution to achieve a result similar to a continuance without adverse tax consequences. This is achieved through the transfer of the Canadian corporation to a U.S. corporation in a three-cornered amalgamation, followed by a distribution of the non-Canadian assets to the U.S. company. The tax treatment of this transaction is thoroughly explained by the author.

The author concludes that emigration of Canadian corporations to the United States, either through corporate continuance or a three-cornered amalgamation, can have both tax and nontax advantages. For Canadian tax purposes, amalgamation is preferable to continuance from the perspective of the Canadian corporation but not that of its shareholders. The determination of the preferred alternative will depend on the particular circumstances, including the nature of the assets of the Canadian corporation and the residence of its shareholders.

[F. Ahmed, 4 J. Int'l Tax'n 81.]

"Indemnification is generally not taxable to corporate officer or director" (1993). When a Canadian corporation reimburses a Canadian resident officer or director for losses or expenses incurred by that individual acting in such a capacity, the issue has arisen as to whether the individual must include the payment in computing Canadian taxable income. While some have taken the position that such payments are taxable income (without offsetting deduction), the author of this article believes that indemnity payments are generally not taxable to an officer or director where the payments reimburse the individual for losses or expenses incurred in the scope of that individual's duties.

After discussing the principal bases for the arguments against his position, the author examines the support for his arguments against taxability of indemnity payments. The author concludes with a summary of his position, noting where indemnity payments should nevertheless be taxable, and a discussion of planning considerations in light of the unsettled state of the law.

[AH Kingissepp, 4 J. Int'l Tax'n 181.]

"New Section 482 regulations create problems for U.S.-Canadian transactions" (1993). The 1993 temporary and proposed regulations under Section 482 may not provide enough flexibility to formulate a transfer pricing policy that complies with both U.S. and foreign law. These regulations create troubling issues for U.S. corporations doing business with their Canadian subsidiaries because Canada closely follows generally accepted international standards for transfer pricing developed by the Organization for Economic Cooperation and Development (OECD).

The authors first explain Canada's transfer pricing rules and compare them with Section 482. Thereafter, they discuss the standards of comparability likely to be of importance in Canada and how the U.S. regulations relate to Canadian standards. The different pricing methodologies of both countries are then compared, along with provisions for compensating adjustments.

The authors then examine the problems that may arise under Canadian law owing to the regulations' periodic adjustments requirement for transfer of intangibles under the "commensurate with income" standard of Section 482. Next, problems caused by the 1993 regulations' adoption of the 1968 regulations' rules on the provision of services without modification are discussed. Last, the authors discuss the use and efficacy of competent authority proceedings in this area.

The authors conclude that as Canadian subsidiaries restructure to integrate into single North American business units, the proportion of intercompany business transactions will increase. Restructurings that started out as cost-cutting measures are now being used as a focal point for revised transfer pricing policies to enhance cost cutting with foreign tax reduction. For tax purposes, transfer pricing policies (as indicated in this article) will only be as defensible as the documentation that supports them.

[MM Levey & PL Barnicke, 4 J. Int'l Tax'n 379.]

"Ontario budget deficit generates higher taxes, fewer breaks" (1993). In May 1993, the Ontario Minister of Finance presented the 1993–1994 budget, which emphasizes revenue generation primarily through increased personal taxes. Thereunder, corporations will be subject to a minimum tax, as well as a number of other changes. A foreign corporation operating in Ontario is especially likely to be affected by the proposed changes to the corporate tax provisions.

In this article, the author discusses these changes, which include the introduction of a corporate minimum tax, revisions to the Ontario capital tax, and the amendment of many of the province's tax rules to conform to recent Canadian federal tax changes. A pilot project requiring large, corporate taxpayers to file corporate income tax returns in electronic form is also discussed.

[AH Kingissepp, 4 J. Int'l Tax'n 368.]

"Borrowing for distributions will change significantly under draft rules" (1992). On December 20, 1991, Canadian Finance Minister Don Mazankowski released long-awaited draft rules on the deductibility of interest. Since the 1987 Canadian Supreme Court decision in *R v. Bronfman Trust,* the deductibility of interest has been less than clear in some circumstances. The draft rules codify many existing administrative practices of Revenue Canada and introduce new limits on the deductibility of interest on money borrowed by corporations and partnerships to make distributions.

The draft legislation will be of concern to nonresident shareholders of Canadian corporations or partners of partnerships carrying on business in Canada. This is because these entities may (in the case of corporations) borrow to pay dividends, to reduce share capital or redeem shares, or (in the case of partnerships) to make distributions of income or capital. These transactions are "distributions" by a "distributor."

As case law has established that interest is generally nondeductible if it is paid on account of capital, interest usually must satisfy the boundaries of Paragraph 20(1)(c) of the Canadian Income Tax Act to be deductible. Under this paragraph, interest on borrowed money generally is deductible only if the money is used to earn income from business or property.

In *Bronfman,* the trustees unsuccessfully argued that money borrowed by the trust to distribute to beneficiaries was used by the trust for income-producing purposes because it allowed the trust to continue to hold income-producing investments. The Court decided that borrowed money must be used directly, rather than indirectly, to earn income in order for the interest on it to be deductible.

The draft legislation deals separately with money borrowed to make a distribution *before* the legislation is released in final form (the implementation date), and money borrowed *after* that. The technical notes released by the Department of Finance with the draft rules refer to the former as "current distributions" and the latter as "future distributions." In each case, however, the effect of draft rules is to treat money borrowed for distributions (and satisfying certain tests described below) as having been used for the purpose of earning income, thus satisfying one of the basic requirements of Paragraph 20(1)(c).

The remainder of this article sets out the tax treatment of current distributions and future distributions.

[SL Scheuermann, 3 J. Int'l Tax'n 44.]

"Canadian income tax considerations relating to management fees" (1992). This article deals with the Canadian federal income tax treatment of fees paid by a corporation incorporated and resident in Canada for income tax purposes (Canco) for management and administration services rendered to it by a related corporation incorporated and resident in the United States (USCo).

There are two key Canadian income tax issues that arise with regard to management and administration fees: (1) the deductibility of the fees in computing the Canadian company's income for purposes of Canada's Income Tax Act (the act) and (2) whether the fees are subject to Canadian withholding tax under Part XIII of the act.

The general rule is that management fees paid or payable by Canco will be deductible in computing Canco's income for purposes of the act if they are deductible in computing Canco's "profit" in accordance with generally accepted business and accounting principles. This general rule is subject to numerous exceptions. Under Paragraph 18(1)(a), deduction of the fees is prohibited except to the extent the fees were "made or incurred by the taxpayer for the purpose of gaining or producing income from [its] business. . . ." Under Paragraph 18(1)(b), the deduction will also be prohibited if the payments are outlays of capital or "on account of capital."

Under Section 245, if there is no business purpose for the payments and they are part of a tax avoidance scheme, the deduction may be disallowed under the general antiavoidance rule.

Section 67 and Subsection 69(2) apply two reasonableness tests. Section 67 is a short and very general provision, which provides that "no deduction shall be made in respect of an outlay or expense . . . except to the extent the outlay or expense was reasonable in the circumstances." Subsection 69(2) is more specific and is directly relevant to the Canco-USCo situation; the deductible amount is the portion of the payment "that would have been *reasonable in the circumstances* if the non-resident person and the taxpayer had been dealing at arm's length."

Revenue Canada has stated in Information Circular No. 87-2, *International Transfer Pricing and Other International Transactions,* dated February 27, 1987 (the circular) that "reasonable in the circumstances" in the context of Subsection 69(2) is presumed to be "fair market value."

Revenue Canada has indicated in the circular that in interpreting Subsection 69(2) of the act, it applies the principles espoused in the 1979 OECD report "Transfer Pricing and Multinational Enterprises." The circular and the OECD approach are addressed in detail.

Subject to Subsection 212(4) and bilateral income tax treaties, payments made by Canco will be subject to a gross 25 percent withholding tax if they are paid on account of, in lieu of, or in satisfaction of a management or administration fee. The author addresses the term "management or administration."

Subsection 212(4) generally exempts two categories of management or administration fees from withholding tax, to the extent the fee is reasonable in the circumstances. The first category covers payment for services performed by a nonresident person if at the time of performance: (1) the service was performed in the ordinary course of a business carried on by the nonresident that included the performance of such a service for a fee and (2) the nonresident person and the payor were dealing with each other at arm's length. Requirement (2) will preclude this exemption from applying in the Canco-USCo situation. The second category covers reimbursement of a specific expense incurred by the nonresident person for the performance of a service that was for the benefit of the payor.

The management fees paid by Canco will generally be part of USCo's business profits and therefore will be exempt from Canadian withholding tax under Article VII, Paragraph 1, of the Canada-U.S. treaty because USCo has no permanent establishment in Canada. Paragraph 6 of Article VII establishes that Article VII defers to other provisions of the Canada-U.S. treaty that apply to the payments, but Paragraph 6 should not apply because fees for management services are not items of income dealt with separately in the other provisions of the Canada-U.S. treaty. Notwithstanding the exemption provided by the Canada-U.S. treaty, there are still certain cases in which Canadian withholding tax may apply to the payment of the management fee by Canco. These cases include three scenarios discussed in the article.

Generally, the Canadian income tax treatment of management fees paid by Canco to USCo is quite favorable, since to the extent that such fees are reasonable in the circumstances, they will generally (1) be deductible by Canco in computing its income and (2) not be subject to any Canadian withholding tax by virtue of Article VII of the Canada-U.S. treaty. It is important, however, that Canco document in detail all of the actual and potential benefits it will receive from the services provided. Also, to the extent that the fees include a profit element, Revenue Canada may disallow the deduction and also subject the profit element to Part XIII withholding tax, unless Canco can clearly justify the reasonableness of the markup (e.g., by reference to open market prices).

[AH Kingissepp, 2 J. Int'l Tax'n 356.]

"How U.S. shareholders can avoid the sting of the Canadian butterfly" (1992). A Canadian "butterfly" divides a single corporation into separate corporations on a tax-free basis. For U.S. tax purposes, dividing a corporation on a tax-free basis is accomplished in a manner radically different from the Canadian butterfly transaction, although the results are the same—the initial corporation has a reduced asset base (and sometimes fewer shareholders), and a new corporation holds assets previously held by the initial corporation (with shareholders that were previously shareholders of the old corporation).

Even if a Canadian butterfly were viewed in form as tax-free for U.S. purposes, the substance-over-form analysis so prevalent in U.S. tax law could be employed by the IRS to recharacterize the butterfly in a more familiar U.S. form—i.e., as though the old corporation transferred assets to a wholly owned subsidiary (the new corporation) and then distributed the stock of the new corporation. Such a transaction would be fully taxable for U.S. purposes if U.S. requirements were not satisfied. While U.S. tax law provides a mechanism for avoiding income or gain on such divisive "D" reorganizations, the form of such reorganizations does not resemble a Canadian butterfly. Fortunately, the IRS issued Letter Ruling 9111053 recharacterizing a Canadian butterfly for U.S. purposes as a divisive D reorganization.

Because that ruling arose in a situation where there was a disagreement among family shareholders of an oil and gas corporation that led to the butterfly transaction, the following comparison of the Canadian butterfly with a divisive D reorganization will consider corporate divisions in the two countries in the oil and gas context.

Many Canadian oil and gas corporations are privately owned by families. Family members of these entrepreneurial clans often wish to divide the corporation's assets and strike out on their own. By negotiating a transactional maze, a departing shareholder may, without recognizing Canadian gain or income, exchange shares of an operating corporation (Opco) for stock in a new corporation (Holdco) that owns Opco assets of equivalent value. This exchange is called a butterfly because of the diagrammatic appearance of the transactions. The authors set out the steps for a butterfly and discuss in detail avoiding capital gains treatment for dividends and the transfer of tax basis.

A U.S. citizen who exchanges stock in a butterfly transaction may recognize income or gain for U.S. purposes even though no income or gain arises for Canadian purposes. For U.S. purposes, the division of a corporation can take three basic forms: a spin-off, a split-up, or a split-off. Corporate divisions to resolve shareholder disputes are usually structured as split-offs. Under a split-off, one shareholder or group of shareholders swaps stock in the old corporation for stock in a new corporation that holds a portion of the assets previously held by the old corporation. A split-off will be tax-free only if the requirements of Section 355 are satisfied.

The single largest obstacle to successfully avoiding both U.S. and Canadian tax consequences of a U.S. shareholder's participation in a Canadian butterfly comes from the way it differs from the U.S. divisive D reorganization. On the Canadian side, there should be no adverse consequences because the transaction can generally be tailored to satisfy the Canadian requirements. On the U.S. side, the analysis is much more difficult because the butterfly's transactional maze does not fit the form of a typical split-off.

Fortunately, U.S. tax law is not as form-bound as is Canadian tax law. Indeed, the general touchstone of U.S. tax law is that the substance, not the form, of a transaction controls its tax treatment and that unnecessary transactional steps are ignored.

In Letter Ruling 9111053, the IRS analyzes the use of a Canadian butterfly to divide a family business. In the ruling, a Canadian oil and gas operating company was owned by Canadian residents—a parent, who was a Canadian citizen, and her two children, who were dual citizens of Canada and the United States. Because of a dispute that could have adversely affected corporate operations, a butterfly transaction was proposed so that one of the children could split off part of the old corporation's assets. Citing Revenue Ruling 77-191, the IRS ruled that for U.S. purposes the Canadian butterfly would be treated in substance as a split-off. Despite the fact Canadian tax law is less malleable than U.S. tax law in terms of its adherence to form rather than substance, there may be a way to structure a transaction on the Canadian side that will fit the form of a split-off in the United States. The authors set out in detail how to set up transactions to receive favorable tax treatment on both sides of the border.

Letter Ruling 9111053 should be welcome news for U.S. citizens resident in Canada or Canadians resident in the United States who wish to participate in the splitting up of a corporate enterprise. This ruling, coupled with Revenue Canada's willingness to grant accommodating butterfly rulings, will permit U.S. citizens resident in Canada or Canadians resident in the United States to ensure that their participation in the transaction is tax-free on both sides of the border.

The principles of Letter Ruling 9111053 are not necessarily limited to the breakup of a family business. A U.S. corporation holding the stock of a Canadian corporation may avail itself of the principles of the ruling by dividing the Canadian corporation on a tax-free basis, both for Canadian and U.S. purposes.

In some circumstances, the breakup of a U.S. corporation's Canadian subsidiary could have favorable U.S. tax ramifications. For example, under Section 902, a U.S. corporation that receives dividends from a 10 percent–owned foreign corporation is entitled to a U.S. tax credit for foreign taxes paid by the foreign corporation. If, as is often the case, the Canadian corporation has available to it significant deductions that substantially reduce or eliminate the current Canadian tax, the payment of a dividend to the U.S. corporation will result in a U.S. tax, but no tax credit (because no Canadian tax was paid). Ultimately, this timing difference in Canadian tax and U.S. tax may result in greater overall tax, because when the corporation later begins paying Canadian tax (and tax credits are available to the U.S. parent), those credits may arise in years when they cannot be carried back to offset U.S. tax.

This potential problem can perhaps be eliminated if the Canadian corporation is restructured through a spin-off so that the portion of the business generating current cash flow and tax is separated from the portion of the business that is generating tax losses. The restructuring on the Canadian side may not be difficult to achieve because of the flexibility that is available to determine the tax basis of assets of Holdco in a butterfly transaction.

Engineering the tax-free split-up of a corporation on either side of the Canada-U.S. border is difficult enough. It is doubly difficult when favorable treatment is desired on both sides of the border. Because of the difficulty of resolving these issues, a transaction of the kind described in Letter Ruling 9111053 should not be implemented unless advance rulings are obtained from Revenue Canada and the IRS.

[BN Lemons & TH Olson, 3 J. Int'l Tax'n 30.]

"Proposals for Canadian tax changes will affect nonresident investment" **(1992).** In recent months, numerous proposals have been made to change the Canadian federal income tax rules. These include the federal budget of February 25, 1992, press releases issued by the Minister of Finance, and proposed technical amendments to the Income Tax Act (Canada) released by the Minister of Finance on December 20, 1991. Key budget changes include modification of dividend withholding rates and corporate tax rates.

The authors briefly discuss the proposed tax changes, including (1) dividend withholding rates; (2) corporate tax rates; (3) aircraft lease payments; (4) discount debt; (5) thin capitalization; (6) share-for-share exchanges; (7) paid-up capital in amalgamations; (8) international reorganizations; (9) nonresident-owned investment corporations; and (10) excess foreign property tax.

[AH Kingissepp & PW Main, 3 J. Int'l Tax'n 106.]

"Structuring tax-efficient software sales to Canada" **(1992).** Nonresidents of Canada who supply computer software to Canadian customers may be subject to Canadian income tax. Canadian income tax treatment of such providers generally depends on the character of the payments made by the Canadian customer, whether the payments (or portions of them) are taxable under the Canadian Income Tax Act (the act), and whether relief under any bilateral income tax treaty is available.

Additionally, payments for software often cause the withholding tax provisions of the act to come into play because products are traditionally distributed by license rather than by sale. Thus, even where mass-marketed software is "purchased" from a distributor, the user is typically only permitted to use the software under a "shrink-wrap license." The enforceability of these licenses has been questioned by at least one court in Canada. License arrangements between the manufacturer, distributor, and customer vary widely and the exact legal relationship among the parties must be ascertained before determining the character of the cross-border payments.

Assuming the software provider is resident in a treaty country and has no Canadian permanent establishment, license fees are usually subject to Canadian withholding tax under Paragraph 212(1)(d) of the act, albeit at a reduced rate. Canadian income tax can be eliminated on payments that (1) are not described in the broad language of Paragraph 212(1)(d) or (2) are not royalties under the relevant treaty and constitute exempt business profits.

The author discusses the U.S.-Canada tax treaty definition of "royalty" and the treatment of software payments thereunder. The author examines copyright protection offered software creators under Canadian law. Thereafter, he discusses which payments to produce software are exempt and how planning can lead to coverage under the exemption. Finally, the author examines the treatment of payments for information and services related to transfer of software. The author concludes that providers can often reduce exposure to Canadian income tax without unduly upsetting commercial arrangements by becoming sensitive to relief under the act and the relevant treaty and by structuring contracts accordingly.

[SL Scheuermann, 3 J. Int'l Tax'n 233.]

"Alternatives for single-project joint ventures in Canada" (1991). Since "joint venture" is not defined under Canadian income tax legislation, its tax treatment in Canada depends on the form in which it is conducted. If the joint venture does not constitute a partnership or a corporation, generally, the venturers are taxed as separate entities.

For purposes of this discussion, assume:

1. The purpose of the joint venture is to carry on a business in Canada;
2. The joint venture is established to pursue one particular project;
3. All the participants in the joint venture are corporations; and
4. At least one of the participating corporations is a nonresident of Canada conducting its own independent enterprise in its country of residence.

Joint ventures are generally treated under Canadian income tax law, including the Income Tax Act (Canada) (the act) and proposed amendments to the act, as either a partnership or a commercial arrangement falling short of a partnership (the contractual joint venture).

In many cases, the determination as to whether a particular relationship constitutes a partnership is a difficult one and in some circumstances cannot be made with complete certainty.

For taxation purposes, the prevailing view in Canada is that where an association between joint venturers does not constitute a partnership, the joint venturers are taxed as separate persons on the basis of the commercial results of the agreement between them.

Since the tax consequences of choosing to carry out a joint venture as a partnership or a contractual joint venture differ substantially, ensuring that the relationship as documented reflects the intention of the parties requires some care. The article continues with a discussion of drafting a joint venture agreement.

The tax treatment in Canada of partnerships, both general and limited, reflects a tension between treating a partnership as an aggregation of persons and as a separate entity. This is reflected in the act in two basic principles of partnership taxation:

1. The income or loss from a partnership business is taxed in the hands of the partners and not at the partnership level.
2. A partner's interest in a partnership is generally treated as capital property, separate and distinct from the underlying partnership property.

In general terms, a partnership is treated under the act as a separate nontransparent entity for the purposes of the computation of net income or loss but is treated as a flow-through or transparent entity for the purposes of calculating the taxable income of the partners.

The author discusses the following areas of Canadian partnership taxation in detail: (1) transactions between a partner and the partnership; (2) direct expenses incurred by partners; (3) allocation of profit and loss; (4) the at-risk rule; (5) partnership interest; (6) nonresident partners; (7) withholding taxes; (8) reporting requirements; and (9) the termination of the partnership.

In the case of a contractual joint venture, there is no separate entity for Canadian income tax purposes. Each venturer continues to own its property and assets dedicated to the joint venture and does not have a separate capital property like a partnership interest representing its interest in the venture. On the assumption that it is carrying on business in Canada, a nonresident is taxed in Canada according to general principles.

Each venturer calculates its own income or loss based on its share of revenues and its own expenses (including capital cost allowances) arising from the joint venture activity. Generally, this calculation would be done by each venturer on the basis of its own fiscal period, but Revenue Canada may permit a joint venture to establish its own fiscal period if all the coventurers agree. Revenue Canada has indicated, however, that a separate fiscal period will not be permitted where the motivation is an attempt to defer or avoid tax.

To the extent that the timing of deductions is discretionary, e.g., capital cost allowance, each venturer has more flexibility in computing income than it would have in a partnership where income is computed at the partnership level. Currently, there are no rules similar to the partnership at-risk rules applicable to contractual joint venturers.

Under income tax treaties concluded between Canada and most industrialized countries, the business profits of a nonresident are not subject to tax under the act, except to the extent such profits are attributable to a permanent establishment in Canada. Since a nonresident venturer involved in a Canadian joint venture would generally also carry on business in Canada, it would likely also have a permanent establishment in Canada. Where, however, the participation of the nonresident venturer is relatively passive (e.g., contributing cash or intellectual property) or the nonresident does not conduct its functions in Canada (e.g., it provides management services for the Canadian business performed in the home jurisdiction), the nonresident venturer may not have a permanent establishment in Canada and therefore may not be subject to Canadian tax by virtue of a treaty. The article continues with its discussion of the taxation of contractual joint ventures in the following areas: (1) the branch tax; (2) the thin capitalization rules; (3) withholding tax; (4) branch accounting; (5) reporting requirements; (6) incorporation; and (7) termination.

An alternative structure for a joint venture would be a single-purpose Canadian corporation to carry out the project. In this case, the interest of each joint venturer, including a nonresident participant, would be represented by respective shareholdings in the joint venture corporation.

The joint venture corporation would be a normal taxable Canadian resident corporation subject to tax on its worldwide income, determined according to the provisions of the act. The nonresident would not be subject to Canadian tax on an ongoing basis merely by being a shareholder of the corporation. Distributions of after-tax profits in the form of dividends to the nonresident, however, would be subject to withholding tax at the statutory rate or a treaty-reduced rate.

Furthermore, payments to the nonresident for such things as interest, rents, or royalties would also be subject to withholding. Depending on the level of ownership of the nonresident in the joint venture corporation, the thin capitalization rules could apply to any interest paid to the nonresident or certain related parties.

While it would also be possible to use a foreign corporation to carry out the joint venture in Canada, such a structure would be tax inefficient from the point of view of Canadian venturers, since the income from the venture would be subject not only to corporate income tax but also likely to branch tax and foreign withholding taxes.

[DR Allgood, 2 J. Int'l Tax'n 92.]

"Canada's goods and services tax (GST) will bring major changes" (1991). On January 1, 1991, the government of Canada implemented the GST. The GST replaces the outdated manufacturer's sales tax (MST), which was payable at varying rates by specified manufacturers, wholesalers, and importers on certain manufactured goods. The new GST has some implications for nonresidents who are, or are contemplating, doing business in Canada.

Overview. The GST is a VAT applied on final consumption and is similar generally to the European VAT. Like the VAT, the GST is a multistage sales tax collected at each stage in the production process that provides an offsetting credit for taxes paid on business inputs by most firms. Unlike the European VAT, the GST will apply to a much broader tax base and will have only one rate.

The GST will be enacted as an amendment to the Excise Tax Act (Canada) (the act). Under the act, GST of 7 percent will be applied on the value of the consideration paid or payable by the purchaser of a taxable supply of property or of services made in Canada. In the case of taxable supplies made in Canada, the GST generally is required to be collected by the vendor (registrant) as an agent of the Crown, although legal liability is imposed on the purchaser. GST will also apply to all imported goods at the time of importation at 7 percent of the duty paid value of the goods. In addition, GST of 7 percent will apply on a self-assessment basis to the importation of intangible personal property or a service that is not used in a commercial activity.

There are many tax issues that nonresidents will face under the GST. These include: (1) integration of provincial retail sales taxes into the GST under a national sales tax with varying provincial rates; (2) transitional rules effective in 1991 affecting the rebate of MST on inventory and residential property and the taxation of pre-1991 transactions; (3) intercorporate charges both in Canada and internationally; (4) changing price effects on Canadian imports and exports; (5) change-of-use rules for capital property; and (6) rebates of GST to nonresidents.

While not an exhaustive list, this does give some indication that the GST will have a significant impact on business operations in Canada. Businesses will have decisions to make about the GST's effect on their accounting procedures, cash flow, pricing decisions, and company organization. Nonresident businesses faced with these decisions would be well advised to contact Canadian tax counsel in order to ensure they are prepared for the GST.

[BM Murray & SC Aylward, 1 J. Int'l Tax'n 300.]

"Financing a Canadian subsidiary through a nonresident-owned investment corporation (NRO)" (1991). In certain circumstances, the use of a nonresident-owned investment corporation may improve the tax efficiency of financing an investment in Canada. This column discusses Canadian income tax considerations when a U.S. parent corporation uses an NRO to finance a Canadian subsidiary carrying on an active business in Canada.

The increased tax efficiency depends on the effect the NRO has on the comparative U.S. taxation of the U.S. parent in respect of its investment in Canada. Accordingly, the use of an NRO requires the close coordination of U.S. and Canadian tax advisors. Moreover, achieving a tax-efficient structure using an NRO imposes constraints on intercorporate cash flow management and distribution policies that must be taken into account from a commercial perspective in assessing such a structure.

An NRO permits a nonresident's Canadian investments to be held by a Canadian corporation financed by the nonresident, while retaining Canadian tax treatment that approximates that applicable to directly held investments. The income of an NRO generally is subject to a special refundable 25 percent tax. This rate is significantly lower than the tax imposed on an ordinary Canadian holding company, and equals the nonresident withholding tax rate generally applied to passive income paid by a Canadian entity to a nonresident, prior to applicable treaty reductions.

The 25 percent tax is generally refundable to the NRO upon sufficient dividends being paid to its nonresident shareholders. The Canadian tax ultimately borne on investments held through an NRO is the applicable treaty-reduced rate of withholding tax on the dividends paid by the NRO.

To qualify as an NRO, a corporation must file an election within ninety days of incorporation in Canada. An NRO must comply continuously from its incorporation with restrictions relating to ownership, business activity, and income, which may be summarized as follows:

1. All of the corporation's issued shares and funded indebtedness must be beneficially owned, directly or indirectly through a trust or through NROs, by nonresident persons.
2. The income of an NRO may be derived only from the ownership of, or trading or dealing in, securities, lending money, rents and certain other forms of property income, and the disposition of capital property.
3. Rents may not exceed 10 percent of the NRO's gross revenue.
4. The NRO's principal business must not be the making of loans or the trading or dealing in enumerated securities or any interest therein.

In considering the use of an NRO in financing a Canadian subsidiary, the prohibition that the principal business of the NRO not be the lending of money is of particular practical importance.

The author discusses the computation of income of an NRO and various special rules in this regard. Next, the author illustrates, in some detail, the potential use of an NRO. The advantages to this structure are then discussed under the following headings: (1) reduced Canadian withholding tax; (2) U.S. tax deferral; (3) improved U.S. tax deferral; (4) accessing U.S. FTCs; and (5) a potential double dip. With respect to this last point, where a nonresident parent uses debt financing to finance its Canadian investments, the use of an NRO may be combined with the deductibility of interest to the nonresident parent in its home jurisdiction. In the case of the U.S. parent, the deductibility of such interest and the effect of debt financing upon accessing FTCs would be subject to the detailed rules under the Code.

The foregoing structure uses an NRO as a sister company of a wholly owned Canadian subsidiary of a U.S. resident corporation. Alternatively, an NRO may hold shares of the Canadian subsidiary in addition to interest-bearing debt. The author analyzes this structure.

The 25 percent tax is refundable to the NRO upon payment of sufficient dividends by the NRO to the U.S. corporation. Thus, the ultimate Canadian tax on investments by the U.S. corporation through the NRO is the Canadian withholding tax on dividends from the NRO. The refundable tax regime applicable to an NRO, however, imposes cash flow constraints because of the need to fund the 25 percent tax until its later refund.

Once NRO status is lost, it cannot be regained, and the NRO will be taxed as an ordinary taxable Canadian corporation. Structures designed to achieve tax-efficient results by using an NRO can suffer adverse tax effects if NRO status is lost.

As is the case for most structures designed to achieve a tax-efficient result, Canadian advisors will have to consider the potential application of Canada's general antiavoidance rule.

[AS McGuffin, 2 J. Int'l Tax'n 235.]

"Minimizing Canadian taxes on repatriated investment capital" (1991). When purchasing shares of an existing Canadian operating company, a nonresident of Canada should consider structures that will maximize flexibility in repatriating funds from the Canadian corporation and eliminate the possibility that the nonresident will be subject to Canadian income tax on the repatriation of its initial invested capital. Other Canadian and U.S. tax considerations not discussed in this column should, of course, also be taken into account.

To illustrate the possible planning techniques, the author relies on a scenario that assumes that a nonresident purchaser is a corporation resident in the United States for purposes of the Income Tax Act (Canada) and the Canada-U.S. Income Tax Convention (1980). The purchaser will acquire 100 percent of the shares of the Canadian corporation from an arm's-length Canadian resident vendor. The Canadian corporation has only one class of shares, common shares, issued and outstanding.

The author discusses the problem that arises from this arrangement and how properly structuring the transaction with a Canadian holding company can alleviate it. Capitalizing holding companies is then addressed. Finally, if the purchaser owns an existing Canadian operating company and wants to finance the acquisition with funds from this company, rather than its own funds, the author suggests a Canadian tax-free structure in order to accomplish this.

This article reviews only some Canadian tax considerations. With proper advance planning, however, a nonresident purchaser of a Canadian company should be able to repatriate its invested capital free of Canadian income tax, including withholding tax. Indeed, where the purchaser owns an existing Canadian operating company, it may even be possible, subject to the potential application of antiavoidance rules, to repatriate additional amounts (in addition to the purchaser's invested capital) free of Canadian withholding tax.

[AH Kingissepp, 1 J. Int'l Tax'n 368.]

"Nonresidents not always subject to Canadian withholding of interest payments" (1991). Part XIII of the Canadian Income Tax Act (the act) generally imposes a 25 percent tax on the gross interest paid or credited to a nonresident of Canada by a resident of Canada. The 25 percent rate may be reduced or even eliminated by a bilateral tax treaty between Canada and the country of residence of the creditor. For example, the Canada-U.S. Income Tax Convention (1980) generally reduces the rate to 15 percent.

The Canadian resident payor, including a paying agent, is obliged to withhold the tax at its source from the gross interest payment and to remit the withheld amount to the Receiver General of Canada.

The withholding tax regime in concept applies where the relevant interest payments constitute passive or investment income of the nonresident person. Where the interest payments relate to a business carried on in Canada by the nonresident, such interest payments may instead be taxed as business income of the nonresident person in accordance with the rules contained in Part I of the act.

There are a variety of exemptions pursuant to which a nonresident lender can lend money to an arm's-length Canadian resident borrower and earn an interest return free of Canadian withholding tax. The most important and widely used of these exemptions is the long-term corporate debt exemption contained in Section 212(1)(b)(vii) of the act. Numerous potential pitfalls may arise in connection with this exemption, which can result in the imposition of withholding tax.

The prerequisites to the availability of the long-term corporate debt exemption are, in general terms, all of the following:

1. It applies only to interest payable by a corporation resident in Canada to a person with whom the issuer is dealing at arm's length.
2. The relevant evidence of indebtedness must be issued after June 23, 1975.
3. The corporation may not, under any circumstances, be obliged to pay more than 25 percent of the principal amount of a single obligation or of an entire issue of identical obligations within five years of the date of issue, except in the case (a) of failure or default under the obligation or any agreement relating thereto; (b) of certain legislative, judicial, or administrative changes; or (c) where the lender exercises a right to convert or exchange the obligation for a prescribed security. The term "prescribed security" includes ordinary common shares of the borrower or a "right or warrant" to acquire such common shares, as defined according to the regulations. The author explains the workings of this exemption in detail.

Interest payable on a bond, debenture, or similar obligation to a holder of a certificate of exemption issued by the Minister of National Revenue is exempt from Canadian withholding tax. The exemption is basically available to foreign pension plans, other employee benefit trusts or corporations, and foreign charitable trusts and corporations that are exempt from income tax in their own country and that would be exempt under the act if they were found to be residents of Canada.

Section 212(1)(b)(viii) of the act provides that interest payable on a mortgage or similar obligation secured by real property situated outside Canada is exempt from withholding tax unless the interest is deductible in computing income from a business carried on in Canada or income from property, as opposed to income from business, other than real property situated outside Canada.

The act provides an exemption from withholding tax for interest payable in a foreign currency where the borrower is at all relevant times a prescribed financial institution and the relevant debt is an amount not repayable in Canadian currency deposited with the prescribed financial institution.

Interest payable in a foreign currency to a lender on an obligation entered into in the course of carrying on business in a country other than Canada is exempt from withholding tax to the extent that the interest payable on the obligation is deductible in computing the income of the borrower, under Part I of the act, from a business carried on by the borrower in that country. Since the act taxes Canadian residents on their worldwide income, this provision may be relevant whenever a borrower carries on a branch business in a foreign country.

Finally, in conjunction with certain incentives granted by the act for an international banking center business carried on in Montreal or in Vancouver, Section 212(1)(b)(xi) of the act provides an exemption for interest payable by a prescribed financial institution on an eligible deposit.

[DR Allgood & AH Kingissepp, 2 J. Int'l Tax'n 42.]

"Canada adopts laws affecting real estate taxes" (1990). The Ontario government has amended the Land Transfer Tax Act (LTTA) and introduced the commercial concentration tax (CCT), and the Canadian federal government introduced the large corporations tax (LCT).

LTTA extends the application of the land transfer tax (LTT) to include most unregistered dispositions of interests in real estate occurring after July 18, 1989. The rate remains unchanged at generally 1.5 percent on transfers of commercial properties. LTT is imposed on any disposition of an interest in real estate, whether or not registered. If an interest in real estate is held in trust, a trustee must, within thirty days of becoming aware of any disposition of such interest, deliver a return setting out the particulars of the disposition. The exemptions that previously applied to registered dispositions now apply to both registered and unregistered dispositions. Under the amendments, where a disposition is made between corporate affiliates, the transferee may apply to the Minister of Revenue to defer tax payable on an unregistered disposition if it

1. Remains an affiliate of the transferor for three years from the date of disposition and the beneficial interest is held during that period by it or a corporate affiliate of both itself and the transferor;
2. Provides a thirty-eight-month letter of credit as security; and
3. Does not register any evidence of the disposition.

If, at the end of the three-year period, these conditions have been met, the tax deferred is no longer owing. If this disposition is subsequently registered, LTT is then payable.

The deferral for certain intercorporate dispositions allows interests in real estate to be transferred on a tax-deferred basis a number of times within a group of corporate affiliates. LTT is generally not payable on transfers of shares and continues not to be payable on an amalgamation. The amendments to LTTA could be interpreted to impose LTT on transfers of interests in trusts or partnerships holding Ontario real estate. However, regulations will exempt from LTT dispositions of "units of mutual funds which are listed on a recognized Canadian Stock Exchange or traded pursuant to a prospectus approved by a Canadian Securities Commission," as well as changes in partnership interest in any one year that do not exceed 5 percent of the right to profits.

Effective January 1, 1990, an annual CCT of $10.75 per square meter is payable on the portion of the gross area of certain commercial buildings in the greater Toronto area exceeding 18,600 square meters, and on the total gross area of certain commercial parking lots, regardless of size. Commercial properties include hotels, office buildings, shopping centers, and similar establishments. Not included and exempt from CCT are warehouses, race tracks, industrial and residential properties, and so forth. Also, property exempt from municipal and school taxes is likewise exempt from CCT. Parking lots in the greater Toronto area are subject to CCT if a fee is charged for parking vehicles and the lots are accessible to the public.

Bill C-28 will amend the Income Tax Act of Canada to introduce an annual corporate capital tax of 0.175 percent of the amount of taxable capital employed in Canada in excess of $10 million. The LCT is effective for tax years ending after June 1989 and is payable monthly beginning in 1990.

The taxable capital of a resident corporation that is not a financial institution is the difference between its capital (indebtedness, capital stock, retained earnings, and so forth) and its investment allowance (shares of, loans to, and bonds of other corporations). Although the LCT is similar to existing provincial capital taxes, the latter are generally deductible in computing income, whereas the LCT is not. The LCT can be credited against any federal surtax on income payable by the corporations. One key issue is whether LCT can be passed on by a landlord to its tenants.

[RF Lindsay, 1 J. Int'l Tax'n 47.]

"Canada—a favorable climate for investment" (1990). As a location for business operations and investment, Canada offers nonresidents valuable tax and business advantages. In this article, the author considers the business and regulatory laws of Canada.

In the first part of the article, the author examines the investment climate of Canada. In so doing, he provides information on its geography, history, population, and resources. Thereafter, he considers the nature of the Canadian economy and the government's economic policy and attitude towards foreign investment. Next, specific government-generated investment incentives are reviewed.

The author then discusses the various forms in which nonresidents may do business in Canada. The legal requirements and responsibilities associated with each of these forms are set forth. Canada's regulatory environment for foreign investment is also addressed. Specific discussion is provided of exchange controls, foreign investment review by the government, monopoly and antitrust laws, import and export laws, and laws for patents, copyrights, and trademarks.

In the last section of this article, the author discusses Canada's financial institutions and banking system, including the laws that govern them. The author concludes with a brief discussion of the Canadian tax system. The topics covered include the income tax system on national and provincial levels and the income base on which such taxes are imposed, as well as other taxes and duties. Included herein is also a discussion of Customs duties, antidumping duties, sales taxes, municipal taxes, LTTs, nonincome business taxes, and death and gift taxes.

[H. Burke, US Tax'n Int'l Operations ¶ 8517.]

"Canada's general antiavoidance rule (GAAR)" (1990). Canada introduced the GAAR to Canadian income tax law under Section 245 of Canada's Income Tax Act in September 1988. An analysis of GAAR must now form the cornerstone of international tax planning involving Canada. There are several possible arguments that taxpayers might make to a Revenue Canada assessment based on GAAR. These arguments are discussed in this article.

The years leading up to the introduction of GAAR saw the Department of Finance becoming increasingly dissatisfied with its attempts to plug specific loopholes in Canada's Income Tax Act on an ad hoc basis. After the Supreme Court of Canada rejected the business purpose test in *Stubart Investments, Ltd.*, the Department of Finance realized no magic solution would be forthcoming from the courts. GAAR represents the Department of Finance's response to the aggressive tax planning that followed the *Stubart* decision.

[RF Lindsay, 1 J. Int'l Tax'n 12.]

"Canada—tax aspects of nonresident investment" (1990). In this article, the author provides an in-depth examination of Canada's tax provisions to the extent relevant for nonresident investment.

The author begins this article by exploring the various ways in which investments may be financed in Canada. He next considers the factors that enter the choice of investment vehicle in Canada. The advantages and disadvantages of using a Canadian branch or subsidiary are compared. Use of partnerships and acquisition of an existing Canadian business are also discussed.

In the second section of this article, the author addresses Canada's system for taxing businesses and their earnings. Included herein are discussions of accounting for profit, allowable deductions and depreciation, and other tax considerations (which include special income inclusions, surtaxes, and the rules for related-party transactions). Then, tax-related business/investment incentives are detailed. Next considered is the Canadian system for taxing nonbusiness earnings, such as capital gains and dividends. The withholding taxes on payments to nonresidents (including dividends, interest, and rental/royalty income) are also discussed, along with the tax on dispositions of capital property located in Canada. The treatment of non-Canadian income and gains is also considered.

In the third section of this article, the author provides an in-depth view of Canadian real estate investment and the special tax aspects of such activity. Analyses are provided for these real estate investment activities: development for resale, acquisition of rent-producing property, and passive holding for appreciation. The treatment of operational income and disposition gains and losses are thoroughly reviewed.

Last, the author discusses other important income tax considerations for investors, including the tax consequences of repatriation of profits and capital, dispositions of investments, liquidation of a Canadian subsidiary, non-arm's-length sales of Canadian stock, corporate reorganizations, and the tax avoidance rules.

[H. Burke, US Tax'n Int'l Operations ¶ 8518.]

"Canadian bill imposes withholding on cross-border security loans" (1990). The 1989 Canadian federal budget resulted in Bill C-28 being introduced to amend the Canadian Income Tax Act (the act) to provide rules governing securities-lending arrangements and repurchase transactions. This article outlines the Canadian tax treatment of cross-border transactions contemplated by the bill.

The bill has imposed constraints on cross-border securities-lending arrangements that could have significant negative effects on participants in these markets. Such participants should examine carefully these transactions with a view to limiting potentially adverse Canadian tax treatment. Also important is the need for ongoing involvement in the development of future legislation in this area. While the Department of Finance (the department) has not agreed with all of the public comment made to date on behalf of Canadian domestic and nonresident securities-lending arrangement market participants, some revisions to the proposals have been made. Given the importance of international capital markets to the Canadian economy as a whole, further scrutiny from the department and further amendments to the act must be expected. Active participation in this process can only benefit all market participants.

[RF Lindsay & PM Meredith, 1 J. Int'l Tax'n 113.]

"Establishing a foreign-owned business in Canada" (1990). If a thriving business enterprise based in another country is planning to expand its operations to Canada, a basic understanding of the Canadian tax regime is essential. This article discusses the tax considerations of nonresidents commencing business operations in Canada in 1990 or thereafter. A summary is provided of the principal tax provisions imposed by Canada and some of its provinces. Particular attention is accorded the following areas: the meaning of "resident," the Canadian withholding tax, the Canadian tax on corporate dividends, the lack of consolidated return provisions, existing tax treaties, the transfer pricing rules for parties not engaging in arm's-length transactions, and specific reporting requirements. In addition, the article discusses special concerns for corporations, including the areas of capital gains and losses, the determination of taxable income, tax rates, and the significant Canadian tax consequences that occur upon acquiring control of a corporation. Finally, some discussion is provided as to the special concerns of individuals.

[JY Lee & SL Scheuermann, 1 J. Int'l Tax'n 176.]

"The appropriate form for a foreign-owned business in Canada" (1990). Once the decision has been made to carry on business in Canada, and a review of the general income tax framework has been made, the nonresident must decide what form the business will take. In addition to federal and provincial income taxes, a nonresident corporation that carries on business in Canada is subject to the branch profits tax (generally 25 percent, unless a lower tax treaty rate prevails) under the Canadian Income Tax Act (the act).

In certain circumstances, when its business is principally carried on in Canada, a nonresident may be deemed under the act to be a resident of Canada so that certain payments made by it to another nonresident are subject to Canadian nonresident withholding tax. The nonresident corporation must file an income tax return with the federal government and may be required to file with one or more provincial governments in which it has a permanent establishment. It is required to keep books and records with respect to its Canadian operations and make these available to audits undertaken by federal and provincial tax authorities.

Since a Canadian subsidiary will be a Canadian corporation, it is not subject to a branch profits tax, but withholding tax of 25 percent (subject to tax treaty reduction) is payable upon repatriation of funds by way of dividends. The thin capitalization rules under the act generally disallow the deduction of interest payable by a Canadian subsidiary on outstanding debts to specified nonresident persons to the extent that the ratio of such debts to the Canadian subsidiary's equity exceeds three to one.

A number of provinces impose a capital tax calculated on the basis of the taxable paid-up capital allocated to the corporation's permanent establishment in the province. Proposed amendments to the act include a new federal-level capital tax, the LCT, levied on capital in excess of $10 million employed in Canada.

The income of a partnership, which is not a separate legal entity subject to ordinary income tax under the act, is allocated among the partners in accordance with the partnership agreement and taxed to them. A nonresident partner in a partnership that carries on business in Canada generally is considered to carry on business in Canada for the purposes of the act. For tax purposes, where a joint venture is determined not to be a partnership, each joint venturer files a separate capital cost allowance claim and is taxed separately.

Sales taxes are imposed by both the federal and provincial governments. Assuming passage of pending legislation, the existing federal sales tax will be replaced on January 1, 1991, with a new multistage VAT imposed at 7 percent on a broad base, including virtually all goods and services consumed in Canada. As a general rule, businesses in the production and distribution chain will charge the GST on their domestic sales and will be able to claim an input tax credit for the tax paid on their purchases. Federal excise taxes are also levied on certain specified goods with rates varying with the class of goods taxed, in addition to any other taxes or duties payable.

Goods imported into Canada may also be subject to federal Customs duties based primarily on the transaction value, which is generally the exporter's free on board selling price. Drawbacks, refunds, or remissions of Customs duties and excise taxes are available, provided certain conditions are met. Customs duties and excise taxes on goods stored in a bonded warehouse are postponed until the stored goods are withdrawn from bond. Goods imported into Canada that were acquired by the importer at a subsidized price or one below market in the country of export and found likely to cause material injury to the production of like goods in Canada may be subject to antidumping or countervailing duties.

On January 1, 1989, the Canada-U.S. Free Trade Agreement completely eliminated duties for many goods imported into the United States from Canada, and vice versa; the duties on importations of most other goods from either country will be eliminated over five or ten years depending on tariff classification.

[JY Lee & SL Scheuermann, 1 J. Int'l Tax'n 236.]

¶ 7.07 CHINA

"China forges a uniform tax system for foreign investors" (1993). Taxation of income of foreign enterprises doing business in the People's Republic of China (PRC) is now governed by the Foreign Investment Enterprise and Foreign Enterprise Income Tax Law, effective July 1, 1991, (the 1991 Act). This law was supplemented by implementation rules also effective July 1, 1991.

The author first discusses nonincome taxes that affect foreign enterprises active in the PRC and the effect of tax treaties on double taxation. Next, the author discusses doing business in the PRC. The author examines doing business in the PRC without an investment vehicle, such as the use of a joint venture, the implementation rules' definition of "permanent establishment," and the taxation of permanent establishments under the 1991 Act. The permanent establishment status of the following activities under the 1991 Act is then examined: sales, employment, barter arrangements, technology transfers, contracting projects, subcontracting to Chinese contractors, consulting services, and use of a representative office.

In the next section of the article, the author examines the special treatment accorded "foreign investment enterprises," which includes Chinese enterprises wholly owned by foreign investors, contractual joint ventures, and equity joint ventures between Chinese and foreign partners. The nature of this special treatment, including taxation on worldwide income and various tax exemptions and reductions for such enterprises, is analyzed. The benefits available for locating an enterprise in certain economic zones is also explored. Last discussed are certain new approaches to investment in PRC businesses, such as foreign ownership in Chinese companies in the PRC through so-called B shares, real estate development in the PRC, use of enterprise leases, and investment in the PRC through holding companies.

The author concludes that certain questions will remain unanswered until clarified through practice. The most important of these questions concerns the omission of a statute of limitations for tax liabilities, claims, or disputes. The net effect of the changes will be to bring China closer to the international markets in which it is seeking to participate.

[S. Stricker, 4 J. Int'l Tax'n 26.]

"PRC tax authorities strengthen enforcement over foreign investment enterprises" (1993). A foreign investment enterprise, upon receiving a license, enjoys certain tax privileges in the PRC, including substantially lower tax rates than Chinese state enterprises as well as import duty exemptions and reductions. If a foreign investment enterprise fails to maintain compliance with the statutory requirements for its status, these privileges will be revoked.

The author discusses some recent PRC cases involving the revocation of foreign investment enterprise status. These cases indicate increased diligence on the part of PRC authorities to halt abuses in the foreign investment enterprise system. Next addressed is the PRC's recent clarification of transfer pricing rules for foreign investment enterprises and their associated enterprises. New rules on the foreign exchange income of foreign investment enterprises are also explained. Last, the author discusses the expansion of trade zones constituting special investment areas entitled to reduced tax rates, the proposed revision of the PRC's tax system for individuals, and the enactment of a statute of limitations on tax claims.

[S. Stricker, 4 J. Int'l Tax'n 366.]

¶ 7.08 CZECH REPUBLIC

"New Czech tax system aims at harmonization with EC" (1993). The Czech legislature has enacted a completely new tax system, effective January 1, 1993. The new law is designed to harmonize the Czech system with those of EC member states, and includes a new personal income tax and a VAT system. In addition, the Administration of Fees and Taxes Act was passed to regulate the administration, assessment, and collection of taxes.

The author first examines the Czech tax on the income of individuals and corporations; the withholding tax on certain types of income is also explained. Next addressed are the Czech real estate tax (whose rates vary depending on use) and the new VAT system. The following other taxes are also explained by the author: the road tax, the real estate transfer tax, the social insurance tax, and gift and inheritance taxes. Last discussed are the Czech treatment of partnerships and available depreciation methods.

The author concludes that the new Czech tax law has greatly modernized and simplified the country's tax system. A major objective has been to make it compatible with those of the EC countries, with a view towards becoming part of the EC. The Czech taxes are among the highest in Europe, requiring careful evaluation by foreign investors.

[M. Bakes, 4 J. Int'l Tax'n 281.]

¶ 7.09 DENMARK

"Denmark's transfer pricing system is attractive to foreign corporations" **(1993).** Denmark has a very attractive transfer pricing policy. This is not the result of a desire to use transfer pricing to attract foreign investment, but more from the difficulty that the Danish Inland Revenue has in enforcing the Danish transfer pricing rules.

A bill, introduced in 1985 but still not enacted, would require enterprises in certain areas largely dominated by foreign enterprises to justify their transfer pricing figures. Until political forces bring such a change about, Denmark will have one of the most lenient transfer pricing policies in Europe.

[U. Fleischer-Michaelsen, 4 J. Int'l Tax'n 226.]

¶ 7.10 DOMINICAN REPUBLIC

"With a new tax code, the Dominican Republic institutionalizes its tax system" **(1993).** The Dominican Republic's new tax code radically changes the Dominican tax system. This revision has reformulated the VAT, added a sales tax on selected goods, eliminated the major protectionist/sector investment incentive laws, and modified other laws. In general, this revision indicates that the Dominican Republic is resisting any efforts to become a tax haven.

The author first discusses administrative provisions that concern the efficacy of private tax rulings, the duties and responsibilities of collection agents, and the use of taxpayer tax payment guarantees. Next, he considers certain tax accounting rules, especially those concerning inventories. Rules on inflation adjustments and currency gains and losses are noted, along with the Dominican sourcing of income provisions.

Thereafter, the author examines the taxation of corporations, taxation of their dividends, and Dominican transfer pricing rules. The treatment of income from exports and imports is also explained. The presumption of minimum net income for certain taxpayers involved in special industries is discussed. Next, the author discusses the deduction of general operating losses, depreciation, interest, and other expenses, such as contributions to employee pension plans, under Dominican law. Also considered are FTC availability, the taxation of capital gains and losses, the tax consequences of business terminations and reorganizations, and bulk sales of business assets.

In conclusion, the author notes that a Tax Court for the Dominican Republic has not been established and regulations for important tax laws have not been issued. The Dominican Republic has shown a desire to develop a more sophisticated tax collection process and has lowered tax rates. In the end, this will encourage businesses looking for labor savings to locate in the country.

[ME Portes, 4 J. Int'l Tax'n 374.]

¶ 7.11 EASTERN AND CENTRAL EUROPE, GENERALLY

"Tax reforms roll out a red carpet for investors looking at Central Europe" (1993). Four Central European countries—Hungary, Poland, and the Czech and Slovak Republics—have become primary targets for foreign investment. They have established a favorable business and tax climate for foreign operations and agreed to a Common Market, creating an increasingly barrier-free economic zone.

The author first discusses the agreements reached by these countries with the EC. Next, he discusses the privatization of businesses and assets previously owned by the Communist governments, in these countries. Thereafter, the author focuses on the existing tax systems in these four countries, for both individuals and corporations. Where appropriate, he discusses other tax matters such as the taxation of persons not engaged in a trade or business within the country, the VAT, import duties, Social Security taxes, and income tax treaties.

The author concludes that, in the last three years, Central European countries have taken substantial steps to adjust their political, social, economic, financial, and business environments to attract foreign investors. The developing Common Market and the arrangements with the EC are beneficial for U.S. businesses establishing operations in Central Europe. By the end of this decade, Central Europe will likely be fully integrated with the Western democracies.

[ZM Mihaly, 4 J. Int'l Tax'n 156.]

"Foreign investment in Eastern Europe" (1991). This piece is a set of charts that compare the tax consequences of foreign investments in four major Eastern European countries. The countries reviewed are Czechoslovakia, Hungary, Poland, and the former U.S.S.R.

The topics of the charts are (1) tax treaties; (2) withholding tax; (3) loss carryforward; (4) foreign investment possibilities (subdivided into areas of activities, legal forms, and partners); (5) corporate tax; (6) joint venture taxation; (7) withholding tax; (8) foreign exchange; and (9) tax reform efforts.

[R. Pollath & J. Toeben, 2 J. Int'l Tax'n 104.]

¶ 7.12 EUROPEAN COMMUNITY

"Directive implementation leaves EC short of full harmonization" (1993). Traditionally, mitigation of double taxation on intragroup profits within the EC has been provided by tax treaties, but this presents serious problems. Out of sixty-six possible tax treaties between the twelve member states, only fifty-seven have been ratified. In nine cases, companies operating in two different member states have no treaty protection, and the relief under domestic law is extremely inadequate in some cases.

Even where a treaty mitigates double taxation, there is never full avoidance. Articles 23A and 23B of the OECD model of 1977 (the model most frequently relied on in treaties between member states) provide two systems of elimination of double taxation, the exemption method and the credit method. Both aim at eliminating "legal" double taxation of the same income in the hands of the same taxpayer, but can do nothing to prevent "economic" double taxation of the same income to two different taxpayers. The commentary to Articles 23A and 23B states that if two states wish to avoid economic double taxation, they must do so by bilateral agreement.

With intragroup profit distributions, legal double taxation occurs when dividends are subject to withholding tax at the source and income tax in the beneficial owner's country of residence. Economic double taxation occurs where income that generates dividends is subject to corporate income tax in the hands of the distributing company, and the dividends are subject to income tax in the hands of the beneficial owner, either through withholding tax or corporate income tax in this owner's country of residence.

The authors first discuss the exemption and tax credit methods of eliminating double taxation. Thereafter, they focus on the 1990 EC Council parent-subsidiary directive, which provides a solution to both legal and economic double taxation. In doing so, they discuss the status of its implementation by member states, the scope of the directive (and its provisions), the distributions covered by the directive, and the territorial scope of the directive.

The authors conclude that tax treaties have not been entirely successful in avoiding double taxation of intragroup profits within the EC. The parent-subsidiary directive attempts to remedy the situation, but differences in implementing legislation and limitations on the scope of the directive have prevented full harmonization.

[A. Fantozzi & A. Manganelli, 4 J. Int'l Tax'n 308.]

"Parent-subsidiary directive changes EC corporate operations" (1993). The EC parent-subsidiary directive, as implemented in Belgium, France, Germany, Italy, Luxembourg, the Netherlands, and the United Kingdom, while attempting to abolish corporate double taxation, presents a number of practical application problems in these countries.

The authors first discuss the directive's withholding tax relief provisions for subsidiaries. Next, they discuss certain problems that may arise thereunder if the parent-company resident in an EC member state holds a qualifying participation in another EC-resident company through a permanent establishment in a third member state. Thereafter, they address the directive's provisions concerning the corporate tax imposed at the parent level. Here, they discuss both the exemption and the credit methods for avoiding double taxation. Problems that may arise in the case of multi-tier entities and companies with permanent establishments in the EC are also examined. General and specific antifraud and antiabuse provisions are considered, including the one aimed at "directive" shopping.

Last, the authors discuss the current dispute among EC member states concerning the development of a common system of taxation for dividends. The two theories or methods for taxing dividends, i.e., the classical and imputation systems, which are the subject of this controversy, are explored. The authors conclude that the suggested extension of the directive's scope to all enterprises and to any percentage of enterprise participation will not eliminate the EC's double taxation problem.

[A. Fantozzi & A. Manganelli, 4 J. Int'l Tax'n 349.]

"Transitional VAT regime simplifies intra-EC transfers of goods" (1993). The creation of a single market on January 1, 1993, abolished the imposition of VAT in cross-border transactions within the EC. Thus, for VAT purposes, the concepts of imports and exports within EC boundaries have been replaced with the concepts of supply and acquisition. Generally, the supply is exempt from VAT in the member state of origin, but the acquisition is taxable in the member state of destination.

The authors first discuss the treatment, for VAT purposes, of internal EC transfers and the exemption from VAT on intra-EC supplies. Next, three-party transactions, transfers without change in ownership, and transfers involving contract work are explored in terms of the application of VAT in the EC. Examples are given to explain application of the EC rules. Then the authors discuss the modifications that must be made to account for the services of trade agents and transportation within the EC.

The new EC regime is transitional. It will expire in 1997 and the final rules will then apply. The authors indicate that such rules will provide that the VAT is no longer payable in the country of destination, only in the country of departure, at that country's applicable rate.

[J. Bouchard & A. Grousset, 4 J. Int'l Tax'n 233.]

"Disposition planning possible under EC 1992 merger directive" (1992). This article examines a number of planning possibilities and obstacles that must be overcome to ensure the avoidance of U.S. and foreign tax by U.S.-based multinational companies considering disposing of their foreign operations after the July 23, 1990, Council of the EC merger directive is implemented. The authors begin by examining three simple strategies: the sale of assets, the sale of stock, and the deemed asset sale election.

The authors then turn to disposition planning under current law. After a general discussion, they focus on the following examples: a broken Section 351, Section 351 boot, and the transfer of assets for stock.

The authors discuss several general points about the EC merger directive before turning to planning possibilities.

When the EC Council directive has been implemented by the member states, new transactions will be possible that involve the transfer of assets without any foreign income taxation but purposely fail the corresponding U.S. nonrecognition requirements. Failing the U.S. requirements permits gain to be recognized with respect to assets so that the gain of a U.S.-incorporated transferor of assets, or the earnings of a foreign-incorporated transferor of assets, can qualify as main-basket for FTC purposes. This could pave the way for the U.S. tax on the disposition to be offset by FTC in various ways.

Article 2(a) of the EC merger directive defines "merger" as a transfer by one or more companies of all their assets and liabilities to either an existing company or a new company, in exchange for the issuance directly to the transferor-share-holders of securities representing the capital of the transferee and cash not exceeding 10 percent of the nominal or par value of those securities. The corporate law of the member states does not yet provide for such cross-border mergers. There is currently circulating a draft for an EC Council directive that would mandate the member state to amend their respective corporate laws to permit such mergers.

The authors address the obstacles to U.S. gain recognition with respect to assets. If the main obstacles have been avoided, it is difficult to see how recasting the transaction would prevent the recognition of gain with respect to assets.

Article 2(d) of the EC merger directive defines an "exchange of shares" as an acquisition of the majority of the target's stock as measured by vote, in exchange for securities representing capital of the acquiror and cash not exceeding 10 percent of the nominal or par value of the securities.

This form of transaction alone will not accomplish the U.S. tax objective. The inclusion of cash in the consideration would violate the "solely voting stock" requirement for a B reorganization, but this would result in gain recognition with respect to the stock. This gain, to the extent not recharacterized under Section 1248, would either be U.S.-source or passive-basket foreign-source income. Even if avoiding B reorganization status means that the stock has been acquired in a Section 338 "qualified stock purchase," Section 338(h)(16) provides that any election pursuant to Section 338 or Section 338(h)(10) will be ignored for purposes of sourcing and basketing the gain. The gain not recharacterized by Section 1248 would thus still be U.S.-source or foreign-source passive income.

Accordingly, this type of transaction would have to be preceded by a transaction that permits the target company to recognize for U.S. tax purposes all of its unrealized appreciation with respect to its assets.

Article 2(c) of the EC merger directive defines a "transfer of assets" as a transfer of the assets comprising one branch, some branches, or all of the branches of the transferor to the transferee in exchange for securities representing the capital of the transferee. The definition does not require other considerations such as cash to be permitted. Also, the transferor is not dissolved under the definition.

No minimum percentages by vote or value of the transferee must be received by the transferor under the directive and, considering the purpose of the provision, implementing legislation of the member states is unlikely to contain any significant minimum percentages. Accordingly, it would appear that U.S. gain recognition would not encounter any obstacles that cannot be overcome. These obstacles are discussed.

Article 2(b) of the EC merger directive defines a "division" as a dissolution of a corporation that transfers all of its assets and liabilities to two or more existing or new companies, in exchange for the pro rata issuance to the transferor's shareholders of securities representing capital of the transferees and cash not exceeding 10 percent of the nominal or par value of the securities. Just as with cross-border mergers, the corporate laws of the member states do not currently permit cross-border divisions. The same EC Council directive that mandates member states amend their respective corporate laws to permit cross-border mergers, also mandates amendments to permit cross-border divisions.

The "division" definition does not require a minimum percentage by vote or value of the transferees to be acquired. It is conceivable, however, that the implementing legislation of the various member states may have such requirements. Where there are no such requirements, or the requirements do not rise to the 80 percent control standard for Section 351 nonrecognition treatment, it should be possible to engineer gain recognition with respect to assets from a U.S. tax perspective. This achieves a fair market value basis in the stock of the transferees for U.S. tax purposes.

A "division" under Article 2(b) of the EC merger directive could qualify as a D/Section 355 "split up" from a U.S. tax perspective and, in addition to the same 80 percent control requirement as required by Section 351, Section 355 contains many other requirements that could be purposely violated.

The article concludes with an explanation of why subsidiary liquidations would not suffice as a planning technique.

[JS Karls & TW Van Den Hoven, 2 J. Int'l Tax'n 279.]

"EC directive attempts to harmonize use of cross-border losses" (1992). While the EC pushes ahead optimistically in 1992 toward its goal of a single market in goods and services, unsuccessful trading activities across the EC can result in losses being bottled up locally and being subject to restrictive rules in relation to their offset against profitable activities.

A wide array of rules for the treatment of losses within member states, combined with limited opportunities for their offset across the borders of member states, calls for ingenuity in ensuring that European groups that have losses in certain areas can make effective use of them. Even with corporate tax rates in the EC dropping generally to around 35 percent, the effect of unrelieved losses may be dramatic on a group's profitability. A survey of domestic law of EC member states indicates a lack of commonality in the rules relating to the offset of losses. Loss carry-forwards are permitted in all member states, but their precise application varies considerably. Only Germany, Ireland, and the United Kingdom provide for indefinite carry-forwards. A number of countries adopt a five-year limit, and the Netherlands applies an eight-year limit. In France, while losses may generally be carried forward five years, because depreciation must be taken up to the amount of straight-line depreciation including loss years, losses may be increased. This increased loss resulting from depreciation may be carried forward indefinitely.

Loss carry-backs are subject to even more rigorous limitations. A majority of countries, including Belgium, Denmark, Greece, Portugal, and Spain provide for no carry-back at all. In those countries that do, the period ranges from one year in Ireland to three years in France and the United Kingdom.

The treatment of capital losses by member states is also diverse. In half the member states, capital losses may be applied in some form against trading income, usually because no distinction is drawn between capital gains and ordinary income. In the other half—namely, Denmark, France, Greece, Ireland, Portugal, and the United Kingdom—restrictions apply to the use of capital losses.

The draft directive released by the European Commission (the commission) proposes common systems to permit enterprises to take account of losses incurred by permanent establishments or subsidiaries situated in other member states. The draft directive adopts the "reincorporation method," which allows foreign losses to be deducted and also taxes any profits subsequently made by the permanent establishment by reincorporating them into the results of the head office to the extent of amounts previously deducted on account of losses.

The draft directive is intended to cover any enterprise of a member state, i.e., an enterprise that is resident for tax purposes under domestic legislation of a member state. It applies to both corporate and unincorporated businesses that are subject to either individual income tax or corporation tax in a member state. It establishes the principle of equal treatment for all legal forms of enterprise. Residence is to be determined by domestic law, although the commission's explanatory memorandum states that account should be taken of the provisions of applicable bilateral treaties.

A subsidiary for the purpose of this directive is any company in which an enterprise of a member state has a minimum capital holding of 75 percent, giving it a majority of voting rights. Member states are free to stipulate a lower minimum holding, should they so choose.

In regard to permanent establishments, member states will be required to permit their enterprises to take into account foreign losses, either by the credit method or the reincorporation method. The credit method includes an enterprise's losses or profits in determining the taxable income in the country of residence and, when appropriate, credits the tax paid by the permanent establishment against any tax payable by the enterprise on the profits of such establishment.

The reincorporation method involves the deduction from the enterprise's taxable profits of losses incurred in the same period by the enterprise's permanent establishment situated in other member states. Subsequent profits of the permanent establishment are incorporated into the enterprise's taxable income to the extent of the losses previously deducted. The directive specifies that the income of permanent establishments is to be determined for this purpose by the laws of the member state in which it is established.

The reincorporation method is the sole method permitted for losses incurred by subsidiaries. The income of such a subsidiary is to be determined in accordance with the law of the member state in which it is situated, and losses will be deductible in proportion to the enterprise's holding in the capital of the subsidiary. The holding to be applied in this respect is the lowest level during the tax period in question.

As is the case with permanent establishments, automatic reincorporation may be required by member states when the loss has not been recovered by the end of the fifth year following that in which it became deductible, or when the subsidiaries were sold, wound up, or converted into permanent establishments. In addition, automatic reincorporation may be required when the enterprise's holding in the capital of the subsidiary has fallen below a minimum level specified by the member state in which the shareholder is situated.

[JS Schwarz, 2 J. Int'l Tax'n 370.]

"Economic interest groupings appeal to EC joint ventures" (1992). Since July 1, 1989, the establishment of European Economic Interest Groupings (EEIGs) under EC law has been possible. Until an "EC" is available under the European Company Statute, the EEIG provides a vehicle for conducting cross-border business within the EC and EC law.

EEIGs were created by regulation rather than by directive. As a result, the rules are self-executing and do not require further enactment into the laws of member states. An EEIG, under Article 3 of the regulation, may be formed to facilitate or develop the economic activities of its members and to improve or increase the results of those activities. It is an instrument of cooperation rather than integration, and is not intended to replace its members or to completely absorb their activities. The regulation specifies that an EEIG's purpose is not to make profits for itself; its activity must be related to the economic activities of its members and must not be more than ancillary to those activities. Because of this limitation, the EEIG has not displaced other forms of joint ventures, including corporate joint ventures, partnerships, and contractual arrangements not constituting an entity for either corporate or tax purposes. It is more simple and flexible than a corporation. It is distinguished from contractual joint ventures by its independent legal capacity and the EC law foundation. As a result, many EEIGs established so far tend to be in sectors providing the services of consultants, lawyers, accountants, or architects, as well as groups making joint bids on certain projects or engaging in joint purchasing or sales activities.

An EEIG can, nevertheless, have rights and obligations of all kinds, make contracts and accomplish other legal acts, and sue and be sued. Members of an EEIG have joint and several liability for the debts of the groupings, however, although creditors must, under Article 24, first seek payment from the EEIG itself before proceeding against its members. Although an EEIG has full legal capacity, the regulation does not automatically grant it the status of a legal person. The question of legal personality is determined by the law of the member state in which the EEIG is established.

Under Article 4 of the regulation, EEIGs may be established only by "persons" located in member states. This includes individuals, partnerships, or companies, but would not extend to the branch of a U.S. corporation, though the European subsidiary of a U.S. corporation would qualify. To constitute a grouping, at least two members must have their central administration in different member states.

Generally, a grouping may not exercise management power over its own members' activities or over the activities of another undertaking, and may not hold shares of any kind in a member undertaking. It may not employ more than 500 individuals and may not be a member of an EEIG itself. It may not make a loan to a director of a company or to anyone connected with him or her if making such a loan directly is prohibited by the law of the member state.

Under regulation Article 19, EEIGs are to be managed by persons appointed by the contract or by decision of the members. Each member is entitled to at least one vote, although more votes may be provided by agreement. No single member may hold a majority of the votes. Decisions that alter objectives, the number of votes allotted to each member, or the conditions for making decisions; or decisions that extend the duration of the grouping beyond any fixed period or change financial contributions, require unanimity.

The central concept relating to direct taxation is set out in regulation Article 40, which provides that profits or losses resulting from the activities of a grouping are taxable only in the hands of its members. Apart from this basic principle, the tax laws of member states apply.

Profits are to be apportioned among members in the ratios laid down in the contract for the formation of the grouping. In the absence of any such provision, Article 21(1) requires that profits are to be divided equally. The precise manner in which groupings are taxed varies throughout the EC.

The grouping is regarded as acting as the agent of its members. Where a trade or profession is carried on by a grouping, taxable income is computed jointly but assessed separately.

The residence of an EEIG is discussed. The position of EEIGs under treaties is far from settled, nor is it certain that an EEIG is a "person" under Article 3(1) of the OECD model convention. Participation in the EEIG will affect the application of treaties to members of an EEIG, however, as then explained with respect to permanent establishments.

Regulation Article 40 does not deal with taxes other than those on profits and losses. As a result, the application to EEIGs of other taxes imposed by member states does vary considerably.

Although the regulation imposes fiscal transparency on member states in the way that they tax groupings, it is not binding outside the EC. The question of classification of EEIGs is therefore determined by the country whose tax is in question.

Despite the fact that the rules relating to the treatment of EEIGs are not uniform throughout the EC and are somewhat unsettled, a grouping is an appropriate vehicle for joint activities both in the EC and for EC persons with activities outside the EC. It is ideal for professional associations and multidisciplinary practices, and the vast majority of EEIGs registered to date are associations of professionals across the EC. A carefully structured EEIG will facilitate such associations on a nontaxable basis by avoiding a permanent establishment and providing for a flow-through of expenses to the joint venture parties.

[JS Schwarz, 3 J. Int'l Tax'n 48.]

"Interim regime brings fundamental change to European VAT system" (1992).
This article begins with a review of the EC's VAT. The complexities of introducing
a system involving VAT deductions across frontiers and revenue compensation
between the treasuries of member states have led the EC to adopt an "interim
regime" expected to operate after 1992 and at least until 1996, when the system
will again be reviewed. The crucial elements of this transitional system are

1. Continuation of zero rating of goods transported from one member state to
another, but in more limited circumstances and
2. "Import" and "export" abolished as concepts of intra-EC trade.

Zero rating for sales to other member states will not be conditional on physical
departure of the goods from the national territory and "acquisition" by a taxable
person in another member state.

Since sales in intra-EC trade after 1992 may be zero-rated only if made to
customers registered for VAT in their own countries, sales to other persons will be
taxable at a positive rate. Purchasers unable to recover input tax in their countries
will not benefit from zero rating on supplies from other member states. Financial
institutions that make significant intra-EC cross-border purchases will have to register for VAT and account for tax on acquisition of goods in their own countries.
This tax will generally not be recoverable but sellers will be permitted to zero-rate
the sales. The minimum annual threshold requiring VAT registration is 10,000 ECU,
though member states may set a higher level.

In sum, goods bought for use in the course of a taxable business will be subject
to tax in the country of the recipient. Goods bought for consumption will be subject
to the VAT rate of the supplier's country. Two exceptions are made to this:

1. If supplies made by mail order firms produce receipts in excess of 100,000
ECU in a member state, VAT is determined by that state.
2. As to new cars and other means of transport, VAT will be collected by the
state where the vehicles are first registered.

After 1992, supplies of services relating to intra-EC transport of goods will be
taxed directly, and no longer as an ancillary operation. Transport services will be
taxed in the member state of departure unless the recipient of the transport services
is established in a member state other than that of departure, in which case the
services will be taxed there. The carrier will generally be liable for the tax if established in the member state where the tax is due, or for any transport service supplied
to a person not identified for VAT purposes. This is the case even if the carrier is
not established in the member state in which tax is due. In all other cases, tax will
be payable by the customer, with the carrier invoicing the transport service exclusive
of tax.

On July 27, 1992, the EC finance ministers agreed to a binding minimum 15
percent standard rate of VAT through 1996. There is no maximum, and the lower
rates, including zero rates, remain unaffected. Although member states must comply

with the Sixth VAT Directive, the manner in which this is done varies from one member state to another. Nevertheless, with the interim VAT regime coming into effect, the move toward uniformity is advancing. Inevitably, the Customs requirements are decreasing, and taxpayers will benefit.

[JS Schwarz, 3 J. Int'l Tax'n 184.]

"Luxembourg takes wide lead in EC mutual funds" (1992). EC investors are an obvious market for U.S. financial services companies. U.S.-managed accounts targeted to foreign investors are, however, limited for tax reasons to "private" fund management, such as accounts for individual clients and investment partnerships.

Because U.S. tax laws governing regulated investment companies (RICs) convert interest and short-term capital gains into dividends, RICs are a tax-disadvantaged investment for EC investors. Therefore, investments that would by statute or income tax treaty be exempt become subject to a 30 percent withholding tax or a reduced rate under a treaty.

In the absence of congressional relief, it appears unlikely that U.S. RICs will attract increasingly greater amounts of foreign capital, particularly in light of the tax-advantaged competing products offered in the EC and elsewhere that are discussed in this article. The article focuses on tax aspects of European mutual funds as well as their investment managers and providers of support services.

The article includes discussion of the EC directive governing investment companies, "Undertakings for Collective Investment in Transferable Securities," which was enacted in 1985.

[RD Lorence, 3 J. Int'l Tax'n 187.]

"Ruding Committee sets EC tax agenda for 1990s" (1992). In September 1990, the EC Commission appointed a committee of independent tax experts under the Chairmanship of Onno Ruding, former Dutch Finance Minister, to examine corporate taxation in the EC and to make recommendations on the future of business taxation in the EC. The committee report's conclusions and recommendations will undoubtedly be the focus of discussions on the European tax system into the next century.

The mandate given to the committee was, first, to evaluate the effect of taxation on business decisions on the location of investments and the international allocation of profits between enterprises. Special attention was to be focused on distortions considered discriminatory. Second, the committee was to consider whether such distortions may be eliminated through the interplay of market forces and tax competition between member states and, if not, whether EC action is required. Third, the committee was to recommend specific measures at the EC level to remove or mitigate these distortions.

Although the Ruding Committee does not purport to provide a comprehensive reform of the tax system in Europe, its proposals are so far-reaching that few areas of business tax would be unaffected. Given that modification of tax law in the EC requires unanimous approval of member states and consultation with the European Parliament, passing changes is likely to be difficult. While some member states are apprehensive, the rate at which tax measures of member states are being found illegal by the European Court is clearly focusing attitudes of administrators and policy makers in a way that has not happened previously. The committee's proposals therefore require serious consideration.

[JS Schwarz, 3 J. Int'l Tax'n 117.]

"EC directives cover cross-border income flows" (1991). Three key categories of income streams (dividends, interest, and royalties) have been lined up as early candidates for tax harmonization within the EC.

The European Commission has now released two directives on the taxation of cross-border financial flows within corporate groups. They include a proposal for a common system of taxation applicable to interest and royalty payments made between parent companies and subsidiaries in different member states as well as a draft directive concerning arrangements for the use of losses by businesses of permanent establishments and subsidiaries located in other member states.

The dividends directive and the draft interest and royalties directive adopt an identical test to determine which entities can benefit under the new regime. They follow the standard in the corporate reorganizations directive, which applies only to companies from member states.

The measures apply only to specific forms of corporation established under the laws of each member state as listed in the schedules to each directive. Although public companies and private limited liability companies in all member states will qualify, not all entities that are subject to the corporate income tax imposed by member states are covered. The second requirement is that the corporation must be resident in a member state for its domestic tax purposes. Third, it may not be resident in a country outside the EC for purposes of any bilateral double taxation treaty. Fourth, the companies must be subject to the corporate income tax imposed in the country of residence, without the possibility of being exempt.

The dividends directive requires parent companies to hold at least 25 percent of the capital of the subsidiary in another member state. In an amendment released in May 1990, however, the commission proposed that the minimum holding be reduced to 10 percent. The commission now takes the view that all withholding taxes on financial flows within the EC should be abolished and that the lower 10 percent threshold is an initial step in this direction.

Under both directives, member states may replace the capital holding criteria with ownership of voting rights. Member states can also introduce a holding period of at least two years to qualify for the relief granted by the directive.

Although commonly referred to as the dividends directive, the word "dividend" is not found anywhere in the document. It refers to the distribution of profits by a subsidiary to a parent. No definition of "profits" or of "dividend" is included in the directive.

Under the dividends directive, profit distributed by a subsidiary to its parent is exempt from withholding in the subsidiary's country. "Withholding tax," however, is not defined in the dividends directive. The directive does not affect the treaty provisions relating to tax credits for dividends in such systems, nor does it affect treaty or domestic rules aimed at eliminating or reducing double taxation. In this regard, it is a minimum standard to which all member states must comply; they remain at liberty to be more generous under their domestic laws or by treaty.

Two methods of avoiding double taxation on profits received by a parent are permitted, as discussed in the article. The rules on how the parent is to receive distributions do not apply to the liquidation of the subsidiary.

Member states are entitled to restrict the deductibility of expenditures based on the capital holding in the subsidiary in computing taxable profits of the parent as well as to prohibit the deductibility of losses resulting from the distribution.

There are important omissions from the scope of the dividends directive. Most important, the directive covers only profit distributions and not capital gains.

The proposed interest and royalty directive exempts from withholding tax interest and royalty payments made between parent companies and subsidiaries. Where interest and royalty payments are made to a permanent establishment of recipient company located in the same member state as the payor, the withholding tax exemption will apply only if the member state does not impose a withholding tax on payments of that kind between resident parent companies and subsidiaries.

"Interest" is defined as income from "debt claims of every kind whether or not carrying a right to participate in the debtor's profit including premiums and prizes attaching to bonds or debentures." Royalties are payments of any kind received as a consideration for the use of or the right to use any copyright of literary, artistic, or scientific work, including cinematographic films, any patent, trademark, or design, or model, secret formula, or process, or for the use of or the right to use industrial, commercial, or scientific equipment, or for information concerning industrial, commercial, or scientific experience.

Both the dividends directive and the draft interest and royalty directive contain identical wording relating to fraud or abuse. In each, domestic law or treaty-based provisions required for the prevention of fraud or abuse are not precluded.

The final discussion in the article concerns implementation issues.

[JS Schwarz, 2 J. Int'l Tax'n 180.]

"New strategies for cross-border mergers, acquisitions, and reorganizations" (1991). After a twenty-year gestation, a council directive finally emerged on July 23, 1990, adopting a common system of taxation applicable to mergers, divisions, transfer of assets, and exchanges of shares concerning companies of different member states.

The requirement in the Treaty of Rome that there be unanimous approval of all member states to introduce tax laws for the EC has made their adoption difficult.

The corporate reorganizations directive is applicable only to companies from a member state. This includes only certain forms of corporation established under the laws of each member state as set out in a schedule to the corporate reorganizations directive. Furthermore, they must be resident in that state for tax purposes, and they may not be resident in a country outside the EC for the purposes of any bilateral double taxation treaty. Finally, the company must be subject to the member state's corporation tax in its home jurisdiction without the possibility of being exempt.

The corporate reorganization directive is to be applied by each member state to mergers, divisions, transfer of assets, and exchanges of shares in which companies from two or more member states are involved. The author discusses the types of mergers, divisions, and share-for-share exchanges to which the rules would apply.

Qualifying mergers or divisions will not give rise to tax on capital gains on appreciated assets transferred as a result of the merger or division. In order to qualify, the assets and liabilities must, as a result of the reorganization, be effectively connected with a permanent establishment of the receiving company in a member state where the transferring company is located. The assets also must be used in generating income for tax purposes.

Subsequent gains and losses are computed as though the merger or division had not taken place, and asset values for capital gains and depreciation purposes are carried over. If member states operate an elective regime that allows different base costs for depreciation and capital gains purposes, the rollover will not apply to assets and liabilities for which such option is exercised. Shareholders will not be subject to income or capital gain tax on merger, division, or exchange of shares, provided that shares received in the exchange carry over the base cost for tax purposes of the securities transferred.

Where a company receiving assets has shares in the transferring company, any gain accruing to the receiving company on the cancellation of its holding is not subject to taxation. Individual member states may deviate from this rule where the receiving company's holding in the capital of the transferring company is under 25 percent.

Provision is made to ensure that loss carry-forwards are not extinguished by the reorganization, as explained by the author.

Some attempt has been made to deal with variations in the system of corporate taxation across the EC, as detailed in the article. Common to these transactions is the ability to receive a cash payment not exceeding 10 percent of the nominal value of the securities received, without the tax-free status of the transaction being jeopardized. Any cash consideration received in such transactions, however, may continue to be taxable. The rules do not permit reorganizations where the consideration includes assets other than securities or cash. A company incorporated in a member state can convert into a permanent establishment of a company in another member state, an important provision, as explained by the author.

Where the member state of the transferring company taxes worldwide profits, it will be entitled to tax any profits or gains of the permanent establishment resulting from the merger on condition that it gives relief for tax that would have been charged on the permanent establishment (in the same way and in the same amount as if that tax had actually been charged and paid).

The benefits of the corporate reorganizations directive may be refused where the transaction has as one of its principal objectives tax evasion or avoidance, as detailed in the article.

In addition, there are matters that the EC has intentionally left to member states, as examples demonstrate.

Where member states fail to implement the laws or where their laws implementing the corporate reorganizations directive do not conform with it, the terms of the corporate reorganizations directive will govern the treatment of the transaction.

The corporate reorganizations directive generally must be implemented by member states not later than January 1, 1992.

Although the corporate reorganizations directive is aimed specifically at European companies, its benefits may be available to U.S. corporations engaging in European transactions. Since the corporate reorganizations directive, when implemented, will become the domestic law of each of the member states, and, since it may discriminate against companies not from member states, the nondiscrimination provision of U.S. tax treaties with the European states may well be applicable to permit similar transactions by U.S. corporations.

[JS Schwarz, 2 J. Int'l Tax'n 51.]

¶ 7.13 FRANCE

"Consolidation holds opportunities for foreign corporations in France" (1993). The current French tax regime for consolidation (*intégration*) of affiliated groups of corporations, enacted in 1988, can only be elected by corporations subject to the French corporation tax. Section 223A of the French tax code indicates that "a corporation with no more than 95% of its ownership being held, directly or indirectly, by another entity subject to corporation tax can be held responsible for the corporate tax with respect to the whole income of the group comprised of that corporation and its subsidiaries in which it owns, directly or indirectly, at least 95% of the stock for an uninterrupted taxable year." The principal advantage of consolidation of affiliated groups under French law is thus aggregation of the group's taxable income at the parent company's level.

To elect consolidated treatment, throughout the consolidation period the parent company (*tête de groupe*) must be either a French corporation or a branch or permanent establishment of a foreign corporation subject to French corporate tax at the standard rate.

The authors first examine the ownership requirements for consolidation under the French tax code. Next, they address the manner in which group taxable income is determined. The computation of taxable income, the carrying forward of losses, and applicable tax rates are specifically discussed. The taxation of group dividend distributions is then explained. Thereafter, the authors address the tax treatment of member departures.

Next, the authors discuss the advantages of consolidation and tax planning in this area. Last, the authors consider consolidation in conjunction with corporate acquisitions by both newly formed and existing groups.

The authors conclude that the French consolidation rules may be used not only to aggregate all profits and losses of French subsidiaries of a foreign group but also to leverage the acquisition of a French or foreign-target company. This seems to have been acknowledged by those corporations (17,600, as of the end of 1991 had created 5,000 groups) that have made the election to consolidate.

[O. Delattre & D. Streiff, 4 J. Int'l Tax'n 113.]

"France proposes laws on taxing foreign trusts" (1993). French law does not provide for trusts as they are known in common-law countries. French courts usually rely on civil law concepts when dealing with foreign trusts with French resident beneficiaries. This is no longer satisfactory, however, in light of the increasing use of trusts by French residents and companies in legal and tax planning. Also, France must enact laws on trusts before it can ratify the Hague Convention of July 1, 1985, on private international law. This is inevitable, as the French government is aware of the need for regulation of trusts in order to facilitate the transfer of estates, particularly those with international business assets. A bill creating the *Fiducie*, a French entity similar to a common-law trust, has been introduced in the French Parliament. The Parliament also recently enacted a supplementary finance bill containing provisions on taxation of foreign trusts.

The author begins this article with a discussion of the current French tax regime with respect to trusts. First examined are provisions concerning estate and gift taxes, both with respect to testamentary trusts and inter vivos trusts. Next addressed is France's net wealth tax on French residents and nonresidents (with respect to their assets in France).

Thereafter, the author discusses the taxation of foreign trusts and foreign trust income prior to the recent change in the law. The effect of tax treaties on France's treatment of foreign trusts is also considered. Specific attention is given to the treatment of U.S. and Canadian trusts under existing tax treaties. Possible renegotiation of certain French tax treaties is addressed. Then the author reviews the advantages of foreign trust use under existing French law.

The author last discusses the anticipated impact of the bill on the *Fiducie*, if passed. He addresses the proposed tax treatment of the *Fiducie* under the estate and gift tax, net wealth tax, and income tax. The author concludes that France is developing legislation on trusts and similar entities. If the proposed bill on the *Fiducie* is enacted, it will be comparable to laws regarding trusts in other countries with, however, less flexibility for practitioners but some planning opportunities.

[AC D'Istria, 4 J. Int'l Tax'n 257.]

"French court changes gain treatment for stock redemptions and liquidations" (1993). The highest French Tax Court issued a decision that substantially narrows the definition of a "dividend distribution" in the context of stock redemptions. As a result, there are significant changes in the tax consequences to both the redeeming corporation and the shareholders. In addition, the decision raises important issues regarding the tax treatment of corporate liquidations.

The authors first describe the principal issue addressed by the court and the applicable provisions of French tax law. Thereafter, they examine the new direction taken by the court in this case. In doing so, they explore the arguments made by the taxpayer and the application of French tax law by the court. The practical consequences of this decision are explored, specifically with regard to parent-subsidiary tax regimes, redemptions involving foreign parties, and corporate liquidations.

The authors conclude that the French court's treatment of taxable gain in stock redemptions departs from the position traditionally taken by the French tax administration. The court has held in a number of recent decisions that such gain is capital gain rather than dividend income, and as such is subject to lower tax rates, except for a qualifying parent company. If not a dividend, the gain does not qualify for the *avoir fiscal*, and the redeeming corporation is not liable for the *précompte* equalization tax. The court's decision can also be applied to complete liquidations of corporations.

[O. Delattre, D. Streiff & C. Fournier, 4 J. Int'l Tax'n 425.]

"French holding companies benefit from French tax system and treaties" **(1992).** Although there is no comprehensive tax system applicable to holding companies, the French tax code *Code Général des Impôrts* (CGI), contains specific measures concerning intercompany dividends and a reduced taxation of long-term capital gains on the transfer of participations. Dividends received by a French company are normally taxable at the standard corporate tax rate, currently 34 percent. French-source dividends receive an *avoir fiscal*, a tax credit equal to half the dividend received. Because of this, the effective tax due by a corporate recipient is one percent of the dividend received.

Foreign-source dividends do not give rise to the *avoir fiscal* and would therefore suffer an effective taxation at the level of a French corporate recipient if not covered by the parent-subsidiary tax system.

Under CGI Article 145, French companies may benefit from the parent-subsidiary system if the following conditions are met:

1. The parent corporation must be subject to corporation tax at the standard rate. French permanent establishments of treaty-based foreign companies qualify. The subsidiary can be either French or foreign.
2. The shares of the subsidiary must be in registered form or must be deposited with one of the financial establishments listed by the tax authorities.
3. The parent must own at least 10 percent of the capital (generally interpreted as financial and voting rights) of the subsidiary or must have acquired the interest for at least Fr 150 million.
4. The French company must commit to keep the shares for at least two years unless they were acquired on issuance.

CGI Article 146 provides, however, that this parent-subsidiary system does not apply in certain situations, such as (1) dividends paid by investment tax-exempt companies, such as venture capital companies, or (2) dividends paid on nonvoting preferred stock.

If a French company owns an interest meeting these conditions, dividends received from the subsidiary are excluded from the taxable income, except for a "service charge" deemed to correspond to the expenses incurred in connection with such dividend income. The service charge is fixed at 5 percent of gross dividends received (dividend received grossed up by the *avoir fiscal*, or FTC when applicable). The amount, however, cannot exceed the amount of expenses actually incurred by the company during that period.

If the French holding company pays a dividend out of the exempt dividend received from qualifying subsidiaries, it will generally have to pay an equalization tax (the *précompte*) equal to the *avoir fiscal*, which its shareholders can use as a credit against their own tax liability. As the distributing company is entitled to deduct from the *précompte* and tax credit attached to the exempt dividends, no *précompte* is paid on redistribution of French-source exempt dividends because of the *avoir fiscal* and, with foreign-source dividends, only the *précompte* net of foreign direct tax credits (corresponding to foreign withholding taxes levied by a treaty country). This appears to be an attractive way to offset such tax credit.

When a French holding company is used in a purely international framework (owning a foreign subsidiary and controlled by foreign shareholders), France allows deducting from the French withholding tax due on outgoing dividends the foreign withholding taxes that may have been imposed by a treaty country on the incoming dividends.

There is no specific exemption of capital gains realized on the transfer of interest in subsidiaries (unless the transfer is part of an exempt reorganization in France or within the EC). There is, however, a reduced rate of taxation (currently 18 percent) provided that:

1. The interest has been held more than two years and
2. The balance of the gain must be set aside in a special reserve for long-term capital gain.

Amounts subsequently distributed from the special reserve are subject to an additional tax to raise the level of effective taxation up to the standard corporate tax. If, however, the special reserve is distributed in the course of the liquidation of the holding company, no additional tax is due except the *précompte*, which allows the shareholder to benefit from the *avoir fiscal*. An equivalent refund is allowed if the shareholder is resident in a treaty country and does not benefit from the transfer of the *avoir fiscal* under the treaty.

The authors conclude their article with a discussion of the planning and miscellaneous other considerations that should come into the decision of whether to locate a holding company in France.

[O. Delattre & D. Streiff, 3 J. Int'l Tax'n 111.]

"French rules on reorganizations are (almost) in line with EC directive" (1992). On July 23, 1990, EC Directive No. 90/434 on the common tax treatment of mergers, divisions, transfers of assets, and share exchanges between corporations located in different EC members was signed. It is expected that the directive will be considered also to apply to domestic reorganizations. The deadline for EC members to implement the directive was December 31, 1991 (1992 for Portugal), although corporate law barriers for cross-border mergers or divisions remain until the publication of a special directive still under discussion.

The French tax regime of mergers and reorganizations already substantially conformed to the directive, but was amended by the Technical Corrections Law of December 30, 1991, to include the EC requirements, which apply to reorganizations in taxable years beginning in 1992.

The three forms of reorganization under French law are (1) merger or *fusion*; (2) division or *scission*; and (3) transfer of assets or *apport partiel d'actif*. Reorganizations can give rise to a corporate tax (currently 34 percent), a tax at the shareholder level on dividends and capital gains, and registration duties. With respect to the corporate tax, taxpayers may elect a special regime that treats reorganizations as intermediary operations, the principal features of which are

1. The transferring company is exempt from corporate tax, which is normally imposed on capital gain arising from the transfer of assets to the receiving company.
2. The receipt of shares of the receiving company by the transferring company's shareholders is tax-exempt. Tax on gain realized on the transfer can be postponed until a subsequent sale of the shares.
3. As to registration duties, a special regime applies under certain conditions, whether or not the special corporate tax regime applies. The special registration-duty regime provides for a 1.2 percent duty on the difference between the transferring company's net assets and its paid-in capital in a merger, and generally no duty in a transfer of assets. Since January 1, 1992, the ordinary regime provides a fixed duty of Fr 5500 on capital contributions and may often be more favorable than the special regime.

The authors discuss the French tax law with regard to mergers. A discussion of both the ordinary regime and the special regime is provided. Specific attention is given to the subjects of retroactive application of merger treatment, the special regime's principal features, the taxation of the transferring company, the obligations of the receiving company, and the rights of the receiving company. Thereafter, they compare the regimes and discuss choosing between the regimes. The taxation of shareholders (individual and corporate), registration duties, and mergers of affiliates are next examined. The second part of this article addresses corporate divisions and asset transfers (including taxation under the special regime of the corporation and shareholders).

The authors conclude that some aspects of French domestic law are still questionable under EC principles, such as

1. The commitment for the transferring company to take a carryover basis in the shares received in the course of a transfer of assets;
2. The requirement to obtain prior administrative agreement for a merger or division involving EC corporations, unless aimed at avoiding abuse of law, and
3. The imposition of the 1.2 percent registration duty.

The special regime registration duty leaves many uncertainties, since it is inconsistent with previous EC directives and the ordinary regime is often more favorable.

The French Administrative Supreme Court has given the courts authority to determine whether a domestic law conforms to an EC directive. Furthermore, a domestic law or a governmental act or decision, such as a prior administrative agreement, which does not conform to an EC directive, will be considered invalid by the courts and therefore will involve the French State's financial responsibility.

[O. Delattre & D. Streiff, 3 J. Int'l Tax'n 209.]

"France adopts new thin capitalization rules" (1991). In 1990, shortly after the United States enacted the earnings stripping provisions, France, among the many foreign countries that criticized the new U.S. rules, passed an amendment to French Tax Code Section 212 that is principally aimed at limiting the deduction of interest paid by a French company to its foreign controlling shareholder.

In order to encourage the shareholders, especially nonresidents, not to finance their French operations through indebtedness, the French legislature enacted three limitations on the deductibility of interest paid to shareholders. The limitations apply to all amounts lent by shareholders, whatever the form.

The first limitation is that interest paid on shareholder loans is deductible only if the share capital of the company has been fully paid up. This rule applies only to stock corporations in which shareholders are entitled to pay up only one quarter of the nominal shares issued for cash upon subscription, the remaining three quarters being paid within a maximum of five years.

The second limitation is that interest on shareholder loans is deductible only up to the average annual rate of private bond issues in France (10.24 percent for 1990). This limitation does not apply if the interest is paid on loans granted as a result of commercial operations between the shareholder and the company.

An example is provided on how to apply this limitation when the loan granted by a nonresident shareholder is denominated in a currency other than the French franc.

In late 1990, the French Parliament amended Tax Code Section 212, effective January 1, 1991, to provide that the limitation of interest deductibility will apply to any shareholder that holds more than 50 percent of the financial rights (i.e., the right to the dividends) or voting rights of the company paying the interest. The exemption for so-called parent companies within the meaning of Tax Code Section 145 still applies. That section provides that the Section 212 limitation does not apply to interest paid to corporate shareholders that (1) qualify as a parent company under Tax Code Section 145, i.e., corporations subject to French corporate tax (thus including French permanent establishments of foreign corporations) and (2) hold at least 10 percent of the capital of the subsidiary or own a participation in such subsidiary at a cost of at least 150 million French francs.

The practical effect of this amendment is to apply more systematically the limitation provided by Tax Code Section 212 to interest paid by French companies to their majority foreign shareholders. The authors analyze this limitation in depth.

Contrary to the U.S. earnings stripping rules under which disallowed interest may be carried forward without limit and still qualify as interest for purposes of U.S. treaties, interest that is not deductible under French Tax Code Section 39.1.3 or Section 212 may not be deducted in the future and is considered a deemed dividend. When the shareholder is a French parent company under Tax Code Section 145, there is no double taxation, in light of the fact that the deemed dividend is exempt from corporate tax, except up to a service charge not exceeding 5 percent of the gross dividend.

When the shareholder is a foreign resident, the deemed dividend generally is subject to a 25 percent withholding tax in France. If the foreign shareholder is a resident of a treaty country, however, the issue arises as to whether under the applicable treaty the deemed dividend is:

1. A dividend subject to a reduced rate of 15 percent or 5 percent above a specified threshold of shares held;
2. An interest generally exempt from withholding tax; and
3. Other income generally taxable only in the other contracting state.

Under recent amendments to treaties, including treaties with Germany and the United States, deemed dividends under French domestic tax law are dividends for purposes of the treaties and therefore subject to withholding tax in France at the applicable treaty rates.

[O. Delattre & D. Streiff, 2 J. Int'l Tax'n 171.]

"France makes little use of its anti–tax haven provisions" (1991). The French government's position on tax havens, *paradis fiscaux*, is not original. The government says that tax havens are reprehensible because they prevent free competition between economic players and deprive treasuries of tax resources. Over the years, provisions dealing with tax evasion through the use of tax havens have been inserted in the CGI, the French equivalent to the U.S. Code.

"Tax haven" is defined in CGI Article 238A as "a low-tax country." Pursuant to Article 238A(2), a person is operating in a country with a privileged tax system if this person is tax-exempt or subject to tax at a much lower rate than in France. Under regulations, a person is taxed at a much lower rate than in France if taxes paid are at least one-third less than taxes that would be paid in similar circumstances in France.

A tentative list of approximately thirty tax haven countries was also established and distributed to the field agents. It was never published. In France, when a regulation or similar text is published, it is binding for the administration as well as for the taxpayers. To retain flexibility, the government kept its list confidential. The list includes islands such as Grand Cayman, Jersey, Guernsey, and Curaçao, as well as inland countries such as Liechtenstein.

The French government takes a more narrow approach to tax havens than the broad definition under the CGI. It favors the notion of evaluating whether each deal is subject to privileged taxation rather than whether the country has a privileged tax system.

Various CGI provisions specifically prohibit certain types of tax planning.

Transfer pricing is generally dealt with in CGI Article 57. It prohibits price manipulation between related corporations with the goal of shifting tax base out of France. If the entity that benefits from the transfer of income is located in a tax haven, transfer pricing may be established even if the two entities are not related. A legal or economic relationship between the two entities is presumed when one of the two is a tax haven–country resident.

Pursuant to CGI Article 209B, the income of a 25 percent or more–owned subsidiary located in a tax haven is taxable in France to the French parent. The income taxable in France is determined by the percentage of participation of the parent in the subsidiary: 45 percent of the income realized by a 45 percent–owned corporation will be taxable in France and so forth.

The CGI includes an earnings stripping provision that is triggered when a tax haven is used in a transaction. CGI Article 238A strictly limits the deduction of expenses paid to a person located in a tax haven.

Remuneration of a foreign entity for services performed in a given country is a common tax planning scheme. Pursuant to CGI Article 155A, any sum paid to a nonresident for services performed in France is taxable in France to the nonresident if this person is controlled by the person who commissioned it or has no other purpose than the performance of this service.

Despite this heavy artillery, there are no more than a few dozen assessments made each year under these provisions. Several possible explanations can be offered for this, which are discussed by the author.

Torn between the need to protect economic growth and the search for tax resources, the French government has scarcely used its anti–tax haven provisions.

[C. Bouvier, 2 J. Int'l Tax'n 240.]

"Using French parent-affiliates can save taxes" (1991). Most developed countries do not intend that there be multiple taxation at the corporate level. If corporations were taxed on dividends received from other corporations, such multiple corporate taxation would occur. Thus, tax laws in many countries provide for devices designed to avoid multiple corporate taxation. The French parent-affiliates tax system is designed to do this. Thus, international structures can improve profitability and minimize tax costs.

Dividends paid by French companies to resident shareholders and certain categories of nonresident shareholders entitle the shareholders to a tax credit called *avoir fiscal* (AF). The purpose of the AF is to alleviate the tax pressure resulting from the taxation of income to the corporation and again to the shareholder. The credit is 50 percent of the dividend from French sources. An example is provided.

An equalization tax called the *précompte mobilier* (PM) is imposed on distributions that (1) have not borne French corporate income tax, e.g., foreign-based income, dividend income, or long-term capital gains, or (2) are made out of profits earned more than five years before the distribution. In such cases, the AF is no longer necessary, since there is no longer any risk of double taxation. Consequently, to restore the equilibrium, the distributing corporation must pay the PM.

This PM is equal to the AF and represents one third of the gross dividend, as further explained by the author.

In France, there are two types of corporations, *societes de capitaux* and *societes de personnes*. The *societes de capitaux* are subject to an independent corporate tax of 34 percent on nondistributed income and 42 percent on distributed income. When *societes de capitaux* distribute dividends, the AF and the PM are taken into account to partially avoid double taxation. Then, the shareholders pay tax (taking the AF into account) on the dividends received.

The *societes de personnes* are different from the *societes de capitaux* in that no tax is levied at the corporate level; the tax is imposed only on the shareholders. Thus, the AF and the PM do not need to be taken into consideration, since there is no risk of double taxation. These corporations can still elect to be treated as *societes de capitaux*, however, in which case the AF and PM rules will be triggered. Thus, *societes de capitaux* can be compared to U.S. corporations. The *societes de personnes* are equivalent to U.S. partnerships.

The French parent-affiliates tax system provides for an exemption of tax at the parent corporation's level on dividends received from an affiliate when the following conditions are met:

1. The parent corporation must be subject to the normal French corporate tax rate; it does not have to be French. French permanent establishments of foreign corporations subject to the normal corporate tax rate qualify.
2. The parent must be either a *societes de capitaux* or a *societes de personnes* that opted to be treated as a *societes de capitaux*.
3. The shares of the affiliate must be registered, must have been subscribed at the time of issue, and must have been owned by the parent for at least two years, or the parent must have promised to hold these shares for at least two years from the date of the acquisition.
4. The affiliate can be either a French or a foreign corporation. A foreign affiliate need not be subject to tax in its own country. Thus, a foreign corporation that is established in a tax haven qualifies.
5. The parent must own at least 10 percent of the shares in the affiliate or must have contributed at least 150 million French francs to the capital of the affiliate.

When all these conditions are met, generally 95 percent of the dividends received are exempt from corporate tax.

When the affiliate is a foreign corporation established in a country that does not have a tax treaty with France, the 95 percent-of-dividends-received exemption is computed on the net dividends received. Any tax withheld in the foreign country is not taken into account, since no FTC is allowed. When there is a tax treaty between France and the foreign country providing for an FTC, the 95 percent exemption is computed on the gross dividends including any tax credit. The tax credit is not lost; it can be imputed from the PM in the event of a subsequent redistribution.

If there is a subsequent redistribution of dividends by the parent to the French shareholders, all the principles discussed above concerning the AF and the PM come into play, as illustrated in several examples.

The general rule is that the AF benefits only French residents. France has signed various tax treaties providing for the transfer of the AF from the French Treasury to nonresidents, however. Most of these tax treaties have been concluded with the United States, Germany, Japan, Luxembourg, United Kingdom, Singapore, and Switzerland. The author discusses how these different treaties work in detail and provides examples.

There can be many situations in which the shareholder does not qualify for a transfer of the AF, e.g., there is no treaty, there is no provision in the treaty, or the recipient shareholder is a parent corporation under the treaty. In such situations, the shareholder will be entitled to a refund of the PM if it is eventually paid by the distributing corporation. An example is provided.

When a French corporation distributes dividends from profits derived from its affiliates, it must not only pay the PM but also withhold any tax on distributions to nonresident beneficiaries. This latter withholding is computed by deducting or subtracting any tax withheld in the original foreign country. This deduction is allowed only if the foreign shareholder is a resident of a country party to a tax treaty with France and if this shareholder cannot benefit from the transfer of the AF. No credit can be imputed from the tax withheld when the AF has been transferred to a foreign shareholder.

This technique, allowed in France, is not followed by most of the other foreign countries. Thus, any structure involving distributions to nonresidents can be more tax advantageous if a French step is provided, as the author then shows.

The French parent-affiliates tax system can effectively improve the profitability of many international tax structures involving France. On the eve of 1992, such system may also represent an efficient European market introduction device. Careful tax planning, however, is required to combine this tax system with the various benefits resulting from French tax credits and refunds.

[JD Chicha, 2 J. Int'l Tax'n 22.]

"France makes stock option plans more attractive" (1990). As a result of amendments to French law in 1984, 1986, and 1987, stock option plans were more widely adopted by French companies on behalf of their employees. However, the French government has recently restructured the tax benefits available to employees under these plans. The following is a review of the French rules governing qualified stock options.

French law allows two types of stock options: (1) options to subscribe to newly issued shares and (2) options to purchase existing shares. Unfortunately, if a company wishes to permit employees to purchase existing shares, it must purchase the shares for which the options are being granted before granting the options to employees. Granting options on existing shares not only ties up available cash, but is also subject to further restrictions. Thus, options permitting employees to subscribe to new shares are generally preferable under current French law.

In France, only French companies that have negotiable shares may offer stock options. This excludes *sociétés à responsabilité limitée* and *sociétés en nom collectif*, both important forms of French companies. Since 1986, non-French companies may offer stock options to employees of a French subsidiary or a French parent company. The regulations also permit a foreign company to grant qualified stock options to employees of its French branch.

In principle, only salaried employees are permitted to participate in a stock option plan. However, since 1987, qualified stock options may be granted to executive officers who are not salaried employees under French law. Under French law, a company is free to select employees who are eligible for its qualified stock option plan. The plan can, for example, be limited to selected top executives. However, there are certain limitations on this freedom.

For options that permit employees to subscribe to newly issued shares of a company, the price of the new shares is determined in accordance with the guidelines set by the shareholders and after consultation with the *commissaire aux comptes*. The method used in determining the value of the shares must be specified. Special rules apply in determining the value of quoted shares that prevent such shares from being over discounted. In general, it is prudent for the company to issue shares at a price equal to the value of those shares without allowing any discount. Once the price is set, it generally cannot be adjusted. There are exceptions if the capital is increased, decreased, or otherwise adjusted. In any event, the option price can never be less than the nominal value of the shares being issued.

Tax benefits. To qualify for the available tax benefits, the shares must be registered shares, and any employee who has been granted a qualified stock option must not sell the shares acquired under the stock option plan less than five years after the option has been granted to the employee and less than one year after the employee has exercised the option.

Under French law, as amended by the Finance Law of 1990, the difference between the value of the shares under the option at the time the option is exercised and the price paid by the employee is additional compensation and is subject to tax at the time the employee resells his shares. This tax is determined under the rules applicable to capital gains. Additionally, under the new rules, at the time the employee exercises his option, he will pay tax at ordinary income rates on the amount of any discount granted to him that exceeds 10 percent of the stock's value when the option was issued. In such event, the basis of the stock is increased by the amount of such excess.

When the employee resells his shares, the full gain is subject to tax as capital gains. In practice, the tax is equal to zero if the shares are not quoted and the employee and his family own less than 25 percent of the outstanding stock of the company granting the options. In general, the tax is 17 percent if the shares are quoted and the total amount realized by the employee from taxable sales of stock exceeds the applicable threshold.

Taxation of companies. The new finance law has not changed the tax rules applicable to the company granting the option. Under these rules, the company is allowed to deduct from its taxable income expenses related to the stock options. If new shares are issued to the employees, no initial loss or deduction is allowed for the difference between the market value of the shares at the time the option is exercised and the price at which the shares are issued to the employees.

If the company (French or foreign) grants options to employees of a subsidiary, parent company, or sister company, it may charge an allocable portion of its allowable expenses to such company. In that case, the company to which the expenses are being recharged may claim a deduction for any amounts that it has paid.

Payroll and Social Security taxes. The additional compensation realized by an employee is exempt from any of the payroll taxes normally assessed on salary. This exemption remains in effect even if the employee sells his shares before the end of the five-year or one-year period discussed previously. The additional compensation is also exempt from all taxes and charges assessed in connection with French Social Security.

[GS Pinkham, 1 J. Int'l Tax'n 180.]

¶ 7.14 GERMANY

"German Parliament approves 1994 Tax Act" (1993). In 1993, the German Parliament approved the 1994 Tax Act. Major changes include lower tax rates, thin capitalization rules, dividend stripping rules, capital gains tax exemption on the sale of shares in a foreign subsidiary, and exemption of certain foreign-source income distributed by German corporations.

In this article, the author discusses these changes. After doing so, he concludes that the measures enacted at this time, particularly the lower tax rates, have been welcomed by the business community. Some progressive corporate tax reform measures were omitted from the final tax act. For example, one proposal would have allowed an individual German shareholder an indirect credit for foreign tax paid on foreign-source income distributed by a German corporation. This proposal is consistent with recommendations by the EC-appointed Ruding Committee for a model neutral corporate tax system for the EC member states.

This tax credit, and a simplification of the corporate imputation system, are likely to be high on the agenda for the next round of reform. In related developments, legislators have released for comments various draft amendments intended to eliminate transactions the government perceives as tax abusive, and to reform and amend the civil and tax code provisions on corporate mergers and acquisitions. The reform measures are intended, among other things, to bring German law further into line with the EC merger directive. Under present German civil law, true cross-border mergers and divisions are not possible. Before the tax code can be changed as required by the merger directive, the appropriate civil law provisions must be enacted.

[RG Minor, 4 J. Int'l Tax'n 431.]

"To stop revenue loss, Germany reconsiders thin capitalization rules" (1993). New proposed rules on thin capitalization of corporations threaten to end Germany's liberal stance on debt financing, especially by foreign shareholders. Following a decision of the German Supreme Tax Court (*Bundesfinanzhof*) in early 1992 invalidating a government ruling that prescribed a debt-equity ratio for corporations, the German government introduced legislation to curb shareholder debt financing.

The author first considers the benefits of debt financing under current German law. The beneficial effects of the German courts' rejection of any specific debt-equity ratio guideline and their recent taxpayer-favorable decision in a case involving the treatment of purported equity invested in a permanent establishment are examined. Additional examples of the German courts' liberal posture on thin capitalization are also considered.

Next, the author examines proposed legislation that would disallow the deduction of interest paid or accrued on certain types of equitylike debt. The triggering requirements of this provision are discussed by the author, along with specific aspects of this provision such as the meaning of the term "substantial interest," the treatment of hybrid instruments, and determination of the debt-equity ratio on a per shareholder basis. The author then examines the proposed law's treatment of a tainted interest payment as a constructive dividend. Last, the author discusses the proposed effective dates and the latest changes made to this legislation while before the German Parliament.

The author concludes that legislation is on its way to limit shareholder debt financing, imposing a more rigid debt-equity ratio on a per shareholder basis. The bill is a direct response to the Supreme Tax Court decisions giving shareholders complete freedom in financing subsidiaries. Since the legislation is only aimed at income taxation, the Supreme Tax Court's liberal holdings on debt financing continue to have importance for net worth tax and trade tax on capital.

[FF Hey, 4 J. Int'l Tax'n 264.]

"Planning around new German passive foreign investment company (PFIC) rules" (1992). German CFC rules (since 1972, copied from U.S. Subpart F) attribute nondistributed "passive" (i.e., not positively listed) income of a "low-tax"

German CFC to its shareholders resident in Germany in proportion to their respective shareholding in the CFC (irrespective of the size of their individual shareholding). In many instances this attribution under German domestic law would be overridden by the respective German income tax treaty under the intercompany dividends received or the permanent establishment (partnership) exemption.

The new passive foreign investment company rules, adopted February 14, 1992, extend that attribution by

1. Waiving the German-control requirement (but replacing it with a 10 percent or more individual participation requirement) and
2. Denying the treaty exemptions for foreign permanent establishments and foreign dividends received.

This extension, however, would be limited to

1. A more narrowly defined subcategory of ''primarily income with a foreign investment character'' of the respective PFIC and
2. Resident shareholders with at least 10 percent participation.

The core of the new PFIC rules is contained in two sets of legislative amendments. The PFIC attribution rule is in Section 7(6) *Aussensteuergeset* (AStG), the German equivalent of the U.S. Subpart F, and the important ''PFIC'' definition is hidden in an addition to Section 10(6)(2). The ''treaty override'' eliminating the intercompany dividends received exemption for PFIC attribution is in Section 10(6)(1). The corresponding explicit treaty override for permanent establishment (permanent agent) income is in Section 20(2) AStG.

The PFIC attribution rule under Section 7(6) AStG provides that if a foreign company is an intermediary company for income with capital investment character (as defined in Section 10(6)(2)), the company's income primarily consists of such income, and a resident taxpayer participates in that company by at least 10 percent, then such income will be taxable to the taxpayer in proportion to the respective shareholding of that resident shareholder even if the company is not German-controlled.

The ''PFIC'' definition under Section 10(6)(2) AStG provides that ''attributable income'' with an investment character is income of the foreign ''attributable company'' derived from holding, administering, value-maintenance or value-appreciation of monetary funds, claims, securities, participations, or similar assets, unless the taxpayer proves that this income is one of the following:

1. Derived from an activity serving an activity of the foreign company pursuant to Section 8(1) Nos. 1 through 6 (positively listed activities like manufacturing, certain trading, etc.) of the act, except activities within the meaning of Section 1(1) No. 6 of the Banking Act;
2. Derived from companies in which the foreign attributable company participates with at least 10 percent;

3. Derived from the financing of foreign permanent establishments or foreign companies belonging to the same group (*Konzern*) as the foreign attributable company; or

4. Correspondent to an arm's-length part of the income allocable to the services rendered by the foreign attributable company.

The treaty exemption for intercompany dividends (provided correspondingly by domestic law under Section 10(5) AStG) does not apply to the extent the attributable amount includes income with an investment character and the foreign attributable company primarily earns such income.

The article concludes with some suggested planning possibilities.

[R. Pollath, 2 J. Int'l Tax'n 362.]

"Tax benefits encourage foreign investment in Germany" (**1992**). Recently, there have been a number of important developments in German tax practice. Among these are treaty provisions and EC directives, both of which affect nonresidents with investments in Germany and German residents with investments abroad.

The author addresses the current treatment of investment in Germany by nonresidents. Included are specific discussions of the proposed 1992 tax cuts, the advantages of locating a holding company in Germany, the tax treatment of so-called conduit companies, withholding taxes, the acquisition of German companies by non-Germans through use of a holding company, a partnership, and a dual-resident company, and the treatment of certain new financial products (e.g., techniques to obtain the corporate tax credit for dividends to nonresidents, the acceleration of interest deductions or interest income deferral on fixed income securities, and the liberalization of the investment fund rules).

The author also addresses investment abroad by German residents. Specific attention is given to PFICs, the elimination of a double exemption under the permanent establishment provision of the new U.S.-German tax treaty, and the treatment of tax-deferred/tax-free financial products.

The new U.S.-German tax treaty is also discussed, including the limitation on treaty shopping benefits and policy trends in the "credit vs. exemption" area. Next, the incorporation of two EC directives into German domestic law (i.e., the EC merger directive and the parent-subsidiary directive) is examined. Specific discussion is also provided on the topic of transfer pricing under the EC rules. Finally, certain changes in German domestic law are discussed. These include the lapsing of the solidarity surcharge in mid-1992, those affecting capital gains (including a recent ruling on the distinction between business and investment real estate), and proposed and existing East German investment incentives.

[R. Pollath, 3 J. Int'l Tax'n 237.]

"Investing in Germany under the new U.S.-German tax treaty" (**1991**). As of the writing of this article, the new German-American double taxation treaty (New Treaty) had not been ratified but was expected to be by the end of August 1991.

The New Treaty does not fundamentally change the tax principles in comparison to the previously existing double taxation treaty (Old Treaty). In particular, the changes are limited with regard to U.S. investors in Germany.

The New Treaty reduces German withholding tax on intercorporate dividends to U.S. parent companies to 5 percent as of 1992. It will then be harmonized with the internal EC rules. The internal rules will become more advantageous, namely, zero percent, in the middle of 1996. The author discusses tax strategies up until 1992.

For profit-dependent interest, e.g., profit participating loans and silent partnerships, the New Treaty raises German-source tax vis-à-vis the Old Treaty. In the future, the full rate according to German tax law (25 percent) applies if, as is usually the case, the German debtor-company can deduct this compensation. To this extent, the entry into force of the New Treaty is also a reason for accelerating such payments.

The New Treaty continues to deny to Germany, as the source country, the right to tax the gain of the U.S. investor from the sale of shares in a German corporation. In comparison to the Old Treaty, however, there is a limitation. Germany can tax such capital gain if the underlying assets of the German corporation predominantly are real estate. German domestic law only makes use of this right to tax under the New Treaty if the direct or indirect interest in the German company has exceeded 25 percent at any point during the last five years before the sale. Both the New Treaty and the Old Treaty leave to Germany the right to tax gains from the sale of German real estate.

The Old Treaty prohibited German taxation of dividends or interest paid by a dual-resident German-American company. For dual-resident individuals, the New Treaty applies the tie-breaker method for determining treaty residency. The New Treaty declined to use this method for dual-resident companies, presumably as a measure against such companies. Their treaty protection is dependent on obtaining a joint determination from both tax authorities, and ultimately upon their goodwill, an extremely dubious provision.

In accordance with U.S. treaty policy, the New Treaty contains a limitation on treaty protection for individually defined instances of treaty shopping. Again, the treaty-shopping clause must be applied to the company claiming treaty protection. For U.S. investors with German investments, that party is the U.S. investor (parent company), not the German subsidiary.

It may be easier to alter the stream of income than to reorganize the company to try to safeguard treaty protection for the U.S. company. In cases of doubt, it is advisable to obtain a binding ruling, preferably in advance, before income is affected.

As requested by Germany, the New Treaty contains special rules on qualification and attribution conflicts. They primarily apply to German investors with U.S. investments.

The New Treaty rules against German investments in the United States are also not pertinent for U.S. investors in Germany. On the other hand, the New Treaty now denies U.S.-source tax relief and German tax exemption to German investors for such investments. The New Treaty retains the German tax exemption for German investors with U.S. financial and permanent establishments, e.g., U.S. finance partnerships. The balance of the article discusses tax strategies in German investments with respect to the New Treaty.

[R. Pollath, 2 J. Int'l Tax'n 175.]

"Outbound financing for German operations" (1991). The tools for financing German outbound transactions largely relate to non-German structures. A German corporate investor is subject to German local business and federal income tax on all net income (current income and capital gains) except for income from another treaty country exempt under a German income tax treaty. The main exemptions are foreign real estate, permanent establishment, and intercompany dividends (from shares of 10 percent or more, frequently requiring voting stock). The intercompany dividends received exemption also eliminates CFC problems under the German equivalent of the U.S. Subpart F, the *Aussensteuergesetz*.

In contrast, German resident individuals do not qualify for the intercompany dividends received exemption unless a German company is interposed. They may protect themselves against German CFC rules only by interposing an active permanent establishment in a treaty country or by employing coventional but rarely used methods, such as pairing.

Although a German corporation may benefit from the intercompany dividends received exemption, it is taxed on capital gains (including capital gains from the sale of intercompany shareholdings). A private individual investor is not taxed on most capital gains (except short-term gains for real estate and capital gains from more than 25 percent direct or indirect shareholdings). The private individual, however, is more vulnerable to CFC and similar rules.

Other exemptions under German income tax treaties are rare. A well-known example is Dutch mortgage interest, a frequently used exemption that may survive longer than expected because the Dutch-German income tax treaty may take longer to be revised than expected. Similar mortgage interest exemptions may be available under a very few other treaties.

Non-German investment companies. Non-German investment companies are subject to the rules for German tax deferral on the income of foreign subsidiaries. These restrictions include requirements that the company must be nonresident (i.e., no German center of management), must not have a German permanent establishment or permanent agent, must not be subject to CFC rules, must not be an abusive base company (mainly a company without nontax substance) and, under several tax treaties, must be engaged in an active business.

German investment companies. A German investor may obtain deferral of German income tax by making financial investments through a German RIC. Single-investor RICs are not usually permitted under regulatory foreign law, however, except for pension fund and similar money.

Zero bonds. Zero bonds (or stripped bonds) do not provide German tax benefits to German corporate or other business investors, because there most probably is no deferral of interest income received (as opposed to the deferral for private investors until redemption or resale). Therefore, again, corporate investors would have to incorporate these investments in non-German financing companies.

Individual investors. Most individual investors make financial investments not so much to obtain benefits from an Irish financial services company, Belgian co-ordination center, and the like, but rather to obtain tax-free capital gains. An exception would be any investment that has a high risk of being characterized as a business rather than as an investment, for instance (1) real estate investments with three or more sales within five years (as a rule of thumb, not a technical rule) or (2) potential buyout, venture capital, or similar investments with low current yield and high turnover (including very speculative futures, options, arbitrage, or other trading of shares or securities). All these investments may have such a high German business characterization risk that it is worth making them in a taxable U.S. structure benefiting from the corresponding German exemption rather than making them in a German structure with the potential of full exemption as private investment but the risk of full tax as a business. It is not easy to make such a U.S. structure subject to U.S. tax as a U.S. trade or business, however, and U.S. trade or business character involves other tax disadvantages (such as U.S. estate tax exposure).

[R. Pollath, 1 J. In'l Tax'n 304.]

"The legal environment for business in eastern Germany" (1991). Because of East Germany's unification with West Germany and the well-publicized factors generally affecting the transition to a Western-style economy, investors in eastern German business enterprises should be aware of certain peculiarities arising in this environment. At this time, crucial considerations for investors are the requirements for owning property, the administration of justice, implementation of the laws, and preferences under tax and other business laws applicable in eastern Germany. In this article, the authors consider property, tax, and other issues of consequence to prospective investors in eastern Germany.

The authors first discuss the current questions concerning the ability of investors to obtain clear title to property located in eastern Germany. Preferences in this regard given to investors over other claimants, under laws enacted in 1991, are thoroughly discussed. Other considerations particularly important when negotiating for property in eastern Germany are also examined by the authors.

Next, the authors explore new tax and nontax incentives available for investment in eastern Germany. Also discussed are existing and proposed U.S. government programs for assisting prospective investors in eastern Germany. Last, new developments in the way business is conducted in eastern Germany are noted by the authors and compared to pre-unification conduct of business operations. In this regard, the authors review the manner in which private enterprise and state-owned enterprise were taxed prior to unification.

[C. Kochinke, H. Reinert & N. Buchbinder, US Tax'n Int'l Operations ¶ 8531.]

"Current events bring rapid changes to East and West German tax laws"
(1990). Much of the applicable tax law in the German Democratic Republic (East
Germany) is old and unused, usually dating back to pre-World War I. This law
consists of pieces of former Reich Law that were not superseded by new law in
areas of interest to the old regime. The Joint Venture Decree of January 25, 1990,
deals with the creation and activity of enterprises with foreign participations in East
Germany. It does not affect the existing legal forms of companies that are controlled
by the Reich Acts.

The Joint Venture Decree is based on an amendment to the East German
Constitution. It introduced a new Article 14a, which permits the creation of enterprises with foreign participation by concerns, businesses, institutions, and so forth,
"on the basis of acts and other legal provisions." This article was the basis for the
Joint Venture Decree, which did not require parliamentary approval. Upon the entry
of a new Constitution, the Joint Venture Decree will be replaced by an act.

Foreign participations in a joint venture are generally limited to 49 percent.
This ceiling may be exceeded in small- and medium-size businesses. Apart from
joint ventures, there continue to be a number of other possibilities for foreign investment, such as the establishment of private businesses by foreigners and foreign
participation in private businesses and the transformation of a people's business into
a corporation.

The creation of a joint venture is clearly separated into two steps even though
this is not legally required. The basic joint venture agreement sets forth all the
particulars of the venture. If made within East Germany, it is subject to East German
law, including the Joint Venture Decree. If made outside, the agreement may be
subject to the laws of any other country and the Joint Venture Decree does not apply,
nor is notarization required under East German law. The second step involves the
articles of association whereby the joint venture company is established by performing the obligations under the agreement.

Reform legislation in East German taxation attempts to create a more reasonable
set of rules, but still has a long way to go in becoming clear in practice. The East
German Income Tax Act is based on the same ground rules as in West Germany,
which include taxation by schedules, and no capital gains tax on long-term capital
gains. Nonresident employees are subject to East German tax after two days, as of
day one; and the revised wage withholding tax system applies equally to blue- and
white-collar workers. All employees of an East German business (including a joint
venture) are subject to East German Social Security taxes.

Corporations and other legal persons are subject to corporate tax, the top rate
being 50 percent on an annual income of 200,000 East German marks. This rate
also applies to businesses with foreign participations and to branches of nonresident
companies. The maximum tax burden from income, corporation, and net worth tax
is an aggregate 75 percent of the income. This does not include local business tax
and the social fund contributions. There is local business tax on income and capital.
Partnerships are transparent for East German tax purposes. A nonresident partner
of an East German partnership therefore has a (pro rata) permanent establishment

in East Germany. Royalties are subject to a 25 percent withholding tax, and this applies to licenses to a joint venture. East Germany does not levy a VAT but rather a general sales tax at 3 percent.

Previously, all transactions with East Germany were required to go through the clearing system of the Berlin treaty. Now, any methods and means of payment are permitted. Direct investments into and from East Germany have been generally approved by the General Approval of the German Federal Bank to the Foreign Exchange Control Acts. This includes the creation of or participation in East German businesses, the creation of branches, capital increases or reduction, and profit transfers.

A resident of West Germany is generally exempt from West German income or corporate tax on all income from East German sources. These are defined by the West German source rules. The West German government has proposed to eliminate some of the disadvantages that were the result of the West German ground rules for taxation of East German income. Losses of an East German branch have been proposed to be deductible from West German income, subject to recapture to the extent that profits arise thereafter. This benefit is limited to active businesses. Start-up losses of an East German subsidiary corporation are deductible by the direct West German shareholder, pro rata to the participation. A transfer of assets from West Germany to East Germany realizes taxable gain. The tax is deferred until the gain is effectively realized at the branch.

The West German VAT system has a regular rate of 14 percent and a reduced rate of 7 percent. This system applies to transactions with East Germany only to the extent that they are carried on outside the framework of the Berlin treaty. Transactions within the Berlin treaty are subject to a special sales tax system. Sales and services from West to East Germany are subject to 6 percent tax, and the East Germans are not entitled to a corresponding input credit. Sales and services from East to West Germany entitle the West German recipient to a deduction of usually 11 percent for sales and 5 percent for services. East Germany does not generally levy Customs, and, therefore does not generally levy an importation sales tax.

[R. Pollath, 1 J. Int'l Tax'n 43.]

"In-bound financing for German operations" (1990). Tax planning for financing is a relatively safe way to achieve predictable and significant tax savings. Germany is a particularly suitable country because of both high statutory tax rates and liberal tax rules in the financing area.

German income tax law is very liberal in characterizing debt as "debt" rather than "equity," even if debt involves profit sharing, is subordinated, or is otherwise hybrid. Second, there is no German interest withholding tax from straight interest or from any interest paid by a non-German debtor. A third favorable item is the absence of German tax on most capital gains of nonresidents such as from the sale of real estate (after two years) or from the sale of shares. Finally, benefits may be derived from inefficiencies in German tax accounting (which is strictly based on commercial accounting).

The most significant relative disadvantage of German taxation of international financing is the German local business tax, especially the add-back rules. Depending on the municipality, local business tax is between 10 percent and 20 percent of adjusted net income and between 0.4 percent and 0.95 percent per annum of adjusted net capital. The main adjustments are add-backs of certain deductible items, including some interest. The 50 percent add-back increases the pre-tax financing costs of a 7–8 percent coupon by one percent. Other disadvantages of the German tax system include stamp taxes (although the one percent tax on equity and profit sharing is scheduled to disappear January 1, 1992) and real estate transfer taxes (frequently to be avoided or reduced).

For a nonresident shareholder, substituting a shareholder loan for an equity contribution reduces the German tax burden from above 60 percent down to approximately 10 percent (the after-tax burden of local business tax due to add-backs). A German borrower is free to choose the currency in which it borrows, hedging the interest cost down to the deutsche mark rate if the lender's currency has significantly higher interest rates than the deutsche mark.

The tax administration holds perpetual debt to be equity, particularly if coupled with other features, such as profit sharing, which might constitute a partnership subjecting the nonresident to full German tax on net income. In contrast, a partnership may be made into a creditor relationship by taking away certain basic rights of a full partner or a share in unrealized appreciation.

Thin capitalization (debt-equity) rules apply only to borrowing between related parties. Thus, if a German company is capitalized with equity by one group of investors and with debt by another unrelated group, there is practically no ceiling on the leverage from a tax viewpoint.

A frequently used way of introducing additional leverage into an existing German corporate structure is decapitalizing the overall investment by interposing a new German holding company, which acquires the shares in the existing German company partly for equity and largely for debt. Such an internal leveraged buyout may drastically reduce the German tax burden.

The leverage produces interest that is effectively deductible from pre-tax German income of the operating company, but this deduction works for local business tax only if there is financial, organizational, and business integration between the new German holding company and its subsidiaries. Integration for federal corporate income tax additionally requires a profit and loss transfer agreement. Interposing a German holding company may allow for a tax-free asset step-up, producing higher depreciation on present fair market values. However, there is no tax-free step-up to the extent that shares of the acquired subsidiary have been held by nonresidents at any time during the last ten years.

A German borrower would deduct the bond interest attributable to each business year, even though it has not been paid and may not (yet) be taxed in the hands of the lender. Original issue discounts are taxable to private investors in Germany, while secondary market discounts are not.

Unlike straight interest, rentals and royalties are subject to the 25 percent withholding under German domestic law, although many tax treaties provide for zero percent withholding. There is no add-back for real estate and none for royalties and similar license fees (as there is for rentals of machinery or equipment), creating a tax incentive to separate real estate and business. While there may be net worth tax disadvantages, an unequivocal advantage from holding real estate separately (i.e., out of a non-German real estate holding company) is the ability of nonresident shareholders to sell real estate tax free after two years. This could be used for an internal asset basis step-up by selling the real estate to an affiliate.

[R. Pollath, 1 J. Int'l Tax'n 232.]

¶ 7.15 HONG KONG

"Doing business in Hong Kong" (1993). In this article, the author provides important background information for U.S. businesses and investors interested in conducting business in or through Hong Kong. The author first discusses Hong Kong's government, its legal system (including significant laws for foreign investors), its currency and exchange control laws, import and export ordinances, and financial institutions. Next, the author reviews and explains Hong Kong's tax system. Specific discussion is provided of its tax structure, property tax, salaries tax, business profits tax, stamp duty, and estate duty.

In the next section of this article, the author examines the permissible entities through which business may be conducted in Hong Kong. He explores both incorporation and acquisition of Hong Kong companies, of a private limited company, and of public companies. The corporate law requirements with respect to each of these corporate forms is also discussed. Hong Kong operations through or using foreign corporations and partnerships are also examined in light of the legal requirements and restrictions imposed on each under Hong Kong law.

In the last section of this article, the author examines Hong Kong law with respect to patents, trademarks, and copyrights. As a separate concluding matter, the author briefly discusses the efforts Hong Kong has made to ensure continuance of its favorable business climate, especially with regard to U.S. investors.

[JP VanderWolk, US Tax'n Int'l Operations ¶ 8508.]

¶ 7.16 ISRAEL

"Israel combines tax and economic incentives to lure investors" (1993). Israel has traditionally been a high-tax country. Its current corporate tax rate is 40 percent. Dividends distributed from Israeli corporations are subject to a 25 percent withholding tax. Nevertheless, a new effort to do away with red tape and recent developments in Israel have made it more attractive for a U.S. corporation engaged in a capital-intensive activity. These new incentives can result in minimal U.S. and Israeli taxes and allow corporations to receive cash grants of up to 38 percent of the amounts they invest in their Israeli operations. Many of these incentives are provided under the Encouragement of Capital Investments Law, enacted by Israel in 1959 and amended in 1990. This amendment added certain benefits such as government guarantees of loans for "Approved Enterprises."

After discussing the qualifications for Approved Enterprise status, the author discusses the system of benefits available for such enterprises. Two systems of benefits are available: the standard set (which focuses primarily on extending government grants to the owner and in lowering its tax rate) and the alternative set (which provides the investor with a complete tax holiday instead of government grants). The author provides an in-depth discussion of both systems of benefits, along with a review of the most recently added rules and benefits affecting Approved Enterprises.

Last, he discuses planning considerations relating to investment in Israel, including valuation of asset issues and the benefits of Dutch registration (that is, using a Dutch company for U.S. investment instead of direct U.S. investment). The author then concludes that Israeli law currently favors the development of foreign investment. No one can predict how long the government will maintain this pro-investment outlook, however. Accordingly, potential investors that want to avail themselves of the favorable grants offered by the Israeli government should consider applying for Approved Enterprise status at this time.

[Al Appel, 4 J. Int'l Tax'n 175.]

¶ 7.17 ITALY

"Italy moves against corporate groups using tax havens" (1993). Italy's Finance Act for 1992 introduced rules to curb tax avoidance through the use or abuse of tax havens. The antiavoidance rules, which apply for tax years starting after 1991, operate in two ways: (1) deductions are disallowed for expenses in transactions with related "tax haven companies" and (2) dividends received from "tax haven–related companies" are taxed at a higher rate than those received from non–tax haven related companies.

The author discusses the deduction disallowance provision and the increased tax rate on tax haven dividends. Additionally, the author discusses the exclusion of EC countries from tax haven classification and the "black list" issued by Italy's Ministry of Finance, which sets forth two different categories of tax havens. Thereafter, the author examines the ways in which exclusion from the antiavoidance rules may be obtained even though a transaction with a tax haven company is involved. The procedure for advance rulings on exclusion is also addressed.

[A. Silvestri, 4 J. Int'l Tax'n 36.]

"Section 482 regulations and Italian transfer pricing rules are often at odds" (1993). The 1993 Section 482 temporary and proposed regulations may not provide enough flexibility for taxpayers to formulate a transfer pricing policy that complies with both U.S. and Italian law. Italy, like many EC countries, adheres closely to the OECD's generally accepted international standards for transfer pricing, which have not appreciably changed since 1979. These principles vary with the concepts and practices in the U.S. and, although the 1993 regulations are more embracing of the OECD standards than the 1992 proposed Section 482 regulations, troubling issues remain.

The authors first describe the statutory basis for Italian transfer pricing in cross-border transactions. Advisory circulars issued by the Italian tax authorities explaining application of the statutory rules are also discussed. Next, the authors focus on the hierarchy of transfer pricing methodologies established under Italian law. A description of each of these methods is provided. The difference in the burden of proof in transfer pricing controversies under U.S. and Italian law is explored. The permissible percentage levels of royalty payments are also considered.

The authors then examine the U.S. "best method" rule under the 1993 transfer pricing regulations and illustrate points of noncompatibility with the Italian rules. Coordination of both countries' methods is then discussed, along with the use of mutual agreement procedures. Certain problem areas are noted, including conflicts in use of the commensurate-with-income standard, the use of Customs valuation, and the treatment of services.

The authors conclude that even though the U.S. and Italian transfer pricing principles have their foundations in the OECD standards, it should not be assumed that application of the U.S. standards will always be appropriate in Italy and vice versa. Significant differences remain in the practices of the tax authorities and application of methods that require planners to consider both systems simultaneously. The best defense to challenges of transfer prices by the Italian authorities is documentation and consistency among entities within the group. A well-reasoned policy that relies on a method other than the comparable uncontrolled price method should be accepted by the Italian authorities.

[MM Levey, LA Oster & F. Greco, 4 J. Int'l Tax'n 456.]

¶ 7.18 JAPAN

"Japan's transfer pricing policies are being more rigorously enforced" (1993).
In recent years, the Japanese National Tax Administration (NTA) has gradually increased its enforcement of the Japanese transfer pricing regulations. These regulations, introduced in 1986, require that a transaction between a Japanese corporation and its "foreign affiliated corporation" must be carried out at arm's length. If the Japanese corporation fails to report income from the transaction on the basis of an arm's-length price and, as a consequence, its taxable income is understated, the NTA can adjust the Japanese corporation's taxable income upward to reflect an arm's-length price. Unlike the U.S. rule under Section 482, the Japanese regulations apply only to international transactions between affiliated corporations.

The author first examines the meaning of "foreign affiliated corporation" under the Japanese regulations. Next, he addresses the different pricing methods under Japan's Special Measures Law, that is: the comparable uncontrolled price method, the resale price method, the cost-plus method, and other "reasonable" methods (including the profit-split method). Each of these methods is explained, along with certain variations permitted under Japanese rulings.

The author then compares the Japanese system and the U.S. system under Section 482. Thereafter, administration of the Japanese transfer pricing policy, along with recent cases, is discussed. Recent regulatory amendments are examined. The author discusses the "correlative downward adjustment" used to avoid double taxation after application of the Japanese transfer pricing regulations. The application of both Japanese law and tax treaties to the procedure for effecting a correlative downward adjustment is explored.

The author concludes that more foreign corporations doing business in Japan will be subject to substantial transfer pricing adjustments. The Japanese rules differ from those in the United States, but not so much that U.S. practitioners will be unable to understand the basic nature of the proceedings. Further changes in the Japanese system, however, might occur in response to overly aggressive actions by the United States in development and enforcement of its own policies.

[A. Fujieda, 4 J. Int'l Tax'n 196.]

"Japan's transfer pricing system is evolving along U.S. lines" (1993). The sophistication and detail of the current Section 482 regulations supersedes the efforts of most other countries in designing transfer pricing regimes. These regulations draw many parallels to current Japanese rules and practices, and their application often assists in complying with the Japanese requirements. This is partly because the tax authorities in Japan and the United States have been "piggybacking" each other's concepts. Because of numerous similarities between the two systems, it should be possible to craft a U.S.-Japan transfer pricing policy that avoids double taxation, as is discussed in this article.

The authors first discuss the existing differences in the way the United States and Japan engage in transfer pricing enforcement. Next, they discuss the transfer pricing methodologies in use in both countries, including comparability standards. The extent to which both countries use the same principles and different principles is highlighted. Differences in how these methodologies may be applied and their theoretical support are also considered and explained. Use of "other reasonable methods" to determine transfer prices is examined for both countries' transfer pricing schemes.

Next, the authors consider differences between the United States and Japan with regard to documentation, disclosure of related-party transactions, imposition of penalties and interest, and enforcement strategies. The authors conclude that, while the U.S. and Japanese methods for determining transfer prices are similar, a similar end result will not always be achieved. If a U.S. taxpayer proceeds under the comparable uncontrolled price method as the most appropriate under the "best method'' rule, it is likely to also be acceptable for Japanese tax purposes. If the taxpayer proceeds under the resale price of cost-plus method as most appropriate under the best method rule, it will also likely be acceptable for Japanese purposes, even if the taxpayer used gross profit margins or gross profit markups from the general industry. If none of these methods is the ''best method'' and the U.S. comparable profits method is applied, while this is not a prescribed method in Japan, at least the Japanese tax authorities have some familiarity with it in the Japanese law and practice. If the comparable profits method analysis is thoroughly and carefully documented, it may be defensible in Japan.

Double taxation may occur despite mutual acceptance of the use of a method. Cultural differences may also result in the tax authorities placing a different emphasis on the value of trade names, advertising, and other marketing intangibles employed in the respective countries. Careful planning and documentation is necessary to alleviate this potential problem.

[MM Levey, T. Dilworth, JE Lanman, M. Inoue & M. Murata, 4 J. Int'l Tax'n 407.]

''Japan introduces thin capitalization rules, other major changes'' (1992). The Japanese Diet has enacted thin capitalization rules for the first time. The new rules permanently disallow as a tax deduction interest paid by a Japanese corporation, or a Japanese branch of a foreign corporation, to a related non-Japanese corporation when the Japanese corporation or branch is thinly capitalized.

An overseas corporation is related to a Japanese corporation if it directly or indirectly owns at least 50 percent of the shares of the Japanese corporation, or if both companies are at least 50 percent owned by a common parent. The new rules also apply even when a 50 percent ownership interest does not exist under conditions set forth in the article.

If a Japanese corporation is paying interest to an overseas related party, the interest disallowed as a deduction is determined by one of several formulas set out by the author. The disallowance rules apply where both (1) the ratio of total interest bearing debt to net equity and (2) the ratio of interest bearing debt to overseas related parties to the net equity investment by such parties, is greater than three to one. Any interest that is disallowed as a deduction is forfeited—there is no carryover available for the disallowed interest.

To encourage foreign investment in Japan, two new incentives have been adopted. The incentives apply to Japanese branches of foreign corporations and to Japanese corporations more than a third of whose equity is owned by a foreign corporation and which meet certain other requirements of the Ministry of International Trade and Investment.

The first incentive permits eligible Japanese taxpayers to claim an additional depreciation deduction equal to 20 percent of the ordinary depreciation deduction for five years.

The second incentive permits eligible Japanese taxpayers an extended net operating loss carry-forward period. Losses incurred during the initial three-year period following the establishment of a company in Japan or the creation of a Japanese branch may be carried forward for seven years, rather than the standard carry-forward period of five years.

Japanese companies have been hampered in structuring their overseas invest-ments because the tax rules permitted an indirect FTC only for taxes paid by first-tier foreign subsidiaries. Under the new legislation, a Japanese company is also treated as having paid taxes incurred by certain second-tier foreign subsidiaries.

For many years, Japanese shareholders have been required to report on a current basis the income of certain foreign subsidiaries formed in tax haven countries. The tax haven countries to which the rules applied were specifically identified. Thus, when a new "tax haven" appeared, Japanese corporations could take advantage of it until the tax authorities got around to issuing a new list of tax havens.

Under the new rules, the system of specifically identifying countries as tax havens has been eliminated. Instead, the tax haven rules applied on the basis of the income tax actually imposed on the foreign subsidiary.

Japanese rules allow a tax-free contribution of assets to a newly formed cor-poration under limited circumstances. If land is involved in the contribution trans-action, 20 percent of any unrealized capital gain is taxed at the time of contribution, and the shares of the corporation that receives the property must be held for at least five years to achieve partial tax-free treatment of the contribution. In the case of a foreign corporation with a direct branch in Japan, these rules may also apply. Re-cently, however, the Japanese tax authorities have been attacking situations where substantial branch activity was not maintained following the contribution of assets on the basis that no Japanese taxpayer remained to which the shares of the new corporation were effectively connected. The new legislation makes it explicit that in the case of a branch transferring land to a new corporation, the branch must be engaged in business up to and following the date of the contribution of assets. Further, when the contributing branch's business is discontinued, any tax-free ben-efit realized at the time of the contribution transaction will be recaptured.

Short discussions on the following tax changes conclude the article: suspension of loss carryback rules, consumption tax rates, interest on certain bonds issued by the Japanese government, and a tax surcharge.

[NW Zimmerman, 3 J. Int'l Tax'n 176.]

"Japan adopts land value tax to curtail spiraling prices" (1991). A number of changes have been made in the Japanese tax rules relating to real estate transactions. Other important changes include the imposition of a temporary tax to fund Japan's contribution to the Gulf War, tightening of the rules applicable to related-party transactions, revisions to the consumption tax, and minimum capitalization require-ments.

A new land value tax, effective in 1992, will apply as of January 1 of each year to both corporate and individual owners of Japanese land or rights to use land. In Japan, buildings are generally not part of the land, and are not subject to the same taxation. In most cases, the value is in the land, not in the buildings. For 1992, the tax rate will be 0.2 percent of the value of Japanese land; it will be 0.3 percent thereafter. Valuation of land is discussed in detail. Certain types of land are exempt from the land value tax. In addition, all taxpayers are entitled to a basic deduction in computing the tax. These items are discussed in detail.

In computing the tax, the exemptions are first applied to exclude appropriate parcels of land, the basic deduction is applied next, and the tax rate is then applied to the balance of the land. The land value tax is deductible in computing corporate income tax in the year the return is filed, and by an individual in determining business or rental income if the land is used for business or rental purposes.

Japan has traditionally had a high tax on the sale of land located in Japan, except when the land has been held for long periods. The holding period is determined as of January 1 of the year in which the land is sold, not the actual date of sale.

For individuals, Japan makes no distinction as to where land is located: The same rates apply to the sale of foreign land as to Japanese land. Although the normal maximum individual rate is 65 percent, individuals pay punitive rates when land with a holding period of five years or less is sold.

Effective in 1992, the rate for property held more than five years will be 39 percent, unless the property is sold to a developer for conversion into residential units, in which case the rate will be only 20 percent. Furthermore, beginning in 1992, an individual with a loss on rental property will not be able to offset the loss against other income to the extent the loss is attributable to interest expense on a loan used to acquire the land.

For corporations, only land located in Japan is subject to punitive tax rates. The author details the tax rates for land held less than two years, between two and five years, and greater than five years.

Japanese tax rules permit the transfer of property to a corporation on a tax-free basis only under very limited circumstances. Japanese tax rules permit a taxpayer that sells land to defer recognition of 80 percent of the gain if the proceeds are reinvested in qualified property. Sale and reinvestment are addressed in detail.

In the past, if land had been held for more than ten years as of January 1 of the year in which it was sold, reinvestment could be in any depreciable property used in a trade or business in Japan. Effective in 1992, this favorable rollover provision is repealed.

A temporary tax on corporations has been introduced to raise funds for Japan's contribution to the Gulf War effort. The tax applies to fiscal years ending between April 1991 and March 1992. The tax is 2.5 percent of the portion of a company's national tax liability that is in excess of 3 million yen ($21,000).

With respect to related-party transactions, the following topics are briefly addressed in the article: statute of limitations, comparable transactions, expanded reporting, donation expense, and tax haven operations.

The minimum capitalization for a Japanese *Kabushiki Kaisha*, the most common form of corporation for business purposes, has been increased to 10 million yen ($71,000). Companies may now transfer retained earnings to capital free of withholding tax to the extent needed to met the new minimum capitalization requirement. Companies formed prior to April 1991 have until March 1996 to comply with the new capitalization requirements.

Japan's version of the VAT, the consumption tax, has been imposed at a 3 percent rate since April 1989. In legislation effective October 1991, the definition of "exempt transactions" is expanded to include residential rents, school entrance fees, textbooks, hospital fees for childbirth, and expenses for burial. Provisions designed to make it easier for small businesses to comply with the law were narrowed so that they will now be available to fewer taxpayers. In addition, if the annual consumption tax liability is greater than 5 million yen ($35,000), quarterly payments will be required to be made instead of semiannual ones.

[NW Zimmerman, 2 J. Int'l Tax'n 167.]

"Japanese import incentives" (1991). As a part of the recently concluded Structural Impediment Initiative talks between the United States and Japan, the Japanese government agreed to enact legislation to promote imports into Japan. Programs to be undertaken include tax incentives, funds for an information network to promote imports, the expansion of low-interest loan facilities for imports, and the elimination of tariffs on over 1,000 products. The tax incentives were put in place even before the Structural Impediment Initiative talks were concluded. These new incentives are effective from April 1990 through March 1993.

The import tax incentives are intended to benefit both manufacturing companies and wholesale or retail companies that import manufactured products into Japan by reducing the taxable income and tax paid in Japan, thus easing to a limited extent the tax planning problems associated with effective tax rates of approximately 52 percent. Fundamental differences between the incentives for manufacturing companies and those for wholesale or retail companies result in quite different benefits for these two groups.

General requirements. The ownership of a company is not a factor in claiming the tax incentives. If the requirements are otherwise met, the company may be Japanese-owned, foreign-owned, or a Japanese branch of a foreign corporation.

Products designated as eligible for the import incentives were included in an official list released by the Ministry of International Trade and Industry. The general categories covered are machinery, electrical instruments, optical instruments, optical industrial products, paper products, vehicles, furniture, and other items that are exempt from Customs duty when imported.

Import computations are made on the basis of the company's accounting years, which include April 1. For 1990, the base period is 1989. For subsequent years, the base period is the year after 1988 with the highest import value. For fiscal years that include periods prior to April 1990 or subsequent to March 1993, the import and tax incentive computations must be prorated. No incentives can be claimed in the first year of existence or if the company is in the process of liquidating.

In order to claim the tax incentives described below for a particular year, the company's eligible imports must have increased by at least 10 percent over the eligible imports in the base period.

Manufacturing company incentives. Manufacturing companies are entitled to a 5 percent tax credit based on the increase in value of their imports of eligible products into Japan over the value of such products imported during the base period. Alternatively, such companies are eligible to take advantage of either a special accelerated depreciation allowance or the establishment of a special tax deductible reserve.

Wholesale and retail company incentives. The new rules also provide an import incentive for companies in the wholesale or retail business. The incentive for such companies is limited to the establishment of a tax deductible reserve, which is then required to be reversed back into taxable income over the five years following the year in which it is established. The reserve that can be established is 20 percent of the increase in the value of eligible imports. Eligible companies are those that derive more than 50 percent of their Japan-source income from the wholesale or retail business.

Conclusion. The new Japanese import incentives have been introduced in an effort to increase imports. Although it is difficult to predict whether these incentives will accomplish the Japanese government's objective, they do provide opportunities for both manufacturing and wholesale and retail companies to currently reduce the tax paid in Japan. In the case of the deductible reserves, the benefit is temporary because of the reversal of the reserves. For a manufacturing company, however, the election of a tax credit yields a permanent reduction in tax.

It generally is accepted that Japanese tax planning opportunities are limited. Thus, the use of these incentives should be considered by any company engaged in manufacturing or wholesale or retail activities in Japan.

[NW Zimmerman, 1 J. Int'l Tax'n 308.]

"Japanese intercompany transfer pricing examinations" (1991). Intercompany transfer pricing legislation applies to cross-border transactions between affiliated companies. There are no formal transfer pricing rules for transactions solely between Japanese entities; however, the tax authorities have other methods that allow them to attack abusive transfer pricing situations. Transactions covered by the cross-border intercompany transfer pricing rules include personal property purchases and sales, loans, services or technical assistance, and other intercompany transactions.

This column discusses the transfer pricing rules, the tax authorities' approach to examinations, the appeals process, and some planning considerations in light thereof. The Japanese tax authorities are actively pursuing audits of cross-border intercompany transfer pricing. Taxpayers with Japanese operations should be aware of the rules and be prepared to support the transfer pricing they have used by having ready for submission to Japanese authorities copies of books of account, records, or other documents to support an arm's-length price.

Affiliation between companies means at least 50 percent direct or indirect ownership of the issued and outstanding shares of one of the following:

1. A Japanese corporation by a foreign corporation;
2. A foreign corporation by a Japanese corporation; and
3. Between a Japanese corporation and its parent and a foreign corporation and the same parent.

Affiliation may also result if control effectively exists by one corporation providing personnel, technology, financing, and the like, to another corporation.

The price that must be charged in intercompany cross-border transactions is an arm's-length price. In the case of inventory purchases and sales, the arm's-length price should be determined by applying one of the following methods: (1) the third-party comparable price method; (2) the resale price method; (3) the cost-plus method; and (4) another method meeting certain criteria. In the case of cross-border transactions not involving inventory, methods similar to the foregoing should be used.

When filing its tax return, a company having cross-border transactions with foreign affiliated companies must attach a schedule disclosing information related to the transactions. If a taxpayer fails to provide requested information at audit, the tax authorities can impute taxable income on the transactions. If the Japanese taxpayer has paid more than the arm's-length price to a foreign affiliate, the excess payment will not be deductible.

The author addresses the applicable penalties and explains the tax appeals process in Japan. He notes that advance clearances are available but that taxpayers do not often request clearances because of the substantial amount of information that must be submitted and the lack of advance clearance from the tax authorities on the other side of the transaction.

The author also looks at tax planning. Because of the high tax rates in Japan, multinational companies based outside Japan will want to keep their transfer prices to their Japanese affiliates as high as possible. Here, care must be taken that prices charged fall within the guidelines of the pricing rules.

Finally, the author observes that in Japan, it is generally not possible to make retroactive changes. He then discusses the problematic amendment of the tax return process. As a result, Japanese companies rarely file amended tax returns. An alternative is to submit an appeal to the tax authorities for a downward tax assessment. This procedure can be used within one year of the filing of the original tax return. The request results in an audit by the tax authorities, but is more commonly used than the amended return approach.

[NW Zimmerman, 1 J. Int'l Tax'n 372.]

"Ways to avoid Japan's high corporate taxes" (1990). Japan's tax rates are among the highest in the world for developed countries. Tax reform in 1988, which became fully implemented for tax years beginning after March 1990, was highly touted as reducing the tax rate for Japanese companies. However, many foreign-owned Japanese subsidiaries distribute substantially all of their earnings each year. For these companies, tax reform's elimination of the preferential tax rate on distributed earnings has actually resulted in a tax increase.

Japanese tax planning starts with a recognition that taxable income is closely tied to the earnings reported in the statutory accounts. Foreign owners of Japanese subsidiaries have an advantage in that it may be possible to adopt accounting methods in the statutory accounts that provide favorable tax results, while at the same time effectively use different accounting methods for worldwide reporting purposes by making adjustments in consolidation. Since approval for changes in accounting methods to be used on the subsidiary's tax returns must be requested before the start of the year in which they will be effective, advance planning is essential.

[NW Zimmerman, 1 J. Int'l Tax'n 118.]

¶ 7.19 KAZAKHSTAN

"Strangers in a new land: U.S. tax lawyers come to Kazakhstan" (1993). Foreign investment in the former republics of the Soviet Union has generated much publicity. Investment opportunities abound in the newly independent republics, including those in the Commonwealth of Independent States. Companies seeking opportunities, however, face numerous obstacles.

One of these obstacles, discussed by the authors of this article, is the lack of legal research tools and the poor compilation of the republics' laws relevant for foreign investors. Nonetheless, the authors, in this article, have pieced together the important provisions of the Kazakh tax law. They also discuss the ways in which the IRS may respond to these provisions in applying the U.S. tax law to Kazakh investors, as for example in the qualification of Kazakh tax for the U.S. FTC. They also examine Kazakhstan's profits and withholding taxes. Last, they explore the business organizations available to foreign investors in Kazakhstan and the way these may be treated under U.S. tax law.

Finally, after discussing the applicable VAT and road taxes, the authors conclude that it is possible to negotiate a feasible tax structure for a Kazakh venture. A clearer general system that reduces the need for negotiation, however, would encourage foreign investors. Kazakh officials have indicated a willingness to consider moving their tax law towards such a system, and several efforts that would do this are under way.

[JM Bedell, D. Horowitz & CA Nordberg, Jr., 4 J. Int'l Tax'n 301.]

¶ 7.20 KOREA

"Korean transfer pricing system broadens its net, but not everyone is caught" (1993). The Korean NTA, becoming alert to the possibility of income-shifting by means of cross-border intercompany transfer pricing arrangements of multinational corporations, began (in 1988) adopting rules and procedures to combat this abuse. The author of this article discusses these rules and procedures, including the reporting requirements adopted in 1990, and further examines the many questions that still remain open on the manner in which these rules and procedures may be interpreted.

The author first addresses the implementation of the arm's-length principle under Korean law, including the specific transactions covered by this principle. Thereafter, he discusses the ways in which the arm's-length price may be determined: the comparable uncontrolled price method, the resale price method, the cost-plus method, and other reasonable methods.

After discussing the reporting requirements imposed on covered transactions, the author concludes that the Korean transfer pricing system is only beginning to develop the sophistication of the U.S. system. Nevertheless, in just a few years, Korean law has broadened the reach of its transfer pricing provisions, specified information reporting requirements, and begun vigorously to scrutinize cross-border transactions where the income may be shifted out of the country.

[Yong S. Oh, 4 J. Int'l Transactions 187.]

¶ 7.21 LATIN AMERICA, GENERALLY

"Mercosur treaty brings most of southern cone into single trade group" (1993). In 1991, the presidents of Argentina, Brazil, Paraguay, and Uraguay signed a treaty creating a Common Market among these four South American nations, i.e., the Mercosur. In this article, the author examines the nature of this treaty agreement and its provisions, including its tax aspects (which concern cross-border movement of products, dispute resolution, and stock markets). Some of the problems in achieving the goals and objectives set forth in the treaty are also discussed by the author.

[MM Valente, 4 J. Int'l Tax'n 372.]

"Latin America eases royalty rules—part I" (1992). Throughout 1991, long-existing restrictions on royalty payments made by companies in certain Latin America countries to companies in the United States and other countries around the world have been dramatically eased. The most exciting recent developments have been the *complete* lifting of royalty restrictions in Mexico and the *partial* lifting of restrictions on related-party royalties in Brazil and the Andean Pact countries, as detailed in the article.

The recent easing of royalty provisions in several major Latin American countries has created new opportunities for worldwide tax savings for many U.S. and foreign companies that license intangible property to subsidiaries in Latin America. Such savings are generally achieved by increasing deductions for royalty remittances in those Latin American countries and by reporting royalty income in the United States. In other cases, the increased remittance of royalties from certain Latin American countries achieves a lower overall effective tax rate through the use of excess FTCs in the United States.

On the less favorable side, the easing of Latin American royalty restrictions may increase tax liabilities in the United States and other countries. In particular, royalty income previously due U.S. companies, which was not included in U.S. taxable income because of the Section 482 blocked-income provision, may now be unblocked and taxed. Hence, it is exceedingly important for U.S. companies to quickly determine true arm's-length royalty rates for licensed intangibles to Latin American countries. Fortunately, increased royalty rates should both decrease U.S. tax exposure while reducing worldwide effective tax rates. Hence, many U.S. companies have a double incentive for raising royalty rates to arm's-length levels. To appropriately determine arm's-length royalty rates, and to justify those rates to both U.S. and Latin American tax authorities, it is advisable in many instances to undertake an economic analysis using appropriate arm's-length comparable information. Without such analysis, significant liability may arise upon scrutiny by revenue authorities, and potential tax savings may be lost.

Part one of this article explores generally the tax opportunities that arise from the easing of Latin American royalty restrictions—especially with regard to royalty payments to related U.S. entities. Potential foreign country and U.S. tax savings have been considered, as well as possible U.S. liabilities. The role of economic analysis in the determination of royalty rates is also discussed.

As related foreign company licenses increase and government supervision of royalty payments is further liberalized, it is expected that Latin American taxing authorities will more closely scrutinize such payments as to the arm's-length standard.

Under the arm's-length standard, royalties paid between related parties should equal royalties that would be set between unrelated parties, i.e., as if they had been negotiated by independent parties under the same terms and conditions. In either related- or unrelated-party situations, license agreements typically allow the full or limited, exclusive or nonexclusive use of intangible assets, such as trade names, trademarks, manufacturing know-how, and manufacturing patents on the part of the licensee. The primary difficulty in the arm's-length standard is the determination of arm's-length royalty rates. The authors examine this in detail.

The lifting of royalty restrictions is likely to translate into reduced tax liabilities for Latin American companies. In particular, Latin American companies operating in countries that now allow royalties paid to foreign related parties to be increased to an arm's-length rate will receive increased tax deductions and will in most cases achieve an overall lowering of local taxes. This includes the avoidance of withholding tax on dividends that might otherwise be remitted abroad. The benefit of these increased deductions, however, will be reduced in part by the withholding tax that is imposed by Latin American countries on the payment of royalties to foreign parties. An exhibit demonstrates the effect of withholding.

In addition to the potential reduction of worldwide tax as a result of the lifting of related-party royalty restrictions in Latin America, as explained in the article, U.S. companies licensing intangibles to Latin American subsidiaries will have to carefully consider the blocked-income provisions under Regulation § 1.482-1(d)(6). Under this regulation, a U.S. company that would be expected to receive income (such as royalty income) at arm's-length from a foreign related party, but cannot, because the country in which that foreign related party is located has enacted restrictions on the remittance of that income, may elect a deferred method of accounting for that income. Under such a deferred method of accounting, income (and corresponding deductions incurred by the parent that relate to the earning of that income) is not includable for U.S. tax purposes until remittance restrictions in the foreign country are lifted. The regulations also allow the election of such a deferred method of accounting even after the commencement of an IRS audit, provided such election is made before the first of certain events.

Now that certain royalty remittances are permitted, the IRS will seek to impute income to U.S. corporations with respect to U.S. intangibles used in Latin America, unless U.S. companies and their Latin American affiliates enter into royalty arrangements or enforce previously existing agreements. The authors discuss the effect of the proposed regulations on different possible situations.

As an important additional consideration, the Section 6662 transfer pricing penalty may apply to situations in which Latin American restrictions have been eased but the U.S. company does not report for tax purposes the proper arm's-length royalty income.

To determine related-party royalty rates (as well as transfer prices for the sale of tangible goods), it is often necessary to conduct an economic analysis. In the United States, this necessity arises because IRS transfer pricing regulations do not provide the sort of guidance that may be used to easily determine arm's-length rates. Rather, the regulations provide a series of methodologies and considerations that must be taken into account to economically derive appropriate arm's-length prices or rates. In addition, new proposed U.S. regulations were issued in January 1992 to ensure that royalty payments made to U.S. companies by related parties meet the commensurate-with-income standard. This standard, originally added by the Tax Reform Act of 1986 (TRA 1986), generally requires that the royalty income derived by a U.S. company from a related party be commensurate with the income derived from the licensed intangibles.

In contrast to the United States, the transfer pricing rules in many Latin American countries are relatively vague and offer little guidance with regard to determining arm's-length royalty rates. Nevertheless, it can be generally assumed that economic studies of the type commonly performed in the United States would be of value in many Latin American countries.

Part one of this article concludes with a brief discussion of the new proposed regulations under Section 482 and the three methodologies set forth therein for determining arm's-length royalty rates.

[SG Sherwood, N. Del Castillo, RW Bitler & MF Solano, 2 J. Int'l Tax'n 334.]

"Latin America eases royalty rules—part II" (1992). This article considers the easing of royalty restrictions in Latin America and summarizes the status of royalties in some of the principal Latin American countries.

Brazilian companies can now remit royalties to controlling foreign corporations in exchange for the license of patents, trademarks, and other intangibles. License agreements, however, must still be registered and approved by the Brazilian patent office (*Instituto Nacional de Propriedad Industrial*) (INPI) and the Brazilian Central Bank. The INPI determines the maximum royalties that can be remitted to the foreign parent. Foreign currency for payment of the royalties can be acquired at the official exchange rate only if the agreement has been registered and approved by both the INPI and the Central Bank. In addition, if these procedures are not followed, the Brazilian company cannot deduct the royalties. The royalty expense deduction is limited by preestablished royalty rates issued by the Brazilian Ministry of Economics (*Ministerio de Economia Fazenda e Planejamento*). Under this schedule, the maximum allowable royalty expense deduction ranges from one percent to 5 percent of net sales, depending on the industry in which the patent or other intangible is used.

Given the disparity between the combined Brazilian corporate and dividend withholding tax rates of approximately 60 percent and the 25 percent withholding tax on royalties paid to nonresident foreign corporations, significant tax savings may result from remitting a Brazilian subsidiary's earnings to its U.S. parent in the form of royalty payments. (The 60 percent rate will be reduced to 54 percent after 1992.)

With regard to Mexico, under the new Law for the Promotion and Protection of Industrial Property, enacted and effective June 1991, license agreements no longer need to be registered or approved, and parties can freely determine the terms of their agreement. A Mexican company may now claim a tax deduction for royalties paid to a nonresident foreign corporation, including foreign parent corporations or other related foreign corporations, as long as the nonresident corporation possesses and renders directly to the Mexican company the appropriate technical expertise.

It is anticipated that the Mexican revenue authorities will begin to scrutinize more closely whether the agreed-upon royalty rate is at arm's length. Under Article 64A of the Mexican income tax law (*Ley del Impuesto Sobre La Renta*), they are given the power to determine the arm's-length royalty rate that the Mexican company can claim as a deductible expense, where the agreed amount differs from the amount charged to unrelated parties.

Under Decision 291 of the Cartagena Accord (promulgated March 22, 1991), most of the Andean Pact countries (Venezuela, Columbia, Ecuador, Peru, and Bolivia) have adopted measures aimed at easing prior restrictions on the remittance of royalty payments to foreign related parties for the licensing of intellectual property. Decisions of the Cartagena Accord are not binding until implementing legislation is adopted by member states. Under Articles 13, 14, and 15 of this decision, local companies may pay royalties to related foreign parties provided certain minimum requirements are satisfied. In general, the licensing agreement must be registered with the appropriate government authorities. The agreement must also comply with certain informational requirements, such as identifying the nature of the technology being transferred, the nationality of the licensor, the royalty rate, and the duration of the agreement. A licensing agreement will not be registered by the local authorities if it does any of the following:

1. Ties the licensing to the acquisition of capital goods, intermediate products, raw materials, or other technologies, or imposes an obligation to employ, on a permanent basis, personnel appointed by the enterprise supplying the technology;

2. Reserves to the licensor the right to set sale or resale prices for the products to be manufactured under the licensed patent;

3. Restricts the volume of production;

4. Prohibits the use of competing technology;

5. Establishes options for the licensor to purchase some or all of the finished goods;

6. Requires the licensee to transfer to the licensor the inventions or improvements obtained through the use of the licensed technology; or

7. Requires royalty payments or unutilized patents.

Licensing agreements that prohibit or limit the export of products manufactured with the use of the licensed technology will not be registered by the local authorities, and in no event are clauses restricting the sale of finished goods in the Andean region permitted.

In practice, the level of scrutiny given to license agreements between local companies and their foreign related parties varies substantially among the member countries. In Peru and Venezuela, for instance, as long as the agreement complies with the above requirements, it is automatically deemed approved on filing with the appropriate authorities, regardless of the royalty rate established under the agreement. In other countries, such as Colombia, an express approval from local authorities is still required. The approval process is fairly liberal, however, and agreements are generally accepted.

The level of scrutiny given to licensing agreements between local companies and their foreign owners varies substantially from one Latin American country to the next. The easing of restrictions on royalty payments is generally beneficial, with some notable exceptions, such as Colombia. With the evolving law in the area, a number of important opportunities are available for American corporations with Latin American affiliates.

[S. Sherwood, N. Del Castillo, R. Bitler & M. Solano, 3 J. Int'l Tax'n 14.]

¶ 7.22 MALTA

"Malta: a base for offshore production and services" (1991). This article examines the considerations associated with investing and doing business in Malta. First, the author sets forth information on the geography and demographics of Malta. Its government, legal system, and infrastructure are reviewed, along with its desirability for banking and foreign exchange operations. The availability of professional services required by business is also set out. Next, the author discusses the corporate and business laws of Malta, particularly those concerning forms of corporate entities, protection of intellectual property, and industrial relations. Its principal industries and cultural activities, are then discussed.

In the next section of this article, the author explores the short- and medium-term outlook for investments in Malta. Included within this discussion is consideration of the business incentives available in Malta and its tax structure, tax incentives for business operations and investment, and procedural requirements. Malta's secrecy laws and corporate registration and fee requirements are also noted.

In the last section of this article, the author considers other benefits of doing business in Malta, such as its access to major markets and its investment protection agreements with other nations. Thereafter, the author discusses Malta's tax treaties, particularly its treaty with the United States. The author concludes his article with a discussion of new developments (as of 1991) in Malta that are of concern to investors.

[C. Kochinke, US Tax'n Int'l Operations ¶ 8529.]

"Maltese tax concessions and immigration preferences form an attractive investment immigration package" (1991). Malta enacted legislation to attract affluent foreign investors. These new incentives link Maltese tax benefits to preferential treatment of foreign real estate ownership and permanent residency. This legislation governs the tax consequences of three investment activities involving either the purchase or lease of a home in Malta and the transfer of foreign-source funds to Malta.

The first activity, called the Holiday Home Program, attracts investors who want a vacation home in Malta. The second activity, called the Temporary Residence Program, entails preferential treatment of income transferred to Malta. The third is called the Permanent Residence Program. In this program, persons with substantial income or assets can stay in Malta for an unlimited period and have their income taxes at only a flat 15 percent rate.

In this article, the author examines these programs and the requirements for their use and coverage. In discussing the Permanent Residence Program, the author also reviews Malta's tax system for personal income. Last, the author includes a discussion of the treatment of expenses associated with the acquisition of real property in Malta.

[C. Kochinke, US Tax'n Int'l Operations ¶ 8506.]

¶ 7.23 MEXICO

"Mexican privatization brings tax costs even with asset purchases" (1993). Mexico's president, in 1989, initiated a privatization program of most businesses wholly or partly owned by the Mexican government. This program has resulted in the creation of many new and unusual tax issues. The type of issue that arises depends on the form of privatization.

In this article, the author considers privatization through the sale of stock in the enterprise and through divestiture of government corporate assets. In addition to discussing the various issues that attach to each form, the author also examines other issues created by Mexican laws regulating the nature of foreign investment, the reservation of certain activities or enterprises to the government, and Mexican labor law.

The author concludes that privatization is in its last stages in Mexico. While it has opened the way for private (including foreign) investment, not all business activities are available to foreigners, and the percentage of foreign investment is often limited. A post-acquisition merger of a Mexican domestic corporation and a foreign corporation solves a number of problems, as noted in this article. Acquisition of assets of government-owned corporations may have tax benefits, but may not erase labor and tax liabilities.

[DJ Kaye, 4 J. Int'l Tax'n 429.]

"New financial products draw investors to Mexican markets" (1993). With the strong encouragement and active involvement of the Salinas administration, Mexico has developed its capital markets and is attracting foreign investment. Economic stability has been of overriding importance, but a regulatory and tax environment that supports a modern financial marketplace and facilitates foreign investment has also been essential. The Salinas government initiatives have included tax reductions, deregulation of the capital markets, privatizations, and opening up of the Mexican market to foreign goods and capital. Moreover, there has been a dramatic decrease in Mexican inflation, virtually a prerequisite to a stable economic environment.

After discussing Mexico's recent economic growth, the authors examine the four principal sovereign fixed-income instruments available in Mexico: (1) Treasury certificates; (2) development bonds; (3) inflation adjusted long-term notes; and (4) dollar-denominated Treasury bonds. The exemption of these instruments and the taxation of other fixed-income investments are also discussed. The authors then address the taxation of accrued interest on the sale of bonds. Last, they discuss Mexico's tax treatment of dividends and gains on the sale of stock.

[RJ Shapiro & RD Lorence, 4 J. Int'l Tax'n 141.]

"Withholding net catches corporations operating in Mexico" (1993). Corporations resident in Mexico, whether or not foreign-owned, are subject to various taxes—income tax, VAT, special taxes on production or services, a tax on assets, payroll taxes, and taxes on international trade. Nonresidents doing business in Mexico are taxed as residents and may be subject to withholding.

The author of this article first provides a general discussion of Mexico's tax law. Thereafter, he provides specific discussion of Mexico's income tax. Issues covered are the effect of tax treaties, persons subject to tax, the meaning of "permanent establishment," and the problematic tax consequences of certain import/export practices. Next, he discusses Mexico's withholding tax system; a table is provided indicating the various Mexican withholding rates. Specific coverage is provided for the withholding tax treatment of wages and salaries; fees; rental income; real estate gains; income from the sale of stock and other securities; dividend income; interest income; royalty income; income from construction, building or maintenance; and income from the exchange of Mexican public debt for capital.

The author concludes that, except for salaries paid from abroad and on the sale of shares abroad, residents making payments to nonresidents must withhold income tax on such payments. As of 1992, the Mexican Ministry of Finance has new powers to estimate nonresidents' taxable income and the value of business activities in Mexico to find any tax evasion.

[DJ Kaye, 4 J. Int'l Tax'n 62.]

"Mexico is no longer hyperinflationary, and tax cost lessens for U.S. investors" **(1992).** TRA 1986 enacted a separate FTC limitation (basket) for dividends received from corporations that do not qualify as CFCs. The separate basket for dividends from each noncontrolled Section 902 corporation adversely affects most U.S. corporations with affiliates in Mexico because the "Mexicanization" program of the early 1970s encouraged majority Mexican ownership of such affiliates.

There is a clear advantage to structuring an investment in Mexico as a CFC even though CFC status triggers current U.S. taxation of the CFC's Subpart F income. On a continuing basis, royalties from the CFC generally fall into the same basket as dividends from it, and the gain on the eventual disposition of the CFC enjoys the deemed-paid credit and foreign-source treatment triggered by Section 1248.

Foreign corporation status and reporting methods have become important because of Mexico's strong economic performance, and will likely become more important if the tax treaty between the United States and Mexico and the North American Free Trade Agreement become final.

For financial reporting purposes, a number of U.S. companies will likely change from the dollar to the peso as the functional currency because it will reduce the volatility of the earnings they report from Mexican affiliates. While it is likely that the IRS would grant permission for a similar change for tax purposes, there are a number of reasons why U.S. taxpayers will continue to report the results of their Mexican affiliates using the dollar under the dollar approximate separate transactions method (DASTM). Regulations probably made DASTM mandatory for operations in hyperinflationary economies because the IRS did not wish to make the mark-to-market regime optional. This is understandable, but the IRS has achieved the same practical result of a mandatory mark-to-market regime under Proposed Regulation § 1.988-2(b)(15) for hyperinflationary financial assets and liabilities.

Unfortunately, the IRS does not have the authority to cure the distortion caused by placing dividends from noncontrolled Mexican affiliates in a separate basket for FTC limitation purposes, but this problem could be cured by a provision in the pending tax treaty between the United States and Mexico that places such dividends in the overall basket subject to the look-through rules. In the alternative, the problem could be partially redressed by placing royalties from the same company in the same basket as dividends from that company.

[DW Dusendschon & ND Hansen, 3 J. Int'l Tax'n 92.]

¶ 7.24 NETHERLANDS

"Netherlands draft bill attempts crackdown on tax haven transactions" (1993). In 1993, the Dutch Ministry of Finance released a draft legislative proposal for the amendment of the Corporate Income Tax Act 1969 (the act). The proposal would introduce anti–tax haven measures and eliminate undesired effects of the Dutch system of determining residence based on incorporation under Dutch law.

The draft bill contains three major changes to the act: (1) a limitation on deemed residence for tax purposes in the Netherlands of companies incorporated under the laws of the Netherlands; (2) a limitation on deductibility of intercompany interest paid to affiliated companies in tax havens; and (3) a reformulation of the subject-to-tax test for participations in companies not resident in the Netherlands for tax purposes, specifically aimed at companies operating in tax havens. Furthermore, the explanatory memorandum to the draft bill announces another proposal, yet to be released, that will restrict use of the exemption method for profits attributable to a foreign permanent establishment of a Dutch resident taxpayer, similar to the proposed change to the participation exemption (item 3, above).

The author first reviews current Dutch law and compares it with the proposed changes. Specific attention is given to residence rules and the proposed limitations on the deductibility of interest charges paid to affiliated companies resident in a foreign country. The proposed tightening of the subject-to-tax test under the participation exemption is then explained, along with the establishment of a new credit system where the participation exemption does not apply. Next, the author considers proposed changes for the exemption system for permanent establishments, including those with regard to unilateral relief decrees and triangular cases.

[SV Weeghel, 4 J. Int'l Tax'n 422.]

"Dutch oil and gas transfers raise corporate tax and profit-sharing issues" (1992). Over the last few months there have been several changes in ownership of exploration and production interests of oil and gas reserves in the Netherlands and the Dutch part of the Continental Shelf (NCS). There are various reasons why companies have sold their interests, one being the relatively small size of the reserves on the NCS, especially in comparison to the prospects in the Commonwealth of former Soviet States. The number of companies with activities on the NCS has decreased, and some of the companies that sold their interests are currently major investors in the eastern region. Certainly, if those transactions involve companies that have not yet used all exploration expenses incurred in the Netherlands, the consolidation of existing properties with the acquired properties is of importance. This consolidation often requires the transfer of exploration and production licenses. This article contains discussion of the corporate income tax under the 1969 Corporate Income Tax Act and the profit share under Royal Decrees issued in 1967 (old-regime profit share) and 1976 (new-regime profit share).

Many of the forementioned transactions involved a sale of all the shares of a company with Netherlands exploration and production activities. The actual sale and transfer of these shares seldom has adverse Netherlands corporate income tax consequences. If the seller is a Netherlands corporate entity, a gain will almost certainly fall under the so-called participation exemption and a loss will not provide any tax relief. A foreign entity selling shares will be confronted with a corporate income tax only in very special circumstances.

The acquisition of all shares in an exploration and production company by a company with similar activities does not result in a consolidation for corporate income tax and profit share purposes of the business of the acquired company with the business of the purchaser. To achieve such consolidation for both levies, a subsequent transfer of one of the businesses, inclusive of the licenses, has to be made. Such transfer will frequently be done on the basis of a corporate income tax– exempt (legal) merger or internal reorganization.

The article addresses Dutch corporate income tax, profit share, and transfers of licenses (especially production licenses), and the differences between the corporate income tax and profit share approach.

[WM Nan, 2 J. Int'l Tax'n 365.]

"The Netherlands provides favorable climate for aircraft leasing" (1992). The Netherlands, traditionally favorable to holding and finance companies, provides specific advantages for aircraft financing and leasing. Nevertheless, some advantages have recently been curtailed. Treaty shopping possibilities should be analyzed, given significant options in Dutch treaties.

The author discusses the Netherlands' taxation of resident companies under the corporate income tax, especially those provisions concerning owners of aircraft. The low–tax haven investment rules are also considered. Next, the author addresses the determination of economic ownership of an aircraft under Netherlands tax law. In this regard, reference is made to several guidelines used to determine who is the economic owner. Finance and operational leases with a Netherlands' lessor are also discussed.

The Netherlands' rules concerning transfer pricing are explained. Obtaining finance rulings and royalty rulings is considered.

The treatment of lease payments made by a lessee in one country to a lessor in another country under tax treaties is considered by the author with regard to treaty provisions concerning shipping and air transport and royalties. Finally, the author examines the treatment under the VAT of both finance and operational leases, including official guidelines defining the features of a typical finance lease agreement. The treatment under the VAT of both finance and operational leases is explained.

The author concludes that although the Netherlands has reduced some of the more extreme benefits of arranging aircraft leasing and financing through Netherlands companies, the climate remains favorable. This is true both from the perspective of the corporate income tax and VAT systems and applies in a variety of leasing and financing arrangements.

[GP Altepost, 3 J. Int'l Tax'n 242.]

"Transfer pricing in the Netherlands" (1991). Netherlands tax law concerning transfer pricing is not laid down in any specific statutory provisions. It is generally accepted, however, that the arm's-length principle is firmly established in the law and applies to the business profits of corporations. This is often referred to as the principle that transactions between related parties must stand the test of comparison with transactions between unrelated parties to be acceptable for tax purposes.

The Netherlands tax authorities will grant advance rulings confirming the arm's-length nature of certain types of transactions. The most common tax rulings relate to financing activities, licensing activities, and support activities that are of a preparatory or auxiliary nature.

Although Netherlands tax law does not contain specific provisions providing for the adjustment of transfer prices between related companies to conform to arm's-length pricing, as far as business profits of corporations are concerned, this power may be derived from the definition of "profit" in Article 7 of the Income Tax Act 1964 (ITA) and from Articles 9 and 10 of the Corporation Income Tax Act 1969. Article 7 of the ITA also applies for purposes of determining profits for corporate income tax purposes.

It is generally assumed in the Netherlands that transfer pricing adjustments may only be made with respect to transactions between a corporation and its shareholder(s) in which a benefit is conferred to the latter.

On several occasions, the Undersecretary of Finance has stated that the Netherlands accepts the methods of determining transfer prices laid down in the OECD reports of 1979 and 1984. These methods are

1. Comparable uncontrolled price method;
2. Cost-plus method;
3. Resale-minus method; and
4. Gross profit method, which compares margins of other companies in the same line of business.

No priority rule has been established concerning the use of one method over another. The Netherlands courts will take into account all aspects of the relevant transactions and all facts and circumstances regarding these transactions.

A Netherlands corporation that has entered in to a non-arm's-length transaction with a related corporation may incur different tax consequences, depending on which company receives and which company confers the benefit. The author also discusses the tax consequences of the following situations: (1) Netherlands subsidiary receives benefits; (2) Netherlands subsidiary confers benefits; (3) Netherlands parent confers benefit; and (4) Netherlands parent receives benefit.

Transfer pricing adjustments may affect the taxation of both the corporation conferring the benefit and the corporation receiving that benefit. A transfer pricing adjustment in another country, however, may not automatically lead to a corresponding adjustment in the Netherlands.

The author also looks into the advance ruling procedure. Areas that the Undersecretary of Finance has identified for which a transfer pricing ruling may be granted are each addressed. These areas are financing activities, licensing activities, and support activities.

The last topic addressed is the obligation to provide information to the Netherlands tax administration to establish that transactions between related corporations are not arm's length. The obligation does not apply if the foreign shareholder or the other entity is a resident of or is established in a country with which the Netherlands has concluded a tax treaty with an adequate provision for the exchange of information or in an EC country. These countries are listed in a decree published on April 10, 1991. The list includes all EC member states (including Portugal, with which the Netherlands has not concluded a tax treaty) and all countries with which the Netherlands has concluded tax treaties, with the exception of Hungary, Japan, Yugoslavia, the former Soviet Union, and Switzerland. The obligation is revived, however, if the required information cannot be obtained through the use of the provision for the exchange of information. In such a case, the Minister of Finance must give prior permission to the tax administration to exercise its right to obtain the information in accordance with the law.

[W. Kapoen, 2 J. Int'l Tax'n 230.]

"VAT recovery denied to Dutch holding company" (1991). The 1991 decision of the European Court of Justice, Luxembourg, in *Polysar*, provides a salutary lesson that planning for European operations requires consideration not only of income taxes but of other types of taxes imposed in the member states.

Of all indirect taxes, VAT is the most important, particularly following agreement by all member states in May 1991 to adopt a 14 percent minimum standard rate. VAT is a truly European tax, since it derives entirely from EC law, and any turnover taxes imposed by member states that do not comply with the various VAT directives are prohibited. VAT legislation of member states must also comply with EC law to maintain its validity.

The *Polysar* case arose from what might be described as a classic Dutch holding company arrangement. Polysar Investment Netherlands, B.V., was a wholly owned subsidiary of Polysar Holdings, Ltd., a Canadian corporation. The Dutch company in turn owned shares in a large number of companies incorporated in a variety of foreign jurisdictions. Dividends were regularly received by it and were in turn paid out to the Canadian parent. The Dutch holding company did not carry on any commercial activity.

Holding companies of this kind are plentiful in the Netherlands and have traditionally been used to route cross-border payments (especially dividends) at reduced withholding rates.

VAT, as its name implies, is a tax on value added. All taxpayers engaged in the making of supplies must charge tax (output tax) on taxable supplies made by them. Where supplies are exempt, no tax is charged. Taxable persons can recover the VAT charged to them (input tax) on any supplies received. Recovery of this input tax is permitted only when taxable supplies are made in the course of business activity of the taxable person. The corollary of this is that the makers of exempt supplies cannot recover the input tax charged to them. The burden of input tax is therefore borne by them and others, e.g., consumers, who cannot recover input tax.

From 1981 to 1985, Polysar Investments Netherlands, B.V., claimed input tax charged on services incurred by it. These included accounting and other expert services and had VAT included in the amount billed to it. The Dutch Inspector of Customs and Excise issued an assessment in order to recover the input tax on the basis that the company was not a taxable person for purposes of the Dutch legislation implementing the EC Sixth VAT Directive, and thus was not entitled to recover input tax on the services it had received.

Article 4(1) of the directive specifies that a "taxable person" is any person who independently carries out in any place any specified economic activity. The crux of the matter arose out of Article 4(2), which provides that "the exploitation of tangible or intangible property for the purpose of obtaining income therefrom on a continuing basis shall also be considered an economic activity."

Polysar argued that the ownership of shares should be included in economic activity. Rejecting this contention, the court stated that VAT applied only to activities of a commercial nature.

The court concluded in *Polysar* that the pure holding of financial participations in other enterprises did not constitute the exploitation of property with a permanent character, because any dividends earned as the fruit of the participation resulted simply from ownership of the property. Thus, the mere ownership of shares and the exercise of rights pertaining thereto does not constitute an economic activity for VAT purposes.

The practical effect of the judgment is that pure holding companies established within the EC cannot recover input tax on services supplied to them. This will mean that the cost of professional services such as those of accountants and lawyers will be increased by the irrecoverable VAT.

Although irrecoverable VAT is generally deductible in computing profits for corporate tax purposes, pure holding companies will not normally have income against which this may be set off. In addition, there may be limitations on the amount deductible by holding companies.

Although it has been suggested by some that *Polysar* might cause some holding companies to move their functions out of Europe, the availability of several strategies, as discussed by the author, to minimize the impact of the case makes this unlikely. In any event, such companies continue to be attractive from a corporate income tax perspective, where the stakes are invariably higher than the potential VAT exposure.

[JS Schwarz, 2 J. Int'l Tax'n 250.]

¶ 7.25 NEW ZEALAND

"New Zealand's foreign investment proposals may discourage outbound investment" (1993). In 1993, New Zealand enacted legislation that imposes on New Zealand residents a comprehensive tax regime for outbound investment. This new law amends the CFC rules and radically changes (and extends) New Zealand's tax on unrealized FIF gains and its foreign dividend withholding tax on repatriations to New Zealand parent companies from offshore subsidiaries.

The authors first discuss New Zealand's taxation of FIFs. The general FIF rules, along with the recent changes made by the 1993 legislation, are considered in-depth. Specific attention is also given to the extent of available exemptions, the effects of the new legislation on investors, and various policy concerns. The authors conclude that the direct impact of the rules is likely to fall on a relatively small number of taxpayers, although indirect effects may have an impact on many others. Moreover, it is important to place them in the context of what is now a remarkably tight set of tax controls on outbound investment from New Zealand.

[AJ Lines & GG Tubb, 4 J. Int'l Tax'n 322.]

"Treaty benefits and tax reforms attract U.S. investors to New Zealand" (1993). New Zealand has overhauled its tax system. This overhaul was in part influenced by its desire to encourage foreign investment. In this article, the author discusses important provisions of the New Zealand tax code and their incentive effect on foreign investment.

The author first considers the interaction of the New Zealand tax law and its tax treaty with the United States. The determination of residency status under both, for corporate and noncorporate entities, is reviewed. Next, the author examines the taxation of business profits, dividends, interest (and the incentive provision that allows zero withholding in certain cases), royalties, and profits from the disposition of capital assets. Investment incentive provisions with respect to each category of income are also discussed.

The author then examines other New Zealand taxes that must be considered, by prospective investors, including the nonresident contractor withholding tax, the GST (consumption tax), and stamp and Customs duties. In addition, New Zealand's counterpart for Section 482, concerning transfer pricing, is also discussed.

The author concludes that, as discussed in this article, there are a number of possible vehicles and methods available to U.S. corporations wishing to invest or carry on business in New Zealand. The recent tax reforms, although reducing rates of tax, have broadened the tax base in many respects. Accordingly, considerable care is required to maintain the value of the investment incentives when basing corporate operations in New Zealand.

[RA Green, 4 J. Int'l Tax'n 355.]

¶ 7.26 NORWAY

"Norwegian tax reform adds new rates for different sources of individual income" (1992). The Norwegian Tax Reform Act, generally effective after 1991, is designed to achieve fairness and simplification, as well as to broaden the tax base and lower tax rates. These objectives are accomplished in part by (1) abolishing most tax credits; (2) restricting tax deferrals on gains from asset sales; and (3) allowing write-downs on inventories. In this article, the author provides a brief summary of the major changes.

The following aspects of the Norwegian Tax Reform Act are discussed: (1) the ordinary income and personal income tax bases (including an examination of the types of income entering personal income, i.e., work income, personal business income, and income of active business owners); (2) certain tax-exempt profits on disposition of stock; (3) the wealth tax on individuals; (4) the treatment of foreign taxpayers (including foreign shareholders in Norwegian corporations, foreign shareholders of foreign corporations doing business in Norway, Norwegian shareholders in Norwegian corporations doing business abroad, Norwegian shareholders in foreign companies, and individuals moving into or out of Norway); (5) the tax treatment of partners and partnerships; (6) the treatment of inventory/commodity contracts (including the write-down provisions on receivables); (7) depreciation generally and depreciation after certain asset acquisitions; (8) the taxation of currency gains and losses; (9) the treatment of gains and losses on stock sales with regard to companies registered in Norway; (10) the treatment of dividends (paid to Norwegian or foreign shareholders); (11) taxation of Norwegian-operated foreign-owned vessels; and (12) the treatment of assets moved into or out of Norway.

At the end of this article, the author briefly discusses a proposal made to assess Norwegian shareholders in Norwegian controlled companies in tax havens for their share of the corporation's income. The author concludes that although fairness and simplification were the objectives of the Norwegian tax reform, many loopholes remain, in part due to the influence of special interest groups. Future changes to the tax law will depend particularly on the evaluation of the split-tax model in calculating the personal income base for 1992 and 1993.

[LM Udjus, 3 J. Int'l Tax'n 226.]

¶ 7.27 ROMANIA

"Romania's tax system evolves with the free market economy" (1993). Since 1989, changes in Romania have required the tax system to adapt to a free market economy, and the law and administration are still evolving. In developing the tax system, new concepts have had to be introduced. The concept of "profit," for instance, did not exist in the former centralized command market economy. A major new change is a law regarding accountancy, and with it the abandonment of the socialist concept of "benefit." Recent legislation provides for taxation of profits, wages, and income from other sources such as real and personal property and intellectual property rights, as well as withholding taxes, Customs duties, and turnover tax. A VAT is expected to take effect in 1993.

The authors first discuss Romania's profits tax. Specific attention is given to provisions of the tax law covering dividends, the law limiting product markups to no more than 30 percent, and the rules for "sole traders" (individuals licensed to engage in commercial or handicraft activities) and commercial companies (including their allowable deductions, losses, tax holidays, and procedural obligations).

Next, the authors examine Romania's tax treatment of foreign investment in Romania, which is generally more favorable than the tax regime applicable to Romanian nationals. Specific attention is given to the law concerning branches and subsidiaries, representative offices, repatriation of profits, the taxation of salaries and wages, and "tax-free zones" for foreign investment. Last discussed are Romania's 18 percent turnover tax (expected to be replaced by a VAT of 18 percent) and Romania's Customs duties.

The authors conclude that Romania has had to develop a new tax system to reflect the change to a free market economy. Romania has a very ambitious economic program for the near future and rapid changes are expected.

[M. Grama & NS Hammond, 4 J. Int'l Tax'n 276.]

¶ 7.28 RUSSIA

"Russia modernizes its tax system, but ghosts of the U.S.S.R. still haunt" (1993). Direct investment in or ownership of Russian enterprises was not possible until 1988. Until enactment of the Enterprise Tax Law by the U.S.S.R. Supreme Soviet in June 1990, the Soviet Union maintained a completely separate tax system for foreign trade and foreign service provider activities. The Enterprise Tax Law contained a large number of favorable provisions applicable only to enterprises with more than 30 percent–foreign ownership. That law applied to (1) "joint enterprises" with foreign participation (at the time the only Russian enterprise in which a foreigner could own an interest); (2) foreign companies earning income from sources in the U.S.S.R.; and (3) U.S.S.R. domestic enterprises. The Enterprise Tax Law also called for a completely new tax system and for a series of tax holidays and other benefits of interest to the foreign business community. It imposed additional taxes—an export-import tax, a turnover tax, and a 90 percent excess profits tax—and greatly strengthened tax enforcement procedures. Many provisions of this law continue in effect.

In December 1990, with the declaration of sovereignty, Russia adopted legislation to replace the U.S.S.R. income tax laws with Russian income tax laws. These were not additional republic-level taxes but an alternative to the all-Union level tax laws within the borders of Russia. For several months it was not clear to whom Russian enterprises were to pay their taxes. The legislation by its terms pertained only to taxation in 1991 and, during that year, it became clear that Russia, not the U.S.S.R., was the taxing authority.

The author of this article examines the Russian Profits Tax. In so doing, he discusses the concept of ''representative office,'' which will trigger this tax if economic activity is carried on through this office. The treatment of operating branches of foreign companies and foreign-owned joint stock societies is also discussed with regard to this tax. Thereafter, the author addresses the applicable tax rates (generally 32 percent, but 45 percent on profits from so-called middleman activities) and certain tax privileges (such as those for the reinvestment of profits into certain activities). The calculation of expenses that can reduce the tax base and the ''Russian alternative minimum tax'' are last examined.

The author then turns to consideration of other taxes imposed by Russia. These include a VAT, an import tax, certain business sector taxes, and the 70 percent ''sin'' tax on revenues from certain activities. The forced sale of 50 percent of hard currency generated by Russian enterprises is also discussed, along with the enforcement procedures and penalties associated with the above taxes.

In the last section of this article the author describes application of the withholding tax on profits paid to foreign investors in Russian enterprises, as well as certain royalties, dividends, and interest payments. A discussion is then provided of certain planning aspects under the Russian taxes. The author concludes that while the Russian system is struggling to encourage foreign investment, old policies and rules have not been completely put to rest and foreign investors must operate in a country that is rapidly changing to adapt to international practices.

[EH Lieberman, 4 J. Int'l Tax'n 32.]

''New Soviet tax laws attract foreign investors'' (1991). This article is a summary of the former Soviet Union's tax laws affecting foreign investors. Momentous economic changes are currently being wrought in the former U.S.S.R. as it moves to a market economy. It is not surprising, therefore, that Soviet taxation of foreign investment in the former U.S.S.R. is also undergoing substantial revision.

Early in 1990, the U.S.S.R. Supreme Soviet enacted two comprehensive income tax laws: the U.S.S.R. Law on Income Tax on Citizens of the U.S.S.R., Foreign Citizens, and Persons Without Citizenship (the personal tax law), and the U.S.S.R. Law on Taxes From Enterprises, Associations, and Organizations (the corporate tax law), which clarify many previous uncertainties concerning the taxation of foreign investments. These two laws also raise myriad new questions, however, for foreign investors in the former Soviet Union. For example, the computation of taxable profit under the corporate tax law needs clarification.

[EH Lieberman, JM Colon & D. Oleszczuk, 1 J. Int'l Tax'n 278.]

¶ 7.29 SINGAPORE

"Singapore becomes popular for Asian regional operations" (1993). Singapore is strategically located for doing business from India to Australia to Mainland China. For many nontax reasons, Singapore is frequently selected as the base for sales into the region, and many multinational companies station regional support staffs in Singapore.

Singapore's tax system is also an important consideration. In this article, the author explains Singapore's tax system. The author first examines Singapore's rules on what constitutes a permanent establishment in that country and its sourcing of income rules. The use of "regional holding companies" is then considered. Singapore's dividend imputation system is discussed and illustrated through an example. Last, the author considers the two generally prevailing methods for using Singapore as a regional base while keeping Singapore taxes at reasonable levels: (1) the operational headquarters incentive and (2) the Singapore service company. Use of a "representative office" in Singapore is also explained.

The author concludes that Singapore is positioning itself as a very desirable location for the regional operations of multinational companies. Whether this is done through a permanent establishment, a regional holding company, a regional headquarters, or a representative office, the tax advantages (as discussed in this article) will generally be favorable. Further, Singapore's twenty-seven treaties, and its ties with Australia and the PRC, allow a rich texture of planning possibilities.

[RD Heyde, 4 J. Int'l Tax'n 399.]

"Singapore strives to be 'Luxembourg of the Pacific Rim' " (1993). In this article, the authors examine the attractiveness of the Pacific Rim as a marketplace for U.S. financial services companies and the tax implications of entering that market. After noting some of the extreme differences peculiar to this market (as compared to EC markets), the authors discuss Singapore as a marketplace for financial services. They first focus on its prevailing tax rates and certain tax incentives available to money managers, traders, and investors. Thereafter, the authors specifically discuss Singapore's taxation of investment companies. Last, they briefly examine the attractiveness of Singapore for non-U.S. financial services companies and some aspects of using Hong Kong and Taiwan as centers for offering financial services.

[RD Lorence & RJ Shapiro, 4 J. Int'l Tax'n 43.]

"Singapore uses tax incentives to become a hub for Asia's expanding economy" **(1993).** Singapore's industrial policy rests upon financial and tax incentives designed to encourage the location of companies valuable to the Singapore economy. This article concerns these incentive packages.

Before discussing the business incentives available to Singapore investors, the author first considers the taxation of business and investment income in Singapore. Specific attention is given to available deductions, the treatment of loss carry-forwards, the taxation of dividends, the availability of FTCs, the application of withholding taxes, transfer pricing restrictions, and the applicability of tax treaties. Thereafter, the author examines the investment incentive system existing in Singapore. He discusses both the agencies supervising these incentive programs and the specific tax incentives for various activities (such as export enterprises, investment allowances, international trade incentives, and expansion incentives).

The author concludes that Singapore is a strategic location for structuring business operations in the Asia Pacific Region. Its tax system essentially taxes only income arising in the geographical area of Singapore. Incentives and other favorable tax arrangements are drawing increasing investment to the country.

[RD Heyde, 4 J. Int'l Tax'n 316.]

¶ 7.30 SPAIN

"Spain is quick to conform its tax system to EC requirements" (1993). Spain has already taken the path toward tax harmonization and was guided by the theory behind EC proposals even before joining the EC in 1986. One objective of the Spanish tax authorities was to approximate Spanish Customs organization with the EC system. In addition to enacting a VAT, Spain has enacted other tax provisions to this end. The most recent enactment, in 1991, adapted certain of Spain's tax provisions to the EC directives and regulations.

The author first discusses Spain's enactment of the EC's "economic interest groupings" concept in its tax and mercantile law. The particular changes made to Spain's law and their effect are examined. The taxation of Spanish economic interest groupings is then discussed. Next, the author addresses the changes made in Spain's corporate provisions for mergers, spin-offs, capital contributions, and securities exchanges. Particular attention is given to asset and stock transfer provisions, provisions concerning parent-subsidiary systems, provisions affecting associated companies, antiabuse and transfer pricing rules, loss carry-forward and corporate tax credit provisions, and rates for corporate tax and withholding on dividends.

Next, the author discusses Spain's VAT provisions, including those pertaining to the residual VAT, Customs issues, and temporary imports. Last, the author examines Spain's tax treatment of "frontier workers," i.e., those who reside every day in one EC member state but work daily in another, and the Canary Islands, whose tax system is slowly being harmonized with EC law while still being subject to special rules.

[CA Garcia-Quintana, 4 J. Int'l Tax'n 164.]

¶ 7.31 SWEDEN

"Sweden reduces taxes while nearly doubling its tax base" (1992). In 1991, Sweden abandoned one of the world's highest rate tax systems (replete with tax gamesmanship of every stripe) for a system that looks much like the U.S. system after TRA 1986.

The new system, effective after 1990, has a top marginal tax rate (national and local) of 51 percent. Income derived from capital, including capital gains, interest, and dividends is subject to a flat national tax of 30 percent. The average local income tax is 31 percent. No national income tax, however, is levied on incomes below 187,000 Kronor, so that only about 15 percent of taxpayers pay the combined national rate (20 percent) and local rate (31 percent). All taxpayers are entitled to a personal allowance of 10,000 to 18,000 Kronor, depending on the level of income from employment or business activities. Under the new system, virtually all benefits, with the principal exception of health care, are taxable at fair market value. The partial indexation under the old system is replaced by taxation of the entire gain, regardless of holding period. Rates are reduced for gains from residential sales.

The corporate tax system is replaced by a new reserve called a tax equalization reserve-*Skatteut jaemningsreserv* (SURV). Corporations can allocate 30 percent of the equity capital (including 70 percent of the year's profits) to a tax-free reserve. The effect of the SURV is a reduction of the tax rate on retained profits from 30 percent to 23 percent. There is an alternative SURV for companies with low equity capital, of 15 percent of payroll. Only minor changes were made to depreciation schedules, which remain generous by U.S. standards—either 30 percent or 25 percent declining balance method for equipment and intangibles.

Reforms included no statutory changes for foreign investors. Nevertheless, foreign investors no longer need to make the kinds of special adaptations to Swedish tax rules that they previously did.

[H. Zahlander, 3 J. Int'l Tax'n 115.]

¶ 7.32 TAIWAN

"Taiwan's tax system offers low rates and business incentives to spur growth" (1993). Taiwan is one of the few countries in the world experiencing significant economic growth. It has enacted tax laws that encourage foreign investment, especially in high-tech industries. This article is a general discussion of Taiwan's tax laws and economic incentive policies.

The authors first discuss the administration of Taiwan's tax system, its advance tax ruling procedure, tax dispute resolution, and tax penalties imposed thereunder. Next, they focus on specific Taiwan taxes. First addressed is the profit-seeking enterprise income tax. Specific discussion is provided on Taiwan taxable income, tax rates, and tax year selection. Next, the different forms in which businesses may be operated and the tax implications of each are discussed (i.e., subsidiary, branch, foreign investment approval status, field/job site office, representative or liaison offices, business agent, exporters, and foreign exchange controls). Taiwan's business and gross sales taxes are next examined. The following other taxes and charges are also discussed: the commodity tax, Customs duties, the harbor construction charge, the land value tax, the land value increment tax, the building tax, and the securities transactions taxes.

The next part of this article addresses business incentives available under Taiwan law for investment in "export processing zones." The authors last discuss Taiwan's taxation of individuals and foreign persons. They conclude that Taiwan's evolution from a manufacturing and agricultural economy to a service-based economy will likely result in additional modifications to its tax system.

[WL Koo & JP Wilson, 4 J. Int'l Tax'n 220.]

"How a Taiwan-based manufacturer should set up U.S. manufacturing operations" (1992). This article discusses the international tax considerations for Taiwan-based businesses planning investment in the United States.

The authors first discuss general tax considerations, including the maximizing of deductions and other charges against U.S. profits, because the United States has a higher effective tax rate on profits than Taiwan. In this regard, the tax regime in Taiwan is examined. Specific discussion is provided of its income taxes, rates, and incentives. Then, U.S. taxation of foreign persons is discussed. Specific attention is given to investment in real property and the taxation of foreign corporations. Next, the authors review and compare the tax consequences of operating a U.S. branch or subsidiary. This discussion covers the branch profits tax, treaty relief, the incorporation of a branch, and inbound transfers of business assets.

Thereafter, the authors discuss transfer pricing problems and the impact of certain treaties on these problems. Particular problem areas discussed are the use of leverage in a subsidiary's capital structure, debt vs. equity classification, earnings and interest stripping limitations, application of the related-party limitations under Section 267, the treatment of excess interest expense, and coverage under treaty relief provisions.

The authors close this article with a discussion of both state tax issues and U.S. estate and gift taxes. They conclude with a summary of the various planning pointers explained throughout the article.

[KW Crawford, J. Tai & JF Wu, US Tax'n Int'l Operations ¶ 8532.]

¶ 7.33 THAILAND

"Thailand's tax system is favorable for foreign investors" (1993). Foreign companies operating in Thailand as of November 25, 1992, are subject to the Alien Business Laws. Alien businesses, whose activities fall into categories established under these laws, are subject to certain limitations.

The author first discusses the application of the Alien Business Laws to U.S. operations in Thailand. He notes that because of the U.S.-Thailand treaty, such laws apply to U.S. operations in a more relaxed manner than other countries' operations. Next, he discusses the ramifications of conducting U.S. business in Thailand through a branch or, alternatively, a subsidiary. Specific attention is given to the tax consequences of branch operations (i.e., corporate income tax, profit remittance tax, and value added tax) and use of a registered Thailand subsidiary (i.e., corporate income tax on the subsidiary and the withholding tax on dividends). Certain benefits, such as those available to Thai Board of Investment–promoted companies, are discussed. Last, the author examines the consequences of using a representative office in Thailand and the formation of joint ventures to carry on business in Thailand.

The author concludes that the treaty between Thailand and the United States affects the application of Thai law to U.S. persons doing business in Thailand. The form of doing business, as well as the residence of the shareholders, may limit the type of business in which a U.S. entity can engage in Thailand. Significant tax and nontax benefits are available to "promoted" companies and joint ventures. Accordingly, consideration of the alternative methods of operation is advisable for tax and nontax reasons.

[M. Hongskrailers, 4 J. of Int'l Tax'n 170.]

¶ 7.34 UNITED KINGDOM

"Foreign debt financing of U.K. entities presents complex issues" (1993). The introduction of legislation in the United Kingdom to deny deductions for interest paid on long-term debt with equity characteristics requires that practitioners review the treatment of interest paid overseas by companies. The provisions included in this legislation affect the planning of debt structuring in the international context.

The author first considers the following issues concerning interest payments by corporations with regard to the corporate tax:

(1) Can interest be paid without withholding tax, and what formalities are required?

(2) Is the interest deductible by the payor?

(3) Is it deductible only against restricted categories of income?

(4) Is it deductible on an accrual basis or only when paid?

(5) If the interest exceeds income, can the resulting loss be used, and in what manner?

Within the context of these questions, the author also explores issues such as Section 482 exposure, the treatment of long-outstanding debt balances, intragroup borrowing, deep discount securities, and what qualifies as a payment of interest.

Next, the author discusses different factors that can affect the foreign lender's treatment of payments received from a U.K. borrower, including whether the lender is related or a nonresident affiliate of the U.K. debtor. In this regard, the author considers the debt-equity ratio used by Inland Revenue to determine if purported debt is in fact equity. Last, the author examines the treatment of hybrid instruments (including "equity notes"), the current administrative review of the U.K. tax treatment of exchange differences, and effective use of treaty relief procedures for problems in this area. The author concludes that given the attraction of generating low-taxed foreign-source income that is general limitation income, U.S. groups are naturally predisposed to lending funds to their U.K. trading subsidiaries. Considerable care is required, however, to achieve the desired result under U.K. law.

[M. Godbee, 4 J. Int'l Tax'n 450.]

"Proposals may entice U.S. multinationals to locate headquarters in the United Kingdom" (1993). In early 1993, the British government announced certain proposals intended to alleviate difficulties for U.K. outbound and inbound investment caused by the U.K.'s integrated system of corporate and shareholder taxation. Before discussing these proposals, the author first explains the U.K.'s imputation system of taxation, which operates to eliminate or relieve double taxation at the corporate and shareholder levels by giving a credit to shareholders for tax paid by the corporation. This in-depth discussion of the U.K. system includes an extensive explanation of the treatment of nonresident shareholders thereunder. Also addressed within this discussion is retaliatory legislation passed by the United Kingdom in reaction to *Barclays Bank International, Ltd. v. Franchise Tax Board*, a California tax case holding that California can apply its worldwide combined reporting method to tax British-owned multinational groups.

Next, the author explains the treatment of surplus corporate tax credits that will arise when a corporation subject to U.K. tax has foreign profits on which the foreign tax is greater than the U.K. tax on such profits. A detailed example of the problems that occur when a surplus of tax credits builds up is provided, along with a number of tax planning arrangements that use up excess credits.

Following the discussion of current U.K. law, the problems it creates, and the means by which tax planners have sought to compensate for these problems, the author discusses the 1993 proposed changes in the U.K.'s taxation of dividends. Included in these changes, explored by the author, are the rate reductions for taxation of dividends, the foreign income dividend scheme (intended to correct the surplus tax credit problem), and the positive effect that the proposed changes would have in encouraging international companies to headquarter their organizations in the United Kingdom. The author illustrates the consequences of these proposals and compares them to the results obtained under existing tax planning techniques.

The author concludes that the foreign income dividend scheme offers a reasonable compromise, but if the proposals become law, U.K. multinationals will face difficult choices. They will have to balance the attractions of reducing their effective tax charge by paying foreign income dividends against the concerns of some of their shareholders to maximize income by reclaiming tax credits.

Whether or not the general foreign income dividends scheme becomes law, the British government has committed itself to a new regime for international headquarter companies. Further clarification is awaited, and draft legislation is promised for the Finance Bill to be published in January 1994.

[MC Hockey, 4 J. Int'l Tax'n 249.]

"Tax reform introduced in 1993 U.K. budget" (1993). In the U.K.'s 1993 budget, a number of tax reforms were proposed. These include a new basis for taxation of dividends and self-employment income and reforms to the Advance Corporation Tax (ACT). This article summarizes the budget's main tax proposals of interest to U.S. and other multinationals.

The author first considers the proposed changes to the corporate tax, including those affecting rate reductions, the treatment for foreign income dividends, ACT carrybacks from acquired companies, capital loss buying, the definition of a "CFC", interest deferral on loans to overseas affiliates, the treatment of deferred gains on corporate takeovers, employer contributions to pensions, pre-trading expenditures, capital allowances on related-party sales, and the oil tax regime.

Next, the author discusses proposed changes to the U.K.'s VAT. These affect the taxation of domestic fuel and power supplies, misdeclaration penalties, VAT payments, bad-debt relief, registration limits, use of VAT cash accounting, and triangular trade in the EC. Proposed changes in employee taxation are thereafter discussed. Areas affected by the proposed changes include the treatment of employee car expenses, the costs of relocation, in-house sports facilities, outplacement counseling, and national insurance contributions.

Next, the proposed changes in personal taxation are examined. These include changes to the rates of income tax and allowances, certain aspects of self-assessment, mortgage interest relief, the taxation of dividends, capital gains tax relief and concessions, the treatment of charitable gifts, the Personal Equity Plan proposals, the determination of residence status, the inheritance tax, and the treatment of Lloyd's Underwriters. In conclusion, the author notes proposed changes in the stamp duty, uniform business rate freezes, and the council tax.

[J. Fox, US Tax'n Int'l Operations ¶ 8535.]

"U.K. Finance Bill includes ACT reduction, foreign exchange, CFC provisions" (1993). The U.K. Finance Bill contains several items of international interest. The author of this article discusses the important aspects of the U.K. Finance Bill, including the reduction of the imputation tax credit, the new treatment of foreign exchange gains and losses, changes made to the treatment of CFCs, changes to the pension contribution provisions, and changes in the determination of U.K.-residency for individuals.

[JB Oliver, 4 J. Int'l Tax'n 328.]

"Refund of tax credits on dividends to U.K. investors available" (1991). Although the United Kingdom has negotiated several treaties under which it has conceded a refund of one half of the tax credit (less a 5 percent withholding tax) on dividends to direct investors in the overseas territory, the current U.S. treaty being the first, until now this treatment has not been reciprocated. Often, this has been due to the lack of compatibility between the respective company tax systems.

There is a similarity between the present Italian system and the U.K. system, however, that has resulted in the first treaty provision giving a refund of the one-half tax credit (less a 5 percent withholding tax) on dividends to a U.K. direct investor in the overseas company. The provision is contained in the new treaty between the United Kingdom and Italy, which entered into force on December 31, 1990. It took effect April 6, 1991, with respect to dividends in the United Kingdom, and in Italy as early as January 1, 1991, for a company with a December 31 accounting year-end, or as late as October 1, 1991, for a company with a September 30 year-end.

An attached exhibit illustrates how the refund mechanism operates and shows that through the refund, the Italian tax on the profits that have been distributed has been reduced from 57.04 percent to 43.52 percent. This brings the Italian tax almost into line with the U.K. tax payable, giving the full benefit to the U.K. direct investor through the reduction of an unusable excess-tax credit. The treaty contains an anti-avoidance rule that is similar to the rule in the U.S.-Swiss treaty.

The author concludes the article with an analysis of the possible impact of the treaty on investment.

[JB Oliver, 2 J. Int'l Tax'n 112.]

"United Kingdom and United States differ on residence requirement for teacher exemption" (1991). Many U.K. treaties contain an article providing a tax exemption for visiting teachers or professors. The interpretation of these provisions was the issue in *Vas*, a 1990 U.K. High Court case that is discussed in this article.

[JB Oliver, 2 J. Int'l Tax'n 246.]

¶ 7.35 VENEZUELA

"Annual inflation adjustments are introduced into Venezuela's tax system" (1993). The law partially amending the Income Tax Law in Venezuela, effective September 1, 1991, had several objectives, including consistency with economic and social development, efficiency in allocating the tax burden, equity among taxpayers, and administrative simplicity. Major changes included:

1. Elimination of tax on income earned abroad, including payments for activities performed abroad in connection with importing goods or services;
2. Taxation of companies owned by national, state, and local governments;
3. Adjustment of assets and liabilities for inflation (rules relating to the initial adjustment and regular annual adjustments for inflation became effective on January 1, 1993); and
4. Taxation at the normal corporate rate of income for mining activities and joint ventures between Venezuelan state-owned companies and domestic or foreign private corporations engaged in extracting and processing crude oil and natural gas where the taxable entity guarantees an international market for the products.

[A. Parra-Febres, 4 J. Int'l Tax'n 270.]

¶ 7.36 VIETNAM

"As the embargo crumbles, Vietnam prepares for U.S. investors" (1993). The embargo against Vietnam was modified in 1992 to allow U.S. companies to open offices, hire staff, and sign contracts, conditioned upon a later lifting of the embargo. Although many companies did business in pre-1975 South Vietnam, the Vietnam of today is a radically new environment for most U.S. investors. Vietnam's tax laws, as with its laws for governing foreign investment, are new and lack the clarity and specificity found in more developed regimes. This article concerns Vietnam's evolving legal framework with regard to the treatment of future U.S. investment in Vietnam.

The author first examines Vietnam's foreign investment law, its personal income tax, its "corporate" (i.e., profits) tax on foreign-owned enterprises, its taxation of petroleum production (through production sharing agreements and profits tax), its "turnover" tax (i.e., a sales tax imposed on enterprises with foreign-owned capital that sell certain products or services), its withholding tax on foreign entities and individuals, and its export and import taxes. The author also discusses Vietnam's set royalties for all foreign resource extractive/exploitive activities and the state rent for land and sea surface use. Last, the author addresses reporting and payment of the Vietnam taxes.

The author concludes that two U.S. tax issues may arise with regard to investment in Vietnam because of the status of the embargo. U.S. citizens violating the provisions of the Foreign Assets Control Regulations, which control travel to Vietnam, can lose their Section 911 exclusion. Also, until the embargo is modified, Vietnam is one of the countries to which Section 901(j) denies an FTC. Individuals and corporations that "jump the gun" face substantial penalties for violating the above regulations, as well as the loss of tax benefits under Sections 911 and 901.

[MJ Scown, 4 J. Int'l Tax'n 12.]

"Vietnam's corporate tax system still requires bartering, but formality is increasing" (1993). A number of major legal changes affecting the taxation of foreign investment have taken place in Vietnam. These include amendments to the law on foreign investment and Vietnam's signing of tax treaties with Thailand, Australia, and France.

The author first discusses the legislative changes made to the Foreign Investment Law, including a 1993 change that revamped the investment incentive procedure in Vietnam and reduced the number of profits tax rates. The preferential rates for certain investments that have not changed are reviewed by the author. Withholding tax and tax holiday provisions are also examined. Changes in the areas of reporting and enforcement of Vietnam taxes are then considered.

The author concludes that Vietnam is in the midst of a massive undertaking to create a modern legal and financial system capable of attracting and sustaining high levels of foreign direct investment. Changes in its laws, including those concerning taxes, are being made at a great speed. Accordingly, investors should consider the goals (as discussed in this article) of the Vietnamese government when planning to make investments in Vietnam.

[MJ Scown, 4 J. Int'l Tax'n 370.]

Table of IRC Sections

[*References are to paragraphs (¶).*]

[References are to paragraphs (¶).]

[References are to paragraphs (¶).]

[References are to paragraphs (¶).]

Table of Treasury Regulations

[References are to paragraphs (¶).]

[References are to paragraphs (¶).]

[References are to paragraphs (¶).]

Table of Revenue Rulings, Revenue Procedures, and Other IRS Releases

[References are to paragraphs (¶).]

Table of Cases

[References are to paragraphs (¶).]

[References are to paragraphs (¶).]

Index

[References are to paragraphs (¶).]

Controlled foreign corporation (CFC)
   (cont'd)
   space or ocean activities, 2.05[6][c][ii]
   stapled stock arrangements, 2.05[6][a]
   stock in CFC, purchase from parent
      by another CFC, 2.07[1]
   taxable year, 2.05[7]
   transfer pricing rules. *See* Transfer
      pricing
   U.S. property, earnings invested in,
      2.05[6][d]
Czech Republic
   tax laws, 7.08
   tax treaties, 6.07[4]

D

Deductions, allocation and
      apportionment of. *See also* Transfer
      pricing
   branch-level taxes, 1.02[2][b], 3.04
   controlled foreign corporation,
      1.02[2][b]
   generally, 1.02[2][a]
   interest
      earnings stripping provisions,
         3.08[1][b]
      effectively connected income,
         1.02[2][b]
      generally, 1.02[2][b]
      U.S. corporations owned by foreign
         persons, 3.08[1][a]
   netting rule, 1.02[2][b]
   notional principal contracts, 1.02[2][b]
   research and experimental
      expenditures, 1.02[2][c]
   state and local taxes, 1.02[2][d]
   stock losses, 1.02[2][e]
   Tax Reform Act of 1986, 1.02[2][b]
Denmark
   tax laws, 7.09
Domestic corporation
   definition of, 2.01[1]
Domestic international sales corporation
   (DISC). *See* United States citizen,
   subhead: foreign corporations
   owned by
Dominican Republic
   tax laws, 7.10

Dual-resident corporations
   dual consolidated loss regulations,
      2.04

E

Eastern and Central Europe, generally
   tax laws, 7.11
Effectively connected income (ECI)
   deductions
      allocation and apportionment of,
         1.02[2][b]
      generally, 3.03[3]
   defined, 3.03[2][a]
   real property income, 3.03[2][b],
      3.03[3]
   "trade or business within United
      States," defined, 3.03[1]
Estate and gift taxation
   marital deduction where surviving
      spouse is not U.S. citizen, 5.02
   nonresident aliens
      generally, 5.01
      generation-skipping transfer tax,
         5.03
   treaties affecting, 6.02, 6.07[5]
   trusts
      foreign trusts, 5.02
      qualified domestic trusts, 5.02
European Community
   tax laws, 7.12
   transfer pricing agreement, 6.08

F

Foreign business entities. *See also*
   specific countries
   classification of, 1.05
   corporations. *See* Foreign
      corporations
   hybrid entities, 1.05
   joint ventures, 1.05
Foreign corporations. *See also* Foreign
   persons
   banks, 3.09
   controlled foreign corporations. *See*
      Controlled foreign corporation
      (CFC)

[References are to paragraphs (¶).]

[References are to paragraphs (¶).]

[References are to paragraphs (¶).]